MySQL 8 Query Performance Tuning

A Systematic Method for Improving Execution Speeds

Jesper Wisborg Krogh

Apress®

MySQL 8 Query Performance Tuning: A Systematic Method for Improving Execution Speeds

Jesper Wisborg Krogh
Hornsby, NSW, Australia

ISBN-13 (pbk): 978-1-4842-5583-4
https://doi.org/10.1007/978-1-4842-5584-1

ISBN-13 (electronic): 978-1-4842-5584-1

Managing Director, Apress Media LLC: Welmoed Spahr
Acquisitions Editor: Jonathan Gennick
Development Editor: Laura Berendson
Coordinating Editor: Jill Balzano

Cover image designed by Freepik (www.freepik.com)

Distributed to the book trade worldwide by Springer Science+Business Media New York, 233 Spring Street, 6th Floor, New York, NY 10013. Phone 1-800-SPRINGER, fax (201) 348-4505, e-mail orders-ny@springer-sbm.com, or visit www.springeronline.com. Apress Media, LLC is a California LLC and the sole member (owner) is Springer Science + Business Media Finance Inc (SSBM Finance Inc). SSBM Finance Inc is a **Delaware** corporation.

For information on translations, please e-mail rights@apress.com, or visit http://www.apress.com/rights-permissions.

Apress titles may be purchased in bulk for academic, corporate, or promotional use. eBook versions and licenses are also available for most titles. For more information, reference our Print and eBook Bulk Sales web page at http://www.apress.com/bulk-sales.

Any source code or other supplementary material referenced by the author in this book is available to readers on GitHub via the book's product page, located at www.apress.com/9781484255834. For more detailed information, please visit http://www.apress.com/source-code.

Printed on acid-free paper

To the MySQL Support team, it has been a pleasure to work with you all.

Table of Contents

About the Author

Jesper Wisborg Krogh has worked with MySQL databases since 2006 both as an SQL developer and a database administrator and for more than eight years as part of the Oracle MySQL Support team. He has spoken at MySQL Connect and Oracle OpenWorld on several occasions, and in addition to his books, he regularly blogs on MySQL topics and has authored around 800 documents in the Oracle Knowledge Base. He has contributed to the sys schema and four Oracle Certified Professional (OCP) exams for MySQL 5.6–8.

He earned a PhD in computational chemistry before changing to work with MySQL and other software development in 2006. Jesper lives in Sydney, Australia, and enjoys spending time outdoors walking, traveling, and reading. His areas of expertise include MySQL Cluster, MySQL Enterprise Backup (MEB), performance tuning, and the Performance and sys schemas.

About the Technical Reviewer

 **Charles Bell** conducts research in emerging technologies. He is a member of the Oracle MySQL development team and is a senior software developer for the MySQL Enterprise Backup team. He lives in a small town in rural Virginia with his loving wife. He received his PhD in engineering from Virginia Commonwealth University in 2005.

Charles is an expert in the database field and has extensive knowledge and experience in software development and systems engineering. His research interests include three-dimensional printers/printing, microcontrollers, database systems, software engineering, high-availability systems, the cloud, and sensor networks. He spends his limited free time as a practicing maker, focusing on microcontroller projects and refinement of three-dimensional printers.

Acknowledgments

I would like to thank all of the people who made this book possible. The Apress team has again been a great help, and I would in particular like to thank Jonathan Gennick, Jill Balzano, and Laura Berendson, the three editors I worked with while getting this book ready for production.

Several people have been invaluable sparring partners in technical discussions. Thanks to Charles Bell for providing a thorough review; his comments were, as always, very useful. The feedback about InnoDB locks from Jakub Lopuszanski has also been invaluable. My work with the MySQL Support team, the countless discussions internally in the team, and the work by my great colleagues have been a great inspiration and source of ideas for this book. Also, a big thank you to Edwin Desouza for his support.

Last but not least, thanks to my wife, Ann-Margrete, for her patience and support while I wrote this book.

Introduction

MySQL performance tuning is a very large subject that takes years to master. The length of this book bears testimony to that, even with the scope reduced to focus on query-related topics. There are no simple recipes for improving performance, and often a solution requires understanding the relationship between various parts not only within MySQL but also for other parts of the stack. If you feel that it is overwhelming to get started, you are far from the first one, but do not despair as it is with performance tuning like with other skills that practice makes perfect.

The aim of this book is to help you to get a good start on the journey to become skilled at improving the performance of the queries executing on your MySQL instances. As said, there are no simple recipes, so the best way forward is to learn how the various components involved in performance tuning work. That is what the bulk of this book tries to do as well as giving examples of what to look for and how to perform common tasks. On the other hand, the scope has been limited to MySQL itself, so there is very limited discussion about the operating system, file system, and hardware levels.

MySQL is famous for its support for storage engines. However, this book exclusively covers the InnoDB storage engine except for the discussion of internal temporary tables. With respect to MySQL versions, only MySQL 8 is considered. That said, most of the discussion also applies to older versions of MySQL, and in general it is mentioned when a feature is new in MySQL 8 or that MySQL 8 has a different behavior compared to older versions.

Book Audience

The book has been written for developers and database administrators who have experience working with MySQL and want to expand their knowledge into the realm of query performance tuning. No prior experience with performance tuning is required.

Examples and the Book's GitHub Repository

I have tried to add as many examples and outputs from examples as possible. Some of the examples are quite short, some are quite long. In either case, I hope you are able to follow them and reproduce the effect or result demonstrated. At the same time, please do bear in mind that by nature there is often randomness involved (sometimes even explicitly as with the index statistics), and the exact outcome of the examples may depend on how the tables and data have been used prior to the example. In other words, you may get different results even if you did everything right. This particularly applies to numbers that relate to index statistics, timings, and the like.

Examples that are long or produce outputs that are either long or wide have been added to this book's GitHub repository. This includes some of the figures that may be hard to read with the image size that the page format allows. The link to the repository can be found from the book's homepage at `www.apress.com/gp/book/9781484255834`.

The GitHub repository will also be the home of the errata for the book once that is created. I will use the errata not only to communicate errors in the book but also to provide updates when bug fixes and new features in MySQL 8 cause changes to book content. If necessary, I will also update the examples in the repository to reflect the behavior in the newer releases. For these reasons, I recommend that you keep an eye on the repository.

Book Structure

The book is divided into six parts with a total of 27 chapters. I have attempted to keep each chapter relatively self-contained with the aim that you can use the book as a reference book. The drawback of this choice is that there is some duplication of information from time to time. An example is Chapter 18 which describes the more theoretical side of locks and how to monitor locks, and Chapter 22 which provides practical examples of investigating lock contention. Chapter 22 naturally draws on the information in Chapter 18, so some of the information is repeated. This was a deliberate choice, and I hope it helps you reduce the amount of page flipping to find the information you need.

The six parts progressively move you through the topics starting with some basic background and finishing with more solution-oriented tasks. The first part starts out discussing the methodology, benchmarks, and test data. The second part focuses on the sources of information such as the Performance Schema. The third part covers the tools such as MySQL Shell used in this book. The fourth part provides the theoretical background used in the last two parts. The fifth part focuses on analyzing queries, transactions, and locks. Finally, the sixth part discusses how to improve performance through the configuration, query optimization, replication, and caching. There are cases where some content is a little out of place, like all replication information is contained in a single chapter.

Part I: Getting Started

Part I introduces you to the concepts of MySQL query performance tuning. This includes some high-level considerations, of which some are not unique to MySQL (but are of course discussed in the context of MySQL). The four chapters are

1. MySQL Performance Tuning – This introductory chapter covers some high-level concepts of MySQL performance tuning such as the importance of considering the whole stack and the lifecycle of a query.

2. Query Tuning Methodology – It is important to work in an effective way to solve performance problems. This chapter introduces a methodology to work effectively and emphasizes the importance of working proactively rather than doing firefighting.

3. Benchmarking with Sysbench – It is often necessary to use benchmarks to determine the effect of a change. This chapter introduces benchmarking in general and specifically discusses the Sysbench tool including how to create your own custom benchmarks.

4. Test Data – The book mostly uses a few standard test databases which are introduced in this chapter.

Part II: Sources of Information

MySQL exposes information about the performance through a few sources. The Performance Schema, the sys schema, the Information Schema, and the SHOW statement are introduced in each their chapter. There are only relatively few examples of using these sources in this part; however, these four sources of information are used extensively in the remainder of the book. If you are not already familiar with them, you are strongly encouraged to read this part. Additionally, the slow query log is covered. The five chapters are

5. The Performance Schema – The main source of performance-related information in MySQL is – as the name suggests – the Performance Schema. This chapter introduces the terminology, the main concepts, the organization, and the configuration.

6. The sys Schema – The sys schema provides reports through predefined views and utilities in stored functions and programs. This chapter provides an overview of what features are available.

7. The Information Schema – If you need metadata about the MySQL and the databases, the Information Schema is the place to look. It also includes important information for performance tuning such as information about indexes, index statistics, and histograms. This chapter provides an overview of the views available in the Information Schema.

8. SHOW Statements – The SHOW statements are the oldest way to obtain information ranging from which queries are executing to schema information. This chapter relates the SHOW statements to the Information Schema and Performance Schema and covers in somewhat more detail the SHOW statements without counterparts in the two schemas.

9. The Slow Query Log – The traditional way to find slow queries is to log them to the slow query log. This chapter covers how to configure the slow query log, how to read the log events, and how to aggregate the events with the mysqldump utility.

Part III: Tools

MySQL provides several tools that are useful when performing the daily work as well as specialized tasks. This part covers three tools ranging from monitoring to simple query execution. This book uses Oracle's dedicated MySQL monitoring solution (requires commercial subscription but is also available as a trial) as an example of monitoring.

Even if you are using other monitoring solutions, you are encouraged to study the examples as there will be a large overlap. These three tools are also used extensively in the remainder of the book. The three chapters in this part are

10. MySQL Enterprise Monitor – Monitoring is one of the most important aspects of maintaining a stable and well-performing database. This chapter introduces MySQL Enterprise Monitor (MEM) and shows how you can install the trial and helps you navigate and use the graphical user interface (GUI).

11. MySQL Workbench – MySQL provides a graphical user interface through the MySQL Workbench product. This chapter shows how you can install and use it. In this book, MySQL Workbench is particularly important for its ability to create diagrams – known as Visual Explain – representing the query execution plans.

12. MySQL Shell – One of the newest tools around from Oracle for MySQL is MySQL Shell which is a second-generation command-line client with support for executing code in both SQL, Python, and JavaScript. This chapter gets you up to speed with MySQL Shell and teaches you about its support for using external code modules, its reporting infrastructure, and how to create custom modules, reports, and plugins.

Part IV: Schema Considerations and the Query Optimizer

In Part IV, there is a change of pace, and the focus moves to the topics more directly related to performance tuning starting with topics related to the schema, the query optimizer, and locks. The six chapters are

13. Data Types – In relational databases, each column has a data type. This data type defines which values can be stored, which rules apply when comparing two values, how the data is stored, and more. This chapter covers the data types available in MySQL and gives guidance on how to decide which data types to use.

14. Indexes – An index is used to locate data, and a good indexing strategy can greatly improve the performance of your queries. This chapter covers the index concepts, considerations about indexes, index types, index features, and more. It also includes a discussion on how InnoDB uses indexes and how to come up with an indexing strategy.

15. Index Statistics – When the optimizer needs to determine how useful an index is and how many rows match a condition on an indexed value, it needs information on the data in the index. This information is index statistics. This chapter covers how index statistics work in MySQL, how to configure them, monitoring, and updating the index statistics.

16. Histograms – If you want the optimizer to know how frequent a value occurs for a given column, you need to create a histogram. This is a new feature in MySQL 8, and this chapter covers how histograms can be used, their internals, and how to query the histogram metadata and statistics.

17. The Query Optimizer – When you execute a query, it is the query optimizer that determines how to execute it. This chapter covers the tasks performed by the optimizer, join algorithms, join optimizations, configuration of the optimizer, and resource groups.

18. Locking Theory and Monitoring – One of the problems that can cause the most frustration is lock contention. The first part of this chapter explains why locks are needed, lock access levels, and lock types (granularities). The second part of the chapter goes into what happens when a lock cannot be obtained, how to reduce lock contention, and where to find information about locks.

Part V: Query Analysis

With the information from Part IV, you are now ready to start analyzing queries. This includes finding the queries for further analysis and then analyzing the query using EXPLAIN or the Performance Schema. You also need to consider how transactions work and investigate lock contention when you have two or more queries fighting for the same locks. The four chapters are

19. Finding Candidate Queries for Optimization – Whether part of the daily maintenance or during an emergency, you need to find the queries that you need to analyze and potentially optimize. This chapter shows how you can use the Performance Schema, the sys schema, MySQL Workbench, your monitoring solution, and the slow query log to find the queries that are worth looking into.

20. Analyzing Queries – Once you have a candidate query, you need to analyze why it is slow or impacts the system too much. The main tool is the EXPLAIN statement which provides information about the query plan chosen by the optimizer. How to generate and read – including examples – the query plans using EXPLAIN is the main focus of the chapter. You can also use the optimizer trace to get more information on how the optimizer arrived at the selected query plan. An alternative way to analyze queries is to use the Performance Schema and sys schema to break queries down into smaller parts.

21. Transactions – InnoDB executes everything as a transaction, and transactions is an important concept. Proper use of transactions ensures atomicity, consistency, and isolation. However, transactions can also be the cause of severe performance and lock problems. This chapter discusses how transactions can become a problem and how to analyze them.

22. Diagnosing Lock Contention – This chapter goes through four scenarios with lock contention (flush locks, metadata locks, record-level locks, and deadlocks) and discusses the symptoms, the cause, how to set up the scenario, the investigation, the solution, and how to prevent problems.

Part VI: Improving Queries

You have found your problem queries and analyzed them and their transaction to understand why they are underperforming. But how do you improve the queries? This chapter goes through the most important configuration options not covered elsewhere, how to change the query plan, schema changes and bulk loading, replication, and caching as means to improve the performance. The five chapters are

23. Configuration – MySQL requires resources when executing a query. This chapter covers the best practices for configuring these resources and the most important configuration options that are not covered in other discussions. There is also an overview of the data lifecycle in InnoDB as background for the discussion of configuring InnoDB.

24. Change the Query Plan – While the optimizer usually does a good job at finding the optimal query execution plan, you will from time to time have to help it on its way. It may be that you end up with full table scans because no indexes exist or the existing indexes cannot be used. You may also wish to improve the index usage, or you may need to rewrite complex conditions or entire queries. This chapter covers these scenarios as well as shows how you can use the SKIP LOCKED clause to implement a queue system.

25. DDL and Bulk Data Load – When you perform schema changes or load large data sets into the system, you ask MySQL to perform a large amount of work. This chapter discusses how you can improve the performance of such tasks including using the parallel data load feature of MySQL Shell. There is also a section on general data load considerations which also applies to data modifications in general and shows the difference between sequential and random order inserts. That discussion is followed by considerations on what this means for the choice of primary key.

26. Replication – The ability to replicate between instances is a popular feature in MySQL. From a performance point of view, replication has two sides: you need to ensure replication performs well, and you can use replication to improve performance. This chapter discusses both sides of the coin including covering the Performance Schema tables that can be used to monitor replication.

27. Caching – One way to improve the performance of queries is to not execute them at all, or at least avoid executing part of the query. This chapter discusses how you can use caching tables to reduce the complexity of queries and how you can use Memcached, the MySQL InnoDB Memcached plugin, and ProxySQL to avoid executing the queries altogether.

PART I

Getting Started

CHAPTER 1

MySQL Performance Tuning

Welcome to the world of MySQL performance tuning. It is a world that sometimes can seem like it is dominated by black magic and luck, but hopefully this book can help you work in a structured way and methodically work your way to a better performance.

This chapter introduces you to MySQL performance tuning by talking about the whole stack as well as the importance of monitoring and basing your actions on data. Since this book is mainly about working with queries, the lifecycle of a query is reviewed before concluding the chapter.

Tip If you need a test instance, whether it is while reading this book or for working on a problem at work, the cloud can be your friend. It allows you to quickly spin up a test instance. If you just need a small instance, for example, to explore examples in this book, you may even be able to use a free instance, such as through Oracle Cloud's free tier (registration and a credit card is still required): `https://mysql.wisborg.dk/oracle_cloude_free_tier`.

Consider the Whole Stack

When you investigate performance problems, it is important that you consider all parts of the system from the end user through the application to MySQL. When someone reports that the application is slow, and you know that MySQL is a central part of the application, then it is easy to jump to the conclusion that "MySQL is slow." That would however rule out a large array of potential causes of the poor performance.

© Jesper Wisborg Krogh 2020
J. W. Krogh, *MySQL 8 Query Performance Tuning*, https://doi.org/10.1007/978-1-4842-5584-1_1

When an application needs the result of the query or needs to store data in MySQL, it sends the request over the network to MySQL, and in order to execute the request, MySQL interacts with the operating system and uses host resources such as memory and disk. Once the result of the request is ready, it is communicated back to the application through the network. This is illustrated in Figure 1-1.

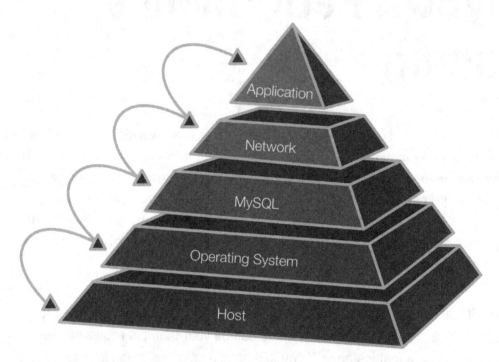

Figure 1-1. *The stack focused around MySQL*

The pyramid is a very simplified picture which leaves out everything beyond the application which may in turn communicate with a user and use its own resources. Communicating over the network also involves both the host and operating system.

To illustrate how the layers can interact, consider a real-world example. A MySQL user reported problems with MySQL experiencing temporary stalls. An investigation using the perf tool on Linux revealed that stalls happened because the memory got extremely fragmented, mainly caused by the I/O cache. When you submit data over the network, Linux requests a contiguous piece of memory (using kmalloc), but because of the severe memory fragmentation, Linux had to defragment (compact) the memory first. While this compaction took place, everything including MySQL stalled, and as it in the worst cases took up to a minute (the server had a large amount of memory available for I/O caching), it caused a severe impact. In this case, changing the MySQL configuration to use direct I/O worked around the issue. While this is an extreme case, it is worth bearing in mind that interactions can cause surprising points of congestion.

A more straightforward real-world example was an application that used a framework to generate queries. There was a bug in the framework that meant that a WHERE clause was omitted for queries against a large table. That meant a cascading list of problems including the application retrying the query and culminating with 50 copies of the query finishing within a few seconds (because the data finally had been read into the buffer pool making the last queries execute much faster than the first) and sending a huge amount of data back to the application causing the network to overload and the application to run out of memory.

This book focuses on MySQL and the aspects affecting queries, but do not forget the rest of your system. That includes when you monitor your system.

Monitoring

If you take just one thing with you from reading this book, then let it be that monitoring is critical to maintain a healthy system. Everything you do should revolve around monitoring. In some cases, monitoring through a dedicated monitoring solution provides all the data you need, and in other cases you need to make ad hoc observations.

Your monitoring should use several sources of information. These include but are not limited to

- The Performance Schema which includes information ranging from low-level mutexes to query and transaction metrics. This is the single most important source of information for query performance tuning. The sys schema provides a convenient interface particularly for ad hoc queries.

- The Information Schema which includes schema information, InnoDB statistics, and more.

- SHOW statements which, for example, include information from InnoDB with detailed engine statistics.

- The slow query log which can record queries matching certain criteria such as taking longer than a predefined threshold.

- The EXPLAIN statement to return the query execution plan. This is an invaluable tool to investigate why a query is not performing well due to missing indexes, the query being written in a suboptimal way, or MySQL choosing a suboptimal way to execute the query. The EXPLAIN statement is mostly used in an ad hoc fashion when investigating a specific query.

- Operating system metrics such as disk utilization, memory usage, and network usage. Do not forget simple metrics such as the amount of free storage as running out of storage will cause an outage.

These sources of information are all discussed and used throughout this book.

When you use monitoring throughout the whole performance tuning process, you can verify what the issue is, find the cause, and prove that you have solved the issue. While working on a solution, it can also be useful to understand the lifecycle of a query.

The Lifecycle of a Query

When you execute a query, it goes through several steps before the result of the query is back at the application or client. Each step takes time and may itself be a complex operation consisting of several subparts.

A simplified overview of the query lifecycle can be seen in Figure 1-2. In practice, there are more steps involved, and if you install plugins such as the query rewriter, it will add steps of their own. The figure does however cover the basic steps, and several of the steps are covered in more detail later.

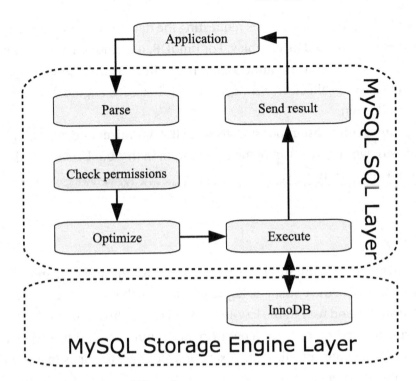

Figure 1-2. *The basic query lifecycle*

MySQL Server can be divided into two layers. There is the SQL layer which, for example, handles the connections and prepares statements for execution. The actual data is stored by storage engines which are implemented as plugins which makes it relatively easy to implement different ways to handle data. The main storage engine – and the only one that will be considered in this book – is InnoDB which is fully transactional and has very good support for high-concurrency workloads. An example of another storage engine is NDBCluster which is also transactional and is used as part of MySQL NDB Cluster.

When the application needs to execute a query, then the first thing is to create a connection (this is not included in the figure as the connection may be reused to execute more queries). When the query arrives, MySQL parses it. This includes splitting the query into tokens, so the query type is known, and there is a list of the tables and columns required by the query. This list is needed during the next step where it is checked whether the user has the necessary permissions to execute the query.

At this time, the query has reached the important step of determining how to execute the query. This is the job of the optimizer and involves rewriting the query as well as determining the order to access the tables and which indexes to use.

The actual execution step includes requesting the data from the storage engine layer. The storage engine may itself be complex. For InnoDB, it includes a buffer pool used to cache data and indexes, redo and undo logs, other buffers, as well as tablespace files. If the query returns rows, these are sent back from the storage engine through the SQL layer to the application.

In query tuning, the most important steps are the optimizer and execution steps including the storage engine. Most of the information in this book relates to these three parts either directly or indirectly.

Summary

This chapter has scratched the surface of performance tuning and prepared you for the journey of the rest of the book. The key takeaways are that you need to consider the whole stack from the end user to the low-level details of the host and operating system and monitoring is an absolute must in performance tuning. Executing a query includes several steps, of which the optimizer and execution steps are the ones that you will learn the most about in this book.

The next chapter will look closer at a methodology that is useful for solving performance issues.

CHAPTER 2

Query Tuning Methodology

There are several approaches to solve problems. At an extreme, you can dive headfirst and try making some changes. While this can seem like a time-saver, more often than not, it just causes frustration, and even when the changes appear to work, you do not know for sure whether you really solved the underlying issue or the issue just temporarily got better.

Instead, the recommendation is to work methodologically by going through analysis and using monitoring to confirm the effect of the changes. This chapter will introduce you to a methodology that can be useful when solving MySQL problems with the focus on performance tuning. The steps in the methodology are first introduced. Then the rest of the chapter discusses each step in more detail as well as why it is important to spend as much time as possible to work proactively.

Note The methodology described here is based on the methodology used in Oracle support to solve the problems reported by customers.

Overview

MySQL performance tuning can be seen as a never-ending process where an iterative approach is used to gradually improve the performance over time. Obviously, there will be times when there is a specific problem like a query taking half an hour to complete, but it is important to keep in mind that performance is not a binary state, so it is necessary to know what good enough performance is. Otherwise, you will never complete even a single task.

© Jesper Wisborg Krogh 2020
J. W. Krogh, *MySQL 8 Query Performance Tuning*, https://doi.org/10.1007/978-1-4842-5584-1_2

Figure 2-1 shows an example of how the performance tuning lifecycle can be described. The cycle starts in the upper left corner and consists of four phases, of which the first is to verify the problem.

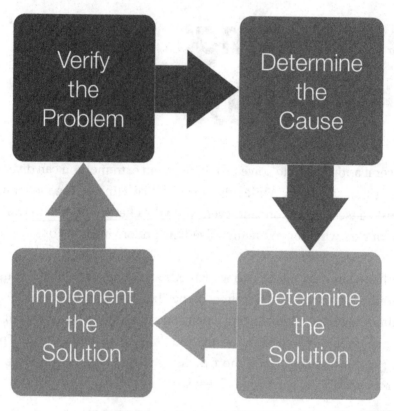

Figure 2-1. *Performance tuning lifecycle*

When you encounter a performance problem, the first phase is to verify what the problem is including collecting evidence of the issue and define what the requirement is to consider the problem solved.

The second phase involves determining the cause of the performance issue, and in the third phase you determine the solution. Finally, in the fourth phase you implement the solution. The implementation of the solution should include verifying the effect of the changes.

Tip   This cycle works both when doing firefighting during a crisis and when working proactively.

You are then ready to start all over, either doing a second iteration to improve the performance further for the problem you have just been looking at, or you may need to work on a second problem. It may also be that there will be a lengthy period between the cycles.

Verify the Problem

Before you try to determine what causes the problem and what the solution is, it is important that you are clear about what problem you are trying to solve. It is not enough to say "MySQL is slow" – what does that mean? A specific problem may be that "The query used in the second section of the front web page takes five seconds" or that "MySQL can only sustain 5000 transactions per second." The more specific you are, the better chance you have solving the problem.

The definition of the problem should also include verifying what the problem is. There can be a difference between what the problem seems to be at first and what the real problem is. Verifying the problem may be as simple as executing a query and observing if the query really takes as long as claimed, or it may involve reviewing your monitoring.

The preparation work should also include collecting a baseline from your monitoring or running a data collection that illustrates the problem. Without the baseline, you may not be able to prove that you have solved the issue at the end of the troubleshooting.

Finally, you need to decide what the goal of the performance tuning is. To quote *The 7 Habits of Highly Effective People* by Stephen R. Covey

Begin with the end in mind.

What is the minimum acceptable target for how quickly the slow query should run, or what is the minimum transaction throughput needed? This will ensure that you know whether the target has been reached when you have made your changes.

When the problem has been clearly defined and verified, you can start analyzing the issue and determine the cause.

Determine the Cause

The second phase is where you determine what the cause of the poor performance is. Make sure you are open-minded and consider the whole stack, so you do not end up staring yourself blind on one aspect that turns out not to have anything to do with the problem.

When you think you know the cause, you also need to argue why that is the cause. You may have an output of the EXPLAIN statement clearly showing that the query performs a full table scan, so that is likely the cause, or you may have a graph showing that the InnoDB redo log was 75% full, so you likely had an asynchronous flush causing temporary performance issues.

Finding the cause is often the hardest part of an investigation. Once the cause is known, you can decide on a solution.

Determine the Solution

It is a two-step process to determine the solution for the issue you investigate. The first step is to find possible solutions; second, you must choose which one to implement.

When you look for possible solutions, it can be useful to do a brainstorm where you write down all the ideas you can think of. It is important that you do not constrain yourself to just consider a narrow area around where the root cause is as often it may be possible to find a solution in a different area. An example are the stalls due to memory fragmentation mentioned in the previous chapter where the solution was to change the configuration of MySQL to use direct I/O to reduce the use of the operating system I/O cache. You should also keep both short-term workarounds and long-term solutions in mind as it may not always be possible to implement the full solution right away, if it requires restarting or upgrading MySQL, changing hardware, or similar.

Tip   A sometimes underappreciated solution is to upgrade MySQL or the operating system to get access to new features. However, of course you need to do careful testing to verify that your application works well with the new version with particular care whether there are any changes by the optimizer that cause poor performance for your queries.

The second part of determining the solution is to choose the candidate solution that will work the best. In order to do that, you must argue for each solution why it works and what the pros and cons are. It is important in this step to be honest with yourself and to carefully consider possible side effects.

Once you have a good understanding of all the possible solutions, you can choose which one to proceed with. You may also choose one solution as a temporary mitigation while you work on a more solid solution. In either case, the next phase is to implement the solution.

Implement the Solution

You implement the solution by a series of steps where you define the action plan, test the action plan, refine the action plan, and so forth until you finally apply the solution to your production system. It is important not to rush this process as this is the last chance to discover problems with the solution. In some cases, the testing may also show that you will need to abandon the solution and go back to the previous phase and choose a different solution. Figure 2-2 illustrates the workflow of implementing the solution.

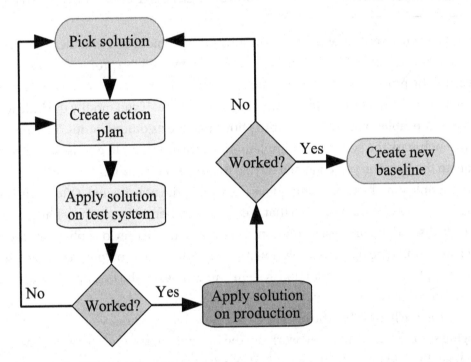

Figure 2-2. *Workflow to implement solution*

You take the solution you picked and create an action plan for it. Here it is important to be very specific, so you can ensure that the action plan you test is also the one you end up applying on your production system. It can be useful to write down the exact commands and statements that will be used, so you can copy and paste them, or to collect them in a script, so they can be applied automatically.

You then need to test the action plan on a test system. It is important that it reflects production as closely as possible. The data you have on the test system must be representative of your production data. One way to achieve this is to copy the production data, optionally using data masking to avoid copying sensitive information such as personal details and credit card information out of your production system.

Tip   The MySQL Enterprise Edition subscription (paid subscription) includes a data masking feature: `www.mysql.com/products/enterprise/masking.html`.

The test should verify that the solution solves the problem and that there are no unexpected side effects. What testing is required depends on the problem you are trying to solve and the proposed solution. If you have a slow query, it involves testing the performance of the query after implementing the solution. If you modify the indexes on one or more tables, you must also verify how that affects other queries. You may also need to benchmark the system after implementing the solution. In all cases, you need to compare to the baseline you collected during the issue verification.

It is possible that the first attempt does not work quite as expected. Often, it is just some refinements of the action plan that are needed, other times you may have to completely discard the proposed solution and go back to the previous phase and pick another solution. If the proposed solution partially solves the problem, you may also choose to apply that to the production system and go back to the beginning and evaluate how you can continue to improve the performance.

When you are happy that the testing shows the solution works, you can apply it to the staging system and, if all is still working, the production system. Once you have done that, you again need to verify that it worked. No matter how careful you are at setting up a test system that represents the production system, it is possible that for one reason or another, the solution does not completely work as expected on production. One possibility that the author of this book has encountered is that the index statistics that are random in nature were different, so an ANALYZE TABLE statement to update the index statistics was necessary when applying the solution on the production system.

If the solution works, you should collect a new baseline that you can use for future monitoring and optimizations. If the solution turns out not to work, you need to decide how to proceed by either rolling back the changes and looking for a new solution or doing a new round of troubleshooting and determining why the solution did not work and applying a second solution.

Work Proactively

Performance tuning is a never-ending process. If you have a fundamentally healthy system, most of the work will be proactively where you work at preventing emergencies and where the urgency is relatively low. This will not bring a lot of attention to your job, but it will make your daily life less stressful and the users will be happier.

Note   This discussion is to some degree based on the habit 3 "Put first things first" in Stephen R. Covey's *The 7 Habits of Highly Effective People*.

Figure 2-3 shows how you can categorize your tasks into how urgent and how important they are. Urgent tasks typically have the attention of other people, whereas other tasks may be important, but they will only become visible if they are not done in a timely matter, so they suddenly become urgent.

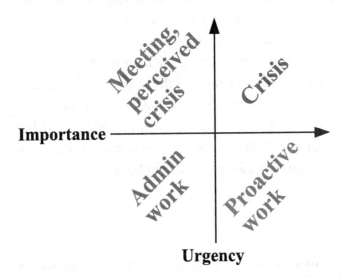

Figure 2-3. *Categorizing tasks according to urgency and importance*

The tasks that are simplest to categorize are those that are related to a crisis such as the production system is down and the company loses revenue, because the customers cannot use the product or make purchases. These tasks are both urgent and important. Spending a lot of time on these tasks may make you feel important, but it is also a very stressful way to work.

The most effective way to work with performance problems is to work on important but not urgent problems. This is the proactive work that prevents crisis from happening and consists of monitoring, making improvements before the problems become visible, and so forth. An important task in this category is also to prepare, so you are ready to handle a crisis. This may, for example, be to set up a standby system that you can fail over to in cases of a crisis or procedures to quickly spin up a replacement instance. This can help reduce the duration of a crisis and bring it back into the important but not so urgent category. The more time you spend working on tasks in this category, typically the more successful you are.

The last two categories include the not so important tasks. Examples of urgent but not important tasks include meetings you cannot reschedule, tasks pushed by other people, and a perceived (but not real) crisis. Nonurgent and non-important tasks include administrative tasks and checking emails. Of course, some of these tasks may be required and important for you to keep your job, but they are not important to keep MySQL performing well. While there will always be tasks in these categories that must be handled, it is important to minimize the time spent here.

Part of avoiding working on non-important tasks includes that you understand how important a task is, for example, by defining when the performance is good enough, so you do not end up overoptimizing a query or the throughput. In practice, it can of course be difficult to push back on non-important tasks if they have the attention of other people in the organization (these often tend to be the urgent tasks), but it is important that you do try as much as possible to shift the work back to the important but not urgent tasks to avoid the crisis tasks to take over at a later time.

Summary

This chapter has discussed a methodology that can be used to solve MySQL performance problems (and other types of problems!) as well as the importance of working proactively.

When a problem is reported, you start out verifying what the problem is and determine what is considered to have solved it. For performance problems that are open-ended by nature, it is important to know what is good enough, or you will risk never to stop performing crisis management and go back to proactive work.

Once you have a clear problem description, you can work on determining the cause; and once the cause is clear, you can determine what you want to do to solve the problem. The last phase is to implement the solution which may require you to revisit the potential solutions, if it turns out that the solution you first chose does not work or have unacceptable side effects. In that connection, it is important to test the solution in as realistic a setup as possible.

The last part of the chapter discussed the importance of spending as much time as possible doing proactive work that prevents a crisis from occurring and that helps you be prepared when a crisis does occur. This will help you have a less stressful job and manage a database in better health.

As this chapter has discussed, it is important to test the impact of your solution before you deploy it to your production system. The next chapter covers benchmarking with focus on the Sysbench benchmark.

## CHAPTER 3

Benchmarking with Sysbench

It is very important to verify the impact of changes before you apply them to your production systems. This applies to both small changes like modifying a query and large changes such as refactoring the application and schema as well as MySQL upgrades. You may think that the optimal performance test is based on your production schema and data using the same queries that the application executes. However, it is not always as simple as it sounds to recreate the right workload, so sometimes it is necessary to use standard benchmark suites.

This chapter starts out with some best practices when executing benchmarks and an overview of some of the most common benchmarks and tools used with MySQL. Then Sysbench which is the most commonly used benchmark will be considered in more detail.

Best Practices

It is easy to install a benchmark program and execute it. The difficult part is to use it right. Performing MySQL benchmark tests shares some of the concepts of performance tuning, and the first and most important point is that you need to work in an "informed way." This means that you must know your tools well and clearly define the goal and success criteria of the tests. For your tools, you need to know how to use them correctly as executing them with default parameters likely will not produce the test that you want.

This is tied together with the goal of the benchmark. What is it you need to determine? For example, you may want to verify the effect of changing some configuration variable in which case you must make sure your tests are set up, so that area is tested. Consider an option such as `innodb_io_capacity` which influences how fast InnoDB writes. If your benchmark is a read-only test, changing `innodb_io_capacity`

19

will not make any difference. In this context, you also need to make sure that you only change one thing at a time and only make relatively small changes – just as you should do when making changes to your production system. Otherwise, if you change several settings at the same time, then some may contribute positively to the result and others negatively, but you have no way to determine which changes to keep and which to revert. If you make large changes, you may overshoot the optimal value, so you end up discarding that change even though there is room for improvements.

When reading the results at the end of the test, you need to understand what the benchmark measures; otherwise, the result is just a meaningless number. This also includes defining which variables to adjust during the tests, and as for performance tuning in general, it is important to keep the number of variables limited, so you easily can identify the effect of each variable. For a result to be valid, you must also ensure that the test is repeatable, that is, if you execute the same test twice, then you get the same result. One requirement for a test to be repeatable is that you have a well-defined starting state of the system.

Tip   Do not assume that one client is enough to generate the load you are aiming at. How many clients are required depends on the number of concurrent queries and the benchmark you are executing.

That leads to the next important point. Your benchmarks should reflect the workload of the application. It does not help you have used an online transaction processing (OLTP) benchmark to prove that your configuration changes work great, if your application has an online analytical processing (OLAP) workload, or that you have a great read-only performance if your application is write-heavy.

You may think that the optimal way to design a benchmark is to capture all queries executed in production and replay them as the benchmark. This definitely has some merits, but there are also challenges. It is expensive to collect all queries executed, though if you already have the MySQL Enterprise Audit log enabled for auditing purposes, that can be used. There may also be data privacy problems of copying the production data to the test system. Finally, it is difficult to scale the test to change the size of the data set (whether down to make it more manageable or up to test growth) or to increase the test workload compared to the current production load. For these reasons, it is often necessary to use artificial benchmarks.

Tip   You can use the MySQL Enterprise Audit log (requires subscription) or the general query log (very high overhead) to capture all queries for a period. This includes timestamps when the queries were executed, so you can use the log to replay the queries in the same order with the same concurrency. It does however require that you create a script yourself to extract the queries and execute them.

The next point is about the benchmark results which also relates to the previous points. When you have the result of a benchmark, it is important to understand what the result means and that you do not discard results just because they look wrong. As such, a benchmark result is "never wrong"; it is the result of some work. If the result is unexpected, it is important to understand why it ended up that way. Maybe, you did not use the parameters you intended or used a different table size than expected, but it may also be that something else interfered with the benchmark, or something third. If something interfered with the benchmark, is it something that could also happen in production? If it can, then the benchmark is very much relevant, and you need to decide how you will handle such a case in production.

To understand what happened during a benchmark, it is also important that you monitor MySQL and the host system. One option is to use the same monitoring solution as that you use for your production system. However, benchmarks on a test or development system are a bit different than a production system as you are typically interested in higher-frequency sampling but for a shorter duration during a benchmark, so it can be useful using a dedicated monitoring solution specifically for benchmarks. One such option is dim_STAT (`http://dimitrik.free.fr/`) developed by Dimitri Kravtchuk who is a performance architect for MySQL and who is behind many of the MySQL Server benchmarks.

In general, understanding the result is not a simple thing. One thing you also need to be aware of is what happens during a benchmark if there is a temporary stall. Does the benchmark hold back on subsequent queries, or does it keep submitting queries? If it holds back, then the subsequent queries will effectively be faster than they should be as in the real world as users do not stop submitting requests just because there is a backlog.

Finally, a benchmark typically produces several metrics, so you need to analyze the result as it makes most relevance for your system. For example, is the latency or throughput the most important? Or do you have requirements to both? Or are you more interested in some third metric?

Standard TPC Benchmarks

There is an almost endless list of benchmarks, but in the end the ones that are commonly used boils down to a handful of tests. This does not mean that you should not consider other benchmarks; in the end the important thing is that the benchmark works for your requirements.

The most commonly used standard benchmarks are defined by TPC (`www.tpc.org/`) with new benchmarks being designed as the hardware and software changes making older benchmarks too simple. The TPC web site includes detailed descriptions and specifications of the benchmarks. Table 3-1 summarizes the current enterprise TPC benchmarks.

Table 3-1. *Common TPC benchmarks*

Name	Type	Description
TPC-C	OLTP	This is maybe the most classic of the TPC benchmarks and dates back to 1992. It simulates the queries of a wholesale supplier and uses nine tables.
TPC-DI	Data Integration	Tests extract, transform, and load (ETL) workloads.
TPC-DS	Decision Support	This benchmark includes complex queries of a data warehouse (star schema).
TPC-E	OLTP	This is meant as a replacement for TPC-C with a more complex schema and queries, so it is more realistic for modern databases. It includes 33 tables.
TPC-H	Decision Support	This is another classic benchmark which is often used to test optimizer features. It consists of 22 complex queries meant to simulate the reporting side of an OLTP database.
TPC-VMS	Virtualization	This uses the TPC-C, TPC-DS, TPS-E, and TPC-H benchmarks to determine performance metrics for virtualized databases.

The advantages of these standard benchmarks are that you are more likely to find tools implementing them and you can compare with results obtained by other people.

> **Tip** If you want to learn more about the TPC benchmarks as well as how to perform database benchmarks the best way, consider the book by Bert Scalzo: *Database Benchmarking and Stress Testing* (Apress), www.apress.com/gp/book/9781484240076.

In the same way as there are standard benchmarks, there are also some common benchmark tools.

Common Benchmarks Tools

Implementing a benchmark is far from trivial, so in most cases it is preferred to use a preexisting benchmark tool that can execute the benchmark for you. Some tools are cross-platform and/or can use several different database systems, whereas others are more specific. You should choose the one that implements the benchmarks you need and work on the platform that you have your production system on.

Table 3-2 summarizes some of the most commonly used benchmark tools to test the performance of MySQL.

Table 3-2. *Common benchmarks used with MySQL*

Benchmark	Description
Sysbench	This is the most commonly used benchmark and the one that will be covered most in this chapter. It has built-in tests for OLTP workloads, non-database tests (such as pure I/O, CPU, and memory tests), and more. Additionally, the latest versions support custom workloads. It is open source and is mostly used on Linux. It can be downloaded from https://github.com/akopytov/sysbench.
DBT2	DBT2 can be used to emulate OLTP workloads using an order system (TPC-C). DBT2 can also be used to automate Sysbench and is available from https://dev.mysql.com/downloads/benchmarks.html.
DBT3	DBT3 implements the TPC-H benchmark and is used to test the performance of complex queries. It is one of the favorite tests used by the MySQL optimizer developers to verify the performance after implementing new optimizer features. A copy of DBT3 is available from https://sourceforge.net/projects/osdldbt/.

(continued)

Table 3-2. (*continued*)

Benchmark	Description
HammerDB	The HammerDB tool is a free cross-database tool with support for both Microsoft Windows and Linux. It has support for the TPC-C and TPC-H benchmarks and is available from `https://hammerdb.com/`.
Database Factory	Database Factory is a powerful benchmark tool for Microsoft Windows that supports several databases and benchmarks. It supports the TPC-H, TPC-C, TPC-D, and TPC-E benchmarks and more. It is a commercial product (free trial available): `www.quest.com/products/benchmark-factory/`.
iiBench	iiBench is testing how fast you can insert data into the database and thus is useful if you regularly need to ingest large amount of data. It can be downloaded from `https://github.com/tmcallaghan/iibench-mysql`.
DVD Store Version 3	The DVD Store combines data for a sample DVD store with a benchmark. It can generate data for any given size with standard sizes being 10 MB, 1 GB, and 100 GB. It is also useful as general test data and can be downloaded from `https://github.com/dvdstore/ds3`. It is based on the older Dell DVD Store Database Test Suite.
`mysqlslap`	The `mysqlslap` tool is special as it is included with the MySQL installation. It can be used to generate a concurrent workload against a table of your choice. It is a very simple tool, so it cannot be used for too many purposes, but it is easy to use. The manual page for `mysqlslap` can be found at `https://dev.mysql.com/doc/refman/en/mysqlslap.html`.

The tool that is most commonly used with MySQL is Sysbench, and the remainder of this chapter covers its installation and example usages.

Sysbench Installation

Since Sysbench is an open source tool, there are several forks available. MySQL maintains one of these forks; however, to get the version with the most recent features, it is recommended to use the fork by Alexey Kopytov. (This is also the fork recommended by MySQL performance architect Dimitri Kravtchuk.) The examples in this chapter all use Kopytov's fork version 1.0.17 (but note the version listed on outputs is 1.1.0), but the examples will be similar for other Sysbench forks as long as the fork is new enough to include the features demonstrated.

There is support for installing Sysbench using native Linux packages, from Homebrew on macOS, or to compile it yourself. While installing using native packages is simpler, it is in general better to compile yourself as it ensures you compile against the MySQL 8 development libraries, and you can compile Sysbench on more platforms than where there are packages available.

Tip   For details about all the installation instructions, including required dependencies and using native packages, see `https://github.com/akopytov/sysbench`. Support for Microsoft Windows has been dropped in Sysbench 1.0. It is currently unknown whether support will be reintroduced. If you are using Microsoft Windows, the recommendation is to install Sysbench through Windows Subsystem for Linux (WSL) (`https://msdn.microsoft.com/en-us/commandline/wsl/about`) in which case the instruction in this chapter should work with minor modifications (depending on the Linux distribution you choose). An alternative is to use a virtual machine, for example, in VirtualBox.

Compiling software may not be very common any longer, but fortunately it is straightforward to compile Sysbench. You will need to download the source code and then configure the build, compile it, and finally install it.

There are some tools you will need to install before you can compile Sysbench. The exact tools required depend on your operating system. See the installation instructions on the project's GitHub page for details. For example, on Oracle Linux 7:

```
shell$ sudo yum install make automake libtool \
                    pkgconfig libaio-devel \
                    openssl-devel
```

You will also need to have the MySQL 8 development libraries installed. The easiest way to do this on Linux is to install the MySQL repository for your Linux distribution from `https://dev.mysql.com/downloads/`. Listing 3-1 shows an example of installing the MySQL 8 development libraries on Oracle Linux 7.

Listing 3-1. Installing the MySQL 8 development libraries

```
shell$ wget https://dev.mysql.com/get/mysql80-community-release-el7-3.
noarch.rpm
...
Saving to: 'mysql80-community-release-el7-3.noarch.rpm'

100%[=================>] 26,024        --.-K/s    in 0.006s

2019-10-12 14:21:18 (4.37 MB/s) - 'mysql80-community-release-el7-3.noarch.
rpm' saved [26024/26024]

shell$ sudo yum install mysql80-community-release-el7-3.noarch.rpm
Loaded plugins: langpacks, ulninfo
Examining mysql80-community-release-el7-3.noarch.rpm: mysql80-community-
release-el7-3.noarch
Marking mysql80-community-release-el7-3.noarch.rpm to be installed
Resolving Dependencies
--> Running transaction check
---> Package mysql80-community-release.noarch 0:el7-3 will be installed
--> Finished Dependency Resolution

Dependencies Resolved

================================================================
 Package
   Arch    Version
           Repository                              Size
================================================================
Installing:
 mysql80-community-release
    noarch el7-3
            /mysql80-community-release-el7-3.noarch  31 k

Transaction Summary
================================================================
Install  1 Package

Total size: 31 k
```

```
Installed size: 31 k
Is this ok [y/d/N]: y
Downloading packages:
Running transaction check
Running transaction test
Transaction test succeeded
Running transaction
  Installing : mysql80-community-release-el7-3.noarc    1/1
  Verifying  : mysql80-community-release-el7-3.noarc    1/1

Installed:
  mysql80-community-release.noarch 0:el7-3

Complete!

shell$ sudo yum install mysql-devel
...
Dependencies Resolved

================================================================
 Package         Arch    Version       Repository        Size
================================================================
Installing:
 mysql-community-client
         x86_64 8.0.17-1.el7 mysql80-community  32 M
     replacing  mariadb.x86_64 1:5.5.64-1.el7
 mysql-community-devel
         x86_64 8.0.17-1.el7 mysql80-community 5.5 M
 mysql-community-libs
         x86_64 8.0.17-1.el7 mysql80-community 3.0 M
     replacing  mariadb-libs.x86_64 1:5.5.64-1.el7
 mysql-community-libs-compat
         x86_64 8.0.17-1.el7 mysql80-community 2.1 M
     replacing  mariadb-libs.x86_64 1:5.5.64-1.el7
 mysql-community-server
         x86_64 8.0.17-1.el7 mysql80-community 415 M
     replacing  mariadb-server.x86_64 1:5.5.64-1.el7
```

```
Installing for dependencies:
 mysql-community-common
         x86_64 8.0.17-1.el7 mysql80-community 589 k

Transaction Summary
============================================================
Install  5 Packages (+1 Dependent package)

Total download size: 459 M
...

Complete!
```

The output depends on what you have already installed. Notice how several other MySQL packages, including mysql-community-server, are pulled in as dependencies. This is because the mysql-community-devel package in this case replaces another preexisting package which triggers a chain of dependency updates.

Note   If you have an older version of MySQL or a fork installed, all related packages will be upgraded. For this reason, it is best to compile Sysbench on a host where you can freely replace packages or the correct MySQL 8 development libraries are already installed.

You are now ready to consider Sysbench itself. You can choose to either clone the GitHub repository or download the source as a ZIP file. To clone the repository, you need to have git installed and then use the git clone command:

```
shell$ git clone https://github.com/akopytov/sysbench.git
Cloning into 'sysbench'...
remote: Enumerating objects: 14, done.
remote: Counting objects: 100% (14/14), done.
remote: Compressing objects: 100% (12/12), done.
remote: Total 9740 (delta 4), reused 5 (delta 2), pack-reused 9726
Receiving objects: 100% (9740/9740), 4.12 MiB | 2.12 MiB/s, done.
Resolving deltas: 100% (6958/6958), done.
```

The ZIP file with the source code can be downloaded from the GitHub repository, for example, using wget:

```
shell$ wget https://github.com/akopytov/sysbench/archive/master.zip
...
Connecting to codeload.github.com (codeload.github.
com)|52.63.100.255|:443... connected.
HTTP request sent, awaiting response... 200 OK
Length: unspecified [application/zip]
Saving to: 'master.zip'

    [ <=>                       ] 2,282,636   3.48MB/s   in 0.6s

2019-10-12 16:01:33 (3.48 MB/s) - 'master.zip' saved [2282636]
```

Alternatively, you can download the ZIP file using your browser as shown in Figure 3-1.

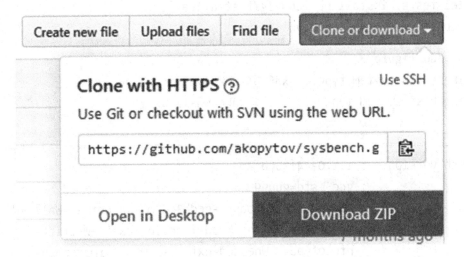

Figure 3-1. *Downloading the Sysbench source code from GitHub in a browser*

Click *Download ZIP* and the file will download. Once the source code is downloaded, unzip it.

You are now ready to configure the compilation. Enter the top-level directory with the source code. The directory listing should look similar to the following output:

```
shell$ ls
autogen.sh    COPYING       Makefile.am      rpm       tests
ChangeLog     debian        missing          scripts   third_party
config        install-sh    mkinstalldirs    snap
configure.ac  m4            README.md        src
```

The configuration is done using the autogen.sh script followed by the configure command as shown in Listing 3-2.

Listing 3-2. Configuring Sysbench for compilation and installation

```
shell$ ./autogen.sh
autoreconf: Entering directory `.'
...
parallel-tests: installing 'config/test-driver'
autoreconf: Leaving directory `.'

shell$ ./configure
checking build system type... x86_64-unknown-linux-gnu
checking host system type... x86_64-unknown-linux-gnu
...

==============================================================================
sysbench version  : 1.1.0-74f3b6b
CC                : gcc -std=gnu99
CFLAGS            : -O3 -funroll-loops -ggdb3  -march=core2 -Wall -Wextra
                    -Wpointer-arith -Wbad-function-cast -Wstrict-
                    prototypes -Wnested-externs -Wno-format-zero-length
                    -Wundef -Wstrict-prototypes -Wmissing-prototypes
                    -Wmissing-declarations -Wredundant-decls -Wcast-align
                    -Wvla   -pthread
CPPFLAGS          : -D_GNU_SOURCE   -I$(top_srcdir)/src -I$(abs_top_
                    builddir)/third_party/luajit/inc -I$(abs_top_
                    builddir)/third_party/concurrency_kit/include
LDFLAGS           : -L/usr/local/lib
LIBS              : -laio -lm
```

```
prefix                 : /usr/local
bindir                 : ${prefix}/bin
libexecdir             : ${prefix}/libexec
mandir                 : ${prefix}/share/man
datadir                : ${prefix}/share

MySQL support          : yes
PostgreSQL support     : no

LuaJIT                 : bundled
LUAJIT_CFLAGS          : -I$(abs_top_builddir)/third_party/luajit/inc
LUAJIT_LIBS            : $(abs_top_builddir)/third_party/luajit/lib/libluajit-
                         5.1.a -ldl
LUAJIT_LDFLAGS         : -rdynamic

Concurrency Kit        : bundled
CK_CFLAGS              : -I$(abs_top_builddir)/third_party/concurrency_kit/
                         include
CK_LIBS                : $(abs_top_builddir)/third_party/concurrency_kit/lib/
                         libck.a
configure flags        :
============================================================================
```

The end of the configuration shows the options that will be used for the compilation. Make sure that MySQL support says yes. The default is to install in /usr/local. You can change that using the --prefix option when executing configure, for example, ./configure --prefix=/home/myuser/sysbench.

The next step is to compile the code which is done using the make command:

```
shell$ make -j
Making all in third_party/luajit
...
make[1]: Nothing to be done for `all-am'.
make[1]: Leaving directory `/home/myuser/git/sysbench'
```

The -j option tells make to compile the source in parallel which can reduce the compilation time. However, Sysbench is in all cases quick to compile, so it is not of great importance in this case.

The final step is to install the compiled version of Sysbench:

```
shell$ sudo make install
Making install in third_party/luajit
...
make[2]: Leaving directory `/home/myuser/git/sysbench'
make[1]: Leaving directory `/home/myuser/git/sysbench'
```

That is it. You are now ready to use Sysbench to perform benchmark.

Executing Benchmarks

Sysbench includes several benchmarks that are ready to use. This ranges from non-database built-in tests to various database tests. The non-database tests are considered built-in as they are defined within the Sysbench source code itself. The other tests are defined in Lua scripts and are installed in the /usr/local/share/sysbench/ directory (assuming you installed into the default location).

Note   This and the next section assume you have a MySQL instance available for testing on the same host as where you have installed Sysbench. If that is not the case, you need to adjust the hostnames as necessary.

You can get general help to understand the Sysbench arguments by invoking sysbench with the --help argument:

```
shell$ sysbench –help
...
Compiled-in tests:
  fileio - File I/O test
  cpu - CPU performance test
  memory - Memory functions speed test
  threads - Threads subsystem performance test
  mutex - Mutex performance test

See 'sysbench <testname> help' for a list of options for each test.
```

At the bottom of the output is a list of the built-in tests and a hint on how to get more information about a given test. You can get a list of the additional tests by listing the files in the shared directory:

```
shell$ ls /usr/local/share/sysbench/
bulk_insert.lua          oltp_update_index.lua
oltp_common.lua          oltp_update_non_index.lua
oltp_delete.lua          oltp_write_only.lua
oltp_insert.lua          select_random_points.lua
oltp_point_select.lua    select_random_ranges.lua
oltp_read_only.lua       tests
oltp_read_write.lua
```

The files with the .lua extension except oltp_common.lua (shared code for the OLTP tests) are the tests available. The Lua language[1] is a lightweight programming language that is often used for embedding code into programs. Working with Lua programs is similar to working with scripting languages such as Python except your code gets executed through another program (Sysbench in this case).

As mentioned, you can get additional help about the tests by providing the name of the test and the help command. For example, to get additional information about the test defined in oltp_read_only.lua, you can use the help command as shown in Listing 3-3.

Listing 3-3. Obtaining help for the oltp_read_only test

```
shell$ sysbench oltp_read_only help
sysbench 1.1.0-74f3b6b (using bundled LuaJIT 2.1.0-beta3)

oltp_read_only options:
  --auto_inc[=on|off]            Use AUTO_INCREMENT column as Primary Key
                                 (for MySQL), or its alternatives in other
                                 DBMS. When disabled, use client-generated
                                 IDs [on]
  --create_secondary[=on|off]    Create a secondary index in addition to the
                                 PRIMARY KEY [on]
  --create_table_options=STRING Extra CREATE TABLE options []
```

---

[1]www.lua.org/ and https://en.wikipedia.org/wiki/Lua_(programming_language)

--delete_inserts=N	Number of DELETE/INSERT combinations per transaction [1]
--distinct_ranges=N	Number of SELECT DISTINCT queries per transaction [1]
--index_updates=N	Number of UPDATE index queries per transaction [1]
--mysql_storage_engine=STRING	Storage engine, if MySQL is used [innodb]
--non_index_updates=N	Number of UPDATE non-index queries per transaction [1]
--order_ranges=N	Number of SELECT ORDER BY queries per transaction [1]
--pgsql_variant=STRING	Use this PostgreSQL variant when running with the PostgreSQL driver. The only currently supported variant is 'redshift'. When enabled, create_secondary is automatically disabled, and delete_inserts is set to 0
--point_selects=N	Number of point SELECT queries per transaction [10]
--range_selects[=on|off]	Enable/disable all range SELECT queries [on]
--range_size=N	Range size for range SELECT queries [100]
--reconnect=N	Reconnect after every N events. The default (0) is to not reconnect [0]
--secondary[=on|off]	Use a secondary index in place of the PRIMARY KEY [off]
--simple_ranges=N	Number of simple range SELECT queries per transaction [1]
--skip_trx[=on|off]	Don't start explicit transactions and execute all queries in the AUTOCOMMIT mode [off]
--sum_ranges=N	Number of SELECT SUM() queries per transaction [1]
--table_size=N	Number of rows per table [10000]
--tables=N	Number of tables [1]

The values in square brackets are the default values.

The help command is just one of several commands available (some tests may not implement all of the commands). The other commands cover the phases of a benchmark test:

- **prepare:** Executes the steps required to set up the test, for example, by creating and populating the tables needed by the test.

- **warmup:** Ensures the buffers and caches are warm, for example, that table data and indexes have been loaded into the InnoDB buffer pool. This is special for the OLTP benchmarks.

- **run:** Executes the test itself. This command is provided by all tests.

- **cleanup:** Removes any tables used by the test.

As an example, consider the read-only OLTP test that you retrieved the help for before. First, create a MySQL user that can execute the required queries. The default is to use the sbtest schema for the benchmark, so a simple solution is to create a user with all privileges on this schema:

```
mysql> CREATE USER sbtest@localhost IDENTIFIED BY 'password';
Query OK, 0 rows affected (0.02 sec)

mysql> GRANT ALL ON sbtest.* TO sbtest@localhost;
Query OK, 0 rows affected (0.01 sec)

mysql> CREATE SCHEMA sbtest;
Query OK, 1 row affected (0.01 sec)
```

In this case, the user is expected to connect from localhost. In general, that will not be the case, so you need to change the hostname part of the account to reflect where the Sysbench user is connecting from. The username was chosen as sbtest as that is the default used by Sysbench. The sbtest schema is also created as the Sysbench tests require it to exist when first connecting.

Note   It is strongly recommended to choose a strong password for the account.

If you want to execute a benchmark that uses four tables each with 20000 rows, then you can prepare that test like it is shown in Listing 3-4.

Listing 3-4. Preparing the test

```
shell$ sysbench oltp_read_only \
        --mysql-host=127.0.0.1 \
        --mysql-port=3306 \
        --mysql-user=sbtest \
        --mysql-password=password \
        --mysql-ssl=REQUIRED \
        --mysql-db=sbtest \
        --table_size=20000 \
        --tables=4 \
        --threads=4 \
        prepare
sysbench 1.1.0-74f3b6b (using bundled LuaJIT 2.1.0-beta3)

Initializing worker threads...

Creating table 'sbtest1'...
Creating table 'sbtest3'...
Creating table 'sbtest4'...
Creating table 'sbtest2'...
Inserting 20000 records into 'sbtest2'
Inserting 20000 records into 'sbtest3'
Inserting 20000 records into 'sbtest1'
Inserting 20000 records into 'sbtest4'
Creating a secondary index on 'sbtest3'...
Creating a secondary index on 'sbtest2'...
Creating a secondary index on 'sbtest4'...
Creating a secondary index on 'sbtest1'...
```

This creates the four tables as sbtest1, sbtest2, sbtest3, and sbtest4 using four threads. The prepare step will be quick in this case as the tables are small; however, if you perform benchmarks using large tables, it can take a significant amount of time to set up the test. As benchmark testing typically involves executing a range of tests, you can speed up the testing by creating a binary backup (copying the tables, either with MySQL shut down or using a tool such as MySQL Enterprise Backup) or a file system snapshot. For each subsequent test, you can restore the backup instead of recreating the tables.

Optionally, you can as the next step go through a warmup phase as shown in Listing 3-5.

Listing 3-5. Warming MySQL up for the test

```
shell$ sysbench oltp_read_only \
        --mysql-host=127.0.0.1 \
        --mysql-port=3306 \
        --mysql-user=sbtest \
        --mysql-password=password \
        --mysql-ssl=REQUIRED \
        --mysql-db=sbtest \
        --table_size=20000 \
        --tables=4 \
        --threads=4 \
        warmup
sysbench 1.1.0-74f3b6b (using bundled LuaJIT 2.1.0-beta3)

Initializing worker threads...

Preloading table sbtest3
Preloading table sbtest1
Preloading table sbtest2
Preloading table sbtest4
```

Here it is important that you include the `--tables` and `--table-size` options as otherwise only the default number of rows (10,000) of the `sbtest1` table will be preloaded. The preloading consists of averaging the `id` column and a simple `SELECT COUNT(*)` query with the rows fetched in a subquery (the queries have been reformatted):

```
SELECT AVG(id)
  FROM (SELECT *
          FROM sbtest1 FORCE KEY (PRIMARY)
          LIMIT 20000
       ) t

SELECT COUNT(*)
  FROM (SELECT *
          FROM sbtest1
          WHERE k LIKE '%0%'
          LIMIT 20000
       ) t
```

So the warmup phase may not be equivalent to running the actual benchmark for a while.

Tip   You can also use the `--warmup-time=N` option when executing the benchmark to disable statistics for the first N seconds.

The benchmark itself is executing using the run command. There are two options to specify the duration of the test:

- **`--events=N`:** The maximum number of events to execute. The default is 0.

- **`--time=N`:** The maximum duration in seconds. The default is 10.

When the value is 0 for one of the options, it means infinite. So, if you set both `--events` and `--time` to 0, the test will run forever. This can, for example, be useful, if you are not interested in the benchmark statistics themselves but want to collect monitoring metrics or want to create a workload while performing some other task.

Tip   The author of this book uses Sysbench with both the number of events and time limits set to 0 to generate a concurrent workload for tests creating backups.

If you, for example, want to execute a test for one minute (60 seconds), you can use a command like the one in Listing 3-6.

Listing 3-6. Executing a Sysbench test for one minute

```
shell$ sysbench oltp_read_only \
        --mysql-host=127.0.0.1 \
        --mysql-port=3306 \
        --mysql-user=sbtest \
        --mysql-password=password \
        --mysql-ssl=REQUIRED \
        --mysql-db=sbtest \
        --table_size=20000 \
        --tables=4 \
```

```
      --time=60 \
      --threads=8 \
      run
sysbench 1.1.0-74f3b6b (using bundled LuaJIT 2.1.0-beta3)

Running the test with following options:
Number of threads: 8
Initializing random number generator from current time

Initializing worker threads...

Threads started!

SQL statistics:
    queries performed:
        read:                    766682
        write:                   0
        other:                   109526
        total:                   876208
    transactions:                54763  (912.52 per sec.)
    queries:                     876208 (14600.36 per sec.)
    ignored errors:              0      (0.00 per sec.)
    reconnects:                  0      (0.00 per sec.)

Throughput:
    events/s (eps):              912.5224
    time elapsed:                60.0128s
    total number of events:      54763

Latency (ms):
        min:                              3.26
        avg:                              8.76
        max:                            122.43
        95th percentile:                 11.24
        sum:                         479591.29

Threads fairness:
    events (avg/stddev):         6845.3750/70.14
    execution time (avg/stddev): 59.9489/0.00
```

Notice that unlike the prepare and warmup phases, the run command was run with eight threads. The number of threads is often one of the things that is varied in a series of tests to determine how concurrent a workload the system can sustain. It is necessary to specify the number of tables and rows that the run command should use as otherwise the default values will be used (there is no state shared between the Sysbench commands).

Once you are done with the tests, you can tell Sysbench to clean up after itself using the cleanup command as shown in Listing 3-7.

Listing 3-7. Cleaning up after a test

```
shell$ sysbench oltp_read_only \
        --mysql-host=127.0.0.1 \
        --mysql-port=3306 \
        --mysql-user=sbtest \
        --mysql-password=password \
        --mysql-ssl=REQUIRED \
        --mysql-db=sbtest \
        --tables=4 \
        cleanup
sysbench 1.1.0-74f3b6b (using bundled LuaJIT 2.1.0-beta3)

Dropping table 'sbtest1'...
Dropping table 'sbtest2'...
Dropping table 'sbtest3'...
Dropping table 'sbtest4'...
```

Notice that it is necessary to specify the number of tables; otherwise, only the first table will be dropped.

The built-in tests are great, but what makes Sysbench a really strong tool is that you can also define your own benchmarks.

Creating Custom Benchmarks

As you saw in the previous section, the database tests that are included with Sysbench are defined in Lua scripts (www.lua.org/). This means that all that you need to do to define your own tests is to create a Lua script with the definition of the test and save it in Sysbench's shared directory. One example where this can be useful is if you want to create a test based on the specific requirements of your application either to test the effect of indexes, refactoring your application, or similar.

This section will put together a small example test script, so you can see the principles of creating your own tests. The test can also be found in sequence.lua in this book's GitHub repository.

Tip A great way to learn how to write your own Sysbench Lua scripts is to study the existing ones. In addition to the example in this chapter, you can look at the Lua scripts shipped with Sysbench and another relatively simple example in https://gist.github.com/utdrmac/92d00a34149565bc155cdef80b6cba12.

Overview of the Custom Script

The example benchmark test will test the performance of a sequence implemented by having a single row per sequence in a table. Such constructs are sometimes used to implement custom sequences in applications. The table definition and an example of the use of the table is shown in Listing 3-8.

Listing 3-8. Using a custom sequence table

```
mysql> SHOW CREATE TABLE sbtest.sbtest1\G
*************************** 1. row ***************************
       Table: sbtest1
Create Table: CREATE TABLE `sbtest1` (
  `id` varchar(10) NOT NULL,
  `val` bigint(20) unsigned NOT NULL DEFAULT '0',
  PRIMARY KEY (`id`)
) ENGINE=InnoDB DEFAULT CHARSET=utf8mb4 COLLATE=utf8mb4_0900_ai_ci
1 row in set (0.00 sec)

mysql> SELECT * FROM sbtest.sbtest1;
+--------+-----+
| id     | val |
+--------+-----+
| sbkey1 |   0 |
+--------+-----+
1 row in set (0.00 sec)
```

```
mysql> UPDATE sbtest1
          SET val = LAST_INSERT_ID(val+1)
        WHERE id = 'sbkey1';
Query OK, 1 row affected (0.01 sec)
Rows matched: 1  Changed: 1  Warnings: 0

mysql> SELECT LAST_INSERT_ID();
+------------------+
| LAST_INSERT_ID() |
+------------------+
|                1 |
+------------------+
1 row in set (0.00 sec)

mysql> SELECT * FROM sbtest.sbtest1;
+--------+-----+
| id     | val |
+--------+-----+
| sbkey1 |   1 |
+--------+-----+
1 row in set (0.00 sec)
```

The LAST_INSERT_ID() function is used in the UPDATE statement to assign the session value for the last inserted id, so it can be fetched afterward in the SELECT statement.

The example test will have the following features:

- Support for the prepare, run, cleanup, and help commands.

- The prepare and run commands can be executed in parallel.

- Support for specifying the number of tables, table size, and whether explicit transactions are used.

- Validation that the number of rows per table is in the range 1–99999. The id column of the tables is created as a varchar(10), and the keys are prefixed with sbkey, so there can be at most five digits.

The functions that will be implemented are summarized in Figure 3-2.

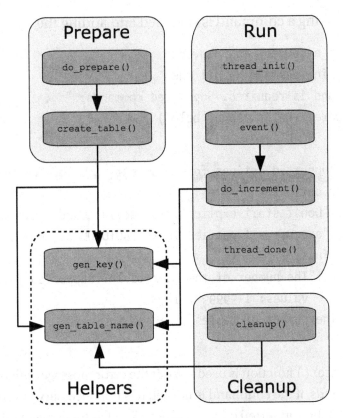

Figure 3-2. *Overview of the functions in the sequence test*

The Prepare, Run, and Cleanup groups represent commands, and the Helpers group contains the two helper functions that will be used from multiple commands. The run and help commands are special as they always exist. The help is automatically generated based on the options that the script adds, so no special consideration is required for that. There is also a little code that is outside functions, of which the first is a sanity check and the options that the script will support.

Defining the Options

The options that the script supports are configured by adding elements to the sysbench. cmdline.options hash. This is one of the built-in features of Sysbench that you can use in your scripts. Another is sysbench.cmdline.command which is the name of the command that has been provided for the execution.

Listing 3-9 shows how you can verify that the command has been set and then add the three options that this script supports.

Listing 3-9. Verifying a command is specified and adding the options

```
-- Validate that a command was provided
if sysbench.cmdline.command == nil then
    error("Command is required. Supported commands: " ..
          "prepare, run, cleanup, help")
end

-- Specify the supported options for this test
sysbench.cmdline.options = {
    skip_trx = {"Don't start explicit transactions and " ..
                "execute all queries in the AUTOCOMMIT mode",
                false},
    table_size = {"The number of rows per table. Supported " ..
                  "values: 1-99999", 1},
    tables = {"The number of tables", 1}
}
```

The built-in error() function is used to emit the error message with a list of supported commands, if the command is not set. It is not necessary to verify whether the command is one of the supported ones as Sysbench will automatically validate that.

The options are added with an array consisting of the help text and the default value. With the definitions in this script, the generated help text becomes:

```
shell$ sysbench sequence help
sysbench 1.1.0-74f3b6b (using bundled LuaJIT 2.1.0-beta3)

sequence options
  --skip_trx[=on|off] Don't start explicit transactions and execute all
    queries in the AUTOCOMMIT mode [off]
  --table_size=N      The number of rows per table. Supported values:
                      1-99999 [1]
  --tables=N          The number of tables [1]
```

The option values are made available in the sysbench.opt hash, for example, to get the number of tables in the test, you can use sysbench.opt.tables. The hash is available globally, so you do not need to do anything before you can use it.

You are now ready to implement the three commands that the script supports. Since the run command is mandatory, it is the first one that will be discussed.

The run Command

The run command is special as it is mandatory and that it always has support for parallel execution. Unlike other commands that are implemented in a single function (optionally invoking other functions), Sysbench uses three functions for the run command. The three functions that must always exist are

- **thread_init():** This is called when Sysbench initializes the script.

- **thread_done():** This is called when Sysbench is done executing the script.

- **event():** This is where the actual test is implemented and is called once per iteration.

For this example, the thread_init() function can be kept very simple:

```
-- Initialize the script
-- Initialize the global variables used in the rest of the script
function thread_init()
    -- Initialize the database driver and connections
    db = sysbench.sql.driver()
    cnx = db:connect()
end
```

For this simple test, all the initialization that is required is to create the connection to MySQL which consists of initializing the database driver and to use that to create the connection. The driver is available from the sysbench object. By creating the connections in the thread_init() function, Sysbench can reuse the connections instead of creating a new connection for each iteration. If you want to simulate creating a new connection for each group of queries, you can also choose to do that by adding the code in the event() function and make the connection object local in the same way as it will be done later for the prepare and cleanup commands.

Similarly, the thread_done() function cleans up after the execution:

```
-- Clean up after the test
function thread_done()
    -- Close the connection to the database
    cnx:disconnect()
end
```

All that is required in this case is to close the connection which is done using the disconnect() method of the connection.

The most interesting of the three required functions is the event() function which defines what is done when executing the test. The code for the example script can be seen in Listing 3-10.

Listing 3-10. The event() function

```
-- Called for each iteration
function event()
    -- Check the --skip_trx option which determines
    -- whether explicit transactions are required.
    if not sysbench.opt.skip_trx then
        cnx:query("BEGIN")
    end

    -- Execute the customer test
    do_increment()

    -- If necessary, commit the transaction
    if not sysbench.opt.skip_trx then
        cnx:query("COMMIT")
    end
end
```

This code uses one option, the --skip_trx option. If --skip_trx is disabled, then the test relies on the auto-commit feature; otherwise, explicit BEGIN and COMMIT are executed.

Note   In the Sysbench Lua scripts, you cannot use START TRANSACTION to begin a transaction.

In this case, the event() function does not actually perform any work itself. That is deferred to the do_increment() function to show how you can add extra functions to separate out the work like in other programs. The do_increment() function together with a couple of helper functions is shown in Listing 3-11.

Listing 3-11. The do_increment() and helper functions

```
-- Generate the table name from the table number
function gen_table_name(table_num)
    return string.format("sbtest%d", table_num)
end

-- Generate the key from an id
function gen_key(id)
    return string.format("sbkey%d", id)
end

-- Increment the counter and fetch the new value
function do_increment()
    -- Choose a random table and id
    -- among the tables and rows available
    table_num = math.random(sysbench.opt.tables)
    table_name = gen_table_name(table_num)
    id = math.random(sysbench.opt.table_size)
    key = gen_key(id)
    query = string.format([[
UPDATE %s
   SET val = LAST_INSERT_ID(val+1)
 WHERE id = '%s']], table_name, key)
    cnx:query(query)
    cnx:query("SELECT LAST_INSERT_ID()")
end
```

The gen_table_name() function generates the table name based on an integer, and the gen_key() function similarly generates a key value based on an integer id. The table name and key value are used in a few other places in the script, so by splitting the logic into helper functions, you can ensure they are generated in the same way throughout the script.

The do_increment() function itself starts out generating the table name and key based on random values based on the number of tables and the number of rows in each table in the test. In a real application, you may not have such a uniform access to the sequences, in which case you can modify the logic in the script. Finally, the UPDATE and

SELECT statements are executed. A possible extension of the script is to use the generated sequence number in some other query, but be careful that you do not end up doing work that is not relevant to what you are trying to benchmark.

That is all that is required for the run command. Notice that nothing was done to implement parallel execution; that is handled automatically by Sysbench unless you do not want to treat all threads the same. An example where the threads should not perform identical work is the prepare command where each thread will be responsible for its own tables.

The prepare Command

The prepare command is an example of a custom command that supports parallel execution. The top-level code for the command is implemented in the do_prepare() function which in turn uses the create_table() function to create one specific table based on the table number passed to the function. The two functions can be seen in Listing 3-12.

Listing 3-12. The do_prepare() and create_table() functions

```
-- Prepare the table
-- Can be parallelized up to the number of tables
function do_prepare()
    -- The script only supports up to 99999 rows
    -- as the id column is a varchar(10) and five
    -- characters is used by 'sbkey'
    assert(sysbench.opt.table_size > 0 and
           sysbench.opt.table_size < 100000,
           "Only 1-99999 rows per table is supported.")

    -- Initialize the database driver and connection
    local db = sysbench.sql.driver()
    local cnx = db:connect()

    -- Create table based on thread id
    for i = sysbench.tid % sysbench.opt.threads + 1,
            sysbench.opt.tables,
            sysbench.opt.threads do
        create_table(cnx, i)
    end
```

```
    -- Disconnect
    cnx:disconnect()
end

-- Create the Nth table
function create_table(cnx, table_num)
    table_name = gen_table_name(table_num)
    print(string.format(
            "Creating table '%s'...", table_name))

    -- Drop the table if it exists
    query = string.format(
        "DROP TABLE IF EXISTS %s", table_name)
    cnx:query(query)

    -- Create the new table
    query = string.format([[
CREATE TABLE %s (
  id varchar(10) NOT NULL,
  val bigint unsigned NOT NULL DEFAULT 0,
  PRIMARY KEY (id)
)]], table_name)
    cnx:query(query)

    -- Insert the rows inside a transaction
    cnx:query("BEGIN")
    for i = 1, sysbench.opt.table_size, 1 do
        query = string.format([[
INSERT INTO %s (id)
VALUES ('%s')]], table_name, gen_key(i))
        cnx:query(query)
    end
    cnx:query("COMMIT")
end
```

The first thing that is done in the do_prepare() function is to verify that the number of rows is within the range 1–99999. This is done using the assert() function where the first argument must evaluate to true; otherwise, the error message given as the second output is printed and the script exists.

The do_prepare() function is called once per thread, so the parallelization is handled for you (more about this at the end of the example), but you need to ensure that each table is only created once. That is done through the for loop where the modulus of sysbench.tid (the Sysbench thread id) with the number of threads is used to determine the table numbers handled by each thread.

The actual table creation is performed in create_table() to separate out the tasks to make it easier to maintain the script. If the table already exists, it is dropped and then created, and finally the table is populated with the number of rows requested. All rows are inserted in a single transaction to improve the performance. If you need to populate larger tables, it is worth committing after every few thousand rows, but since the maximum number of rows in this table is 99999 and the rows are very small, it is fine to keep things simple and just use a single transaction per table.

The cleanup Command

The last command that must be implemented is cleanup which is an example of a single-threaded command. The work for the command is done in the cleanup() function as shown in Listing 3-13.

Listing 3-13. The cleanup() function

```
-- Cleanup after the test
function cleanup()
    -- Initialize the database driver and connection
    local db = sysbench.sql.driver()
    local cnx = db:connect()

    -- Drop each table
    for i = 1, sysbench.opt.tables, 1 do
        table_name = gen_table_name(i)
        print(string.format(
                "Dropping table '%s' ...", table_name))
```

```
    query = string.format(
        "DROP TABLE IF EXISTS %s", table_name)
    cnx:query(query)
  end

  -- Disconnect
  cnx:disconnect()
end
```

The cleanup() function only supports serial execution, so it can just loop over the tables and drop them one by one.

This leaves a question: How does Sysbench know that the prepare command can be run on parallel, but the cleanup command cannot?

Registering Commands

By default, all commands except run execute in serial, and the function implementing the command is named the same as the command. So, for the prepare command, it is necessary to set the prepare object in the script to point to the do_prepare() function with an additional argument that do_prepare() should be called once per thread:

```
-- Specify the actions other than run that support
-- execution in parallel.
-- (Other supported actions are found based on the
-- function name except 'help' that is built-in.)
sysbench.cmdline.commands = {
    prepare = {do_prepare, sysbench.cmdline.PARALLEL_COMMAND}
}
```

The sysbench.cmdline.PARALLEL_COMMAND constant is built-in and specifies that the command should be executed in parallel. It is important that this code is after the definition of do_prepare() as otherwise a nil value is assigned. In practice, it is convenient to add the code at the end of the script.

That concludes the script. You can now use it in the same way as the tests that ship with Sysbench provided that you have copied it into the shared Sysbench directory (/usr/local/share/sysbench/ with the default installation directory when you compile Sysbench yourself). Assuming you have saved the script as sequence.lua, an example use of the script is shown – without output – in Listing 3-14.

Listing 3-14. Example commands for the sequence test

```
shell$ sysbench sequence \
        --mysql-host=127.0.0.1 \
        --mysql-port=3306 \
        --mysql-user=sbtest \
        --mysql-password=password \
        --mysql-ssl=REQUIRED \
        --mysql-db=sbtest \
        --table_size=10 \
        --tables=4 \
        --threads=4 \
        prepare

shell$ sysbench sequence \
        --mysql-host=127.0.0.1 \
        --mysql-port=3306 \
        --mysql-user=sbtest \
        --mysql-password=password \
        --mysql-ssl=REQUIRED \
        --mysql-db=sbtest \
        --table_size=10 \
        --tables=4 \
        --time=60 \
        --threads=8 \
        run

shell$ sysbench sequence \
        --mysql-host=127.0.0.1 \
        --mysql-port=3306 \
        --mysql-user=sbtest \
        --mysql-password=password \
        --mysql-ssl=REQUIRED \
        --mysql-db=sbtest \
        --tables=4 \
        cleanup
```

Note that as for the `oltp_read_only` test, the `sbtest` schema must exist before executing the `prepare` command. It is left as an exercise to the reader to try the script with different values for `--threads`, `--tables`, `--table_size`, and `--skip_trx`.

Summary

This chapter has discussed how benchmarks can be used with MySQL. First, some general best practices using benchmarks were discussed. The single most important things are that you have determined what to benchmark and what is considered the success criteria. This is not all that different from performance tuning in general. It is also important that you understand the tests the benchmark performs and what the result means. Often, you will need to collect additional metrics either through your normal monitoring solution or through specialized scripts to determine whether the benchmark was a success.

Next, the standard TPC benchmarks were covered. The TPC-C and TPC-E benchmarks are good for testing OLTP workloads with TPC-C being the most used as it is the oldest, but TPC-E being the most realistic for modern applications. The TPC-H and TPC-DS use complex queries that can be great, for example, to explore changes that can affect the query plan.

While you can choose to implement a benchmark from scratch yourself, it is more likely you will use a preexisting benchmark tool. The most commonly used tool with MySQL is Sysbench which was covered in some detail. First, Sysbench was installed by compiling it. Then it was shown how the standard Sysbench benchmarks can be executed. The real strength of Sysbench, though, is that you can define your own custom tests. A simple example was shown in the last section.

In the same way as it is not always possible to use a real-world benchmark, it is not always possible to use read-world data for general testing. The next chapter explores some generic data sets often used with MySQL and of which several are also used in this book.

CHAPTER 4

Test Data

Testing is a very important part of the performance tuning work as it is important that you have verified that your changes work before you apply them to your production system. The best data for verification of your changes closely relates to your production data; however, for exploring how MySQL works, it can be better to use some generic test data. This chapter introduces four standard data sets with installation instructions as well as a few other data sets that are available.

Tip The `world`, `world_x`, and `sakila` databases are used as test data in the remainder of this book.

First, however, you need to know how you can download the databases.

Downloading the Example Databases

Common for the example databases that are discussed in detail in this chapter is that they can be downloaded from `https://dev.mysql.com/doc/index-other.html` or there is a link to where they can be downloaded from. For several of the databases, there is also online documentation and PDF files linked from this page. The relevant part of the page is shown in Figure 4-1.

© Jesper Wisborg Krogh 2020
J. W. Krogh, *MySQL 8 Query Performance Tuning*, https://doi.org/10.1007/978-1-4842-5584-1_4

Example Databases

Title	Download DB	HTML Setup Guide	PDF Setup Guide
employee data (large dataset, includes data and test/verification suite)	GitHub	View	US Ltr | A4
world database	Gzip | Zip	View	US Ltr
world_x database	TGZ | Zip		
sakila database	TGZ | Zip	View	US Ltr | A4
menagerie database	TGZ | Zip		

Figure 4-1.   *The table with links to the example databases*

The employee data (the employees database) is downloaded from Giuseppe Maxia's (also known as The Data Charmer) GitHub repository, whereas the other databases are downloaded from Oracle's MySQL's site. The download with the employee data also includes a copy of the sakila database. For the employee data, the world database, and the sakila database, there is also documentation available.

Note   If you are not using the latest version of the data, you may see warnings about deprecated features, when you install the test databases. You can ignore those warnings, however, it is recommended to get the latest version of the data.

The menagerie database is a tiny two-table database with a total of fewer than 20 rows that was created for the tutorials section in the MySQL manual. It will not be discussed further.

The world Database

The world sample database is one of the most commonly used databases for simple tests. It consists of three tables with a few hundred to a few thousand rows. This makes it a small data set which means it can easily be used even on small test instances.

Schema

The database consists of the city, country, and countrylanguage tables. The relationship between the tables is shown in Figure 4-2.

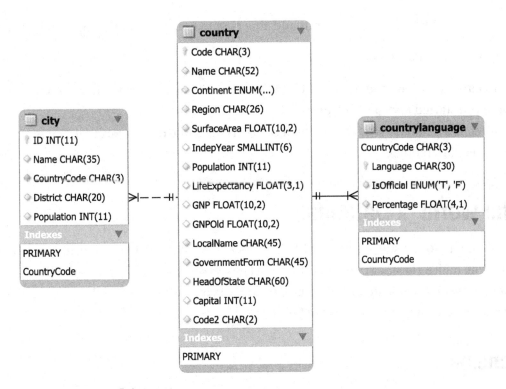

Figure 4-2. *The* world *database*

The country table includes information about 239 countries and serves as the parent table in foreign keys from the city and countrylanguage tables. There are a total of 4079 cities in the database and 984 combinations of country and language.

Installation

The downloaded file consists of a single file named world.sql.gz or world.sql.zip depending on whether you chose the Gzip or Zip link. In either case, the downloaded archive contains a single file world.sql. The installation of the data is straightforward as all that is required is to execute the script.

If you use MySQL Shell with a copy of the world database from around January 2020 or before, you will need to use the traditional protocol as the X Protocol (the default) requires UTF-8 and the world database used Latin 1. You use the \source command to load the data from MySQL Shell:

```
MySQL [localhost ssl] SQL> \source world.sql
```

If you use the legacy `mysql` command-line client, use the SOURCE command instead:

```
mysql> SOURCE world.sql
```

In either case, add the path to the `world.sql` file if it is not located in the directory where you started MySQL Shell or `mysql`.

A related database is `world_x` which contains the same data as `world`, but it is organized differently.

The world_x Database

MySQL 8 has added support for the MySQL Document Store which supports storing and retrieving data as JavaScript Object Notation (JSON) documents. The `world_x` database stores some of the data in JSON documents to give you a test database that can readily be used for tests that include the use of JSON.

Schema

The `world_x` database includes the same three tables as the `world` database, though the columns are a little different, for example, the `city` table includes the JSON column `Info` with the population instead of the `Population` column and the `country` table has omitted several columns. Instead, there is the `countryinfo` table which is a pure Document Store–type table with the information otherwise removed from the `country` table. The schema diagram is shown in Figure 4-3.

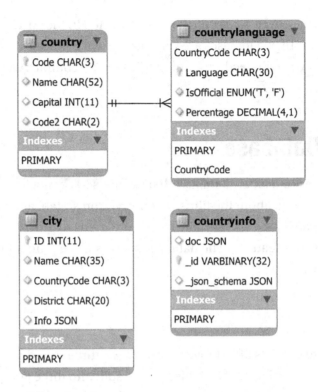

Figure 4-3. *The* world_x *database*

While there are no foreign keys from the city and countryinfo tables, they can be joined to the country table using the CountryCode column and doc->>'$.Code' value, respectively. The _id column of the countryinfo table is an example of a stored generated column where the value is extracted from the JSON document in the doc column.

Installation

The installation of the world_x database is very similar to the world database. You download either the world_x-db.tar.gz or world_x-db.zip file and extract it. The extracted files include a file named world_x.sql as well as a README file. The world_x. sql file includes all the statements required to create the schema.

Since the world_x schema uses UTF-8, you can install it using either of the MySQL protocols. For example, using MySQL Shell:

```
MySQL [localhost+ ssl] SQL> \source world_x.sql
```

Add the path to the `world_x.sql` file if it is not located in the current directory.

The `world` and `world_x` databases are very simple which makes them easy to use; however, sometimes you will need something a little more complex which the `sakila` database can deliver.

The sakila Database

The `sakila` database is a realistic database that contains a schema for a film rental business with information about the films, inventory, stores, staff, and customers. It adds a full text index, a spatial index, views, and stored programs to provide a more complete example of using MySQL features. The database size is still very moderate making it suitable for small instances.

Schema

The `sakila` database consists of 16 tables, seven views, three stored procedures, three stored functions, and six triggers. The tables can be split into three groups, customer data, business, and inventory. For brevity, not all columns are included in the diagrams and most indexes are not shown. Figure 4-4 shows a complete overview of the tables, views, and stored routines.

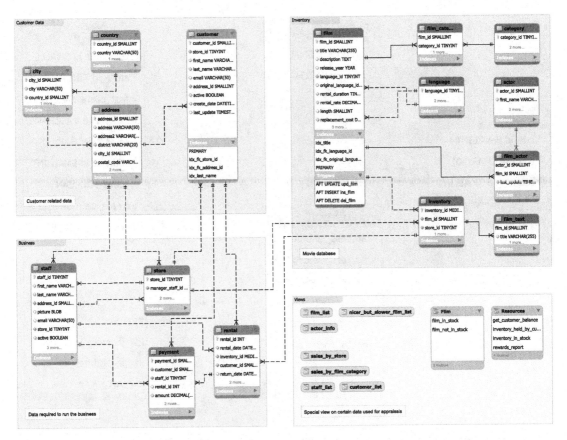

Figure 4-4. *Overview of the* sakila *database*

The tables with customer-related data (plus addresses for staff and stores) are in the area in the top-left corner. The area in the lower left includes data related to the business, and the area in the top right contains information about the films and inventory. The lower right is used for the views and stored routines.

Tip   You can view the entire diagram (though formatted differently) by opening the sakila.mwb file included with the installation in MySQL Workbench. This is also a good example of how you can use enhanced entity-relationship (EER) diagrams in MySQL Workbench to document your schema.

As there is a relatively large number of objects, they will be split into five groups (each of the table groups, views, and stored routines) when discussing the schema. The first group is the customer-related data with the tables shown in Figure 4-5.

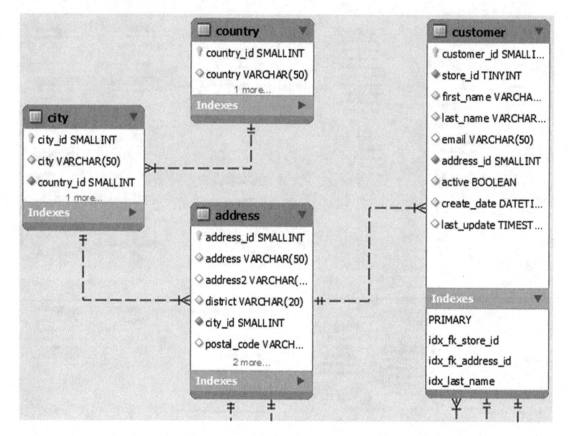

Figure 4-5. *The tables with customer data in the* `sakila` *database*

There are four tables with data related to the customers. The `customer` table is the main table, and the address information is stored in the `address`, `city`, and `country` tables.

There are foreign keys between the customer and business groups with a foreign key from the `customer` table to the `store` table in the business group. There are also four foreign keys from tables in the business group to the `address` and `customer` tables. The business group is shown in Figure 4-6.

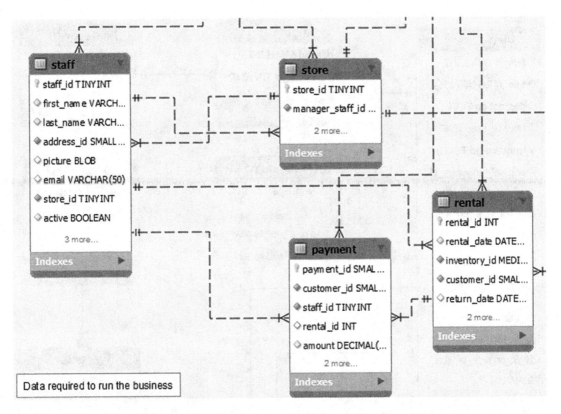

Figure 4-6. *The tables with business data in the* `sakila` *database*

The business tables contain information about the stores, staff, rentals, and payments. The `store` and `staff` tables have foreign keys in both directions with staff belonging to a store and a store having a manager that is part of the staff. Rentals and payments are handled by a staff member and thus indirectly linked to a store, and payments are for a rental.

The business group of tables is the one with the most relations to other groups. The `staff` and `store` tables have foreign keys to the `address` table, and the `rental` and payment tables reference the customer. Finally, the `rental` table has a foreign key to the `inventory` table which is in the inventory group. The diagram for the inventory group is shown in Figure 4-7.

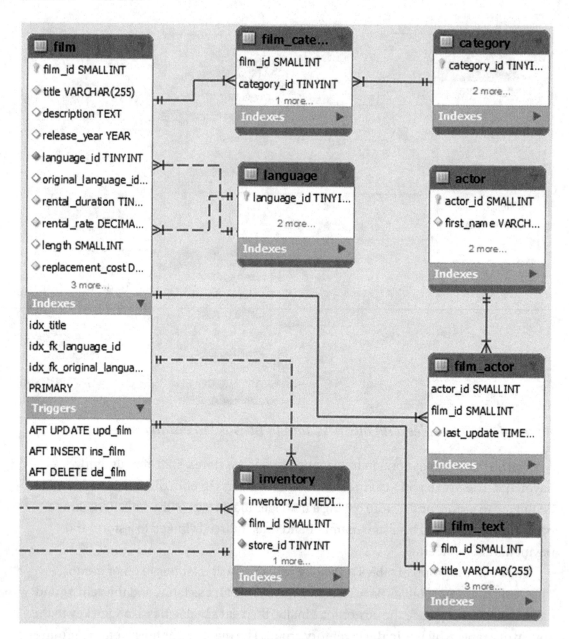

Figure 4-7. *The tables with inventory data in the sakila database*

The main table in the inventory group is the `film` table which contains the metadata about the films the stores offer. Additionally, there is the `film_text` table with the title and description with a full text index.

There is a many-to-many relationship between the `film` and the `category` and `actor` tables. Finally, there is a foreign key from the `inventory` table to the `store` table in the business group.

That covers all the tables in the `sakila` database, but there are also some views as shown in Figure 4-8.

Figure 4-8. *The views in the* `sakila` *database*

The views can be used like reports and can be divided into two categories. The `film_list`, `nicer_but_slower_film_list`, and `actor_info` views are related to the films stored in the database. The second category contains information related to the stores in the `sales_by_store`, `sales_by_film_category`, `staff_list`, and `customer_list` views.

To complete the database, there are also the stored functions and procedures shown in Figure 4-9.

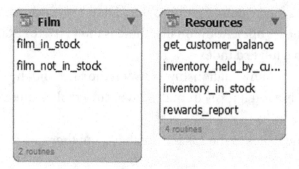

Figure 4-9. *The stored routines in the* sakila *database*

The film_in_stock() and film_not_in_stock() procedures return a result set consisting of the inventory ids for a given film and store based on whether the film is in stock or not. The total number of inventory entries found is returned as an out parameter. The rewards_report() procedure generates a report based on minimum spends for the last month.

The get_customer_balance() function returns the balance for a given customer on a given data. The two remaining functions check the status of an inventory id with inventory_held_by_customer() returning customer id of the customer currently renting that item (and NULL if no customer is renting it), and if you want to check whether a given inventory id is in stock, you can use the inventory_in_stock() function.

Installation

The downloaded file expands into a directory with three files, of which two create the schema and data and the last file contains the ETL diagram in the format used by MySQL Workbench.

Note   This section and the examples later in the book use the copy of the sakila database that is downloaded from MySQL's homepage.

The files are

- **sakila-data.sql:** The INSERT statements needed to populate the tables as well as the trigger definitions.

- **sakila-schema.sql:** The schema definition statements.

- **sakila.mwb:** The MySQL Workbench ETL diagram. This is similar to that shown in Figure 4-4 with details in Figures 4-5 to 4-9.

You install the sakila database by first sourcing the sakila-schema.sql file and then the sakila-data.sql file. For example, the following is using MySQL Shell:

```
MySQL [localhost+ ssl] SQL> \source sakila-schema.sql
MySQL [localhost+ ssl] SQL> \source sakila-data.sql
```

Add the path to the files if they are not located in the current directory.

Common for the three data sets thus far is that they contain little data. While this is in many cases a nice feature as it makes it easier to work with, in some cases you need a bit more data to explore the difference in query plans. The employees database is an option with more data.

The employees Database

The employees database (called employee data on the MySQL documentation download page; the name of the GitHub repository is test_db) was originally created by Fusheng Wang and Carlo Zaniolo and is the largest of the test data sets linked from MySQL's homepage. The total size of the data files is around 180 MiB for the non-partitioned version and 440 MiB for the partitioned version.

Schema

The employees database consists of six tables and two views. You can optionally install two more views, five stored functions, and two stored procedures. The tables are shown in Figure 4-10.

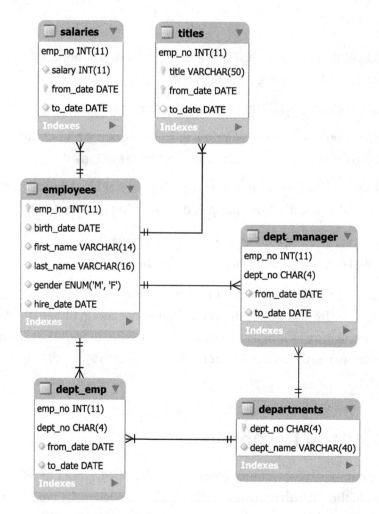

Figure 4-10. *The tables, views, and routines in the* employees *database*

It is possible to choose to have the salaries and titles tables partitioned by the year of the from_date column as shown in Listing 4-1.

Listing 4-1. The optional partitioning of the salaries and titles tables

```
PARTITION BY RANGE  COLUMNS(from_date)
(PARTITION p01 VALUES LESS THAN ('1985-12-31') ENGINE = InnoDB,
 PARTITION p02 VALUES LESS THAN ('1986-12-31') ENGINE = InnoDB,
 PARTITION p03 VALUES LESS THAN ('1987-12-31') ENGINE = InnoDB,
 PARTITION p04 VALUES LESS THAN ('1988-12-31') ENGINE = InnoDB,
 PARTITION p05 VALUES LESS THAN ('1989-12-31') ENGINE = InnoDB,
```

```
PARTITION p06 VALUES LESS THAN ('1990-12-31') ENGINE = InnoDB,
PARTITION p07 VALUES LESS THAN ('1991-12-31') ENGINE = InnoDB,
PARTITION p08 VALUES LESS THAN ('1992-12-31') ENGINE = InnoDB,
PARTITION p09 VALUES LESS THAN ('1993-12-31') ENGINE = InnoDB,
PARTITION p10 VALUES LESS THAN ('1994-12-31') ENGINE = InnoDB,
PARTITION p11 VALUES LESS THAN ('1995-12-31') ENGINE = InnoDB,
PARTITION p12 VALUES LESS THAN ('1996-12-31') ENGINE = InnoDB,
PARTITION p13 VALUES LESS THAN ('1997-12-31') ENGINE = InnoDB,
PARTITION p14 VALUES LESS THAN ('1998-12-31') ENGINE = InnoDB,
PARTITION p15 VALUES LESS THAN ('1999-12-31') ENGINE = InnoDB,
PARTITION p16 VALUES LESS THAN ('2000-12-31') ENGINE = InnoDB,
PARTITION p17 VALUES LESS THAN ('2001-12-31') ENGINE = InnoDB,
PARTITION p18 VALUES LESS THAN ('2002-12-31') ENGINE = InnoDB,
PARTITION p19 VALUES LESS THAN (MAXVALUE) ENGINE = InnoDB)
```

Table 4-1 shows the number of rows and size of the tablespace files for the tables in the employees database (note that the size may vary a little when you load the data). The size assumes you load the non-partitioned data; the partitioned tables are somewhat larger.

Table 4-1. *The size of each table in the employees database*

Table	# Rows	Tablespace Size
departments	9	128 kiB
dept_emp	331603	25600 kiB
dept_manager	24	128 kiB
employees	300024	22528 kiB
salaries	2844047	106496 kiB
titles	443308	27648 kiB

By today's standards, it is still a relatively small amount of data, but it is big enough that you can start to see some performance differences for different query plans.

The views and routines are summarized in Figure 4-11.

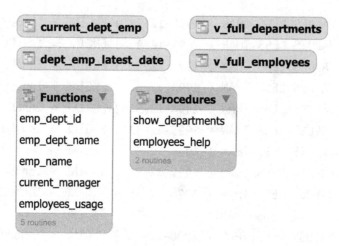

Figure 4-11. *The views and routines in the employees database*

The dept_emp_latest_date and current_dept_emp views are installed together with the tables, whereas the rest of the objects are installed separately in the objects.sql file. The stored routines come with their own built-in help which you can obtain by using the employees_usage() function or the employees_help() procedure. The latter is shown in Listing 4-2.

Listing 4-2. The built-in help for the stored routines in the employees database

```
mysql> CALL employees_help()\G
*************************** 1. row ***************************
info:
    == USAGE ==
    ====================

    PROCEDURE show_departments()

        shows the departments with the manager and
        number of employees per department

    FUNCTION current_manager (dept_id)

        Shows who is the manager of a given departmennt

    FUNCTION emp_name (emp_id)

        Shows name and surname of a given employee
```

```
FUNCTION emp_dept_id (emp_id)

    Shows the current department of given employee

1 row in set (0.00 sec)

Query OK, 0 rows affected (0.02 sec)
```

Installation

You can download a ZIP file with the files required for the installation, or you can clone the GitHub repository at https://github.com/datacharmer/test_db. At the time of writing, there is only a single branch named master. If you have downloaded the ZIP file, it will unzip into a directory named test_db-master.

There are several files. The two relevant for installing the employees database in MySQL 8 are employees.sql and employees_partitioned.sql. The difference is whether the salaries and titles tables are partitioned. (There is also employees_partitioned_5.1.sql which is meant for MySQL 5.1 where the partitioning scheme used in employees_partitioned.sql is not supported.)

The data is loaded by sourcing the .dump files using the SOURCE command. At the time of writing, the SOURCE command is not supported in MySQL Shell, so you will need to use the legacy mysql command-line client to import the data. Go to the directory with the source files, and choose the employees.sql or employees_partitioned.sql file, depending on whether you want to use partitioning or not, for example:

```
mysql> SOURCE employees.sql
```

The import takes a little time and completes by showing how long it took:

```
+---------------------+
| data_load_time_diff |
+---------------------+
| 00:01:51            |
+---------------------+
1 row in set (0.44 sec)
```

Optionally, you can load some extra views and stored routines by sourcing the objects.sql file:

```
mysql> SOURCE objects.sql
```

In addition to the data sets discussed here, there are some other choices to obtain example data to work with.

Other Databases

It can happen that you need to perform testing that requires data with some requirements that are not fulfilled by the standard example databases discussed thus far. Fortunately, there are other options available.

Tip   Do not discount the possibility to create your own custom example database, for example, by using data masking on your production data.

If you are looking for a very large real-world example, then you can download the Wikipedia database as described at https://en.wikipedia.org/wiki/Wikipedia:Database_download. The English Wikipedia dump from September 20, 2019, is 16.3 GiB in bzip2 compressed XML format.

If you are looking for JSON data, then an option is the earthquake information from the United States Geological Survey (USGS) which is provided in GeoJSON format with options to download information for earthquakes for the last hour, day, week, or month optionally filtered by the strength of the earthquake. The format description and links to the feeds can be found at https://earthquake.usgs.gov/earthquakes/feed/v1.0/geojson.php. Since the data includes geographic information in the GeoJSON format, it can be useful for testing that requires spatial indexes.

The benchmark tools described in the previous chapter also include test data or support creating test data. This data may also be useful for your own testing.

There are other example databases available if you search the Internet. In the end, the important things to consider are whether the data has a good size for your testing and whether it uses the features you require.

Summary

This chapter has introduced four standard example databases and some other examples of test data. The four standard databases that were discussed were `world`, `world_x`, `sakila`, and `employees`. These can all be found through the MySQL manual at `https://dev.mysql.com/doc/index-other.html`. Except for `employees`, these databases are used for the examples in this book unless stated otherwise.

The `world` and `world_x` databases are the simplest with the difference that `world_x` uses JSON to store some of the information, whereas the `world` database is purely relational. These databases do not contain much data, but because of their small size and simplicity, they are useful for simple tests and examples. Particularly the `world` database is used extensively in this book.

The `sakila` database has a much more complex schema including different index types, views, and stored routines. This makes it more realistic and allows for more complex tests. Yet, the size of the data is still small enough to use it on even small MySQL instances. It is also used extensively in this book.

The `employees` database has a schema that is in between the `world` and `sakila` databases in complexity, but has significantly more data making it better for testing the difference between various query plans. It is also useful if you need to generate some load on the instance, for example, using table scans. The `employees` database is not directly used in this book, but if you want to reproduce some of the examples where some load is required, then this is the best of the four standard test databases to use.

You should not limit yourself to consider the standard test databases. You may be able to create your own, create one using a benchmark tool, or find data made available on the Internet. Wikipedia's database and the earthquake data from the United States Geological Survey (USGS) are examples of data that can be downloaded.

This completes the introduction to MySQL query performance tuning. Part II goes through the common sources of information in connection with diagnosing performance problems starting with the Performance Schema.

PART II

Sources of Information

CHAPTER 5

The Performance Schema

The Performance Schema is the main source of diagnostics information related to performance in MySQL. It was first introduced in MySQL in version 5.5, then heavily modified to its current structure in version 5.6, and since then gradually improved in 5.7 and 8.

This chapter introduces and provides an overview of the Performance Schema, so it is clear how it works when the Performance Schema is used throughout the remainder of the book. Close relatives to the Performance Schema are the sys schema which will be discussed in the next chapter and the Information Schema which is the topic of Chapter 7.

The chapter discusses the concepts unique to the Performance Schema with particular focus on threads, instruments, consumers, events, digests, and dynamic configuration. First, however, it is necessary to become familiar with the terminology used in the Performance Schema.

Terminology

One of the things that can be difficult when studying a new subject is the terminology, and the Performance Schema is no exception. Since there is an almost cyclic relationship between the terms, there is no clear order to describe them. Instead, this section will provide a brief overview of the most important terms used in this chapter, so you have an idea what the terms mean. By the end of the chapter, you should understand better what the concepts mean and how they relate to each other.

Table 5-1 summarizes the most important terms in the Performance Schema.

© Jesper Wisborg Krogh 2020
J. W. Krogh, *MySQL 8 Query Performance Tuning*, https://doi.org/10.1007/978-1-4842-5584-1_5

Table 5-1. *The MySQL Performance Schema terminology*

Term	Description
Actor	A combination of a username and hostname (an account).
Consumer	The process collecting the data generated by the *instruments*.
Digest	A checksum of a normalized query. The digest is used to aggregate statistics for similar queries.
Dynamic configuration	The Performance Schema can be configured at runtime which is called dynamic configuration. This is done through *setup tables* rather than by changing system variables.
Event	An event is what comes out of a *consumer* collecting the data from an *instrument*. Thus, an event contains metrics and information on when and where the metrics were collected.
Instrument	The code points where the measurements are done.
Object	A table, event, function, procedure, or trigger.
Setup table	The Performance Schema has several tables used for *dynamic configuration*. These are called setup tables, and the table name starts with `setup_`.
Summary table	A table with aggregate data. The table name includes the word summary, and the rest of the name indicates the type of data and what it is grouped by.
Thread	A thread corresponds to a connection or a background thread. There is a one-to-one correspondence between Performance Schema threads and operating system threads.

As you read this chapter, it can be useful to refer back to this table if you encounter terms that you are not sure what they mean.

Threads

A thread is a fundamental concept in the Performance Schema. When anything is done in MySQL, whether it is handling a connection or performing background work, the work is done by a thread. MySQL has several threads at any given time as it allows MySQL to perform work in parallel. For a connection, there is a single thread.

> **Note**   The introduction of support for performing parallel reads of the clustered index and partitions in InnoDB has somewhat muddied the picture of one thread for one connection. However, since the threads that perform the parallel scans are considered background threads, for this discussion you can consider the connection single threaded.

Each thread has an id which is what uniquely identifies the thread, and the column storing this id in the Performance Schema tables is called THREAD_ID. The main table for inspecting threads is the threads table with Listing 5-1 showing a typical example of the type of threads that exist in MySQL 8. The number of threads and exact thread types available depend on your configuration and usage of the instance at the time of querying the threads table.

Listing 5-1. Threads in MySQL 8

```
mysql> SELECT THREAD_ID AS TID,
              SUBSTRING_INDEX(NAME, '/', -2) AS THREAD_NAME,
              IF(TYPE = 'BACKGROUND', '*', '') AS B,
              IFNULL(PROCESSLIST_ID, '') AS PID
          FROM performance_schema.threads;
+-----+--------------------------------------+---+-----+
| TID | THREAD_NAME                          | B | PID |
+-----+--------------------------------------+---+-----+
|   1 | sql/main                             | * |     |
|   2 | mysys/thread_timer_notifier          | * |     |
|   4 | innodb/io_ibuf_thread                | * |     |
|   5 | innodb/io_log_thread                 | * |     |
|   6 | innodb/io_read_thread                | * |     |
|   7 | innodb/io_read_thread                | * |     |
|   8 | innodb/io_read_thread                | * |     |
|   9 | innodb/io_read_thread                | * |     |
|  10 | innodb/io_write_thread               | * |     |
|  11 | innodb/io_write_thread               | * |     |
|  12 | innodb/io_write_thread               | * |     |
|  13 | innodb/io_write_thread               | * |     |
```

```
|  14 | innodb/page_flush_coordinator_thread | * |      |
|  15 | innodb/log_checkpointer_thread       | * |      |
|  16 | innodb/log_closer_thread             | * |      |
|  17 | innodb/log_flush_notifier_thread     | * |      |
|  18 | innodb/log_flusher_thread            | * |      |
|  19 | innodb/log_write_notifier_thread     | * |      |
|  20 | innodb/log_writer_thread             | * |      |
|  21 | innodb/srv_lock_timeout_thread       | * |      |
|  22 | innodb/srv_error_monitor_thread      | * |      |
|  23 | innodb/srv_monitor_thread            | * |      |
|  24 | innodb/buf_resize_thread             | * |      |
|  25 | innodb/srv_master_thread             | * |      |
|  26 | innodb/dict_stats_thread             | * |      |
|  27 | innodb/fts_optimize_thread           | * |      |
|  28 | mysqlx/worker                        |   | 9    |
|  29 | mysqlx/acceptor_network              | * |      |
|  30 | mysqlx/acceptor_network              | * |      |
|  31 | mysqlx/worker                        | * |      |
|  34 | innodb/buf_dump_thread               | * |      |
|  35 | innodb/clone_gtid_thread             | * |      |
|  36 | innodb/srv_purge_thread              | * |      |
|  37 | innodb/srv_purge_thread              | * |      |
|  38 | innodb/srv_worker_thread             | * |      |
|  39 | innodb/srv_worker_thread             | * |      |
|  40 | innodb/srv_worker_thread             | * |      |
|  41 | innodb/srv_worker_thread             | * |      |
|  42 | innodb/srv_worker_thread             | * |      |
|  43 | innodb/srv_worker_thread             | * |      |
|  44 | sql/event_scheduler                  |   | 4    |
|  45 | sql/compress_gtid_table              |   | 6    |
|  46 | sql/con_sockets                      | * |      |
|  47 | sql/one_connection                   |   | 7    |
|  48 | mysqlx/acceptor_network              | * |      |
|  49 | innodb/parallel_read_thread          | * |      |
|  50 | innodb/parallel_read_thread          | * |      |
```

```
|  51 | innodb/parallel_read_thread              | * |     |
|  52 | innodb/parallel_read_thread              | * |     |
+-----+------------------------------------------+---+-----+
49 rows in set (0.0615 sec)
```

The TID column is the THREAD_ID for each thread, the THREAD_NAME column includes the two last components of the thread name (the first component is thread for all threads), the B column has an asterisk for the background threads, and the PID column has the process list id for the foreground threads.

Note   Unfortunately, the term thread is overloaded in MySQL and is in some places used as a synonym for a connection. In this book, a connection refers to a user connection, and a thread refers to a Performance Schema thread, that is, it can either be a background or foreground (including connections) thread. The exception is when discussing a table that explicitly violates that convention.

The list of threads shows several important concepts for threads. The process list id and the thread id are not related. In fact, the thread with thread id = 28 has a higher process list id (9) than the thread with thread id 44 (4). So it is not even guaranteed that the order is the same (though for non-mysqlx threads it is in general the case).

For the mysqlx/worker threads, one is a foreground thread and the other a background thread. This reflects how MySQL handles connections using the X Protocol which is considerably different from how classic connections are handled.

There are also "hybrid" threads that are not fully a background nor fully a foreground thread. An example is the sql/compress_gtid_table thread which compresses the mysql.gtid_executed table. It is a foreground thread, yet if you execute SHOW PROCESSLIST, then it will not be included.

Tip   The performance_schema.threads table is very useful and also includes all the information displayed by SHOW PROCESSLIST. As there is less overhead querying this table compared to executing SHOW PROCESSLIST or querying the information_schema.PROCESSLIST table, using the threads table along with the sys.processlist and sys.session views is the recommended way to get a list of connections.

It can sometimes be useful to obtain the thread id for a connection. There are two functions for this:

- **PS_THREAD_ID():** Get the Performance Schema thread id for the connection id provided as an argument.

- **PS_CURRENT_THREAD_ID():** Get the Performance Schema thread id for the current connection.

In MySQL 8.0.15 and earlier, use sys.ps_thread_id() instead and give an argument of NULL to get the thread id for the current connection. An example of using the functions is

```
mysql> SELECT CONNECTION_ID(),
              PS_THREAD_ID(13),
              PS_CURRENT_THREAD_ID()\G
*************************** 1. row ***************************
      CONNECTION_ID(): 13
     PS_THREAD_ID(13): 54
PS_CURRENT_THREAD_ID(): 54
1 row in set (0.0003 sec)
```

Using these functions is equivalent to querying the PROCESSLIST_ID and THREAD_ID columns in the performance_schema.threads table to link a connection id with a thread id. Listing 5-2 shows an example of using the PS_CURRENT_THREAD_ID() function to query the threads table for the current connection.

Listing 5-2. Querying the threads table for the current connection

```
mysql> SELECT *
         FROM performance_schema.threads
        WHERE THREAD_ID = PS_CURRENT_THREAD_ID()\G
*************************** 1. row ***************************
          THREAD_ID: 54
               NAME: thread/mysqlx/worker
               TYPE: FOREGROUND
     PROCESSLIST_ID: 13
   PROCESSLIST_USER: root
   PROCESSLIST_HOST: localhost
     PROCESSLIST_DB: performance_schema
```

```
PROCESSLIST_COMMAND: Query
   PROCESSLIST_TIME: 0
  PROCESSLIST_STATE: statistics
   PROCESSLIST_INFO: SELECT *
         FROM threads
        WHERE THREAD_ID = PS_CURRENT_THREAD_ID()
   PARENT_THREAD_ID: 1
               ROLE: NULL
       INSTRUMENTED: YES
            HISTORY: YES
    CONNECTION_TYPE: SSL/TLS
      THREAD_OS_ID: 31516
     RESOURCE_GROUP: SYS_default
1 row in set (0.0005 sec)
```

There are several of the columns that provide useful information in the context of performance tuning and will be used in later chapters. Worth noting here are the columns whose names start with PROCESSLIST_. These are equivalent of the information returned by SHOW PROCESSLIST, but querying the threads table causes less impact on the connections. The INSTRUMENTED and HISTORY columns specify whether instrumentation data is collected for the thread and whether the history of events is kept for the thread. You can update these two columns to change the behavior of a thread, or you can define the default behavior for the threads based on the thread type in the setup_threads table or based on the account using the setup_actors table. That begs the question what instruments and events are. The three next sections discuss that as well as how the instrumentations are consumed.

Instruments

Instruments are the code points where the measurements are done. There are two types of instruments: those that can be timed and those that cannot. The timed instruments are events and the idle instrument (measuring when the thread is idle), whereas the untimed instruments count errors and memory usage.

The instruments are grouped by their names which forms a hierarchy with the components separated by /. There is no rule as to how many components a name has, and some have as little as one component, whereas others have up to five components.

An example of an instrument name is `statement/sql/select` which represents a `SELECT` statement executed directly (i.e., not from within a stored procedure). Another instrument is `statement/sp/stmt` which is a statement executed inside a stored procedure.

The number of instruments is ever increasing as new features are added, and more instrumentation points are inserted into the existing code. In MySQL 8.0.18, there are around 1229 instruments when no extra plugins or components have been installed (the exact number of instruments depends on the platform as well). These instruments are split among the top-level components listed in Table 5-2. The *Timed* column shows whether the instruments can be timed, and the *Count* column shows the total number of instruments for that top-level component and how many of them are enabled by default in 8.0.18.

Table 5-2. *The top-level instrument components in MySQL 8.0.18*

Component	Timed	Count	Description
error	No	Total: 1 Enabled: 1	Whether to collect information about errors and warnings encountered. There are no subcomponents.
idle	Yes	Total: 1 Enabled: 1	Used to instrument when threads are idle. There are no subcomponents.
memory	No	Total: 511 Enabled: 511	Collects the number and size of the memory allocations and deallocations. The names have three components: memory, the code area, and the instrument name.
stage	Yes	Total: 119 Enabled: 16	Collects information about the query stage events. The names have three components: stage, the code area, and the stage name.
statement	Yes	Total: 212 Enabled: 212	Collects information about statement events. There are one to two subcomponents.
transaction	Yes	Total: 1 Enabled: 1	Collects information about transaction events. There are no subcomponents.
wait	Yes	Total: 384 Enabled: 52	Collects information about wait events which are the lowest-level events. This, for example, includes obtaining locks and mutexes and doing I/O. There are up to three subcomponents

The naming scheme makes it relatively easy to determine what an instrument measures. You can find all the available instruments in the `setup_instruments` table which also allows you to configure whether the instruments are enabled and timed. For some of the instruments, there is also a short documentation of what data the instrument collects.

If you want to enable or disable instruments at the time MySQL is started, you can use the `performance-schema-instrument` option. It works differently than most options as you can specify it several times to change the setting of several instruments, and you can use the % wildcard to match a pattern. Examples of how you can use the option are

```
[mysqld]
performance-schema-instrument = "stage/sql/altering table=ON"
performance-schema-instrument = "memory/%=COUNTED"
```

The first option enables both counting and timing of the `stage/sql/altering table` instrument, whereas the second enables counting of all memory instruments (which is also the default).

Caution   It may seem tempting to enable all instruments (and consumers that are discussed next). However, the more that is instrumented and consumed, the larger the overhead. Enabling everything can effectively cause an outage (the author of this book has seen that happen). Particularly, the `wait/synch/%` instruments and `events_waits_%` consumers add overhead. As a rule of thumb, the finer grained the monitoring is, the more overhead it adds. In most cases, the default settings in MySQL 8 provide a good compromise between observability and overhead.

The data generated by the instruments must be consumed in order for the data to be available in the Performance Schema tables. This is done by consumers.

Consumers

The consumers are what processes the data generated by the instruments and make it available in the Performance Schema tables. The consumers are defined in the `setup_consumers` table which in addition to the consumer name has a column to specify whether the consumer is enabled.

The consumers form a hierarchy as shown in Figure 5-1. The figure is split into two parts with the high-level consumers above the dashed line and the event consumers below the dashed line. The green (light colored) consumers are enabled by default, and the red (dark) are disabled by default.

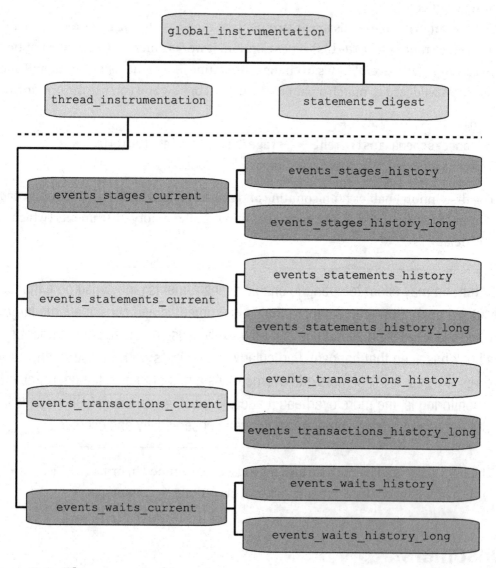

Figure 5-1. *The consumers hierarchy*

That the consumers form a hierarchy means that a consumer is only consuming events if both itself and all consumers higher up in the hierarchy are enabled. Thus, disabling the global_instrumentation consumer effectively disables all consumers.

You can use the sys schema function ps_is_consumer_enabled() to determine if the consumer and the consumers it depend on are enabled, for example:

```
mysql> SELECT sys.ps_is_consumer_enabled(
                'events_statements_history'
            ) AS IsEnabled;
+-----------+
| IsEnabled |
+-----------+
| YES       |
+-----------+
1 row in set (0.0005 sec)
```

The statements_digest consumer is the one responsible for collecting the data grouped by statement digests that, for example, is made available through the events_statements_summary_by_digest table. For query performance tuning, this is possibly the most important consumer. It only depends on the global consumer. The thread_instrumentation consumer determines whether threads are collecting thread-specific instrumentation data. It also controls whether any of the event consumers collect data.

For the consumers, there is one configuration option per consumer with the option name consisting of the performance-schema-consumer- prefix followed by the consumer name, for example:

```
[mysqld]
performance-schema-consumer-events-statements-history-long = ON
```

This will enable the events_statements_history_long consumer.

You will rarely need to consider disabling any of the three high-level consumers. The event consumers are more often configured specifically and will be discussed with the concept of events.

Events

An event is the result of a consumer recording the data collected by an instrument and is what you can use to observe what is going on in MySQL. There are several event types, and events are linked such that in general an event both has a parent and one or more child events. This section covers how events work.

Event Types

There are four event types covering the various levels of details ranging from transactions to waits. An event type also groups events of similar type, and the information collected for an event depends on its type. For example, events representing the execution of statements include the query and how many rows are examined, whereas an event for a transaction has information such as the requested transaction isolation level. The event types are illustrated in Figure 5-2.

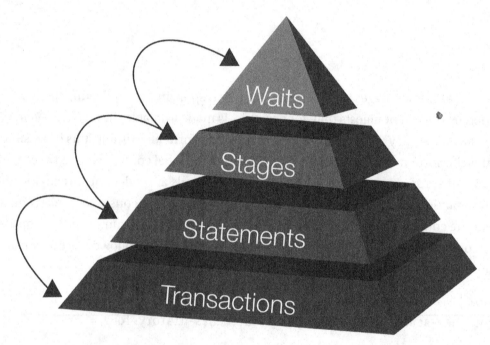

Figure 5-2. *The four event types*

The events correspond to different levels of details with the transactions being the highest level (lowest details) and the wait events the lowest level (highest details):

- **Transactions:** The events describe the transactions and include details such as the transaction isolation level requested (but not necessarily used), transaction status, and so on. By default, the current and the last ten transactions for each thread are collected.

- **Statements:** This is the most commonly used event type with information about the queries executed. It also includes information about statements executed within a stored procedure. This includes such information as the number of examined rows, rows returned, whether indexes were used, and execution time. By default, the current and the last ten statements for each thread are collected.

- **Stages:** This roughly corresponds to the states reported by SHOW PROCESSLIST. These are not enabled by default (with InnoDB progress information partially being an exception).

- **Waits:** These are the low-level events and include I/O and waiting for mutexes. These are very specific and very useful for low-level performance tuning, but they are also the most expensive. None of the wait event consumers are enabled by default.

There is also the question of how long to keep the recorded events.

Event Scopes

For each event type, there are three consumers which specify the lifetime of the consumed events. The scopes are

- **current:** Events currently in progress and for idle threads the last completed event. In some circumstances, there may be more than one event of the same level at the same time. An example is when a stored procedure is executed where there are both the statement event for the procedure itself and the statement currently executing within the procedure.

- **history:** The last ten (by default) events for each thread. The events are discarded when the thread is closed.

- **history_long:** The last 10,000 (by default) events irrespective of the thread generating the event. Events are kept even after a thread is closed.

The event type and scope combine to form the 12 event consumers. There is a Performance Schema table corresponding to each of the event consumers with the table name being the same as the consumer name as shown in Listing 5-3.

Listing 5-3. The correspondence between consumer and table names

```
mysql> SELECT TABLE_NAME
         FROM performance_schema.setup_consumers c
           INNER JOIN information_schema.TABLES t
              ON t.TABLE_NAME = c.NAME
        WHERE t.TABLE_SCHEMA = 'performance_schema'
            AND c.NAME LIKE 'events%'
        ORDER BY c.NAME;
+----------------------------------+
| TABLE_NAME                       |
+----------------------------------+
| events_stages_current            |
| events_stages_history            |
| events_stages_history_long       |
| events_statements_current        |
| events_statements_history        |
| events_statements_history_long   |
| events_transactions_current      |
| events_transactions_history      |
| events_transactions_history_long |
| events_waits_current             |
| events_waits_history             |
| events_waits_history_long        |
+----------------------------------+
12 rows in set (0.0323 sec)
```

As Figure 5-2 hinted with the arrows between the event types, there is a relationship between the types beyond the level of detail they represent. This relationship is not a hierarchy but rather consists of event nesting.

Event Nesting

In general, events are generated by other events, so the events form a tree with each event having one parent event and possibly a number of child events. While it can seem like the event types form a hierarchy with, for example, the transactions being parents of statements, the relationship is more complicated than that and goes both ways. Take the

START TRANSACTION statement which begins a transaction, so the statement becomes the parent of the transaction which in turn is the parent of other statements. Another example is a CALL statement invoking a stored procedure which becomes the parent of the statements executing in the procedure.

The nesting can become quite complex. Figure 5-3 shows an example of a chain of events including all four event types.

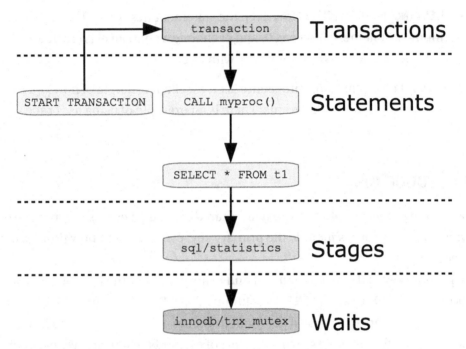

Figure 5-3. *Example of a chain of events*

For the statement events, an actual query is shown, while for the other event types, the event name or part of the event name is shown. The chain starts with the START TRANSACTION statement which starts a transaction. Inside the transaction the myproc() procedure is called which makes it the parent of the SELECT statement which goes through several stages including stage/sql/statistics, and the stage in turn includes requesting the trx_mutex in InnoDB.

The event tables have two columns to keep track of the relationship between the events:

- **NESTING_EVENT_ID:** The parent event id

- **NESTING_EVENT_TYPE:** The event type (TRANSACTION, STATEMENT, STAGE, or WAIT) of the parent event

The statement event tables have some additional columns related to nested statement events:

- **OBJECT_TYPE:** The object type of the parent statement event.

- **OBJECT_SCHEMA:** The schema the parent statement object is stored in.

- **OBJECT_NAME:** The name of the parent statement object.

- **NESTING_EVENT_LEVEL:** How deep the statement nesting is. The topmost statement has level 0, and each time a child level is created, NESTING_EVENT_LEVEL increments with one.

The sys.ps_trace_thread() procedure is an excellent example of how you can automate generating a tree of the events. There is an example of using ps_trace_thread() in Chapter 20.

Event Properties

There are some properties of events that are shared among all events irrespective of their type. These properties include the primary key, event ids, and how timings of the events work.

The primary key of the events' current and history (but not the long history) tables consists of the THREAD_ID and EVENT_ID columns. The EVENT_ID column increments as the thread creates more events, so if you want to get the events in order, you must order by EVENT_ID. Each thread has its own sequence of event ids. There are two event id columns in each of the event tables:

- **EVENT_ID:** This is the main event id of the event and is set when the event starts.

- **END_EVENT_ID:** This id is set when the event ends. This means you can determine whether an event is in progress by checking whether the END_EVENT_ID column is NULL.

Additionally, the column EVENT_NAME has the name of the instrument responsible for the event, and the SOURCE column for statements, stages, and waits has the filename and line number from the source code where the instrument triggered.

There are three columns related to the timings of events recording the start, end, and duration of events:

- **TIMER_START:** When MySQL starts, the internal timer counter is set to 0 and incremented every picosecond. When an event starts, the value of the counter is taken and assigned to TIMER_START.

  However, since the unit is picoseconds, the counter may reach the maximum supported value (this happens after around 30.5 weeks) in which case the counter starts at 0 again.

- **TIMER_END:** For events in progress, this is the current time, and for completed events it is the time when the event completed.

- **TIMER_WAIT:** This is the duration of the event. For events still in progress, it is the amount of time since the event started.

An exception is transactions which do not include the timings.

Note   Different event types use different timers, so you cannot use the TIMER_ START and TIMER_END columns to order events of different types.

Timings are done in picoseconds (10^{-12} seconds). The unit has been chosen for performance reason as it allows MySQL to use multiplications (the cheapest mathematical operation together with addition) in as many cases as possible. The timing columns are 64-bit unsigned integers which means they will overflow after around 30.5 weeks at which time the values start from 0 again.

While it is good to work with picoseconds from a computational perspective, it is less practical for humans. For this reason, the function FORMAT_PICO_TIME() exists to convert picoseconds into a human-readable format, for example:

```
SELECT FORMAT_PICO_TIME(111577500000);
+--------------------------------+
| FORMAT_PICO_TIME(111577500000) |
+--------------------------------+
| 111.58 ms                      |
+--------------------------------+
1 row in set (0.0004 sec)
```

The function was added in MySQL 8.0.16. In earlier versions, you need to use the sys.format_time() function instead.

Actors and Objects

The Performance Schema lets you configure which user accounts and schema objects that by default should be instrumented. The accounts are configured through the setup_actors table and the objects through the setup_objects table. By default, all accounts and all schema objects except objects in the mysql, information_schema, and performance_schema system schemas are instrumented.

Digests

The Performance Schema generates statistics for the statements that are executed based on a statement digest. This is a SHA-256 hash based on the normalized query. Statements with the same digest are considered the same query.

The normalization consists of removing comments (but not optimizer hints), changing whitespace to a single-space character, replacing values in WHERE clauses with a question mark, and similar. You can use the function STATEMENT_DIGEST_TEXT() to obtain the normalized query, for example:

```
mysql> SELECT STATEMENT_DIGEST_TEXT(
                'SELECT *
                   FROM city
                  WHERE ID = 130'
              ) AS DigestText\G
*************************** 1. row ***************************
DigestText: SELECT * FROM `city` WHERE `ID` = ?
1 row in set (0.0004 sec)
```

Similarly, you can use the STATEMENT_DIGEST() function to get the SHA-256 hash for the query:

```
mysql> SELECT STATEMENT_DIGEST(
                'SELECT *
                   FROM city
                  WHERE ID = 130'
              ) AS Digest\G
```

```
*************************** 1. row ***************************
Digest: 26b06a0b2f651e04e61751c55f84d0d721d31041ea57cef5998bc475ab9ef773
1 row in set (0.0004 sec)
```

The STATEMENT_DIGEST() function can, for example, be useful if you want to query one of the statement event tables, the events_statements_histogram_by_digest table or the events_statements_summary_by_digest table, to find information about the queries that have the same digest.

Note   It is not guaranteed that the digest for a given query remains the same when you upgrade MySQL. This means that you should not compare digests for different MySQL releases.

When MySQL calculates the digest, the query is tokenized and in order to avoid excessive memory usage, the amount of memory per connection that is allowed for this process is capped. This means that if you have large queries (in terms of the query text), the normalized queries (called the digest text) will be truncated. You can configure how much memory the connection is allowed to use for the tokens during the normalization with the max_digest_length variable (defaults to 1024 and requires a restart of MySQL). If you have large queries, you may need to increase this avoid collisions between queries longer than max_digest_length bytes. If you increase max_digest_length you may also want to increase the performance_schema_max_digest_length option which specifies the maximum length of the digest texts stored in the Performance Schema. However, be careful as it will increase the size of all digest text values stored in the Performance Schema, and since the Performance Schema tables are stored in memory, it can cause a significant increase in memory usage. The author has seen several support tickets where MySQL failed to start because the digest lengths were set too high, so MySQL ran out of memory.

Caution   Do not blindly increase the digest length options as you may end up running out of memory.

Table Types

You have already encountered some of the tables available in the Performance Schema. The tables can be grouped according to the type of information they contain with the setup tables and event tables encountered earlier in this chapter forming two of the groups. Table 5-3 summarizes the types of tables available as of MySQL 8.0.18.

Table 5-3. *Performance Schema table types*

Table Type	Description
Setup	The tables with the dynamic configuration. This includes the setup_consumers and setup_instruments. All the setup tables have names starting with setup_.
Event	The tables storing the individual events either currently in progress or the history. This includes the events_statements_current. All the tables have the same name as one of the event consumers. Common is also that the table name starts with events_ but does not include summary or histogram.
Instance	The instance tables contain information about instances ranging from mutexes to prepared statements. The most commonly used instance table is prepared_statements_instances which includes statistics for server-side prepared statements. The instance tables all have table names ending in _instances with the exception of table_handles.
Summary	The summary tables can be considered as a kind of reports. They aggregate the events from the events tables, so you can get a longer-term overview. The most commonly used summary table is events_statements_summary_by_digest which groups the statement event data by the default schema and digest of the statements. Another example of a summary table is file_summary_by_instance which groups file-related statistics by the file instance. All table names include _summary_ or start with status_. The table names also include _by_ followed by a description of what the data is grouped by. As of 8.0.18 there are 45 summary tables, which makes it the largest group of tables.
Histogram	The histogram tables are report tables like the summary tables but provide histogram statistics for the statement latencies. There are currently two histogram tables: events_statements_histogram_by_digest and events_statements_histogram_global.

(continued)

Table 5-3. (*continued*)

Table Type	Description
Connections and threads	Various tables with information about the connections and threads. This includes the threads, session_account_connect_attrs, session_connect_attrs, accounts, host_cache, hosts, and users tables.
Replication	Information about the replication configuration and status both for traditional asynchronous replication and Group Replication. All the table names except log_status start with replication_.
Lock	This group includes three tables with information about data and metadata locks: data_locks, data_lock_waits, and metadata_locks.
Variable	The variable tables contain information about system and status variables (both for the global and session scopes) and user variables. All the table names include the word variables or status.
Clone	Information about the status and progress when using the clone plugin. The tables include clone_progress and clone_status.
Miscellaneous	The keyring_keys and performance_timers tables.

The tables that are most used are the summary tables as they provide easy access to data that on their own can be used as reports similar to what you will see in the next chapter with the sys schema views.

Dynamic Configuration

In addition to the traditional MySQL configuration options that can be set with SET PERSIST_ONLY or in a configuration file, the Performance Schema also features its own unique dynamic configuration through setup tables. This section explains how the dynamic configuration works.

Table 5-4 lists the setup tables available in MySQL 8. For the tables that allow inserts and deletes, all columns can be changed, but only the non-key columns are listed for settable columns.

Table 5-4. *Performance Schema setup tables*

Setup Table	Key Columns	Settable Columns	Description
setup_actors	HOST USER ROLE	ENABLED HISTORY	This table is used to determine whether foreground threads are instrumented and has history collected by default based on the account. The ROLE column is currently unused. You can insert rows into and delete rows from this table.
setup_consumers	NAME	ENABLED	This table defines which consumers are enabled.
setup_instruments	NAME	ENABLED TIMED	This table defines which instruments are enabled and timed.
setup_objects	OBJECT_TYPE OBJECT_SCHEMA OBJECT_NAME`	ENABLED TIMED	This table defines which schema objects are enabled and timed. You can insert rows into and delete rows from this table.
setup_threads	NAME	ENABLED HISTORY	This table defines which thread types are instrumented and have history collected by default.

For the tables with a HISTORY column, the history can only be recorded if instrumentation is also enabled. In the same way for the TIMED column, it only is relevant if the instrument or object is enabled. For setup_instruments, note that not all instruments support being timed in which case the TIMED column is always NULL.

The setup_actors and setup_objects tables are special among the setup tables as you can insert and delete rows for them. This includes using the TRUNCATE TABLE statement to remove all rows. Since the tables are stored in memory, you cannot freely insert as many rows as you want. Instead, the maximum number of rows is defined by the performance_schema_setup_actors_size and performance_schema_setup_objects_size configuration options. Both options are autosized by default. It requires restarting MySQL for a change to the table sizes to take effect.

You use regular UPDATE statements to manipulate the configuration. For the setup_ actors and setup_objects tables, you can also use INSERT, DELETE, and TRUNCATE TABLE. An example of enabling the events_statements_history_long consumer is

```
mysql> UPDATE performance_schema.setup_consumers
          SET ENABLED = 'YES'
       WHERE NAME = 'events_statements_history_long';
Query OK, 1 row affected (0.2674 sec)

Rows matched: 1   Changed: 1   Warnings: 0
```

This configuration is not persistent when restarting MySQL, so if you want to change the configuration of these tables for the cases where there are no configuration options, add the SQL statements required to an init file and execute it through the init_file option.

That concludes the introduction to the Performance Schema, but you will see many examples of using the tables in the remainder of the book.

Summary

This chapter has covered the most important concepts of the Performance Schema. MySQL is a multi-threaded process, and the Performance Schema includes information for all threads, both foreground threads (connections) and background threads.

The instruments correspond to the instrumented code points in the source code and thus determine which data is collected. When an instrument is enabled, it can optionally also be timed with the exception of memory and error instruments.

The consumers take the data collected by the instruments and process it and make it available through the Performance Schema tables. Twelve of the consumers represent the four event types with three scopes for each type.

The four event types are transactions, statements, stages, and waits which cover different detail levels. The three event scopes are current for the current or last completed events, history for the ten last events for each thread that still exists, and the last 10,000 events irrespective of the thread generating them. Events can trigger other events, so they form a tree.

An important concept is also the digests which allow MySQL to aggregate data grouping by the normalized queries. This is a feature that will prove particularly useful when you will be looking for candidates for query tuning.

At the end, the various types of tables in the Performance Schema were summarized. The most commonly used group of tables is the summary tables which are essentially reports that make it easy to access aggregate data from the Performance Schema. Another example of reports based on the Performance Schema – and in several cases of summary tables – is the information made available in the sys schema which is the topic of the next chapter.

## CHAPTER 6

The sys Schema

The sys schema is the brainchild of Mark Leith, who has also for long been part of the team that develops MySQL Enterprise Monitor. He started the ps_helper project to experiment with monitoring ideas and to showcase what the Performance Schema was able to do while making it simpler at the same time. The project was later renamed to the sys schema and moved into MySQL. There have since been contributions from several other people, including the author of this book.

The sys schema is available for MySQL Server 5.6 and later. In MySQL 5.7 it became part of the standard installation, so you do not need to do anything to install the sys schema or upgrade it. As of MySQL 8.0.18, the sys schema source code is part of the MySQL Server source.

The sys schema is used throughout the book for analyzing queries, locks, and more. This chapter will give the high-level overview of the sys schema including how to configure it, formatting functions, how the views work, and various helper routines.

Tip The sys schema source code (`https://github.com/mysql/mysql-server/tree/8.0/scripts/sys_schema` and for older MySQL versions `https://github.com/mysql/mysql-sys/`) is also a useful resource to learn how to write queries against the Performance Schema.

---

sys Schema Configuration

The sys schema uses its own configuration system as it was originally implemented independent of MySQL Server. There are two ways to change the configuration depending on whether you want to change the setting permanently or just for the session.

© Jesper Wisborg Krogh 2020
J. W. Krogh, *MySQL 8 Query Performance Tuning*, https://doi.org/10.1007/978-1-4842-5584-1_6

The persisted configuration is stored in the sys_config table which includes the name of the variable, its value, and when the value was last set and by which user. Listing 6-1 shows the default content (the set_time will depend on when the sys schema was last installed or upgraded).

Listing 6-1. The sys schema persisted configuration

```
mysql> SELECT * FROM sys.sys_config\G
*************************** 1. row ***************************
variable: diagnostics.allow_i_s_tables
   value: OFF
set_time: 2019-07-13 19:19:29
  set_by: NULL
*************************** 2. row ***************************
variable: diagnostics.include_raw
   value: OFF
set_time: 2019-07-13 19:19:29
  set_by: NULL
*************************** 3. row ***************************
variable: ps_thread_trx_info.max_length
   value: 65535
set_time: 2019-07-13 19:19:29
  set_by: NULL
*************************** 4. row ***************************
variable: statement_performance_analyzer.limit
   value: 100
set_time: 2019-07-13 19:19:29
  set_by: NULL
*************************** 5. row ***************************
variable: statement_performance_analyzer.view
   value: NULL
set_time: 2019-07-13 19:19:29
  set_by: NULL
```

```
*********************** 6. row **************************
variable: statement_truncate_len
   value: 64
set_time: 2019-07-13 19:19:29
  set_by: NULL
6 rows in set (0.0005 sec)
```

Currently the set_by column is always NULL unless the @sys.ignore_sys_config_ triggers user variable is set to a value that evaluated to FALSE but is not NULL.

The option you are most likely to change is statement_truncate_len which specifies the maximum length the sys schema will use for statements in the formatted views (more about these later). The default of 64 was chosen to increase the probability that querying views will fit in the width of your console; however, sometimes it is too little to get enough useful information about the statement.

You can update the configuration settings by updating the value in sys_config. This will persist the change and apply immediately to all connections unless they have set their own session value (this happens implicitly when using something in the sys schema that formats statements). As sys_config is a normal InnoDB table, the change will also remain after restarting MySQL.

Alternatively, you can change the setting just for the session. This is done by taking the name of the configuration variable and prepending sys. and turning it into a user variable. Listing 6-2 shows examples both of using the sys_config table and a user variable to change the configuration of statement_truncate_len. The result is tested with the format_statement() function which is what the sys schema uses to truncate statements.

Listing 6-2. Changing the sys schema configuration

```
mysql> SET @query = 'SELECT * FROM world.city INNER JOIN world.city ON
country.Code = city.CountryCode';
Query OK, 0 rows affected (0.0003 sec)

mysql> SELECT sys.sys_get_config(
                'statement_truncate_len',
                NULL
            ) AS TruncateLen\G
```

```
*************************** 1. row ***************************
TruncateLen: 64
1 row in set (0.0007 sec)

mysql> SELECT sys.format_statement(@query) AS Statement\G
*************************** 1. row ***************************
Statement: SELECT * FROM world.city INNER ... ountry.Code = city.CountryCode
1 row in set (0.0019 sec)

mysql> UPDATE sys.sys_config SET value = 48 WHERE variable = 'statement_
truncate_len';
Query OK, 1 row affected (0.4966 sec)

mysql> SET @sys.statement_truncate_len = NULL;
Query OK, 0 rows affected (0.0004 sec)

mysql> SELECT sys.format_statement(@query) AS Statement\G
*************************** 1. row ***************************
Statement: SELECT * FROM world.ci ... ode = city.CountryCode
1 row in set (0.0009 sec)

mysql> SET @sys.statement_truncate_len = 96;
Query OK, 0 rows affected (0.0003 sec)

mysql> SELECT sys.format_statement(@query) AS Statement\G
*************************** 1. row ***************************
Statement: SELECT * FROM world.city INNER JOIN world.city ON country.Code =
          city.CountryCode
1 row in set (0.0266 sec)
```

First, a query is set in the @query user variable. This is purely for convenience, so it is easy to keep referencing the same query. The sys_get_config() function is used to get the current configuration value for the statement_truncate_len option. This takes into account whether the @sys.statement_trauncate_len user variable is set. The second argument provides the value to return if the provided option does not exist.

The format_statement() function is used to demonstrate formatting the statement in @query, first with the default value of 64 for statement_truncate_len, then updating sys_config to have a value of 48, and finally setting the value for the session to 96. Notice how the @sys.statement_truncate_len user variable is set to NULL after updating the sys_config table to make MySQL apply the updated setting to the session.

Note   There are a few configuration options supported by some of the sys schema features that are not in the sys_config table by default, for example, the debug option. The documentation of the sys schema objects (https://dev.mysql.com/doc/refman/en/sys-schema-reference.html) includes information on which configuration options are supported.

The format_statement() function is not the only formatting function in the sys schema, so let's take a look at all of them.

Formatting Functions

The sys schema includes four functions to help you format the output of the queries against the Performance Schema to make the result easier to read or take up less space. Two of the functions have been deprecated in MySQL 8.0.16 as native Performance Schema functions have been added to replace them.

Table 6-1 summarizes the four functions and the new native functions that replace them for the case of format_time() and format_bytes().

Table 6-1. sys *schema formatting functions*

sys Schema Function	Native Function	Description
format_bytes()	FORMAT_BYTES()	Converts a value in bytes into a string with a unit (1024-based).
format_path()		Takes a path to a file and replaces the data directory, temporary directory, and so on with a string representing the corresponding global variable.
format_ statement()		Truncates a statement to at most the number of characters set by the statement_truncate_ len configuration option by replacing the middle of the statement with ellipses (...).
format_time()	FORMAT_PICO_TIME()	Converts a time in picoseconds to a human-readable string.

Listing 6-3 shows an example of using the formatting functions, and for format_bytes() and format_time(), the results will be compared to the native Performance Schema functions.

Listing 6-3. Using the formatting functions

```
mysql> SELECT sys.format_bytes(5000) AS SysBytes,
              FORMAT_BYTES(5000) AS P_SBytes\G
*************************** 1. row ***************************
SysBytes: 4.88 KiB
P_SBytes: 4.88 KiB
1 row in set, 1 warning (0.0015 sec)
Note (code 1585): This function 'format_bytes' has the same name as a
                native function

mysql> SELECT @@global.datadir AS DataDir,
              sys.format_path(
                  'D:\\MySQL\\Data_8.0.18\\ib_logfile0'
              ) AS LogFile0\G
*************************** 1. row ***************************
 DataDir: D:\MySQL\Data_8.0.18\
LogFile0: @@datadir\ib_logfile0
1 row in set (0.0027 sec)

mysql> SELECT sys.format_statement(
                  'SELECT * FROM world.city INNER JOIN world.city ON
                  country.Code = city.CountryCode'
              ) AS Statement\G
*************************** 1. row ***************************
Statement: SELECT * FROM world.city INNER ... ountry.Code = city.CountryCode
1 row in set (0.0016 sec)

mysql> SELECT sys.format_time(123456789012) AS SysTime,
              FORMAT_PICO_TIME(123456789012) AS P_STime\G
*************************** 1. row ***************************
SysTime: 123.46 ms
P_STime: 123.46 ms
1 row in set (0.0006 sec)
```

Notice that the use of `sys.format_bytes()` triggers a warning (but only the first time a connection uses it) because the `sys` schema function name is the same as the native function name. The `format_path()` function expects backslashes for path names on Microsoft Windows and forward slashes on other platforms. The result of the `format_statement()` function assumes the value of the `statement_truncate_len` option has been reset to its default value of 64.

Tip   While the `sys` schema implementations of `format_time()` and `format_bytes()` still exist, it is best to use the new native functions as the `sys` schema implementations are likely to get removed in a future version and the native functions are much faster.

These functions are not only useful on their own, they are also used by the `sys` schema to implement views that return formatted data. As it is in some cases necessary to work with the unformatted data, there exist two implementations of most `sys` schema views as you will see next.

The Views

The `sys` schema provides a number of views that work as predefined reports. The views mostly use the Performance Schema tables, but a few also use the Information Schema. The views are there both to make it easy to get information out of the Performance Schema and to serve as examples of how to query the Performance Schema.

As the views are ready-made reports that you can use as a database administrator or developer, they are defined with a default ordering. This means that a typical way of using the views is to do a plain `SELECT * FROM <view name>`, for example:

```
mysql> SELECT *
         FROM sys.schema_tables_with_full_table_scans\G
*************************** 1. row ***************************
    object_schema: world
      object_name: city
rows_full_scanned: 4079
          latency: 269.13 ms
```

```
*************************** 2. row ***************************
   object_schema: sys
     object_name: sys_config
rows_full_scanned: 18
         latency: 328.80 ms
2 rows in set (0.0021 sec)
```

The result depends on which tables have been used with a full table scan. Notice how the latencies have been formatted like with the FORMAT_PICO_TIME() or sys. format_time() function.

Most of the sys schema views exist in two forms with one having statements, paths, byte values, and timings formatted and the other returning the raw data. The formatted views are very useful if you query a view at the console and look at the data yourself, whereas the unformatted views work better if you need to process the data in a program or want to change the default sorting. The performance reports in MySQL Workbench use the unformatted views, so you can change the ordering from within the user interface.

You can distinguish between the formatted and unformatted views from the name. If a view contains formatting, there will also be an unformatted view with the same name, but with x$ prepended to the name. For example, for the schema_tables_with_full_table_scans view that was used in the previous example, the unformatted view is named x$schema_tables_with_full_table_scans:

```
mysql> SELECT *
       FROM sys.x$schema_tables_with_full_table_scans\G
*************************** 1. row ***************************
   object_schema: world
     object_name: city
rows_full_scanned: 4079
         latency: 269131954854
*************************** 2. row ***************************
   object_schema: sys
     object_name: sys_config
rows_full_scanned: 18
         latency: 328804286013
2 rows in set (0.0017 sec)
```

The last topic for the sys schema is the helper functions and procedures that are provided.

Helper Functions and Procedures

The sys schema provides several utilities that can help you when working with MySQL. These include the ability to execute dynamically created queries, manipulating lists, and more. The most important of the helper functions and procedures are summarized in Table 6-2.

Table 6-2. *Helper functions and procedures in the sys schema*

Routine Name	Routine Type	Description
extract_schema_ from_file_name	Function	Extracts the schema name from a path for a file-per-table InnoDB tablespace file.
extract_table_ from_file_name	Function	Extracts the table name from a path for a file-per-table InnoDB tablespace file.
list_add	Function	Adds an element to a list unless it already exists in the list. This is, for example, useful if you need to change the SQL mode.
list_drop	Function	Removes an element from a list.
quote_ identifier	Function	Quotes an identifier (e.g., table name) with backticks (`).
version_major	Function	Returns the major version for the instance you are querying. For example, it returns 8 for 8.0.18.
version_minor	Function	Returns the minor version for the instance you are querying. For example, it returns 0 for 8.0.18.
version_patch	Function	Returns the patch release version for the instance you are querying. For example, it returns 18 for 8.0.18.
execute_ prepared_stmt	Procedure	Executes a query given as a string. The query is executed using a prepared statement, and the procedure deallocates the prepared statement after the execution has completed.
table_exists	Procedure	Returns whether a table exists and if so whether it is a base table, temporary table, or a view.

Several of these utilities are also used internally in the sys schema. The most common use of the routines is in stored programs where you need to handle data and queries dynamically.

Tip   The sys schema functions and procedures come with built-in help in the form of routine comments. You can obtain the help by querying the ROUTINE_COMMENT column of the information_schema.ROUTINES view.

Summary

This chapter has provided a brief introduction to the sys schema, so you know what it is and how to use it when you see examples in later chapters. The sys schema is a useful addition that provides ready-made reports and utilities that can simplify your daily tasks and investigations. The sys schema is a system schema in MySQL 5.7 and later, so no action is required from your side to start using it.

First, the sys schema configuration was discussed. The global configuration is stored in the sys.sys_config table which can be updated, if you prefer different default values than what is provided when MySQL is installed. You can also change the configuration option for a session by setting a user variable with sys. prefixed to the name of the configuration option.

Then the sys schema formatting functions were covered with mention of the cases where native Performance Schema functions have been added as replacement for the sys schema functions. The formatting functions are also used in several of the views to help make the data easier to read for humans. For the views using the formatting functions, there is also a corresponding unformatted view with x$ prefixed to the name.

Finally, several helper functions and procedures were discussed. These can help you when you try to do work dynamically, such as executing a query generated in a stored procedure.

The next chapter is about the Information Schema.

CHAPTER 7

The Information Schema

When you need to optimize a query, it is common that you need information about the schema, indexes, and the like. In that case, the Information Schema is a good resource of data. This chapter introduces the Information Schema together with an overview of the views it contains. The Information Schema is used on several occasions in the rest of the book.

What Is the Information Schema?

The Information Schema is a schema common to several of the relational databases including MySQL where it was added in MySQL 5.0. MySQL mostly follows the SQL:2003 standard for *F021 Basic information schema* with the changes necessary to reflect the unique features of MySQL and with additional views that are not part of the standard.

Note The Information Schema is virtual in the sense that no data is stored in it. For this reason, this chapter refers to all views and tables as views even if a SHOW CREATE TABLE displays it as if it was a regular table. This is also in line with the `information_schema.TABLES` view that has the table type set to SYSTEM VIEW for all the objects.

After the introduction of the Performance Schema in MySQL 5.5, the aim is to make relatively static data such as schema information available through the Information Schema and more volatile data belonging to the Performance Schema. That said, it is not always clear-cut what belongs where, for example, index statistics are relatively volatile, but are also part of the schema information. There is also some information such as the InnoDB metrics that for historical reasons still reside in the Information Schema.

© Jesper Wisborg Krogh 2020
J. W. Krogh, *MySQL 8 Query Performance Tuning*, https://doi.org/10.1007/978-1-4842-5584-1_7

As such, you can consider the Information Schema a collection of data describing the MySQL instance. In MySQL 8 with the relational data dictionary, several of the views are simple SQL views on the underlying data dictionary tables. This means that the performance of many Information Schema queries in MySQL 8 will be vastly superior to what you may have experienced in older versions. This is particularly the case when querying schema data that does not require retrieving information from the storage engine.

Caution   If you are still using MySQL 5.7 or earlier, be careful with queries against views such as the TABLES and COLUMNS views in the Information Schema. They can take a long time if the tables they contain data for are not yet in the table definition cache or if the cache is not large enough to hold all tables. An example of the performance difference of the Information Schema between MySQL 5.7 and 8 is discussed in a blog by the MySQL Server team: `https://mysqlserverteam.com/mysql-8-0-scaling-and-performance-of-information_schema/`.

Privileges

The Information Schema is a virtual database, and the access to the views works a little different from other tables. All users will see that the `information_schema` schema exists, and they will see all views. However, the result of querying the views depends on the privileges assigned to the account. For example, an account that has no other privileges than the global USAGE privilege will only see the Information Schema views when querying the `information_schema.TABLES` view.

Some views require additional privileges in which case an ER_SPECIFIC_ACCESS_DENIED_ERROR (error number 1227) error is returned with a description of which privilege is missing. For example, the INNODB_METRICS view requires the PROCESS privilege, so if a user without the PROCESS privilege queries that view, the following error occurs:

```
mysql> SELECT *
        FROM information_schema.INNODB_METRICS;
ERROR: 1227: Access denied; you need (at least one of) the PROCESS
privilege(s) for this operation
```

Now, it is time to look at what kind of information you can find in the Information Schema views.

Views

The data that is available in the Information Schema ranges from high-level information about the system to low-level InnoDB metrics. This section provides an overview of the views but will not go into detail as the most important of the views from a performance tuning perspective are discussed in the relevant parts of later chapters.

Note   Some plugins add their own views to the Information Schema. The extra plugin views are not considered here.

System Information

The highest level of information that is available in the Information Schema concerns the whole MySQL instance. This includes such information as which character sets are available and which plugins are installed.

The views with system information are summarized in Table 7-1.

Table 7-1. *Information Schema views with system information*

View Name	Description
CHARACTER_SETS	The character sets available.
COLLATIONS	The collations available for each character set. This includes the id of the collation which in some cases (e.g., in the binary log) is used to uniquely specify both the collation and character set.
COLLATION_CHARACTER_ SET_APPLICABILITY	The mapping of collations to character sets (the same as the first two columns of COLLATIONS).
ENGINES	The storage engines that are known and whether they are loaded.
INNODB_FT_DEFAULT_ STOPWORD	A list of the default stopwords that are used when creating a full text index on an InnoDB table.
KEYWORDS	A list of the keywords in MySQL and whether the keyword is reserved.

(continued)

Table 7-1. (*continued*)

View Name	Description
PLUGINS	The plugins known to MySQL including the status.
RESOURCE_GROUPS	The resource groups that are used by threads to do their work. A resource group specifies the priority of a thread and which CPUs it can use.
ST_SPATIAL_REFERENCE_ SYSTEMS	A list of the spatial reference systems including the SRS_ID column which contains the id used to specify a reference system for spatial columns.

The system-related views largely work as reference views with the RESOURCE_GROUPS table being somewhat a difference as it is possible to add resource groups as it will be discussed in Chapter 17.

The KEYWORDS view is, for example, useful when testing an upgrade as you can use it to verify whether any of your schema, table, column, routine, or parameter names matches a keyword in the new version. If that is the case, you will need to update the application to quote the identifier, if that is not already the case. To find all column names matching a keyword:

```
SELECT TABLE_SCHEMA, TABLE_NAME,
       COLUMN_NAME, RESERVED
  FROM information_schema.COLUMNS
       INNER JOIN information_schema.KEYWORDS
         ON KEYWORDS.WORD = COLUMNS.COLUMN_NAME
 WHERE TABLE_SCHEMA NOT IN ('mysql',
                            'information_schema',
                            'performance_schema',
                            'sys'
                           )
 ORDER BY TABLE_SCHEMA, TABLE_NAME, COLUMN_NAME;
```

The query uses the COLUMNS view to find all column names except for the system schemas (you can choose to include those, if you use those in your application or in scripts). The COLUMNS view is one of several views describing the schema objects.

Schema Information

The views with information about the schema objects are among the most useful views in the Information Schema. These are also the source for several of the SHOW statements. You can use the views to find information from everything from parameters for a stored routine to database names. The views with schema information are summarized in Table 7-2.

Table 7-2. Information Schema views with schema information

View Name	Description
CHECK_CONSTRAINTS	This view contains information about the CHECK constraints and is available in MySQL 8.0.16 and later.
COLUMN_STATISTICS	The definition of histograms including the statistics. This is a very useful view for query performance tuning.
COLUMNS	The column definitions.
EVENTS	The definitions of the stored events.
FILES	Information about InnoDB tablespace files.
INNODB_COLUMNS	Metadata information for columns in InnoDB tables.
INNODB_DATAFILES	This view links the InnoDB tablespace ids to the file system paths.
INNODB_FIELDS	Metadata for columns included in InnoDB indexes.
INNODB_FOREIGN	Metadata for the InnoDB foreign keys.
INNODB_FOREIGN_COLS	Lists the child and parent columns of InnoDB foreign keys.
INNODB_FT_BEING_DELETED	A snapshot of the INNODB_FT_DELETED view during an OPTIMIZE TABLE statement for the InnoDB table specified in the innodb_ft_aux_table option.
INNODB_FT_CONFIG	Configuration information for full text indexes on the InnoDB table specified in the innodb_ft_aux_table option.
INNODB_FT_DELETED	Rows that have been deleted from full text indexes for the InnoDB table specified in the innodb_ft_aux_table option. InnoDB uses this extra list for performance reasons to avoid having to update the index itself for each DML statement.

(continued)

Table 7-2. (*continued*)

View Name	Description
INNODB_FT_INDEX_CACHE	Newly inserted rows into the full text indexes for the InnoDB table specified in the `innodb_ft_aux_table` option. InnoDB uses this extra list for performance reasons to avoid having to update the index itself for each DML statement.
INNODB_FT_INDEX_TABLE	The inverted full text index for the InnoDB table specified in the `innodb_ft_aux_table` option.
INNODB_INDEXES	Information about indexes on InnoDB tables. This includes internal information such as the page number of the root page and the merge threshold.
INNODB_TABLES	Metadata for the InnoDB tables.
INNODB_TABLESPACES	Metadata for the InnoDB tablespaces.
INNODB_TABLESPACES_BRIEF	This view combines the `SPACE`, `NAME`, `FLAG`, and `SPACE_TYPE` columns from `INNODB_TABLESPACES` with the `PATH` column from `INNODB_DATAFILES` to provide a summary of the InnoDB tablespace.
INNODB_TABLESTATS	Table statistics for InnoDB tables. Some of these statistics are updated at the same time as index statistics; others are maintained at an ongoing basis.
INNODB_TEMP_TABLE_INFO	Metadata for InnoDB temporary tables (both internal and explicit).
INNODB_VIRTUAL	Internal metadata information about virtual generated columns on InnoDB tables.
KEY_COLUMN_USAGE	Information about the primary keys, unique keys, and foreign keys.
PARAMETERS	Information about the parameters for stored functions and stored procedures.
PARTITIONS	Information about table partitions.
REFERENTIAL_CONSTRAINTS	Information about foreign keys.

(*continued*)

Table 7-2. (*continued*)

View Name	Description
ROUTINES	The definition of stored functions and stored procedures.
SCHEMATA	Information about the schemas (databases). (Schemata is technically the correct word for the plural form of schema, but most use schemas nowadays.)
ST_GEOMETRY_COLUMNS	Information about columns with a spatial data type.
STATISTICS	The index definitions and statistics. This is one of the most useful views when it comes to query performance turning.
TABLE_CONSTRAINTS	Summary of the primary, unique, and foreign keys and CHECK constraints.
TABLES	Information about tables and views and their properties.
TABLESPACES	This view is only used for NDB Cluster tablespaces.
TRIGGERS	The trigger definitions.
VIEW_ROUTINE_USAGE	Lists the stored functions used in views. This table was added in 8.0.13.
VIEW_TABLE_USAGE	Lists the tables referenced by views. This view was added in 8.0.13.
VIEWS	The view definitions.

Several of the views are closely related, for example, the columns are in tables which are in schemas and constraints refer to tables and columns. This means that some of the column names are present in several of the views. The most commonly used column names that relate to these views are

- **TABLE_NAME:** Used in the views not specific to InnoDB for the table name.

- **TABLE_SCHEMA:** Used in the views not specific to InnoDB for the schema name.

- **COLUMN_NAME:** Used in the views not specific to InnoDB for the column name.

- **SPACE:** Used in the InnoDB-specific views for the tablespace id.

- **TABLE_ID:** Used in the InnoDB-specific views to uniquely identify the table. This is also used internally in InnoDB.

- **NAME:** The InnoDB-specific views use a column called NAME to give the name of the object irrespective of the object type.

In addition to the use of the names as in this list, there are also examples where these column names are slightly modified like in the view KEY_COLUMN_USAGE where you find the columns REFERENCED_TABLE_SCHEMA, REFERENCED_TABLE_NAME, and REFERENCED_COLUMN_NAME that are used in the description of foreign keys. As an example, if you want to use the KEY_COLUMN_USAGE view to find the tables with foreign keys referencing the sakila.film table, you can use a query like this:

```
mysql> SELECT TABLE_SCHEMA, TABLE_NAME
    FROM information_schema.KEY_COLUMN_USAGE
   WHERE REFERENCED_TABLE_SCHEMA = 'sakila'
     AND REFERENCED_TABLE_NAME = 'film';
+--------------+----------------+
| TABLE_SCHEMA | TABLE_NAME     |
+--------------+----------------+
| sakila       | film_actor     |
| sakila       | film_category  |
| sakila       | inventory      |
+--------------+----------------+
3 rows in set (0.0078 sec)
```

This shows that the film_actor, film_category, and inventory tables all have foreign keys where the film table is the parent table. For example, if you look at the table definition for film_actor:

```
mysql> SHOW CREATE TABLE sakila.film_actor\G
*************************** 1. row ***************************
       Table: film_actor
Create Table: CREATE TABLE `film_actor` (
  `actor_id` smallint(5) unsigned NOT NULL,
  `film_id` smallint(5) unsigned NOT NULL,
```

```
`last_update` timestamp NOT NULL DEFAULT CURRENT_TIMESTAMP ON UPDATE
CURRENT_TIMESTAMP,
PRIMARY KEY (`actor_id`,`film_id`),
KEY `idx_fk_film_id` (`film_id`),
CONSTRAINT `fk_film_actor_actor` FOREIGN KEY (`actor_id`) REFERENCES
`actor` (`actor_id`) ON DELETE RESTRICT ON UPDATE CASCADE,
CONSTRAINT `fk_film_actor_film` FOREIGN KEY (`film_id`) REFERENCES `film`
(`film_id`) ON DELETE RESTRICT ON UPDATE CASCADE
) ENGINE=InnoDB DEFAULT CHARSET=utf8
1 row in set (0.0097 sec)
```

The fk_film_actor_film constraint references the film_id column in the film table. You can use this as the starting point for finding the full chain of foreign keys either by manually executing the query for each table returned in the query against the KEY_COLUMN_USAGE view or by creating a recursive common table expression (CTE). This is left as an exercise for the reader.

Tip   For an example where the KEY_COLUMN_USAGE view is used in a recursive common table expression to find the chain of foreign key dependencies, see `https://mysql.wisborg.dk/tracking-foreign-keys`.

For completeness, a visual representation of the tables depending on the film table through foreign keys can be found in Figure 7-1.

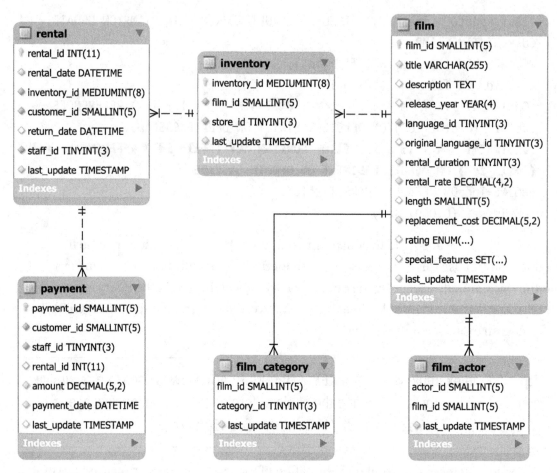

Figure 7-1. *A visual representation of the foreign key chain from* `sakila.film`

The diagram is created using the reverse engineering feature of MySQL Workbench.

The views with information specific to InnoDB use the SPACE and TABLE_ID to identify the tablespace and table. Each tablespace has a unique id with ranges reserved for different tablespace types. For example, the data dictionary tablespace file (`<datadir>/mysql.ibd`) has space id 4294967294, the temporary tablespace has id 4294967293, undo log tablespaces start with 4294967279 and decrement, and user tablespaces start at 1.

The views with information about InnoDB full text indexes are special as they require you to set the `innodb_ft_aux_table` global variable with the name of the table you want to get information for. For example, to get the full text index configuration of the `sakila.film_text` table:

```
mysql> SET GLOBAL innodb_ft_aux_table = 'sakila/film_text';
Query OK, 0 rows affected (0.0685 sec)

mysql> SELECT *
          FROM information_schema.INNODB_FT_CONFIG;
+---------------------------+-------+
| KEY                       | VALUE |
+---------------------------+-------+
| optimize_checkpoint_limit | 180   |
| synced_doc_id             | 1002  |
| stopword_table_name       |       |
| use_stopword              | 1     |
+---------------------------+-------+
4 rows in set (0.0009 sec)
```

The values in the INNODB_FT_CONFIG view may differ for you.

InnoDB also includes views with information that relates to performance. These will be discussed together with a few other performance-related tables.

Performance Information

The group of views that relate to performance are those that you will likely use the most in your performance tuning work together with the COLUMN_STATISTICS and STATISTICS views from the previous group of views. The views with performance-related information are listed in Table 7-3.

Table 7-3. *Information Schema views with performance-related information*

View Name	Description
INNODB_BUFFER_PAGE	A list of the pages in the InnoDB buffer pool which can be used to determine which tables and indexes are currently cached. **Warning:** There is a high overhead of querying this table particularly for large buffer pools and many tables and indexes. It is best used on test systems.
INNODB_BUFFER_PAGE_LRU	Information about the pages in the InnoDB buffer pool and how they are ordered in the least recently used (LRU) list. **Warning:** There is a high overhead of querying this table particularly for large buffer pools and many tables and indexes. It is best used on test systems.
INNODB_BUFFER_POOL_STATS	Statistics about the usage of the InnoDB buffer pool. The information is similar to what can be found in the SHOW ENGINE INNODB STATUS output in the BUFFER POOL AND MEMORY section. This is one of the most useful views.
INNODB_CACHED_INDEXES	A summary of the number of index pages cached in the InnoDB buffer pool for each index.
INNODB_CMP INNODB_CMP_RESET	Statistics about operations related to compressed InnoDB tables.
INNODB_CMP_PER_INDEX INNODB_CMP_PER_INDEX_RESET	The same as INNODB_CMP but grouped by the index.
INNODB_CMPMEM INNODB_CMPMEM_RESET	Statistics about compressed pages in the InnoDB buffer pool.
INNODB_METRICS	Similar to the global status variables but specific to InnoDB.
INNODB_SESSION_TEMP_TABLESPACES	Metadata including the connection id, file path, and size for InnoDB temporary tablespace files (each session gets its own file in MySQL 8.0.13 and later). It can be used to link a session to a tablespace file which is very useful if you notice one file becoming large. The view was added in 8.0.13.

(continued)

Table 7-3. (*continued*)

View Name	Description
INNODB_TRX	Information about InnoDB transactions.
OPTIMIZER_TRACE	When the optimizer trace is enabled, the trace can be queried from this view.
PROCESSLIST	The same as SHOW PROCESSLIST.
PROFILING	When profiling is enabled, the profiling statistics can be queried from this view. This is deprecated, and it is recommended to use the Performance Schema instead.

For the views with information about InnoDB compressed tables, the table with _ RESET as the suffix returns the operation and timing statistics as deltas since the last time the view was queried.

The INNODB_METRICS view includes metrics similar to the global status variables but specific to InnoDB. The metrics are grouped into subsystems (the SUBSYSTEM column), and for each metric there is a description of what the metric measures in the COMMENT column. You can enable, disable, and reset the metrics using global system variables:

- **innodb_monitor_disable:** Disable one or more metrics.

- **innodb_monitor_enable:** Enable one or more metrics.

- **innodb_monitor_reset:** Reset the counter for one or more metrics.

- **innodb_monitor_reset_all:** Reset all statistics including the counter, minimum, and maximum values for one or more metrics.

The metrics can be turned on and off as needed with the current status found in the STATUS column. You specify the name of the metric as the value to the innodb_monitor_ enable or innodb_monitor_disable variable, and you can use % as a wildcard. The value all works as a special value to affect all metrics. Listing 7-1 shows an example of enabling and using all the metrics matching %cpu% (which happens to be the metrics in the cpu subsystem). The counter values depend on the workload you have at the time of the query.

Listing 7-1. Using the INNODB_METRICS view

```
mysql> SET GLOBAL innodb_monitor_enable = '%cpu%';
Query OK, 0 rows affected (0.0005 sec)

mysql> SELECT NAME, COUNT, MIN_COUNT,
              MAX_COUNT, AVG_COUNT,
              STATUS, COMMENT
         FROM information_schema.INNODB_METRICS
         WHERE NAME LIKE '%cpu%'\G
*************************** 1. row ***************************
     NAME: module_cpu
    COUNT: 0
MIN_COUNT: NULL
MAX_COUNT: NULL
AVG_COUNT: 0
   STATUS: enabled
  COMMENT: CPU counters reflecting current usage of CPU
*************************** 2. row ***************************
     NAME: cpu_utime_abs
    COUNT: 51
MIN_COUNT: 0
MAX_COUNT: 51
AVG_COUNT: 0.4358974358974359
   STATUS: enabled
  COMMENT: Total CPU user time spent
*************************** 3. row ***************************
     NAME: cpu_stime_abs
    COUNT: 7
MIN_COUNT: 0
MAX_COUNT: 7
AVG_COUNT: 0.05982905982905983
   STATUS: enabled
  COMMENT: Total CPU system time spent
```

```
*************************** 4. row ***************************
     NAME: cpu_utime_pct
    COUNT: 6
MIN_COUNT: 0
MAX_COUNT: 6
AVG_COUNT: 0.05128205128205128
   STATUS: enabled
  COMMENT: Relative CPU user time spent
*************************** 5. row ***************************
     NAME: cpu_stime_pct
    COUNT: 0
MIN_COUNT: 0
MAX_COUNT: 0
AVG_COUNT: 0
   STATUS: enabled
  COMMENT: Relative CPU system time spent
*************************** 6. row ***************************
     NAME: cpu_n
    COUNT: 8
MIN_COUNT: 8
MAX_COUNT: 8
AVG_COUNT: 0.06837606837606838
   STATUS: enabled
  COMMENT: Number of cpus
6 rows in set (0.0011 sec)

mysql> SET GLOBAL innodb_monitor_disable = '%cpu%';
Query OK, 0 rows affected (0.0004 sec)
```

First, the metrics are enabled using the innodb_monitor_enable variable; then
the values are retrieved. In addition to the values shown, there is also a set of columns
with the _RESET suffix which are reset when you set the innodb_monitor_reset (only
the counter) or innodb_monitor_reset_all system variable. Finally, the metrics are
disabled again.

Caution   The metrics have varying overheads, so you are recommended to test with your workload before enabling metrics in production.

The InnoDB metrics are also included in the sys.metrics view together with the global status variables and a few other metrics and when the metrics are retrieved.

The remaining Information Schema views contain information about privileges.

Privilege Information

MySQL uses privileges assigned to the accounts to determine which accounts can access which schemas, tables, and columns. The common way to determine the privileges for a given account is to use the SHOW GRANTS statement, but the Information Schema also includes views that allow you to query the privileges.

The Information Schema privilege views are summarized in Table 7-4. The views are ordered from global privileges to column privileges.

Table 7-4. *Information Schema tables with privilege information*

Table Name	Description
USER_PRIVILEGES	The global privileges.
SCHEMA_PRIVILEGES	Privileges to access schemas.
TABLE_PRIVILEGES	Privileges to access tables.
COLUMN_PRIVILEGES	Privileges to access columns.

In all views, the account is called GRANTEE and is in the form 'username'@'hostname' with the quotes always present. Listing 7-2 shows an example of retrieving the privileges for the mysql.sys@localhost account and comparing it to the output of the SHOW GRANTS statement.

Listing 7-2. Using the Information Schema privilege views

```
mysql> SHOW GRANTS FOR 'mysql.sys'@'localhost'\G
*************************** 1. row ***************************
Grants for mysql.sys@localhost: GRANT USAGE ON *.* TO `mysql.
sys`@`localhost`
*************************** 2. row ***************************
Grants for mysql.sys@localhost: GRANT TRIGGER ON `sys`.* TO `mysql.
sys`@`localhost`
*************************** 3. row ***************************
Grants for mysql.sys@localhost: GRANT SELECT ON `sys`.`sys_config` TO
`mysql.sys`@`localhost`
3 rows in set (0.2837 sec)

mysql> SELECT *
         FROM information_schema.USER_PRIVILEGES
         WHERE GRANTEE = '''mysql.sys''@''localhost'''\G
*************************** 1. row ***************************
      GRANTEE: 'mysql.sys'@'localhost'
 TABLE_CATALOG: def
PRIVILEGE_TYPE: USAGE
  IS_GRANTABLE: NO
1 row in set (0.0006 sec)

mysql> SELECT *
         FROM information_schema.SCHEMA_PRIVILEGES
         WHERE GRANTEE = '''mysql.sys''@''localhost'''\G
*************************** 1. row ***************************
      GRANTEE: 'mysql.sys'@'localhost'
 TABLE_CATALOG: def
  TABLE_SCHEMA: sys
PRIVILEGE_TYPE: TRIGGER
  IS_GRANTABLE: NO
1 row in set (0.0005 sec)

mysql> SELECT *
         FROM information_schema.TABLE_PRIVILEGES
         WHERE GRANTEE = '''mysql.sys''@''localhost'''\G
```

```
*************************** 1. row ***************************
       GRANTEE: 'mysql.sys'@'localhost'
 TABLE_CATALOG: def
  TABLE_SCHEMA: sys
    TABLE_NAME: sys_config
PRIVILEGE_TYPE: SELECT
  IS_GRANTABLE: NO
1 row in set (0.0005 sec)

mysql> SELECT *
          FROM information_schema.COLUMN_PRIVILEGES
         WHERE GRANTEE = '''mysql.sys''@''localhost'''\G
Empty set (0.0005 sec)
```

Notice how the single quotes around the username and hostname are escaped by doubling the quotes.

While the views with the privilege information are not directly usable for performance tuning, they are very useful for maintaining a stable system as you can use them to easily identify whether any accounts have privileges that they do not need.

Tip   It is best practice to limit accounts to have just the privileges they need and no more. That is one of the steps to keep the system secure.

The last topic to consider about the Information Schema is how data related to index statistics are cached.

Caching of Index Statistics Data

One thing that is important to understand is where the information in the index statistics–related views (and the equivalent SHOW statements) comes from. Most of the data comes from the MySQL data dictionary. In MySQL 8, the data dictionary is stored in an InnoDB table, so the views are just normal SQL views on top of the data dictionary. (You can, for example, try to execute SHOW CREATE VIEW information_schema. STATISTICS to get the definition of the STATISTICS view.)

The index statistics themselves are however still originating from the storage engine layer, so it is relatively expensive to query those. To improve the performance, the statistics are cached in the data dictionary. You can control how old the statistics are allowed to be before MySQL refreshes the cache. This is done with the `information_schema_stats_expiry` variable which defaults to 86400 seconds (one day). If you set the value to 0, you will always get the latest values available from the storage engine; this is the equivalent of the MySQL 5.7 behavior. The variable can be set both at the global and session scopes, so you can set it to 0 for the session, if you are investigating an issue where it is important to see the current statistics, for example, if the optimizer is not using the index you expect.

Tip   Use the `information_schema_stats_expiry` variable to control how long index statistics can be cached in the data dictionary. This is only for displaying purposes – the optimizer always uses the latest statistics. Setting `information_schema_stats_expiry` to 0 to disable caching can, for example, be useful when investigating an issue with the wrong index being used by the optimizer. You can change the value both at the global and session scopes as needed.

The caching affects the columns listed in Table 7-5. The SHOW statements displaying the same data are also affected.

Table 7-5. *Columns affected by information_schema_stats_expiry*

View Name	Column Name	Description
STATISTICS	CARDINALITY	The estimate for the number of unique values for the part of the index up and including to the column in the same row.
TABLES	AUTO_INCREMENT	The next value for the auto-increment counter for the table.
	AVG_ROW_LENGTH	The estimated data length divided with the estimated number of rows.
	CHECKSUM	The table checksum. It is not used by InnoDB, so the value is NULL.
	CHECK_TIME	When the table was last checked (CHECK TABLE). For partitioned tables, InnoDB always returns NULL.
	CREATE_TIME	When the table was created.
	DATA_FREE	An estimate of the amount of free space in the tablespace the table belongs to. For InnoDB, this is the size of completely free extents minus a safety margin.
	DATA_LENGTH	The estimated size of the row data. For InnoDB, it is the size of the clustered index, which is found as the number of pages in the clustered index multiplied with the page size.
	INDEX_LENGTH	The estimated size of secondary indexes. For InnoDB, this is the sum of pages in non-clustered indexes times the page size.
	MAX_DATA_LENGTH	The maximum allowed size of the data length. It is not used by InnoDB, so the value is NULL.
	TABLE_ROWS	The estimated number of rows. For InnoDB tables, this comes from the cardinality of the primary key or clustered index.
	UPDATE_TIME	When the tablespace file was last updated. For tables in the InnoDB system tablespace, the value is NULL. As data is written to the tablespace asynchronously, the time will not in general reflect the time of the last statement changing the data.

You can force an update of this data for a given table by executing ANALYZE TABLE for the table.

There are times when querying the data does not update the cached data:

- When the cached data has not yet expired, that is, it was refreshed less than information_schema_stats_expiry seconds ago

- When information_schema_stats_expiry is set to 0

- When MySQL or InnoDB is running in a read-only mode, that is, when one of the modes, read_only, super_read_only, transaction_read_only, or innodb_read_only, is enabled.

- When the query also includes data from the Performance Schema

Summary

This chapter introduced the Information Schema by first discussing what the Information Schema is and how the user privileges work. The remainder of the chapter walked through the standard views and how caching works. The Information Schema views can be grouped by the type of information they contain: system, schema, performance, and privilege information.

The system information includes the character sets and collations, resource groups, keywords, and information related to spatial data. This is useful as an alternative to using the reference manual.

The schema information is the largest group of views and includes all the information available from schema data down to columns, indexes, and constraints. These views together with the performance views that have information such as metrics and InnoDB buffer pool statistics are the most commonly used views in performance tuning. The privilege-related views are not so often used for performance tuning, but they are very useful to help maintain a stable system.

A common shortcut to obtain information from the Information Schema views is to use a SHOW statement. These will be discussed in the next chapter.

CHAPTER 8

SHOW Statements

The SHOW statements are the good old workhorse in MySQL for database administrators to obtain information about the schema objects and what happens on the system. While today most of the information can be found in the Information Schema or Performance Schema, the SHOW command is still very popular for interactive use due to its short syntax.

Tip It is recommended to query the underlying Information Schema views and Performance Schema tables. This particularly applies to noninteractive access to the data. Querying the underlying sources is also more powerful as it allows you to join to other views and tables.

This chapter starts out with an overview of how the SHOW statements match up with the Information Schema views and Performance Schema tables. The remainder of the chapter covers SHOW statements that do not have views or tables in the Information Schema and Performance Schema including obtaining engine status information with a little more in-depth view of the InnoDB monitor output provided by the SHOW ENGINE INNODB STATUS statement as well as getting replication and binary log information.

Relationship to the Information Schema

For the SHOW statements returning information about the schema objects or privileges, the same information that can be found in the Information Schema. Table 8-1 lists the SHOW statements that get the information from Information Schema views and which views the information can be found in.

© Jesper Wisborg Krogh 2020
J. W. Krogh, *MySQL 8 Query Performance Tuning*, https://doi.org/10.1007/978-1-4842-5584-1_8

Table 8-1. *Correlation between SHOW statements and the Information Schema*

SHOW Statement	I_S Views	Comments
CHARACTER SET	CHARACTER_SETS	
COLLATION	COLLATIONS	
COLUMNS	COLUMNS	
CREATE DATABASE	SCHEMATA	
CREATE EVENT	EVENTS	
CREATE FUNCTION	ROUTINES	ROUTINE_TYPE = 'FUNCTION'
CREATE PROCEDURE	ROUTINES	ROUTINE_TYPE = 'PROCEDURE'
CREATE TABLE	TABLES	
CREATE TRIGGER	TRIGGERS	
CREATE VIEW	VIEWS	
DATABASES	SCHEMATA	
ENGINES	ENGINES	
EVENTS	EVENTS	
FUNCTION STATUS	ROUTINES	ROUTINE_TYPE = 'FUNCTION'
GRANTS	COLUMN_PRIVILEGES SCHEMA_PRIVILEGES TABLE_PRIVILEGES USER_PRIVILEGES	
INDEX	STATISTICS	SHOW INDEXES and SHOW INDEXES are synonyms for SHOW INDEX.
PLUGINS	PLUGINS	
PROCEDURE STATUS	ROUTINES	ROUTINE_TYPE = 'PROCEDURE'
PROCESSLIST	PROCESSLIST	It is recommended to use performance_ schema.threads instead.
PROFILE	PROFILING	Deprecated – use the Performance Schema instead.

(continued)

Table 8-1. (*continued*)

SHOW Statement	I_S Views	Comments
PROFILES	PROFILING	Deprecated – use the Performance Schema instead.
TABLE STATUS	TABLES	
TABLES	TABLES	
TRIGGERS	TRIGGERS	

The information will not always be identical between the SHOW statement and the corresponding Information Schema views. In some cases, there is more information available using the views, and in general the views are more flexible.

There are also several SHOW statements where the underlying data can be found in the Performance Schema.

Relationship to the Performance Schema

After the Performance Schema was introduced, some of the information that was originally placed in the Information Schema has been moved to the Performance Schema where it logically belongs. That is also reflected in the relationship to the SHOW statements where there are now several tables as shown in Table 8-2 that get their data from Performance Schema tables.

Table 8-2. *Correlation between SHOW statements and the Performance Schema*

SHOW Statement	Performance Schema Tables
MASTER STATUS	log_status
SLAVE STATUS	log_status
	replication_applier_configuration
	replication_applier_filters
	replication_applier_global_filters
	replication_applier_status
	replication_applier_status_by_coordinator
	replication_applier_status_by_worker
	replication_connection_configuration
	replication_connection_status
STATUS	global_status
	session_status
	events_statements_summary_global_by_event_name
	events_statements_summary_by_thread_by_event_name
VARIABLES	global_variables
	session_variables

The SHOW MASTER STATUS includes information about what filtering is enabled when writing events to the binary log. This information is not available from the Performance Schema, so if you are using the binlog-do-db or binlog-ignore-db option (not recommended as they can prevent point-in-time recoveries), then you still need to use SHOW MASTER STATUS.

There are a few columns in the SHOW SLAVE STATUS output that cannot be found in the Performance Schema tables. Some of those can be found in the slave_master_info and slave_relay_log_info tables in the mysql schema (if master_info_repository and relay_log_info_repository have been set to TABLE which is the default).

For SHOW STATUS and SHOW VARIABLES, one difference is that the SHOW statements returning session scope values will include the global values if there is no session value. When querying the session_status and session_variables, only the values belonging to the requested scope are returned. Additionally, the SHOW STATUS statement includes the Com_% counters, whereas when querying the Performance Schema directly, these counters correspond to events in the `events_statements_summary_global_by_event_name` and `events_statements_summary_by_thread_by_event_name` tables (depending on whether the global or session scope is queried).

There are also some `SHOW` statements that do not have any corresponding tables. The first group of these that will be discussed is for the engine status.

Engine Status

The `SHOW ENGINE` statement can be used to get storage engine–specific information. It is currently implemented for the InnoDB, Performance_Schema, and NDBCluster engines. For all three engines, it is possible to request the status, and for the InnoDB engine, it is also possible to get mutex information.

The `SHOW ENGINE PERFORMANCE_SCHEMA STATUS` statement can be useful to get some status information about the Performance Schema including the size of the tables and their memory usage. (The memory usage can also be obtained from the memory instrumentation.)

By far, the most used engine status statement is `SHOW ENGINE INNODB STATUS` which provides a comprehensive report called the InnoDB monitor report which includes some information that cannot be obtained from other sources. The rest of this section introduces the InnoDB monitor report.

Tip   You can also make InnoDB output the monitor report to the error log at regular intervals by enabling the `innodb_status_output` system variable. When the `innodb_status_output_locks` option is set, the InnoDB monitor (whether generated because of `innodb_status_output = ON` or using `SHOW ENGINE INNODB STATUS`) includes additional lock information.

The InnoDB monitor report starts out with the header and a note saying how long the averages cover:

```
mysql> SHOW ENGINE INNODB STATUS\G
*************************** 1. row ***************************
  Type: InnoDB
  Name:
Status:
```

```
=====================================
2019-09-14 19:52:40 0x6480 INNODB MONITOR OUTPUT
=====================================
```
Per second averages calculated from the last 59 seconds

The report itself is divided into several sections, including

- **BACKGROUND THREAD:** The work done by the main background thread.

- **SEMAPHORES:** Semaphore statistics. The section is most important in cases where contention causes long semaphore waits in which case the section can be used to get information about the locks and who holds them.

- **LATEST FOREIGN KEY ERROR:** If a foreign key error has been encountered, this section includes details of the error. Otherwise, the section is omitted.

- **LATEST DETECTED DEADLOCK:** If a deadlock has occurred, this section includes details of the two transactions and the locks that caused the deadlock. Otherwise, the section is omitted.

- **TRANSACTIONS:** Information about the InnoDB transactions. Only transactions that have modified InnoDB tables are included. If the innodb_status_output_locks option is enabled, the locks held for each transaction are listed; otherwise, it is just locks involved in lock waits. It is in general better to use the information_schema. INNODB_TRX view to query the transaction information and for lock information to use the performance_schema.DATA_LOCKS and performance_schema.DATA_LOCK_WAITS tables.

- **FILE I/O:** Information about the I/O threads used by InnoDB including the insert buffer thread, log thread, read threads, and write threads.

- **INSERT BUFFER AND ADAPTIVE HASH INDEX:** Information about the change buffer (this was formerly called the insert buffer) and the adaptive hash index.

- **LOG:** Information about the redo log.

- **BUFFER POOL AND MEMORY:** Information about the InnoDB buffer pool. This information is better obtained from the `information_schema.INNODB_BUFFER_POOL_STATS` view.

- **INDIVIDUAL BUFFER POOL INFO:** If `innodb_buffer_pool_instances` is greater than 1, this section includes information about the individual buffer pool instances with the same information as for the global summary in the previous section. Otherwise, the section is omitted. This information is better obtained from the `information_schema.INNODB_BUFFER_POOL_STATS` view.

- **ROW OPERATIONS:** This section shows various information about InnoDB including the current activity, what the main thread is doing, and the row activity for inserts, updates, deletes, and reads.

Several of the sections will be used in later chapters when their content is used to analyze performance or lock problems.

Replication and Binary Logs

The SHOW statements have always been important when working with replication. While the Performance Schema replication tables have now largely replaced the SHOW SLAVE STATUS and SHOW MASTER STATUS statements, if you want to see which replicas are connected and inspect events in the binary log or relay log from inside MySQL, then you still need to use SHOW statements.

Listing Binary Logs

The SHOW BINARY LOGS statement is useful to check which binary logs exist. This can be useful if you want to know how much space the binary logs occupy, whether they are encrypted, and for position-based replication whether the logs required by a replica still exist.

An example of what the output can look like is

```
mysql> SHOW BINARY LOGS;
+----------------+-----------+-----------+
| Log_name       | File_size | Encrypted |
+----------------+-----------+-----------+
| binlog.000044  |      2616 | No        |
| binlog.000045  |       886 | No        |
| binlog.000046  |       218 | No        |
| binlog.000047  |       218 | No        |
| binlog.000048  |       218 | No        |
| binlog.000049  |       575 | No        |
+----------------+-----------+-----------+
6 rows in set (0.0018 sec)
```

The Encrypted column was added in MySQL 8.0.14 together with the support for encrypted binary logs.

In general, the file size will be larger than in the example as the autorotation of the binary log files happens when the size exceeds max_binlog_size (defaults to 1 GiB) after writing a transaction. Since transactions are not split between files, if you have large transactions, the file can become somewhat larger than max_binlog_size.

Viewing Log Events

The SHOW BINLOG EVENTS and SHOW RELAYLOG EVENTS statements read the binary log and relay log, respectively, and return the events matching the arguments. There are four arguments, of which one only applies to relay log events:

- **IN:** The name of the binary log or relay log file to read events from.

- **FROM:** The position in bytes to start reading from.

- **LIMIT:** The number of events to include with an optional offset. The syntax is the same as for SELECT statements: [offset], row_count.

- **FOR CHANNEL:** For relay logs, the replication channel to read events for.

All arguments are optional. If the IN argument is not given, events from the first log are returned. An example of using SHOW BINLOG EVENTS is shown in Listing 8-1. If you want to try the example, you will need to replace the binary log filename, position, and limit.

Listing 8-1. Using SHOW BINLOG EVENTS

```
mysql> SHOW BINLOG EVENTS IN 'binlog.000049' FROM 195 LIMIT 5\G
*************************** 1. row ***************************
    Log_name: binlog.000049
         Pos: 195
  Event_type: Gtid
   Server_id: 1
 End_log_pos: 274
        Info: SET @@SESSION.GTID_NEXT= '4d22b3e5-a54f-11e9-8bdb-ace2d35785be:603'
*************************** 2. row ***************************
    Log_name: binlog.000049
         Pos: 274
  Event_type: Query
   Server_id: 1
 End_log_pos: 372
        Info: BEGIN
*************************** 3. row ***************************
    Log_name: binlog.000049
         Pos: 372
  Event_type: Table_map
   Server_id: 1
 End_log_pos: 436
        Info: table_id: 89 (world.city)
*************************** 4. row ***************************
    Log_name: binlog.000049
         Pos: 436
  Event_type: Update_rows
   Server_id: 1
 End_log_pos: 544
        Info: table_id: 89 flags: STMT_END_F
```

```
*************************** 5. row ***************************
    Log_name: binlog.000049
         Pos: 544
  Event_type: Xid
   Server_id: 1
End_log_pos: 575
        Info: COMMIT /* xid=44 */
5 rows in set (0.0632 sec)
```

The example illustrates some of the limitations of using SHOW statements to inspect binary and relay logs. The result is a normal result set from a query, and since the files typically are around 1 GiB in size, it means the result can be equally large. You can do as in the example where only specific events are chosen, but it is not always trivial to know where the interesting events start, and you cannot filter by the event types or which tables they affect. Finally, the default event format (the binlog_format option) is the row format, and as it can be seen from the third and fourth rows in the result, all you can see from SHOW BINGOG EVENTS is that the transaction updated the world.city table. You cannot see which rows were updated and what the values are.

In practice, if you have access to the file system, it is in most cases better to use the mysqlbinlog utility that is shipped with MySQL. (The SHOW BINLOG EVENTS and SHOW RELAYLOG EVENTS statements can still be useful in controlled testing or when replication stops and you quickly want to inspect the event that caused the error.) The equivalent command using the mysqlbinlog utility to the previous SHOW BINLOG EVENTS statement is shown in Listing 8-2. That example also uses the verbose flag to show the before and after images of the row-based event that updates the world.city table.

Listing 8-2. Inspecting the binary log using the mysqlbinlog utility

```
shell> mysqlbinlog -v --base64-output=decode-rows --start-position=195
--stop-position=575 binlog.000049
/*!50530 SET @@SESSION.PSEUDO_SLAVE_MODE=1*/;
/*!50003 SET @OLD_COMPLETION_TYPE=@@COMPLETION_TYPE,COMPLETION_TYPE=0*/;
DELIMITER /*!*/;
# at 124
#190914 20:38:43 server id 1  end_log_pos 124 CRC32 0x751322a6  Start:
binlog v 4, server v 8.0.18 created 190914 20:38:43 at startup
```

```
# Warning: this binlog is either in use or was not closed properly.
ROLLBACK/*!*/;
# at 195
#190915 10:18:45 server id 1  end_log_pos 274 CRC32
0xe1b8b9a1  GTID     last_committed=0          sequence_number=1
rbr_only=yes    original_committed_timestamp=1568506725779031
immediate_commit_timestamp=1568506725779031      transaction_length=380
/*!50718 SET TRANSACTION ISOLATION LEVEL READ COMMITTED*//*!*/;
# original_commit_timestamp=1568506725779031 (2019-09-15 10:18:45.779031
AUS Eastern Standard Time)
# immediate_commit_timestamp=1568506725779031 (2019-09-15 10:18:45.779031
AUS Eastern Standard Time)
/*!80001 SET @@session.original_commit_timestamp=1568506725779031*//*!*/;
/*!80014 SET @@session.original_server_version=80018*//*!*/;
/*!80014 SET @@session.immediate_server_version=80018*//*!*/;
SET @@SESSION.GTID_NEXT= '4d22b3e5-a54f-11e9-8bdb-ace2d35785be:603'/*!*/;
# at 274
#190915 10:18:45 server id 1  end_log_pos 372 CRC32 0x2d716bd5  Query
thread_id=8      exec_time=0      error_code=0
SET TIMESTAMP=1568506725/*!*/;
SET @@session.pseudo_thread_id=8/*!*/;
SET @@session.foreign_key_checks=1, @@session.sql_auto_is_null=0,
@@session.unique_checks=1, @@session.autocommit=1/*!*/;
SET @@session.sql_mode=1168113696/*!*/;
SET @@session.auto_increment_increment=1, @@session.auto_increment_
offset=1/*!*/;
/*!\C utf8mb4 *//*!*/;
SET @@session.character_set_client=45,@@session.collation_connection=45,
@@session.collation_server=255/*!*/;
SET @@session.lc_time_names=0/*!*/;
SET @@session.collation_database=DEFAULT/*!*/;
/*!80011 SET @@session.default_collation_for_utf8mb4=255*//*!*/;
BEGIN
/*!*/;
# at 372
```

```
#190915 10:18:45 server id 1  end_log_pos 436 CRC32 0xb62c64d7  Table_map:
`world`.`city` mapped to number 89
# at 436
#190915 10:18:45 server id 1  end_log_pos 544 CRC32 0x62687b0b
Update_rows: table id 89 flags: STMT_END_F
### UPDATE `world`.`city`
### WHERE
###    @1=130
###    @2='Sydney'
###    @3='AUS'
###    @4='New South Wales'
###    @5=3276207
### SET
###    @1=130
###    @2='Sydney'
###    @3='AUS'
###    @4='New South Wales'
###    @5=3276208
# at 544
#190915 10:18:45 server id 1  end_log_pos 575 CRC32 0x149e2b5c  Xid = 44
COMMIT/*!*/;
SET @@SESSION.GTID_NEXT= 'AUTOMATIC' /* added by mysqlbinlog */ /*!*/;
DELIMITER ;
# End of log file
/*!50003 SET COMPLETION_TYPE=@OLD_COMPLETION_TYPE*/;
/*!50530 SET @@SESSION.PSEUDO_SLAVE_MODE=0*/;
```

The -v arguments request verbose mode and can be given up to two times to increase the amount of information included. A single -v is what generates the comment with the pseudo query in the event starting at position 436. The --base64-output=decode-rows argument tells mysqlbinlog not to include a base64 encoded version of the events in row format. The --start-position and --stop-position arguments specify the start and stop offsets in bytes.

The most interesting event in the transaction is the one starting with the comment # at 436 which means the event starts at offset 436 (in bytes). It is written as a pseudo update statement with the WHERE part showing the values before the change and the SET part the values after the update. This is also known as the before and after images.

Note   If you use encrypted binary logs, you cannot directly use mysqlbinlog to read the files. One option is to make mysqlbinlog connect to the server and read them which returns the logs unencrypted. Another option if you use the keyring_file plugin to store the encryption key is to use Python or standard Linux tools to decrypt the file. These methods are described in https://mysql.wisborg.dk/decrypt-binary-logs and https://mysqlhighavailability.com/how-to-manually-decrypt-an-encrypted-binary-log-file/.

Show Connected Replicas

Another useful command is to ask a source of replication to list all replicas connected to it. This can be used for auto-discovering a replication topology in monitoring tools.

The command to list the connected replicas is SHOW SLAVE HOSTS, for example:

```
mysql> SHOW SLAVE HOSTS\G
*************************** 1. row ***************************
 Server_id: 2
      Host: replica.example.com
      Port: 3308
 Master_id: 1
Slave_UUID: 0b072c80-d759-11e9-8423-ace2d35785be
1 row in set (0.0003 sec)
```

If no replicas are connected at the time the statement is executed, the result will be empty. The Server_id and Master_id columns are the values of the server_id system variable on the replica and source, respectively. The Host is the hostname of the replica as specified with the report_host option. Similarly, the Port column is the replica's report_port value. Finally, the Slave_UUID column is the value of @@global.server_uuid on the replica.

The only group of SHOW statements left consists of various statements to get information about privileges, users, open tables, warnings, and errors.

Miscellaneous Statements

There are a few SHOW statements that are useful but that do not fit into any of the groups that have been discussed thus far. They can be used to list the available privileges, return the CREATE USER statement for an account, list the open tables, and list warnings or errors after executing a statement. The statements are summarized in Table 8-3.

Table 8-3. *Miscellaneous SHOW statements*

SHOW Statement	Description
PRIVILEGES	Lists the available privileges, which context they apply to, and for some privileges a description of what the privilege controls.
CREATE USER	Returns the CREATE USER statement for an account.
GRANTS	Lists the assigned privileges for the current account or another account.
OPEN TABLES	Lists the tables in the table cache, the number of table locks or lock requests, and whether the name of the table is locked (happens during DROP TABLE or RENAME TABLE).
WARNINGS	Lists the warnings and errors and if sql_notes is enabled (the default) notes for the last executed statement.
ERRORS	Lists the errors for the last executed statement.

The three most commonly used of the miscellaneous SHOW statements are SHOW CREATE USER, SHOW GRANTS, and SHOW WARNINGS.

The SHOW CREATE USER statement can be used to retrieve the CREATE USER statement for an account. This is useful for inspecting metadata for the account without querying the underlying mysql.user table directly. All users are allowed to execute the statement for the current user. For example:

```
mysql> SET print_identified_with_as_hex = ON;
Query OK, 0 rows affected (0.0200 sec)
```

```
mysql> SHOW CREATE USER CURRENT_USER()\G
*************************** 1. row ***************************
CREATE USER for root@localhost: CREATE USER 'root'@'localhost' IDENTIFIED
WITH 'caching_sha2_password' AS 0x24412430303524377B743F5E176E1A77494F574
D216C41563934064E58364E385372734B77314E43587745314F506F59502E747079664957
776F4948346B526B59467A642F30 REQUIRE NONE PASSWORD EXPIRE DEFAULT ACCOUNT
UNLOCK PASSWORD HISTORY DEFAULT PASSWORD REUSE INTERVAL DEFAULT PASSWORD
REQUIRE CURRENT DEFAULT
1 row in set (0.0003 sec)
```

The print_identified_with_as_hex variable (available in 8.0.17 and later) is enabled to return the password digest in hexadecimal notation. This is the preferred when returning the value to the console as the digest may include unprintable characters. The SHOW CREATE USER output is equivalent to how the user was created and can be used to create a new user with the same settings, including password.

Note Specifying the authentication digest in hexadecimal notation when creating a user is only supported in MySQL 8.0.17 and later.

The SHOW GRANTS statement complements SHOW CREATE USER by returning the privileges assigned to the account. The default is to return for the current user, but if you have the SELECT privilege for the mysql system database, you can also obtain the privileges assigned to other accounts. For example, to list the privileges for the root@ localhost account:

```
mysql> SHOW GRANTS FOR root@localhost\G
*************************** 1. row ***************************
Grants for root@localhost: GRANT SELECT, INSERT, UPDATE, DELETE, CREATE,
DROP, RELOAD, SHUTDOWN, PROCESS, FILE, REFERENCES, INDEX, ALTER, SHOW
DATABASES, SUPER, CREATE TEMPORARY TABLES, LOCK TABLES, EXECUTE,
REPLICATION SLAVE, REPLICATION CLIENT, CREATE VIEW, SHOW VIEW, CREATE
ROUTINE, ALTER ROUTINE, CREATE USER, EVENT, TRIGGER, CREATE TABLESPACE,
CREATE ROLE, DROP ROLE ON *.* TO `root`@`localhost` WITH GRANT OPTION
```

```
*************************** 2. row ***************************
Grants for root@localhost: GRANT APPLICATION_PASSWORD_ADMIN,AUDIT_
ADMIN,BACKUP_ADMIN,BINLOG_ADMIN,BINLOG_ENCRYPTION_ADMIN,CLONE_
ADMIN,CONNECTION_ADMIN,ENCRYPTION_KEY_ADMIN,GROUP_REPLICATION_
ADMIN,INNODB_REDO_LOG_ARCHIVE,PERSIST_RO_VARIABLES_ADMIN,REPLICATION_
APPLIER,REPLICATION_SLAVE_ADMIN,RESOURCE_GROUP_ADMIN,RESOURCE_GROUP_
USER,ROLE_ADMIN,SERVICE_CONNECTION_ADMIN,SESSION_VARIABLES_ADMIN,SET_USER_
ID,SYSTEM_USER,SYSTEM_VARIABLES_ADMIN,TABLE_ENCRYPTION_ADMIN,XA_RECOVER_
ADMIN ON *.* TO `root`@`localhost` WITH GRANT OPTION
*************************** 3. row ***************************
Grants for root@localhost: GRANT PROXY ON "@" TO 'root'@'localhost' WITH
GRANT OPTION
3 rows in set (0.0129 sec)
```

The SHOW WARNINGS statement is one of the most underused statements in MySQL. If MySQL encounters a problem but is able to continue, it will generate a warning but otherwise complete the execution of the statement. While the statement completes without error, the warning may be a sign of a larger problem, and it is best practice to always check for warnings and aim at never having warnings in the queries executed by your application.

Note   MySQL Shell does not support the SHOW WARNINGS statement as it will automatically fetch warnings if the \W mode has been enabled (the default) and otherwise not make the warnings available. The statement is however still useful in the legacy mysql command-line client and from some connectors such as MySQL Connector/Python.

Listing 8-3 shows an example where SHOW WARNINGS is used with the legacy mysql command-line client to identify that the schema definition and data do not match.

Listing 8-3. Using SHOW WARNINGS to identify problems

```
mysql> SELECT @@sql_mode\G
*************************** 1. row ***************************
@@sql_mode: ONLY_FULL_GROUP_BY,STRICT_TRANS_TABLES,NO_ZERO_IN_DATE,
NO_ZERO_DATE,ERROR_FOR_DIVISION_BY_ZERO,NO_ENGINE_SUBSTITUTION
1 row in set (0.0004 sec)
```

```
mysql> SET sql_mode = sys.list_drop(
                        @@sql_mode,
                        'STRICT_TRANS_TABLES'
                      );
Query OK, 0 rows affected, 1 warning (0.00 sec)

mysql> SHOW WARNINGS\G
*************************** 1. row ***************************
  Level: Warning
   Code: 3135
Message: 'NO_ZERO_DATE', 'NO_ZERO_IN_DATE' and 'ERROR_FOR_DIVISION_BY_ZERO'
sql modes should be used with strict mode. They will be merged with strict
mode in a future release.
1 row in set (0.00 sec)

mysql> UPDATE world.city
          SET Population = Population/0
        WHERE ID = 130;
Query OK, 0 rows affected, 2 warnings (0.00 sec)
Rows matched: 1  Changed: 0  Warnings: 2

mysql> SHOW WARNINGS\G
*************************** 1. row ***************************
  Level: Warning
   Code: 1365
Message: Division by 0
*************************** 2. row ***************************
  Level: Warning
   Code: 1048
Message: Column 'Population' cannot be null
2 rows in set (0.00 sec)

mysql> SELECT *
          FROM world.city
        WHERE ID = 130\G
```

```
*************************** 1. row ***************************
         ID: 130
       Name: Sydney
CountryCode: AUS
   District: New South Wales
 Population: 0
1 row in set (0.03 sec)
```

The example starts with the SQL mode set to the default in MySQL 8. First, the SQL mode is changed using the sys.list_drop() function to remove the STRICT_TRANS_TABLES mode which triggers a warning as disabling the strict mode should be done together with other modes as they will be merged together at a later date. Then the population of one of the cities in the world.city table is updated, but the calculation ends up dividing with 0 which triggers two warnings. One warning is for division by 0 which is not defined, so MySQL uses a NULL value which causes the second warning as the Population column is a NOT NULL column. The result is that a population of 0 is assigned to the city, which is probably not what is expected in the application. This also illustrates why it is important to enable the strict SQL mode as that would have made the division by zero an error and prevented the update.

Caution   Do not disable the STRICT_TRANS_TABLES SQL mode as it makes it more likely that you end up with invalid data in your tables.

Summary

This chapter introduced the SHOW statements which date back to before the Information Schema and Performance Schema were implemented. Nowadays, it is often better to use the underlying data sources in the Information Schema and Performance Schema. The mapping between the SHOW statements and data sources was given in the first two sections.

There are also some SHOW statements that return data that cannot be accessed through other sources. A commonly used feature is the InnoDB monitor report from InnoDB obtained with the SHOW ENGINE INNODB STATUS statement. The report is split into several sections, of which some will be used when investigating performance and lock issues.

There are also some statements for replication and the binary logs that are useful. The most commonly used statement of these is SHOW BINARY LOGS which lists the binary logs that MySQL knows of for that instance. The information includes the size and whether the log is encrypted. You can also list events in the binary logs or relay logs, but in practice the mysqlbinlog utility is usually a better option.

Finally, a group of miscellaneous SHOW statements were covered. The three most used of these are SHOW CREATE USER to display a statement that can be used to recreate the user, SHOW GRANTS that returns the privileges assigned to a user, and SHOW WARNINGS which lists the errors, warnings, and by default notes that occurred for the last executed query. Checking the warnings is an often-overlooked aspect of executing queries as warnings can be an indication that the result of a query is not what you expect. It is recommended to always check for warnings and to enable the STRICT_TRANS_TABLES SQL mode.

The final chapter about sources of information is about the slow query log.

CHAPTER 9

The Slow Query Log

In the days before it was possible to get query statistics from the Performance Schema, the slow query log was the main source of information to find queries that are candidates for optimization. Even today, the slow query log should not be completely dismissed.

The slow query log has three main advantages over the statement digest information in the Performance Schema. The logged queries are persisted, so you can review the information after MySQL has been restarted, the queries are logged with timestamps, and the actual queries are logged. For these reasons, the slow query log is often used together with the Performance Schema.

Tip A monitoring solution like MySQL Enterprise Monitor (`https://dev.mysql.com/doc/mysql-monitor/en/mem-qanal-using.html`) can overcome these limitations of the Performance Schema, so if you have a monitoring solution that includes detailed query information, you are less likely to need the slow query log.

There are also disadvantages of the slow query log. The overhead is higher than for the Performance Schema as the queries are written to a plain text file and there is no concurrency support when writing the events. There is also only limited support for querying the log (you can store the slow query log in a table, but that has its own disadvantages) which makes it less practical to use it during an investigation.

This chapter will look at how you can configure the slow query log, how the raw log events look, and how you can use the `mysqldumpslow` (`mysqldumpslow.pl` on Microsoft Windows) script to aggregate the log.

© Jesper Wisborg Krogh 2020
J. W. Krogh, *MySQL 8 Query Performance Tuning*, https://doi.org/10.1007/978-1-4842-5584-1_9

Configuration

There are several options that you can use to configure the slow query log and which queries are logged. As the overhead of having the log enabled goes up with the number of queries you log, a well-configured slow query log is important. Logging "just the right amount" of queries also makes it easier to identify queries of interest.

The slow query log is not enabled by default, and when the log is enabled, the default is only to log nonadministrative queries executed directly on the local instance and where the query takes more than 10 seconds to execute. Table 9-1 summarizes the configuration options you have at your disposal for fine-tuning this behavior. The information includes the default value and whether the option is used in the global scope or session scope or both. The options are listed alphabetically.

***Table 9-1.** Configuration options for the slow query log*

Option/Default Value/Scope	Description
`min_examined_row_limit` Default: 0 Scope: Global, Session	Only queries examining more rows than this value will be logged. This can particularly be useful when enabling logging of all queries doing full scans.
`log_output` Default: FILE Scope: Global	Controls whether the slow query log and general query log are logged to a file, a table, or both or not at all.
`log_queries_not_using_indexes` Default: OFF Scope: Global	When enabled, all queries that perform a full table or index scan are logged irrespective of how long they take.
`log_short_format` Default: OFF Scope: Global	When enabled, less information is logged. This option can only be set in the configuration file.
`log_slow_admin_statements` Default: OFF Scope: Global	When enabled, administrative statements like ALTER TABLE and OPTIMIZE TABLE are eligible for logging.

(continued)

Table 9-1. (*continued*)

Option/Default Value/Scope	Description
log_slow_extra Default: OFF Scope: Global	When enabled, there is extra information such as the value of the Handler_% status variables for the query. It is only supported when logging to a file and in MySQL 8.0.14 and later. The main reason to not enable log_slow_extra is if you have scripts that require the old format.
log_slow_slave_statements Default: OFF Scope: Global	When enabled, replicated statements are also eligible for logging. This only applies for binary log events in statement format.
log_throttle_queries_not_using_indexes Default: 0 Scope: Global	When you have enabled logging of all queries doing a full scan, this option can throttle the maximum number of times the query can be logged per minute.
log_timestamps Default: UTC Scope: Global	Whether to use UTC or the system time zone for the timestamps. This option also applies to the error log and general query log. It only applies when logging to a file.
long_query_time Default: 10 Scope: Global, Session	The minimum query latency in seconds before a query is logged (unless it is doing full scans and you have enabled logging those queries). Fractional seconds are supported. Set to 0 to log all queries. **Warning:** Logging all queries has a significant overhead and is best done on test systems or for short periods of time.
slow_query_log Default: OFF Scope: Global	Whether to enable the slow query log.
slow_query_log_file Default: <hostname>-slow.log Scope: Global	The path and filename of the slow query log file. The default location is in the data directory and is named from the hostname of the system.

It is recommended to leave `log_output` at the default and log the events to the file set by `slow_query_log_file`. It may seem attractive to get the slow query log as a table; however, the data is in that case saved as comma-separated values (CSV), and queries against the table cannot use indexes. There are also some features such as `log_slow_extra` that are not supported with `log_output` = `TABLE`.

The options mean that you have fine-grained control of which queries are logged. All the options except `log_short_format` can be changed dynamically, so you can make changes as the situation requires. If you feel it can be hard to determine how the options interact, then Figure 9-1 shows a flowchart of the decision process determining whether a query should be logged. (The flowchart is illustrative only – the actual code path is different.)

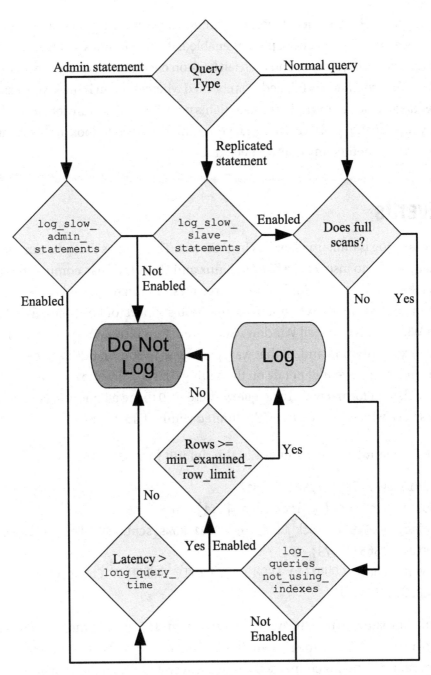

Figure 9-1. *Flowchart to determine whether a query is logged to the slow log*

The flow starts with the query type. For administrative and replicated statements, they only proceed if the respective option is enabled. Regular queries first check whether they qualify as not using indexes and then fall back on checking the query execution time (latency). If either condition is fulfilled, it is checked whether enough rows were examined. Some finer details such as throttling of statements not using indexes are left out of the figure.

Once you have the query settings that you want, you need to look at the events in the log to determine whether any queries need attention.

Log Events

The slow query log is built up of events in plain text. This means that you can use any text viewer that you like to inspect the file. On Linux and Unix, the `less` command is a good option as it has good support for handling large files. On Microsoft Windows, Notepad++ is a common choice, but there is not the same good support for large files. Another option on Windows is to install Windows Subsystem for Linux (WSL) which allows you to install a Linux distribution and, in that way, get access to commands like `less`.

The format of the event depends on the settings. Listing 9-1 shows an example of an event in the default format with `long_query_time = 0` to log all queries. Note that some of the lines have wrapped because of the limited width of the page.

Listing 9-1. A slow query log event in the default format

```
# Time: 2019-09-17T09:37:53.269881Z
# User@Host: root[root] @ localhost [::1]  Id:    22
# Query_time: 0.032531  Lock_time: 0.000221 Rows_sent: 10  Rows_examined: 4089
SET timestamp=1568713073;
SELECT CountryCode, COUNT(*) FROM world.city GROUP BY CountryCode ORDER BY
COUNT(*) DESC LIMIT 10;
```

The first line shows when the query was executed. This is the timestamp where you can control whether UTC or the system time is used with the `log_timestamp` option. The second line shows which account executed the query and the connection id. The third line includes some basic statistics for the query: the query execution time, the time spent waiting for a lock, the number of rows returned to the client, and the number of rows examined.

The SET timestamp query sets the timestamp of the query measured in the number of seconds since epoch (January 1, 1970 00:00:00 UTC), and finally the slow query is in the last line.

In the statistics, the query time and the ratio between the number of examined rows and sent rows are of particular interest. The more rows that are examined compared to the number of returned rows, the less effective indexes are in general. However, you should always look at the information in context of the query. In this case, the query finds the ten country codes with the most cities. There is no way that can be found without performing a full table or index scan, so in this case there is a good reason for the poor ratio of examined rows to the number of sent rows.

If you enable log_slow_extra in versions 8.0.14 and later, then you get additional information for the query as shown in Listing 9-2.

Listing 9-2. Using log_slow_extra with the slow query log

```
# Time: 2019-09-17T10:09:50.054970Z
# User@Host: root[root] @ localhost [::1]  Id:     22
# Query_time: 0.166589  Lock_time: 0.099952 Rows_sent: 10  Rows_examined:
  4089 Thread_id: 22 Errno: 2336802955 Killed: 0 Bytes_received: 0 Bytes_
  sent: 0 Read_first: 1 Read_last: 0 Read_key: 1 Read_next: 4079 Read_
  prev: 0 Read_rnd: 0 Read_rnd_next: 0 Sort_merge_passes: 0 Sort_range_
  count: 0 Sort_rows: 10 Sort_scan_count: 1 Created_tmp_disk_tables:
  0 Created_tmp_tables: 0 Start: 2019-09-17T10:09:49.888381Z End:
  2019-09-17T10:09:50.054970Z
SET timestamp=1568714989;
SELECT CountryCode, COUNT(*) FROM world.city GROUP BY CountryCode ORDER BY
COUNT(*) DESC LIMIT 10;
```

The statistics of main interest from a performance perspective are the ones starting with Bytes_received and finishing with Created_tmp_tables. Several of these statistics are the equivalent of the Handler_% status variables for the query. In this case, you can see that it is the Read_next counter that is the main contributor to the large number of examined rows. Read_next is used when scanning an index to find rows, so it can be concluded that the query performs an index scan.

Viewing the raw events can be very useful if you need to know what was executed at a given time. If you are more interested in knowing which queries are in general contributing the most to the load on the system, you need to aggregate the data.

Aggregation

It is possible to aggregate the data in the slow query log using the `mysqldumpslow` (`mysqldumpslow.pl` on Microsoft Windows) script that is included in the MySQL installation. `mysqldumpslow` is a Perl script that by default normalizes the queries in the log by replacing numeric values with `N` and string values with `'S'`. This allows the script to aggregate the queries in a similar way to what is done in the `events_statements_summary_by_digest` table in the Performance Schema.

Note   The script requires Perl to be installed on your system. This is not a problem on Linux and Unix where Perl is always present, but on Microsoft Windows, you will need to install Perl yourself. One option is to install Strawberry Perl from `http://strawberryperl.com/`.

There are a few options to control the behavior of `mysqldumpslow`. These are summarized in Table 9-2. Additionally, the slow query log file can be given as an argument without an option name.

Table 9-2. *Command-line arguments for* `mysqldumpslow`

Option	Default Value	Description
`-a`		Do not replace number and string values with `N` and `'S'`.
`--debug`		Execute in debug mode.
`-g`		Perform pattern matching (using the same syntax as for `grep`) on the queries and only include matching queries.
`-h`	`*`	By default, `mysqldumpslow` searches for files in the `datadir` set in the MySQL configuration file. This option specifies the hostnames that the files should match assuming the default slow query log filename is used. Wildcards can be used.
`--help`		Display a help text.
`-i`		The instance name in the `mysql.server` startup script to use in the automatic algorithm to look for slow query log files.
`-l`		Do not extract the lock time for the queries.

(continued)

Table 9-2. (*continued*)

Option	Default Value	Description
-n	0	The minimum number of digits that must be in numbers before they are abstracted to N.
-r		Reverse the order the queries are returned.
-s	at	How to sort the queries. The default is to sort according to the average query time. The full list of sort options will be covered separately.
-t	(All)	The maximum number of queries to return in the result.
--verbose		Print additional information during the execution of the script.

The -s, -t, and -r options are the most commonly used. While mysqldumpslow can search for the slow query log using the MySQL configuration file in the default paths and hostname, it is more common to specify the path to the slow query log file as an argument on the command line.

The -s option is used to specify how to sort the queries included in the result. For some of the sorting options, there is the choice between using the total and the average for the sorting. The sorting options are listed in Table 9-3 and are also available from the mysqldumpslow --help output. The *Total* column specifies the option to use to sort by the total, and the *Average* column shows the option to sort by the average.

Table 9-3. *The sorting options for* mysqldumpslow

Total	Average	Description
c		Sort by the number of times (count) the query has been executed.
l	al	Sort by the lock time.
r	ar	Sort by the number of rows sent.
t	at	Sort by the query time.

It can sometimes be useful to generate several reports using different sorting options to get a better picture of the queries being executed on the instance.

As a case study, consider an instance starting out with an empty slow query log file; then the queries in Listing 9-3 are executed. These queries are executed with long_query_time set to 0 for the session to record all queries which is useful to avoid having to spend a long time executing the queries.

Listing 9-3. The queries used to create slow query log events for a case study

```
SET GLOBAL slow_query_log = ON;
SET long_query_time = 0;
SELECT * FROM world.city WHERE ID = 130;
SELECT * FROM world.city WHERE ID = 131;
SELECT * FROM world.city WHERE ID = 201;
SELECT * FROM world.city WHERE ID = 2010;
SELECT * FROM world.city WHERE ID = 1;
SELECT * FROM world.city WHERE ID = 828;
SELECT * FROM world.city WHERE ID = 131;
SELECT * FROM world.city WHERE CountryCode = 'AUS';
SELECT * FROM world.city WHERE CountryCode = 'CHN';
SELECT * FROM world.city WHERE CountryCode = 'IND';
SELECT * FROM world.city WHERE CountryCode = 'GBR';
SELECT * FROM world.city WHERE CountryCode = 'USA';
SELECT * FROM world.city WHERE CountryCode = 'NZL';
SELECT * FROM world.city WHERE CountryCode = 'BRA';
SELECT * FROM world.city WHERE CountryCode = 'AUS';
SELECT * FROM world.city WHERE CountryCode = 'DNK';
SELECT * FROM world.city ORDER BY Population DESC LIMIT 10;
SELECT * FROM world.city ORDER BY Population DESC LIMIT 4;
SELECT * FROM world.city ORDER BY Population DESC LIMIT 9;
```

There are three basic queries with different values for the WHERE clause or LIMIT clause. First, the city is found by the primary key which will search one row in order to return one row. Second, cities are found by the CountryCode which is a secondary index, so several rows are found but still the same number of rows are examined as returned. Third, all cities are examined to return the most populous cities.

Assuming the slow query log file is named mysql-slow.log and you are executing mysqldumpslow from the same directory where the file is located, then you can group the queries and order them by the number of times the queries have been executed as shown in Listing 9-4. The -t option is used to limit the report to include three (normalized) queries.

Listing 9-4. Using mysqldumpslow to sort the queries by count

```
shell$ mysqldumpslow -s c -t 3 mysql-slow.log

Reading mysql slow query log from mysql-slow.log
Count: 9  Time=0.00s (0s)  Lock=0.00s (0s)  Rows=150.1 (1351), root[root]
@localhost
  SELECT * FROM world.city WHERE CountryCode = 'S'

Count: 7  Time=0.02s (0s)  Lock=0.00s (0s)  Rows=1.0 (7), root[root]
@localhost
  SELECT * FROM world.city WHERE ID = N

Count: 3  Time=0.00s (0s)  Lock=0.00s (0s)  Rows=7.7 (23), root[root]
@localhost
  SELECT * FROM world.city ORDER BY Population DESC LIMIT N
```

Notice how the WHERE and LIMIT clauses have been modified to use N and 'S'. The query time is listed as Time=0.00s (0s) which has the average query time first (0.00s) and the total time in parenthesis. Similar for the lock and row statistics.

Since the mysqldumpslow script is written in Perl, it is relatively easy to modify the script if you want to include support for new sorting options or to change the output. For example, if you want to include more decimals for the average execution time, you can modify the printf statement just before the usage subroutine (lines 168–169 in the script included with MySQL 8.0.18) like

```
printf "Count: %d  Time=%.6fs (%ds)  Lock=%.2fs (%ds)  Rows=%.1f (%d),
$user\@$host\n%s\n\n",
      $c, $at,$t, $al,$l, $ar,$r, $_;
```

The change is in the Time=%.6fs part of the first line. That will print the average execution time with microseconds.

Summary

This chapter has shown how the slow query log can be used to collect information about the queries executed on the MySQL instance. The slow query log is focused on capturing queries based on the execution time and whether they use indexes (in practice whether they perform full table or index scans). The main advantages of the slow query log over the Performance Schema are that the log includes the exact statements executed and that it is persisted. The disadvantages are the overhead and that it is harder to get a report returning the queries you are interested in.

First, the configuration options used to configure the slow query log were discussed. There are options to control the minimum execution time, whether queries not using indexes should be logged irrespective of the execution time, the types of queries to log, and more. In MySQL 8.0.14 and later, you can use the log_slow_extra to include more detailed information about the slow queries.

Second, two examples of the slow query log events were discussed. There was an example with the default information and one with log_slow_extra enabled. The raw events can be useful if you are looking for information of the queries executing at a given point in time. For more general queries, aggregating the data with the mysqldumpslow script is more useful. The use of mysqldumpslow was discussed in the last section.

The next part covers some tools that are useful in performance tuning starting with a discussion of monitoring using MySQL Enterprise Monitor as an example.

PART III

Tools

CHAPTER 10

MySQL Enterprise Monitor

Monitoring is one of the keystones of performance tuning whether you are looking at improving the performance at the system or query level. This chapter will look at one of the monitoring solutions available for MySQL, MySQL Enterprise Monitor, also known as MEM.

This chapter will start out with an overview of the architecture and principles of MySQL Enterprise Monitor. Then there is a section with installation instructions if you want to try MySQL Enterprise Monitor followed by a discussion of starting and stopping the Service Manager and how to add MySQL instances to the list of monitored instances. Finally, there is a tour of the user interface.

The rest of the book uses graphs and reports from MySQL Enterprise Monitor to illustrate the use of a monitoring tool, but you can also use other monitoring solutions. If you have no interest in MySQL Enterprise Monitor, you can skip this chapter.

Overview

MySQL Enterprise Monitor is Oracle's monitoring solution that is dedicated to MySQL. It is available for customers as a companion to MySQL Server and is developed by the MySQL development team.

Note   MySQL Enterprise Monitor requires a MySQL Enterprise Edition or MySQL Cluster CGE (Carrier Grade Edition) subscription to be used beyond the 30-day trial version (see also the download instructions in the next section). You can review the MySQL commercial features at `www.mysql.com/products/enterprise/`.

© Jesper Wisborg Krogh 2020
J. W. Krogh, *MySQL 8 Query Performance Tuning*, https://doi.org/10.1007/978-1-4842-5584-1_10

MySQL Enterprise Monitor consists of components which each serves its role in the overall monitoring solution. In version 8, there are two main components:

- **Service Manager:** This component stores the collected metrics and provides the front-end interface to view the data and manage the configuration. The Service Manager consists of two parts which are a Tomcat server that is the application side of the Service Manager and the *repository* which is a MySQL database storing the data.

- **Agent:** MySQL Enterprise Monitor uses Agents to connect to the MySQL instances that are monitored. The Service Manager includes a built-in Agent that by default monitors the repository. An Agent can monitor the local operating system as well as both local and remote MySQL instances.

Note   This book follows the convention from the MySQL Enterprise Monitor manual (`https://dev.mysql.com/doc/mysql-monitor/en/`) to write Service Manager and Agent in title case.

Since the Agent can only monitor the operating system on which it runs – metrics such as CPU and memory usage, disk capacity, and so on – it is best to install an Agent on each host where you monitor MySQL instances. This will allow you to correlate the host metrics with the MySQL activities. If you are not able to install the Agent locally, for example, if you are using a cloud solution that does not give you access to the operating system, you can use an Agent installed on another host to monitor the MySQL metrics. One option in this case is to use the built-in Agent in the Service Manager. Figure 10-1 shows an example of a setup with three hosts, of which one is used for the Service Manager and two hosts have the monitored MySQL instances installed.

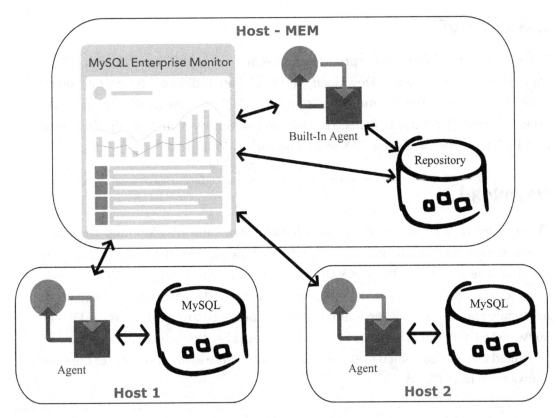

Figure 10-1. *Overview of the MySQL Enterprise Monitor components*

The host at the top is the one with the MySQL Enterprise Monitor Service Manager installed. It consists of the front end – here depicted with a web page with a graph – and the built-in Agent and the repository. The built-in Agent monitors the repository and can optionally be used to monitor other MySQL instances as well (not shown in the figure) which can be useful if you do not have access to the host, as is the case for some cloud products, or if you are testing and want to monitor a second MySQL instance on the same host as where the Service Manager is installed.

Host 1 and Host 2 are two hosts with MySQL Server installed. There is a MySQL Enterprise Monitor Agent installed on each host. The Agents query the MySQL instance for metrics and send the metrics to the Service Manager which stores them in the repository. The Service Manager can also send requests to the Agents, for example, to run an ad hoc report or to change the frequency the Agent collects metrics.

The installation process is similar for the Service Manager and the Agent and uses a customer installation program. The next section covers how to install the Service Manager. It is left as an exercise for the reader to install the Agent, if you want to try that.

Installation

The installation of MySQL Enterprise Monitor is quite straightforward though different from other MySQL products. Downloading the software is different from what you may be used to if you use the community editions of MySQL, and the installation is always done through a dedicated installer. This section will guide you through the download, installation process, and setup of MySQL Enterprise Monitor.

Download

The first step of the installation is to download MySQL Enterprise Monitor. There are two places you can download MySQL Enterprise Monitor. Existing MySQL customers can download it from the Patches & Updates tab in My Oracle Support (MOS). This is the recommended location for customers as Patches & Updates gets updated more frequently and includes all versions since 2011. The alternative location is the Oracle Software Delivery Cloud at `https://edelivery.oracle.com/` which also allows registered users to download a 30-day trial version. These instructions cover the Oracle Software Delivery Cloud.

Note   New accounts and accounts that have not been used for a while may need to undergo export validation which can take a few days.

You start out at the "homepage" as shown in Figure 10-2.

Figure 10-2. *The Oracle Software Delivery Cloud homepage*

If you do not have a login, you need to create a new user using the *New User? Register Here* icon. Once you have logged in, you get to the search page. Figure 10-3 shows part of the search form.

Figure 10-3.   *The Oracle Software Delivery Cloud search form*

Choose *Release* in the drop box to the left of the text field. If you are interested in other products as well, you leave it on the default value which is *All Categories* which includes software packages. In the text field, enter *MySQL Enterprise Monitor* and click *MySQL Enterprise Monitor* in the search list that shows up or click the *Search* button to the right of the text field (neither the list nor button is shown in the figure). Then click *Add to Cart* next to the result for MySQL Enterprise Monitor.

When the product has been added to the cart, you can click the *Checkout* link near the top right of the page (also not shown in the figure). The next screen is shown in Figure 10-4 and allows you to choose which platforms to download for.

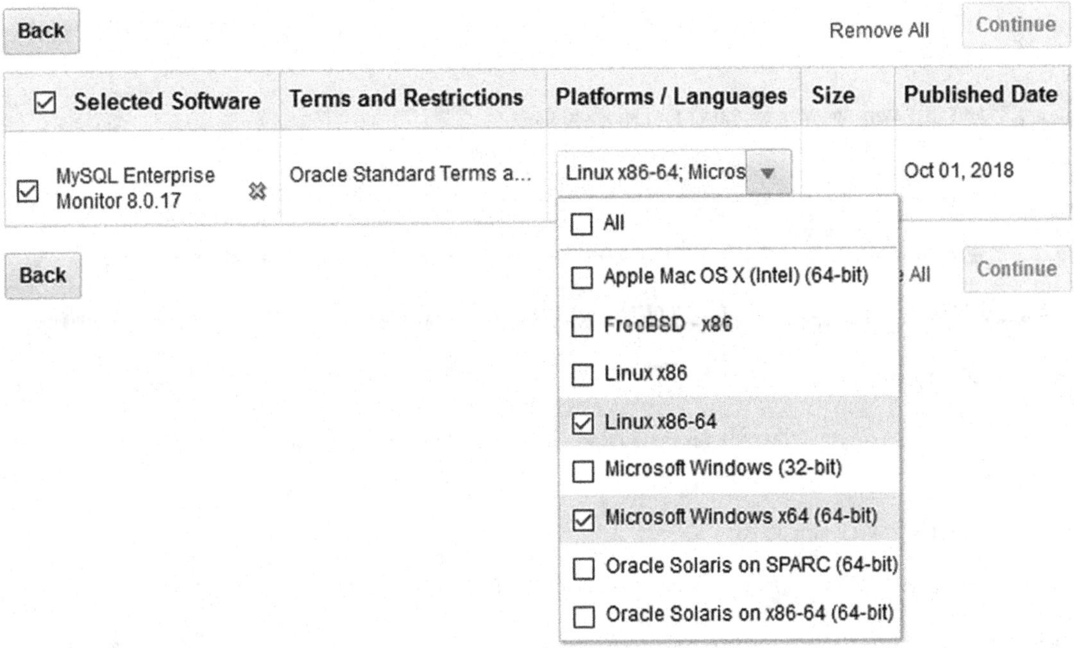

Figure 10-4. *Choose the platforms to download for*

Choose the platforms you are interested in. If you plan on having the Service Manager on one platform while monitoring instances with an Agent installed on another platform, you need to choose both platforms. When you have decided which platforms you want to download for, click *Continue*.

The next step is to accept the license agreement. Please read carefully before accepting it. The Oracle Trial License Agreement is at the end of the document. Once you have accepted the terms and conditions, click *Continue*.

Note   You may be asked to complete a survey about the usability of Oracle Software Delivery Cloud as one of the steps.

The last step is to choose which parts of MySQL Enterprise Monitor you want to download. This is shown in Figure 10-5.

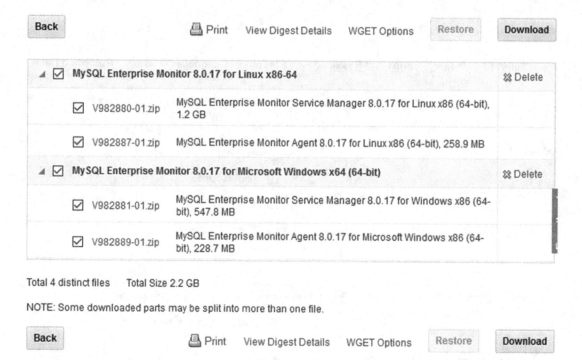

Figure 10-5. *Choose which parts of MySQL Enterprise Monitor to download*

There are two packages for each platform with one package for the Service Manager and one for the Agent. Optionally (recommended), you can click the *View Digest Details* link at the center bottom of the screenshot to show the SHA-1 and SHA-256 checksums for each file. You can use these to validate the download completed successfully.

You can download the files in two ways. If you click the filename, you download the files one by one. Alternatively, check the files you want and click the *Download* button to start the download using a download manager. If you do not have the download manager installed, you will be guided through installing it before the download commences.

Tip Oracle Software Delivery Cloud uses generic filenames such as V982880-01.zip. It is useful to rename the file to a name that includes information about the product, platform, and version you have downloaded.

Once the download has completed, you can start the installation process.

Installation Process

MySQL Enterprise Monitor uses its own installer which works the same on all platforms. There is support for performing the installation using a wizard mode either through a graphical user interface or in text mode, or you can provide all the arguments on the command line and use the unattended mode.

The names of the downloaded files depend on which platform you have downloaded for and the version of MySQL Enterprise Monitor. For example, the Service Manager version 8.0.17 for Microsoft Windows is named V982881-01.zip. The names for other files are similar. If you unpack the ZIP file, you will find several files:

```
PS> ls | select Length,Name

   Length Name
   ------ ----
  6367299 monitor.a4.pdf
  6375459 monitor.pdf
  5275639 mysql-monitor-html.tar.gz
  5300438 mysql-monitor-html.zip
281846252 mysqlmonitor-8.0.17.1195-windows64-installer.exe
281866739 mysqlmonitor-8.0.17.1195-windows64-update-installer.exe
      975 README_en.txt
      975 READ_ME_ja.txt
```

The exact filenames and sizes depend on the platform and MySQL Enterprise Monitor version. Notice that there are two executables, in this case mysqlmonitor-8.0.17.1195-windows64-installer.exe and mysqlmonitor-8.0.17.1195-windows64-update-installer.exe. The former is for installing MySQL Enterprise Monitor from scratch, while the other (also sometimes called the update installer) is for performing an upgrade of an existing installation. The PDF and HTML files are the manual, but you are usually better off using the online manual at https://dev.mysql.com/doc/mysql-monitor/en/ as that is updated regularly.

Tip   If you want to use the text-based wizard or the unattended mode, invoke the installer with the --help argument to get a list of supported arguments.

This discussion will continue using the graphical user interface for the installation. You start the installation by executing the installer without any arguments. The first step is to choose the language (English, Japanese, and Simplified Chinese are available). Then you are told that you need to make sure you keep the usernames and passwords you enter during the installation in a secure location.

After passing the welcome screen, the configuration starts in proper by specifying the installation location. On Microsoft Windows, the default location is `C:\Program Files\ MySQL\Enterprise\Monitor`, and on Linux it is `/opt/mysql/enterprise/monitor` when installing as the `root` user or `mysql/enterprise/monitor` relative to the home directory when installing as a non-privileged user.

The next screen shown in Figure 10-6 asks you to choose how large a system you will monitor.

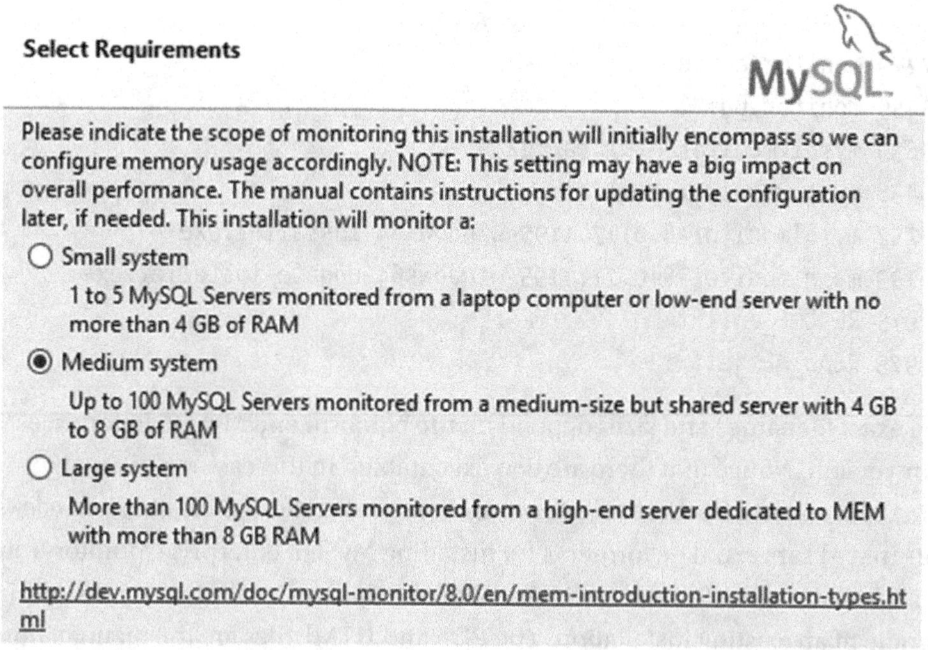

Figure 10-6. *Choosing the size of the system*

The system size determines the default settings for things like the memory configuration of the Service Manager. You can tune the memory settings manually after the installation has completed, but choosing the correct system size means you do not have to worry about these settings initially. Unless you just want to try MySQL Enterprise Monitor with a few instances, choose the medium or large system.

Next, you need to specify the port numbers to use. MySQL Enterprise Monitor uses Tomcat server for the front end with port 18080 as the default unencrypted port and 18443 as the default SSL port. You will always be using the SSL port. (The non-SSL port is there for legacy reasons but cannot be used for the front end.)

At this point, if you are installing on Linux using the root account, you will be asked which user account you want to run the Tomcat processes under (the MySQL Server repository process will use the mysql user). The default is mysqlmem. If you are installing on Linux with a non-root account, you will be notified that it is not possible for the installer to set up auto-start.

The Service Manager uses a MySQL instance to store the data including the collected metrics. You have a choice (see Figure 10-7) between using the MySQL instance bundled with the installer and using an existing MySQL instance.

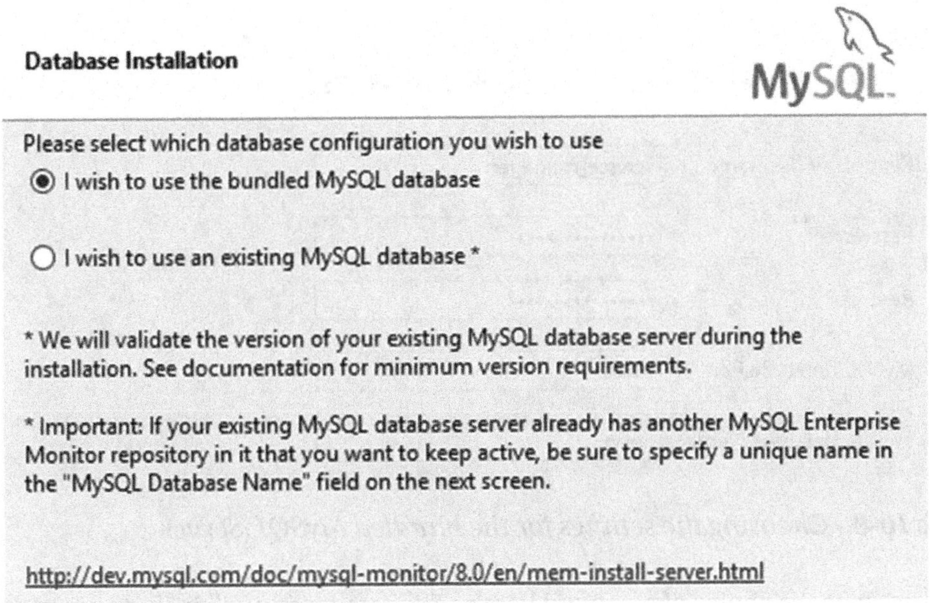

Database Installation   MySQL

Please select which database configuration you wish to use
◉ I wish to use the bundled MySQL database

○ I wish to use an existing MySQL database *

* We will validate the version of your existing MySQL database server during the installation. See documentation for minimum version requirements.

* Important: If your existing MySQL database server already has another MySQL Enterprise Monitor repository in it that you want to keep active, be sure to specify a unique name in the "MySQL Database Name" field on the next screen.

http://dev.mysql.com/doc/mysql-monitor/8.0/en/mem-install-server.html

Figure 10-7. Choose which MySQL instance to use

Unless you have very good reasons to choose otherwise, it is recommended to use the bundled MySQL database. This not only allows the installer to use a base configuration that is known to work well with the Service Manager, it also simplifies upgrades.

> **Caution**   Do not be tempted to use the MySQL instance you want to monitor as the repository for the Service Manager. MySQL Enterprise Monitor does cause a significant amount of database activity, and if you use your production database, your monitoring will stop working if the database it is supposed to monitor shuts down.

You now get to choose the username and password for the connection the Service Manager uses to the MySQL instance as well as the port number and schema name. This is shown in Figure 10-8.

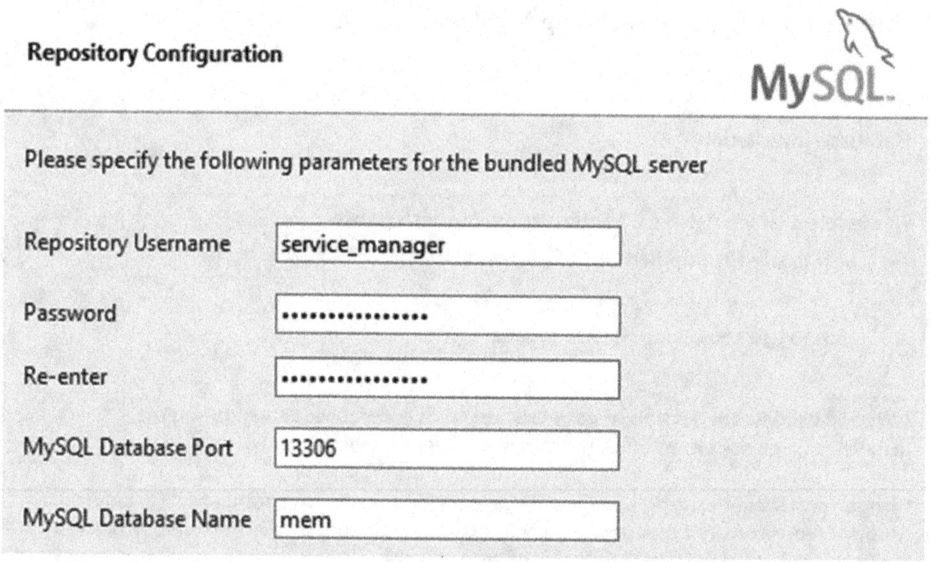

Repository Configuration   MySQL

Please specify the following parameters for the bundled MySQL server

Repository Username	service_manager
Password	••••••••••••••••
Re-enter	••••••••••••••••
MySQL Database Port	13306
MySQL Database Name	mem

Figure 10-8. *Choosing the settings for the bundled MySQL Server*

Do not take the choice of password lightly. The monitoring will include many details about your system including the hostnames and queries. This means it is important to choose a strong password.

That is the end of the configuration, and the installer is ready to commence the actual installation step. The installation takes a little while as it includes both installing a MySQL Server instance and the Tomcat server front end. When the installation is done, a confirmation screen is shown followed by the warning in Figure 10-9.

Completed installing files

WARNING: To improve security, all communication with the Service Manager uses SSL. Because only a basic self-signed security certificate is included when the Service Manager is installed, it is likely that your browser will display a warning about an untrusted connection. Please either install your own certificate or add a security exception for the Service Manager URL to your browser. See the documentation for more information.

http://dev.mysql.com/doc/mysql-monitor/8.0/en/mem-ssl-installation.html

Figure 10-9. *Warning about the self-signed certificates used by default*

The installer creates a self-signed certificate for the SSL connections. This will encrypt the communication just fine, but it does not allow for validating that you are connected to the correct server. You can choose to purchase a certificate signed by a trusted provider and make MySQL Enterprise Monitor use that. If you continue to use the default self-signed certificate (which is assumed here), the browser will complain the first time you connect to the Service Manager that you cannot trust the connection (this is harmless in this case).

That completes the installation. The final screen shows a confirmation that you have completed the wizard, and you can choose to open the readme file and launch the browser. The installer has started the Service Manager in the background, so you do not need to do anything else than open the URL to the Service Manager in the browser. If your browser is on the same host as where you installed the Service Manager and you chose the default SSL port (18443), the URL is `https://localhost:18443/`.

Note   It can take a little while for Tomcat to be ready to respond to the connections which can make the first connection attempt take a while to complete.

As mentioned, if you use the default self-signed certificate, the browser will warn you that there is a potential security risk. An example of this from Firefox is shown in Figure 10-10.

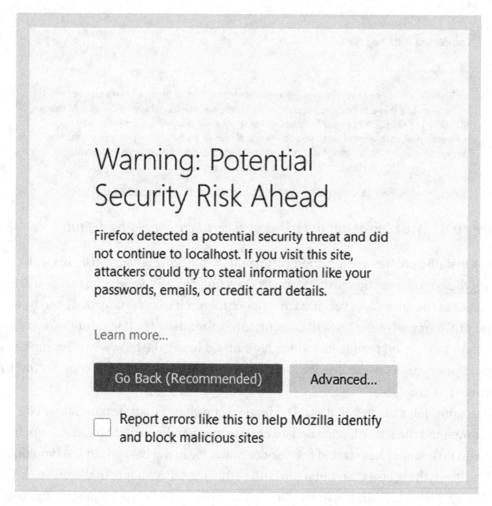

Figure 10-10. *The warning by Firefox that the site cannot be verified*

You will need to accept this risk. How to do this depends on your browser and version. In the case of Firefox 68, you go to the *Advanced* option and choose *Accept the Risk and Continue*.

The first step when you connect to the Service Manager is a little more configuration. Most of this is collected in one screen as shown in Figure 10-11.

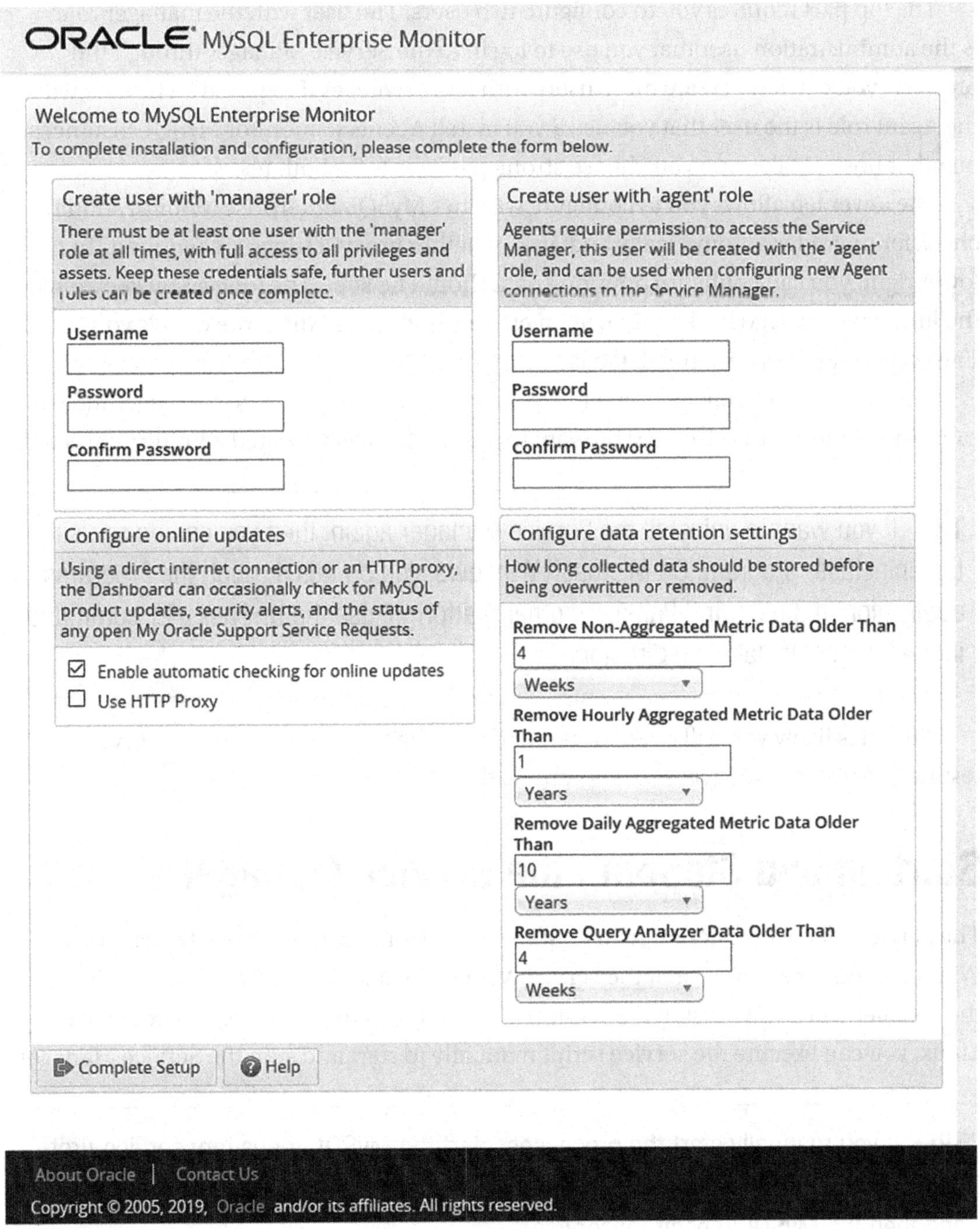

ORACLE MySQL Enterprise Monitor

Welcome to MySQL Enterprise Monitor

To complete installation and configuration, please complete the form below.

Create user with 'manager' role

There must be at least one user with the 'manager' role at all times, with full access to all privileges and assets. Keep these credentials safe, further users and roles can be created once complete.

Username

Password

Confirm Password

Create user with 'agent' role

Agents require permission to access the Service Manager, this user will be created with the 'agent' role, and can be used when configuring new Agent connections to the Service Manager.

Username

Password

Confirm Password

Configure online updates

Using a direct internet connection or an HTTP proxy, the Dashboard can occasionally check for MySQL product updates, security alerts, and the status of any open My Oracle Support Service Requests.

☑ Enable automatic checking for online updates
☐ Use HTTP Proxy

Configure data retention settings

How long collected data should be stored before being overwritten or removed.

Remove Non-Aggregated Metric Data Older Than

4

Weeks ▾

Remove Hourly Aggregated Metric Data Older Than

1

Years ▾

Remove Daily Aggregated Metric Data Older Than

10

Years ▾

Remove Query Analyzer Data Older Than

4

Weeks ▾

⏏ Complete Setup   ❓ Help

Figure 10-11. *The Service Manager configuration screen*

The top part requires you to configure two users. The user with the manager role is the administration user that you use to log in to the Service Manager through the browser (you can later create more users with less privileges if required). The user with the Agent role is the user that you use if you install Agents to monitor MySQL instances on other hosts. Make sure you choose strong passwords for both users.

The lower left allows you to configure whether MySQL Enterprise Monitor should check for upgrades automatically and, if so, whether proxy settings are required. To the lower right, you can configure how long data should be kept. The longer you keep data, the further you can go back in time to investigate issues, and the more details you keep. The cost is that the size of the database increases.

Once you have completed the setup, you will be taken to a What's New page, and you can set the time zone and locale you want to use for the newly created administration user.

Tip   If you want to uninstall the Service Manager again, then you can do so using the uninstaller program. On Microsoft Windows, you do this through the Programs application in the Control Panel. On other platforms, use the `uninstall` command in the topmost installation directory.

Since it is likely you will need to start and stop the Service Manager during you testing, the next section will show how to do that.

Starting and Stopping the Service Manager

The Service Manager is designed to be started and stopped as a service. On Microsoft Windows and when you install the Service Manager using the `root` account on Linux, the installer will always install the services for you. If you install it as a non-root user on Linux, you can execute the service script manually to start and stop the Service Manager.

Tip   If you manually start the processes, start the MySQL repository service first and then Tomcat. When stopping it, it is the other way around, first stop Tomcat and then the MySQL repository service.

Microsoft Windows

On Microsoft Windows, the installer always requires the administrator privilege to run, which means it can also install the Service Manager processes as services. By default, the services are set to automatically start and stop when you boot and shut down the computer.

You can edit the settings for the services by opening the Services application. On Windows 10, the easiest way to do this is to use the Windows key on the keyboard (alternatively open the Start menu by clicking the Windows icon in the lower-left corner) and type *Services* as shown in Figure 10-12.

Figure 10-12. *Opening the Services application*

The search result may look different to some degree compared to the screenshot. Click the *Services app* match under *Best match*. This opens the application where you can control the services. From the Services application, you can control the services by starting, stopping, pausing, or restarting the service. The repository service is named *MySQL Enterprise MySQL,* and the Tomcat service is named *MySQL Enterprise Tomcat* as shown in Figure 10-13.

Services (Local)					
MySQL Enterprise MySQL	Name ^	Description	Status	Startup Type	Log On As
	MySQL Enterprise MySQL		Running	Automatic	Local Syste...
Stop the service	MySQL Enterprise Tomcat	Apache To...	Running	Automatic	Local Syste...
Pause the service	MySQL			Manual	Local Syste...
Restart the service					

Figure 10-13. *Controlling the services*

When you click a service, you get the basic control actions in the pane to the left of the services list. You can also right-click the service to get the actions as well as the option to edit the properties of the service. These properties include whether to automatically start and stop the service.

Linux

How you start and stop MySQL Enterprise Monitor on Linux depends on whether you performed the installation using the root operating system user. If you used the root user, you start and stop the processes using the service command (there is no native support for systemd) with the mysql-monitor-server service; otherwise, you use the mysqlmonitorctl.sh script that is to the base of the installation directory. Either way, you can add the tomcat or mysql argument to just change the status of one of the processes.

Listing 10-1 shows how to use the service command to start, restart, and stop MySQL Enterprise Monitor.

Listing 10-1. Changing the status of the services with the service command

```
shell$ sudo service mysql-monitor-server start
Starting mysql service  [ OK ]
2019-08-24T06:45:43.062790Z mysqld_safe Logging to '/opt/mysql/enterprise/
monitor/mysql/data/ol7.err'.
2019-08-24T06:45:43.168359Z mysqld_safe Starting mysqld daemon with
databases from /opt/mysql/enterprise/monitor/mysql/data
Starting tomcat service  [ OK ]

shell$ sudo service mysql-monitor-server restart
Stopping tomcat service . [ OK ]
Stopping mysql service 2019-08-24T06:47:57.907854Z mysqld_safe mysqld from
pid file /opt/mysql/enterprise/monitor/mysql/runtime/mysqld.pid ended
. [ OK ]
Starting mysql service  [ OK ]
2019-08-24T06:48:04.441201Z mysqld_safe Logging to '/opt/mysql/enterprise/
monitor/mysql/data/ol7.err'.
2019-08-24T06:48:04.544643Z mysqld_safe Starting mysqld daemon with
databases from /opt/mysql/enterprise/monitor/mysql/data
Starting tomcat service  [ OK ]
```

```
shell$ sudo service mysql-monitor-server stop tomcat
Stopping tomcat service . [ OK ]
```

```
shell$ sudo service mysql-monitor-server stop mysql
Stopping mysql service 2019-08-24T06:48:54.707288Z mysqld_safe mysqld from
pid file /opt/mysql/enterprise/monitor/mysql/runtime/mysqld.pid ended
. [ OK ]
```

First, both services are started and then restarted, and finally the services are stopped one by one. It is not necessary to stop the services one by one, but it can be useful, for example, if you need to do maintenance on the repository.

Listing 10-2 shows the same example using the mysqlmonitorctl.sh script.

Listing 10-2. Changing the status of the services with mysqlmonitorctl.sh

```
shell $ ./mysqlmonitorctl.sh start
Starting mysql service  [ OK ]
2019-08-24T06:52:34.245379Z mysqld_safe Logging to '/home/myuser/mysql/
enterprise/monitor/mysql/data/ol7.err'.
2019-08-24T06:52:34.326811Z mysqld_safe Starting mysqld daemon with
databases from /home/myuser/mysql/enterprise/monitor/mysql/data
Starting tomcat service  [ OK ]
```

```
shell$ ./mysqlmonitorctl.sh restart
Stopping tomcat service . [ OK ]
Stopping mysql service 2019-08-24T06:53:08.292547Z mysqld_safe mysqld from
pid file /home/myuser/mysql/enterprise/monitor/mysql/runtime/mysqld.pid
ended
. [ OK ]
Starting mysql service  [ OK ]
2019-08-24T06:53:15.310640Z mysqld_safe Logging to '/home/myuser/mysql/
enterprise/monitor/mysql/data/ol7.err'.
2019-08-24T06:53:15.397898Z mysqld_safe Starting mysqld daemon with
databases from /home/myuser/mysql/enterprise/monitor/mysql/data
Starting tomcat service  [ OK ]
```

```
shell$ ./mysqlmonitorctl.sh stop tomcat
Stopping tomcat service . [ OK ]
```

```
shell$ ./mysqlmonitorctl.sh stop mysql
Stopping mysql service 2019-08-24T06:54:39.592847Z mysqld_safe mysqld from
pid file /home/myuser/mysql/enterprise/monitor/mysql/runtime/mysqld.pid
ended
. [ OK ]
```

The steps are very similar to the previous example with the service command. In fact, the script invoked by the service command is the same as the mysqlmonitorctl. sh script except that the paths and usernames in it depend on the operating user used to install the Service Manager and the installation path.

Adding MySQL Instances

If you just want to play around with MySQL Enterprise Monitor, you do not need to do any more than you already have. The built-in Agent of the Service Manager will automatically monitor the repository instance, so already when you log in to the user interface the first time, there is monitoring data available. If you have installed an Agent, the Agent will also register the instance it is monitoring automatically. The last option, which will be discussed in this section, is to add an instance from the user interface.

If the MySQL instance you want to add monitoring for is installed on the same host as the Service Manager or an existing Agent, it will be detected automatically, and the icon with a dolphin and a question mark in the upper-right part of the page will be highlighted as it is shown in Figure 10-14.

Figure 10-14. *One instance is shown as unmonitored*

Notice how it says 1 to the right of the dolphin with a question mark in a (yellow) circle. This is the number of MySQL instances that have been found but are not monitored. When you hover over the icon, a tooltip with the number of unmonitored instances will be displayed. If you click the dolphin or the number, it will take you to the MySQL instance configuration screen which you can also access through the menu in the left-hand pane.

Note   Instances added through the user interface will be monitored by an existing Agent (the built-in Agent if you did not install any Agents yourself). Only those systems with the Agent installed will have their operating system monitored.

The instance configuration screen both includes the option of adding new instances, a list of unmonitored instances found by MySQL Enterprise Monitor, and a list of the monitored instances. Figure 10-15 shows part of the page related to start monitoring new and unmonitored instances.

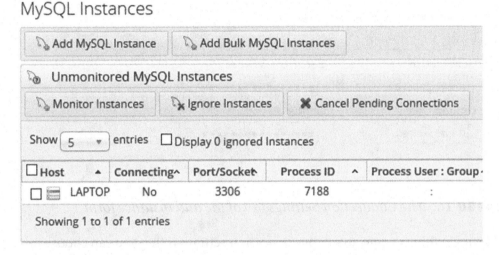

Figure 10-15. The instance configuration page

You can add monitoring of any MySQL instance by using the *Add MySQL Instance* or *Add Bulk MySQL Instances* button at the top of the page. If the instance you want to monitor is listed in the Unmonitored MySQL Instances list, you can also choose it there and click the *Monitor Instances* button which will take you to the same form as *Add MySQL Instance* with the difference that the known connection settings have been prefilled. The form has several tabs, of which the Connection Settings tab is shown in Figure 10-16.

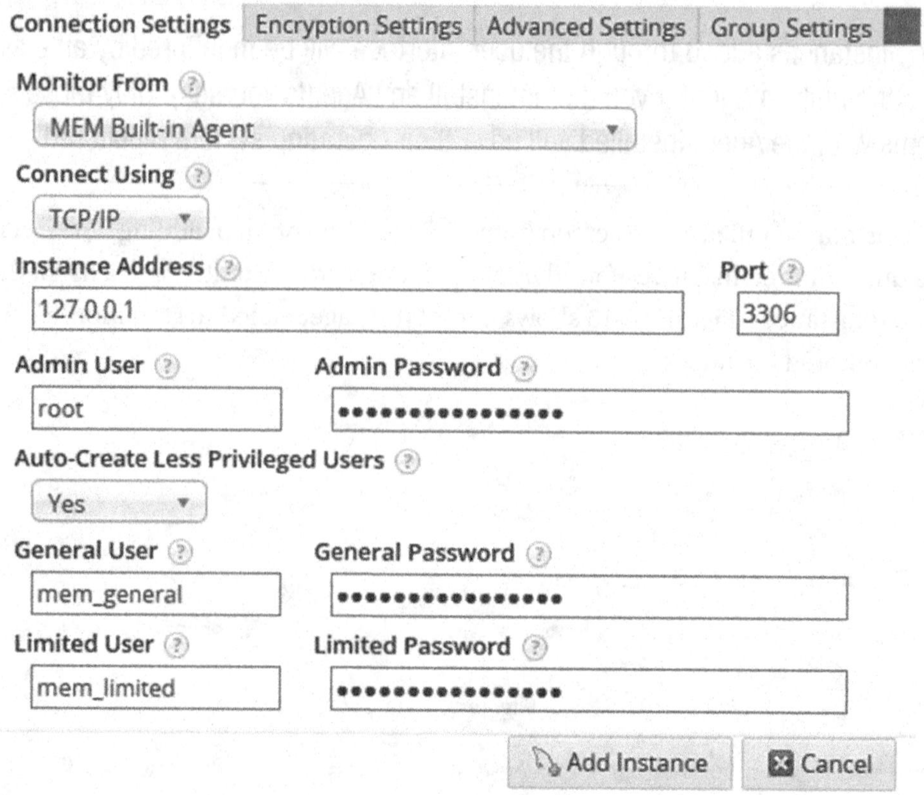

Figure 10-16. *The Connection Settings tab of the add instance form*

The main thing to note about the connection settings is that you can choose to have MySQL Enterprise Monitor auto-create users with fewer privileges than the administration user that is used to set up the monitoring. It is recommended to allow these users to be created as it allows the Agent to use a user with as few privileges as possible for the task it performs.

If you have encryption requirements, you can edit those in the Encryption Settings tab. The Advanced Settings tab is rarely needed. If you are setting up monitoring of several instances, you may want to specify a group for the instance in the Group Settings tab. These settings can also be changed after the instance has been added.

It will take a little time to add the instance. When it is ready, you can start exploring the rest of the user interface.

The Graphical User Interface

The user interface provided by the Service Manager's Tomcat server is where you will spend most of the time using MySQL Enterprise Monitor. As you have already seen, it can be used to add new instances. This section will dive further into the user interface and discuss general navigation, advisors, timeseries graphs, and the Query Analyzer.

General Navigation

The MySQL Enterprise Monitor user interface divides the features into logical groups with support for filtering by the group, host, Agent, or instance. This section will give a brief tour of the interface with the aim that when graphs or reports are mentioned later in the book, you can find them in the interface, if you want to explore it closer.

Figure 10-17 shows the top-left part of the page in the user interface. This is where you choose which feature to access and for which targets you want data to be displayed.

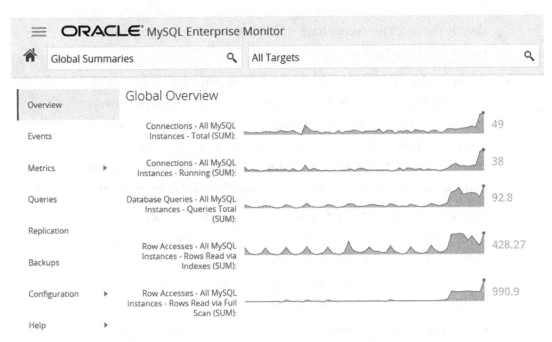

Figure 10-17. *The top left of the page in MySQL Enterprise Monitor*

The navigation to the features is centered on the left-hand pane with the filters applied in the two search fields at the top of the page. The search field with the label *Global Summaries* in the screenshot allows you to choose a group of instances. Groups can be created manually but are also created automatically for instances that are replicating between each other. *Global Summaries* is a special group that includes all instances. The right-hand search field allows you to limit the instances, Agents, or hosts included from the group.

The features include dashboards, graphs, reports, and more. The list of available features depends on which filters you have applied. The menu items are

- **Overview:** This is a high-level dashboard.

- **Topology:** This option is only available when a replication group has been chosen. It takes you to a diagram showing the topology of the group with the status of the replication for each instance.

- **Events:** Returns a report of the monitoring events for the instances. The events are raised when some condition set by the advisors (more shortly) is met. The events have different severities ranging from a notice to an emergency.

- **Metrics:** This takes you to the reports displaying metrics collected by the Agents. No matter the filter, the timeseries graphs are always available (but which graphs depends on the filter). For individual instances, there are also reports for table statistics, user statistics, memory usage, database file I/O, the InnoDB buffer pool, processes, and lock waits. Several of these reports will be used in later chapters.

- **Queries:** This is the MySQL Query Analyzer which allows you to investigate which queries are executed on the instance. The timeseries graphs are linked to the Query Analyzer, so you can go from examining the graphs to seeing which queries were executing during the period being investigated.

- **Replication:** The replication dashboard and other replication-related reports.

- **Backups:** Information about backups created by MySQL Enterprise Backup (MEB).

- **Configuration:** Configuration of the various aspects of MySQL Enterprise Monitor including instances and advisors.

- **Help:** The documentation including What's New that you have already seen and access to download a diagnostic report that can be used to troubleshoot problems. The diagnostic report is mostly used if you have a MySQL support contract and need to provide diagnostics in a support ticket.

One term that is necessary to explain further is advisors.

Advisors

Advisor is the name MySQL Enterprise Monitor uses for the rules that define how often data is collected, which conditions trigger events, and which severity the event is. This is an important concept that you should take some time to understand and configure.

One of the most important steps to get a useful monitoring solution is to ensure you get the right events (alerts) at the right time but avoid unnecessary events. This includes ensuring that each alert is set to the appropriate severity. You may at first think that the more events the better, so that you know everything that goes on. However, that is not how you best use a monitoring system. If you have many false positives when you examine the events or you get woken up unnecessarily at 3:00 a.m. for an issue that easily can wait until the morning, then you start ignoring events, and that is the sure recipe to miss an important event sooner or later. In short, your work with the advisors should be ongoing to keep improving them to trigger "just the right" events at "just the right" time.

Tip   An important part of the work with monitoring is to ensure the monitoring system triggers an event with a severity that matches the urgency of the issue. The goal should be never to ignore an event and that you always get alerted at a time and in a way that is appropriate for the urgency.

The advisors can be configured under the *Configuration* item in the left-hand pane. The advisors are organized in groups as shown in Figure 10-18.

Manage Advisors

Create Advisor	Import/Export	

Edit Selected	All Advisors ☆ ▼	New ▼	▽
Disable Selected	Select All Expand All Collapse All		

Administration	Count: 22	▼
Agent	Count: 2	▼
Availability	Count: 5	▼
Backup	Count: 1	▼
Graphing	Count: 81	▼
Memory Usage	Count: 6	▼
Monitoring and Support Services	Count: 9	▼
NDB Cluster	Count: 8	▼
Operating System	Count: 5	▼
Performance	Count: 22	▼
Query Analysis	Count: 4	▼
Replication	Count: 19	▼
Schema	Count: 17	▼
Security	Count: 26	▼

Edit Selected	Disable Selected	Select All	Expand All	Collapse All

Figure 10-18.   *The advisors are organized into groups*

Each group covers advisors of similar type, for example, there is the Performance group with 22 advisors such as Excessive Number of Locked Processes and Indexes Not Being Used Efficiently.

By default, all advisors are enabled with the thresholds for the severity levels set to values that work well in many cases. However, as no two systems are the same, you will need to fine-tune the settings which you do by expanding the group and clicking the menu icon to the left of the name of the advisor as shown in Figure 10-19.

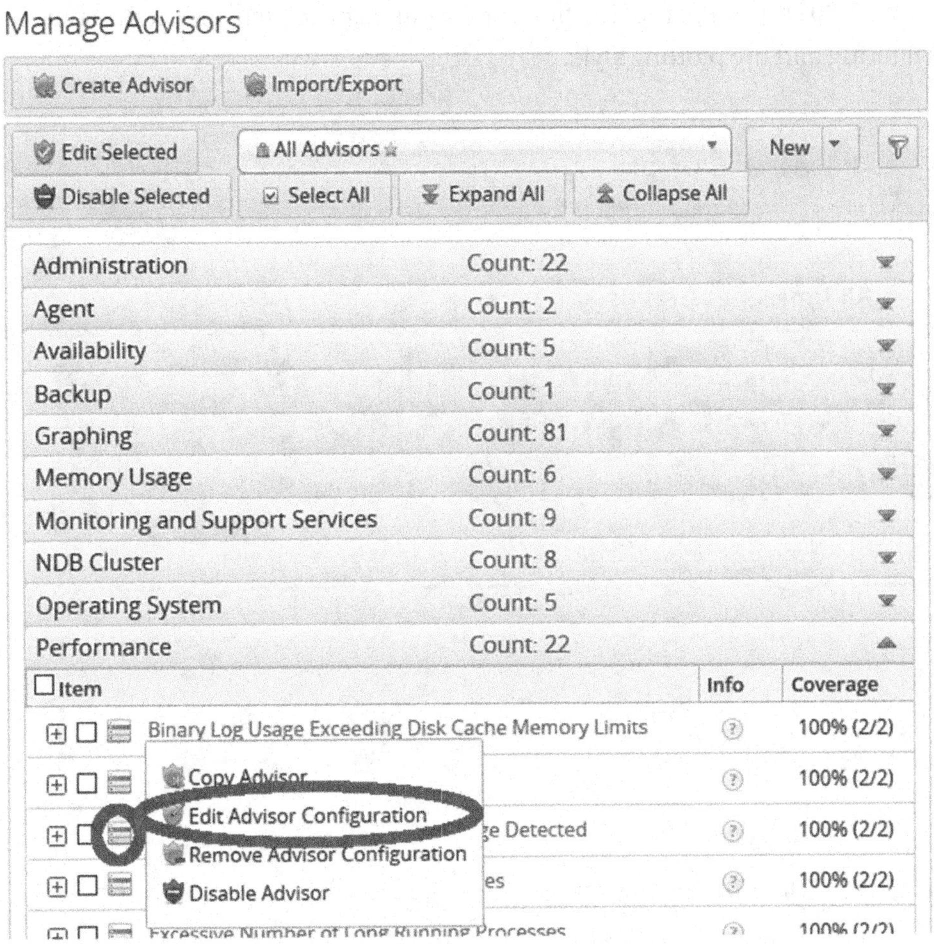

Manage Advisors

🐢 Create Advisor	🐢 Import/Export

| Edit Selected | 🛡 All Advisors ⭐ | ▼ | New ▼ | 🔻 |
| Disable Selected | ☑ Select All | 🔻 Expand All | 🔺 Collapse All | |

Administration	Count: 22	▼
Agent	Count: 2	▼
Availability	Count: 5	▼
Backup	Count: 1	▼
Graphing	Count: 81	▼
Memory Usage	Count: 6	▼
Monitoring and Support Services	Count: 9	▼
NDB Cluster	Count: 8	▼
Operating System	Count: 5	▼
Performance	Count: 22	🔺

☐ Item		Info	Coverage
⊞ ☐ ▦ Binary Log Usage Exceeding Disk Cache Memory Limits		⑦	100% (2/2)
⊞ ☐ ▦ 🐢 Copy Advisor		⑦	100% (2/2)
⊞ ☐ ▦ ✓ Edit Advisor Configuration	...ge Detected	⑦	100% (2/2)
⊞ ☐ ▦ 🐢 Remove Advisor Configuration	...es	⑦	100% (2/2)
🛡 Disable Advisor			
⊞ ☐ ▦ Excessive Number of Long Running Processes		⑦	100% (2/2)

Figure 10-19. *Menu to edit an advisor configuration*

You can also expand the advisor using the + icon to the left of the advisor item which allows you to edit the advisor for a specific group of instances or a single instance. The ? icon in the *Info* column provides additional information such as the expression evaluated or the source of the data for the advisor. There is additional information available which is not shown in the figure.

Timeseries Graphs

The timeseries graphs are the graphs that show the metrics over time. This is a standard feature of all monitoring solutions. You can filter which graphs to display and change the time frame to plot as well as the plotting style.

Figure 10-20 shows a part of the timeseries graphs page focusing on the controls to access filtering and the plotting style.

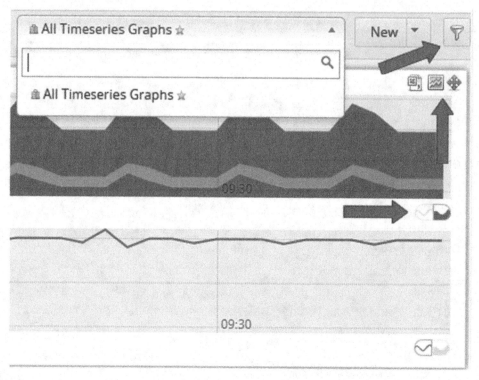

Figure 10-20. *The timeseries graphs*

Above the graphs are the options to choose which graphs to display and the time frame of the graphs. The search field to the left in the screenshot allows you to choose between saved timeseries groups. By default, there is a single group called *All Timeseries Graphs* that – as the name suggests – includes all timeseries graphs appropriate for the instance filtering in place.

You access the options for the timeseries graphs by using the funnel icon in the top-right corner of the screenshot. This will open a frame that allows you to choose which graphs to display and the time frame to cover.

The two small buttons below each graph allow you to toggle between using the line and stacked plotting modes. The screenshot shows an example of the stacked mode in the topmost graph and the line mode in the lower graph. The line mode is the default. You can also change the height of the graphs using a slider (not included in the screenshot) to the left of the field to select between saved graph groups.

The three icons above the graph become visible when you hover above the graph and allows you to export the data for the graph in CSV format, open the graph as a PNG image, or move the graph which allow you to reorder the graphs as it suits you best. In this case where there are two graphs grouped together, the controls apply to both graphs.

An alternative way to change the time frame of the graphs is to highlight the part of a graph that is of interest and zoom in on that part. This also allows you to go to the Query Analyzer to examine which queries were executed during that period. Figure 10-21 shows an example of highlighting a time frame in a graph.

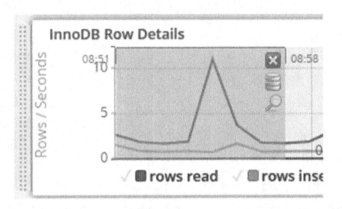

Figure 10-21. *Selecting a part of a timeseries graph*

Notice that in the upper-right part of the highlighted area, there are three icons to control what to do with the selection. The X in the box discards the selection, the database cylinder opens the graph for the selected time frame in the Query Analyzer, and the magnifying glass zooms the timeseries graphs to use the selected time frame.

The Query Analyzer

The Query Analyzer is a feature that makes MySQL Enterprise Monitor stand out from other monitoring solutions. It allows you to see which queries execute on the instance in a given period which is invaluable when investigating performance problems.

The Query Analyzer page is divided into three areas. At the top there is access to filtering options, then optionally there is one or more graphs, and the rest of the page is a list of statements. Figure 10-22 shows an example of this.

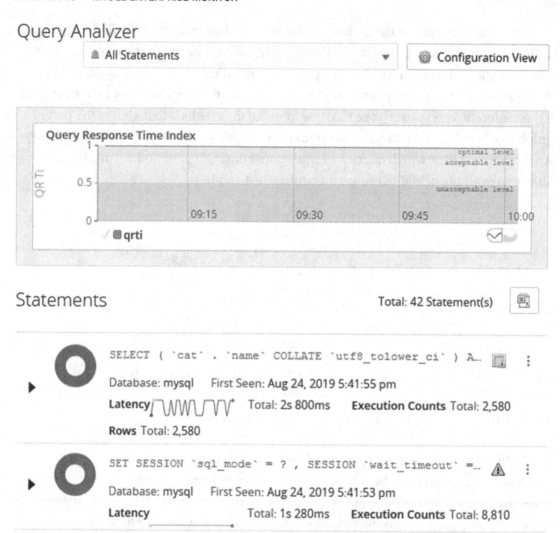

Figure 10-22. *The Query Analyzer*

The drop box at the top saying *All Statements* in the screenshot allows you to choose the statement type to show statements for. The default is to include all statements. To the right there is the *Configuration View* button which takes you to a page where you can configure how the Query Analyzer page should be configured. This includes the time frame to cover, which graphs to display, filtering options, and which information to include for each statement.

By default, the Query Analyzer includes the graph for the Query Response Time index (QRTi). The definition of the Query Response Time index and how to use it will be covered in Chapter 19 when the Query Analyzer is used to find candidates for optimization.

That concludes the tour of MySQL Enterprise Monitor. You are encouraged to explore the user interface further on your own.

Summary

This chapter has provided a brief introduction to MySQL Enterprise Monitor with the aim at allowing you to get it installed and monitor a MySQL instance. First, an overview of the architecture and principles was discussed. MySQL Enterprise Monitor consists of a Service Manager where the data is aggregated, and you can access the monitoring system through the user interface. The monitoring of the hosts and instances is done by the Agent. There is a built-in Agent in the Service Manager, and you can install additional Agents on the hosts of your MySQL instances.

The overview was followed by download and installation instructions. Since MySQL Enterprise Monitor is a commercial-only product, you download it either from Oracle Software Delivery Cloud or My Oracle Support. The installation is done using an installer. This chapter showed how to use the graphical user interface of the installer for the Service Manager.

Starting and stopping the Service Manager is based on having it installed as a service. On Linux and Unix, you can also have the Service Manager installed as a non-root user in which case the same script that the `service` command uses can be invoked directly from the installation directory.

There are two main ways to add an instance to be monitored. If you install an Agent to monitor the instance, the Agent will register the instance. You can also add an instance from the user interface of the Service Manager.

Finally, there was a quick tour of the graphical user interface of the Service Manager. The focus was on the filtering of the instances you see data for and the list of features, the timeseries graphs, and the Query Analyzer. Several of these features will be used to demonstrate monitoring in the remainder of the book.

The next chapter will look at another useful tool that is used in the later chapters: MySQL Workbench.

## CHAPTER 11

MySQL Workbench

MySQL Workbench is Oracle's graphical user interface for querying and managing MySQL Server. It can be seen as one of the two Swiss army knives for working with MySQL, with the other being MySQL Shell that is discussed in the next chapter.

The main feature of MySQL Workbench is the query mode where you can execute queries. There are however also several other features such as the performance reports, Visual Explain, the ability to manage the configuration and inspect the schema, and more.

If you compare MySQL Workbench with MySQL Enterprise Monitor, then MySQL Enterprise Monitor is dedicated to monitoring and is a server solution, whereas MySQL Workbench is a desktop solution which is primarily a client for working with MySQL Server. Similarly, the monitoring that is included in MySQL Workbench is all ad hoc monitoring, whereas MySQL Enterprise Monitor as a server solution includes support for storing historical data.

This chapter will introduce MySQL Workbench and go through installation, basic usage, and how to create EER diagrams. The performance reports and Visual Explain will be covered in later chapters.

Tip If you are already familiar MySQL Workbench, you can consider skipping this chapter or skim it.

Installation

You install MySQL Workbench in the same way as other MySQL programs except there is only support for using the package manager (thus no standalone installations). The MySQL Workbench version numbers follow the MySQL Server versions so that MySQL Workbench 8.0.18 is released at the same time as MySQL Server 8.0.18. A MySQL

199

© Jesper Wisborg Krogh 2020
J. W. Krogh, *MySQL 8 Query Performance Tuning*, https://doi.org/10.1007/978-1-4842-5584-1_11

Workbench version supports the MySQL Server versions that are still being maintained at the time of release, so MySQL Workbench 8.0.18 supports connecting to MySQL Server 5.6, 5.7, and 8.

Tip   It is best to use the latest MySQL Workbench release. You can see the compatibility of the MySQL tools at `https://dev.mysql.com/doc/mysql-compat-matrix/en/`.

This section will show examples of how to install MySQL Workbench on Microsoft Windows, on "Enterprise Linux 7" (Oracle Linux, Red Hat Enterprise Linux, and CentOS), and on Ubuntu 19.10. Other Linux platforms are similar in concept to the two Linux examples.

Tip   If you are a MySQL customer, it is recommended to download MySQL Workbench from Patches & Updates in My Oracle Support (MOS). This will give you access to the commercial version of MySQL Workbench which has some extra features such as an audit log inspector and a graphical user interface for MySQL Enterprise Backup (MEB).

Microsoft Windows

On Microsoft Windows, the preferred way to install MySQL Workbench is to use MySQL Installer for Windows. If you have other MySQL products installed, you may already have MySQL Installer installed in which case you can skip the first steps of these instructions and instead click *Add* on the main screen which takes you to the point of Figure 11-5.

You can download MySQL Installer from `https://dev.mysql.com/downloads/installer/`. Figure 11-1 shows the download section.

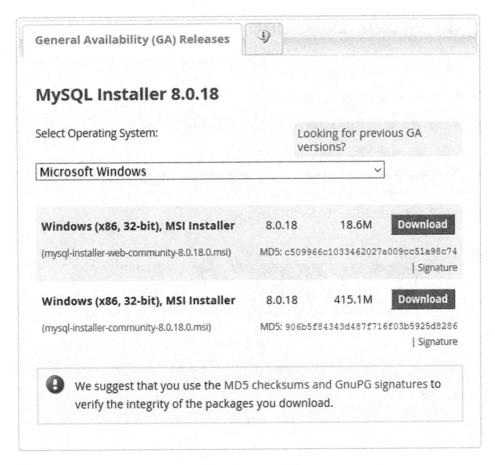

Figure 11-1. *The MySQL Workbench download page*

There are two choices for the installer. The first called the web installer (`mysql-installer-web-community-8.0.18.0.msi`) is just MySQL Installer, whereas the second (`mysql-installer-community-8.0.18.0.msi`) also includes MySQL Server. If you plan to install MySQL Server as well, it makes sense to choose the download that includes both MySQL Installer and MySQL Server as you avoid waiting for the installer to download the MySQL Server installation files later. This example assumes you choose the web installer.

You click the *Download* button to access the download. If you are not logged in, it will take you to the Begin Your Download page where you can choose between logging in and starting the download straight away. This is shown in Figure 11-2.

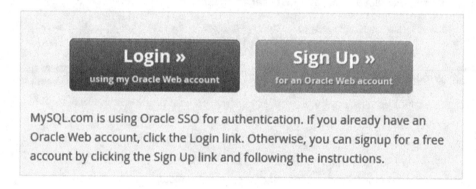

Figure 11-2. *The second step in downloading MySQL Workbench*

If you already have an account, you can sign in. Otherwise, you can choose to sign up to an Oracle account. You can also choose to download the installer without logging in by clicking the *No thanks, just start my download* link.

When the download has completed, launch the downloaded file. Other than confirming that you will allow the installer and MySQL Installer to modify the installed programs, there are no actions required to install MySQL Installer. Once the installation has completed, MySQL Installer automatically launches and detects MySQL programs already installed using an MSI installer as shown in Figure 11-3.

Figure 11-3. *The MySQL Installer detects previously installed MySQL programs*

If you do not have any MySQL programs installed, you are taken to a screen that asks you to confirm that you agree with the license terms. Please read the license terms carefully before proceeding. If you can accept the license, tick the *I accept the license terms* check box and click the button labelled *Next* ➤ to continue.

The next step is to choose what to install. The setup type selection screen is shown in Figure 11-4.

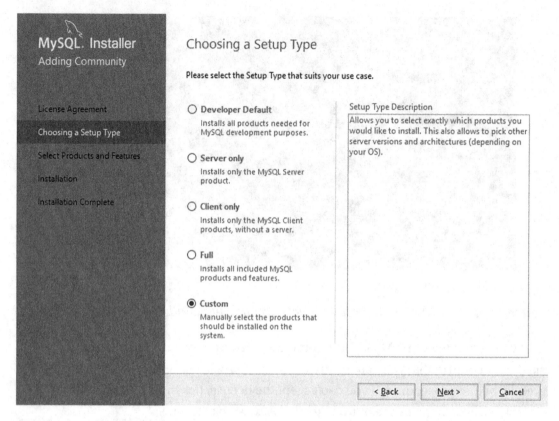

Figure 11-4. *The MySQL Installer setup type chooser*

You can choose between several bundles such as the developer bundle (called *Developer Default*) which installs the products typically used in a development environment. When you choose a setup type, the description in the right of the screen includes a list of the products that will be installed. For this example, the custom installation type will be used.

The next step is to choose which products to install. That uses the selector shown in Figure 11-5.

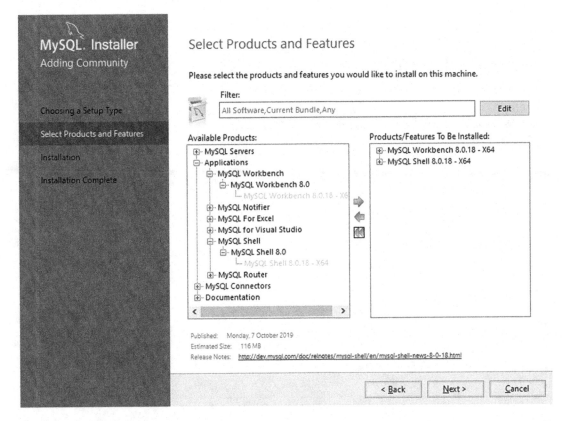

Figure 11-5. *Select what to install*

You find MySQL Workbench in the available products list under Applications. Click the arrow pointing to the right to add MySQL Workbench to the list of products and features to be installed. Feel free to choose additional products; for this book, it is recommended to also include MySQL Shell. When you have added all the products you need, click *Next* ➤ to proceed.

The following screen provides a summary of the products that will be installed. Click *Execute* to start the installation. The installation process includes downloading the product if MySQL Installer does not already have a local copy. The installation may take a little while to complete. When it has completed, click *Next* ➤ to continue. The final screen lists the installed programs and gives you the option to launch MySQL Workbench and MySQL Shell. Click *Finish* to close MySQL Installer.

If you later want to install more products or perform upgrades or remove products, you can launch MySQL Installer again which takes you to the main MySQL Installer screen as shown in Figure 11-6.

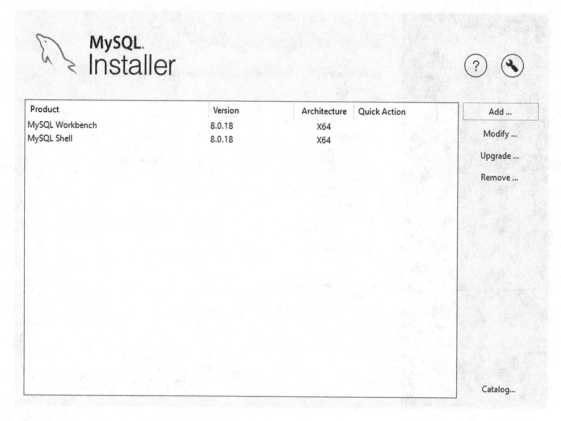

Figure 11-6. *The main MySQL Installer screen*

You choose the action you want to perform in the rightmost part of the screen. The actions are

- **Add:** Install products and features.

- **Modify:** Change the installation of an existing product. This is mainly useful for MySQL Server.

- **Upgrade:** Upgrade a product that is already installed.

- **Remove:** Uninstall a product.

- **Catalog:** Update MySQL Installer's list of available MySQL products.

These five actions allow you to perform all steps required during the lifecycle of the MySQL products.

Enterprise Linux 7

If you are using Linux, you install MySQL Workbench using the package manager. On Oracle Linux, Red Hat Enterprise Linux, and CentOS 7, the preferred package manager is yum as it will help resolve dependencies of the packages that you install or upgrade. MySQL has a yum repository for its community products. This example will show how to install that and use it to install MySQL Workbench.

You can find the URL to the repository definition at `https://dev.mysql.com/downloads/repo/yum/`. There are also repositories for APT and SUSE. Choose the file that corresponds to your Linux distribution and click *Download*. Figure 11-7 shows the file for Enterprise Linux 7.

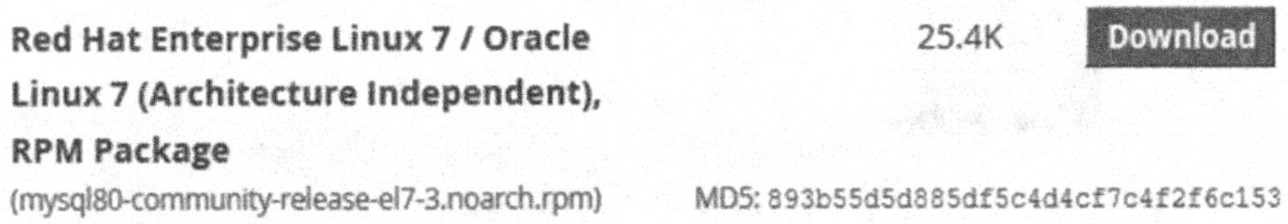

Red Hat Enterprise Linux 7 / Oracle	25.4K	Download
Linux 7 (Architecture Independent),		
RPM Package		
(mysql80-community-release-el7-3.noarch.rpm)	MD5: 893b55d5d885df5c4d4cf7c4f2f6c153	

Figure 11-7. *The repository definition download for Enterprise Linux 7*

If you are not logged in, it will take you to a second screen like in the example of installing MySQL Workbench on Microsoft Windows. This will allow you to log in to your Oracle Web account, create an account, or download without logging in. Either download the RPM file and save it in the directory you want to install it from or right-click the *Download* button (if you are logged in) or the *No thanks, just start my download* link and copy the URL as shown in Figure 11-8.

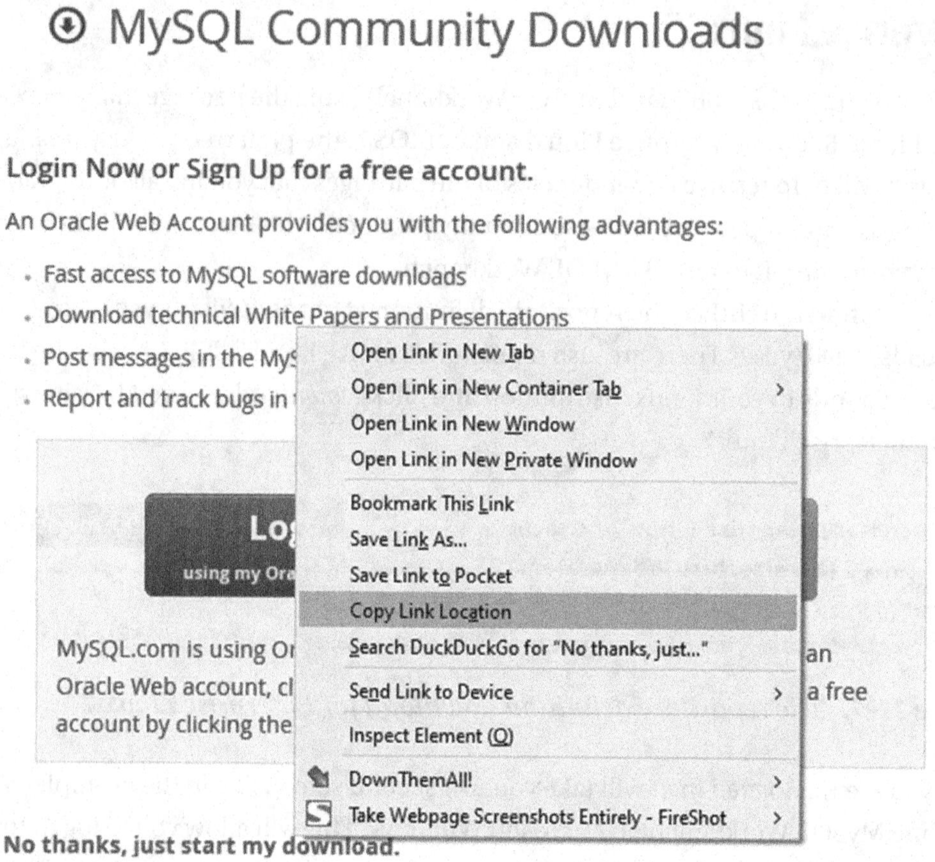

⊙ MySQL Community Downloads

Login Now or Sign Up for a free account.

An Oracle Web Account provides you with the following advantages:

- Fast access to MySQL software downloads
- Download technical White Papers and Presentations
- Post messages in the My~~~~
- Report and track bugs in ~~~~

Open Link in New Tab
Open Link in New Container Tab >
Open Link in New Window
Open Link in New Private Window
Bookmark This Link
Save Link As...
Save Link to Pocket
Copy Link Location
Search DuckDuckGo for "No thanks, just..."
Send Link to Device >
Inspect Element (Q)
DownThemAll! >
Take Webpage Screenshots Entirely - FireShot >

Lo~~

using my Ore~~

MySQL.com is using Or~~~~ an
Oracle Web account, cl~~~~ a free
account by clicking the~~~~

No thanks, just start my download.

***Figure 11-8.** Copying the link to the repository installation file*

You can now install the repository definition as shown in Listing 11-1.

***Listing 11-1.** Installing the MySQL community repository*

```
shell$ wget https://dev.mysql.com/get/mysql80-community-release-el7-3.
noarch.rpm
...
HTTP request sent, awaiting response... 200 OK
Length: 26024 (25K) [application/x-redhat-package-manager]
Saving to: 'mysql80-community-release-el7-3.noarch.rpm'

100%[=========================>] 26,024      --.-K/s   in 0.001s

2019-08-18 12:13:47 (20.6 MB/s) - 'mysql80-community-release-el7-3.noarch.rpm'
saved [26024/26024]
```

shell$ **sudo yum install mysql80-community-release-el7-3.noarch.rpm**
Loaded plugins: langpacks, ulninfo
Examining mysql80-community-release-el7-3.noarch.rpm: mysql80-community-
release-el7-3.noarch
Marking mysql80-community-release-el7-3.noarch.rpm to be installed
Resolving Dependencies
--> Running transaction check
---> Package mysql80-community-release.noarch 0:el7-3 will be installed
--> Finished Dependency Resolution

Dependencies Resolved

```
================================================================
 Package
     Arch    Version
                   Repository                            Size
================================================================
Installing:
 mysql80-community-release
        noarch el7-3 /mysql80-community-release-el7-3.noarch  31 k

Transaction Summary
================================================================
Install  1 Package

Total size: 31 k
Installed size: 31 k
Is this ok [y/d/N]: y
Downloading packages:
Running transaction check
Running transaction test
Transaction test succeeded
Running transaction
  Installing : mysql80-community-release-el7-3.noarch         1/1
  Verifying  : mysql80-community-release-el7-3.noarch         1/1
```

```
Installed:
  mysql80-community-release.noarch 0:el7-3
```

```
Complete!
```

MySQL Workbench requires some packages from the EPEL repository. On Oracle Linux 7, you can enable it like

```
sudo yum install oracle-epel-release-el7
```

On Red Hat Enterprise Linux and CentOS, you need to download the repository definition from Fedora:

```
wget https://dl.fedoraproject.org/pub/epel/epel-release-latest-7.noarch.rpm
```

```
sudo yum install epel-release-latest-7.noarch.rpm
```

You are now able to install MySQL Workbench as shown in Listing 11-2.

Listing 11-2. Installing MySQL Workbench on Enterprise Linux 7

```
shell$ sudo yum install mysql-workbench
...
Dependencies Resolved

================================================================
 Package         Arch    Version        Repository          Size
================================================================
Installing:
 mysql-workbench-community
                 x86_64 8.0.18-1.el7 mysql-tools-community  26 M

Transaction Summary
================================================================
Install  1 Package

Total download size: 26 M
Installed size: 116 M
Is this ok [y/d/N]: y
Downloading packages:
```

```
warning: /var/cache/yum/x86_64/7Server/mysql-tools-community/packages/
mysql-workbench-community-8.0.18-1.el7.x86_64.rpm: Header V3 DSA/SHA1
Signature, key ID 5072e1f5: NOKEY
Public key for mysql-workbench-community-8.0.18-1.el7.x86_64.rpm is not
installed
mysql-workbench-community-8.0.18-1.         |  31 MB  00:14
Retrieving key from file:///etc/pki/rpm-gpg/RPM-GPG-KEY-mysql
Importing GPG key 0x5072E1F5:
 Userid     : "MySQL Release Engineering <mysql-build@oss.oracle.com>"
 Fingerprint: a4a9 4068 76fc bd3c 4567 70c8 8c71 8d3b 5072 e1f5
 Package    : mysql80-community-release-el7-3.noarch (@/mysql80-community-
              release-el7-3.noarch)
 From       : /etc/pki/rpm-gpg/RPM-GPG-KEY-mysql
Is this ok [y/N]: y
Running transaction check
Running transaction test
Transaction test succeeded
Running transaction
  Installing : mysql-workbench-community-8.0.18-1.el7.x86    1/1
  Verifying  : mysql-workbench-community-8.0.18-1.el7.x86    1/1

Installed:
  mysql-workbench-community.x86_64 0:8.0.17-1.el7

Complete!
```

Your output will likely look different, for example, depending on which packages you already have installed, dependencies may be pulled in. The first time you install a package from the MySQL repository, you will be asked to accept the GPG key used to validate the downloaded packages. If you installed the EPEL repository from Fedora, then you will also need to accept the GPG key from that repository.

Debian and Ubuntu

Installing MySQL Workbench on Debian and Ubuntu follows the same principles as in the previous example. For the steps demonstrated here, Ubuntu 19.10 will be used.

Tip   See `https://dev.mysql.com/doc/mysql-apt-repo-quick-guide/en/` for the full documentation on using the MySQL APT repository.

For Debian and Ubuntu, you need to install the MySQL APT repository for which the definition file can be downloaded from `https://dev.mysql.com/downloads/repo/apt/`. At the time of writing, there is just one file available – see Figure 11-9 – which is architecture independent and works for all supported Debian and Ubuntu versions.

Ubuntu / Debian (Architecture Independent), DEB Package	34.7K	Download
(mysql-apt-config_0.8.14-1_all.deb)	MD5: 5cc94c7720fcd3124449b3e789441b98	

Figure 11-9. *The APT repository configuration file*

If you are not logged in, you will be taken to the screen where you can choose between logging in and starting the download straight away. Either download the DEB package or right-click the *Download* button (if you are logged in) or the *No thanks, just start my download* link and copy the URL as shown in Figure 11-10.

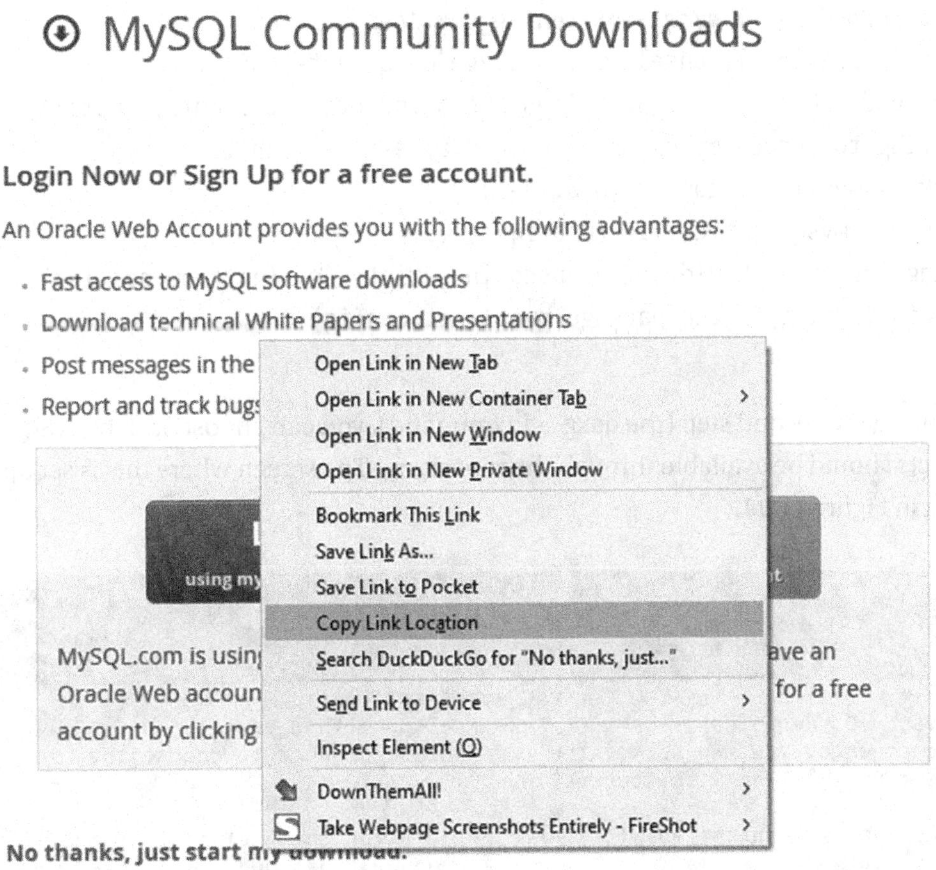

⊕ MySQL Community Downloads

Login Now or Sign Up for a free account.

An Oracle Web Account provides you with the following advantages:

- Fast access to MySQL software downloads
- Download technical White Papers and Presentations
- Post messages in the
- Report and track bug

Open Link in New **T**ab	
Open Link in New Container Ta**b**	>
Open Link in New **W**indow	
Open Link in New **P**rivate Window	
Bookmark This **L**ink	
Save Lin**k** As...	
Save Link t**o** Pocket	
Copy Link Loc**a**tion	
Search DuckDuckGo for "No thanks, just..."	
Se**n**d Link to Device	>
Inspect Element (**Q**)	
DownThemAll!	>
Take Webpage Screenshots Entirely - FireShot	>

MySQL.com is usin~~g~~   ~~h~~ave an
Oracle Web accoun~~t~~   for a free
account by clicking

No thanks, just start my download.

Figure 11-10. *Copying the link to the repository installation file*

You can now install the MySQL repository as shown in Listing 11-3.

Listing 11-3. Installing the DEB package definition

```
shell$ wget https://dev.mysql.com/get/mysql-apt-config_0.8.14-1_all.deb
...
Connecting to repo.mysql.com (repo.mysql.com)|23.202.169.138|:443... connected.
HTTP request sent, awaiting response... 200 OK
Length: 35564 (35K) [application/x-debian-package]
Saving to: 'mysql-apt-config_0.8.14-1_all.deb'

mysql-apt-config_0. 100%[===================>]   34.73K  --.-KB/s    in 0.02s

2019-10-26 17:16:46 (1.39 MB/s) - 'mysql-apt-config_0.8.14-1_all.deb' saved
[35564/35564]
```

shell$ **sudo dpkg -i mysql-apt-config_0.8.14-1_all.deb**
Selecting previously unselected package mysql-apt-config.
(Reading database ... 161301 files and directories currently installed.)
Preparing to unpack mysql-apt-config_0.8.14-1_all.deb ...
Unpacking mysql-apt-config (0.8.14-1) ...
Setting up mysql-apt-config (0.8.14-1) ...
Warning: apt-key should not be used in scripts (called from postinst
maintainerscript of the package mysql-apt-config)
OK

During the second step (the dpkg -i command), you can choose which MySQL
products should be available through the repository. The screen where this is set up is
shown in Figure 11-11.

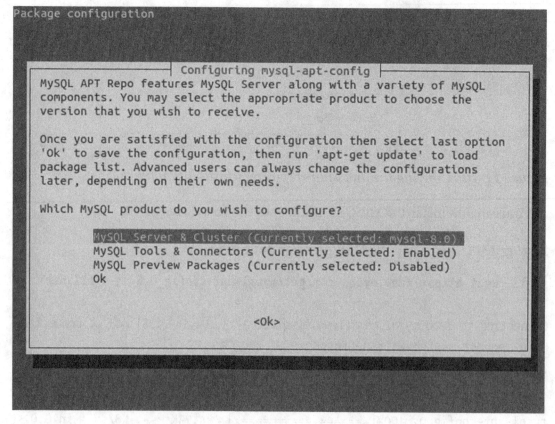

Figure 11-11. *Package configuration for the MySQL APT repository*

The default is to enable MySQL Server and Cluster as well as the tools and connectors. For MySQL Server and Cluster, you can also choose which version you want to use with the default being 8. In order to install MySQL Shell, you need to ensure that *MySQL Tools & Connectors* is set to be enabled. Select *Ok* when you have made your changes.

Before you can start to use the repository, you need to execute the update command for apt-get:

```
shell$ sudo apt-get update
Hit:1 http://repo.mysql.com/apt/ubuntu eoan InRelease
Hit:2 http://au.archive.ubuntu.com/ubuntu eoan InRelease
Hit:3 http://au.archive.ubuntu.com/ubuntu eoan-updates InRelease
Hit:4 http://au.archive.ubuntu.com/ubuntu eoan-backports InRelease
Hit:5 http://security.ubuntu.com/ubuntu eoan-security InRelease
Reading package lists... Done
```

You can now install MySQL products using the install command for apt-get. Listing 11-4 shows an example of installing MySQL Workbench (notice that the package name is mysql-workbench-community – the "-community" at the end is important).

Listing 11-4. Installing MySQL Workbench from the APT repository

```
shell$ sudo apt-get install mysql-workbench-community
Reading package lists... Done
Building dependency tree
Reading state information... Done
...
Setting up mysql-workbench-community (8.0.18-1ubuntu19.10) ...
Setting up libgail-common:amd64 (2.24.32-4ubuntu1) ...
Processing triggers for libc-bin (2.30-0ubuntu2) ...
Processing triggers for man-db (2.8.7-3) ...
Processing triggers for shared-mime-info (1.10-1) ...
Processing triggers for desktop-file-utils (0.24-1ubuntu1) ...
Processing triggers for mime-support (3.63ubuntu1) ...
Processing triggers for hicolor-icon-theme (0.17-2) ...
Processing triggers for gnome-menus (3.32.0-1ubuntu1) ...
```

The output is quite verbose and includes a list of changes to other packages that are required to install MySQL Workbench. The list of packages depends on what you have installed already.

You are now ready to start using MySQL Workbench.

Creating Connections

The first time you launch MySQL Workbench, you will need to define the connection to the MySQL Server instance. If you have MySQL Notifier[1] installed, MySQL Workbench will automatically create a connection for the root user to each instance monitored by MySQL Notifier.

You can also create connections as needed. One option is to do this from the MySQL Workbench connections screen which is shown in Figure 11-12.

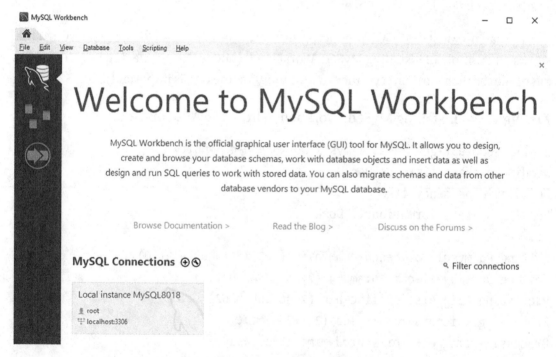

Figure 11-12. *The MySQL Workbench connections screen*

---

[1] www.mysql.com/why-mysql/windows/notifier/

The connections screen is accessed by clicking the icon at the upper left showing a database with a dolphin. The icon below with the tables connected by lines takes you to the database modeling feature, and the last of the three icons opens a tab for the data migration feature.

The screenshot shows the connections screen with the welcome message and with one connection already present. You can right-click the connection to access the options for the connection – these include opening the connection (creating a connection to the MySQL instance), editing the connection, adding it to a group, and more.

You add a new connection by clicking + to the right of *MySQL Connections*. The dialog for configuring a connection is shown in Figure 11-13. The dialogs for creating a new connection and editing an existing one are very similar.

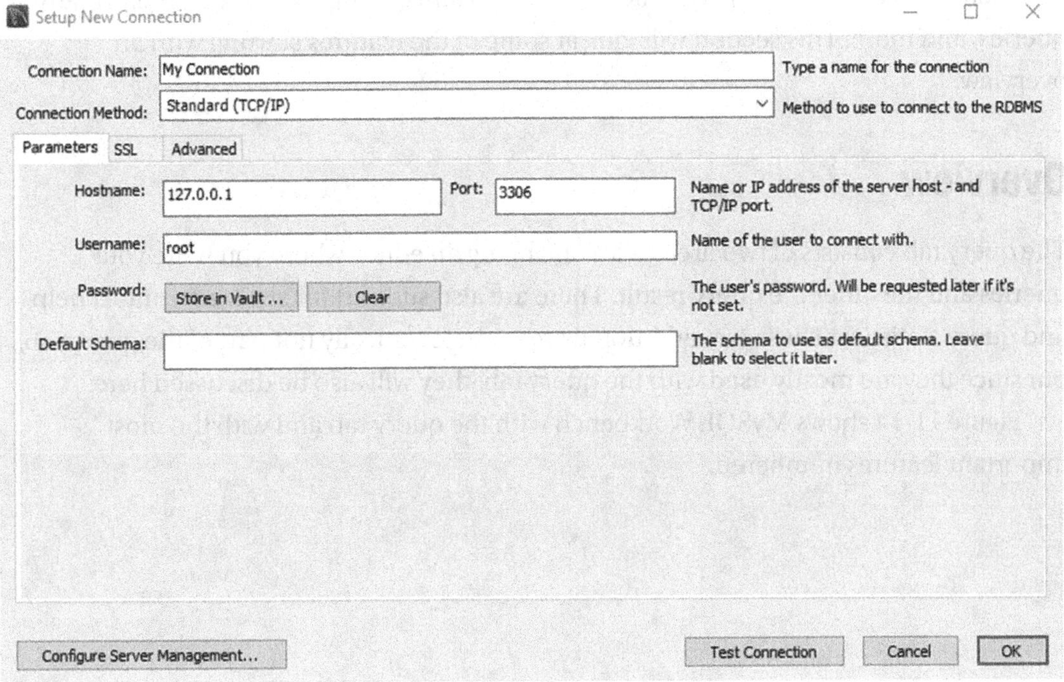

Figure 11-13. The dialog for creating a new connection

You can name the connection with a name of your choice. It is a free-form string that is just used to make it easier to identify the purpose of the connection. The rest of the options are the usual connection options.

Once you have your connection, you can double-click it from the connections screen to create a connection.

Using MySQL Workbench

The most used feature in MySQL Workbench is the ability to execute queries. This is done from the query tab which includes several features in addition to the ability to execute the queries. These features include showing the result set, obtaining a visual representation of the query plan called Visual Explain, getting context help, reformatting queries, and more. This section will look at some of the features starting with an overview.

Overview

The query tab consists of two areas with one being an editor where you write your queries and the other the query result. There are also support for showing context help and query statistics. These two additional areas are technically not part of the query tab, but since they are mostly used with the query tab, they will also be discussed here.

Figure 11-14 shows MySQL Workbench with the query tab and with the most important features numbered.

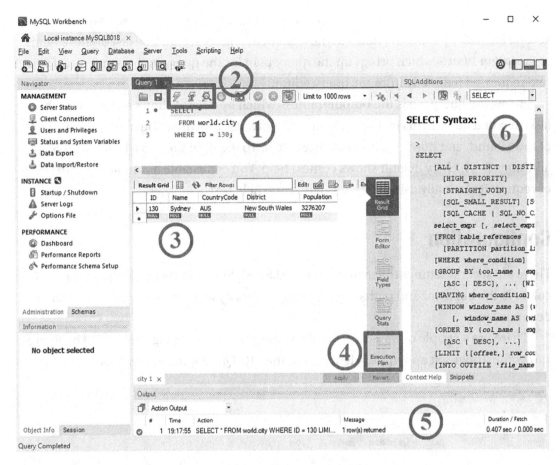

Figure 11-14. *MySQL Workbench and the query tab*

The area marked as ① is where you write your queries. You can keep several queries here, and MySQL Workbench will save them, so they are restored when you open the connection again. This makes it convenient as a scratch pad to store your most frequently used queries.

You execute the query or queries using one of the three lightning icons marked as ②. The left icon is a plain lightning symbol and executes the query or queries selected in the query editor part. This is the same as using the keyboard shortcut Ctrl+Shift+Enter. The middle icon with the lightning symbol and a cursor executes the query where the cursor is. Using this icon is the same as using shortcut Ctrl+Enter while in the editor. The third icon has a magnifier in front of the lightning symbol and creates the query plan in form for the query where the cursor is currently placed. The default way to display the query plan is as a Visual Explain diagram. You can also obtain the query plan by using the keyboard shortcut Ctrl+Alt+X.

The result is displayed below the query editor ③, and you can choose between several formats by using the items to the right of the query result. The last of these items is *Execution Plan* ④ which brings up the query plan for the query in the same way if you had requested it directly from the query editor.

Below the query tab is the output frame ⑤ which by default shows statistics for the last executed query. This includes when the query was executed, the query, the number of rows found, and how long it took to execute it. To the right there is a frame with SQL additions ⑥ which by default shows context help. You can enable automatic context help or request it manually using the icons above the help text.

Configuration

There are several settings that can be changed for MySQL Workbench ranging from the colors to the behavior and paths to programs such as `mysqldump` that MySQL Workbench depends on.

There are a couple of ways to get to the settings as shown in Figure 11-15. The figure shows the upper-left and upper-right part of the MySQL Workbench window.

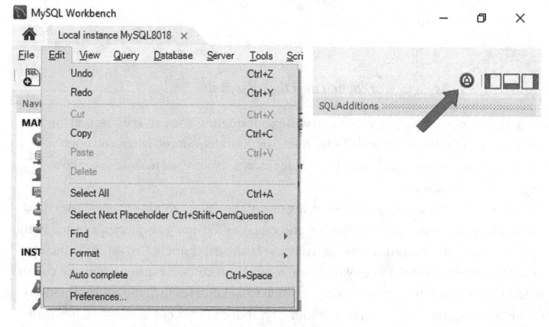

Figure 11-15. *Accessing the MySQL Workbench preferences*

In the left-hand side, you can get the preferences from the menu by using *Edit* and go to the *Preferences* item at the bottom. Alternatively, you can click the gear icon in the right-hand side of the window. Either way, you get to the preferences pop-up that is shown in Figure 11-16.

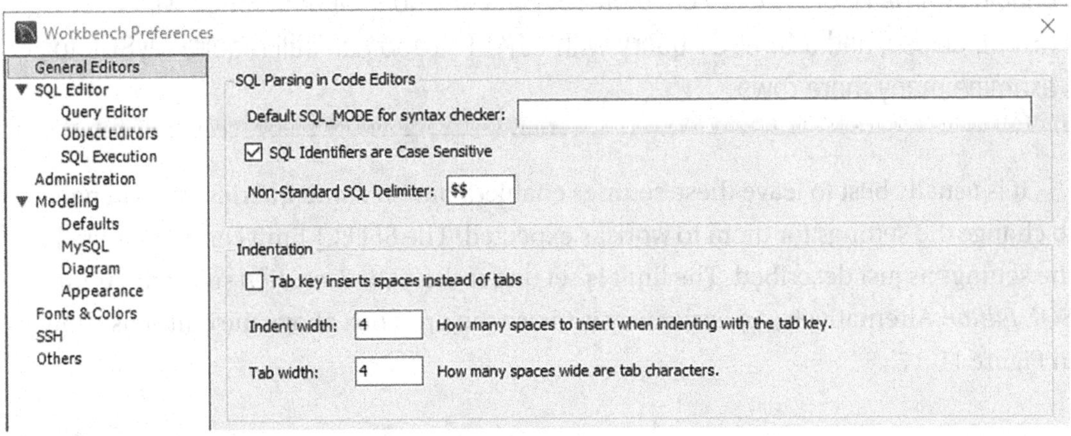

Figure 11-16. *The MySQL Workbench preferences*

The *General Editors* settings include settings such as the SQL mode to consider for the syntax checker and whether to use spaces or tabs for indentation. The *SQL Editor* settings include whether to use the safe settings, whether to save the editors, and the general behavior of the editor and query tab. The *Administration* settings specify the paths to use including for mysqldump if you do not want to use the bundled binary. The *Modeling* settings are for the database modeling feature. The *Fonts & Colors* settings allow you to change the visual appearance of MySQL Workbench. The *SSH* settings are used when you use a feature that requires an SSH connection to a remote host. Finally, the *Others* settings include a few settings that do not fit in the other categories such as whether the welcome message should be displayed on the start screen with the connections.

The settings include safe settings. What are those?

Safe Settings

MySQL Workbench has two safe settings enabled by default to help prevent changing or deleting all rows in a table and to avoid fetching too many rows. The safety settings mean that UPDATE and DELETE statements are blocked if they do not have a WHERE clause, and SELECT statements have LIMIT 1000 added (the maximum number of rows can be configured). The WHERE clause for UPDATE and DELETE statements cannot be a trivial one.

Caution   Do not become complacent just because the safety settings are enabled. UPDATE and DELETE statements can still do a lot of damage with a WHERE clause, and a SELECT query with LIMIT 1000 can still require MySQL to examine many more rows.

It is usually best to leave these settings enabled, but for some queries you will need to change the settings for them to work as expected. The SELECT limit can be changed in the settings as just described. The limit is set under the *SQL Execution* submenu under *SQL Editor*. Alternatively, an easier way is to use the drop box above the editor as shown in Figure 11-17.

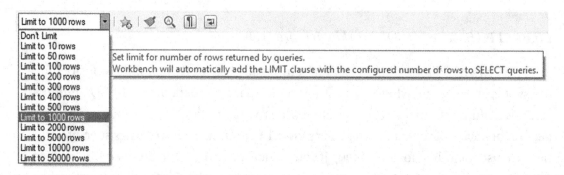

Figure 11-17. *Changing the SELECT limit*

Changing the limit this way updates the same setting as if you go through the preferences.

The UPDATE and DELETE safe setting can be changed in the *SQL Editor* settings furthest down. It is recommended to keep it on unless you really need to update or delete all rows in a table. Note that disabling the setting requires reconnecting.

Reformatting Queries

One nice feature of MySQL Workbench that does not usually get a lot of attention is the query beautifier tool. This can also be useful for query tuning as a well-formatted query can make it easier to understand what the query is doing.

The query beautifier takes a query and splits the select list, tables, and filters into separate lines and adds indentation. An example of this is shown in Figure 11-18.

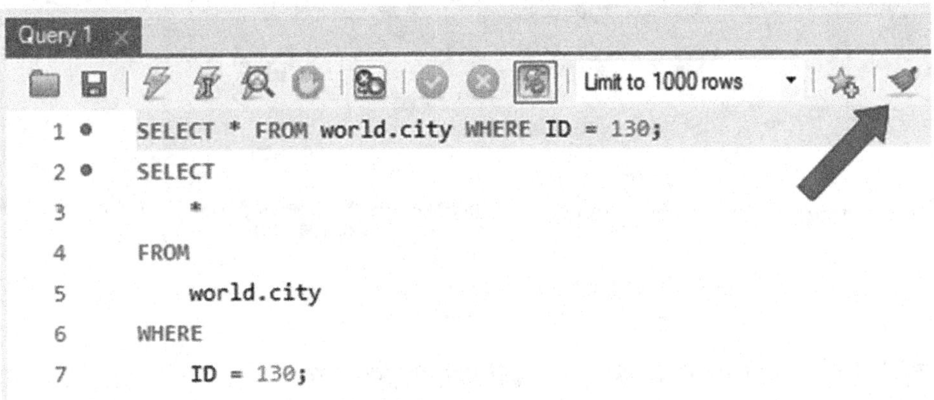

Figure 11-18. *The query beautifier feature*

The first query is the original query with the whole query in a single line. The second query is the reformatted query. For a simple query like in this example, the beautification is of little value, but for a more complex query, it can make the query much easier to read.

The beautification by default includes changing SQL keywords to uppercase. You can change whether that should happen in the *Query Editor* submenu of the *SQL Editor* settings in the preferences.

EER Diagrams

The last feature that will be explored is the support for reverse engineering a schema and creating an enhanced entity-relationship (EER) diagram. This is a useful way to get an overview of the schema you are working with. If foreign keys have been defined, MySQL Workbench will use the definitions to link the tables together.

You can start the reverse engineering wizard from the *Database* menu option and then choose *Reverse Engineering*. Alternatively, the Ctrl+R keyboard combination will also take you there. This is shown in Figure 11-19.

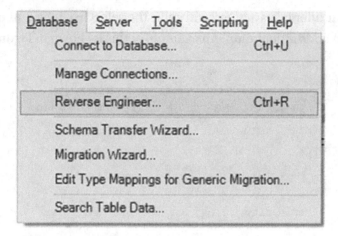

Figure 11-19. *Opening the reverse engineering feature*

The wizard will take you through the steps to import the schema starting with choosing which of your stored connections to use or optionally configuring the connection manually. The next step connects and imports a list of the available schemas which are shown in the third step. Here you choose one or more schemas to reverse engineer as shown in Figure 11-20.

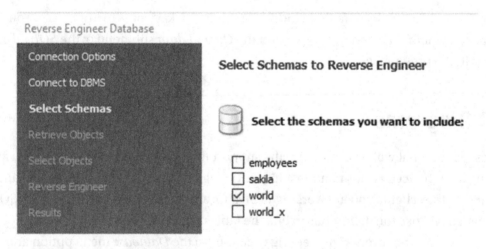

Figure 11-20. *Choosing which schemas to reverse engineer*

In this example, the world schema has been chosen. The next steps fetch the schema objects and allow you to filter which objects to include. Finally, the objects are imported and placed in the diagram, and a confirmation is shown. The resulting EER diagram is shown in Figure 11-21.

Tip   If MySQL Workbench crashes when creating the diagram, try opening Edit ➤ Configuration… ➤ Modelling in the menu and check the *Force use of software based rendering for EER diagrams* option.

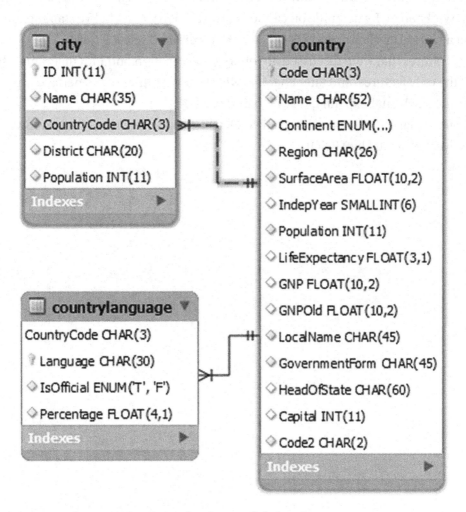

Figure 11-21. The EER diagram for the world database

The diagram shows the three tables in the `world` database. When you hover over a table, the relations to the other tables will be highlighted in green for a child table and in blue for a parent table. This allows you to quickly explore the relations between the tables to give you knowledge that can be crucial when you need to tune queries.

Summary

This chapter introduced MySQL Workbench which is MySQL's graphical user interface solution. It was shown how to install MySQL Workbench and create connections. Then an overview of the main query view was given, and it was shown how you can configure MySQL Workbench. By default, you cannot execute `UDPATE` and `DELETE` statements without a real `WHERE` clause, and `SELECT` queries are limited to 1000 rows.

Two features that were discussed are query beautification and EER diagrams. These are not the only features, and later chapters will show examples of the performance reports and the Visual Explain query plan diagrams.

The next chapter will discuss MySQL Shell which is the second of the two "Swiss army knives" provided by MySQL.

## CHAPTER 12

MySQL Shell

MySQL Shell is the second-generation command-line client which stands out compared to the traditional `mysql` command-line client by supporting the X Protocol as well as the Python and JavaScript languages. It also comes with several utilities and is highly extensible. This makes it a great tool for not only day-to-day tasks but also when investigating performance issues.

This chapter starts out with an overview of what the MySQL Shell offers including the built-in help and the rich prompt. The second part of the chapter covers how you can extend the functionality of MySQL Shell through the use of external code modules, the reporting infrastructure, and plugins.

Overview

The first MySQL Shell release with the status of general availability was in 2017, so it is still a very new tool in the MySQL toolbox. Yet, it already has a large array of features well beyond what the traditional `mysql` command-line client has. These features are not limited to those required to use MySQL Shell as part of the MySQL InnoDB Cluster solution; there are also several features that are useful for day-to-day database administration tasks and performance optimization.

An advantage of MySQL Shell over the `mysql` command-line client is that the MySQL Shell editor behaves the same on Linux and Microsoft Windows, so if you work on both platforms, you get a consistent user experience. This means that Ctrl+D exists the shell both on Linux, macOS, and Microsoft Windows, Ctrl+W deletes the previous word, and so forth.

© Jesper Wisborg Krogh 2020
J. W. Krogh, *MySQL 8 Query Performance Tuning*, https://doi.org/10.1007/978-1-4842-5584-1_12

> **Tip**   Charles Bell (the technical reviewer of this book and a MySQL developer)
> has written the book *Introducing MySQL Shell* (Apress) with a comprehensive
> introduction to MySQL Shell: `www.apress.com/gp/book/9781484250822`.
> Additionally, the author of this book has published several blogs about MySQL
> Shell. See `https://mysql.wisborg.dk/mysql-shell-blogs/`.

This section will look at installing MySQL Shell, invoking it, and some of the basic
features. It is however not possible to go into details with all features of MySQL Shell. You
are encouraged to consult the online manual at `https://dev.mysql.com/doc/mysql-shell/en` for more information as you are using MySQL Shell.

Installing MySQL Shell

MySQL Shell is installed in the same way as other MySQL products (except for MySQL
Enterprise Monitor). You can download it from `https://dev.mysql.com/downloads/shell/`; and it is available for Microsoft Windows, Linux, and macOS and as a source
code. For Microsoft Windows, you can also install it through MySQL Installer.

If you install MySQL Shell using a native package format and MySQL Installer for
Microsoft Windows, the installation instructions are the same as for MySQL Workbench
except for the names. Please see the previous chapter for details.

You can also install MySQL Shell using a ZIP archive on Microsoft Windows or a
TAR archive on Linux and macOS. If you choose that option, you simply unpack the
downloaded file, and you are done.

Invoking MySQL Shell

MySQL Shell is invoked using the `mysqlsh` (or `mysqlsh.exe` on Microsoft Windows)
binary which is in the `bin` directory of the installation directory. When you install MySQL
Shell using a native package, the binary will be in your PATH environment variable, so the
operating system can find it without you explicitly providing the path.

This means that the simplest way to start MySQL Shell is just to execute `mysqlsh`:

```
shell> mysqlsh
MySQL Shell 8.0.18

Copyright (c) 2016, 2019, Oracle and/or its affiliates. All rights
reserved.
Oracle is a registered trademark of Oracle Corporation and/or its
affiliates.
Other names may be trademarks of their respective owners.

Type '\help' or '\?' for help; '\quit' to exit.
MySQL JS>
```

The prompt will look different than in this output as the default prompt cannot be fully represented in plain text. Unlike the `mysql` command line, MySQL Shell does not require a connection to be present, and by default none is created.

Creating Connections

There are several ways to create a connection for MySQL Shell including from the command line and from inside MySQL Shell.

If you add any connection-related argument when invoking `mysqlsh`, then MySQL Shell will create a connection as part of starting up. Any connection options that are not specified will use their default values. For example, to connect as the `root` MySQL user to a MySQL instance on the local host using the default port (and on Linux and macOS socket) values, you just need to specify the `--user` argument:

```
shell> mysqlsh --user=root
Please provide the password for 'root@localhost': ********
Save password for 'root@localhost'? [Y]es/[N]o/Ne[v]er (default No): yes
MySQL Shell 8.0.18

Copyright (c) 2016, 2019, Oracle and/or its affiliates. All rights
reserved.
```

```
Oracle is a registered trademark of Oracle Corporation and/or its
affiliates.
Other names may be trademarks of their respective owners.

Type '\help' or '\?' for help; '\quit' to exit.
Creating a session to 'root@localhost'
Fetching schema names for autocompletion... Press ^C to stop.
Your MySQL connection id is 39581 (X protocol)
Server version: 8.0.18 MySQL Community Server - GPL
No default schema selected; type \use <schema> to set one.
MySQL  localhost:33060+ ssl  JS >
```

The first time you connect, you will be asked to enter the password for the account.
If MySQL Shell finds the mysql_config_editor command in the path or you are on
Microsoft Windows where MySQL Shell can use the Windows keyring service, MySQL
Shell will offer to save the password for you, so you do not need to enter it in the future.

Alternatively, you can use a URI to specify the connection options, for example:

```
shell> mysqlsh root@localhost:3306?schema=world
```

After MySQL Shell has started up, notice how the prompt has changed. MySQL Shell
features an adaptive prompt that changes to reflect the status of your connection. The
default prompt includes the port number you are connected to. If you connect to MySQL
Server 8, then the default port used is 33060 instead of port 3306 as MySQL Shell by
default uses the X Protocol when the server supports it rather than the traditional MySQL
protocol. That is the reason the port number is not what you may expect.

You can also create (or change) the connection from within MySQL Shell. You can
even have multiple connections, so you can work on two or more instances concurrently.
There are several ways to create a session, including those listed in Table 12-1. The table
also includes how to set and retrieve a global session. The *Language Commands* column
shows the commands or methods to invoke depending on the language mode in use.

Table 12-1. *Various ways to create and work with a connection*

Method	Language Commands	Description
Global session	**All modes:** `\connect` (or `\c` for short)	Creates a global session (the default session). This is the equivalent of a connection in the `mysql` command-line client.

General session	**JavaScript:**
	`mysqlx.getSession()`
	Python:
	`mysqlx.get_session()`
		Returns the session so it can be assigned to a variable. Can be used both for a connection using the X Protocol and the classic protocol.

Classic session	**JavaScript:**
	`mysql.getClassicSession()`
	Python:
	`mysql.get_classic_session()`
		Similar to a general session, but always returns a classic session.

Set global session	**JavaScript:**
	`shell.setSession()`
	Python:
	`shell.set_session()`
		Sets the global session from a variable containing a session.

Get global session	**JavaScript:**
	`shell.getSession()`
	Python:
	`shell.get_session()`
		Returns the global session, so it can be assigned to a variable.

Reconnect	**All modes:** `\reconnect`	Reconnects using the same arguments as for the existing global connection.

All the commands and methods to create a session support a URI in the format `[scheme://][user[:password]@]<host[:port]|socket>[/schema][?option=value&option=value...]`. The methods also support supplying the options in a dictionary. If you do not include the password and MySQL Shell does not have a stored password for the account, you will be prompted to enter the password interactively (unlike the traditional command-line client, MySQL Shell can prompt for information during the execution of a command). For example, to connect as the `myuser` user to `localhost`

```
MySQL JS> \connect myuser@localhost
Creating a session to 'myuser@localhost'
Please provide the password for 'myuser@localhost': *******
```

The language mode has been mentioned a few times. The next subsection will look at how you work with it.

Language Modes

One of the biggest features of MySQL Shell is that you are not restricted to executing SQL statements. You have the full power of both JavaScript and Python at your disposal – and of course SQL statements. This makes MySQL Shell very powerful for automating tasks.

You work in one language mode at a time, though it is possible to execute queries through the API in both JavaScript and Python. Table 12-2 summarizes how you can choose the language mode you want to use from the command line and from within MySQL Shell.

Table 12-2. *Choosing the MySQL Shell language mode*

Mode	Command-Line	MySQL Shell
JavaScript	--js	\js
Python	--py	\py
SQL	--sql	\sql

The default mode is JavaScript. The prompt reflects which language mode you are in, so you always know which mode you are using.

Tip   In MySQL Shell 8.0.16 and later, you can in the Python and JavaScript modes prefix a command with \sql which makes MySQL Shell execute the command as an SQL statement.

One thing to be aware of that also was hinted when listing how to create connections is that MySQL Shell like the X DevAPI tries to keep the naming convention normally used for the language. This means that in JavaScript mode, the functions and methods use camel case (e.g., getSession()), whereas in Python mode snake case (get_session()) is used. If you use the built-in help, the help will reflect the names used for the language mode you are in.

Built-in Help

It can be hard to keep on top of all of the features of MySQL Shell and how to use them. Fortunately, there is an extensive built-in help feature that lets you get information on the features without having to go back to the online manual each time.

If you execute mysqlsh with the --help argument, you will get information about all the supported command-line arguments. After starting a shell, you can also get help about the commands, objects, and methods. The topmost help is obtained using the \h, \? or \help command which is available from all language modes. This lists the commands and the global objects and how to get further help.

The second level of help is for the commands and global objects. You can specify the name of a command of a global object with one of the help commands to get more information about the command or object. For example:

```
mysql-js> \h \connect
NAME
        \connect - Connects the shell to a MySQL server and assigns the global
        session.

SYNTAX
        \connect [<TYPE>] <URI>

        \c [<TYPE>] <URI>

DESCRIPTION
...
```

The final level of help is for the features of the global objects. The global objects and modules of global objects all have a help() method that provides help for the object or module. The help() method can also take the name of a method of the module or object as a string which will return help for that method. Some examples are (the output is omitted as it is quite verbose – it is recommended to try the commands for yourself to see the help text that is returned):

```
MySQL JS> \h shell
```

```
MySQL JS> shell.help()
```

```
MySQL JS> shell.help('reconnect')
```

```
MySQL JS> shell.reports.help()
```

```
MySQL JS> shell.reports.help('query')
```

The two first commands retrieve the same help text. It is worth familiarizing yourself with the help feature as it can greatly improve how efficiently you can work with MySQL Shell.

The context awareness of the help goes further than to detect whether a global object exists and whether a method name follows the JavaScript or Python convention. Consider a request for help about "select." There are several possibilities of what you mean by that. It can be one of the select() methods in the X DevAPI, or you may think of the SELECT SQL statement. If you request the help in the SQL mode, MySQL Shell assumes you mean the SQL statement. However, in the Python and JavaScript modes, you will be asked which one you mean:

```
MySQL Py> \h select
Found several entries matching select

The following topics were found at the SQL Syntax category:

- SQL Syntax/SELECT

The following topics were found at the X DevAPI category:

- mysqlx.Table.select
- mysqlx.TableSelect.select

For help on a specific topic use: \? <topic>

e.g.: \? SQL Syntax/SELECT
```

The reason MySQL Shell can provide the help for the SELECT statement in the SQL mode without considering the X DevAPI is that the X DevAPI methods can only be accessed from Python and JavaScript. On the other hand, all three meanings of "select" make sense in the Python and JavaScript modes.

As noted earlier, there exist several global objects. What are those?

Built-in Global Objects

MySQL Shell uses global objects to group features. Much of the functionality that makes MySQL Shell so powerful can be found in the global objects. As you will see in the "Plugins" section, it is also possible to add your own global objects.

The built-in global objects include

- **db:** When a default schema has been set, db holds the X DevAPI schema object for the default schema. X DevAPI table objects can be found as properties of the db object (unless the table or view name is the same as an existing property). The session object can also be obtained from the db object.

- **dba:** For administrating MySQL InnoDB Cluster.

- **mysql:** For connecting to MySQL using the classic MySQL protocol.

- **mysqlx:** For working with MySQL X Protocol sessions.

- **session:** For working with the current global session (connection to a MySQL instance).

- **shell:** Various general-purpose methods and properties.

- **util:** Various utilities such as the upgrade checker, importing JSON data, and importing data in CSV files to relational tables.

That concludes the general overview of MySQL Shell. Next, you will learn more about the prompt and how to customize it.

The Prompt

One of the features setting MySQL Shell apart from the traditional command-line client is the rich prompt which not only makes it easy to see which host and schema you are working with but also can add information such as whether you are connected to a production instance, whether SSL is used, and custom fields.

Built-in Prompts

The MySQL Shell installation comes with several predefined prompt templates that you can choose from. The default is to use a prompt that provides information about the connection and supports 256 colors, but there are also simpler prompts.

The location of the prompt definition templates depends on how you installed MySQL Shell. Examples of the location include

- **ZIP and TAR archives:** The share/mysqlsh/prompt directory in the archive.

- **RPM on Oracle Linux 7:** /usr/share/mysqlsh/prompt/

- **MySQL Installer on Microsoft Windows:** C:\Program Files\MySQL\ MySQL Shell 8.0\share\mysqlsh\prompt

The prompt definitions are JSON files with the definitions that are included as of MySQL Shell 8.0.18 being

- **prompt_16.json:** A colored prompt limited to use 16/8 color ANSI colors and attributes.

- **prompt_256.json:** The prompt uses 256 indexed colors. This is the one that is used by default.

- **prompt_256inv.json:** Like the prompt_256.json, but with an "invisible" background color (it just uses the same as for the terminal) and with different foreground colors.

- **prompt_256pl.json:** Same as prompt_256.json but with extra symbols. This requires a Powerline patched font such as the one that is installed with the Powerline project. This will add a padlock with the prompt when you use SSL to connect to MySQL and use "arrow" separators. An example of installing the Powerline font is shown later.

- **prompt_256pl+aw.json:** Same as `prompt_256pl.json` but with "awesome symbols." This additionally requires the awesome symbols to be included in the Powerline font. An example of installing the awesome symbols is shown later.

- **prompt_classic.json:** This is a very basic prompt that just shows `mysql-js>`, `mysql-py>`, or `mysql-sql>` based on the mode in use.

- **prompt_dbl_256.json:** A two-line version of the `prompt_256.json` prompt.

- **prompt_dbl_256pl.json:** A two-line version of the `prompt_256pl.json` prompt.

- **prompt_dbl_256pl+aw.json:** A two-line version of the `prompt_256pl+aw.json` prompt.

- **prompt_nocolor.json:** Gives the full prompt information, but completely without colors. An example of a prompt is `MySQL [localhost+ ssl/world] JS>`.

The two-line templates are particularly useful if your shell window is of limited width as they will put the information on one line and allow you to type your command on the next without having it preceded by the full prompt.

There are two ways to specify which prompt you want to use. MySQL Shell first looks for the file `prompt.json` in the user's MySQL Shell directory. The default location depends on your operating system:

- **Linux and macOS:** `~/.mysqlsh/prompt.json` – that is in the `.mysqlsh` directory in the user's home directory.

- **Microsoft Windows:** `%AppData%\MySQL\mysqlsh\prompt.json` – that is in `AppData\Roaming\MySQL\mysqlsh` directory from the user's home directory.

You can change the directory by setting the `MYSQLSH_HOME` environment variable. If you prefer a different prompt than the default, you can copy that definition into the directory and name the file `prompt.json`.

The other way to specify the location of the prompt definition is to set the MYSQLSH_PROMPT_THEME environment variable, for example, on Microsoft Windows using the command prompt:

```
C:\> set MYSQLSH_PROMPT_THEME=C:\Program Files\MySQL\MySQL Shell 8.0\share\
mysqlsh\prompt\prompt_256inv.json
```

In PowerShell the syntax is a little different:

```
PS> $env:MYSQLSH_PROMPT_THEME = "C:\Program Files\MySQL\MySQL Shell 8.0\
share\mysqlsh\prompt\prompt_256inv.json";
```

On Linux and Unix:

```
shell$ export MYSQLSH_PROMPT_THEME=/usr/share/mysqlsh/prompt/prompt_256inv.
json
```

This can be useful if you temporarily want to use a different prompt than your usual prompt.

As it has already been hinted, there are several parts to most of the prompt definitions. The easiest way is to take a look at an example of the prompt such as the default (prompt_256.json) prompt shown in Figure 12-1.

Figure 12-1. The default MySQL Shell prompt

There are several parts to the prompt. First, it says PRODUCTION on a red background which is to warn you that you are connected to a production instance. Whether an instance is considered a production instance is based on whether the hostname you are connected to is included in the PRODUCTION_SERVERS environment variable. The second element is the MySQL string which does not have any special meaning.

Third is the host and port you are connected to, whether you use the X Protocol, and whether SSL is used. In this case, there is a + after the port number which indicates that the X Protocol is in use. The fourth element is the default schema.

The fifth and last element (not counting the > at the end) is the language mode. It will show SQL, Py, or JS depending on whether you have enabled the SQL, Python, or JavaScript mode, respectively. The background color of this element also changes with the language. SQL uses orange, Python blue, and JavaScript yellow.

In general, you will not see all elements of the prompt as MySQL Shell only includes those that are relevant. For example, the default schema is only included when you have set a default schema, and the connection information is only present when you are connected to an instance.

As you work with MySQL Shell, you may realize that you would like to make some changes to the prompt definition. Let's look at how you can do that.

Custom Prompt Definition

The prompt definitions are JSON files, and there is nothing that prevents you from editing a definition to change according to your preferences. The best way to do this is to copy the template that is closest to what you want and then make your changes.

Tip The best source for help to create your own prompt definition is the README.prompt file that is located in the same directory as the template files.

Instead of going through the specification in details, it is easier to look at the prompt_256.json template and discuss some parts of it. Listing 12-1 shows the end of the file is where the elements of the prompt are defined.

Listing 12-1. The definition of the elements of the prompt

```
"segments": [
  {
    "classes": ["disconnected%host%", "%is_production%"]
  },
  {
    "text": " My",
    "bg": 254,
    "fg": 23
  },
  {
    "separator": "",
    "text": "SQL ",
    "bg": 254,
```

```
    "fg": 166
  },
  {
    "classes": ["disconnected%host%", "%ssl%host%session%"],
    "shrink": "truncate_on_dot",
    "bg": 237,
    "fg": 15,
    "weight": 10,
    "padding" : 1
  },
  {
    "classes": ["noschema%schema%", "schema"],
    "bg": 242,
    "fg": 15,
    "shrink": "ellipsize",
    "weight": -1,
    "padding" : 1
  },
  {
    "classes": ["%Mode%"],
    "text": "%Mode%",
    "padding" : 1
  }
]
```

There are a few things that are interesting to note here. First, notice that there is an object with the classes disconnected%host% and %is_production%. The names within the percentage signs are variables defined in the same file or that come from MySQL Shell itself (it has variables such as the host and port). For example, is_production is defined as

```
"variables" : {
  "is_production": {
    "match" : {
      "pattern": "*;%host%;*",
      "value": ";%env:PRODUCTION_SERVERS%;"
    },
```

```
        "if_true" : "production",
        "if_false" : ""
    },
```

So a host is considered to be a production instance if it is included in the environment variable `PRODUCTION_SERVERS`.

The second thing to note about the list of elements is that there are some special fields such as `shrink` which can be used to define how the text is kept relatively short. For example, the host element uses `truncate_on_dot`, so only the part before the first dot in the hostname is displayed if the full hostname is too long. Alternatively `ellipsize` can be used to add ... after the truncated value.

Third, the background and foreground colors are defined using the `bg` and `fg` elements, respectively. This allows you to completely customize the prompt to your liking with respect to colors. The color can be specified in one of the following ways:

- **By Name:** There are a few colors that are known by name: black, red, green, yellow, blue, magenta, cyan, and white.

- **By Index:** A value between 0 and 255 (both inclusive) where 0 is black, 63 light blue, 127 magenta, 193 yellow, and 255 white.

- **By RGB:** Use a value in the #rrggbb format. This requires that the terminal supports TrueColor colors.

One group of built-in variables that deserve an example are the ones that in some way depend on the environment or the MySQL instance you are connected to. These are

- **%env:varname%:** This uses an environment variable. The way it is determined whether you are connected to a production server is an example of using an environment variable.

- **%sysvar:varname%:** This uses the value of a global system variable from MySQL, that is, the value returned by `SELECT @@global. varname`.

- **%sessvar:varname%:** Similar to the previous but using a session system variable.

- **%status:varname%:** This uses the value of a global status variable from MySQL, that is, the value returned by SELECT VARIABLE_VALUE FROM performance_schema.global_status WHERE VARIABLE_NAME = 'varname'.

- **%status:varname%:** Similar to the previous, but using a session status variable.

If you, for example, want to include the MySQL version of the instance you are connected to in the prompt, you can add an element like

```
{
    "separator": "",
    "text": "%sysvar:version%",
    "bg": 250,
    "fg": 166
},
```

You are encouraged to play around with the definition until you get a color scheme and the elements that work best for you. An alternative way to improve the prompt on Linux is to install the Powerline and Awesome fonts.

Powerline and Awesome Fonts

If you feel that the normal MySQL Shell prompts are too square and you use MySQL Shell on Linux, you can consider using one of the templates that rely on the Powerline and the Awesome fonts. The fonts are not installed by default.

This example will show you how to do a minimal installation of the Powerline fonts[1] and install the Awesome font using the patching-strategy branch of gabrielelana's awesome-terminal-fonts project on GitHub.[2]

---

[1]https://powerline.readthedocs.io/en/latest/index.html
[2]https://github.com/gabrielelana/awesome-terminal-fonts/tree/patching-strategy

---

Tip   Another option is the Fantasque Awesome Powerline fonts (`https://github.com/ztomer/fantasque_awesome_powerline`) which include both the Powerline and Awesome fonts. These fonts look a little different from those installed in this example. Choose those that you prefer.

You install the Awesome fonts by cloning the GitHub repository and change to the patching-strategy branch. Then it is a matter of copying the required files to `.local/share/fonts/` under the home directory and rebuilding the font information cache files. The steps are shown in Listing 12-2. The output is also available in `listing_12_2.txt` in this book's GitHub repository to make it easier to copy the commands.

Listing 12-2. Installing the Awesome fonts

```
shell$ git clone https://github.com/gabrielelana/awesome-terminal-fonts.git
Cloning into 'awesome-terminal-fonts'...
remote: Enumerating objects: 329, done.
remote: Total 329 (delta 0), reused 0 (delta 0), pack-reused 329
Receiving objects: 100% (329/329), 2.77 MiB | 941.00 KiB/s, done.
Resolving deltas: 100% (186/186), done.

shell$ cd awesome-terminal-fonts

shell$ git checkout patching-strategy
Branch patching-strategy set up to track remote branch patching-strategy
from origin.
Switched to a new branch 'patching-strategy'

shell$ mkdir -p ~/.local/share/fonts/

shell$ cp patched/SourceCodePro+Powerline+Awesome+Regular.* ~/.local/share/
fonts/

shell$ fc-cache -fv ~/.local/share/fonts/
/home/myuser/.local/share/fonts: caching, new cache contents: 1 fonts,
0 dirs
/usr/lib/fontconfig/cache: not cleaning unwritable cache directory
```

```
/home/myuser/.cache/fontconfig: cleaning cache directory
/home/myuser/.fontconfig: not cleaning non-existent cache directory
/usr/bin/fc-cache-64: succeeded
```

This requires that you have git installed. The next part is to install the Powerline fonts which is shown in Listing 12-3. The output is also available in listing_12_3.txt in this book's GitHub repository to make it easier to copy the commands.

Listing 12-3. Installing the Powerline font

```
shell$ wget --directory-prefix="${HOME}/.local/share/fonts" https://github.
com/powerline/powerline/raw/develop/font/PowerlineSymbols.otf
...
2019-08-25 14:38:41 (5.48 MB/s) - '/home/myuser/.local/share/fonts/
PowerlineSymbols.otf' saved [2264/2264]

shell$ fc-cache -vf ~/.local/share/fonts/
/home/myuser/.local/share/fonts: caching, new cache contents: 2 fonts,
0 dirs
/usr/lib/fontconfig/cache: not cleaning unwritable cache directory
/home/myuser/.cache/fontconfig: cleaning cache directory
/home/myuser/.fontconfig: not cleaning non-existent cache directory
/usr/bin/fc-cache-64: succeeded

shell$ wget --directory-prefix="${HOME}/.config/fontconfig/conf.d" https://
github.com/powerline/powerline/raw/develop/font/10-powerline-symbols.conf
...
2019-08-25 14:39:11 (3.61 MB/s) - '/home/myuser/.config/fontconfig/
conf.d/10-powerline-symbols.conf' saved [2713/2713]
```

This does not do a full installation of the Powerline font, but it is all that is required if you just want to use the Powerline font with MySQL Shell. The two wget commands download the font and configuration files, and the fc-cache command rebuilds the font information cache files. You will need to restart Linux for the changes to take effect.

Once the restart has completed, you can copy one of the pl+aw templates to become your new prompt, for example:

```
shell$ cp /usr/share/mysqlsh/prompt/prompt_dbl_256pl+aw.json ~/.mysqlsh/
prompt.json
```

The resulting prompt can be seen in Figure 12-2.

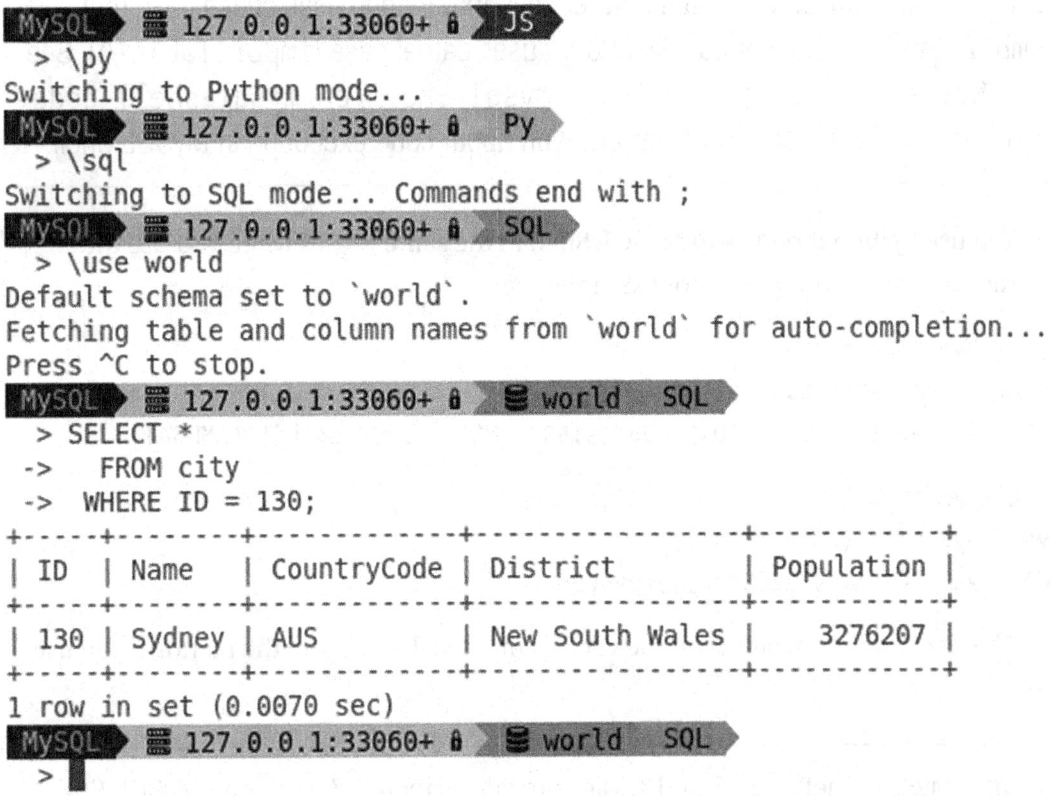

```
MySQL    127.0.0.1:33060+ ⓐ   JS
   > \py
Switching to Python mode...
MySQL    127.0.0.1:33060+ ⓐ   Py
   > \sql
Switching to SQL mode... Commands end with ;
MySQL    127.0.0.1:33060+ ⓐ   SQL
   > \use world
Default schema set to `world`.
Fetching table and column names from `world` for auto-completion...
Press ^C to stop.
MySQL    127.0.0.1:33060+ ⓐ   world   SQL
   > SELECT *
  ->    FROM city
  ->    WHERE ID = 130;
+-----+--------+-------------+-------------------+------------+
| ID  | Name   | CountryCode | District          | Population |
+-----+--------+-------------+-------------------+------------+
| 130 | Sydney | AUS         | New South Wales   |    3276207 |
+-----+--------+-------------+-------------------+------------+
1 row in set (0.0070 sec)
MySQL    127.0.0.1:33060+ ⓐ   world   SQL
   >
```

Figure 12-2. *The double-line Powerline + Awesome fonts prompt*

This example also shows how the prompt changes as you change the language mode and set a default schema. Regarding support for multiple modules, then that is largely why MySQL Shell is such a powerful tool, so the next section will look at how you can use external modules in MySQL Shell.

Using External Modules

The support for JavaScript and Python makes it easy to perform tasks in MySQL Shell. You are not limited to the core functionality but can also import both standard modules and your own custom modules. This section will start out with the basics of using external modules (as opposed to the built-in MySQL Shell modules). The next section will go into the reporting infrastructure, and after that plugins will be covered.

Note   The discussion in this book focuses on Python. If you prefer JavaScript, the usage is very similar. One main difference is that Python uses snake case (e.g., `import_table()`), whereas JavaScript uses camel case (`importTable()`). See also `https://dev.mysql.com/doc/mysql-shell/en/mysql-shell-code-execution.html` for general information about code execution in MySQL Shell.

You use Python modules in MySQL Shell in the same way as when you use the interactive Python interpreter, for example:

```
mysql-py> import sys
mysql-py> print(sys.version)
3.7.4 (default, Sep 13 2019, 06:53:53) [MSC v.1900 64 bit (AMD64)]

mysql-py> import uuid
mysql-py> print(uuid.uuid1())
fd37319e-c70d-11e9-a265-b0359feab2bb
```

The exact output depends on the version of MySQL Shell and the platform you use it on.

Note   MySQL Shell 8.0.17 and earlier provide Python 2.7, whereas MySQL Shell 8.0.18 and later come with Python 3.7.

The MySQL Shell interpreter allows you to import all the usual modules included with Python. If you want to import your own modules, you will need to adjust the search path. You can do this directly in the interactive session, for example:

```
mysql-py> sys.path.append('C:\MySQL\Shell\Python')
```

Modifying the path this way is fine for a one-off use of a module; however, it is inconvenient if you have created a module you will be using on a regular basis.

When MySQL Shell starts, it reads two configuration files, one for Python and one for JavaScript. For Python the file is `mysqlshrc.py` and for JavaScript `mysqlshrc.js`. MySQL Shell searches in four places for the files. On Microsoft Windows, the paths are in the order they are searched:

1. `%PROGRAMDATA%\MySQL\mysqlsh\`

2. `%MYSQLSH_HOME%\shared\mysqlsh\`

3. `<mysqlsh binary path>\`

4. `%APPDATA%\MySQL\mysqlsh\`

On Linux and Unix:

1. `/etc/mysql/mysqlsh/`

2. `$MYSQLSH_HOME/shared/mysqlsh/`

3. `<mysqlsh binary path>/`

4. `$HOME/.mysqlsh/`

All four paths are always searched, and if the file is found in multiple locations, each file will be executed. This means that the last found file takes precedence if the files affect the same variables. If you make changes meant for you personally, the best place to make the changes is in the fourth location. The path in step 4 can be overridden with the `MYSQLSH_USER_CONFIG_HOME` environment variable.

If you add modules that you want to use on a regular basis, you can modify the search path in the `mysqlshrc.py` file. That way, you can import the module as any other Python module.

Tip   A great example of the power of the support for external modules is the MySQL Shell port of Innotop (`https://github.com/lefred/mysql-shell-innotop`). It also reveals two of the limitations. Because the reporting part of Innotop is implemented using the `curses` library, it does not work on Microsoft Windows, and because the implementation uses Python, it requires that you execute Innotop in the Python language mode. The reporting infrastructure and plugins discussed later in the chapter avoid these limitations.

As a simple example, consider a very simple module which has a function to roll a virtual dice and return a value between one and six:

```
import random

def dice():
    return random.randint(1, 6)
```

The example is also available from the file example.py in this book's GitHub repository. If you save the file to the directory C:\MySQL\Shell\Python, add the following code to the mysqlshrc.py file (adjust the path in the sys.path.append() line according to where you save the file):

```
import sys
sys.path.append('C:\MySQL\Shell\Python')
```

The next time you start MySQL Shell, you can use the module, for example (since the dice() function returns a random value, your output will vary):

```
mysql-py> import example
mysql-py> example.dice()
5
mysql-py> example.dice()
3
```

This is the simplest way of extending MySQL Shell. Another way is to add reports to the reporting infrastructure.

Reporting Infrastructure

Starting with MySQL Shell 8.0.16, there is a reporting infrastructure available that you can use with both built-in reports and your own custom reports. This is a very powerful way to use MySQL Shell to monitor a MySQL instance and collect information when you encounter performance problems.

Tip   Since the reporting infrastructure is still very new, it is recommended to check each new release for new built-in reports.

This section will start out showing how you get help about the available reports and then discuss how to execute the reports and finally how to add your own reports.

Report Information and Help

The built-in help of MySQL Shell also extends to the reports, so you can easily obtain help of how to use the reports. You can start out using the \show command without any arguments to get a list of available reports. If you add a report name as an argument together with the --help option, you get detailed help for that report. Listing 12-4 shows an example of both uses.

Listing 12-4. Obtaining a list of reports and help for the query report

```
mysql-py> \show
Available reports: query, thread, threads.

mysql-py> \show query --help
NAME
      query - Executes the SQL statement given as arguments.

SYNTAX
      \show query [OPTIONS] [ARGS]
      \watch query [OPTIONS] [ARGS]

DESCRIPTION
      Options:

      --help, -h  Display this help and exit.

      --vertical, -E
                  Display records vertically.

      Arguments:

      This report accepts 1-* arguments.
```

The output of the \show command shows there are three reports available. These are the built-in reports as of version 8.0.18. The second command returns the help for the query report which shows it takes one or more arguments and has two options: --help for returning the help text and --vertical or -E to return the query result in the vertical format.

The built-in reports are

- **query:** Execute the query provided as an argument.

- **thread:** Return information about the current connection.

- **threads:** Return information about all connections for the current user, foreground threads, or background threads.

Another thing that you should notice in the help output is that it lists two ways to execute the report. You can either use the \show command that was also used to generate the help, or you can use the \watch command. You can get more help about each command using the usual built-in help:

```
mysql-py> \h \show
```

```
mysql-py> \h \watch
```

The help output is rather verbose, so it has been omitted here. Instead, the next subsection will discuss how to use the two commands.

Executing Reports

There are two different ways to execute a report. You can either ask for the report to be executed a single time, or you can request the report to be executed over and over at a fixed interval.

There are two commands available to execute a report:

- **\show:** Execute the report a single time.

- **\watch:** Keep executing the report at the interval provided like the watch command on Linux.

Both commands can be used from either of the language modes. The \show command does not have any arguments of its own (but a report may add arguments specific to it). The \watch command has two options that specify when and how to output the report. These options are

- **--interval=float, -i float:** The number of seconds to wait between each execution of the report. The value must be in the range 0.1–86400 (one day) seconds. The default is 2 seconds.

- **--nocls:** Do not clear the screen when outputting the result of the report. This appends the new result below the previous ones and allows you to see the history of the report results until the oldest scroll out of view.

When you execute a report with the \watch command, you stop the execution with Ctrl+C.

As an example of executing a report, consider the query report which you give a query that will be executed. If you want the result to be returned in a vertical format, you can use the --vertical argument. Listing 12-5 shows an example of the result of first executing the report fetching active queries from the sys.session view with the \show command and then with the \watch command refreshing every 5 seconds and without clearing the screen. To ensure that there is some data returned, you can, for example, execute the query SELECT SLEEP(60) in a second connection.

Listing 12-5. Using the query report

```
mysql-sql> \show query --vertical SELECT conn_id, current_statement AS
stmt, statement_latency AS latency FROM sys.session WHERE command = 'Query'
AND conn_id <> CONNECTION_ID()
*************************** 1. row ***************************
conn_id: 34979
   stmt: SELECT SLEEP(60)
latency: 32.62 s

mysql-sql> \watch query --interval=5 --nocls --vertical SELECT conn_id,
current_statement AS stmt, statement_latency AS latency FROM sys.session
WHERE command = 'Query' AND conn_id <> CONNECTION_ID()
*************************** 1. row ***************************
conn_id: 34979
   stmt: SELECT SLEEP(60)
latency: 43.02 s
*************************** 1. row ***************************
conn_id: 34979
   stmt: SELECT SLEEP(60)
latency: 48.09 s
```

```
*************************** 1. row ***************************
conn_id: 34979
   stmt: SELECT SLEEP(60)
latency: 53.15 s
*************************** 1. row ***************************
conn_id: 34979
   stmt: SELECT SLEEP(60)
latency: 58.22 s
Report returned no data.
```

If you execute the same commands, your output will depend on which statements are executing in other threads at the time the report is run. The query used for the report adds a condition that the connection id must be different from the one for the connection generating the report. The \show command with the query report has little value on its own as you could just as well execute the query. It is more useful with other reports and to check the query before using it with \watch command.

The \watch command is more interesting as it allows you keep getting the result updated. In the example, the report runs five times before it is stopped. The four first times, there is another connection executing a query, and the fifth time the report generates no data. Notice that more than five seconds are added to the statement latency for the query between successive executions. That is because the 5 seconds is the time MySQL Shell waits from the result of one iteration has been displayed until it starts executing the query again. So the overall time between two outputs is the interval plus the query execution time plus the time it takes to process the result.

The reporting infrastructure not only allows you to use the built-in reports. You can also add your own reports.

Adding Your Own Reports

The real power of the reporting infrastructure is that it is easily extendable, so both the MySQL development team and you can add more reports. While you can use the support for external modules to add reports as it is done with Innotop, that approach requires you to implement the reporting infrastructure yourself, and you must use the language mode of the modules to execute the report. When you use the reporting infrastructure, that is all handled for you, and the report is available for all language modes.

Note   The report code in this section is not meant to be executed in a MySQL Shell session (and it will cause errors if you copy and paste it as the code stands because blank lines inside a block are used by MySQL Shell in interactive mode to exit the block). Instead, the code must be saved to a file that is loaded when invoking MySQL Shell. Instructions how to install the code follow at the end of the example.

A good way to discuss how to create your own reports is to create a simple report and discuss the various parts that make it up. Listing 12-6 shows the code necessary to create a report that queries the sys.session view. The code is also available from the file listing_12_6.py in this book's GitHub repository. Where to save the code so it becomes available as a report in MySQL Shell will be discussed later.

Listing 12-6. Report querying the sys.session view

```
'''Defines the report "sessions" that queries the sys.x$session view
for active queries. There is support for specifying what to order by
and in which direction, and the maximum number of rows to include in
the result.'''

SORT_ALLOWED = {
    'thread': 'thd_id',
    'connection': 'conn_id',
    'user': 'user',
    'db': 'db',
    'latency': 'statement_latency',
    'memory': 'current_memory',
}

def sessions(session, args, options):
    '''Defines the report itself. The session argument is the MySQL
    Shell session object, args are unnamed arguments, and options
    are the named options.'''
    sys = session.get_schema('sys')
    session_view = sys.get_table('x$session')
    query = session_view.select(
```

```
        'thd_id', 'conn_id', 'user', 'db',
        'sys.format_statement(current_statement) AS statement',
        'sys.format_time(statement_latency) AS latency',
        'format_bytes(current_memory) AS memory')

    # Set what to sort the rows by (--sort)
    try:
        order_by = options['sort']
    except KeyError:
        order_by = 'latency'

    if order_by in ('latency', 'memory'):
        direction = 'DESC'
    else:
        direction = 'ASC'
    query.order_by('{0} {1}'.format(SORT_ALLOWED[order_by], direction))

    # If ordering by latency, ignore those statements with a NULL latency
    # (they are not active)
    if order_by == 'latency':
        query.where('statement_latency IS NOT NULL')

    # Set the maximum number of rows to retrieve is --limit is set.
    try:
        limit = options['limit']
    except KeyError:
        limit = 0
    if limit > 0:
        query.limit(limit)

    result = query.execute()
    report = [result.get_column_names()]
    for row in result.fetch_all():
        report.append(list(row))

    return {'report': report}
```

The code first defines a dictionary with the supported values for sorting the result. This will be used later in the code both inside the sessions() function and when registering the report. The `sessions()` function is where the report is created. The function takes three arguments:

- **session:** This is a MySQL Shell `Session` object (what defines the connection to the MySQL instance).

- **args:** A list with the unnamed arguments passed to the report. This is what is used for the query report where you just specify the query without adding an argument name before the query.

- **options:** A dictionary with the named arguments for the report.

The sessions report uses named options, so the `args` argument is not used.

The next eight lines use the X DevAPI to define the base query. First, the schema object for the `sys` schema is obtained from the session. Then the `sessions` view is obtained from the schema object (you use `get_table()` both to fetch a view and a table). Finally, a select query is created with the arguments specifying which columns that should be retrieved and which aliases to use for the columns.

Next, the `--sort` argument is handled which is available as the `sort` key in the `options` dictionary. If the key does not exist, the report falls back to sorting by latency. The sort order is defined as descending in case the output is sorted according to the latency or memory usage; otherwise, the sort order is ascending. The `order_by()` method is used to add the sorting information to the query. Additionally, when sorting by latency, only sessions where the latency is not `NULL` are included.

The `--limit` argument is handled in a similar fashion, and a value of 0 is taken to mean all matching sessions. Finally, the query is executed. The report is generated as a list with the first item being the column headers and the rest the rows in the result. The report returns a dictionary with the report list in the `report` item.

This report returns the result formatted as a list. There are two other formats as well. Overall, the following result formats are supported:

- **List Type:** The result is returned as a list with the first item the headers and the remaining the rows in the order they should be displayed. The headers and the rows are themselves lists.

- **Report Type:** The result is a list with a single item. MySQL Shell uses YAML to display the result.

- **Print Type:** The result is printed directly to the screen as is.

All that remains is to register the report. That is done using the register_report() method of the shell object as shown in Listing 12-7 (this is also included in the file listing_12-6.py).

Listing 12-7. Registering the sessions report

```
# Make the report available in MySQL Shell.
shell.register_report(
    'sessions',
    'list',
    sessions,
    {
        'brief': 'Shows which sessions exist.',
        'details': ['You need the SELECT privilege on sys.session view and ' +
                    'the underlying tables and functions used by it.'],
        'options': [
            {
                'name': 'limit',
                'brief': 'The maximum number of rows to return.',
                'shortcut': 'l',
                'type': 'integer'
            },
            {
                'name': 'sort',
                'brief': 'The field to sort by.',
                'shortcut': 's',
                'type': 'string',
                'values': list(SORT_ALLOWED.keys())
            }
        ],
        'argc': '0'
    }
)
```

The `register_report()` method takes four arguments that define the report and provides the help information returned by MySQL Shell's built-in help feature. The arguments are

- **name:** The name of the report. You can choose the name relatively freely as long as it is a single word and it is unique for all reports.

- **type:** The result format: `'list'`, `'report'`, or `'print'`.

- **report:** The object of the function generating the report, in this case `sessions`.

- **description:** An optional argument that describes the report. If you provide the description, you use a dictionary as described shortly.

The description is the most complex of the arguments. It consists of a dictionary with the following keys (all items are optional):

- **brief:** A short description of the report.

- **details:** A detailed description of the report provided as a list of strings.

- **options:** The named arguments as a list of dictionaries.

- **argc:** The number of unnamed arguments. You specify that either as an exact number like in this example, an asterisk (*) for any number of arguments, a range with exact numbers (like `'1-3'`), or a range with a minimum number of arguments (`'3-*'`).

The `options` element is used to define the named arguments of the report. Each dictionary object of the list must include the name of the argument, and there is support for several optional arguments to provide more information about the argument. Table 12-3 lists the dictionary keys along with their default values and a description. The `name` key is required; the rest are optional.

Table 12-3. *The dictionary keys used to define the report argument*

Key	Default Value	Description
name		The argument name which is used with double dashes (e.g., `--sort`) when invoking the report.
brief		A short description of the argument.
details		A detailed description of the argument provided as a list of strings.
shortcut		A single alphanumeric character that can be used to access the argument.
type	string	The argument type. Supported values at the time of writing are string, bool, integer, and float. When a Boolean is chosen, the argument works as a switch defaulting to `False`.
required	False	Whether the argument is mandatory.
values		The allowed values for a string argument. If values are not provided, all values are supported. This is what is used in the example to restrict the allowed sorting options.

The typical way you import a report is to save the report definition and registration code in the `init.d` directory under the user configuration path which defaults to %AppData%\MySQL\mysqlsh\ on Microsoft Windows and $HOME/.mysqlsh/ on Linux and Unix (the same as the fourth path searched for the configuration files). All scripts with the filename extension `.py` will be executed as a Python script (and `.js` for JavaScript) when starting up MySQL Shell.

Tip   If there are errors in the scripts, information about the problems will be logged to the MySQL Shell log which is stored in the file `mysqlsh.log` in the user configuration path.

If you copy the `listing_12_6.py` file into this directory and restart MySQL Shell (make sure you connect using the MySQL X port – by default port 33060), you can use the sessions report as shown in Listing 12-8. The result of the report varies, so you will not see the same if you execute the report.

Listing 12-8. Using the sessions report

mysql-py> \show
Available reports: query, sessions, thread, threads.

mysql-py> \show sessions --help
NAME
      sessions - Shows which sessions exist.

SYNTAX
      \show sessions [OPTIONS]
      \watch sessions [OPTIONS]

DESCRIPTION
      You need the SELECT privilege on sys.session view and the underlying
      tables and functions used by it.

      Options:

      --help, -h Display this help and exit.

      --vertical, -E
                  Display records vertically.

      --limit=integer, -l
                  The maximum number of rows to return.

      --sort=string, -s
                  The field to sort by. Allowed values: thread, connection,
                  user, db, latency, memory.

mysql-py> \show sessions --vertical
```
*************************** 1. row ***************************
   thd_id: 81
  conn_id: 36
     user: mysqlx/worker
       db: NULL
statement: SELECT `thd_id`,`conn_id`,`use ... ER BY `statement_latency` DESC
  latency: 40.81 ms
   memory: 1.02 MiB
```

```
mysql-py> \js
Switching to JavaScript mode...
```

mysql-js> \show sessions --vertical
```
*************************** 1. row ***************************
   thd_id: 81
  conn_id: 36
     user: mysqlx/worker
       db: NULL
statement: SELECT `thd_id`,`conn_id`,`use ... ER BY `statement_latency` DESC
  latency: 71.40 ms
   memory: 1.02 MiB
```

```
mysql-js> \sql
Switching to SQL mode... Commands end with ;
```

mysql-sql> \show sessions --vertical
```
*************************** 1. row ***************************
   thd_id: 81
  conn_id: 36
     user: mysqlx/worker
       db: NULL
statement: SELECT `thd_id`,`conn_id`,`use ... ER BY `statement_latency` DESC
  latency: 44.80 ms
   memory: 1.02 MiB
```

The new sessions report shows up in the same way as the built-in reports, and you have the same features as for the built-in report, for example, support for displaying the result in the vertical output. The reason the vertical output is supported is because the report returns the result as a list, so MySQL Shell handles the formatting. Notice also how the report can be used in all three language modes even though it was written in Python.

There is an alternative way to import the report. Instead of saving the file to the init.d directory, you can include the report as part of a plugin.

Plugins

MySQL Shell added support for plugins in version 8.0.17. A plugin consists of one or more code modules which can include reports, utilities, or anything else that may be of use to you and that can be executed as Python or JavaScript code. This is the most powerful way to extend MySQL Shell. The price is that it is also relatively complex, but the benefit is that it is easier to share and import a package of features. Another benefit of plugins is that not only can reports be executed from any language mode; the rest of your code can also be used from both Python and JavaScript.

> **Tip**   For all the details of adding plugins including the description of the parameters for the methods used to create plugin objects and register them, see `https://dev.mysql.com/doc/mysql-shell/en/mysql-shell-plugins.html`. There is also an example plugin available at Mike Zinner's (MySQL development manager whose team includes the MySQL Shell developers) GitHub repository that is worth studying: `https://github.com/mzinner/mysql-shell-ex`.

You create a plugin by adding a directory with the name of the plugin to the `plugins` directory under the user configuration path which defaults to `%AppData%\MySQL\mysqlsh\` on Microsoft Windows and `$HOME/.mysqlsh/` on Linux and Unix (the same as the fourth path searched for the configuration files). The plugin can consist of any number of files and directories, but all files must use the same programming language.

> **Note**   All code within a plugin must use the same programming language. If you need to use both Python and JavaScript, you must split the code into two different plugins.

An example plugin called `myext` is included in the directory `Chapter_12/myext` in this book's GitHub repository. It includes the directories and files depicted in Figure 12-3. The light-colored (yellow) rectangles with rounded corners represent directories, and the darker (red) document shapes are a list of files in a directory.

Note   The example plugin is very basic with the aim at demonstrating how the plugin infrastructure works. If you use plugins in productions, make sure to add appropriate validation and error handling to your code.

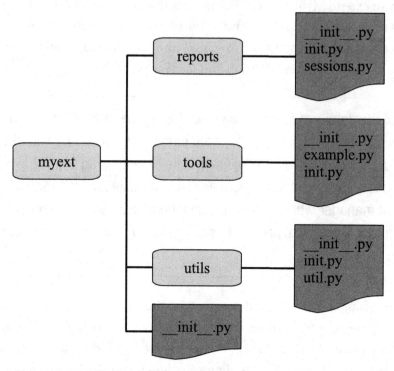

Figure 12-3. *The directories and files for the* myext *plugin*

You can view the structure of the plugin like Python packages and modules. Two important things to be aware of are that there must be a __init__.py file in each directory and when the plugin is imported, only the init.py files (init.js for a JavaScript module) are executed. This means that you must include the code that is necessary to register the public parts of the plugin in init.py files. In this example plugin, all the __init__.py files are empty.

Note   Plugins are not meant to be created interactively. Make sure you save the code to files and at the end restart MySQL Shell to import the plugin. More details are given in the remainder of this section.

The `sessions.py` file in the `reports` directory is the same as the `sessions` report that was generated in Listing 12-6 except that the registration of the report is done in `reports/init.py` and the report is renamed to `sessions_myext` to avoid two reports with the same name.

The `utils` directory includes a module with the `get_columns()` function that is used by the `describe()` function in `tools/example.py`. The `get_columns()` function is also registered as `util.get_columns()` in `utils/init.py`. Listing 12-9 shows the `get_columns()` function from `utils/util.py`.

Listing 12-9. The `get_columns()` function from utils/util.py

```
'''Define utility functions for the plugin.'''

def get_columns(table):
    '''Create query against information_schema.COLUMNS to obtain
    meta data for the columns.'''
    session = table.get_session()
    i_s = session.get_schema("information_schema")
    i_s_columns = i_s.get_table("COLUMNS")

    query = i_s_columns.select(
        "COLUMN_NAME AS Field",
        "COLUMN_TYPE AS Type",
        "IS_NULLABLE AS `Null`",
        "COLUMN_KEY AS Key",
        "COLUMN_DEFAULT AS Default",
        "EXTRA AS Extra"
    )
    query = query.where("TABLE_SCHEMA = :schema AND TABLE_NAME = :table")
    query = query.order_by("ORDINAL_POSITION")

    query = query.bind("schema", table.schema.name)
    query = query.bind("table", table.name)

    result = query.execute()
    return result
```

The function takes a table object and uses the X DevAPI to construct a query against the information_schema.COLUMNS view. Notice how the function obtains the session and schema through the table object. At the end, the result object of executing the query is returned.

Listing 12-10 shows how to register the get_columns() function, so it is available as util.get_columns() in the myext plugin. The registration happens in utils/init.py.

Listing 12-10. Registering the get_columns() function as util.get_columns()

```python
'''Import the utilities into the plugin.'''
import mysqlsh
from myext.utils import util

shell = mysqlsh.globals.shell
# Get the global object (the myext plugin)
try:
    # See if myext has already been registered
    global_obj = mysqlsh.globals.myext
except AttributeError:
    # Register myext
    global_obj = shell.create_extension_object()
    description = {
        'brief': 'Various MySQL Shell extensions.',
        'details': [
            'More detailed help. To be added later.'
        ]
    }
    shell.register_global('myext', global_obj, description)

# Get the utils extension
try:
    plugin_obj = global_obj.utils
except IndexError:
    # The utils extension does not exist yet, so register it
    plugin_obj = shell.create_extension_object()
    description = {
```

```
        'brief': 'Utilities.',
        'details': ['Various utilities.']
    }
    shell.add_extension_object_member(global_obj, "util", plugin_obj,
                                        description)

definition = {
    'brief': 'Describe a table.',
    'details': ['Show information about the columns of a table.'],
    'parameters': [
        {
            'name': 'table',
            'type': 'object',
            'class': 'Table',
            'required': True,
            'brief': 'The table to get the columns for.',
            'details': ['A table object for the table.']
        }
    ]
}

try:
    shell.add_extension_object_member(plugin_obj, 'get_columns',
                                        util.get_columns, definition)
except SystemError as e:
    shell.log("ERROR", "Failed to register myext util.get_columns ({0})."
            .format(str(e).rstrip()))
```

The first important observation is that the mysqlsh module is imported. Both the shell and the session objects can be obtained through the mysqlsh module, so this is an important module when working with extensions in MySQL Shell. Notice also how the util module is imported. It is always required to use full paths starting from the plugin name to import plugin modules.

In order to register the function, first, it is checked whether the myext plugin already exists in mysqlsh.globals. If not, it is created with shell.create_extension_object() and registered using the shell.register_global() method. This dance is necessary as there are multiple init.py files and you should not rely on the order they are executed.

Next, the utils module is registered in a similar fashion using the shell.create_ extension_object() and shell.add_extension_object_member() methods. There is potential for ending up duplicating code and performing similar steps a lot if you have a large plugin, so you can consider creating utility functions to avoid repeating yourself.

Finally, the function itself is registered using the shell.add_extension_object_ member() method. Since the table argument takes an object, it is possible to specify the type of object that is required.

For the registration of the module and function, there is no requirement that the name in the code and the registered name are the same. The registration of the report in reports/init.py includes an example of changing the name, if you are interested. However, in most cases, it is the preferred way to keep the names the same to make it easier to find the code behind a feature.

The tools/example.py file adds two functions that are both registered. There is the dice() function from earlier as well as the describe() function that uses get_columns() to get the column information. The part of the code relevant for the describe() function is shown in Listing 12-11.

Listing 12-11. The describe() function in tools/example.py

```
import mysqlsh
from myext.utils import util

def describe(schema_name, table_name):
    shell = mysqlsh.globals.shell
    session = shell.get_session()
    schema = session.get_schema(schema_name)
    table = schema.get_table(table_name)
    columns = util.get_columns(table)
    shell.dump_rows(columns)
```

The most important thing to notice is that the shell object is obtained as mysqlsh. globals.shell and from there the session, schema, and table objects can be obtained. The shell.dump_rows() method is used to generate the output of the result. The method takes a result object and optionally the format (defaults to the table format). In the process of outputting the result, the result object is consumed.

You are now ready to try the plugin. You need to copy the whole myext directory into the plugins directory and restart MySQL Shell. Listing 12-12 shows the global objects from the help content.

Tip   If MySQL Shell encounters errors importing the plugin, a line like WARNING: Found errors loading plugins, for more details look at the log at: C:\Users\myuser\AppData\Roaming\MySQL\mysqlsh\ mysqlsh.log will be generated when starting MySQL Shell.

Listing 12-12. The global objects in the help content

```
mysql-py> \h
...
GLOBAL OBJECTS

The following modules and objects are ready for use when the shell starts:

- dba      Used for InnoDB cluster administration.
- myext    Various MySQL Shell extensions.
- mysql    Support for connecting to MySQL servers using the classic MySQL
           protocol.
- mysqlx   Used to work with X Protocol sessions using the MySQL X DevAPI.
- session  Represents the currently open MySQL session.
- shell    Gives access to general purpose functions and properties.
- util     Global object that groups miscellaneous tools like upgrade checker
           and JSON import.

For additional information on these global objects use: <object>.help()
```

Notice how the myext plugin shows up as a global object. You can use the myext plugin just as any of the built-in global objects. This includes obtaining help for the subparts of the plugin such as shown in Listing 12-13 for myext.tools.

Listing 12-13. Obtaining help for `myext.tools`

```
mysql-py> myext.tools.help()
NAME
      tools - Tools.

SYNTAX
      myext.tools

DESCRIPTION
      Various tools including describe() and dice().

FUNCTIONS
      describe(schema_name, table_name)
            Describe a table.

      dice()
            Roll a dice

      help([member])
            Provides help about this object and it's members
```

As a last example, consider how the `describe()` and `get_columns()` methods can be used. Listing 12-14 uses both methods for the `world.city` table in the Python language mode.

Listing 12-14. Using the `describe()` and `get_columns()` methods in Python

```
mysql-py> myext.tools.describe('world', 'city')
+-------------+----------+------+-----+---------+----------------+
| Field       | Type     | Null | Key | Default | Extra          |
+-------------+----------+------+-----+---------+----------------+
| ID          | int(11)  | NO   | PRI | NULL    | auto_increment |
| Name        | char(35) | NO   |     |         |                |
| CountryCode | char(3)  | NO   | MUL |         |                |
| District    | char(20) | NO   |     |         |                |
| Population  | int(11)  | NO   |     | 0       |                |
+-------------+----------+------+-----+---------+----------------+
```

```
mysql-py> \use world
Default schema `world` accessible through db.

mysql-py> result = myext.util.get_columns(db.city)

mysql-py> shell.dump_rows(result, 'json/pretty')
{
    "Field": "ID",
    "Type": "int(11)",
    "Null": "NO",
    "Key": "PRI",
    "Default": null,
    "Extra": "auto_increment"
}
{
    "Field": "Name",
    "Type": "char(35)",
    "Null": "NO",
    "Key": "",
    "Default": "",
    "Extra": ""
}
{
    "Field": "CountryCode",
    "Type": "char(3)",
    "Null": "NO",
    "Key": "MUL",
    "Default": "",
    "Extra": ""
}
{
    "Field": "District",
    "Type": "char(20)",
    "Null": "NO",
    "Key": "",
```

```
    "Default": "",
    "Extra": ""
}
{
    "Field": "Population",
    "Type": "int(11)",
    "Null": "NO",
    "Key": "",
    "Default": "0",
    "Extra": ""
}
5
```

First, the `describe()` method is used. The schema and table are provided as strings using their names, and the result is printed as a table. Then, the current schema is set to the `world` schema which allows you to access the tables as properties of the `db` object. The `shell.dump_rows()` method is then used to print the result as pretty printed JSON.

Tip   Because MySQL Shell detects if you use a method interactively, if you do not assign the result of `get_columns()` to a variable, MySQL Shell will output it directly to the console.

That concludes the discussion of MySQL Shell. If you do not already take advantage of the features it provides, you are encouraged to start using it.

Summary

This chapter has introduced MySQL Shell. It started out with an overview of how to install and use MySQL Shell, including working with connections; the SQL, Python, and JavaScript language modes; the built-in help; and the global objects. The rest of the chapter covered customization of MySQL Shell, reports, and extending MySQL.

The MySQL Shell prompt is more than a static label. It adapts according to the connection and default schema, and you can customize it to include information such as the version of MySQL you are connected to, and you can change the theme that is used.

The power of MySQL Shell comes from the built-in complex features and its support for creating complex methods. The simplest way to extend the features is to use external modules for JavaScript or Python. You can also use the reporting infrastructure including creating your own custom reports. Finally, MySQL Shell 8.0.17 and later have support for plugins which you can use to add your features in a global object. The reporting infrastructure and plugins have the advantage that the features you add become language independent.

All examples that use a command-line interface in the remainder of the book are created with MySQL Shell unless noted otherwise. To minimize the space used, the prompt has been replaced with just `mysql>` unless the language mode is important in which case the language mode is included, for example, `mysql-py>` for Python mode.

That concludes the discussion about tools for performance turning. Part IV covers schema considerations and the query optimizer with the next chapter discussing data types.

PART IV

Schema Considerations and the Query Optimizer

CHAPTER 13

Data Types

When you create a table in MySQL (and other relational databases), you specify the data type for each column. Why not just store everything as strings? After all, when the number 42 is used in this book, it is represented as a string, so why not just use strings for everything and allow all kinds of values for every column? There is some merit to that idea. This is partly how NoSQL databases work (though there is more to it than that), and the author of this book has seen tables with all columns defined as varchar(255) strings. Why bother with integers, decimals, floats, dates, strings, and so on? There are several reasons for this, and that is the topic of this chapter.

First, the benefits of using different data types for different types of values will be discussed. Then there will be an overview of the data types supported in MySQL. Finally, it will be discussed how data types affect query performance and how to choose the data type for a column.

Why Data Types?

The data type of a column defines what type of values can be stored and how the values are stored. Additionally, there may be meta properties associated with the data type, such as the size (e.g., number of bytes used for numbers and maximum number of characters in strings) and for strings the character set and collation. While the data type properties may seem like an unnecessary restriction, they also have benefits. These benefits include

- Data validation
- Documentation
- Optimized storage
- Performance
- Correct sorting

The rest of this section will discuss these benefits.

275

© Jesper Wisborg Krogh 2020
J. W. Krogh, *MySQL 8 Query Performance Tuning*, https://doi.org/10.1007/978-1-4842-5584-1_13

Data Validation

At their core, data types define what kind of values are allowed. A column defined as an integer data type can only store integer values. This is also a safeguard. If you make a mistake and try to store a value into a column with a different data type than what was defined, it is possible to reject it or convert the value.

Tip   Whether assigning a value of a wrong data type to a column results in an error or the data type being converted depends on whether you have the STRICT_TRANS_TABLES (for transactional storage engines) and STRICT_ALL_TABLES (for all storage engines) SQL modes enabled and whether it is considered safe to convert the data type. Some conversions that are considered safe are always allowed, for example, converting '42' to 42 and vice versa. It is recommended to always enable strict mode which makes DML queries fail when an unsafe conversion or a truncation of data is attempted.

When you can be sure the data stored in your tables always have the expected data types, it makes life easier for you. If you query a column with an integer, you know it is safe to do arithmetic operations on the returned value. Likewise, if you know the value is a string, you can safely perform string operations. It requires a little more planning up front, but once it is done, you will learn to appreciate that you know the data type of your data.

There is one more consideration about the data type and data validation. In general, there are properties associated with the data type. In the simplest case, you have the maximum size. An integer can, for example, be 1, 2, 3, 4, or 8 bytes in size. This affects the range of values that can be stored. Additionally, integers can be signed or unsigned. A more complex example is strings which not only have a limit on how much text they store but also need a character set to define how the data is encoded and a collation to define how the data sorts.

Listing 13-1 shows an example of how MySQL validates the data against the data type.

Listing 13-1. Data validation based on data type

```
mysql> SELECT @@sql_mode\G
*************************** 1. row ***************************
@@sql_mode: ONLY_FULL_GROUP_BY,STRICT_TRANS_TABLES,NO_ZERO_IN_DATE,
NO_ZERO_DATE,ERROR_FOR_DIVISION_BY_ZERO,NO_ENGINE_SUBSTITUTION
1 row in set (0.0003 sec)

mysql> SHOW CREATE TABLE t1\G
*************************** 1. row ***************************
       Table: t1
Create Table: CREATE TABLE `t1` (
  `id` int(10) unsigned NOT NULL AUTO_INCREMENT,
  `val1` int(10) unsigned DEFAULT NULL,
  `val2` varchar(5) DEFAULT NULL,
  PRIMARY KEY (`id`)
) ENGINE=InnoDB DEFAULT CHARSET=utf8mb4 COLLATE=utf8mb4_0900_ai_ci
1 row in set (0.0011 sec)

mysql> INSERT INTO t1 (val1) VALUES ('abc');
ERROR: 1366: Incorrect integer value: 'abc' for column 'val1' at row 1

mysql> INSERT INTO t1 (val1) VALUES (-5);
ERROR: 1264: Out of range value for column 'val1' at row 1

mysql> INSERT INTO t1 (val2) VALUES ('abcdef');
ERROR: 1406: Data too long for column 'val2' at row 1

mysql> INSERT INTO t1 (val1, val2) VALUES ('42', 42);
Query OK, 1 row affected (0.0825 sec)
```

The SQL mode is set to the default which includes STRICT_TRANS_TABLES. The table has two columns in addition to the primary key, of which one column is an unsigned integer and the other is a varchar(5) meaning it can store up to five characters. When it is attempted to insert a string or a negative integer into the val1 column, the value is rejected as it cannot be converted safely to an unsigned integer. Similarly, attempting to store a string with six characters into the val2 column fails. However, storing the string '42' into val1 and the integer 42 into val2 is considered safe and is thus allowed.

A side effect of the data validation is that you also describe what data you expect – this is an implicit documentation of the column.

Documentation

When you design a table, you know what the expected usage of the table is. This is however not necessarily clear when you or someone else uses the table later. There are several ways to document the columns: use a column name that describes the values, the COMMENT column clause, CHECK constraints, and the data type.

While not the most detailed way to document a column – and it certainly should not stand on its own – the data type does help to describe what kind of data you expect. If you choose the date column instead of datetime, you are clearly only intending for the date part to be stored. Similarly, using tinyint instead of int shows you only expect relatively small values. This all helps for yourself or others to understand what kind of data can be expected. The better understanding of the data, the better change you have to succeed when you need to optimize queries, so in that way it can indirectly help in query optimization.

Tip   The best way to provide documentation within the table is to use the COMMENT clause and CHECK constraints. These are however often not visible in table diagrams which is where the data type helps to give a better mental picture of the kind of data that is expected.

On the topic of performance, there are benefits of explicitly choosing the data type as well. One of them is related to how the values are stored.

Optimized Storage

MySQL does not store all data in the same way. The storage format for a given data type is chosen to be as compact as possible to reduce the storage needed. As an example, consider the value 123456. If this is stored as a string, it will require at least 6 bytes plus possible 1 byte to store the length of the string. If you instead choose an integer, you only need 3 bytes (for integers, all values are always using the same number of bytes depending on the maximum storage allowed for the column). Additionally, reading an integer from storage does not require any interpretation of the value,[1] whereas for a string it is necessary to decode the value using its character set.

Choosing the correct maximum size of a column can reduce the amount of storage needed. If you need to store integers and know that you never need values that need more than 4 bytes of storage, you can use the int data type instead of bigint which uses 8 bytes of storage. This is half the amount of storage needed for the column. If you work with big data, the storage (and memory) savings may become large enough to be significant. However, be careful not to overoptimize. Changing the data type or size of a column in many cases requires rebuilding the whole table which can be an expensive operation, if the table is large. In that way, it can be better to use a little more storage now to save work later.

Tip   As with other types of optimization, be careful not to overoptimize the data types. A relatively small saving in storage now can cause pain later.

How the data is stored also affects the performance.

Performance

Not all data types are created equal. Integers are very cheap to use in computations and comparisons, whereas strings where the bytes stored must be decoded using a character set are relatively expensive. By choosing the correct data type, you can significantly improve the performance of your queries. Particularly, if you need to compare values in two columns (possibly in different tables), make sure they have the same data type including character set and collation for strings. Otherwise, the data in one of the columns will have to be converted before it can be compared with the other column.

While it is simple to understand why an integer performs better than a string, exactly what makes one data type perform better or worse than another is relatively complex and depends on how the data type is implemented (stored on disk). Thus, further discussion of performance will be deferred until after the walkthrough of the MySQL data types in the next section.

The last benefit that will be discussed is sorting.

---

[1]This is not strictly true, but the interpretation is at a lower level, for example, the endianness that is used.

Correct Sorting

The date type has a major impact on how values are sorted. While the human brain usually can make sense of the data intuitively, a computer needs some help understanding how two values compare to each other. The data type and for strings the collation are the key properties that are used to ensure your data is sorted correctly.

Why is sorting important? There are a couple of reasons for this:

- Correct sorting requires knowledge of whether two values are equal or whether a value is in a given range. This is essential to have WHERE clauses and join conditions work as expected.

- When you create indexes, the sorting is used to ensure that MySQL quickly can find the row(s) with the value you are looking for.[2] Indexes are covered in detail in the next chapter.

Consider the values 8 and 10. How do they sort? If you consider them to be integers, 8 comes before 10. However, if you consider them as strings, then '10' (ASCII: 0x3130) comes before '8' (ASCII: 0x38). Whether you expect one or the other depends on your application, but unless there are also values with non-numeric parts, you likely expect the integer behavior which requires the data type to be of an integer type.

Now that it has been discussed what the benefits of explicit data types are, it is time to go through the data types that MySQL supports.

MySQL Data Types

There are more than 30 different data types in MySQL. Several of these can be fine-tuned with respect to the size, precision, and whether they accept signed values. It can at first seem overwhelming, but if you group the data types into categories, you can do a stepwise approach to select the correct data type for your data.

---

[2]There are several different index types, and the implementation of them differs a lot. Not all index types use sorting; most notable hash indexes calculate a hash of the value.

The data types in MySQL can be considered as part of one of the following categories:

- **Numeric:** This includes integers, fixed precision decimal types, approximate precision floating point types, and bit types.

- **Temporal:** This includes years, dates, times, datetime, and timestamp values.

- **Strings:** This includes both binary objects and strings with a character set.

- **JSON:** The JSON data type can store JSON documents.

- **Spatial:** These types are used to store values that describe one or more points in a coordinate system.

- **Hybrid:** MySQL has two data types that both can be used as integers and as strings.

Tip   The MySQL reference manual has a comprehensive discussion about data types in `https://dev.mysql.com/doc/refman/8.0/en/data-types.html` and references therein.

The rest of this section will go through the data types and discuss their specifics.

Numeric Data Types

Numeric data types are the simplest of the data types supported by MySQL. You can choose between integers, fixed precision decimal values, and approximate floating point values.

Table 13-1 summarizes the numeric data types including their storage requirements in bytes and the supported range of values. For integers, you can choose whether the values are signed or unsigned which affects the range of supported values. For the supported values, both the start and end values are included in the range of allowed values.

Table 13-1. *The numeric data types (integers, fixed point, and floating point)*

Data Type	Bytes Stored	Range
tinyint	1	Signed: -128–127 Unsigned: 0–255
smallint	2	Signed: -32768–32767 Unsigned: 0–65535
mediumint	3	Signed: -8388608–8388607 Unsigned: 0–16777215
int	4	Signed: -2147483648–2147483647 Unsigned: 0–4294967295
bigint	8	Signed: -2^{63}–2^{63}-1 Unsigned: 0–2^{64}-1
decimal(M, N)	1–29	Depends on M and N
float	4	Variable
double	8	Variable
bit(M)	1–8	

The integer data types are the simplest with a fixed storage requirement and fixed ranges of supported values. A synonym for tinyint is bool (for a Boolean value).

The decimal data type (numeric is a synonym) takes two arguments, M and N, which define the precision and scale of the values. If you have decimal(5,2), the values will have at most five digits, of which two are decimals (to the right of the decimal point). That means that values between -999.99 and 999.99 are allowed. Up to 65 digits are supported. The amount of storage for decimals depends on the number of digits with each multiple of nine digits using 4 bytes and the remaining digits using 0–4 bytes.

The float and double data types store approximate values. These types are efficient for numeric calculations, but at the cost that there is an uncertainty in their values. They use 4 and 8 bytes, respectively, for storage.

Tip   Never use floating point data types to store exact data, such as monetary amounts. Use the exact precision decimal data type instead. For approximate floating point data types, you should never use the equal (=) and not equal (<>) operators as comparing two approximate values will in general not return that they are equal even if they are meant to be.

The final numeric data type is the bit type. It can store between 1 and 64 bits in one value. This can, for example, be used for bit masks. The storage required depends on the number of bits required (the M value); it can be approximated as FLOOR((M+7)/8) bytes.

A category of data types related to the numeric types are temporal data types, which are the next category that will be covered.

Temporal Data Types

Temporal data defines a point in time. The precision can range from a year to a microsecond. Except for the year data type, values are entered as strings, but internally an optimized format is used, and the values will sort correctly according to the point in time the values represent.

Table 13-2 shows the temporal data types supported by MySQL, the amount of storage in bytes each type uses, and the range of values supported.

Table 13-2. *The temporal data types*

Data Type	Bytes Stored	Range
year	1	1901–2155
date	3–6	'1000-01-01' to '9999-12-31'
datetime	5–8	'1000-01-01 00:00:00.000000' to '9999-12-31 23:59:59.999999'
timestamp	4–7	'1970-01-01 00:00:01.000000' to '2038-01-19 03:14:07.999999'
time	3–6	'-838:59:59.000000' to '838:59:59.000000'

The datetime, timestamp, and time types all support fractional seconds up to microsecond resolution. The storage requirement for the fractional seconds is 0–3 bytes depending on the number of digits (1 byte per two digits).

The datetime and timestamp columns differ in a subtle way. When you store a value in a datetime column, MySQL stores it as you specify it. For a timestamp column on the other hand, the value is converted to UTC using the time zone MySQL has been configured to use – the @@session.time_zone variable (by default the system time zone). In the same way, when you retrieve the data, datetime values are returned as you originally specified them, whereas timestamp columns are converted to the time zone set in the @@session.time_zone variable.

Tip   When using datetime columns, store the data in the UTC time zone and convert to the time zone required when using the data. By always storing the value in UTC, there is less chance of problems if the operating system time zone or MySQL Server time zone is changed, or you share data with users from different time zones.

While you enter and retrieve dates and times using a string, they are stored internally in a dedicated format. What about actual strings? Let's take a look at the string and binary data types.

String and Binary Data Types

Strings and binary data types are very flexible types for storing arbitrary data. The difference between a binary value and a string is that the string has a character set associated with it, so MySQL knows how to interpret the data. Binary values on the other hand store raw data which means you can use them for any kind of data including images and custom data formats.

While strings and binary data are very flexible, they come with a cost. For strings, MySQL needs to interpret the bytes to determine which characters they represent. This is relatively expensive in terms of the computational power required. Some character sets, including UTF-8 which is the default character set in MySQL 8, are variable width, that is, a character uses a variable number of bytes; for UTF-8 it ranges from 1 to 4 bytes per character. This means that if you request the first four characters of a string, it can require reading between 4 and 16 bytes depending on which characters it is, so MySQL will need to analyze the bytes to determine when four characters have been found. For binary strings, the interpretation of the meaning of the data is put back on the application.

Table 13-3 shows the data types in MySQL representing strings and binary data. The table includes the maximum amount of data that can be stored as well as a description of the storage requirements. For the data types, (M) is the maximum number of characters that the column must be able to store, and in bytes stored L is the number of bytes required to represent the string value in character set used for the encoding.

Table 13-3. *The string and binary data types*

Data Type	Bytes stored	Max Length
char(M)	M*char width	255 chars
varchar(M)	L+1 or L+2	16383 chars for utf8mb4 and 65532 for latin1
tinytext	L+1	255 bytes
text	L+2	65535 bytes
mediumtext	L+3	16777216 bytes
longtext	L+4	4294967296 bytes
binary(M)	M	255 bytes
varbinary(M)	L+1 or L+2	65532 bytes
tinyblob	L+1	255 bytes
blob	L+2	65536 bytes
mediumblob	L+3	16777216 bytes
longblob	L+4	4294967296 bytes

The storage requirements for strings and binary objects depend on the length of the data. L is the number of bytes required to store the value; for text strings, the character set must be taken into account as well. For variable width types, 1–4 bytes are used to store the length of the value. For char(M) columns, the required storage may be less than M times the character width when the compact family of InnoDB storage formats is used and the string is encoded with a variable width character set.

For all but char and varchar, the maximum supported length of the strings is specified in bytes. This means that the number of characters that can be stored in string types depends on the character set. Additionally, char, varchar, binary, and varbinary columns count toward the row width which in total must be less than 64 kiB, which in practice means that it rarely is possible to create columns using the theoretical maximum length. (This is also the reason that varchar and varbinary columns at most can store 65532 characters/bytes.) For longtext and longblob columns, it should be noted that while they in principle can store up to 4 GiB of data, in practice the storage is limited by the max_allowed_packet variable which at most can be 1 GiB.

One additional consideration for the data types that store strings is that you must choose a character set and collation for the column. If you do not choose one explicitly, then the default for the table will be used. In MySQL 8, the default character set is utf8mb4 using the utf8mb4_0900_ai_ci collation. What does utf8mb4 and utf8mb4_0900_ai_ci mean?

The utf8mb4 character set is UTF-8 supporting up to 4 bytes per character (required, e.g., for some emojis). Originally, MySQL only supported up to 3 bytes per character for UTF-8, and later utf8mb4 was added to extend the support. Today, you should not use utf8mb3 (at most 3 bytes per character) or its utf8 alias (deprecated, so it later can be changed to mean utf8mb4). When you use UTF-8, always choose the 4-byte variant as there is little benefit from the 3-byte variant and it has been deprecated. In MySQL 5.7 and earlier, Latin 1 was the default character set, but with the improvements for UTF-8 in MySQL 8, it is recommended to use utf8mb4 unless you have a specific reason to choose another character set.

The utf8mb4_0900_ai_ci collation is a general-purpose collation for utf8mb4. A collation defines the sorting and comparison rules, so when you compare two strings they compare correctly. The rules can be quite complex and include that some character sequences compare as equal to other single characters (e.g., the German sharp ß is the same as "ss" in some collations). The collation name consists of several parts which are

- **utf8mb4:** The character set the collation belongs to.

- **0900:** This means the collation is one of the Unicode Collation Algorithm (UCA) 9.0.0–based collations. These were introduced in MySQL 8 and provide a significant performance improvement compared to older UTF-8 collations.

- **ai:** A collation can be accent insensitive (ai) or accent sensitive (as). When a collation is accent insensitive, an accented character like à is considered equal to the non-accented character a. In this case, it is accent insensitive.

- **ci:** A collation can be case insensitive (ci) or case sensitive (cs). In this case, it is case insensitive.

The name can include other parts as well, and other character sets have other collations. Particularly, there are several country-specific character sets to take local sorting and comparison rules into account; for those, the country code is added to the name. It is recommended to use one of the UCA 9.0.0 collations as these have better performance and are more modern than the other collations. The `information_schema.COLLATIONS` view includes all collations supported by MySQL with support for filtering by the character set. As of 8.0.18, there are 75 collations available for utf8mb4, of which 49 are UCA 9.0.0 collations.

Tip   Character sets and collations are a large and interesting topic on their own. If you would like to dive further into that topic, a starting point is the following blog by the author of this book and the references therein: `https://mysql.wisborg.dk/mysql-8_charset`.

A special kind of strings is JSON documents. MySQL has a dedicated data type for them.

JSON Data Type

A popular format for storing data with more flexibility than relational tables is the JavaScript Object Notation (JSON) format. This is also the format that has been chosen for the MySQL Document Store that is available in MySQL 8. Support for the `json` data type was introduced in MySQL 5.7.

A JSON document is a combination of JSON objects (keys and values), JSON arrays, and JSON values. A simple example of a JSON document can be seen in the following:

```
{
    "name": "Sydney",
    "demographics": {
        "population": 5500000
    },
    "geography": {
        "country": "Australia",
        "state": "NSW"
    },
    "suburbs": [
        "The Rocks",
        "Surry Hills",
        "Paramatta"
    ]
}
```

As a JSON document is a string (or binary object) as well, it can also be stored in a string or binary object column. However, by having a dedicated data type, it is possible to add validation, and the storage is optimized for accessing specific elements in the document.

One great performance-related feature of JSON documents in MySQL 8 is that there is support for partial updates. That makes the change in-place which reduces not only the amount of work done during the update, but it is also possible to write just the partial change to the binary log. There are some requirements for a partial in-place update to be possible. These are as follows:

- Only the JSON_SET(), JSON_REPLACE(), and JSON_REMOVE() functions are supported.

- Only updates within a column are supported. That is, setting a column to the return value of one of the three JSON functions working on another column is not supported.

- It must be an existing value that is replaced. Adding new object or array elements causes the whole document to be rewritten.

- The new value must at most be the same size as the value that is replaced. The exceptions are cases where space freed by a previous partial update can be reused.

In order to log the partial updates to the binary log as partial updates, you need to set the `binlog_row_value_options` option to `PARTIAL_JSON`. The option can be set dynamically both at the session and global levels.

Internally, the document is stored as a long binary object (`longblob`) with the text interpreted using the `utf8mb4` character set. The maximum storage is limited to 1 GiB. The storage requirements are similar to those for `longblob`, but it is necessary to take the overhead of metadata and the dictionaries used for lookups into account.

Thus far, numbers, temporal data, strings, binary objects, and JSON documents have been covered. What about data specifying a point in space? This is the next category of data types to cover.

Spatial Data Types

Spatial data specifies one or more points in a coordinate system, possibly forming an object such as a polygon. This is useful, for example, to specify the location of an item on a map.

MySQL 8 added support for specifying which reference system is used; this is called the Spatial Reference System Identifier (SRID). The reference systems supported can be found in the `information_schema.ST_SPATIAL_REFERENCE_SYSTEMS` view (the `SRS_ID` column has the value to use for the SRID); there are more than 5000 to choose from. Each spatial value has a reference system associated with it in order to make it possible for MySQL to correctly identify the relation between two values, for example, to calculate the distance between two points. To use Earth as the reference system, set the SRID to 4326.

There is support for eight different spatial data types, of which four are single-value types and four are collections of values. Table 13-4 summarizes the spatial types with the required storage listed in bytes.

Table 13-4. *The spatial data types*

Data Type	Bytes Stored	Description
geometry	Variable	A single spatial object of any type.
point	25	A single point, for example, the location of a person.
linestring	9+16*#points	A set of points that form a line, that is, it is not a closed object.
polygon	13+16*#points	A set of points that encloses an area. One polygon can include several such sets, for example, to create an inner and outer ring of a donut-shaped object.
multipoint	13+21*#points	A collection of points.
multilinestring	Variable	A collection of linestring values.
multipolygon	Variable	A collection of polygons.
geometrycollection	Variable	A collection of geometry values.

MySQL uses a binary format to store the data. The storage requirements for the geometry, multilinestring, multipolygon, and geometrycollection types depend on the size of the objects contained in the value. The storage for these collections of objects is a little larger than storing the objects in individual columns. You can use the LENGTH() function to get the size of the spatial object and then add 4 bytes to store the SRID to get the total storage required for the data.

That leaves one category of data types to be discussed: hybrids between numeric and string data types.

Hybrid Data Types

There are two special data types that combine the properties of integers and strings: enum and set. Both can be considered a collection of possible values with the difference that the enum data type allows you to choose exactly one of the possible values, whereas the set data type allows you to choose any of the possible values.

What makes the enum and set data types hybrid is that you can both use them as integers and as strings. The latter is the most common and the most user-friendly. Internally, the values are stored as integers which gives compact and efficient storage while still allowing to use strings when setting or querying the columns. Both data types can as an alternative be implemented using lookup tables.

The enum data type is the most commonly used of the two. When you create the column, you specify a list of allowed values, for example:

```
CREATE TABLE t1 (
    id int unsigned NOT NULL PRIMARY KEY,
    val enum('Sydney', 'Melbourne', 'Brisbane')
);
```

The numeric value is the position in the list starting with 1. That is, Sydney has the integer value 1, Melbourne 2, and Brisbane 3. The total storage requirement is just 1 or 2 bytes depending on the number of members in the list, and up to 65535 members are supported.

The set data type works similarly to enum except you can select more than one of the options. To create it, list the members you want to be available, for example:

```
CREATE TABLE t1 (
    id int unsigned NOT NULL PRIMARY KEY,
    val set('Sydney', 'Melbourne', 'Brisbane')
);
```

Each member in the list gets a numeric value in the series 1, 2, 4, 8, and so on based on the member's position in the list. In the example, Sydney has the value 1, Melbourne 2, and Brisbane 4. What does the value 3 then represent? It is Sydney and Melbourne. If you want to include multiple values, you sum their individual values. In this way, the set data type works the same as the bit type. It is simpler when you specify the value as a string, as you include the members for the value in a comma-separated list. Listing 13-2 shows two examples of inserting set values with each example inserting the same value twice using both the numeric and string values.

Listing 13-2. Working with set values

```
mysql> INSERT INTO t1
        VALUES (1, 4),
               (2, 'Brisbane');
Query OK, 2 rows affected (0.0812 sec)
```

```
Records: 2  Duplicates: 0  Warnings: 0

mysql> INSERT INTO t1
       VALUES (3, 7),
              (4, 'Sydney,Melbourne,Brisbane');
Query OK, 2 rows affected (0.0919 sec)

Records: 2  Duplicates: 0  Warnings: 0

mysql> SELECT *
          FROM t1\G
*************************** 1. row ***************************
 id: 1
val: Brisbane
*************************** 2. row ***************************
 id: 2
val: Brisbane
*************************** 3. row ***************************
 id: 3
val: Brisbane,Melbourne,Sydney
*************************** 4. row ***************************
 id: 4
val: Brisbane,Melbourne,Sydney
4 rows in set (0.0006 sec)
```

First, the value of 'Brisbane' is inserted. Since it is the third element in the set, it has a numeric value of 4. Then the sets Sydney, Melbourne, and Brisbane are inserted. Here you need to sum 1, 2, and 4. Notice in the SELECT query that the order of the elements is not the same as in the set definition.

A set column uses 1, 2, 3, 4, or 8 bytes of storage depending on the number of members in the set. It is possible to have up to 64 members in a set.

This concludes the discussion of the available data types. How does the data type influence the performance of your queries? Potentially quite a lot, so that is worth some consideration.

Performance

The choice of data type is not only important with respect to the data integrity and to tell what kind of data is expected, but also different data types have different performance characteristics. This section will discuss how the performance varies when comparing data types.

In general, the simpler the data type, the better it performs. Integers have the best performance, and floating point (approximate values) follows closely. Decimal (exact) values have a higher overhead than the approximate floating point values. Binary objects perform better than text strings as binary objects do not have the overhead of character sets.

When it comes to a data type like JSON, you may think it performs worse than using a binary object as JSON documents have some storage overhead as described earlier in the chapter. However, exactly this storage overhead means that a JSON data type will perform better than storing the same data as a blob. The overhead consists of metadata and a dictionary for lookups, and that means accessing the data is faster. Additionally, JSON documents support in-place updates, whereas the text and blob data types replace the entire object even if only a single character or byte is replaced.

Within a given family of data types (e.g., `int` versus `bigint`), the smaller data type performs better than the larger; however, in practice, there are also considerations about the alignment within the registers of the hardware, so for in-memory workloads the difference may be negligible or even the reverse.

So which data types should you use? That's the final topic of the chapter.

Which Data Type Should You Choose?

In the beginning of the chapter, it was discussed how it could seem like a good idea just to store all data in strings or binary objects to have the greatest flexibility. During the course of the chapter, it has been discussed how there are benefits from using specific data types, and in the previous section the performance of different data types was discussed. So which data type should you choose?

You can start asking yourself some questions about the data you need to store in the column. Some examples of questions are as follows:

- What is the native format for the data?

- How large values can be expected initially?

- Will the size of the values grow over time? If so, how much and how quickly?

- How often will the data be retrieved in queries?

- How many unique values do you expect?

- Do you need to index the values? Particularly, is it the primary key of the table?

- Do you need to store the data, or can it, for example, be fetched through a foreign key in another table (using an integer reference column)?

You should choose a data type that is native for the data you need to store. If you need to store integers, choose an integer data type, usually `int` or `bigint` depending on how large values you need. You can choose a smaller integer type if you want to restrict the values; for example, the number of children for a table storing data about parents need not be a `bigint`, but a `tinyint` suffices. Similarly, if you want to store JSON documents, use the `json` type instead of `longtext` or `longblob`.

For the size of the data type, you need to consider both the current need and the future need. If you expect within long to need larger values, it is likely best to choose the larger data type right away. That saves changing the table definition at a later date. However, if the expected change is years away, it may be better to go with the smaller data type now and reevaluate your needs over time. For the `varchar` and `varbinary`, you can also change the width in-place as long as you do not change the number of bytes required to store the length of the string or the character set.

When you work with strings and binary objects, you can also consider storing the data in a separate table and reference the values using an integer. This will add a join when you need to retrieve the values; however, if you only rarely need the actual string values, it may be an overall win to keep the main table small. The benefit of this approach also depends on the number of rows in the table and how you query the rows; large scans retrieving many rows will benefit more than single-row lookups, and using `SELECT *` even when not all columns are needed will benefit more than selecting just the columns needed.

If you only have a few unique string values, it can also be worth considering using the enum data type. It works similar to a lookup table but saves the join and allows you to retrieve the string values directly.

For non-integer numeric data, you have the choice between the exact decimal data type and the approximate float and double data types. If you need to store data such as monetary values that must be exact, you should always choose the decimal data type. This is also the type to choose if you need to do equality and non-equality comparisons. If you do not need the data to be exact, the float and double data types perform better.

With respect to string values, then the char, varchar, tinytext, text, mediumtext, and longtext data types require a character set and a collation. In general, it is recommended to choose utf8mb4 with one of the UCA 9.0.0–based collations (the collations with _0900_ in the name). The default utf8mb4_0900_ai_ci is a good choice, if you do not have specific requirements. Latin 1 will perform marginally better, but rarely enough to warrant the added complexity of having different character sets for different needs. The UCA 9.0.0 collations also provide more modern sorting rules than those collations that are available for Latin 1.

When you need to decide how large values to allow, go for the smallest data type or width that supports the values you need now and in the near future. Smaller data types also mean that less space is used toward the row size limit (64 kiB) and more data can fit into an InnoDB page. As the InnoDB buffer pool can store a certain number of pages according the size of the buffer pool and the pages, it in turn means more data can fit into the buffer pool and thus help to reduce disk I/O. At the same time, remember that optimization is also about knowing when you have optimized enough. Do not spend a long time to shave off a few bytes, just to end up having to do an expensive table rebuild in a year.

A last thing to consider is whether the value is included in indexes. The larger the values, the larger the index also becomes. This is a particular issue for the primary key. InnoDB organizes the data according to the primary key (as the clustered index), so when you add a secondary index, the primary key is added to the end of the index to provide the link to the row. Additionally, this organization of the data means that in general monotonically increasing values perform best for the primary key. If the column with the primary key changes randomly over time and/or it is large, you may likely be better off adding a dummy column with an auto-increment integer and using that as the primary key.

Indexes are themselves an important and large topic which will be discussed in the next chapter.

Summary

This chapter has gone through the concept of data types. There are several benefits from using data types: data validation, documentation, optimized storage, performance, and correct sorting.

MySQL supports a large range of data types, from simple integers over strings and spatial objects to complex JSON documents. Each data type was discussed with focus on the supported values, the supported size of the values, and the amount of storage required.

The final part of the chapter discussed how the data type can impact performance and how to determine which data type to choose for a column. This included considerations of whether the column will be indexed, which also relates to one of the benefits of data types: correct sorting. Indexes is a very important topic, and indeed the next chapter will be covering them.

CHAPTER 14

Indexes

Adding indexes to a table is a very powerful way to improve the query performance. An index allows MySQL to quickly find the data needed for a query. When the right indexes are added to your tables, query performance can potentially be improved by several orders of magnitude. The trick is to know which indexes to add. Why not just add indexes on all columns? Indexes have overhead as well, so you need to analyze your needs before adding random indexes.

This chapter starts out discussing what an index is, some index concepts, and what drawbacks adding an index can have. Then the various index types and features supported by MySQL are covered. The next part of the chapter starts out discussing how InnoDB uses indexes particularly related to index-organized tables. Finally, it is discussed how to choose which indexes you should add to your tables and when to add them.

What Is an Index?

In order to be able to use indexes to properly improve performance, it is important to understand what an index is. This section will not cover different index types – that will be discussed in the section "Index Types" later in the chapter – but rather the higher-level idea of an index.

The concept of an index is nothing new and existed well before computer databases became known. As a simple example, consider this book. At the end of the book, there is an index of some words and terms that have been selected as the most relevant search terms for the text in this book. The way that book index works is similar in concept to how database indexes work. It organizes the "terms" in the database, so your queries can find the relevant data more quickly than by reading all of the data and checking whether it matches the search criteria. The word terms is quoted here as it is not necessarily human-readable words that the index is made up of. It is also possible to index binary data such as spatial data.

© Jesper Wisborg Krogh 2020
J. W. Krogh, *MySQL 8 Query Performance Tuning*, https://doi.org/10.1007/978-1-4842-5584-1_14

In short, an index organizes your data in such a way that it is possible to narrow down the number of rows queries need to examine. The speedup from well-chosen indexes can be tremendous – several order of magnitudes. Again consider this book: if you want to read about B-tree indexes, you can either start from page 1 and keep reading the whole book or look up the term "B-tree index" in the book's index and jump straight to the pages of relevance. When querying a MySQL database, the improvements are similar with the difference that queries can be much more complex than looking for information about something in a book, and thus the importance of indexes increases.

Clearly then, you just need to add all possible indexes, right? No. Other than the administrative complexity of adding the indexes, indexes themselves not only improve performance when used right; they also add overhead. So you need to pick your indexes with care.

Another thing is that even when an index can be used, it is not always more efficient than scanning the whole table. If you want to read significant parts of this book, looking up each term of interest in the index to find out where the topic is discussed and then going to read it will eventually become slower than just reading the whole book from cover to cover. In the same say, if your query anyway needs to access a large part of the data in the table, it will become faster to just read the whole table from one end to the other. Exactly what the threshold is where it becomes cheaper to scan the whole table depends on several factors. These factors include the disk type, the performance of sequential I/O compared to random I/O, whether the data fits in memory, and so on.

Before diving into the details of indexes, it is worth taking a quick look at some key indexing concepts.

Index Concepts

Given how big a topic indexes are, it is no surprise that there are several terms used to describe indexes. There are of course the names of the index types such as B-tree, full text, spatial, and so on, but there are also more general terms that are important to be aware of. The index types will be covered later in this chapter, so here the more general terms will be discussed.

Key Versus Index

You may have noticed that sometimes the word "index" is used and other times the word "key" is used. What is the difference? An index is a list of keys. However, in MySQL statements, the two terms are often interchangeable.

An example where it does matter is "primary key" – in that case, "key" must be used. On the other hand, when you add an index, you can write ALTER TABLE table_name ADD INDEX ... or ALTER TABLE table_name ADD KEY ... as you wish. The manual uses "index" in that case, so for consistency it is recommended to stick with index.

There are several terms to describe which kind of an index you are using. The first of these that will be discussed is a unique index.

Unique Index

A unique index is an index that only allows one row for each value in the index. Consider a table with data about people. You may include the social security number or a similar identifier for the person. No two persons should share social security numbers, so it makes sense to define a unique index on the column storing the social security number.

In this sense, "unique" more refers to a constraint than an indexing feature. However, the index part is critical for MySQL to be able to quickly determine whether a new value already exists.

An important consideration when using unique indexes in MySQL is how NULL values are handled. Comparing two NULL values is undefined (or in other words NULL does not equal NULL), so a unique index on a column that allows NULL values does not put any limit on how many rows can have NULL for the column. If you want to restrict your unique constraint to only allow a single NULL value, use a trigger to check whether there is already a NULL value and raise an error with the SIGNAL statement. An example of a trigger can be seen in Listing 14-1.

Listing 14-1. Trigger checking for unique constraint violations

```
CREATE TABLE my_table (
  Id int unsigned NOT NULL,
  Name varchar(50),
  PRIMARY KEY (Id),
  UNIQUE INDEX (Name)
);
```

```
DELIMITER $$
CREATE TRIGGER befins_my_table
BEFORE INSERT ON my_table
   FOR EACH ROW
BEGIN
   DECLARE v_errmsg, v_value text;
   IF EXISTS(SELECT 1 FROM my_table WHERE Name <=> NEW.Name) THEN
       IF NEW.Name IS NULL THEN
           SET v_value = 'NULL';
       ELSE
           SET v_value = CONCAT('''', NEW.Name, '''');
     END IF;
       SET v_errmsg = CONCAT('Duplicate entry ',
                             v_value,
                           ' For key ''Name''');
     SIGNAL SQLSTATE '23000'
       SET MESSAGE_TEXT = v_errmsg,
          MYSQL_ERRNO = 1062;
  END IF;
END$$
DELIMITER ;
```

This handles any kind of duplicate values for the Name column. It uses the NULL safe equal operator (<=>) to determine whether the new value for Name already exists in the table. If it does, it quotes the value if it is not NULL and otherwise does not quote it, so it is possible to distinguish between the string "NULL" and the NULL value. Finally, a signal with SQL state 23000 and the MySQL error number 1062 is emitted. The error message, SQL state, and error number are the same as the normal duplicate key constraint error.

A special kind of unique index is the primary key.

Primary Key

The primary key for a table is an index which uniquely defines the row. NULL values are never allowed for a primary key. If you have multiple NOT NULL unique indexes on your table, either can serve the purpose of being the primary key. For reasons that will be explained shortly when discussing the clustered index, you should choose one or more columns with immutable values for the primary key. That is, aim at never changing the primary key for a given row.

The primary key is very special for InnoDB, while for other storage engines, it may more be a matter of convention. However, in all cases, it is best to always have some value that uniquely identifies a row as that, for example, allows replication to quickly determine which row to modify (more on this in Chapter 26), and the Group Replication feature explicitly requires all tables to have a primary key or a not NULL unique index. In MySQL 8.0.13 and later, you can enable the `sql_require_primary_key` option to require that all new tables must have a primary key. The restriction also applies if you change the structure of an existing table.

Tip   Enable the `sql_require_primary_key` option (disabled by default). Tables without a primary key can cause performance problems, sometimes in unexpected and subtle ways. This also ensures your tables are ready, if you want to use Group Replication in the future.

If there are primary keys, are there secondary keys as well?

Secondary Indexes

The term "secondary index" is used for an index that is not a primary key. It does not have any special meaning, so the name is just used to make it explicit that the index is not the primary key whether it is a unique or nonunique index.

As mentioned, the primary key has a special meaning for InnoDB as it is used for the clustered index.

Clustered Index

The clustered index is specific to InnoDB and is the term used for how InnoDB organizes the data. If you are familiar with Oracle DB, you may know of index-organized tables; that describes the same thing.

Everything in InnoDB is an index. The row data is in the leaf pages of a B-tree index (B-tree indexes will be described shortly). This index is called the clustered index. The name comes from the fact that index values are clustered together. The primary key is used for the clustered index. If you do not specify an explicit primary key, InnoDB will look for a unique index that does not allow NULL values. If that does not exist either, InnoDB will add a hidden 6-byte integer column using a global (for all InnoDB tables) auto-increment value to generate a unique value.

The choice of primary key also has performance implications. These will be discussed in the section "Index Strategies" later in the chapter. The clustered index can also be seen as a special case of a covering index. What is this? You are about to find out.

Covering Index

An index is said to be a covering index if it includes all the columns that are required from the indexed table for a given query. That is, whether the index is covering depends on the query you are using the index for. An index may be covering for one query but not for another. Consider an index that indexes the columns (a, b) and a query selecting those two columns:

```
SELECT a, b
  FROM my_table
 WHERE a = 10;
```

In this case, the query just needs the columns a and b, so it is not necessary to look up the rest of the row – the index is enough to retrieve all the required data. On the other hand, if the query also needs column c, the index is no longer covering. When you analyze a query using the EXPLAIN statement (this will be covered in Chapter 20) and a covering index is used for the table, the Extra column in the EXPLAIN output will include "Using index."

A special case of a covering index is InnoDB's clustered index (though EXPLAIN will not say "Using index" for it). The clustered index includes all the row data in the leaf node (even though in general only a subset of columns is actually indexed), so the index will always include all required data. Some databases support an include clause when creating indexes that can be used to simulate how the clustered index works.

Clever creation of indexes so they can be used as covering indexes for the most executed queries can greatly improve performance as it will be discussed in the "Index Strategies" section.

When you add indexes, there are some limitations you need to adhere to. These limitations are the next thing to cover.

Index Limitations

There are a few limitations with respect to InnoDB indexes. These range from the index size to the number of indexes allowed on a table. The most important limitations are as follows:

- The maximum width of a B-tree index is 3072 bytes or 767 bytes depending on the InnoDB row format. The maximum size is based on 16 kiB InnoDB pages with lower limits for smaller page sizes.

- Blob- and text-type columns can only be used in an index other than full text indexes when a prefix length is specified. Prefix indexes are discussed later in the chapter in the section "Index Features."

- Functional key parts count toward the limit of 1017 columns in a table.

- There can be at most 64 secondary indexes on each table.

- A multicolumn index can include at most 16 columns and functional key parts.

The limitation you are likely to encounter is the maximum index width for B-tree indexes. No index can be more than 3072 bytes when you use the DYNAMIC (the default) or COMPRESSED row format and no more than 767 bytes for the REDUNDANT and COMPACT row formats. The limit for tables using the DYNAMIC and COMPRESSED row formats is reduced to the half (1536 bytes) for 8 KiB pages and to a quarter (768 bytes) for 4 KiB pages. This is particularly a restriction for indexes on string and binary columns as not only are these values by nature often large, it is also the maximum possible amount of storage required that is used in the size calculation. That means that a varchar(10) using the utf8mb4 character set contributes 40 bytes to the limit even if you never store anything by single-byte characters in the column.

When you add a B-tree index to a text- or blob-type column, you must always provide a key length specifying how much of a prefix of the column you want to include in the index. This applies even for tinytext and tinyblob that only support 256 bytes of data. For char, varchar, binary, and varbinary columns, you only need to specify a prefix length if the maximum size of the values in bytes exceeds the maximum allowed index width for the table.

Tip   For text- and blob-type columns, instead of using a prefix index, it is often better to index using a full text index (more later), to add a generated column with the hash of the blob, or to optimize the access in some other way.

If you add functional indexes to a table, then each functional key part counts toward the limit for columns on a table. If you create an index with two functional parts, then this counts as two columns toward the table limit. For InnoDB there can be at most 1017 columns in a table.

The final two limitations are related to the number of indexes that can be included in a table and the number of columns and functional key parts you can have in a single index. You can have at most 64 secondary indexes on a table. In practice, if you are getting close to this limit, you can probably benefit from rethinking your indexing strategy. As it will be discussed in "What Are the Drawbacks of Indexes?" later in this chapter, there are overheads associated with indexes, so in all cases it is best to limit the number of indexes to those really benefitting queries. Similarly, the more parts you add to an index, the larger the index becomes. The InnoDB limit is that you can at most add 16 parts.

What do you do if you need to add an index to a table or remove a superfluous index? Indexes can be created together with the table or later, and it is also possible to drop indexes as discussed next.

SQL Syntax

When you first create your schema, you will in general have some ideas which indexes to add. Then as time passes, your monitoring may determine that some indexes are no longer needed but others should be added instead. These changes to indexes may be due to a misconception of the required indexes; the data may have changed, or the queries may have changed.

There are three distinct operations when it comes to changing the indexes on a table: creating indexes when the table itself is created, adding indexes to an existing table, or removing indexes from a table. The index definition is the same whether you add the index together with the table or as a following action. When dropping an index, you just need the index name.

This section will show the general syntax for adding and removing indexes. Throughout the rest of the chapter, there will be further examples based on the specific index types and features.

Creating Tables with Indexes

When you create a table, you can add the index definition to the CREATE TABLE statement. The indexes are defined right after the columns. You can optionally specify the name of the index; if you do not, the index will be named after the first column in the index.

Listing 14-2 shows an example of a table where several indexes are created. Do not worry if you do not know what all the index types are doing – that will be discussed later in the chapter.

Listing 14-2. Example of creating a table with indexes

```
CREATE TABLE db1.person (
  Id int unsigned NOT NULL,
  Name varchar(50),
  Birthdate date NOT NULL,
  Location point NOT NULL SRID 4326,
  Description text,
  PRIMARY KEY (Id),
  INDEX (Name),
  SPATIAL INDEX (Location),
  FULLTEXT INDEX (Description)
);
```

This creates the table person with four indexes in the db1 schema (which must exist beforehand). The first is a primary key which is a B-tree index (more about that shortly) on the Id column. The second is also a B-tree index, but it is a so-called secondary index and indexes the Name column. The third index is a spatial index on the Location column. The fourth is a full text index on the Description column.

You can also create an index that includes more than a single column. This is useful if you need to put conditions on more than one column, put a condition on the first column and sort by the second, and so on. To create a multicolumn index, specify the column names as a comma-separated list:

```
INDEX (Name, Birthdate)
```

The order of the columns is very important as it will be explained in "Index Strategies." In short, MySQL will only be able to use the index from the left, that is, the Birthdate part of the index can only be used if Name is also used. That means that the index (Name, Birthdate) is not the same index as (Birthdate, Name).

The indexes on a table will not in general remain static, so what do you do if you want to add an index to an existing table?

Adding Indexes

You can add indexes to an existing table, if you determine that is needed. To do this, you need to use the ALTER TABLE or CREATE INDEX statement. Since ALTER TABLE can be used for all modifications of the table, you may want to stick to that; however, the work made is the same with either statement.

Listing 14-3 shows two examples of how to create indexes using ALTER TABLE. The first example adds a single index; the second adds two indexes on one statement.

Listing 14-3. Adding indexes using ALTER TABLE

```
ALTER TABLE db1.person
  ADD INDEX (Birthdate);

ALTER TABLE db1.person
  DROP INDEX Birthdate;

ALTER TABLE db1.person
  ADD INDEX (Name, Birthdate),
  ADD INDEX (Birthdate);
```

The first and last ALTER TABLE statements use the ADD INDEX clause to tell MySQL that an index should be added to the table. The third statement adds two such clauses separated by a comma to add both indexes in one statement. In between, the index is dropped as it is bad practice to have duplicate indexes, and MySQL will also warn against it.

Does it make a difference if you use two statements to add two indexes or add both indexes with one statement? Yes, there can potentially be a big difference. When an index is added, it is necessary to perform a full table scan to read all the values needed for the index. A full table scan is an expensive operation for a large table, so in that sense, it is better to add both indexes in one statement. On the other hand, it is considerably faster to create the index as long as the index can be kept fully in the InnoDB buffer pool. Splitting the creation of the two indexes into two statements can reduce the pressure on the buffer pool and thus improve the index creation performance.

The last action is to remove indexes that are no longer needed.

Removing Indexes

The act of removing an index is similar to adding one. You can use the ALTER TABLE or DROP INDEX statement. When you use ALTER TABLE, you can combine dropping an index with other data definition manipulations of the table.

When you drop an index, you will need to know the name of the index. There are several ways to do this as shown in Listing 14-4.

Listing 14-4. Find the index names for a table

```
mysql> SHOW CREATE TABLE db1.person\G
*************************** 1. row ***************************
       Table: person
Create Table: CREATE TABLE `person` (
  `Id` int(10) unsigned NOT NULL,
  `Name` varchar(50) DEFAULT NULL,
  `Birthdate` date NOT NULL,
  `Location` point NOT NULL /*!80003 SRID 4326 */,
  `Description` text,
  PRIMARY KEY (`Id`),
  KEY `Name` (`Name`),
  SPATIAL KEY `Location` (`Location`),
  KEY `Name_2` (`Name`,`Birthdate`),
  KEY `Birthdate` (`Birthdate`),
  FULLTEXT KEY `Description` (`Description`)
) ENGINE=InnoDB DEFAULT CHARSET=utf8mb4 COLLATE=utf8mb4_0900_ai_ci
1 row in set (0.0010 sec)
```

```
mysql> SELECT INDEX_NAME, INDEX_TYPE,
              GROUP_CONCAT(COLUMN_NAME
                          ORDER BY SEQ_IN_INDEX) AS Columns
         FROM information_schema.STATISTICS
        WHERE TABLE_SCHEMA = 'db1'
          AND TABLE_NAME = 'person'
        GROUP BY INDEX_NAME, INDEX_TYPE;
+-------------+------------+-----------------+
| INDEX_NAME  | INDEX_TYPE | Columns         |
+-------------+------------+-----------------+
| Birthdate   | BTREE      | Birthdate       |
| Description | FULLTEXT   | Description     |
| Location    | SPATIAL    | Location        |
| Name        | BTREE      | Name            |
| Name_2      | BTREE      | Name,Birthdate  |
| PRIMARY     | BTREE      | Id              |
+-------------+------------+-----------------+
6 rows in set (0.0013 sec)
```

The indexes may be listed in a different order in your case. The first query uses the SHOW CREATE TABLE statement to get the full table definition which also includes the indexes and their names. The second query queries the information_schema. STATISTICS view. This view is very useful to obtain information about indexes and will be discussed in detail in the next chapter. Once you have decided which index you want to drop, you can use ALTER TABLE as shown in Listing 14-5.

Listing 14-5. Dropping an index using ATLER TABLE

```
ALTER TABLE db1.person DROP INDEX name_2;
```

This drops the index named name_2 – that is, the index on the (Name, Birthdate) columns.

The rest of this chapter will cover various details of what indexes are, and at the end of the chapter, the section "Index Strategies" discusses how to choose which data to index. First, it is important to understand why indexes have overhead.

What Are the Drawbacks of Indexes?

Very few things in life come for free – indexes are no exception. While indexes are great for improving query performance, they also need to be stored and kept up to date. Additionally, a less obvious overhead is when you execute a query, the more indexes you have, the more work the optimizer needs to do. This section will go through these three drawbacks of indexes.

Storage

One of the most obvious costs of adding an index is that the index needs to be stored, so it is readily available when it is needed. You do not want to first create the index each time it is needed as that would kill the performance benefit of the index.[1] The storage overhead is twofold: the index is stored on disk to persist it, and it requires memory in the InnoDB buffer pool for queries to use it.

The disk storage means that you may need to add disks or block storage to your system. If you use a backup solution such as MySQL Enterprise Backup (MEB) that copies the raw tablespace files, your backups will also become larger and take longer to complete.

InnoDB always uses its buffer pool to read the data needed for a query. If the data does not already exist in the buffer pool, it is first read into it and then used for the query. So, when you use an index, both the index and the row data will in general be read into the buffer pool (one exception is when covering indexes are used). The more you need to fit into the buffer pool, the less room there is for other indexes and data – unless you make the buffer pool larger. It is of course more complex than that as avoiding a full table scan also prevents reading the whole table into the buffer pool which relieves the pressure on the buffer pool. The overall benefit versus overhead comes back to how much of the table you avoid examining by using the index and whether other queries anyway read the data the index otherwise avoids accessing.

All in all, you will need extra disk as you add indexes, and in general you will need a larger InnoDB buffer pool to keep the same buffer pool hit rate. Another overhead is that an index is only useful if it is kept up to date. That adds work when you update the data.

---

[1] Actually, there are cases where MySQL will auto-generate indexes specific to a single query. More about this later when discussing index features.

Updating the Index

Whenever you make changes to your data, the indexes will have to be updated. This ranges from adding or removing links to rows as data is inserted or deleted to modifying the index as values are updated. You may not think much of this, but it can be a significant overhead. In fact, during bulk data loads such as restoring a logical backup (a file that typically includes SQL statements for creating the data, e.g., created with the `mysqlpump` program), the overhead of keeping the indexes updated is often what limits the insert rate.

Tip   The overhead of keeping indexes up to date can be so high that it is generally recommended to remove the secondary indexes while doing a large import into an empty table and then recreate the indexes when the import has completed.

For InnoDB, the overhead also depends on whether the secondary indexes fit into the buffer pool or not. As long as the whole index is in the buffer pool, it is relatively cheap to keep the index up to date, and it is not very likely to become a severe bottleneck. If the index does not fit, InnoDB will have to keep shuffling the pages between the tablespace files and the buffer pool which is when the overhead becomes a major bottleneck causing severe performance problems.

There is one less obvious performance overhead as well. The more indexes, the more work for the optimizer to determine the optimal query plan.

The Optimizer

When the optimizer analyzes a query to determine what it believes is the optimal query execution plan, it needs to evaluate the indexes on each table to determine if the index should be used and possibly whether to do an index merge of two indexes. The goal is of course to have the query evaluate as quickly as possible. However, the time spent in the optimizer is in general non-negligible and in some cases can even become a bottleneck.

Consider an example of a really simple query, selecting some rows from a single table:

```
SELECT ID, Name, District, Population
  FROM world.city
 WHERE CountryCode = 'AUS';
```

In this case, if there are no indexes on the table city, it is clear that a table scan is required. If there is one index, it is also necessary to evaluate the query cost using the index, and so forth. If you have a complex query involving many tables each with a dozen possible indexes, it will make for so many combinations that it will be reflected in the query execution time.

Tip   If the time spent in the optimizer becomes a problem, you can add optimizer and join order hints as discussed in Chapters 17 and 24 to help the optimizer, so it does not need to evaluate all possible query plans.

While these pages describing the overhead of adding indexes can make it sound like indexes are bad, do not avoid indexes. An index that has a great selectivity for queries that are executed frequently will be a great benefit. However, do not add indexes for the sake of adding indexes. It will be discussed at the end of the chapter in the section "Index Strategies" what some ideas to choosing indexes are, and there will also be examples in the rest of the book where indexes are discussed. Before getting that far, it is worth discussing the various index types supported by MySQL as well as other index features.

Index Types

The optimal type of index is not the same for all uses. An index optimized to find rows in a given range of values, for example, all dates in the year 2019, needs to be vastly different from an index that searches a large amount of text for a given word or phrase. This means that when you choose to add an index, you must decide which index type is needed. MySQL currently supports five different index types:

- B-tree indexes

- Full text indexes

- Spatial indexes (R-tree indexes)

- Multi-valued indexes

- Hash indexes

This section will go through these five index types and discuss what type of questions they can be used to speed up.

B-Tree Indexes

B-tree indexes are by far the most commonly used index type in MySQL. In fact, all InnoDB tables include at least one B-tree index as the data is organized in a B-tree index (the clustered index).

A B-tree index is an ordered index, so it is good at finding rows where you are looking for a column that is equal to some value, where a column is greater than or less than a given value, or where the column is between two values. This makes it a very useful index for many queries.

Another good feature of B-tree indexes is that they have predictable performance. As the name suggests, the index is organized as a tree starting with the root page and finishing with the leaf pages. InnoDB uses an extension of the B-tree index which is called B+-tree. The + means that the nodes at the same level are linked, so it is easy to scan the index without the need to go back up to the parent node when reaching the last record in a node.

Note   In MySQL the terms B-tree and B+-tree are used interchangeably.

An example of the index tree for an index with city names can be seen in Figure 14-1. (The figure is oriented left to right for the index levels which is different from the top-to-bottom orientation by some other illustrations of B-tree indexes. This is done largely because of space reasons.)

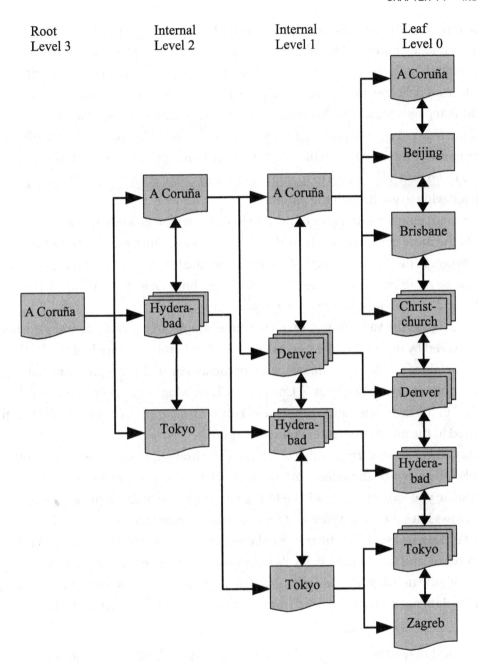

Figure 14-1. *Example of a B+-tree index*

In the figure, the document shapes represent an InnoDB page, and the shapes with multiple documents stacked on top of each other (e.g., the one in Level 0 labeled "Christchurch") represent several pages. The arrows going from the left to the right go from the root page toward the leaf pages. The root page is where the index search starts, and the leaf pages are where the index records exist. Pages in between are typically called internal pages or branch pages. Pages may also be called nodes. The double arrows connecting the pages at the same level are what distinguishes a B-tree and a B+-tree index and allow InnoDB to quickly move to the previous or next sibling page without having to go through the parent.

For small indexes, there may only be a single page serving both as the root and leaf page. In the more general case, the index has a root page illustrated in the leftmost part of the figure. In the rightmost part of the figure are the leaf pages. For large indexes, there may also be more levels in between. The leaf nodes have Level 0, their parent pages Level 1, and so forth until the root page is reached.

In the figure, the value noted for a page, for example, "A Coruña," denotes the first value covered by that part of the tree. So, if you are at Level 1 and are looking for the value "Adelaide," you know it will be in the topmost page of the leaf pages as that page contains the values starting with "A Coruña" and finishing with the last value earlier than "Beijing" in the order the values are sorted. This is an example of where the collation discussed in the previous chapter comes into play.

A key feature is that irrespective of which of the branches you traverse, the number of levels will always be the same. For example, in the figure, that means no matter which value you look for, there will be four pages read, one for each of the four levels (if several rows have the same value and for range scans, more pages in the leaf level may be read). Thus, it is said that the tree is balanced. It is this feature that gives predictable performance, and the number of levels scales well – that is, the number of levels grows slowly with the number of index records. That is a property that is particularly important when the data needs to be accessed from relatively slow storage such as disks.

Note   You may have heard of T-tree indexes as well. While B-tree indexes are optimized for disk access, T-tree indexes are similar to B-tree indexes except they are optimized for in-memory access. Therefore, the `NDBCluster` storage engine which stores all indexed data in memory uses T-tree indexes even when they at the SQL level are called B-tree indexes.

In the beginning of this section, it was stated that B-tree indexes are by far the most commonly used index type in MySQL. In fact, if you have any InnoDB tables, even if you never added any indexes yourself, you are using B-tree indexes. InnoDB stores the data index organized – using the clustered index – which really just means the rows are stored in a B+-tree index. B-tree indexes are also not just used in relational databases, for example, several file systems organize their metadata in a B-tree structure.

One property of B-tree indexes that is important to be aware of is that they can only be used for comparing the whole value of the indexed column(s) or a left prefix. This means that if you want to check if the month of an indexed date is May, the index cannot be used. This is the same if you want to check whether an indexed string contains a given phrase.

When you include multiple columns in an index, the same principle applies. Consider the index (`Name, Birthdate`): in this case, you can use the index to search for a given name or a combination of a name and a birthday. However, you cannot use the index to search for a person with a given birthdate without knowing the name.

There are several ways to handle this limitation. In some cases, you can use functional indexes, or you can extract information about the column into a generated column that you can index. In other cases, another index type can be used. As discussed next, a full text index can, for example, be used to search for columns with the phrase "query performance tuning" somewhere in the string.

Full Text Indexes

Full text indexes are specialized at answering questions such as "Which document contains this string?" That is, they are not optimized to find rows where a column exactly matches a string – for that, a B-tree index is a better choice.

A full text index works by tokenizing the text that is being indexed. Exactly how this is done depends on the parser used. InnoDB supports using a custom parser, but typically the built-in parser is used. The default parser assumes the text uses whitespace as the word separator. MySQL includes two alternative parsers: the ngram parser[2] which supports Chinese, Japanese, and Korean and the MeCab parser which supports Japanese.

---

[2]https://dev.mysql.com/doc/refman/en/fulltext-search-ngram.html

InnoDB links the full text index to the rows using a special column named
FTS_DOC_ID which is a bigint unsigned NOT NULL column. If you add a full text index
and the column does not already exist, InnoDB will add it as a hidden column. Adding
the hidden column requires a table rebuild, so you need to take that into consideration if
you are adding a full text index to a large table. If you know that you intend to use full text
indexes for a table, you can add the column yourself up front together with the unique
index FTS_DOC_ID_INDEX for the column. You can also choose to use the FTS_DOC_ID
column as your primary key, but be aware that FTS_DOC_ID values are not allowed to be
reused. An example of preparing the table yourself is as follows:

```
DROP TABLE IF EXISTS db1.person;

CREATE TABLE db1.person (
  FTS_DOC_ID bigint unsigned NOT NULL auto_increment,
  Name varchar(50),
  Description text,
  PRIMARY KEY (FTS_DOC_ID),
  FULLTEXT INDEX (Description)
);
```

If you do not have the FTS_DOC_ID column and you add a full text column to an existing
table, MySQL will return a warning to tell the table has been rebuilt to add the column:

```
Warning (code 124): InnoDB rebuilding table to add column FTS_DOC_ID
```

If you are planning to use full text indexes, it is recommended from a performance
perspective to explicitly add the FTS_DOC_ID column and either set it as the primary
key on the table or create a secondary unique index for it. The downside of creating the
column yourself is that you must manage the values yourself.

Another specialized index type is for spatial data. Where full text indexes are for text
documents (or strings), spatial indexes are for spatial data types.

Spatial Indexes (R-Tree)

Historically, spatial features have not been used much in MySQL. However, with support
for spatial indexes in InnoDB in version 5.7 and additional improvements such as
support for specifying a Spatial Reference System Identifier (SRID) for spatial data in
MySQL 8, chances are that you may need spatial indexes at some point.

A typical use case for spatial indexes is a table with points of interest with the location of each point stored together with the rest of the information. The user may, for example, ask to get all electrical vehicle charging stations within 50 kilometers of their current location. To answer such a question as efficiently as possible, you will need a spatial index.

MySQL implements spatial indexes as R-trees. The R stands for rectangle and hints at the usage of the index. An R-tree index organizes the data such that points that are close in space are stored close to each other in the index. This is what makes it effective to determine whether a spatial value fulfills some boundary condition (e.g., a rectangle).

Spatial indexes can only be used if the column is declared NOT NULL and the Spatial Reference System Identifier has been set. The spatial condition is specified using one of the functions such as MBRContains() which takes two spatial values and returns whether the first value contains the other. Otherwise, there are no special requirements for using spatial indexes. Listing 14-6 shows an example of a table with a spatial index and a query that can use the index.

Listing 14-6. Using a spatial index

```
mysql> CREATE TABLE db1.city (
          id int unsigned NOT NULL,
          Name varchar(50) NOT NULL,
          Location point SRID 4326 NOT NULL,
          PRIMARY KEY (id),
          SPATIAL INDEX (Location));
Query OK, 0 rows affected (0.5578 sec)

mysql> INSERT INTO db1.city
          VALUES (1, 'Sydney',
                  ST_GeomFromText('Point(-33.8650 151.2094)',
                                  4326));
Query OK, 1 row affected (0.0783 sec)

mysql> SET @boundary = ST_GeomFromText('Polygon((-9 112, -45 112, -45 160,
-9 160, -9 112))', 4326);
Query OK, 0 rows affected (0.0004 sec)
```

```
mysql> SELECT id, Name
          FROM db1.city
          WHERE MBRContains(@boundary, Location);
+----+--------+
| id | Name   |
+----+--------+
|  1 | Sydney |
+----+--------+
1 row in set (0.0006 sec)
```

In the example, a table with city locations has a spatial index on the `Location` column. The Spatial Reference System Identifier (SRID) is set to 4326 to represent Earth. For this example, a single row is inserted, and a boundary is defined (if you are curious, then the boundary contains Australia). You can also specify the polygon directly in the `MBRContains()` function, but here it is done in two steps to make the parts of the query stand out clearer.

So spatial indexes help to answer if some geometrical shape is within some boundary. Similarly, a multi-valued index can help answer whether a given value is in a list of values.

Multi-valued Indexes

MySQL introduced support for the JSON data type in MySQL 5.7 and extended the feature with the MySQL Document Store in MySQL 8. You can use indexes on generated columns or functional indexes to create indexes on JSON documents; however, a use case that is not covered by the index types discussed thus far is to search for documents where a JSON array includes some value. An example is a collection of cities, and for each city there is an array of suburbs. The example JSON document from the previous chapter had just that:

```
{
    "name": "Sydney",
    "demographics": {
        "population": 5500000
    },
```

```
    "geography": {
        "country": "Australia",
        "state": "NSW"
    },
    "suburbs": [
        "The Rocks",
        "Surry Hills",
        "Paramatta"
    ]
}
```

If you want to search all of the cities in your city collection and return those cities that have a suburb called "Surry Hills," then you need a multi-valued index. MySQL 8.0.17 has added support for multi-valued indexes.

The easiest way to explain how multi-valued indexes are useful is to look at an example. Listing 14-7 takes the `countryinfo` table from the `world_x` example database, copies it to the `mvalue_index` table, and modifies it so each JSON document includes an array of cities with their population and the district they are located in. Finally, a query is included to show an example of retrieving all the city names for Australia (`_id = 'AUS'`). The queries are also available in the file `listing_14_7.sql` from this book's GitHub repository and can be executed in MySQL Shell using the command `\source listing_14_7.sql`.

Listing 14-7. Preparing the mvalue_index table for multi-valued indexes

```
mysql> \use world_x
Default schema set to `world_x`.
Fetching table and column names from `world_x` for auto-completion...
Press ^C to stop.

mysql> DROP TABLE IF EXISTS mvalue_index;
Query OK, 0 rows affected, 1 warning (0.0509 sec)
Note (code 1051): Unknown table 'world_x.mvalue_index'

mysql> CREATE TABLE mvalue_index LIKE countryinfo;
Query OK, 0 rows affected (0.3419 sec)
```

```
mysql> INSERT INTO mvalue_index (doc)
       SELECT doc
         FROM countryinfo;
Query OK, 239 rows affected (0.5781 sec)

Records: 239  Duplicates: 0  Warnings: 0

mysql> UPDATE mvalue_index
          SET doc = JSON_INSERT(
                  doc,
                  '$.cities',
                  (SELECT JSON_ARRAYAGG(
                          JSON_OBJECT(
                              'district', district,
                              'name', name,
                              'population',
                                  Info->'$.Population'
                          )
                      )
                     FROM city
                    WHERE CountryCode = mvalue_index.doc->>'$.Code'
                  )
              );
Query OK, 239 rows affected (3.6697 sec)

Rows matched: 239  Changed: 239  Warnings: 0

mysql> SELECT JSON_PRETTY(doc->>'$.cities[*].name')
          FROM mvalue_index
         WHERE doc->>'$.Code' = 'AUS'\G
*************************** 1. row ***************************
JSON_PRETTY(doc->>'$.cities[*].name'): [
  "Sydney",
  "Melbourne",
  "Brisbane",
  "Perth",
```

```
    "Adelaide",
    "Canberra",
    "Gold Coast",
    "Newcastle",
    "Central Coast",
    "Wollongong",
    "Hobart",
    "Geelong",
    "Townsville",
    "Cairns"
]
1 row in set (0.0022 sec)
```

The listing starts out making the world_x schema the default, then drops the mvalue_index table if it exists, and creates it again using the same definition as for the countryinfo table and with the same data. You can also modify the countryinfo table directly, but by working on the mvalue_index copy, you can easily reset the world_x schema by dropping the mvalue_index table. The table consists of a JSON document column named doc and a generated column named _id which is the primary key:

```
mysql> SHOW CREATE TABLE mvalue_index\G
*************************** 1. row ***************************
       Table: mvalue_index
Create Table: CREATE TABLE `mvalue_index` (
  `doc` json DEFAULT NULL,
  `_id` varbinary(32) GENERATED ALWAYS AS
  (json_unquote(json_extract(`doc`,_utf8mb4'$._id'))) STORED NOT NULL,
  `_json_schema` json GENERATED ALWAYS AS (_utf8mb4'{"type":"object"}')
  VIRTUAL,
  PRIMARY KEY (`_id`)
) ENGINE=InnoDB DEFAULT CHARSET=utf8mb4 COLLATE=utf8mb4_0900_ai_ci
1 row in set (0.0006 sec)
```

The UPDATE statement uses the JSON_ARRAYAGG() function to create a JSON array with three JSON objects, the district, name, and population, for each country. Finally, a SELECT statement is executed to return the names of the Australian cities.

You can now add a multi-valued index for the city names:

```
ALTER TABLE mvalue_index
  ADD INDEX (((CAST(doc->>'$.cities[*].name'
                    AS char(35) ARRAY))));
```

The index extracts the name object from all elements of the cities array at the root of the doc document. The resulting data is casted to an array of char(35) values. The data type was chosen as the city table where the city names originate from is char(35). In the CAST() function, you use char for both the char and varchar data types.

The new index can be used for WHERE clauses using the MEMBER OF operator and the JSON_CONTAINS() and JSON_OVERLAPS() functions. The MEMBER OF operator asks whether a given value is a member of the array. JSON_CONTAINS() is very similar, but requires a range search compared to a reference search for MEMBER OF. JSON_OVERLAPS() can be used to find documents that contain at least one of several values. Listing 14-8 shows an example of using the operator and each of the functions.

Listing 14-8. Queries taking advantage of a multi-valued index

```
mysql> SELECT doc->>'$.Code' AS Code, doc->>'$.Name'
          FROM mvalue_index
          WHERE 'Sydney' MEMBER OF (doc->'$.cities[*].name');
+------+-----------------+
| Code | doc->>'$.Name' |
+------+-----------------+
| AUS  | Australia       |
+------+-----------------+
1 row in set (0.0032 sec)

mysql> SELECT doc->>'$.Code' AS Code, doc->>'$.Name'
          FROM mvalue_index
          WHERE JSON_CONTAINS(
                  doc->'$.cities[*].name',
                  '"Sydney"'
                );
```

```
+------+----------------+
| Code | doc->>'$.Name' |
+------+----------------+
| AUS  | Australia      |
+------+----------------+
1 row in set (0.0033 sec)

mysql> SELECT doc->>'$.Code' AS Code, doc->>'$.Name'
          FROM mvalue_index
        WHERE JSON_OVERLAPS(
               doc->'$.cities[*].name',
               '["Sydney", "New York"]'
              );
+------+----------------+
| Code | doc->>'$.Name' |
+------+----------------+
| AUS  | Australia      |
| USA  | United States  |
+------+----------------+
2 rows in set (0.0060 sec)
```

The two queries using MEMBER OF and JSON_CONTAINS() both look for countries that have a city named Sydney. The last query using JSON_OVERLAPS() looks for countries that have a city named Sydney or New York or both.

There is one index type left in MySQL: hash indexes.

Hash Indexes

If you want to search for rows where a column is exactly equal to some value, you can use a B-tree index as discussed earlier in the chapter. There is an alternative though: create a hash for each of the column values and use the hash to search for the matching rows. Why would you want to do that? The answer is that it is a very fast way to look up rows.

Hash indexes are not used much in MySQL. A notable exception is the NDBCluster storage engine that uses hash indexes to ensure uniqueness for the primary key and unique indexes and also uses them to provide fast lookups using those indexes. In terms of InnoDB, there is no direct support for hash indexes; however, InnoDB has a feature called adaptive hash indexes which is worth considering a little more.

The adaptive hash index feature works automatically within InnoDB. If InnoDB detects that you are using a secondary index frequently and adaptive hash indexes are enabled, it will build a hash index on the fly of the most frequently used values. The hash index is exclusively stored in the buffer pool and thus is not persisted, when you restart MySQL. If InnoDB detects that the memory can be used better for loading more pages into the buffer pool, it will discard part of the hash index. This is what is meant when it is said that it is an adaptive index: InnoDB will try to adapt it to be optimal for your queries. You can enable or disable the feature using the innodb_adaptive_hash_index option.

In theory, the adaptive hash index is a win-win situation. You get the advantages of having a hash index without the need to consider which columns you need to add it for, and the memory usage is all automatically handled. However, there is an overhead of having it enabled, and not all workloads benefit from it. In fact, for some workloads, the overhead can become so large that there are severe performance issues.

There are two ways to monitor the adaptive hash index: the INNODB_METRICS table in the Information Schema and the InnoDB monitor. The INNODB_METRICS table includes eight metrics for the adaptive hash index with two of them enabled by default. Listing 14-9 shows the eight metrics included in INNODB_METRICS.

Listing 14-9. The metrics for the adaptive hash index in INNODB_METRICS

```
mysql> SELECT NAME, COUNT, STATUS, COMMENT
          FROM information_schema.INNODB_METRICS
          WHERE SUBSYSTEM = 'adaptive_hash_index'\G
*************************** 1. row ***************************
   NAME: adaptive_hash_searches
  COUNT: 10717
 STATUS: enabled
COMMENT: Number of successful searches using Adaptive Hash Index
*************************** 2. row ***************************
   NAME: adaptive_hash_searches_btree
  COUNT: 29515
 STATUS: enabled
COMMENT: Number of searches using B-tree on an index search
```

```
*************************** 3. row ***************************
   NAME: adaptive_hash_pages_added
  COUNT: 0
 STATUS: disabled
COMMENT: Number of index pages on which the Adaptive Hash Index is built
*************************** 4. row ***************************
   NAME: adaptive_hash_pages_removed
  COUNT: 0
 STATUS: disabled
COMMENT: Number of index pages whose corresponding Adaptive Hash Index
entries were removed
*************************** 5. row ***************************
   NAME: adaptive_hash_rows_added
  COUNT: 0
 STATUS: disabled
COMMENT: Number of Adaptive Hash Index rows added
*************************** 6. row ***************************
   NAME: adaptive_hash_rows_removed
  COUNT: 0
 STATUS: disabled
COMMENT: Number of Adaptive Hash Index rows removed
*************************** 7. row ***************************
   NAME: adaptive_hash_rows_deleted_no_hash_entry
  COUNT: 0
 STATUS: disabled
COMMENT: Number of rows deleted that did not have corresponding Adaptive
        Hash Index entries
*************************** 8. row ***************************
   NAME: adaptive_hash_rows_updated
  COUNT: 0
 STATUS: disabled
COMMENT: Number of Adaptive Hash Index rows updated
8 rows in set (0.0015 sec)
```

The number of successful searches using the adaptive hash index (adaptive_hash_searches) and the number of searches completed using the B-tree index (adaptive_hash_searches_btree) are enabled by default. You can use those to determine how often InnoDB resolves queries using the hash index compared to the underlying B-tree index. The other metrics are less often needed and thus disabled by default. That said, if you want to explore the usefulness of the adaptive hash index in more detail, you can safely enable the six metrics.

The other way to monitor the adaptive hash index is to use the InnoDB monitor as shown in Listing 14-10. The data in the output will be different in your case.

Listing 14-10. Using the InnoDB monitor to monitor the adaptive hash index

```
mysql> SHOW ENGINE INNODB STATUS\G
*************************** 1. row ***************************
  Type: InnoDB
  Name:
Status:
=====================================
2019-05-05 17:22:14 0x1a7c INNODB MONITOR OUTPUT
=====================================
Per second averages calculated from the last 16 seconds
-----------------
BACKGROUND THREAD
-----------------
srv_master_thread loops: 52 srv_active, 0 srv_shutdown, 25121 srv_idle
srv_master_thread log flush and writes: 0
----------
SEMAPHORES
----------
OS WAIT ARRAY INFO: reservation count 8
OS WAIT ARRAY INFO: signal count 11
RW-shared spins 12, rounds 12, OS waits 0
RW-excl spins 102, rounds 574, OS waits 8
RW-sx spins 0, rounds 0, OS waits 0
Spin rounds per wait: 1.00 RW-shared, 5.63 RW-excl, 0.00 RW-sx
...
```

```
----------------------------------------
INSERT BUFFER AND ADAPTIVE HASH INDEX
----------------------------------------
Ibuf: size 1, free list len 0, seg size 2, 0 merges
merged operations:
 insert 0, delete mark 0, delete 0
discarded operations:
 insert 0, delete mark 0, delete 0
Hash table size 2267, node heap has 2 buffer(s)
Hash table size 2267, node heap has 1 buffer(s)
Hash table size 2267, node heap has 2 buffer(s)
Hash table size 2267, node heap has 1 buffer(s)
Hash table size 2267, node heap has 1 buffer(s)
Hash table size 2267, node heap has 1 buffer(s)
Hash table size 2267, node heap has 2 buffer(s)
Hash table size 2267, node heap has 3 buffer(s)
0.00 hash searches/s, 0.00 non-hash searches/s
...
```

The first point to check is the semaphores section. If the adaptive hash index is a major source of contention, there will be semaphores around the btr0sea.ic file (where the adaptive hash index is implemented in the source code). If you once in a while – but rarely – see semaphores, it is not necessarily a problem, but if you see frequent and long semaphores, you are likely better off disabling the adaptive hash index.

The other part of interest is the section for the insert buffer and adaptive hash index. This includes the amount of memory used for the hash indexes and the rate queries are answered using hash and non-hash searches. Be aware that these rates are for the period listed near the top of the monitor output – in the example, for the last 16 seconds prior to 2019-05-05 17:22:14.

That concludes the discussion of the supported index types. There is still more to indexes as there are several features that are worth familiarizing yourself with.

Index Features

It is one thing to know which types of indexes exist, but another thing is to be able to get the full advantage of them. For that to happen, you need to know more about the index-related features that are available in MySQL. These range from sorting the values in the index in reverse order to functional indexes and auto-generated indexes. This section will go through these features, so you can use them in your daily work.

Functional Indexes

Thus far, the indexes have been applied directly to the columns. It is the most common way to add indexes, but there are cases where you need to work with derived values. An example is a query that requests all persons with a birthday in May:

```
DROP TABLE IF EXISTS db1.person;

CREATE TABLE db1.person (
  Id int unsigned NOT NULL,
  Name varchar(50),
  Birthdate date NOT NULL,
  PRIMARY KEY (Id)
);
SELECT *
  FROM db1.person
 WHERE MONTH(Birthdate) = 5;
```

If you add an index on the `Birthdate` column, this cannot be used to answer that query as the dates are stored according to their full value and you are not matching against the leftmost part of the column. (On the other hand, searching for all born in 1970 can use a B-tree index on the `Birthdate` column.)

One way to do this is to have a generated column with the derived values. In MySQL 5.7 and later, you can tell MySQL to keep the column up to date automatically, for example:

```
CREATE TABLE db1.person (
  Id int unsigned NOT NULL,
  Name varchar(50) NOT NULL,
  Birthdate date NOT NULL,
```

```
BirthMonth tinyint unsigned
            GENERATED ALWAYS AS (MONTH(Birthdate))
            VIRTUAL NOT NULL,
  PRIMARY KEY (Id),
  INDEX (BirthMonth)
);
```

In MySQL 8.0.13 there is a more direct way to achieve this. You can directly index the result of a function:

```
CREATE TABLE db1.person (
  Id int unsigned NOT NULL,
  Name varchar(50) NOT NULL,
  Birthdate date NOT NULL,
  PRIMARY KEY (Id),
  INDEX ((MONTH(Birthdate)))
);
```

The advantage of using the functional index is that is it more explicit what you want to index, and you do not have the extra BirthMonth column. Otherwise, the two ways of adding functional indexes work the same way.

Prefix Indexes

It is not uncommon for the index part of a table to become larger than the table data itself. This can particularly be the case if you index large string values. There are also limitations on the maximum length of the indexed data for B-tree indexes – 3072 bytes for InnoDB tables using the DYNAMIC or COMPRESSED row format and smaller for other tables. This effectively means you cannot index a text column, not to mention a longtext column. One way to mitigate large string indexes is to only index the first part of the value. That is called a prefix index.

You create a prefix index by specifying the number of characters for strings or number of bytes for binary objects you want to index. If you want to index the first ten characters of the Name column in the city table (from the world database), you can do it like

```
ALTER TABLE world.city ADD INDEX (Name(10));
```

Notice how the number of characters to index has been added in parenthesis. As long as you choose enough characters to give a good selectivity, this index will work almost as good as indexing the whole name, and on the upside, it uses less storage and memory. How many characters do you need to include? That entirely depends on the data you are indexing. You can query the data to get an idea of how unique a prefix is. Listing 14-11 shows an example of examining how many city names share the first ten characters.

Listing 14-11. The frequency of city names based on the first ten characters

```
mysql> SELECT LEFT(Name, 10), COUNT(*),
             COUNT(DISTINCT Name) AS 'Distinct'
         FROM world.city
       GROUP BY LEFT(Name, 10)
       ORDER BY COUNT(*) DESC, LEFT(Name, 10)
       LIMIT 10;
+----------------+----------+----------+
| LEFT(Name, 10) | COUNT(*) | Distinct |
+----------------+----------+----------+
| San Pedro      |        6 |        6 |
| San Fernan     |        5 |        3 |
| San Miguel     |        5 |        3 |
| Santiago d     |        5 |        5 |
| San Felipe     |        4 |        3 |
| San José       |        4 |        1 |
| Santa Cruz     |        4 |        4 |
| São José d     |        4 |        4 |
| Cambridge      |        3 |        1 |
| Ciudad de      |        3 |        3 |
+----------------+----------+----------+
10 rows in set (0.0049 sec)
```

This shows that with this index prefix, you will at most read six cities to find a match. While that is more than a complete match, it is still much better than scanning all the table. In this comparison, you of course also need to verify whether the number of prefix matches is due to prefix collisions, or the city names are the same. For example, for "Cambridge," there are three cities with that name, so whether you index the first ten characters or the whole name makes no difference. You can do this kind of analysis for different prefix lengths to get an idea for the threshold where increasing the size of the index gives a diminutive return. In many cases, you do not need all that many characters for the index to work well.

What do you do if you believe you can delete an index or you want to roll out an index but not let it take effect immediately? The answer is invisible indexes.

Invisible Indexes

MySQL 8 has introduced a new feature called *invisible indexes*. It allows you to have an index that is maintained and ready for use, but the optimizer will ignore the index until you decide to make it visible. This allows you to roll out a new index in a replication topology or to disable an index you believe is not required or similar. You can quickly enable or disable the index as it only requires an update of the metadata for the table, so the change is "instant."

If you, for example, believe an index is not needed, making it invisible first allows you to monitor how the database works without it before telling MySQL to drop the index. Should it turn out that some queries – for example, monthly reporting queries that just had not been executed in the period you monitored – do need the index, you can quickly reenable it.

You mark an index as invisible with the INVISIBLE keyword and make an invisible index visible again with the VISIBLE keyword. For example, to create an index on the Name column of the world.city table as invisible and to make it visible later, you can use

```
mysql> ALTER TABLE world.city ADD INDEX (Name) INVISIBLE;
Query OK, 0 rows affected (0.0649 sec)

Records: 0  Duplicates: 0  Warnings: 0

mysql> ALTER TABLE world.city ALTER INDEX Name VISIBLE;
Query OK, 0 rows affected (0.0131 sec)

Records: 0  Duplicates: 0  Warnings: 0
```

If you disable an index and a query uses an index hint that refers to the hidden index, the query will return an error:

```
ERROR: 1176: Key 'Name' doesn't exist in table 'city'
```

You can override the invisibility of an index by enabling the optimizer switch `use_invisible_indexes` (defaults to `off`). This can be useful if you experience problems because an index has been made invisible and you cannot reenable it immediately or if you want to test with a new index before making it generally available. An example of temporarily enabling invisible indexes for a connection is

```
SET SESSION optimizer_switch = 'use_invisible_indexes=on';
```

Even with the `use_invisible_indexes` optimizer switch enabled, you are not allowed to refer to the index in an index hint.

Another new feature in MySQL 8 is descending indexes.

Descending Indexes

In MySQL 5.7 and older, when you added a B-tree index, it was always sorted in ascending order. This is great for finding exact matches, retrieving rows in ascending order of the index, and so on. However, while ascending indexes can speed up queries looking for rows in descending order, they are not as effective. MySQL 8 added descending indexes to help with those use cases.

There is nothing particular you need to do to take advantage of descending indexes. All that is required is that the `DESC` keyword is used with the index, for example:

```
ALTER TABLE world.city ADD INDEX (Name DESC);
```

If there are multiple columns in the index, the columns do not all need to be included in ascending or descending order. You can mix ascending and descending columns as it works best in your queries.

Partitioning and Indexes

If you create a partitioned table, the partitioning column must be part of the primary key and all unique keys. The reason for this is that MySQL does not have a concept of global indexes, so it must be ensured that uniqueness checks only need to consider a single partition.

With respect to performance tuning, then partitions can be used to effectively use two indexes to resolve a query without using index merging. When the column that is used for partitioning is used in a condition in a query, MySQL will prune the partitions, so only the partitions that can be matched by the condition are searched. Then an index can be used to resolve the rest of the query.

Consider a table t_part that is partitioned according to the Created column which is a timestamp and with one partition per month. If you query for all rows with a value of the val column less than 2 in the month of March 2019, then the query will first prune the partitions on the value of Created and then use the index on val. Listing 14-12 shows an example of this.

Listing 14-12. Combining partition pruning and filtering using an index

```
mysql> CREATE TABLE db1.t_part (
  id int unsigned NOT NULL AUTO_INCREMENT,
  Created timestamp NOT NULL,
  val int unsigned NOT NULL,
  PRIMARY KEY (id, Created),
  INDEX (val)
) ENGINE=InnoDB
  PARTITION BY RANGE (unix_timestamp(Created))
(PARTITION p201901 VALUES LESS THAN (1548939600),
 PARTITION p201902 VALUES LESS THAN (1551358800),
 PARTITION p201903 VALUES LESS THAN (1554037200),
 PARTITION p201904 VALUES LESS THAN (1556632800),
 PARTITION p201905 VALUES LESS THAN (1559311200),
 PARTITION p201906 VALUES LESS THAN (1561903200),
 PARTITION p201907 VALUES LESS THAN (1564581600),
 PARTITION p201908 VALUES LESS THAN (1567260000),
 PARTITION pmax VALUES LESS THAN MAXVALUE);
1 row in set (5.4625 sec)

-- Insert random data
-- 1546261200 is 2019-01-01 00:00:00 UTC
-- The common table expression (CTE) is just
-- a convenient way to quickly generate 1000 rows.
mysql> INSERT INTO db1.t_part (Created, val)
        WITH RECURSIVE counter (i) AS (
          SELECT 1
           UNION SELECT i+1
            FROM counter
           WHERE i < 1000)
```

```
       SELECT FROM_UNIXTIME(
                FLOOR(RAND()*(1567260000-1546261200))
                +1546261200
            ), FLOOR(RAND()*10) FROM counter;
Query OK, 1000 rows affected (0.0238 sec)

Records: 1000  Duplicates: 0  Warnings: 0

mysql> EXPLAIN
       SELECT id, Created, val
         FROM db1.t_part
        WHERE Created BETWEEN '2019-03-01 00:00:00'
                          AND '2019-03-31 23:59:59'
            AND val < 2\G
*************************** 1. row ***************************
           id: 1
  select_type: SIMPLE
        table: t_part
   partitions: p201903
         type: range
possible_keys: val
          key: val
      key_len: 4
          ref: NULL
         rows: 22
     filtered: 11.110000610351562
        Extra: Using where; Using index
1 row in set, 1 warning (0.0005 sec)
```

The t_part table is partitioned by range using the Unix timestamp of the Created column. The EXPLAIN output (EXPLAIN is covered in detail in Chapter 20) shows that only the p201903 partition will be included in the query and that the val index will be used as the index. The exact output of EXPLAIN may differ given the example uses random data.

Thus far, everything that has been discussed about indexes has been for explicitly created indexes. For certain queries, MySQL will also be able to auto-generate indexes. That is the last index feature to discuss.

Auto-generated Indexes

For queries that include subqueries joined to other tables or subqueries, the join can be expensive as subqueries cannot include explicit indexes. To avoid doing full table scans on these temporary tables generated by subqueries, MySQL can add an automatically generated index on the join condition.

As an example, consider the film table from the sakila sample database. It has a column called release_year with the year the film was released. If you want to query how many films were released in each of the years there are data for, you can use the following query (yes, this query can be written better without the subquery, but it is written this way to demonstrate the auto-generated index feature):

```
SELECT release_year, COUNT(*)
  FROM sakila.film
       INNER JOIN (SELECT DISTINCT release_year
                     FROM sakila.film
                  ) release_years USING (release_year)
 GROUP BY release_year;
```

MySQL chooses to do a full table scan on the film table and add an auto-generated index on the subquery. When MySQL adds an auto-generated index, the EXPLAIN output will include <auto_key0> (or 0 replaced with a different value) as the possible key and used key.

Auto-generated indexes can drastically improve the performance of queries that include subqueries that the optimizer cannot rewrite as normal joins. The best of it all is that it happens automatically.

That concludes the discussion of index features. Before discussing how you should use indexes, it is also necessary to understand how InnoDB uses indexes.

InnoDB and Indexes

The way InnoDB has organized its tables since its first versions in the mid-1990s has been to use a clustered index to organize the data. This fact has led to the common saying that everything in InnoDB is an index. The organization of the data is literally an index. By default, InnoDB uses the primary key for the clustered index. If there is no primary key, it will look for a unique index not allowing NULL values. As a last resort, a hidden column will be added to the table using a sort of auto-increment counter.

With index-organized tables, it is true that everything in InnoDB is an index. The clustered index is itself organized as a B+-tree index with the actual row data in the leaf pages. This has some consequences when it comes to query performance and indexes. The next sections will look at how InnoDB uses the primary key and what it means for secondary keys, provide some recommendations, and look at the optimal use cases for index-organized tables.

The Clustered Index

Since the data is organized according to the clustered index (the primary key or substitutes thereof), the choice of primary key is very important. If you insert a new row with a primary key value between existing values, InnoDB will have to reorganize the data to make room for the new row. In the worst case, InnoDB will have to split existing pages into two as the pages are fixed size. Page splits can cause the leaf pages to be out of order on the underlying storage causing more random I/O which in turn leads to worse query performance. Page splits will be discussed as part of the DDL and bulk data loading in Chapter 25.

Secondary Indexes

The leaf pages of a secondary index store the reference to the row itself. Since the row is stored in a B+-tree index according to the clustered index, all secondary indexes must include the value of the clustered index. If you have chosen a column where the values require many bytes, for example, a column with long and potentially multi-byte strings, this greatly adds to the size of the secondary indexes.

It also means that effectively when you perform a lookup using a secondary index, then two index lookups are made: first is the expected secondary key lookup, and then from the leaf page, the primary key value is fetched and used for a primary key lookup to get the actual data.

For nonunique secondary indexes, if you have an explicit primary key or a NOT NULL unique index, it is the columns used for the primary key that are added to the index. MySQL knows about these extra columns even though they have not been explicitly made part of the index, and MySQL will use them if it will improve the query plan.

Recommendations

Because of the way InnoDB uses the primary key and how it is added to the secondary indexes, it is best to use a monotonical incrementing primary key that uses as few bytes as possible. An auto-incrementing integer fulfills these properties and thus makes a good primary key.

The hidden column used for the clustered index if the table does not have any suitable indexes uses an auto-increment–like counter to generate new values. However, as that counter is global for all InnoDB tables in the MySQL instance with a hidden primary key, it can become a contention point. The hidden key also cannot be used in replication to locate the rows that are affected by an event, and Group Replication requires a primary key or NOT NULL unique index for its conflict detection. The recommendation is therefore always to explicitly choose a primary key for all tables.

An UUID on the other hand is not monotonical incrementing and is not a good choice. An option in MySQL 8 is to use the UUID_TO_BIN() function with a second argument set to 1 which will make MySQL swap the first and third groups of hexadecimal digits. The third group is the high field of the timestamp part of the UUID, so bringing that up to the beginning of the UUID helps ensure the IDs keep increasing and storing them as binary data requires less than half the amount of storage compared to hexadecimal values.

Optimal Use Cases

Index-organized tables are particularly useful for queries that use that index. As the name "clustered index" suggests, rows that have similar values for the clustered index are stored near each other. Since InnoDB always reads entire pages into memory, it also means that two rows with similar values for the primary key are likely read in together. If you need both in your query or in queries executed shortly after each other, the second row is already available in the buffer pool.

You should now have a good background knowledge of indexes in MySQL and how InnoDB uses indexes including its organization of data. It is time to put it all together and discuss index strategies.

Index Strategies

The big question when it comes to indexes is what to index and secondly what kind of index and which index features to use. It is not possible to create ultimate step-by-step instructions to ensure the optimal indexes; for that, experience and good understanding of the schema, data, and queries are required. It is however possible to give some general guidelines as it will be discussed in this section.

The first thing to consider is when you should add the indexes; whether you should do it at the time you originally create the table or later. Then there is the choice of primary key and the considerations how to choose it. Finally, there are the secondary indexes including how many columns to add to the index and whether the index can be used as a covering index.

When Should You Add or Remove Indexes?

Index maintenance is a never-ending task. It starts when you first create the table and continues throughout the lifetime of the table. Do not take index work lightly – as mentioned, the difference between great and poor indexing can be several orders of magnitude. You cannot buy yourself out of a situation with poor indexes by pouring more hardware resources at it. Indexes affect not only the raw query performance but also locking (as will be further discussed in Chapter 18), memory usage, and CPU usages.

When you create the table, you should particularly spend time on choosing a good primary key. The primary key will typically not change during the life of the table, and if you do decide to change the primary key, with index-organized tables it will necessarily require a full rebuild of the table. Secondary indexes can to a larger degree be tuned over time. In fact, if you plan on importing a large amount of data for the initial population of the table, it is best to wait to add the secondary indexes until after the data has been loaded. A possible exception is unique indexes as they are required for data validation.

Once the table has been created and populated with its initial data, you need to monitor the usage of the table. There are two views in the sys schema that can be used to find tables and statements with full table scans:

- **schema_tables_with_full_table_scans:** This view shows all tables where rows are read without using an index and ordered in descending order by that number. If a table has a large number of rows read without using an index, you can look for queries using this table and see if indexes can help. The view is based on the `table_io_waits_summary_by_index_usage` Performance Schema table which can also be used directly, for example, if you want to do a more advanced analysis, such as finding the percentage of rows read without using an index.

- **statements_with_full_table_scans:** This view shows the normalized version of the statements that do not use an index at all or do not use a good index. The statements are ordered by the number of times they have been executed without using an index at all and then by the number of times they have not been using a good index – both in descending order. The view is based on the `events_statements_summary_by_digest` Performance Schema table.

Chapters 19 and 20 will cover the use of these views and the underlying Performance Schema tables in more detail.

When you identify that queries can benefit from additional indexes, then you need to evaluate whether the cost of having an extra benefit is worth the gain when executing the query.

At the same time, you also need to keep an eye on whether you have indexes that are no longer used. The Performance Schema and the `sys` schema are particularly useful to find indexes that are unused or not used very much. Three `sys` schema views that are useful are

- **schema_index_statistics:** This view has statistics for how often an index is used to read, insert, update, and delete rows using a given index. Like the `schema_tables_with_full_table_scan` view, `schema_index_statistics` is based on the `table_io_waits_summary_by_index_usage` Performance Schema table.

- **schema_unused_indexes:** This view will return the names of the indexes that have not been used since the data was last reset (no longer than since the last restart). This view is also based on the `table_io_waits_summary_by_index_usage` Performance Schema table.

- **schema_redundant_indexes:** If you have two indexes covering the same columns, you double the amount of effort for InnoDB to keep the indexes up to date and add a burden on the optimizer, but do not gain anything. The schema_redundant_indexes view can as the name suggests be used to find redundant indexes. The view is based on the STATISTICS Information Schema table.

When you use the first two of these views, you must remember that the data comes from in-memory tables in the Performance Schema. If you have some queries that are only executed very occasionally, the statistics may not reflect what your overall index needs are. This is one of the cases where the invisible index feature can come in handy as it allows you to disable the index and at the same time keep the index until you are sure it is safe to drop it. If it turns out some rarely executed queries need the index, you can easily enable the index again.

As mentioned, the first consideration is what to choose as the primary key. Which columns should you include? That is the next thing to discuss.

Choice of the Primary Key

When you work with index-organized tables, the choice of the primary index is very important. The primary key can impact the ratio between random and sequential I/O, the size of secondary indexes, and how many pages need to be read into the buffer pool. The primary key for InnoDB tables is always a B+-tree index.

An optimal primary key with respect to the clustered index is as small (in bytes) as possible, keeps increasing monotonically, and groups the rows you query frequently and within short time of each other. In practice, it may not be possible to fulfill all of this in which case you need to make the best possible compromise. For many workloads, an auto-incrementing unsigned integer, either int or bigint depending on the number of rows that are expected for the table, is a good choice; however, there may be special considerations such as requirements for uniqueness across multiple MySQL instances. The most important feature of the primary key is that it should be as sequential as possible and immutable. If you change the value of the primary key for a row, it requires moving the whole row to the new position in the clustered index.

Tip   An unsigned integer that auto-increments is often a good choice as a primary key. It keeps incrementing monotonically, it does not require much storage, and it groups recent rows together in the clustered index.

You may think that the hidden primary key may be as good a choice for the clustered index as any other column. After all, it is an auto-incrementing integer. However, there are two major drawbacks of the hidden key: it only identifies the row for that local MySQL instance, and the counter is global to all InnoDB tables (in the instance) without a user-defined primary key. That the hidden key is only useful locally means that in replication, the hidden value cannot be used to identify which row to update on replicas. That the counter is global means that it can become a point of contention and cause performance degradation when inserting data.

The bottom line is that you should always explicitly define what you want as your primary key. For secondary indexes, there are more choices as it will be seen next.

Adding Secondary Indexes

Secondary indexes are all those indexes that are not the primary key. They can be either unique or not unique, and you can choose between all the supported index types and features. How do you choose which indexes to add? This section will make it easier for you to make that decision.

Be careful not to add too many indexes to a table up front. Indexes have overhead, so when you add indexes that end up not being used, queries and the system overall will perform worse. This does not mean you should not add any secondary indexes when you create the table. It's just that you need to put some thought into it.

Secondary indexes can be used in several ways when executing queries. Some of these are as follows:

- **Reduce the rows examined:** This is used when you have a WHERE clause or join condition to find the required rows without scanning the whole table.

- **Sort data:** B-tree indexes can be used to read the rows in the order the query needs allowing MySQL to bypass the ordering step.

- **Validate data:** This is what the uniqueness in unique indexes is used for.

- **Avoid reading the row:** Covering indexes can return all the required data without reading the whole row.

- **Find `MIN()` and `MAX()` values:** For `GROUP BY` queries, the minimum and maximum values for an indexed column can be found by just checking the first and last records in the index.

The primary key can obviously also be used for all these purposes. From a query perspective, there is no difference between a primary key and a secondary key.

When you need to decide whether to add an index, you need to ask yourself which of the purposes the index is needed for and whether it will be able to fulfill them. Once you have confirmed that it is the case, you can look at which order columns should be added in for multicolumn indexes and whether additional columns should be added. The next two subsections will discuss this in more detail.

Multicolumn Index

You can add up to 16 columns or functional parts to an index as long as you do not exceed the maximum width of the index. This applies both for the primary key and for secondary indexes. InnoDB has a limit of 3072 bytes per index. If you include strings using variable width character sets, then it is the maximum possible width that counts toward the index width.

An advantage of adding multiple columns to an index is that it allows you to use the index for multiple conditions. This is a very effective way to improve the query performance. Consider, for example, a query looking for cities in a given country with a minimum requirement of the population of the city:

```
SELECT ID, Name, District, Population
  FROM world.city
 WHERE CountryCode = 'AUS'
       AND Population > 1000000;
```

You can use an index on the `CountryCode` column to look for cities with the country code set to AUS, and you can use an index on the `Population` column to look for cities with a population greater than 1 million. Even better, you can combine it into one index that includes both columns.

How you do this is important. The country code uses an equal reference, whereas the population is a range search. Once a column in an index is used for a range search or for sorting, no more columns in the index can be used except as part of a covering index. For this example, you need to add the `CountryCode` column before the `Population` column in order to use the index for both conditions:

```
ALTER TABLE world.city
  ADD INDEX (CountryCode, Population);
```

In this example, the index can even be used to order the result using the population.

If you need to add several columns that all are used for equality conditions, then there are two things to consider: which columns are most often used and how well does the column filter the data. When there are multiple columns in an index, MySQL will only use a left prefix of the index. If you, for example, have an index (`col_a`, `col_b`, `col_c`), you can only use the index to filter on `col_b`, if you also filter on `col_a` (and that must be an equality condition). So you need to choose the order carefully. In some cases, it can be necessary to add more than one index for the same columns where the column order differs between the indexes.

If you cannot decide in which order to include the columns based on the usage, then add them with the most selective column first. The next chapter will discuss selectivity of indexes, but in short, the more distinct values a column has, the more selective it is. By adding the most selective columns first, you will more quickly narrow down the number of rows that the part of the index contains.

You may also want to include columns that are not used for filtering. Why would you want to do that? The answer is that it can help form a covering index.

Covering Indexes

A covering index is an index on a table where the index for a given query includes all columns needed from that table. This means that when InnoDB reaches the leaf page of the index, it has all the information it needs, and it does not need to read the whole row. Depending on your table, this can potentially give a good improvement in query performance, particularly if you can use it to exclude large parts of the row such as large text or blob columns.

You can also use a covering index to simulate a secondary clustered index. Remember that the clustered index is just a B+-tree index with the whole row included in the leaf pages. A covering index has a complete subset of the rows in the leaf pages and thus emulates a clustered index for that subset of columns. Like for a clustered index, any B-tree index groups similar values together, and thus it can be used to reduce the number of pages read into the buffer pool, and it helps doing sequential I/O when you perform an index scan.

There are a couple of limitations for a covering index compared to a clustered index though. A covering index only emulates a clustered index for reads. If you need to write data, the changes always must access the clustered index. Another thing is that due to InnoDB's multi-version concurrency control (MVCC), even when you use a covering index, it is necessary to check the clustered index to verify whether another version of the row exists.

When you add an index, it is worth considering which columns will be needed for the queries the index is intended for. It may be worth adding any extra columns used in the select part even if the index will not be used for filtering or sorting on those columns. You need to balance the benefit of the covering index with the added size of the index. Thus, this strategy is mostly useful if you just miss one or two small columns. The more queries the covering index benefits, the more extra data you can accept adding to the index.

Summary

This chapter has been a journey through the world of indexes. A good indexing strategy can mean the difference of a database coming to a grinding halt and a well-oiled machine. Indexes can help reduce the number of rows examined in queries, and additionally covering indexes can avoid reading the whole row. On the other hand, there are overheads associated with indexes both in terms of storage and ongoing maintenance. It is thus necessary to balance out the need for indexes and the cost of having them.

MySQL supports several different index types. The most important is B-tree indexes which are also what InnoDB uses to organize the rows in its index-organized tables using a clustered index. Other index types include full text indexes, spatial (R-tree) indexes, multi-valued indexes, and hash indexes. The latter type is special in InnoDB as it is only supported using the adaptive hash index feature which decides which hash indexes to add automatically.

There is a range of index features that have been discussed. Functional indexes can be used to index the result of using a column in an expression. Prefix indexes can be used to reduce the size of indexes for text and binary data types. Invisible indexes can be used during a rollout of new indexes or when soft deleting existing indexes. Descending indexes improve the effectiveness of traversing the indexed values in descending order. Indexes also play a role in connection with partitioning, and you can use partitioning to effectively implement support for using two indexes for a single table in a query. Finally, MySQL is able to auto-generate indexes in connection with subqueries.

The final part of the chapter started out with the specifics of InnoDB and the considerations of using index-organized tables. These are optimal for primary key–related queries but work less well for data inserted in random primary key order and querying data by secondary indexes.

The last section discussed indexing strategies. Choose your primary key carefully when you first create the table. Secondary indexes can to a larger extent be added and removed over time based on observations of metrics. You can use multicolumn indexes to use the index to filter on multiple columns and/or for sorting. Finally, covering indexes can be used to emulate secondary clustered indexes.

This concludes the discussion of what indexes are and when to use them. There is a little more to indexes as will be seen in the next chapter when index statistics are discussed.

CHAPTER 15

Index Statistics

In the previous chapter, you learned about indexes. It was mentioned that the optimizer evaluates each index to decide whether to use the index or not. How does it do that? That is largely the topic of this chapter where index statistics, how to view information about the index statistics, and how to maintain the statistics are covered.

The chapter starts out with a discussion of what index statistics are and how InnoDB works with index statistics. Then you will learn about transient and persistent statistics. The rest of the chapter covers how you can monitor the statistics and update them.

What Are Index Statistics?

When MySQL decides whether to use an index or not use it, it boils down to how effective MySQL thinks the index is for the query. Remember that when you use a secondary index, there will effectively be an extra primary key lookup to get to the data. Secondary indexes are also not ordered in the same way as the rows, so using the index will in general mean random I/O (this can be helped using covering indexes). A table scan on the other hand is to a larger degree sequential I/O. So, row for row, doing a table scan is cheaper than finding the same row using a secondary index.

This means that for an index to be effective, it must filter out a large part of the table. Exactly how much must be filtered out depends on the performance characteristics of your hardware, how much of the table is in the buffer pool, the table definition, and more. In the days of the old spinning disks, the rule of thumb used to be that if more than 30% of the rows were needed, then a table scan is preferred. The more of the rows that are in memory and the better the random I/O performance of your disks, the higher this threshold will be.

Note Covering indexes changes this picture as they reduce the amount of random I/O required from jumping to the actual row data.

© Jesper Wisborg Krogh 2020
J. W. Krogh, *MySQL 8 Query Performance Tuning*, https://doi.org/10.1007/978-1-4842-5584-1_15

This is where index statistics come into the picture. The optimizer – which is the part of MySQL that decides which query plan to use – needs some simple way to determine how good an index is for a given query plan. The optimizer obviously knows which columns the index includes, but additionally it needs some measure of how well the index filters the rows. This information is what the index statistics provide. Thus, index statistics are a measure of the selectivity of the index. There are two main statistics: the number of unique values and the number of values in some range.

The number of unique values is what is most often thought of when discussing index statistics. That is known as the *cardinality* of the index. The higher the cardinality, the more unique values. For the primary key and other unique indexes not allowing NULL values, the cardinality is the number of rows in the table as all values must be unique.

The number of rows in a given range is requested by the optimizer on a query-by-query basis. This is useful for range conditions such as WHERE val > 5 as well as IN() conditions or a series of OR conditions. One exception that this information is collected ad hoc for a single query is histograms which MySQL 8 supports. Histograms will be discussed in the next chapter.

In short, index statistics are approximate information about the distribution of data in an index. In MySQL it is the storage engines that are responsible for providing the index statistics. So it is worth looking more into how InnoDB handles index statistics.

InnoDB and Index Statistics

It is the storage engine that provides the index statistics to the server layer and the optimizer. Thus, it is important to understand how InnoDB determines its statistics. InnoDB supports two ways to store the statistics: persistent and transient. Either way, the statistics are determined the same way. This section will start out with a discussion of how the statistics are collected and then go through the specifics of persistent and transient statistics.

How Statistics Are Collected

InnoDB calculates its index statistics by analyzing random leaf pages of the index. It may, for example, be that 20 random index pages are sampled (this is also called 20 index dives), and it is examined which index values those pages consist of. InnoDB then scales this based on the total size of the index.

An important implication of this is that InnoDB index statistics are not exact. When you see that a given query condition means that 100 rows will be read, it is only an estimate based on the samples analyzed. This even includes the primary key and other unique indexes as well as the total number of rows reported in the information_schema. TABLES view. The estimated number of rows in the table is the same as the estimated cardinality of the primary key.

Another consideration is how to handle NULL values as NULL has the property that it does not equal NULL. So, when you collect statistics, should you group all NULL values into one bucket or consider them separate? The optimal solution depends on your queries. Treating all NULL values as different values increases the cardinality of the index, particularly if you have many rows with NULL for the indexed column. This is good for queries looking for non-NULL values. On the other hand, if you treat all NULLs as the same, it reduces the cardinality which makes sense for queries where NULL is included. You can choose how InnoDB should handle NULL values using the innodb_stats_method option. It can take one of three values:

- **nulls_equal:** In this case, all NULL values are considered the same. This is the default. If you are not sure which value to choose, choose nulls_equal.

- **nulls_unequal:** In this case, NULL values are considered different values.

- **nulls_ignored:** In this case, NULL values are ignored when collecting the statistics.

Why are estimates used instead of exact statistics (meaning a full index scan)? The reason is performance. For large indexes, it will take a long time to perform complete index scans. It will in general also include disk I/O which makes the performance issue even worse. To avoid that calculating the index statistics has an adverse effect on the query performance, it has been chosen to limit the scans to a relatively small number of pages.

Sample Pages

The downside of using approximate statistics is that they are not always a good representation of the actual distribution of values. When this happens, the optimizer may choose the wrong index or the wrong join order causing slower than necessary queries. However, it is also possible to adjust the number of random index dives to make. How to do this depends on whether persistent or transient statistics are used:

- Persistent statistics use the innodb_stats_persistent_sample_pages option as the default number of pages to sample. The table option STATS_SAMPLE_PAGES can be used to specify the number of pages for a given table.

- Transient statistics use the number of pages specified by the innodb_stats_transient_sample_pages option for all tables.

The two subsections on persistent and transient statistics have more details for the specifics of the two ways to handle index statistics.

What does it mean to set the number of sample pages to a given value? It depends on the number of columns in the index. If there is just a single column, the value literally means that that number of leaf pages is sampled. However, for multicolumn indexes, the number of pages is per column. If you, for example, set the number of sample pages to 20 and have four columns in an index, a total of 4*20=80 pages are sampled.

Note   In practice, index statistics sampling is more complex than described in this chapter. For example, it is not always necessary to descend all the way to the leaf pages. Consider when two neighboring non-leaf nodes have the same value. Then it can be concluded that all leaf pages of the leftmost (as per the ordering) part have the same value. If you are interested in learning more, a good starting point is the comment at the top of the storage/innobase/ dict/dict0stats.cc file in the source code: https://github.com/mysql/mysql-server/blob/8.0/ storage/innobase/dict/dict0stats.cc.

How many pages must be examined to get a good estimate? That depends on the table. If the data is uniform, that is, roughly the same number of rows per index value, then only a relatively small number of pages need to be examined and the default number of pages is usually enough. On the other hand, if you have data that has a very irregular distribution, you may need to increase the number of pages sampled. An example of data that is very irregular is the status of tasks in a queue. Over time, most tasks will be in a completed status. In the worst case, you may experience that all the random dives see the same status making InnoDB conclude there is only one value and the index is worthless as a filter.

> **Tip** For data with just a few rows with the values used for filtering, histograms as discussed in the next chapter can be very useful to improve the query plan.

The table size is also a factor to consider. The larger the table, in general the more pages must be examined to get a good estimate. The reason is that the larger the table, the more likely entire leaf pages point to rows with the same index value. This lowers the value of each sampled page, so to compensate, it is necessary to sample more pages.

A special case is when InnoDB has been configured to make more index dives than there are leaf pages. In that case, InnoDB examines all the leaf pages and stops at that point. This will give as accurate statistics as possible. If there are no active transactions for the duration of the analysis, the statistics will be exact for that point in time. That includes the number of pages in the table. You will learn how to find the number of leaf pages in the index and table for tables using persistent statistics later in this chapter.

In practice, it is impossible to use exact values. InnoDB supports multi-versioning to allow for high concurrency of transactions even if they involve writes. Since each transaction has its own view of the data, exact statistics would imply each transaction has its own index statistics. That is not feasible, so how does InnoDB handle that? That's the next thing to consider.

Transaction Isolation Level

A related question is what transaction isolation level is used when collecting the statistics. InnoDB supports four isolation levels: read uncommitted, read committed, repeatable read (the default), and serializable. When collecting index statistics, the choice has been made to use read uncommitted. This makes sense as it is a good assumption that most transactions end up being committed or if they fail that they are retried. The statistics are for future queries, so there is little reason to add overhead of maintaining a read view while gathering the statistics.

However, this does have implications for transactions that make large changes to a table. For an extreme (but not unlikely) case, consider a cache table where the data is refreshed by a transaction consisting of two steps:

1. Delete all existing data from the table.

2. Rebuild the table with updated data.

Index statistics are by default updated when "a large part" of the table has changed. (What constitutes "a large part" will be covered in the "Persistent Index Statistics" and "Transient Index Statistics" sections later in the chapter.) This means that when step 1 completes, InnoDB will recalculate the statistics. This is easy – the table is empty, so there are none. If a query executes just at that point, the optimizer will see the table as empty. However, unless the query is executed in the read uncommitted transaction isolation level, the query will still read all the old rows, and it is likely the query plan causes inefficient query execution.

For issues like the one that has just been discussed, you need persistent statistics as there are better configuration options to deal with special cases. Before getting to discuss the details of persistent statistics, it is worth learning how to choose between persistent and transient statistics.

Configuring Statistics Type

As mentioned, there are two ways for InnoDB to store the index statistics. It can either use persistent storage, or it can use transient storage. You can set the default method for tables using the innodb_stats_persistent option. When this is set to 1 or ON (the default), then persistent statistics are used; setting it to 0 or OFF changes the method to transient statistics. You can also configure the method for each table using the STATS_PERSISTENT table option. For example, to enable persistent statistics for the world.city table, you can use ALTER TABLE like

```
ALTER TABLE world.city
    STATS_PERSISTENT = 1;
```

The STATS_PERSISTENT option can also be set when a new table is created using the CREATE TABLE statement. For STATS_PERSISTENT only 0 and 1 can be used as values.

Persistent index statistics have been the default since they got introduced and are also the recommended choice unless you encounter problems that testing shows that transient statistics work around. There are some differences between persistent and transient statistics that are important to understand. These differences are discussed next.

Persistent Index Statistics

Persistent index statistics were introduced in MySQL 5.6 to make query plans more stable than for the older transient index statistics. As the name suggests, with persistent index statistics enabled, then the statistics are saved so they are not lost when MySQL is restarted. There are more differences than the persistence alone though as will become clear.

Other than stable query plans, persistent statistics allow detailed configuration of the number of pages to sample and have good monitoring, and you can even directly query the tables where the statistics are saved. Since monitoring has a large overlap with transient statistics, that is deferred until later in the chapter, so this section will focus on the configuration of persistent statistics and the tables storing the statistics.

Configuration

Persistent statistics can be configured to give a good balance between the cost of collecting statistics and the accuracy of the statistics. Unlike transient statistics, it is possible to configure the behavior both at the global level and per table. The global configuration serves as the default when table-specific options are not set.

There are three global options that are specific to persistent statistics. These are

- **innodb_stats_persistent_sample_pages:** The number of pages to sample. The more pages, the more accurate statistics but also the higher the cost. If the value is larger than the number of leaf pages for an index, the whole index is sampled. The default value is 20.

- **innodb_stats_auto_recalc:** Whether to automatically update the statistics when more than 10% of the rows in the table have been changed. The default is enabled (ON).

- **innodb_stats_include_delete_marked:** Whether to include rows that are marked as deleted but not yet committed in the statistics. This option will be discussed more shortly. The default is disabled (OFF).

The innodb_stats_persistent_sample_pages and innodb_stats_auto_recalc options can also be set per table. This allows you to fine-tune the requirements based on the size, data distribution, and workload associated with specific tables. While micromanaging is not recommended, it can be used to handle cases such as the cache table scenario discussed earlier as well as other tables that cannot be covered by a general default value.

The recommendation is to try to find a good compromise for `innodb_stats_persistent_sample_pages` that gives good enough statistics so the optimizer can determine the best query plan while avoiding excessive scans to calculate the statistics. If you find that your queries perform badly because inaccurate index statistics cause the optimizer to choose an inefficient plan, then you need to increase the number of sampled pages. On the other hand, you can consider decreasing the number of sampled pages, if `ANALYZE TABLE` takes too long. You can then use the table-specific options as described shortly to decrease or increase the number of sampled pages for specific tables as required.

For most tables, it is recommended to enable `innodb_stats_auto_recalc`. This will help ensure the statistics are not outdated due to a large amount of changes. The auto-recalculation occurs in the background, so it does not delay the response to the application that triggered the update. The table will be queued for an index statistics update when more than 10% of the table has changed. To avoid constantly recalculating statistics for small tables, there is also a requirement that there must be at least 10 seconds between each index statistics update.

There are of course exceptions where automatically recalculating the statistics is not desired, for example, if you have a cache table to make reporting queries execute faster and the data in the cache table is completely recreated from time to time but otherwise does not change. In that case, it can be an advantage to disable auto-recalculation of the statistics and explicitly recalculate them when the rebuild is done. Another option is to include delete marked rows in the statistics.

Remember that index statistics are calculated using the read uncommitted transaction isolation level. While this is in most cases what gives the best statistics, there is an exception. When a transaction temporarily completely changes the distribution of data, it can lead to incorrect statistics. A complete rebuild of a table is the most extreme case and where the issue is most often seen. It was for cases like that the `innodb_stats_include_delete_marked` option was introduced. Instead of considering uncommitted deleted rows as deleted, InnoDB will still include them in the statistics. The option only exists as a global option, so it will affect all tables even if you only have one table that suffers from the issue. As mentioned, an alternative is to disable auto-recalculation of statistics for the affected tables and handle it yourself.

> **Tip**   If you have transactions that make large changes to a table such as deleting all rows and then rebuilding the table, consider disabling automatic recalculation of index statistics for the table or enable `innodb_stats_include_delete_marked`.

Thus far, only the global options have been mentioned. How do you change the index statistics settings for a table? As you can use the STATS_PERSISTENT table option to override the global value of `innodb_stats_persistent` for a table, there are options to control how persistent statistics behave for the table. The table options are

- **STATS_AUTO_RECALC:** Overwrites whether automatic recalculation of index statistics is enabled for the table.

- **STATS_SAMPLE_PAGES:** Overwrites the number of pages sampled for the table.

You can set these options either when you create the table using CREATE TABLE or later using ALTER TABLE as it is shown in Listing 15-1.

Listing 15-1. Setting the persistent statistics options for a table

```
mysql> CREATE SCHEMA IF NOT EXISTS chapter_15;
Query OK, 1 row affected (0.4209 sec)

mysql> use chapter_15
Default schema set to `chapter_15`.
Fetching table and column names from `chapter_15` for auto-completion...
Press ^C to stop.

mysql> CREATE TABLE city (
        City_ID int unsigned NOT NULL auto_increment,
        City_Name varchar(40) NOT NULL,
        State_ID int unsigned DEFAULT NULL,
        Country_ID int unsigned NOT NULL,
        PRIMARY KEY (City_ID),
        INDEX (City_Name, State_ID, City_ID)
      ) STATS_AUTO_RECALC = 0,
        STATS_SAMPLE_PAGES = 10;
Query OK, 0 rows affected (0.0637 sec)
```

```
mysql> ALTER TABLE city
              STATS_AUTO_RECALC = 1,
              STATS_SAMPLE_PAGES = 20;
Query OK, 0 rows affected (0.0280 sec)

Records: 0  Duplicates: 0  Warnings: 0
```

First, the table city is created with auto-recalculation disabled and ten sample pages. Then the settings are changed to enable auto-recalculation and increase the number of sample pages to 20. Notice how the ALTER TABLE returns 0 rows affected. Changing the persistent stats options only changes the metadata for the table, so they occur instantly and do not affect the data. This means you can change the settings as needed without worrying about performing an expensive operation. For example, you may want to disable auto-recalculation during bulk operations.

With the opportunities to tune the index statistics, it is important to be able to look into the data collected. There are some general methods for this that will be discussed in the "Monitoring" section after the discussion of transient statistics. However, what makes persistent statistics persistent is that they are stored in tables and those also provide valuable information.

Index Statistics Tables

InnoDB uses two tables in the mysql schema for storing the data related to persistent statistics. These can be useful not only to investigate the statistics and the data that was sampled but also to learn more about the indexes in general.

The table that is most often useful to look at is the innodb_index_stats table. This table has several rows per B-tree index providing information about the number of unique values (the cardinality) for each part of the index, the number of leaf pages in the index, and the total size of the index. Table 15-1 summarizes the columns in the table.

Table 15-1. *The innodb_index_stats table*

Column Name	Data Type	Description
database_name	varchar(64)	The schema where the table with the index is located.
table_name	varchar(199)	The name of the table with the index.
index_name	varchar(64)	The name of the index.
last_update	timestamp	When the index statistics were last updated.
stat_name	varchar(64)	The name of the statistic that the stat_value is for. See also after this table.
stat_value	bigint unsigned	The value for the statistic.
sample_size	bigint unsigned	How many pages that were sampled.
stat_description	varchar(1024)	A description of the statistic. For the cardinalities, it is the columns included in calculating the cardinality.

The primary key consists of the columns database_name, table_name, index_name, and stat_name. The database, table, and index name define which index the statistics are for. The last_update column is useful to see how long time has passed since the statistics were last updated. The stat_name and stat_value are what give you the actual statistics. The sample_size is the number of leaf pages that were examined to determine the statistics. This will be the smaller of the number of leaf pages in the index and the sample pages set for the table. Finally, the stat_description column gives some more information about the statistic. For the cardinalities, the description shows which columns in the index were included and there will be one row per column (an example is provided shortly).

As mentioned, there are several statistics included in the innodb_index_stats table. The name can have one of the following values:

- **n_diff_pfxNN:** The cardinality for the first NN columns in the index. NN is 1-based, so for an index with two columns, n_diff_pfx01 and n_diff_pfx02 exist. For the rows with these statistics, stat_description includes the columns included for the statistic.

- **n_leaf_pages:** The total number of leaf pages in the index. You can compare this to the sample size for the n_diff_pfxNN statistics to determine the fraction of the index that has been sampled.

- **size:** The total number of pages in the index. This includes non-leaf pages.

It can be useful to look at an example to get a better understanding of what this data represents. The world.city table has two indexes: the primary key which is on the ID column and the CountryCode index which is on the CountryCode column. Listing 15-2 shows the statistics for the two indexes. Note that the statistics values may be different if you execute the same query, and if you still have the extra indexes added in Chapter 14, there will be more rows.

Listing 15-2. The innodb_index_stats table for the world.city table

```
mysql> SELECT index_name, stat_name,
              stat_value, sample_size,
              stat_description
         FROM mysql.innodb_index_stats
        WHERE database_name = 'world'
          AND table_name = 'city'\G
*************************** 1. row ***************************
       index_name: CountryCode
        stat_name: n_diff_pfx01
       stat_value: 232
      sample_size: 7
 stat_description: CountryCode
*************************** 2. row ***************************
       index_name: CountryCode
        stat_name: n_diff_pfx02
       stat_value: 4079
      sample_size: 7
 stat_description: CountryCode,ID
```

```
*************************** 3. row ***************************
      index_name: CountryCode
       stat_name: n_leaf_pages
      stat_value: 7
     sample_size: NULL
stat_description: Number of leaf pages in the index
*************************** 4. row ***************************
      index_name: CountryCode
       stat_name: size
      stat_value: 8
     sample_size: NULL
stat_description: Number of pages in the index
*************************** 5. row ***************************
      index_name: PRIMARY
       stat_name: n_diff_pfx01
      stat_value: 4188
     sample_size: 20
stat_description: ID
*************************** 6. row ***************************
      index_name: PRIMARY
       stat_name: n_leaf_pages
      stat_value: 24
     sample_size: NULL
stat_description: Number of leaf pages in the index
*************************** 7. row ***************************
      index_name: PRIMARY
       stat_name: size
      stat_value: 25
     sample_size: NULL
stat_description: Number of pages in the index
7 rows in set (0.0007 sec)
```

Rows 1–4 are for the CountryCode index, whereas rows 5–7 are for the primary key. The first thing to notice is that there are both the n_diff_pfx01 and n_diff_pfx02 statistics for the CountryCode index. How come, considering the index only included one column? Remember that InnoDB uses a clustered index and that nonunique indexes always get the primary key appended since it is anyway needed to locate the actual rows. That is what you see here with n_diff_pfx01 representing the CountryCode column and n_diff_pfx02 the combination of the CountryCode and ID columns.

The CountryCode index is eight pages large, of which seven pages are leaf nodes. That means that the index has two levels with the leaf nodes being level 0 and the root node being level 1. You are encouraged to go back to the discussion in the previous chapter about B-tree indexes and review it while looking at the size statistics for some of the indexes in your tables.

The primary key is simpler as it just consists of one column. Here there are 24 leaf pages, so only a subset of the index has been sampled. (Remember, for the primary key, the index is the table.) A consequence of this is that the statistics are not exact. The n_diff_pfx01 for the primary key predicts 4188 unique values. Since it is the primary key, that is also the estimate for the total number of rows. However, if you look at the statistics for CountryCode, it is predicted that there are 4079 different combinations of the CountryCode and ID values. Since the CountryCode index only has seven leaf pages, all pages have been examined, and the row estimate is exact.

The other table related to persistent statistics is the innodb_table_stats table. It is similar to innodb_index_stats, except that it is aggregate statistics for the whole table that is included. The columns of innodb_table_stats are summarized in Table 15-2.

Table 15-2. *The innodb_table_stats table*

Column Name	Data Type	Description
database_name	varchar(64)	The schema where the table is located.
table_name	varchar(199)	The name of the table.
last_update	timestamp	When the statistics for the table were last updated.
n_rows	bigint unsigned	The estimated number of rows in the table.
clustered_index_size	bigint unsigned	The number of pages in the clustered index.
sum_of_other_index_sizes	bigint unsigned	The total number of pages for secondary indexes.

The primary key consists of the columns database_name and table_name. An important point to note with the table statistics is that they are as approximate as the index statistics. The number of rows in the table is simply the estimated cardinality of the primary key. Similarly, the clustered index size is the same as the size of the primary key from the innodb_index_stats table. The number of secondary index pages is the sum of the size of each of the secondary indexes. Listing 15-3 shows an example of the content of the innodb_table_stats table for the world.city table using the same index statistics as in the previous example.

Listing 15-3. The innodb_table_stats table for the world.city table

```
mysql> SELECT *
         FROM mysql.innodb_table_stats
        WHERE database_name = 'world'
          AND table_name = 'city'\G
*************************** 1. row ***************************
        database_name: world
           table_name: city
          last_update: 2019-05-25 13:51:40
               n_rows: 4188
  clustered_index_size: 25
sum_of_other_index_sizes: 8
1 row in set (0.0005 sec)
```

Tip   The innodb_index_stats and innodb_table_stats are regular tables. It is useful to include the tables in backups, so you can go back and compare the statistics if the query plan suddenly changes.

It is also possible to update the table for users with the UPDATE privilege. This can seem like a very useful property, but be careful. If you do not know the correct statistics, you will end up with very poor query plans. Manually modifying the index statistics should almost never be done. If done, the changes only take effect after flushing the table.

If you feel the discussion of the information that is available in the `innodb_index_stats` and `innodb_table_stats` sounds similar to what you may be used to see with the `SHOW INDEX` statement and the `TABLES` and `STATISTICS` Information Schema tables, then you are right. There is some overlap. Since these sources also apply to transient statistics, discussion of them will be deferred until after the transient index statistics have been covered.

Transient Index Statistics

Transient index statistics is the original method implemented in InnoDB to handle index statistics. As the name suggests, the statistics are not persistent, that is, they do not persist when MySQL is restarted. Instead, the statistics are calculated when the table is first opened (among other times) and kept only in memory. Since the statistics are not persisted, they are less stable, and thus it is more likely to see changes to the query plans.

There are two configuration options to influence the behavior of transient statistics. These are

- **innodb_stats_transient_sample_pages:** The number of pages to sample when updating the index statistics. The default is 8.

- **innodb_stats_on_metadata:** Whether to recalculate the statistics when metadata for the table is queried. The default is `OFF` and has been so since MySQL 5.6.

The `innodb_stats_transient_sample_pages` option is equivalent to `innodb_stats_persistent_sample_pages` except it applies to tables using transient statistics. Tables using transient statistics not only have the statistics recalculated when they are first opened but also when just 6.25% (1/16) of the rows have changed with a requirement that at least 16 updates have occurred. Additionally, transient statistics do not use background threads when the statistics are auto-recalculated, so updates are more likely to impact the performance. For this reason, the default value of `innodb_stats_transient_sample_pages` is just eight pages.

If you want to have the transient index statistics updated more often, you can enable the `innodb_stats_on_metadata` option. When that is enabled, querying the `TABLES` and `STATISTICS` tables in the Information Schema or using their equivalent `SHOW` statements triggers an update of the index statistics. In practice, there is rarely any reason for this, and it is safe to leave the option turned off.

There are no special tables available for transient statistics. There are however the tables and statements that are available for all tables in MySQL.

Monitoring

The index statistics are important for the optimizer to help determine the optimal way to execute a query. Thus, it is also important to know how you can check the index statistics for your tables. It has already been discussed that for persistent statistics there are the `mysql.innodb_index_stats` and `mysql.innodb_table_stats` tables. There are however also general methods, and those are the ones that will be discussed here.

Tip   Remember that the `information_schema_stats_expiry` variable affects how often the data dictionary refreshes its view of the data related to index statistics.

Information Schema STATISTICS View

The main table for getting detailed information about the index statistics is the `STATISTICS` view in the Information Schema. The view not only contains the index statistics themselves but also meta-information about the indexes. In fact, you can recreate the index definitions based on the data in the `STATISTICS` view. This is the view that was used in the previous chapter to look up the index names on a table.

Table 15-3 contains a summary of the columns in the view. You will often only need a subset of the columns, but it is convenient to have access to all the information for the cases when it is needed. The `CARDINALITY` column is the only one affected by the `information_schema_stats_expiry` variable.

Table 15-3. *The STATISTICS Information Schema view*

Column Name	Data Type	Description
TABLE_ CATALOG	varchar(64)	The catalogue the table belongs to. The value will always be def.
TABLE_SCHEMA	varchar(64)	The schema where the table is located.
TABLE_NAME	varchar(64)	The table where the index is located.
NON_UNIQUE	int	Whether the index is unique (0) or not unique (1).
INDEX_SCHEMA	varchar(64)	The same as TABLE_SCHEMA (as indexes are always co-located with the table).
INDEX_NAME	varchar(64)	The name of the index.
SEQ_IN_INDEX	int unsigned	The position in the index the column has. For single-column indexes, this is always 1.
COLUMN_NAME	varchar(64)	The name of the column.
COLLATION	varchar(1)	How the index is sorted. Values can be NULL (not sorted), A (ascending), or D (descending).
CARDINALITY	bigint	The estimate for the number of unique values for the part of the index up and including to the column in the row.
SUB_PART	bigint	For prefix indexes, it is the number of characters or bytes that is indexed. If the whole column is indexed, the value is NULL.
PACKED	binary(0)	For InnoDB tables, this is always NULL.
NULLABLE	varchar(3)	Whether NULL values are allowed. The column will either be an empty string or YES.
INDEX_TYPE	varchar(11)	The index type, for example, BTREE for B-tree indexes.
COMMENT	varchar(8)	Extra information about the index. This is not used for InnoDB tables.
INDEX_COMMENT	varchar(2048)	The comment specified when the index was added.
IS_VISIBLE	varchar(3)	Whether the index is visible (YES) or invisible (NO).
EXPRESSION	longtext	For functional indexes, this column contains the expression used to generate the indexed values. For nonfunctional indexes, the value is always NULL.

The STATISTICS view is not only useful in relation to index statistics but also for the indexes themselves, and it includes information about all indexes irrespective of the index type. You can, for example, use it to find invisible indexes and the expressions used for functional indexes. With respect to index statistics, the most interesting column is CARDINALITY which is the number of unique values estimated to exist in the index.

When you query the STATISTICS view, it is recommended to order the result by the TABLE_SCHEMA, TABLE_NAME, INDEX_NAME, and SEQ_IN_INDEX columns. That will group related rows together, and for multicolumn indexes, the rows will be returned in the order of the columns in the index. Listing 15-4 shows an example for the indexes on the world.countrylanguage table. In this case, ordering is only on the index name and the sequence in the index as the table schema and table name are fixed. As the values are inexact in nature, your result may differ.

Listing 15-4. The STATISTICS view for the world.countrylanguage table

```
mysql> SELECT INDEX_NAME, NON_UNIQUE,
              SEQ_IN_INDEX, COLUMN_NAME,
              CARDINALITY, INDEX_TYPE,
              IS_VISIBLE
         FROM information_schema.STATISTICS
        WHERE TABLE_SCHEMA = 'world'
          AND TABLE_NAME = 'countrylanguage'
        ORDER BY INDEX_NAME, SEQ_IN_INDEX\G
*************************** 1. row ***************************
   INDEX_NAME: CountryCode
   NON_UNIQUE: 1
 SEQ_IN_INDEX: 1
  COLUMN_NAME: CountryCode
  CARDINALITY: 233
   INDEX_TYPE: BTREE
   IS_VISIBLE: YES
*************************** 2. row ***************************
   INDEX_NAME: PRIMARY
   NON_UNIQUE: 0
 SEQ_IN_INDEX: 1
  COLUMN_NAME: CountryCode
```

```
  CARDINALITY: 233
   INDEX_TYPE: BTREE
   IS_VISIBLE: YES
*************************** 3. row ***************************
   INDEX_NAME: PRIMARY
   NON_UNIQUE: 0
SEQ_IN_INDEX: 2
  COLUMN_NAME: Language
  CARDINALITY: 984
   INDEX_TYPE: BTREE
   IS_VISIBLE: YES
3 rows in set (0.0010 sec)
```

The countrylanguage table has two indexes. There is a primary key on the CountryCode and Language columns, and there is a secondary index on the CountryCode alone. Unlike the mysql.innodb_index_stats table where there also was a row for when the primary key was appended to the secondary nonunique index, the STATISTICS view does not include that information.

Note   The secondary index on the CountryCode column alone is redundant as the CountryCode column is the first column in the primary key. This means the primary key could just as well be used as the secondary index. Best practice is to avoid redundant indexes.

You may want to keep a record of the data in the STATISTICS view and compare how the data changes over time. A sudden change may indicate that there is something unexpected happening to the data or that the latest recalculation of the index statistics can lead to different query plans.

Some of the information in the STATISTICS view is also available through the SHOW INDEX statement.

The SHOW INDEX Statement

The SHOW INDEX statement was the original way to obtain information about indexes in MySQL. Today it gets the data from the same source as information_schema. STATISTICS, so you can use either as it works best for you. One major advantage of the

STATISTICS view is that you can choose what information you want and how to order it; with the SHOW INDEX statement, you always get indexes for a single table and ordered with an option to filter based on the available fields.

The columns returned by SHOW INDEX are the same as in the STATISTICS view, except that the table catalogue, table schema, and index schema are omitted. On the other hand, SHOW INDEX optionally takes the EXTENDED keyword which includes information about hidden parts of the indexes. This should not be confused with invisible indexes but is rather additional parts such as the primary key appended to the secondary indexes. The standard and extended outputs have the same information for the rows that are in common.

Listing 15-5 shows an example of the output of SHOW INDEX for the world.city table (the result assumes the indexes from Chapter 14 have been removed). First, the standard output is returned, followed by the extended output. As the extended output is several pages long, it has been abbreviated by removing some of the columns and rows. To see the full output, execute the statement yourself or see the listing_15_5.txt file available from this book's GitHub repository.

Listing 15-5. The SHOW INDEX output for the world.city table

```
mysql> SHOW INDEX FROM world.city\G
*************************** 1. row ***************************
        Table: city
   Non_unique: 0
     Key_name: PRIMARY
 Seq_in_index: 1
  Column_name: ID
    Collation: A
  Cardinality: 4188
     Sub_part: NULL
       Packed: NULL
         Null:
   Index_type: BTREE
      Comment:
Index_comment:
      Visible: YES
   Expression: NULL
```

```
*************************** 2. row ***************************
        Table: city
   Non_unique: 1
     Key_name: CountryCode
 Seq_in_index: 1
  Column_name: CountryCode
    Collation: A
  Cardinality: 232
     Sub_part: NULL
       Packed: NULL
         Null:
   Index_type: BTREE
      Comment:
Index_comment:
      Visible: YES
   Expression: NULL
2 rows in set (0.0013 sec)

mysql> SHOW EXTENDED INDEX FROM world.city\G
*************************** 1. row ***************************
   Non_unique: 0
     Key_name: PRIMARY
 Seq_in_index: 1
  Column_name: ID
  Cardinality: 4188
*************************** 2. row ***************************
   Non_unique: 0
     Key_name: PRIMARY
 Seq_in_index: 2
  Column_name: DB_TRX_ID
  Cardinality: NULL
*************************** 3. row ***************************
   Non_unique: 0
     Key_name: PRIMARY
 Seq_in_index: 3
  Column_name: DB_ROLL_PTR
  Cardinality: NULL
```

```
*************************** 4. row ***************************
    Non_unique: 0
      Key_name: PRIMARY
  Seq_in_index: 4
   Column_name: Name
   Cardinality: NULL
...
*************************** 8. row ***************************
    Non_unique: 1
      Key_name: CountryCode
  Seq_in_index: 1
   Column_name: CountryCode
   Cardinality: 232
*************************** 9. row ***************************
    Non_unique: 1
      Key_name: CountryCode
  Seq_in_index: 2
   Column_name: ID
   Cardinality: NULL
9 rows in set (0.0013 sec)
```

Notice how the column names are not identical to what the STATISTICS view uses. The order of the columns is however the same and the names similar, so it is easy to map the two outputs to each other.

In the extended output, the primary key has two hidden columns internal to InnoDB: DB_TRX_ID which is the 6-byte transaction identifier and DB_ROLL_PTR which is a 7-byte roll pointer pointing to an undo log record written to the rollback segment. These are part of the InnoDB multi-versioning support.[1] After the two internal fields, each of the remaining columns in the table is added. This reflects that InnoDB uses a clustered index for its rows, so the primary key is the row.

For the secondary index on the CountryCode, the primary key now appears as a second part of the index. This is expected and reflects what was also seen in the mysql. innodb_index_stats table.

---

[1]If you are interested in reading more about the InnoDB multi-versioning control, see https:// dev.mysql.com/doc/refman/en/innodb-multi-versioning.html

While the extended output is usually not of great interest when investigating performance issues, it is of value when exploring how InnoDB works.

Another Information Schema view that is useful when working with index statistics is the `INNODB_TABLESTATS` view.

The Information Schema INNODB_TABLESTATS View

The `INNODB_TABLESTATS` view in the Information Schema is a view on top of the InnoDB internal memory structures holding information about the indexes. It does not contain any information that can be used to verify the cardinality and sizes of the indexes that is not included in the tables and views already described. It does however provide some insight into the status of the index statistics and the number of modifications since the table was last analyzed. The view includes information for all InnoDB tables irrespective of whether they use persistent or transient statistics. Table 15-4 summarizes the columns of the `INNODB_TABLESTATS` view.

Table 15-4. *The INNODB_TABLESTATS Information Schema view*

Column Name	Data Type	Description
TABLE_ID	bigint unsigned	The internal InnoDB table ID. You can, for example, use this to look up the table in the INNODB_ TABLES Information Schema view.
NAME	varchar(193)	The table name in the format `<schema>/<table>`, for example, `world/city`.
STATS_INITIALIZED	varchar(193)	Whether the memory structure has been initialized for the table. This is not the same as whether the index statistics exist. Possible values are `Uninitialized` and `Initialized`.
NUM_ROWS	bigint unsigned	The estimated number of rows in the table.
CLUST_INDEX_SIZE	bigint unsigned	The number of pages in the clustered index.
OTHER_INDEX_SIZE	bigint unsigned	The sum of the number of pages for secondary indexes.

(continued)

Table 15-4. (*continued*)

Column Name	Data Type	Description
MODIFIED_COUNTER	bigint unsigned	The number of rows changed using DML statements since the last update of the index statistics.
AUTOINC	bigint unsigned	The value of the auto-increment counter if it exists. For tables without an auto-increment column, the value is 0.
REF_COUNT	int	How many references there are to the metadata. When the reference counter reached zero, InnoDB may evict the data, and the initialized status returns to Uninitialized.

The initialized status can cause confusion. This shows whether the index statistics and related metadata (as exposed in this view) have been loaded into memory. The status always starts out as Uninitialized even if the statistics exist. When some connection or a background thread needs the data, InnoDB loads it into memory, and the status becomes Initialized. Whenever no threads hold a reference to the table, InnoDB is free to evict the information again, and the status becomes Uninitialized. This can, for example, happen when the table is flushed or ANALYZE TABLE is executed for the table.

The modified counter is interesting as it can be used to see how many rows have been changed since the index statistics were last updated. The counter only increases when a DML query affects an index. This means that if you update a non-indexed column and otherwise leave the row as it is, the counter will not increment. The counter is related to the automatic updates that are triggered when a given amount of changes have been made.

Listing 15-6 has an example output from the INNODB_TABLESTATS view for the world.city table. The table ID, number of rows, and reference count may be different, if you execute the same query.

Listing 15-6. The INNODB_TABLESTATS view for the world.city table

```
mysql> SELECT *
         FROM information_schema.INNODB_TABLESTATS
        WHERE NAME = 'world/city'\G
*************************** 1. row ***************************
         TABLE_ID: 1670
             NAME: world/city
STATS_INITIALIZED: Initialized
         NUM_ROWS: 4188
 CLUST_INDEX_SIZE: 25
 OTHER_INDEX_SIZE: 8
 MODIFIED_COUNTER: 0
          AUTOINC: 4080
        REF_COUNT: 2
1 row in set (0.0009 sec)
```

The output shows that the index statistics are up to date as there have been no rows modified since the last analysis. The number of rows and the size of the clustered and secondary indexes are the same as have been found using the mysql.innodb_index_ stats table. These table size–related numbers are also used for the information_ schema.TABLES view and the SHOW TABLE STATUS statement.

The Information Schema TABLES View and SHOW TABLE STATUS

The index statistics collection is also what is used to populate some of the columns in the tables used by the information_schema.TABLES view and the SHOW TABLE STATUS statement. This includes the estimate for the number of rows and the size of the data and indexes.

Table 15-5 shows a summary of the columns in the TABLES view. The SHOW TABLE STATUS statement has the same columns in its output except for the TABLE_CATALOG, TABLE_SCHEMA, TABLE_TYPE, and TABLE_COMMENT columns, and a few columns have slightly different names. The columns marked with an asterisk (*) are affected by the information_schema_stats_expiry variable.

Table 15-5. *The TABLES Information Schema view*

Column Name	Data Type	Description
TABLE_CATALOG	varchar(64)	The catalogue the table belongs to. The value will always be def.
TABLE_SCHEMA	varchar(64)	The schema where the table is located.
TABLE_NAME	varchar(64)	The name of the table.
TABLE_TYPE	enum	What kind of table it is. Possible values are BASE TABLE, VIEW, and SYSTEM VIEW. A base table is created with CREATE TABLE and a view with CREATE VIEW, and system views are views such as the Information Schema views created by MySQL.
ENGINE	varchar(64)	The storage engine used by the table.
VERSION	int	Unused in MySQL 8 as it was related to the .frm files in MySQL 5.7 and earlier. The version value is now hardcoded to 10.
ROW_FORMAT	enum	The row format used for the table. Possible values are Fixed, Dynamic, Compressed, Redundant, Compact, and Paged.
TABLE_ROWS*	bigint unsigned	The estimated number of rows. For InnoDB tables, this comes from the cardinality of the primary key or clustered index.
AVG_ROW_LENGTH*	bigint unsigned	The estimated data length divided with the estimated number of rows.
DATA_LENGTH*	bigint unsigned	The estimated size of the row data. For InnoDB, it is the size of the clustered index, which is found as the number of pages in the clustered index multiplied with the page size.
MAX_DATA_LENGTH*	bigint unsigned	The maximum allowed size of the data length. Not used by InnoDB, so the value is NULL.

(continued)

Table 15-5. (*continued*)

Column Name	Data Type	Description
INDEX_LENGTH*	bigint unsigned	The estimated size of secondary indexes. For InnoDB, this is the sum of pages in non-clustered indexes times the page size.
DATA_FREE*	bigint unsigned	An estimate of the amount of free space in the tablespace the table belongs to. For InnoDB, this is the size of completely free extents minus a safety margin.
AUTO_INCREMENT*	bigint unsigned	The next value for the auto-increment counter for the table.
CREATE_TIME*	timestamp	When the table was created.
UPDATE_TIME*	datetime	When the tablespace file was last updated. For tables in the InnoDB system tablespace, the value is NULL. As data is written to the tablespace asynchronously, the time will not in general reflect the time of the last statement changing the data.
CHECK_TIME*	datetime	When the table was last checked (CHECK TABLE). For partitioned tables, InnoDB always returns NULL.
TABLE_COLLATION	varchar(64)	The default collation used for sorting and comparisons of values for string columns (where it is not explicitly set for the column).
CHECKSUM	bigint	The table checksum. Not used by InnoDB, so the value is NULL.
CREATE_OPTIONS	varchar(256)	Table options, such as STATS_AUTO_RECALC and STATS_SAMPLE_PAGES.
TABLE_COMMENT	text	The comment specified when the table was created.

Of the information available, the number of rows and the size of the data and indexes are the most closely related to the index statistics. The TABLES view is not only useful for querying estimates of the table size, but it can also be used to query which tables have the persistent statistics variables set explicitly. Listing 15-7 shows an example chapter_15.t1 table, populating it with exactly 1 million rows and then querying the content of the TABLES view for the table.

Listing 15-7. The TABLES view for the table chapter_15.t1

```
mysql> CREATE TABLE chapter_15.t1 (
          id int unsigned NOT NULL auto_increment,
          val varchar(36) NOT NULL,
          PRIMARY KEY (id)
       ) STATS_PERSISTENT=1,
         STATS_SAMPLE_PAGES=50,
         STATS_AUTO_RECALC=1;
Query OK, 0 rows affected (0.5385 sec)

mysql> SET SESSION cte_max_recursion_depth = 1000000;
Query OK, 0 rows affected (0.0003 sec)

mysql> START TRANSACTION;
Query OK, 0 rows affected (0.0002 sec)

mysql> INSERT INTO chapter_15.t1 (val)
       WITH RECURSIVE seq (i) AS (
         SELECT 1
          UNION ALL
         SELECT i + 1
           FROM seq WHERE i < 1000000
       )
       SELECT UUID()
         FROM seq;
Query OK, 1000000 rows affected (15.8552 sec)

Records: 1000000  Duplicates: 0  Warnings: 0

mysql> COMMIT;
Query OK, 0 rows affected (0.8306 sec)
```

```
mysql> SELECT *
          FROM information_schema.TABLES
         WHERE TABLE_SCHEMA = 'chapter_15'
           AND TABLE_NAME = 't1'\G
*************************** 1. row ***************************
  TABLE_CATALOG: def
   TABLE_SCHEMA: chapter_15
     TABLE_NAME: t1
     TABLE_TYPE: BASE TABLE
         ENGINE: InnoDB
        VERSION: 10
     ROW_FORMAT: Dynamic
     TABLE_ROWS: 996442
 AVG_ROW_LENGTH: 64
    DATA_LENGTH: 64569344
MAX_DATA_LENGTH: 0
   INDEX_LENGTH: 0
      DATA_FREE: 7340032
 AUTO_INCREMENT: 1048561
    CREATE_TIME: 2019-11-02 11:48:28
    UPDATE_TIME: 2019-11-02 11:49:25
     CHECK_TIME: NULL
TABLE_COLLATION: utf8mb4_0900_ai_ci
       CHECKSUM: NULL
 CREATE_OPTIONS: stats_sample_pages=50 stats_auto_recalc=1 stats_
                 persistent=1
  TABLE_COMMENT:
1 row in set (0.0653 sec)
```

The table is populated with random data using a recursive common table expression to ensure exactly 1 million rows are inserted. For this to work, it is necessary to set cte_max_recursion_depth to 1000000 as otherwise the common table expression will fail with a too high recursion depth.

Notice how the estimated number of rows is only 996442 rows, or around 0.3% less than the actual number of rows. This is within the expected range – differences up to 10% or more are not unusual. The table also has several table options set to explicitly configure that persistent statistics are used for the table with auto-recalculation enabled and 50 sample pages used.

If you prefer to use the SHOW TABLE STATUS statement instead, you can use it without an argument in which case the table status for all tables in the default schema is returned. Alternatively, you can add a LIKE clause to only include a subset of tables. To retrieve the table status for tables in a non-default schema, use a FROM clause to specify the schema name. For example, consider the world schema being the default, and then the following queries will all return the table status for the city table:

```
mysql> use world
mysql> SHOW TABLE STATUS LIKE 'city';
mysql> SHOW TABLE STATUS LIKE 'ci%';
mysql> SHOW TABLE STATUS FROM world LIKE 'city';
```

The two first queries rely on the default schema to know where to look for tables. The third query explicitly looks for the city table in the world schema.

If the index statistics are out of data, how can you update them? That is the last topic to explore before rounding off this chapter.

Updating the Statistics

Up-to-date index statistics are important in order for the optimizer to arrive at the optimal query execution plans. There are two ways for the indexes to update: automatic because there have been enough changes to the table to trigger a recalculation of the statistics and manually triggering an update.

Automatic Updates

The automatic update mechanism has already been discussed to some degree when covering persistent and transient statistics. Table 15-6 summarizes the feature based on the index statistics type.

Table 15-6. *Summary of auto-recalculation of InnoDB index statistics*

Property	Persistent	Transient
Rows changed	10% of table	6.25% of table
Minimum time between updates due to changed rows	10 seconds	16 updates
Other actions triggering changes		First opening of table, optionally when querying table metadata.
Background updates	Yes	No
Configuration	The `innodb_stats_auto_recalc` variable and the `STATS_AUTO_RECALC` table option	None

The summary shows that persistent statistics are in general updated less frequently and have less impact as the automatic updates happen in the background. Persistent statistics also have better configuration options.

It is also possible to manually trigger updates of the index statistics. You can use either the `ANALYZE TABLE` statement or the `mysqlcheck` command-line program as discussed in the next sections.

The ANALYZE TABLE Statement

The `ANALYZE TABLE` statement is convenient to use when you are working in the `mysql` command-line client or MySQL Shell or the update is to be triggered by a stored procedure. The statement can both update index statistics and histograms. The latter will be discussed in the next chapter, so here only updates of index statistics are covered.

There is one argument to `ANALYZE TABLE` which is whether to log the statement to the binary log or not. If you specify either `NO_WRITE_TO_BINLOG` or `LOCAL` between `ANALYZE` and `TABLE`, the statement will only be applied to the local instance and not written to the binary log.

When you execute `ANALYZE TABLE`, it forces a refresh of the index statistics and table cache values that are otherwise subject to the `information_schema_stats_expiry` variable. So, if you force an update of the index statistics, you do not need to change information_schema_stats_expiry to have the information_schema.STATISTICS view and similarly reflect the updated values.

You can optionally specify multiple tables to have their index statistics updated. You achieve this by listing the tables in a comma-separated list. An example of updating the statistics of three tables in the world schema can be seen in Listing 15-8.

Listing 15-8. Analyzing the index statistics for the tables in the world schema

```
mysql> ANALYZE LOCAL TABLE
                world.city, world.country,
                world.countrylanguage\G
*************************** 1. row ***************************
   Table: world.city
      Op: analyze
Msg_type: status
Msg_text: OK
*************************** 2. row ***************************
   Table: world.country
      Op: analyze
Msg_type: status
Msg_text: OK
*************************** 3. row ***************************
   Table: world.countrylanguage
      Op: analyze
Msg_type: status
Msg_text: OK
3 rows in set (0.0248 sec)
```

In the example, the LOCAL keyword is used to avoid logging the statement to the binary log. If you do not specify the schema name together with the table name (e.g., city instead of world.city), MySQL looks for the table in the current default schema.

> **Note**   While it is possible to query the tables concurrently with the ANALYZE TABLE, do be aware that as a last step (after returning to the client), the analyzed tables are flushed (an implicit FLUSH TABLES statement). The table flush can only happen after all queries in progress have completed, so you should not use ANALYZE TABLE (or mysqlcheck) while you have long-running queries.

The ANALYZE TABLE statement is great for ad hoc updates and when you know exactly which tables you want to analyze. It is less useful for analyzing all tables in a given schema or all tables in the instance. For that, mysqlcheck which is discussed next is a better option.

The mysqlcheck Program

The mysqlcheck program is convenient, if you, for example, want to trigger the update from a shell script, through the cron daemon, or Windows Task Scheduler. It can be used not only to update the index statistics on a single table or multiple tables like ANALYZE TABLE, but you can also tell mysqlcheck to update the index statistics on all tables in a schema or all tables in the instance altogether. What mysqlcheck does is to execute ANALYZE TABLE for the tables matching your criteria, so from an index statistics point of view, there is no difference between manually executing ANAYZE TABLE and using mysqlcheck.

> **Note**   The mysqlcheck program can do much more than just analyzing tables to update the index statistics. Only the analyze feature is covered here. To read the full documentation of the mysqlcheck program, see https://dev.mysql.com/doc/refman/en/mysqlcheck.html.

You use the --analyze option to make mysqlcheck update index statistics and the --write-binlog/--skip-write-binlog arguments to tell whether you want the statements logged to the binary log. The default is to log the statements. You will also need to tell how to connect to MySQL; for that you use the standard connection options.

There are three ways to specify which tables to analyze. The default is to analyze one or more tables in the same schema, like for the ANALYZE TABLE statement. If you choose that, you do not need to add any extra options, and the first value specified is interpreted as the schema name and optional arguments as table names. Listing 15-9 shows how to analyze all tables in the world schema in two ways: by explicitly listing the table names and without listing the tables.

Listing 15-9. Using mysqlcheck to analyze all tables in the world schema

```
shell$ mysqlcheck --user=root --password --host=localhost --port=3306
--analyze world city country countrylanguage
Enter password: ********
world.city                OK
world.country             OK
world.countrylanguage     OK

shell$ mysqlcheck --user=root --password --host=localhost --analyze world
Enter password: ********
world.city                OK
world.country             OK
world.countrylanguage     OK
```

In both cases, the output lists the three tables that were analyzed.

If you want to analyze all tables in more than one schema, but still list which schemas to include, you can use the --databases argument. When that is present, all the object names listed on the command line are interpreted as schema names. Listing 15-10 shows an example of analyzing all tables in the sakila and world schemas.

Listing 15-10. Analyze all tables in the sakila and world schemas

```
shell$ mysqlcheck --user=root --password --host=localhost --port=3306
--analyze --databases sakila world
Enter password: ********
sakila.actor              OK
sakila.address            OK
sakila.category           OK
sakila.city               OK
sakila.country            OK
sakila.customer           OK
sakila.film               OK
sakila.film_actor         OK
sakila.film_category      OK
```

```
sakila.film_text           OK
sakila.inventory           OK
sakila.language            OK
sakila.payment             OK
sakila.rental              OK
sakila.staff               OK
sakila.store               OK
world.city                 OK
world.country              OK
world.countrylanguage      OK
```

The final option is to use the --all-databases option to analyze all tables irrespective of the schema they are located in. This will include system tables as well except for the Information Schema and Performance Schema. Listing 15-11 shows an example of using mysqlcheck with --all-databases.

Listing 15-11. Analyzing all tables

```
shell$ mysqlcheck --user=root --password --host=localhost --port=3306
--analyze --all-databases
Enter password: ********
mysql.columns_priv           OK
mysql.component              OK
mysql.db                     OK
mysql.default_roles          OK
mysql.engine_cost            OK
mysql.func                   OK
mysql.general_log
note      : The storage engine for the table doesn't support analyze
mysql.global_grants          OK
mysql.gtid_executed          OK
mysql.help_category          OK
mysql.help_keyword           OK
mysql.help_relation          OK
mysql.help_topic             OK
mysql.innodb_index_stats     OK
```

```
mysql.innodb_table_stats          OK
mysql.password_history            OK
mysql.plugin                      OK
mysql.procs_priv                  OK
mysql.proxies_priv                OK
mysql.role_edges                  OK
mysql.server_cost                 OK
mysql.servers                     OK
mysql.slave_master_info           OK
mysql.slave_relay_log_info        OK
mysql.slave_worker_info           OK
mysql.slow_log
note     : The storage engine for the table doesn't support analyze
mysql.tables_priv                 OK
mysql.time_zone                   OK
mysql.time_zone_leap_second       OK
mysql.time_zone_name              OK
mysql.time_zone_transition        OK
mysql.time_zone_transition_type   OK
mysql.user                        OK
sakila.actor                      OK
sakila.address                    OK
sakila.category                   OK
sakila.city                       OK
sakila.country                    OK
sakila.customer                   OK
sakila.film                       OK
sakila.film_actor                 OK
sakila.film_category              OK
sakila.film_text                  OK
sakila.inventory                  OK
sakila.language                   OK
sakila.payment                    OK
sakila.rental                     OK
sakila.staff                      OK
```

```
sakila.store                      OK
sys.sys_config                    OK
world.city                        OK
world.country                     OK
world.countrylanguage             OK
```

Notice how there are two tables that reply that their storage engine does not support analyze. The mysqlcheck program tries to analyze all tables irrespective of their storage engine, so messages like in the example are expected. The mysql.general_log and mysql.slow_log tables both use the CSV storage engine by default which does not support indexes and thus neither ANALYZE TABLE.

Summary

This chapter picked up where the previous ended by looking at how InnoDB handles index statistics. There are two ways for InnoDB to store the statistics: either persistent in the mysql.innodb_index_stats and mysql.innodb_table_stats tables or transient in memory. Persistent statistics are in general preferred as they give more consistent query plans, allow to sample more pages, update in the background, and can be configured to a larger degree including support for table-level options.

There are several tables, views, and SHOW statements that can be used to investigate and learn about InnoDB indexes and their statistics. Of particular interest is the information_schema.STATISTICS view which has details of all indexes in MySQL. The information_schema.INNODB_TABLESTATS and information_schema.TABLES views, the SHOW INDEX, and the SHOW TABLE STATUS statements were also discussed.

You can update the index statistics in two ways: either using the ANALYZE TABLE statement or the mysqlcheck program. The former is useful from an interactive client or inside a stored procedure, whereas the latter is more useful for shell scripts and to update all tables in one or more schemas. Both methods also force an update of cached values of the table metadata and the index cardinality in the MySQL data dictionary.

When discussing the ANALYZE TABLE statement, it was mentioned that MySQL also supports histograms. These are related to indexes and are the topic of the next chapter.

CHAPTER 16

Histograms

In the previous two chapters, you learned about indexes and index statistics. The purpose of indexes is to reduce the reads required to access the row required for the query and for index statistics to help the optimizer determine the optimal query plan. That is all great, but indexes are not for free and there are cases where indexes are not very effective and do not warrant the overhead, but you still need the optimizer to be aware of the data distribution. That is where histograms can be useful.

This chapter starts out discussing what histograms are and for which workloads histograms are useful. Then the more practical side of working with histograms is covered including adding, maintaining, and inspecting histogram data. Finally, there is an example of a query where the query plan changes as a histogram is added.

What Are Histograms?

The support for histograms is a new feature in MySQL 8. It makes it possible to analyze and store information about the distribution of data in a table. While histograms have some similarity with indexes, they are not the same, and you can have histograms for columns that do not have any index.

When you create a histogram, you tell MySQL to divide the data into buckets. This can be done either by putting one value into each bucket or having values for a roughly equal number of rows in each bucket. The knowledge about the distribution of the data can help the optimizer estimate more accurately how much of the data in the table a given WHERE clause or join condition will filter out. Without this knowledge, the optimizer may, for example, assume a condition returns a third of the table, whereas a histogram may tell that only 5% of the rows match the condition. That knowledge is critical for the optimizer to choose the best query plan.

© Jesper Wisborg Krogh 2020
J. W. Krogh, *MySQL 8 Query Performance Tuning*, https://doi.org/10.1007/978-1-4842-5584-1_16

At the same time, it is important to realize that a histogram is not the same as an index. MySQL cannot use the histogram to reduce the number of rows examined for the table with the histogram compared to the same query plan executing without the histogram. However, by knowing how much of a table will be filtered, the optimizer can do a better job to determine the optimal join order.

One advantage of histograms is that they only have a cost when they are created or updated. Unlike indexes, there are no changes to the histograms when you change the data. You may from time to time recreate the histogram to ensure the statistics are up to date, but there is no overhead for the DML queries. In general, histograms should be compared to index statistics rather than with indexes.

Note   It is important to understand a fundamental difference between indexes and histograms. Indexes can be used to reduce the work required to access the required rows, histograms cannot. When a histogram is used for the query, it does not reduce the number of examined rows directly, but it can help the optimizer to choose a more optimal query plan.

Just like for indexes, you should choose with care which column you add histograms for. So let's discuss which columns should be considered as good candidates.

When Should You Add Histograms?

The important factor for the benefit of adding histograms is that you add them to the right columns. In short, histograms are most beneficial for columns that are not the first column in an index, that has a non-uniform distribution of values, and where you apply conditions to these columns. This may sound like a very limited use case, and indeed histograms are not quite as useful in MySQL as in some other databases. This is because MySQL is efficient in estimating the number of rows in a range for indexed columns and thus histograms are not used together with an index on the same column. Note also that while histograms are particularly useful for columns with a nonuniform data distribution, they can also be useful for a uniform data distribution in cases where it is not worth adding an index.

Tip   Do not add a histogram to a column that is the first column in an index. For columns that appear later in indexes, a histogram can still be of value for queries where the index cannot be used for the column due to the requirement of using a left prefix of the index.

That said, there are still cases where histograms can greatly improve the query performance. A typical use case is a query with one or more joins and some secondary conditions on columns with a nonuniform distribution of the data. In this case, a histogram can help the optimizer determine the optimal join order so as much of the rows are filtered out as early as possible.

Some examples of data with a nonuniform data distribution are status values, categories, time of day, weekday, and price. A status column may have the vast number of rows in a terminal state such as "completed" or "failed" and a few values in a working state. Similarly, a product table may have more products in some categories than others. Time of day and weekday values may not be uniform as certain events are more likely to happen at certain times or days than others. For example, the weekday a ball game occurs may (depending on the sport) be much more likely to occur during a weekend than on a weekday. For the price, you may have most products in a relatively narrow price range, but the minimum and maximum prices are well outside this range. Examples of columns with low selectivity are columns of the enum data type, Boolean values, and other columns with just a few unique values.

One benefit of histograms compared to indexes is that histograms are cheaper than index dives to determine the number of rows in a range, for example, for long IN clauses or many OR conditions. The reason for this is that the histogram statistics are readily available for the optimizer, whereas the index dives to estimate the number of rows in a range are done while determining the query plan and thus repeated for each query.

Tip   For indexed columns, the optimizer will switch from doing the relatively expensive but very accurate index dives to just using the index statistics to estimate the number of matching rows when there are eq_range_index_dive_limit (defaults to 200) or more equality ranges.

You can argue why bother with histograms when you can add an index, but remember it is not without a cost to maintain indexes as data changes. They need to be maintained when you execute DML queries, and they add to the size of the tablespace files. Additionally, statistics for the number of values in a range (including equality range) are calculated on the fly during the optimization stage of executing a query. That is, they are calculated as needed for each query. Histograms on the other hand just store the statistics, and they are only updated when explicitly requested. The histogram statistics are also always readily available for the optimizer.

In summary, the best candidates for histograms are the columns that match the following criteria:

- Has a nonuniform distribution of data or has so many values that the optimizer's rough estimates (discussed in the next chapter) are not good estimates of the selectivity of the data.

- Has a poor selectivity (otherwise an index is likely a better choice).

- Is used to filter the data in the table in either a WHERE clause or a join condition. If you do not filter on the column, the optimizer cannot use the histogram.

- Has a stable distribution of data over time. The histogram statistics are not updated automatically, so if you add a histogram on a column where the distribution of data changes frequently, the histogram statistics are likely to be inaccurate. A prime example where a histogram is a poor choice is a column storing the date and time of an event.

One exception to these rules is if you can use the histogram statistics to replace expensive queries. The histogram statistics can be queried as it will be shown in the "Inspecting Histogram Data" section, so if you only need approximate results for the distribution of data, you may be able to query the histogram statistics instead.

Tip   If you have queries that determine the number of values in a given range and you only need approximate values, then you can consider creating a histogram even if you do not intend to use the histogram to improve the query plans.

Since the histograms store values from the column, it is not allowed to add histograms to encrypted tables. Otherwise, encrypted data can inadvertently end up being written unencrypted to disk. Additionally, there is no support for histograms on temporary tables.

In order to apply histograms in the most optimal way, you need to know a little of the internals of how histograms work, including the supported histogram types.

Histogram Internals

There are a couple of internals around histograms that are necessary to know in order to use them efficiently. The concepts that you should understand are buckets, the cumulative frequency, and the histogram types. This section will go through each of these concepts.

Buckets

When a histogram is created, the values are distributed to buckets. Each bucket may contain one or more distinct values, and for each bucket, MySQL calculates the cumulative frequency. Thus, the concept of a bucket is important as it is tightly related to the accuracy of the histogram statistics.

MySQL supports up to 1024 buckets. The more buckets you have, the less values are in each bucket, and so the more buckets, the more accurate statistics you have for each value. In the best case, you have just one value per bucket, so you know "exactly" (to the extent the statistics are accurate) the number of rows for that value. If you have more than one value per bucket, the number of rows for the range of values is calculated.

It is important to understand in this context what constitutes a distinct value. For strings, only the first 42 characters are considered in the comparison of values, and for binary values the first 42 bytes are considered. If you have long strings or binary values with the same prefix, histograms may not work well for you.

Note   Only the first 42 characters for strings and the first 42 bytes for binary objects are used to determine the values that exist for a histogram.

Values are added in order, so if you order the buckets from left to right and inspect a given bucket, then you know that all buckets to the left have smaller values and all buckets to the right have larger values. The concept of buckets is illustrated in Figure 16-1.

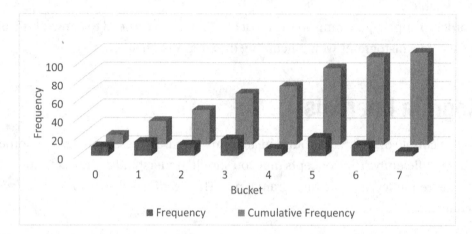

Figure 16-1. *Values distributed into buckets and the cumulative frequency*

In the figure, the dark columns in the front are the frequency of values in each bucket. The frequency is the percentage of the rows having that value. In the background (the brighter-colored columns) is the cumulative frequency which has the same value as the count column for bucket 0 and then increases gradually until it reaches 100 for bucket 7. What are cumulative frequencies? That is the second concept of histograms that you should understand.

Cumulative Frequencies

The cumulative frequency of a bucket is the percentage of rows that is in the current bucket and the previous buckets. If you are looking at bucket number 3 and the cumulative frequency is 50%, then 50% of the rows fit into buckets 0, 1, 2, and 3. This makes it very easy for the optimizer to determine the selectivity of a column with a histogram.

There are two scenarios to consider when the selectivity is calculated: an equality condition and a range condition. For an equality condition, the optimizer determines which bucket the value of the condition is in, then takes the cumulative frequency for that bucket, and subtracts the cumulative frequency of the previous bucket (for bucket 0, nothing is subtracted). If there is just one value in the bucket, that is all that is needed. Otherwise, the optimizer assumes each value in the bucket occurs at the same frequency, so the frequency for the bucket is divided with the number of values in the bucket.

For a range condition, it works in a very similar way. The optimizer finds the bucket where the edge condition is located. For example, for val < 4, the bucket with the value 4 is located. The cumulative frequency used depends on the number of values in the bucket and the condition type. As for equality conditions, for multi-valued buckets, the cumulative frequency is found by assuming an equal distribution of the values in the bucket. Depending on the condition type, the cumulative frequency is used as follows:

- **Less Than:** The cumulative frequency for the previous value is used.

- **Less Than or Equal:** The cumulative frequency of the value in the condition is used.

- **Greater Than or Equal:** The cumulative frequency of the previous value subtracted from 1.

- **Greater Than:** The cumulative frequency of the value in the condition is subtracted from 1.

This means that by using the cumulative frequency, it is at most necessary to consider two buckets to determine how well the condition will filter the rows in the table. It can be useful to look at an example to better understand exactly how the cumulative frequencies work. Table 16-1 shows an example of a histogram with one value per bucket with the cumulative frequency per bucket.

Table 16-1. *Histogram with one value per bucket*

Bucket	Value	Cumulative Frequency
0	0	0.1
1	1	0.25
2	2	0.37
3	3	0.55
4	4	0.63
5	5	0.83
6	6	0.95
7	7	1.0

In this example, the values are the same as the bucket numbers, but that is in general not the case. The cumulative frequency starts out with 0.1 (10%) and increases with the percentage of rows in each bucket until 100% is reached in the last bucket. This distribution is the same as that seen in Figure 16-1.

If you look at the five condition types compared to the value 4, then the number of rows estimated for each type is as follows:

- **val = 4:** The cumulative frequency of bucket 3 is subtracted from the cumulative frequency of bucket 4: estimate = 0.63 - 0.55 = 0.08. So 8% of the rows are estimated to be included.

- **val < 4:** The cumulative frequency of bucket 3 is used, so 55% of the rows are estimated to be included.

- **val <= 4:** The cumulative frequency of bucket 4 is used, so 63% of the rows are estimated to be included.

- **val >= 4:** The cumulative frequency of bucket 3 is subtracted from 1, so 45% of the rows are estimated to be included.

- **val > 4:** The cumulative frequency of bucket 4 is subtracted from 1, so 37% of the rows are estimated to be included.

It becomes a little more complex when more than one value is included in each bucket. Table 16-2 shows the same table and distribution of values, but this time the histogram only has four buckets, so on average there are two values per bucket.

***Table 16-2.** Histogram with more than one value per bucket*

Bucket	Values	Cumulative Frequency
0	0-1	0.25
1	2-3	0.55
2	4-5	0.83
3	6-7	1.0

In this case, there happens to be two values in each bucket, but in general that is not the case (more about that when discussing histogram types). Evaluating the same five conditions now needs to take into account that each bucket includes estimates for the number of rows of more than one value:

- **val = 4:** The cumulative frequency of bucket 1 is subtracted from the cumulative frequency of bucket 2; then the result is divided with the number of values in bucket 2: $estimate = (0.83 - 0.55)/2 = 0.14$. So 14% of the rows are estimated to be included. This is higher than the more accurate estimate with one value per bucket as the frequencies for the values 4 and 5 are considered together.

- **val < 4:** The cumulative frequency of bucket 1 is the only one that is required as buckets 0 and 1 include all values less than 4. Thus, it is estimated that 55% of the rows will be included (this is the same as for the previous example since in both cases the estimate only needs to consider complete buckets).

- **val <= 4:** This is more complex as half the values in bucket 2 are included in the filtering and half are not. So the estimate will be the cumulative frequency for bucket 1 plus the frequency for bucket 2 divided with the number of values in the bucket: $estimate = 0.55 + (0.83 - 0.55)/2 = 0.69$ or 69%. This is higher and less accurate than the estimate using one value per bucket. The reason this estimate is less accurate is that it is assumed that values 4 and 5 have the same frequency.

- **val >= 4:** This condition requires all values in buckets 2 and 3, so the estimate is to include 1 minus the cumulative frequency of bucket 1; that is 45% – the same as the estimate for the case with one value per bucket.

- **val > 4:** This case is similar to val <= 4, just that the values to include are the opposite, so you can take the 0.69 and subtract from 1 which gives 0.31 or 31%. Again, since two buckets are involved, the estimate is not as accurate as for the single value per bucket.

As you have seen, there are two different scenarios when distributing the values into buckets: either there are at least as many buckets as values and each value can be assigned its own bucket or multiple values will have to share a bucket. These are two different types of histograms, and the specifics of those are discussed next.

Histogram Types

There are two types of histograms in MySQL 8. The histogram type is chosen automatically when creating or updating the histogram based on whether there are more values than buckets. The two histogram types are

- **Singleton:** For singleton histograms, there is exactly one value per bucket. These are the most accurate histograms as there is an estimate for every value that exists at the time the histogram is created.

- **Equi-height:** When there are more values for the column than there are buckets, MySQL will distribute the values, so each bucket roughly has the same number of rows – that is, each bucket will be roughly the same height. Since all rows with the same value are distributed to the same bucket, the buckets will not be exactly the same height. For equi-height histograms, there are a different number of values represented for each bucket.

You have already encountered both histogram types when the cumulative frequencies were explored. The singleton histograms are the simplest and most accurate, but equi-height histograms are the most flexible as they can work with any data set.

To demonstrate a singleton and equi-height histogram, you can create the `city_histogram` table from the `world.city` table with a subset of cities based on eight country codes. The table can be created using the following queries:

```
use world

CREATE TABLE city_histogram LIKE city;

INSERT INTO city_histogram
SELECT *
  FROM city
```

```
WHERE CountryCode IN
        ('AUS', 'BRA', 'CHN', 'DEU',
         'FRA', 'GBR', 'IND', 'USA');
```

Figure 16-2 shows an example of a singleton histogram on the CountryCode column. Since there are eight values, the histogram has eight buckets. (You will learn later in the chapter how to create and retrieve the histogram statistics.)

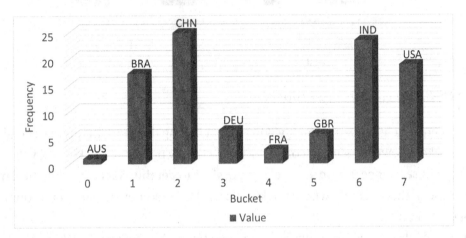

Figure 16-2. *A singleton histogram*

The histogram has exactly one value per bucket. The frequencies range from 1.0% for Australia (AUS) to 24.9% for China (CHN). This is an example where a histogram can greatly help giving more accurate estimates of the filtering if there is no index on the CountryCode column. The original world.city table has 232 distinct CountryCode values, so a singleton histogram works well.

Figure 16-3 shows the equi-height histogram for the same data but with just four buckets for the statistics.

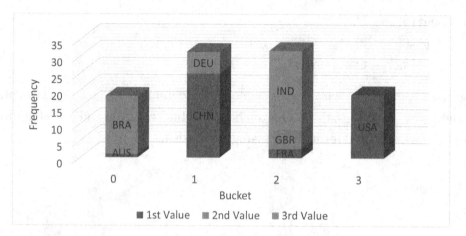

Figure 16-3. *An equi-height histogram*

For an equi-height histogram, MySQL aims at having the same frequency (height) of each bucket. However, since a column value will fully be in one bucket and values are distributed in sequence, it is in general not possible to get the exact same height. This is also the case in this example where buckets 0 and 3 have somewhat smaller frequencies than buckets 1 and 2.

The graph also shows a disadvantage of equi-height histograms. The high frequency of cities in Brazil (BRA), China (CHN), and India (IND) is somewhat masked by the low frequency of the countries they share buckets with. Thus, the accuracy of equi-height histograms is not as great as for singleton histograms. This is particularly the case when the frequencies of the values vary a lot. The reduced accuracy is in general a bigger issue for equality conditions than for range conditions, so equi-height histograms are best suited for columns mainly used for range conditions.

Before you can use the histogram statistics, you will need to create them, and once created you need to maintain the statistics. How to do that is the topic of the next section.

Adding and Maintaining Histograms

Histograms only exist as statistics unlike indexes that have a physical presence in the tablespaces. It is not too surprising then that histograms are created, updated, and dropped using the ANALYZE TABLE statement that is also used to update index statistics. There are two variants of the statement: to update and to drop the statistics. When creating and updating histograms, you also need to be aware of the sampling rate. This section goes through each of these topics.

Create and Update Histograms

You create or update a histogram by adding the UPDATE HISTOGRAM clause to the ANALYZE TABLE statement. If there are no statistics and a request to update is made, then the histogram is created; otherwise, the existing histogram is replaced. You will need to specify how many buckets that you want to divide the statistics into.

To add histograms to the length column of the sakila.film table using at most 256 buckets (length is in minutes, so 256 buckets should be enough to ensure a singleton histogram), you can use a statement like the following example:

```
mysql> ANALYZE TABLE sakila.film
       UPDATE HISTOGRAM ON length
         WITH 256 BUCKETS\G
*************************** 1. row ***************************
   Table: sakila.film
      Op: histogram
Msg_type: status
Msg_text: Histogram statistics created for column 'length'.
1 row in set (0.0057 sec)
```

Optionally, you can add the NO_WRITE_TO_BINLOG or LOCAL keyword between ANALYZE and TABLE to avoid writing the statement to the binary log. This works the same way as when updating index statistics.

Tip   If you do not want to write the ANALYZE TABLE statement to the binary log, add the NO_WRITE_TO_BINLOG or LOCAL keyword, for example, ANALYZE LOCAL TABLE ....

When the ANALYZE TABLE completes the creation of the histogram without error, the Msg_type will be equal to status, and the Msg_text shows that the histogram statistics have been created and for which column. If an error occurs, the Msg_type is equal to Error with Msg_text explaining the issue. For example, if you try to create a histogram for a nonexistent column, the error will look similar to this example:

```
mysql> ANALYZE TABLE sakila.film
       UPDATE HISTOGRAM ON len
         WITH 256 BUCKETS\G
```

```
*************************** 1. row ***************************
   Table: sakila.film
      Op: histogram
Msg_type: Error
Msg_text: The column 'len' does not exist.
1 row in set (0.0004 sec)
```

You can also update the histograms for several columns in the same table using the same statement. For example, if you want to update the histograms on the `length` and `rating` columns of the `sakila.film` table, you can use a statement like the one in Listing 16-1.

Listing 16-1. Updating histograms for multiple columns

```
mysql> ANALYZE TABLE sakila.film
       UPDATE HISTOGRAM ON length, rating
          WITH 256 BUCKETS\G
*************************** 1. row ***************************
   Table: sakila.film
      Op: histogram
Msg_type: status
Msg_text: Histogram statistics created for column 'length'.
*************************** 2. row ***************************
   Table: sakila.film
      Op: histogram
Msg_type: status
Msg_text: Histogram statistics created for column 'rating'.
2 rows in set (0.0119 sec)
```

How many buckets should you choose? If you have fewer than 1024 unique values, it is recommended to have enough buckets to create a singleton histogram (i.e., at least as many buckets as unique values). If you choose more buckets than there are values, MySQL will just use the buckets needed to store the frequencies for each value. In this sense, the number of buckets should be taken as the maximum number of buckets to use.

If there are more than 1024 distinct values, you need enough buckets to get a good representation of the data. Between 25 and 100 buckets is often a good starting point. With 100 buckets, an equi-height histogram will on average have 1% of the rows in each bucket. The more uniform a distribution of the rows, the less buckets are needed, and the larger the difference in distribution, the more buckets are needed. Aim at having the most frequently occurring values in their own bucket. For example, for the subset of the `world.city` table used in the previous section, five buckets place China (CHN), India (IND), and the USA in their own buckets.

The histogram is created by sampling the values. How that is done depends on the amount of memory available.

Sampling

When MySQL creates a histogram, it needs to read the rows to determine the possible values and their frequencies. This is done in a similar but yet different way to sampling for index statistics. When the index statistics are calculated, the number of unique values is determined, which is a simple task as it just requires counting. Thus, all you need to specify is how many pages you want to sample.

For histograms, MySQL must determine not only the number of different values but also their frequency and how to distribute the values into buckets. For this reason, the sampled values are read into memory and then used to create the buckets and calculate the histogram statistics. This means that it is more natural to specify the amount of memory that can be used for the sampling rather than the number of pages. Based on the amount of memory available, MySQL will determine how many pages can be sampled.

Tip   In MySQL 8.0.18 and earlier, a full table scan is always required. In MySQL 8.0.19 and later, InnoDB can directly perform the sampling itself, so it can skip pages that will not be used in the sampling. This makes the sampling much more efficient for large tables. The `sampled_pages_read` and `sampled_pages_skipped` counters in `information_schema.INNODB_METRICS` provide statistics about the sampled and skipped pages for InnoDB.

The memory available during an `ANALYZE TABLE .. UPDATE HISTOGRAM ...` statement is specified with the `histogram_generation_max_mem_size` option. The default is 20,000,000 bytes. The `information_schema.COLUMN_STATISTICS` view that is discussed in the "Inspecting Histogram Data" section includes information about the resulting sampling rate. If you do not get the expected accuracy of the filtering, you can check the sample rate, and if it is low, you can increase the value of histogram_generation_max_ mem_size. The number of pages sampled scales linearly with the amount of memory available, whereas the number of buckets does not have any impact on the sampling rate.

Dropping a Histogram

If you determine that you no longer need a histogram, you can drop it again. Like for updating histogram statistics, you drop the statistics using the ANALYZE TABLE statement using the DROP HISTOGRAM clause. You can drop one or more histograms in one statement. An example of dropping the histograms on the length and rating columns of the sakila.film table is shown in Listing 16-2. The section with examples later in the chapter includes a query that you can use to find all existing histograms.

Listing 16-2. Dropping histograms

```
mysql> ANALYZE TABLE sakila.film
          DROP HISTOGRAM ON length, rating\G
*************************** 1. row ***************************
   Table: sakila.film
      Op: histogram
Msg_type: status
Msg_text: Histogram statistics removed for column 'length'.
*************************** 2. row ***************************
   Table: sakila.film
      Op: histogram
Msg_type: status
Msg_text: Histogram statistics removed for column 'rating'.
2 rows in set (0.0120 sec)
```

The output of the ANALYZE TABLE statement is similar to creating statistics. You can also optionally add the NO_WRITE_TO_BINLOG or LOCAL keyword between ANALYZE and TABLE to avoid writing the statement to the binary log.

Once you have histograms, how do you inspect the statistics and the metadata of them? You can use the Information Schema for this as discussed next.

Inspecting Histogram Data

Knowing what information is available to the optimizer is important when the query plan is not what you expect. Like you have various views for the index statistics, the Information Schema also contains a view, so you can review the histogram statistics. The data is available through the information_schema.COLUMN_STATISTICS view. The next section includes examples of using this view to retrieve information about the histograms.

The COLUMN_STATISTICS view is a view on the part of the data dictionary that contains the histogram information. Table 16-3 summarizes the four columns.

Table 16-3. *The COLUMN_STATISTICS view*

Column Name	Data Type	Description
SCHEMA_NAME	varchar(64)	The schema in which the table is located.
TABLE_NAME	varchar(64)	The table in which the column for the histogram is located.
COLUMN_NAME	varchar(64)	The column with the histogram.
HISTOGRAM	json	The details of the histogram.

The first three columns (SCHEMA_NAME, TABLE_NAME, COLUMN_NAME) form the primary key and allow you to query the histograms you are interested in. The HISTOGRAM column is the most interesting as it stores the metadata for the histogram as well as the histogram statistics.

The histogram information is returned as a JSON document with several objects that include information such as when the statistics were created, the sampling rate, and the statistics themselves. Table 16-4 shows the fields that are included in the document. The fields are listed alphabetically and may be different from the order they are included, when you query the COLUMN_STATISTICS view.

Table 16-4. *The fields in the JSON document for the HISTOGRAM column*

Field Name	JSON Type	Description
buckets	Array	An array with one element per bucket. The information available for each bucket depends on the histogram type and is described later.
collation-id	Integer	The id for the collation of the data. This is only relevant for string data types. The id is the same as the ID column in the INFORMATION_SCHEMA.COLLATIONS view.
data-type	String	The data type of the data in the column the histogram has been created for. This is not a MySQL data type but rather a more generic type such as "string" for string types. Possible values are int, uint (unsigned integer), double, decimal, datetime, and string.
histogram-type	String	The histogram type, either singleton or equi-height.
last-updated	String	When the statistics were last updated. The format is YYYY-mm-dd HH:MM:SS.uuuuuu.
null-values	Decimal	The fraction of the sampled values that is NULL. The value is between 0.0 and 1.0.
number-of-buckets-specified	Integer	The number of buckets requested. For singleton histograms, this may be larger than the actual number of buckets.
sampling-rate	Decimal	The fraction of pages in the table that were sampled. The value is between 0.0 and 1.0. When the value is 1.0, the whole table was read, and the statistics are exact.

The view is not only useful to determine the histogram statistics, but you can also use it to check metadata, for example, to determine how long it has been since the statistics were last updated and use that to ensure the statistics are updated regularly.

The buckets field deserves some more attention as it is where the statistics are stored. It is an array with one element per bucket. The per bucket elements are themselves JSON arrays. For singleton histograms, there are two elements per bucket, whereas for equi-height histograms there are four elements.

The elements that are included for singleton histograms are

- **Index 0:** The column value for the bucket.

- **Index 1:** The cumulative frequency.

The information for equi-height statistics is similar, but there are a total of four elements to account for the fact that each bucket may contain information for more than one column value. The elements are

- **Index 0:** The lower bound of the column values included in the bucket.

- **Index 1:** The upper bound of the column values included in the bucket.

- **Index 2:** The cumulative frequency.

- **Index 3:** The number of values included in the bucket.

If you go back and consider the examples of calculating the expected filtering effect of various conditions, you can see that the bucket information includes everything that is necessary, but also it does not include any extra information.

Since the histogram data is stored as a JSON document, it is worth having a look at a few example queries that retrieve various information.

Histogram Reporting Examples

The COLUMN_STATISTICS view is very useful for querying the histogram data. Since the metadata and statistics are stored in a JSON document, it is useful to consider some of the JSON manipulating functions that are available, so you can retrieve histogram reports. This section will show several examples of generating reports for the histograms you have in your system. All examples are also available from this book's GitHub repository, for example, the query in Listing 16-3 is available in the file listing_16_3.sql.

List All Histograms

A basic report is to list all histograms in your MySQL instance. Some relevant information to include is the schema information for the histogram, the histogram type, when the histogram was last updated, the sampling rate, the number of buckets, and so on. Listing 16-3 shows the query and the output for one histogram (you may see a different list of histograms depending on which histograms you have created).

Listing 16-3. Listing all histograms

```
mysql> SELECT SCHEMA_NAME, TABLE_NAME, COLUMN_NAME,
       HISTOGRAM->>'$."histogram-type"' AS Histogram_Type,
       CAST(HISTOGRAM->>'$."last-updated"'
           AS DATETIME(6)) AS Last_Updated,
       CAST(HISTOGRAM->>'$."sampling-rate"'
           AS DECIMAL(4,2)) AS Sampling_Rate,
       JSON_LENGTH(HISTOGRAM->'$.buckets')
           AS Number_of_Buckets,
       CAST(HISTOGRAM->'$."number-of-buckets-specified"'AS UNSIGNED)
       AS Number_of_Buckets_Specified
   FROM information_schema.COLUMN_STATISTICS\G
*************************** 1. row ***************************
                SCHEMA_NAME: sakila
                 TABLE_NAME: film
                COLUMN_NAME: length
             Histogram_Type: singleton
               Last_Updated: 2019-06-02 08:49:18.261357
              Sampling_Rate: 1.00
          Number_of_Buckets: 140
Number_of_Buckets_Specified: 256
1 row in set (0.0006 sec)
```

The query gives a high-level view of the histograms. The -> operator extracts a value from the JSON document, and the ->> operator additionally unquotes the extracted value which can be useful when extracting strings. From the example output, you can, for example, see that the histogram on the length column in the sakila.film table has 140 buckets but 256 buckets were requested. You can also see it is a singleton histogram, which is not surprising since not all requested buckets were used.

List All Information for a Single Histogram

It can be useful to take a look at the entire output of a histogram. As an example, consider the world.city_histogram table that was created and populated with data for eight countries earlier in the chapter. You can create an equi-height histogram with four buckets on the CountryCode column like

```
ANALYZE TABLE world.city_histogram
 UPDATE HISTOGRAM ON CountryCode
   WITH 4 BUCKETS;
```

Listing 16-4 queries the data for this histogram. This is the same histogram that was used for Figure 16-3 when equi-histograms were discussed.

Listing 16-4. Retrieving all data for a histogram

```
mysql> SELECT JSON_PRETTY(HISTOGRAM) AS Histogram
         FROM information_schema.COLUMN_STATISTICS
        WHERE SCHEMA_NAME = 'world'
              AND TABLE_NAME = 'city_histogram'
              AND COLUMN_NAME = 'CountryCode'\G
*************************** 1. row ***************************
Histogram: {
  "buckets": [
    [
      "base64:type254:QVVT",
      "base64:type254:QlJB",
      0.1813186813186813,
      2
    ],
    [
      "base64:type254:Q0hO",
      "base64:type254:REVV",
      0.4945054945054945,
      2
    ],
    [
      "base64:type254:R1JB",
      "base64:type254:SU5E",
      0.8118131868131868,
      3
    ],
```

```
    [
        "base64:type254:VVNB",
        "base64:type254:VVNB",
        1.0,
        1
    ]
  ],
  "data-type": "string",
  "null-values": 0.0,
  "collation-id": 8,
  "last-updated": "2019-06-03 10:35:42.102590",
  "sampling-rate": 1.0,
  "histogram-type": "equi-height",
  "number-of-buckets-specified": 4
}
1 row in set (0.0006 sec)
```

There are a couple of interesting things for this query. The JSON_PRETTY() function is used to make it easier to read the histogram information. Without the JSON_PRETTY() function, the whole document would be returned as a single line.

Notice also that the lower and upper bounds for each are returned as base64-encoded strings. This is to ensure that any value in string and binary columns can be handled by the histograms. Other data types have their values stored directly.

List Bucket Information for a Singleton Histogram

In the previous example, the raw data for the histogram was queried. It is possible to handle the bucket information nicer by using the JSON_TABLE() function to convert the array into a table output. The table used in the example is city_histogram which is a copy of the world.city table for eight countries to avoid an excessive amount of output. There is a singleton histogram on the CountryCode column:

```
ANALYZE TABLE world.city_histogram
 UPDATE HISTOGRAM ON CountryCode
   WITH 8 BUCKETS;
```

This is the same histogram that was used for the example in Figure 16-2 when singleton histograms were discussed. Listing 16-5 shows an example of doing this for a singleton histogram.

Listing 16-5. Listing the bucket information for a singleton histogram

```
mysql> SELECT (Row_ID - 1) AS Bucket_Number,
              SUBSTRING_INDEX(Bucket_Value, ':', -1) AS
                 Bucket_Value,
              ROUND(Cumulative_Frequency * 100, 2) AS
                 Cumulative_Frequency,
              ROUND((Cumulative_Frequency - LAG(Cumulative_Frequency, 1, 0)
              OVER()) * 100, 2) AS Frequency
          FROM information_schema.COLUMN_STATISTICS
              INNER JOIN JSON_TABLE(
                 histogram->'$.buckets',
                 '$[*]' COLUMNS(
                      Row_ID FOR ORDINALITY,
                      Bucket_Value varchar(42) PATH '$[0]',
                      Cumulative_Frequency double PATH '$[1]'
                 )
              ) buckets
         WHERE SCHEMA_NAME  = 'world'
              AND TABLE_NAME = 'city_histogram'
              AND COLUMN_NAME = 'CountryCode'
         ORDER BY Row_ID\G
*************************** 1. row ***************************
     Bucket_Number: 0
      Bucket_Value: AUS
Cumulative_Frequency: 0.96
         Frequency: 0.96
*************************** 2. row ***************************
     Bucket_Number: 1
      Bucket_Value: BRA
Cumulative_Frequency: 18.13
         Frequency: 17.17
```

```
*************************** 3. row ***************************
      Bucket_Number: 2
       Bucket_Value: CHN
Cumulative_Frequency: 43.06
           Frequency: 24.93
*************************** 4. row ***************************
      Bucket_Number: 3
       Bucket_Value: DEU
Cumulative_Frequency: 49.45
           Frequency: 6.39
*************************** 5. row ***************************
      Bucket_Number: 4
       Bucket_Value: FRA
Cumulative_Frequency: 52.2
           Frequency: 2.75
*************************** 6. row ***************************
      Bucket_Number: 5
       Bucket_Value: GBR
Cumulative_Frequency: 57.76
           Frequency: 5.56
*************************** 7. row ***************************
      Bucket_Number: 6
       Bucket_Value: IND
Cumulative_Frequency: 81.18
           Frequency: 23.42
*************************** 8. row ***************************
      Bucket_Number: 7
       Bucket_Value: USA
Cumulative_Frequency: 100
           Frequency: 18.82
8 rows in set (0.0008 sec)
```

The query joins the COLUMN_STATISTICS view on the JSON_TABLE() function[1] to convert the JSON document into an SQL table. The function takes two arguments, of which the first is the JSON document and the second is the path to the values and a column definition for the resulting table. The column definition includes three columns that are created for each bucket:

- **Row_ID:** This column has a FOR ORDINALITY clause which makes it a 1-based auto-increment counter, so it can be used for the bucket number by subtracting 1.

- **Bucket_Value:** The column value used with the bucket. Notice that the value is returned after it has been decoded from its base64 encoding, so the same query works for strings and numeric values.

- **Cumulative_Frequency:** The cumulative frequency for the bucket as a decimal number between 0.0 and 1.0.

The result of the JSON_TABLE() function can be used in the same way as a derived table. The cumulative frequency is in the SELECT part of the query converted to a percentage, and the LAG() window function[2] is used to calculate the frequency (also as a percentage) for each bucket.

List Bucket Information for an Equi-height Histogram

The query to retrieve the bucket information for an equi-height histogram is very similar to the query just discussed for a singleton histogram. The only difference is that an equi-height histogram has two values (the start and end of the interval) defining the bucket and the number of values in the bucket.

For example, you can create a histogram on the CountryCode column in the world. city_histogram table with four buckets:

```
ANALYZE TABLE world.city_histogram
 UPDATE HISTOGRAM ON CountryCode
   WITH 4 BUCKETS;
```

---

[1]https://dev.mysql.com/doc/refman/en/json-table-functions.html#function_json-table
[2]https://dev.mysql.com/doc/refman/en/window-function-descriptions.html#function_lag

Listing 16-6 shows an example of extracting the bucket information for CountryCode column in the world.city_histogram table with four buckets.

Listing 16-6. Listing the bucket information for an equi-height histogram

```
mysql> SELECT (Row_ID - 1) AS Bucket_Number,
              SUBSTRING_INDEX(Bucket_Value1, ':', -1) AS
                 Bucket_Lower_Value,
              SUBSTRING_INDEX(Bucket_Value2, ':', -1) AS
                 Bucket_Upper_Value,
              ROUND(Cumulative_Frequency * 100, 2) AS
                 Cumulative_Frequency,
              ROUND((Cumulative_Frequency - LAG(Cumulative_Frequency, 1, 0)
              OVER()) * 100, 2) AS Frequency,
              Number_of_Values
         FROM information_schema.COLUMN_STATISTICS
         INNER JOIN JSON_TABLE(
             histogram->'$.buckets',
             '$[*]' COLUMNS(
                 Row_ID FOR ORDINALITY,
                 Bucket_Value1 varchar(42) PATH '$[0]',
                 Bucket_Value2 varchar(42) PATH '$[1]',
                 Cumulative_Frequency double PATH '$[2]',
                 Number_of_Values int unsigned PATH '$[3]'
             )
         ) buckets
        WHERE SCHEMA_NAME  = 'world'
              AND TABLE_NAME = 'city_histogram'
              AND COLUMN_NAME = 'CountryCode'
        ORDER BY Row_ID\G
*************************** 1. row ***************************
      Bucket_Number: 0
  Bucket_Lower_Value: AUS
  Bucket_Upper_Value: BRA
Cumulative_Frequency: 18.13
           Frequency: 18.13
    Number_of_Values: 2
```

```
*************************** 2. row ***************************
      Bucket_Number: 1
 Bucket_Lower_Value: CHN
 Bucket_Upper_Value: DEU
Cumulative_Frequency: 49.45
           Frequency: 31.32
    Number_of_Values: 2
*************************** 3. row ***************************
      Bucket_Number: 2
 Bucket_Lower_Value: FRA
 Bucket_Upper_Value: IND
Cumulative_Frequency: 81.18
           Frequency: 31.73
    Number_of_Values: 3
*************************** 4. row ***************************
      Bucket_Number: 3
 Bucket_Lower_Value: USA
 Bucket_Upper_Value: USA
Cumulative_Frequency: 100
           Frequency: 18.82
    Number_of_Values: 1
4 rows in set (0.0011 sec)
```

Now you have some tools to inspect the histogram data, all that is left is to show an example of how histograms can change a query plan.

Query Example

The main goal of histograms is to help the optimizer to realize the optimal way to execute a query. It can be useful to see an example of how a histogram can influence the optimizer to change the query plan, so to round off this chapter, a query that changes the plan when a histogram is added to one of the columns in the WHERE clause will be discussed.

The query uses the sakila sample database and queries for films that are shorter than 55 minutes and features an actor with the first name Elvis. This may seem like a contrived example, but similar queries are common, for example, to find orders for customers fulfilling some conditions. This example query can be written as follows:

```
SELECT film_id, title, length,
       GROUP_CONCAT(
           CONCAT_WS(' ', first_name, last_name)
       ) AS Actors
  FROM sakila.film
       INNER JOIN sakila.film_actor USING (film_id)
       INNER JOIN sakila.actor USING (actor_id)
 WHERE length < 55 AND first_name = 'Elvis'
 GROUP BY film_id;
```

The film_id, title, and length columns come from the film table and the first_name and last_name columns from the actor table. The GROUP_CONCAT() function is used in case there is more than one actor in the movie that is named Elvis. (An alternative for this query is to use EXISTS(), but this way the full name of the actors with first name Elvis is included in the query result.)

There are no indexes on the length and first_name columns, so the optimizer cannot know how well the conditions on these columns filter. By default, it assumes that the condition on length returns around a third of the rows in the film table and that the condition on first_name returns 10% of the rows. (The next chapter includes where these default filter values come from.)

Figure 16-4 shows the query plan when no histograms exist. The query plan is shown as a *Visual Explain* diagram which will be discussed in Chapter 20.

Tip   You can create a Visual Explain diagram by executing the query in MySQL Workbench and clicking the *Execution Plan* button to the right of the query result.

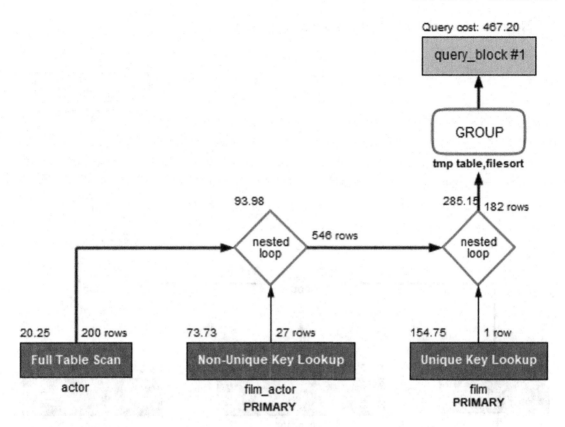

Figure 16-4. *The query plan without a histogram*

The important thing to notice in the query plan is that the optimizer has chosen to start with a full table scan on the actor table, then goes through the film_actor table, and finally joins on the film table. The total query cost (in the upper-right corner of the figure) is calculated as 467.20 (the query cost numbers in the diagram may differ from what you get as they depend on the index – and histogram – statistics).

As mentioned, the optimizer by default estimates that around a third of the films have a length less than 55 minutes. Just given the range of possible values for the length, it suggests this is a poor estimate (but the optimizer does not know anything about movies, so it cannot see that). In fact, only 6.6% of the films have a length in that range. This makes the length column a good candidate for a histogram which you can add like it was previously shown:

```
ANALYZE TABLE sakila.film
 UPDATE HISTOGRAM ON length
   WITH 256 BUCKETS;
```

Now the query plan changes as shown in Figure 16-5.

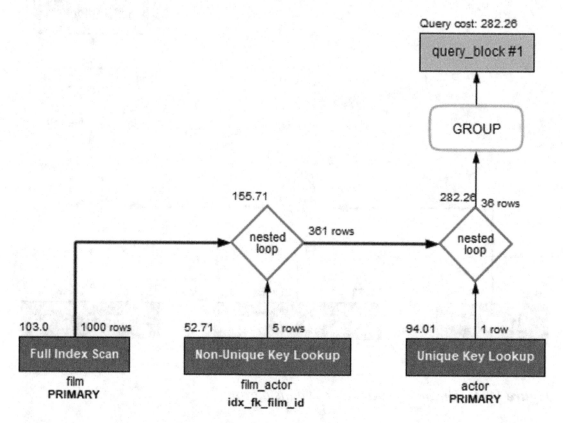

Figure 16-5. *The query plan with a histogram on the* length *column*

The histogram means that now the optimizer knows exactly how many rows will be returned if the film table is scanned first. This reduces the total cost of the query to 282.26 which is a good improvement. (Again, depending on your index statistics, you may see a different change. The important thing in the example is that the histogram changes the query plan and the estimated cost.)

Note   In practice, there are so few rows in the tables used for this example that it hardly matters which order the query executes. However, in real-world examples, using a histogram can provide large gains, in some cases more than an order of magnitude.

What is also interesting with this example is that if you change the condition to look for movies shorter than 60 minutes, then the join order changes back to first scanning the `actor` table. The reason is that with that condition, enough films will be included based on the length that it is better to start finding candidate actors. In the same way, if you additionally add a histogram on the `first_name` of the actor table, the optimizer will realize the first name is a rather good filter for the actors in this database; particularly, there is only one actor named Elvis. It is left as an exercise for the reader to try to change the `WHERE` clause and the histograms and see how the query plan changes.

Summary

This chapter has shown how histograms can be used to improve the information the optimizer has available when it tries to determine the optimal query plan. Histograms divide the column values into buckets, either one value per bucket called a singleton histogram or multiple values per bucket called an equi-height histogram. For each bucket, it is determined how frequent the values are encountered, and the cumulative frequency is calculated for each bucket.

Histograms are mainly useful for columns that are not candidate to have indexes, but they are still used for filtering in queries featuring joins. In this case, the histogram can help the optimizer determine the optimal join order. An example was given at the end of the chapter showing how a histogram changes the join order for a query.

The metadata and statistics for a histogram can be inspected in the `information_schema.COLUMN_STATISTICS` view. The information includes all the data for each bucket that the optimizer uses as well as metadata such as when the histogram was last updated, the histogram type, and the number of buckets requested.

During the query example, it was mentioned that the optimizer has some defaults for the estimated filtering effect of various conditions. Thus far, in the discussion of indexes and histograms, the optimizer has mostly been ignored. It is time to change that: the next chapter is all about the query optimizer.

CHAPTER 17

The Query Optimizer

When you submit a query to MySQL for execution, it is not as simple as just reading the data and returning it. True, for simple queries requesting all data from a single table, there are not many options how to retrieve the data. However, most queries are more complex – some much more complex – and executing the query exactly as it is written is by no means given to be the most efficient way to get to the result. You already touched on some of this complexity when reading about indexes. You can add to the choice of index, the join order, the algorithm used to execute the joins, various join optimizations, and more. That is where the optimizer comes into play.

The main job of the optimizer is to prepare the query for execution and determine the optimal query plan. The first stage involves making transformations to the query with the aim that the rewritten query can be executed at a lower cost than the original query. The second stage consists of calculating the cost of the various ways the query can be executed and determining the cheapest option.

Note It is important to realize that the work done by the optimizer is not exact science because of the variations in data and its distribution. The transformations the optimizer chooses and the costs calculated are both to some degree based on estimates. Usually these estimates are good enough to get a good query plan, but occasionally you will need to provide hints. How to configure the optimizer is discussed in the "Configuring the Optimizer" section later in this chapter.

This chapter starts out discussing the transformations and the cost-based optimization. The chapter then continues to discuss the basic join algorithms followed by other optimization features such as batch key access. The final part of the chapter covers how to configure the optimizer and how to use resource groups to prioritize queries.

© Jesper Wisborg Krogh 2020
J. W. Krogh, *MySQL 8 Query Performance Tuning*, https://doi.org/10.1007/978-1-4842-5584-1_17

Transformations

The way a human finds it natural to write a query may not be the same as the optimal way to execute it inside MySQL. The optimizer knows of several transformations that can be used to change the query while still returning the same result, so the query becomes more optimal for MySQL.

It is of course paramount that the original and rewritten queries return the same result. Fortunately, relational databases are based on the mathematical set theory, so many of the transformations can use standard mathematical rules which ensure the two versions of the query return the same result (bar implementation bugs).

One of the simplest types of transformations the optimizer does is constant propagation. As an example, consider the following query:

```
SELECT *
  FROM world.country
       INNER JOIN world.city
          ON city.CountryCode = country.Code
 WHERE city.CountryCode = 'AUS';
```

This query has two conditions: the city.CountryCode column must be equal to "AUS", and the CountryCode column of the city table must be equal to the Code column of the country table. From those two conditions, it can be derived that the country.Code column also must equal "AUS". The optimizer uses this knowledge to filter the country table directly. Since the Code column is the primary key of the country table, it means the optimizer knows that there will only be a single row matching the condition, and the optimizer can treat the country table as a constant. Effectively, the query ends up being executed with the column values from the country table as constants in the select list and a scan over the entries in the city table with CountryCode = 'AUS':

```
SELECT 'AUS' AS `Code`,
       'Australia' AS `Name`,
       'Oceania' AS `Continent`,
       'Australia and New Zealand' AS `Region`,
       7741220.00 AS `SurfaceArea`,
       1901 AS `IndepYear`,
       18886000 AS `Population`,
       79.8 AS `LifeExpectancy`,
       351182.00 AS `GNP`,
```

```
     392911.00 AS `GNPOld`,
     'Australia' AS `LocalName`,
     'Constitutional Monarchy, Federation' AS `GovernmentForm`,
     'Elisabeth II' AS `HeadOfState`,
     135 AS `Capital`,
     'AU' AS `Code2`,
     city.*
  FROM world.city
 WHERE CountryCode = 'AUS';
```

This is a safe transformation from a performance point of view. Other transformations are more complicated and do not always improve the performance. For that reason, it can be configured whether the optimization is enabled or not. The configuration is done using the `optimizer_switch` option and optimizer hints which are discussed when covering optimizations and how to configure the optimizer.

Once the optimizer has decided which transformations to do, it needs to determine how to execute the rewritten query as will be discussed next.

Cost-Based Optimization

MySQL uses cost-based optimization of the queries. That means that the optimizer calculates a cost for the various operations required to execute the query, then combines these partial costs to calculate the overall query cost for the possible query plans, and chooses the cheapest plan. This section covers the principles of estimating the cost of the query plans.

The Basics: Single Table SELECT

The principles of calculating the cost are the same irrespective of the query, but obviously the more complex the query, the more complex the cost estimation becomes. As a simple example, consider a query that queries a single table with a WHERE clause on an indexed column:

```
SELECT *
  FROM world.city
 WHERE CountryCode = 'IND';
```

There `world.city` table has a secondary nonunique index on the `CountryCode` column as can be seen from the table definition:

```
mysql> SHOW CREATE TABLE world.city\G
*************************** 1. row ***************************
       Table: city
Create Table: CREATE TABLE `city` (
  `ID` int(11) NOT NULL AUTO_INCREMENT,
  `Name` char(35) NOT NULL DEFAULT ",
  `CountryCode` char(3) NOT NULL DEFAULT ",
  `District` char(20) NOT NULL DEFAULT ",
  `Population` int(11) NOT NULL DEFAULT '0',
  PRIMARY KEY (`ID`),
  KEY `CountryCode` (`CountryCode`),
  CONSTRAINT `city_ibfk_1` FOREIGN KEY (`CountryCode`) REFERENCES `country`
  (`Code`)
) ENGINE=InnoDB AUTO_INCREMENT=4080 DEFAULT CHARSET=utf8mb4
COLLATE=utf8mb4_0900_ai_ci
1 row in set (0.0008 sec)
```

There are two ways the optimizer can choose to fetch the matching rows. One way is to use the index on `CountryCode` to find the matching rows in the index and then look up the row values requested. The other way is to do a full table scan and check each row to determine whether it meets the filter condition.

Which of these access methods has the lowest cost (is the fastest) is not as straightforward to determine as it may seem. It depends on several factors:

- **How selective is the index?** Reading a row through the secondary index involves first finding the row in the index and then possibly (see the next item) doing a primary key lookup to get the row. This means that it is more expensive to examine and retrieve a row using the secondary index than reading the row directly, and for the index access to become overall cheaper than a table scan, the index must significantly reduce the number of rows to examine. The more selective the index, the relatively cheaper it is to use it.

- **Is the index a covering index?** If the index includes all columns required for the query, it is possible to skip reading in the actual row making it more favorable to use the index.

- **How expensive is it to read records?** This again depends on several factors such as whether the index and row data are already in the buffer pool and, if not, how fast the records can be read from disk. Using the index will require more random I/O given the switching between reading the index and reading the clustered index, so the seek times involved to locate the records become very important.

One of the new features in MySQL 8 is that the optimizer can ask InnoDB whether the records required for the query can be expected to be found in the buffer pool or if it is necessary to read it from disk. This can greatly help improve the query plans.

The question of the cost involved to read the records is more complicated as MySQL does not know the performance characteristics of the hardware. MySQL 8 by default assumes that it is four times as expensive to read from disk than memory. This can be configured as discussed in "Engine Costs" in the "Configuring the Optimizer" section.

As soon as you introduce a second table into the query, the optimizer also needs to decide in which order to join the tables.

Table Join Order

For more complicated queries than a single table SELECT statement, the optimizer not only needs to take the cost of accessing each table into account but also needs to consider the order each table is included and which index to use for each table.

For outer and straight joins, the join order is fixed, but for inner joins the optimizer is free to choose the order, so the optimizer must calculate the cost of each combination. The number of possible combinations is N! (factorial) which scales very poorly. If you have five tables participating in inner joins, the optimizer has a choice of five tables as the first table, then four tables for the second table, three tables for the third table, two tables for the fourth table, and finally one table for the last table:

```
Combinations = 5 * 4 * 3 * 2 * 1 = 5! = 120
```

MySQL supports joining up to 61 tables in which case there are potentially 5.1E83 combinations to calculate the cost which is cost prohibitive and will likely take longer than executing the query itself. For this reason, the optimizer by default prunes the query plans based on partial evaluations of the cost, so only the most promising plans are fully evaluated. It is also possible to tell the optimizer to stop evaluating the cost after including a given number of tables. The pruning and search depth are configured with the `optimizer_prune_level` and `optimizer_search_depth` options, respectively, as it will be discussed in the "Configuring the Optimizer" section.

The optimal join order is related to how large the tables are and how well the filters work on reducing the number of rows included from each table.

Default Filtering Effects

When you join two or more tables, the optimizer needs to know how many rows are included from each table to be able to determine the optimal join order. It is by no means always a trivial task.

When an index is used, the optimizer can estimate very accurately how many rows will match for the index when the filter is not relating to other tables. If there is no index, histogram statistics can be used to get a good filtering estimate. The difficulties arise when there are no statistics for the filtered columns. In that case, the optimizer falls back on built-in default estimates. Table 17-1 includes examples of default filtering effects that are used when there are no index or histogram statistics that can be used.

Table 17-1. *Default filtering effects for conditions without statistics*

Type	Filter %	Notes/Example
All	100	This is used when filtering by index or there is no filtering condition.
Equality	10	`Name = 'Sydney'`
Not Equal	90	`Name <> 'Sydney'`
Inequality	33.33	`Population > 4000000`
Between	11.11	`Population BETWEEN 1000000 AND 4000000`
IN	min(#items * 10, 50)	`Name IN ('Sydney', 'Melbourne')`

The filtering effects are based on the article "Access path selection in a relational database management system" by Selinger et al.[1] You will sometimes see different filtering values. Some examples include

- **Distinct values are known:** This includes enum and bit data types. Consider the Continent column in the world.country table. This is an enum with seven values, so the optimizer will estimate the filtering effect to be 1/7 for a WHERE clause like Continent = 'Europe'.

- **Few rows:** If there are fewer than ten rows in a table and you add an equality condition, the filtering estimate will be 1/number_of_rows and similar for the not equal filter estimate.

- **Combination of filters:** If you combine filters on several non-indexed columns, the estimated filtering effect is the combined effect. For example, for the world.city table, the filter Name = 'Sydney' AND Population > 3000000 is estimated to take 10% of the rows due to the equality on Name and 33% because of the inequality on Population, so the combined effect is P(Equality on Name) * P(Inequality on Population) = 0.1 * 0.33 = 0.0333 = 3.33%.

This list is not exhaustive, but it should give you a good idea of how MySQL arrives at the filtering estimates. The default filtering effects are obviously not very accurate, particularly for large tables as the data does not follow such rigid rules. That is why indexes and histograms are so important to get good query plans.

At the end of determining the query plan, there are cost estimates for both the individual parts and the whole query. These can be informative to understand how the optimizer arrived at the query execution plan.

The Query Cost

If you want to examine the costs the optimizer has found, you will need to use the tree-(including EXPLAIN ANALYZE) or JSON-formatted EXPLAIN output, a MySQL Workbench Visual Explain diagram, or the optimizer trace. These are all described in detail in Chapter 20.

---

[1] https://dl.acm.org/citation.cfm?id=582099 (requires membership/subscription)

As a simple example, consider a query joining the country and city tables of the world sample database:

```
SELECT *
  FROM world.country
       INNER JOIN world.city
          ON CountryCode = Code;
```

Figure 17-1 shows the Visual Explain diagram for the query including extra details for the city table.

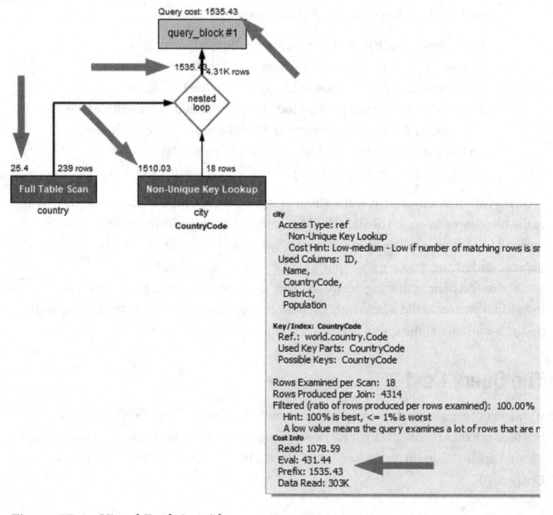

Figure 17-1. *Visual Explain with cost estimates*

The figure shows how the optimizer has decided to execute the query. How to read the diagram will be discussed in Chapter 20. Here the important part are the figures pointed to by the arrows. These are the cost estimates that the optimizer has arrived at for the various parts of the query execution with the lower cost, the better. The example shows that the cost estimates are calculated for very specific tasks such as reading the data, evaluating the filter condition, and so on. At the top of the diagram, the total query cost is estimated to be 1535.43.

Note   Since the calculated cost depends on such things as the index statistics, and the index statistics are not exact, the cost will not be the same over time. This also means that you may see different cost estimates, if you execute the same query compared to what is shown in the examples in this book.

After you have executed a query, you can also get the estimated cost from the Last_query_cost status variable. Listing 17-1 shows an example of doing this for the same query as in Figure 17-1.

Listing 17-1. Obtaining the estimated query cost after executing a query

```
mysql> SELECT *
         FROM world.country
             INNER JOIN world.city
                 ON CountryCode = Code;
...

mysql> SHOW SESSION STATUS LIKE 'Last_query_cost';
+-----------------+-------------+
| Variable_name   | Value       |
+-----------------+-------------+
| Last_query_cost | 1535.425669 |
+-----------------+-------------+
1 row in set (0.0013 sec)
```

The result of the query has been removed from the output as it is not important for this discussion. An important thing to note about Last_query_cost is that it is the estimated cost which is why it shows the same value as the total cost in the Visual

Explain diagram. If you want information about the actual cost of executing the query, you need to use EXPLAIN ANALYZE.

The Visual Explain diagram mentions the query is executed using a *nested loop*. That is just one of the join algorithms MySQL supports.

Join Algorithms

A join is a very broad concept in MySQL – so much that you can argue that everything is a join. Even querying a single table is considered a join. That said, the most interesting joins are those between two or more tables. In this discussion a table can also be a derived table.

When a query is executed, and two tables need to be joined, MySQL has support for three different algorithms. The algorithms are

- Nested loop

- Block nested loop

- Hash join

Note   The timings shown in this section are for illustrative purposes only. The timings you see on your system will be different, and there may also be differences in the timings relative to each other.

This section and the next will reference several names of optimizer switches and optimizer hints. The optimizer switches refer to the optimizer_switch configuration option, and the optimizer hints refer to the /*+ ... */ comments that can be added to queries to tell the optimizer how you would like the query to be executed. Both concepts and how to use them will be discussed further in the section "Configuring the Optimizer" later in this chapter.

Nested Loop

The nested loop algorithm is the simplest of the algorithms used in MySQL. Until MySQL 5.6 it was also the only algorithm available. As the name suggests, it works by nesting loops with one loop for each table in the join. Not only is the nested join algorithm very simple; it also works well for index lookups.

Consider a query on the `world.country` table joining on the `world.city` table querying for countries and cities in Asia. You can write the query in the following way:

```
SELECT CountryCode, country.Name AS Country,
       city.Name AS City, city.District
  FROM world.country
       INNER JOIN world.city
             ON city.CountryCode = country.Code
 WHERE Continent = 'Asia';
```

It will be executed using a nested loop with a table scan on the country table where the filter in the WHERE clause is applied followed by an index lookup on the city table. In a tree notation, the query looks like

```
-> Nested loop inner join
    -> Filter: (country.Continent = 'Asia')
        -> Table scan on country
    -> Index lookup on city using CountryCode
                    (CountryCode=country.`Code`)
```

You can also write this as pseudo code. Using a Python-like syntax, the nested loop join can be written like the following code snippet:

```
result = []
for country_row in country:
    if country_row.Continent == 'Asia':
        for city_row in city.CountryCode['country_row.Code']:
            result.append(join_rows(country_row, city_row))
```

In the pseudo code, `country` and `city` represent the `country` and `city` tables, respectively, `city.CountryCode` is the CountryCode index on the city table, and `country_row` and `city_row` represent a single row. The `join_rows()` function is used to represent the process of combining the columns needed from the two rows to a row in the result set.

Figure 17-2 shows the same nested loop join using a diagram. For simplicity and to focus on the join, only the primary key values of the matching rows are included even though all rows are read from the `country` table.

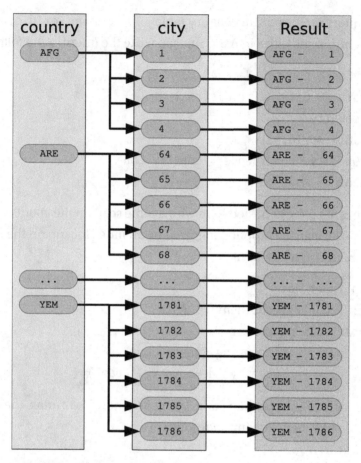

Figure 17-2. *An example of a nested loop join*

The diagram shows that MySQL scans the country table until it finds a row matching the WHERE clause. In the diagram, the first matching row is AFG (for Afghanistan). Then all rows in the city table for CountryCode = AFG are found (ID equal to 1, 2, 3, and 4), and each combination is used to form a row in the result. This continues with the country code equaling ARE (for United Arab Emirates) and so forth until YEM (for Yemen).

The exact order the rows are scanned in the country table and within the CountryCode index in the city table depends on the index definitions as well as internals in the optimizer, executor, and storage engine. You should never rely on the ordering to stay the same unless you have an explicit ORDER BY clause.

In general, a join may be more complex than in this example as there may be additional filters. Yet the concept remains the same.

While being simple is usually a good property, the nested loop join has some limitations. It cannot be used to execute a full outer join as the nested loop join requires the first table to return rows which is not always the case for a full outer join. The workaround is to write a full outer join as a union of a left and a right outer join. Consider a query looking for all countries and cities including those cases where there are no cities for a country and there is no country for a city. That can be written as a full outer join (not valid in MySQL):

```
SELECT *
  FROM world.country
       FULL OUTER JOIN world.city
             ON city.CountryCode = country.Code;
```

In order to execute that in MySQL, you can use a union of country LEFT JOIN city and country RIGHT JOIN city like

```
SELECT *
  FROM world.country
       LEFT OUTER JOIN world.city
             ON city.CountryCode = country.Code
 UNION
SELECT *
  FROM world.country
       RIGHT OUTER JOIN world.city
             ON city.CountryCode = country.Code;
```

Another limitation is that a nested loop join is not very effective for joins that cannot use indexes. Since nested loop joins work on one row at a time from the first table in the join, it is necessary with a full table scan of the second table for each row included from the first table. That quickly becomes too expensive. Consider the query examined a little earlier where all cities in Asia were found:

```
mysql> SELECT PS_CURRENT_THREAD_ID();
+------------------------+
| PS_CURRENT_THREAD_ID() |
+------------------------+
|                     30 |
+------------------------+
1 row in set (0.0017 sec)
```

```
SELECT CountryCode, country.Name AS Country,
        city.Name AS City, city.District
  FROM world.country
        INNER JOIN world.city
            ON city.CountryCode = country.Code
 WHERE Continent = 'Asia';
```

With a table scan on the country table (239 rows) and an index lookup on the city table, a total of 2005 rows will be examined (execute this query in a second connection):

```
mysql> SELECT rows_examined, rows_sent,
            last_statement_latency AS latency
        FROM sys.session
        WHERE thd_id = 30\G
*********************** 1. row ***************************
rows_examined: 2005
   rows_sent: 1766
     latency: 4.36 ms
1 row in set (0.0539 sec)
```

The filter on thd_id needs to match the Performance Schema thread id of the connection that executed the query (this can be found with the PS_CURRENT_THREAD_ID() function in MySQL 8.0.16 and later). The 2005 examined rows come from examining the 239 rows in the country table doing a full table scan followed by reading the 1766 rows in the city table for the Asian countries.

If MySQL cannot use an index for the join, then the query performance changes drastically. You can execute the query using a nested loop join without using an index in the following way (the NO_BNL(city) comment is an optimizer hint):

```
SELECT /*+ NO_BNL(city) */
        CountryCode, country.Name AS Country,
        city.Name AS City, city.District
  FROM world.country IGNORE INDEX (Primary)
```

```
        INNER JOIN world.city IGNORE INDEX (CountryCode)
             ON city.CountryCode = country.Code
 WHERE Continent = 'Asia';
```

The IGNORE INDEX () clause is an index hint that tells MySQL to ignore the index given between the parentheses. The query statistics for this version of the query show that now more than 200,000 rows are examined and the query takes around ten times longer to execute than before (perform this test in the same way as the previous where the query finding the Asian cities is executed in one connection and the following query against sys.session is executed in another connection and thd_id = 30 is changed to use the thread id of the first connection):

```
mysql> SELECT rows_examined, rows_sent,
              last_statement_latency AS latency
         FROM sys.session
        WHERE thd_id = 30\G
*************************** 1. row ***************************
rows_examined: 208268
    rows_sent: 1766
      latency: 44.83 ms
```

There are 51 countries with Continent = 'Asia' which means that there are 51 full table scans of the city table. Since there are 4079 rows in the city table, that gives a total of $51 * 4079 + 239 = 208268$ rows that must be examined. The extra 239 come from the table scan on the country table with 239 rows.

Why was it necessary to add the comment with NO_BNL(country,city) in the example? BNL stands for block nested loop which can help improve joins without indexes, and the comment disables that optimization. Usually, you do want to keep it enabled as will be explained next.

Block Nested Loop

The block nested loop algorithm is an extension of the nested loop algorithm. It is also known as the BNL algorithm. Instead of submitting the rows from the first table in a join one by one, the join buffer is used to collect as many rows as possible and compare them all in one scan of the second table. This can greatly improve the performance for some queries over the nested loop algorithm.

If you consider the same query that was used as the example for the nested loop algorithm but disabling the use of indexes (to simulate two tables without indexes) and not allowing a hash join (in 8.0.18 and later), you have a query that can take advantage of the block nested loop algorithm. The query is

```
SELECT /*+ NO_HASH_JOIN(country,city) */
       CountryCode, country.Name AS Country,
       city.Name AS City, city.District
  FROM world.country IGNORE INDEX (Primary)
       INNER JOIN world.city IGNORE INDEX (CountryCode)
           ON city.CountryCode = country.Code
 WHERE Continent = 'Asia';
```

In MySQL 8.0.17 and earlier, remove the comment with the NO_HASH_JOIN() optimizer hint.

Listing 17-2 shows an example of a pseudo code implementation of the block nested loop algorithm using Python-like code.

Listing 17-2. Pseudo code representing a block nested loop join

```
result = []
join_buffer = []
for country_row in country:
    if country_row.Continent == 'Asia':
        join_buffer.append(country_row.Code)

        if is_full(join_buffer):
            for city_row in city:
                CountryCode = city_row.CountryCode
```

```
            if CountryCode in join_buffer:
                country_row = get_row(CountryCode)
                result.append(
                    join_rows(country_row, city_row))
        join_buffer = []

if len(join_buffer) > 0:
    for city_row in city:
        CountryCode = city_row.CountryCode
        if CountryCode in join_buffer:
            country_row = get_row(CountryCode)
            result.append(join_rows(country_row, city_row))
    join_buffer = []
```

The join_buffer list represents the join buffer storing the columns needed for
the join. In the pseudo code, the columns are extracted with the required_columns()
function. For the query used as the example, only the Code column from the country
table is needed. This is an important thing to note and will shortly be discussed further.
When the join buffer is full, a table scan is performed on the city table; and if there is a
match of the CountryCode column of the city table with one of the Code values stored in
the join buffer, the result row is constructed.

Figure 17-3 shows a diagram representing the join. For simplicity, only the primary
key values of the rows required for the join are included even though a full table scan is
performed for both tables.

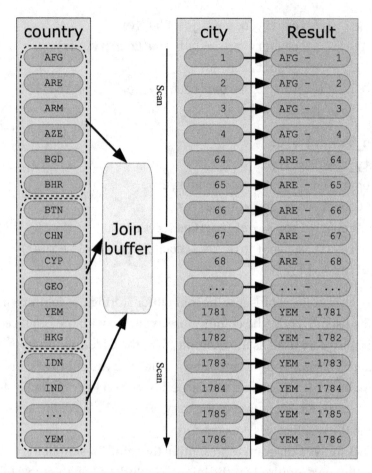

Figure 17-3. *An example of a block nested loop join*

The figure shows how rows from the country table are read together and stored in the join buffer. Each time the join buffer is full, a full table scan is performed for the city table, and the result is built incrementally. In the figure, six rows fit into the join buffer at a time. As the Code column only requires 3 bytes per row, in practice the join buffer will be able to hold all the country codes except when using the smallest possible settings of join_buffer_size.

How does the use of the join buffer to buffer several country codes affect the query statistics? As for the previous examples, first, execute the query finding the Asian cities in one connection:

```
SELECT /*+ NO_HASH_JOIN(country,city) */
       CountryCode, country.Name AS Country,
       city.Name AS City, city.District
```

```
FROM world.country IGNORE INDEX (Primary)
     INNER JOIN world.city IGNORE INDEX (CountryCode)
          ON city.CountryCode = country.Code
WHERE Continent = 'Asia';
```

Then in another connection, query `sys.session` to get the number of examined rows and the query latency (change `thd_id = 30` to use the thread id of the first connection):

```
mysql> SELECT rows_examined, rows_sent,
             last_statement_latency AS latency
         FROM sys.session
        WHERE thd_id = 30\G
*************************** 1. row ***************************
rows_examined: 4318
    rows_sent: 1766
      latency: 16.87 ms
1 row in set (0.0490 sec)
```

The result assumes the default value for `join_buffer_size`. The statistics show that block nested loop performs significantly better than the nested loop algorithm without using an index. By comparison, executing the query with an index examined 2005 rows and took around 4 ms, whereas using a nested loop join without index examined 208268 rows and took around 45 ms. This may seem like irrelevant differences in the query execution time, but both the `country` and `city` tables are very small. For large tables, the difference will grow nonlinearly and can mean the difference between a query completing and seemingly running forever.

There are some points about the block nested loop that you should be aware of as it helps you use it optimally. These points include

- Only the columns required for the join are stored in the join buffer. This means that you will need less memory for the join buffer than you may at first expect.

- The size of the join buffer is configured with the `join_buffer_size` variable. The value of `join_buffer_size` is the minimum size of the buffer! Even if less than 1 KiB of country code values will be stored in the join buffer in the discussed example, if `join_buffer_size` is set to 1 GiB, then 1 GiB will be allocated. For this reason, keep the value of `join_buffer_size` low and only increase it as needed. The section "Configuring the Optimizer" includes information on how to change the size of the join buffer just for the single query.

- One join buffer is allocated per join using the block nested loop algorithm.

- Each join buffer is allocated for the entire duration of the query.

- The block nested loop algorithm can be used for full table scans, full index scans, and range scans.

- The block nested loop algorithm will never be used for constant tables as well as the first nonconstant table. This means that it requires a join between two tables with more than one row after filtering by unique indexes to use the block nested loop algorithm.

You can configure whether the optimizer is allowed to choose the block nested loop algorithm by setting the `block_nested_loop` optimizer switch. The default is to have it enabled. For a single query, you can use the `BNL()` and `NO_BNL()` optimizer hints to enable or disable the block nested loop for specific joins.

While the block nested loop is a great improvement for non-indexed joins, it is in most cases possible to do even better by using a hash join.

Hash Join

The hash join algorithm is a very recent addition to MySQL and is supported in MySQL 8.0.18 and later. It marks a significant break with the tradition of nested loop joins including the block nested loop variant. It is particularly useful for large joins without indexes but can in some cases even outperform an index join.

MySQL implements a hybrid between a classic in-memory hash join and the on-disk GRACE hash join algorithm.[2] If it is possible to store all the hashes in memory, then the pure in-memory implementation is used. The join buffer is used for the in-memory part, so the amount of memory that can be used for the hashes is limited by `join_buffer_size`. When the join does not fit in memory, the join spills over to disk, but the actual join operations are still performed in memory.

---

[2] https://dev.mysql.com/worklog/task/?id=2241

The in-memory hash join algorithm consists of two steps:

1. One of the tables in the join is chosen as the *build table*. The hash is calculated for the columns required for the join and loaded into memory. This is known as the *build phase*.

2. The other table in the join is the *probe input*. For this table, rows are read one at a time, and the hash is calculated. Then a hash key lookup is performed on the hashes calculated from the build table, and the result of the join is generated from the matching rows. This is known as the *probe phase*.

When the hashes of the build table do not fit into memory, MySQL automatically switches to use the on-disk implementation (based on the GRACE hash join algorithm). The switch from the in-memory to the on-disk algorithm happens if the join buffer becomes full during the build phase. The on-disk algorithm consists of three steps:

1. Calculate the hashes of all rows in both the build and probe tables and store them on disk in several small files partitioned by the hash. The number of partitions is chosen to make each partition of the probe table fit into the join buffer but with a limit of at most 128 partitions.

2. Load the first partition of the build table into memory and iterate over the hashes from the probe table in the same way as for the probe phase for the in-memory algorithm. Since the partitioning in step 1 uses the same hash function for both the build and probe tables, it is only necessary to iterate over the first partition of the probe table.

3. Clear the in-memory buffer and continue with the rest of the partitions one by one.

Both the in-memory and on-disk algorithms use the xxHash64 hash function which is known as being fast while still providing hashes of good quality (reducing the number of hash collisions). For the optimal performance, the join buffer needs to be large enough to fit all the hashes from the build table. That said, the same considerations for join_buffer_size exist for hash joins as for block nested loop joins.

MySQL will use the hash join whenever the block nested loop would otherwise be chosen, and the hash join algorithm is supported for the query. At the time of writing, the following requirements exist for the hash join algorithm to be used:

- The join must be an inner join.

- The join cannot be performed using an index, either because there is no available index or because the indexes have been disabled for the query.

- All joins in the query must have at least one equi-join condition between the two tables in the join, and only columns from the two tables as well as constants are referenced in the condition.

- As of 8.0.20, anti, semi, and outer joins are also supported.[3] If you join the two tables t1 and t2, then examples of join conditions that are supported for hash join include

  - `t1.t1_val = t2.t2_val`

  - `t1.t1_val = t2.t2_val + 2`

  - `t1.t1_val1 = t2.t2_val AND t1.t1_val2 > 100`

  - `MONTH(t1.t1_val) = MONTH(t2.t2_val)`

If you consider the recurring example query for this section, you can execute it using a hash join by ignoring the indexes on the tables that can be used for the join:

```
SELECT CountryCode, country.Name AS Country,
       city.Name AS City, city.District
  FROM world.country IGNORE INDEX (Primary)
       INNER JOIN world.city IGNORE INDEX (CountryCode)
           ON city.CountryCode = country.Code
 WHERE Continent = 'Asia';
```

The pseudo code for performing this join is similar to that of a block nested loop except that the columns needed for the join are hashed and that there is support for overflowing to disk. The pseudo code is shown in Listing 17-3.

---

[3]https://twitter.com/lefred/status/1222916855150600192

Listing 17-3. Pseudo code representing a hash join

```
result = []
join_buffer = []
partitions = 0
on_disk = False
for country_row in country:
    if country_row.Continent == 'Asia':
        hash = xxHash64(country_row.Code)
        if not on_disk:
            join_buffer.append(hash)

            if is_full(join_buffer):
                # Create partitions on disk
                on_disk = True
                partitions = write_buffer_to_disk(join_buffer)
                join_buffer = []
        else
            write_hash_to_disk(hash)

if not on_disk:
    for city_row in city:
        hash = xxHash64(city_row.CountryCode)
        if hash in join_buffer:
            country_row = get_row(hash)
            city_row = get_row(hash)
            result.append(join_rows(country_row, city_row))
else:
    for city_row in city:
        hash = xxHash64(city_row.CountryCode)
        write_hash_to_disk(hash)

    for partition in range(partitions):
        join_buffer = load_build_from_disk(partition)
        for hash in load_hash_from_disk(partition):
```

```
        if hash in join_buffer:
            country_row = get_row(hash)
            city_row = get_row(hash)
            result.append(join_rows(country_row, city_row))
    join_buffer = []
```

The pseudo code starts out reading the rows from the country table and calculates the hash for the Code column and stores it in the join buffer. If the buffer becomes full, then the code switches to the on-disk algorithm and writes out the hashes from the buffer. This is also where the number of partitions is determined. After this the rest of the country table is hashed.

In the next part, for the in-memory algorithm, there is a simple loop over the rows in the city table comparing the hashes to those in the buffer. For the on-disk algorithm, the hashes of the city table are first calculated and stored on disk; then the partitions are handled one by one.

Note   The algorithm as described is a little simplified compared to the actual algorithm used. The real algorithm will have to take hash collisions into account, and for the on-disk algorithm, it is possible for some partitions to become too large to fit into the join buffer, in which case they are handled in chunks to avoid using more memory to be used than configured.

Figure 17-4 shows a diagram for the in-memory hash join algorithm. For simplicity, only the primary key values of the rows required for the join are included even though a full table scan is performed for both tables.

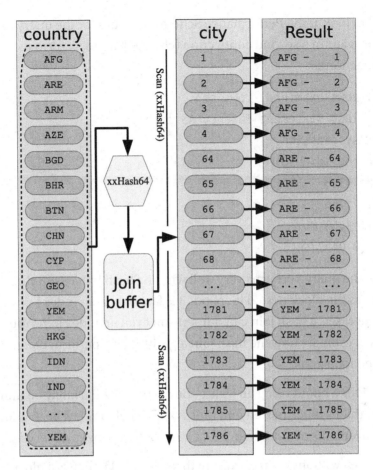

Figure 17-4. *An example of an in-memory hash join*

The values of the Code column for the matching rows from the country table are hashed and stored in the join buffer. Then a table scan is executed for the city table with the hash calculated of CountryCode for each row, and the result is constructed from the matching rows.

You can check the statistics for the query in the same way as for the previous algorithms by first executing the query in one connection:

```
SELECT CountryCode, country.Name AS Country,
       city.Name AS City, city.District
  FROM world.country IGNORE INDEX (Primary)
       INNER JOIN world.city IGNORE INDEX (CountryCode)
           ON city.CountryCode = country.Code
 WHERE Continent = 'Asia';
```

Then you can look at the Performance Schema statistics for the query by querying the sys.session view in a second connection (change thd_id = 30 to use the thread id of the first connection):

```
mysql> SELECT rows_examined, rows_sent,
              last_statement_latency AS latency
         FROM sys.session
        WHERE thd_id = 30\G
rows_examined: 4318
    rows_sent: 1766
      latency: 3.53 ms
1 row in set (0.0467 sec)
```

You can see the query performs very well with the hash join examining the same number of rows as the block nested loop, but it is faster than an index join. This is not a mistake: in some cases, a hash join can outperform even an index join. You can use the following rules to estimate how the hash join algorithm will perform compared to index and block nested loop joins:

- For a join without using an index, the hash join will usually be much faster than a block nested join unless a LIMIT clause has been added. Improvements of more than a factor of 1000 have been observed.[4]

- For a join without an index where there is a LIMIT clause, a block nested loop can exit when enough rows have been found, whereas a hash join will complete the entire join (but can skip fetching the rows). If the number of rows included due to the LIMIT clause is small compared to the total number of rows found by the join, a block nested loop may be faster.

- For joins supporting an index, the hash join algorithm can be faster if the index has a low selectivity.

The biggest benefit using the hash joins is by far for joins without an index and without a LIMIT clause. In the end, only testing can prove which join strategy is the optimal for your queries.

---

[4]https://mysqlserverteam.com/hash-join-in-mysql-8/ and www.slideshare.net/NorvaldRyeng/mysql-8018-latest-updates-hash-join-and-explain-analyze

You can enable and disable support for hash joins using the `hash_join` optimizer switch. Additionally, the `block_nested_loop` optimizer switch must be enabled. Both are enabled by default. If you want to configure the use of hash joins for specific joins, you can use the `HASH_JOIN()` and `NO_HASH_JOIN()` optimizer hints.

That concludes the discussion about the three high-level join strategies supported in MySQL. There are some lower-level optimizations as well that are worth considering.

Join Optimizations

The join optimizations can be used by MySQL to improve the basic concepts of the join algorithms discussed in the previous section or to decide how to execute parts of the query. This section will cover the index merge, Multi-Range Read (MRR), and Batched Key Access (BKA) optimization in detail. These three optimizations are the ones most likely to need you to help the optimizer to get the query plan to be the most optimal. The remaining configurable optimizations are covered at the end of the section but in less detail.

Index Merge

Usually MySQL will only use a single index per table. However, that is not optimal if you have conditions on multiple columns from the same table and you do not have a single index covering all columns. For those cases, MySQL supports index merges.

Tip   A multicolumn index covering the columns with filter conditions is more efficient than using the index merge optimization. You should weigh that performance difference up against possibly having an extra index.

There is support for three index merge algorithms. Table 17-2 summarizes the algorithms, when the algorithms are used, and the information included in the query plans.

Table 17-2. *The index merge algorithms*

Algorithm	Use Case	EXPLAIN Extra Colum	EXPLAIN JSON Key Field
Intersection	AND	Using intersect(...)	intersect(...)
Union	OR	Using union(...)	union(...)
Sort-Union	OR with ranges	sort_union(...)	sort_union(...)

In addition to the EXPLAIN information listed in the table, the access type is set to index_merge.

The use case specifies the operator joining the conditions. The difference between the union and sort-union algorithms is that the union algorithm is for equality conditions and the sort-union algorithm is for range conditions. For the EXPLAIN outputs, the names of the indexes used with the index merge are listed inside the parentheses.

When discussing the three algorithms, it can be useful to consider real queries that use each algorithm. The payment table in the sakila database is useful for this purpose. The table definition of sakila.payment is

```
CREATE TABLE `payment` (
  `payment_id` smallint unsigned NOT NULL,
  `customer_id` smallint unsigned NOT NULL,
  `staff_id` tinyint unsigned NOT NULL,
  `rental_id` int(DEFAULT NULL,
  `amount` decimal(5,2) NOT NULL,
  `payment_date` datetime NOT NULL,
  `last_update` timestamp NULL,
  PRIMARY KEY (`payment_id`),
  KEY `idx_fk_staff_id` (`staff_id`),
  KEY `idx_fk_customer_id` (`customer_id`),
  KEY `fk_payment_rental` (`rental_id`)
) ENGINE=InnoDB DEFAULT CHARSET=utf8
```

The default values, auto-increment information, and foreign key definitions have been removed from the table to focus on the columns and the indexes. The table has four indexes, all on a single column, which makes it a good candidate for the index merge optimizations.

The rest of the index merge discussion will go through each of the index merge algorithms as well as performance considerations and how to configure the use of index merges. The examples all include conditions on just two columns, but the algorithms do support index merges involving more columns.

Note   Whether the optimizer chooses an index merge or not depends on the index statistics. This means that for the same query, different values in the WHERE clause may cause different query plans, and changes to the index statistics can make the query execute differently even with the exact same conditions between using index merges and not using them – or vice versa.

Intersection Algorithm

The intersection algorithm is used when you have conditions on several index columns separated by AND. Two examples of queries using the intersection index merge algorithm are

```
SELECT *
  FROM sakila.payment
 WHERE staff_id = 1
       AND customer_id = 75;

SELECT *
  FROM sakila.payment
 WHERE payment_id > 10
       AND customer_id = 318;
```

The first query has an equality condition on two secondary indexes, and the second query has a range condition on the primary key and an equality condition on the secondary index. The index merge optimization with the second query exclusively works with InnoDB tables. Listing 17-4 shows the EXPLAIN output using the first of the two queries using two different formats.

Listing 17-4. Example of an EXPLAIN output for an intersection merge

```
mysql> EXPLAIN
        SELECT *
          FROM sakila.payment
         WHERE staff_id = 1
               AND customer_id = 75\G
*************************** 1. row ***************************
           id: 1
  select_type: SIMPLE
        table: payment
   partitions: NULL
         type: index_merge
possible_keys: idx_fk_staff_id,idx_fk_customer_id
          key: idx_fk_customer_id,idx_fk_staff_id
      key_len: 2,1
          ref: NULL
         rows: 20
     filtered: 100
        Extra: Using intersect(idx_fk_customer_id,idx_fk_staff_id); Using
               where 1 row in set, 1 warning (0.0007 sec)

mysql> EXPLAIN FORMAT=TREE
        SELECT *
          FROM sakila.payment
         WHERE staff_id = 1
               AND customer_id = 75\G
*************************** 1. row ***************************
EXPLAIN: -> Filter: ((sakila.payment.customer_id = 75) and (sakila.payment.
staff_id = 1))  (cost=14.48 rows=20)
    -> Index range scan on payment using intersect(idx_fk_customer_id,idx_
    fk_staff_id)  (cost=14.48 rows=20)

1 row in set (0.0004 sec)
```

Notice the Using intersect(...) message in the Extra column and for the index range scan in the tree-formatted output. This shows that the idx_fk_customer_id and idx_fk_staff_id indexes are used for the index merge. The traditional output also includes two indexes in the key column and provides two key lengths in the key_len column.

Union Algorithm

The union algorithm is used when there is a series of equality conditions for a table separated with OR. Two examples of queries that can use the union algorithm are

```
SELECT *
  FROM sakila.payment
 WHERE staff_id = 1
       OR customer_id = 318;

SELECT *
  FROM sakila.payment
 WHERE payment_id > 15000
       OR customer_id = 318;
```

The first query has two equality conditions on secondary indexes, whereas the second query has a range condition on the primary key and an equality condition on a secondary index. The second query will only use an index merge for InnoDB tables. Listing 17-5 shows an example of the corresponding EXPLAIN output for the first of the queries.

Listing 17-5. The EXPLAIN output for a union merge

```
mysql> EXPLAIN
        SELECT *
          FROM sakila.payment
         WHERE staff_id = 1
               OR customer_id = 318\G
*************************** 1. row ***************************
           id: 1
  select_type: SIMPLE
        table: payment
   partitions: NULL
```

```
        type: index_merge
possible_keys: idx_fk_staff_id,idx_fk_customer_id
          key: idx_fk_staff_id,idx_fk_customer_id
      key_len: 1,2
          ref: NULL
         rows: 8069
     filtered: 100
        Extra: Using union(idx_fk_staff_id,idx_fk_customer_id); Using where
               1 row in set, 1 warning (0.0008 sec)

mysql> EXPLAIN FORMAT=TREE
       SELECT *
         FROM sakila.payment
        WHERE staff_id = 1
              OR customer_id = 318\G
*************************** 1. row ***************************
EXPLAIN: -> Filter: ((sakila.payment.staff_id = 1) or (sakila.payment.
customer_id = 318))  (cost=2236.18 rows=8069)
    -> Index range scan on payment using union(idx_fk_staff_id,idx_fk_
    customer_id)  (cost=2236.18 rows=8069)

1 row in set (0.0010 sec)
```

Notice the Using union(...) in the Extra column and for the index range scan in the tree-formatted output. This shows that the idx_fk_staff_id and idx_fk_customer_id indexes are used for the index merge.

Sort-Union Algorithm

The sort-union algorithm is used for queries similar to those where the union algorithm is used, but where the conditions are range conditions instead of equality conditions. Two examples of queries that can use the sort-union algorithm are

```
SELECT *
  FROM sakila.payment
 WHERE customer_id < 30
       OR rental_id < 10;
```

```
SELECT *
  FROM sakila.payment
 WHERE customer_id < 30
       OR rental_id > 16000;
```

Both queries have range conditions on two secondary indexes. Listing 17-6 shows the corresponding EXPLAIN output using the traditional and tree format for the first of the queries.

Listing 17-6. The EXPLAIN output using a sort-union merge

```
mysql> EXPLAIN
        SELECT *
          FROM sakila.payment
         WHERE customer_id < 30
               OR rental_id < 10\G
*************************** 1. row ***************************
           id: 1
  select_type: SIMPLE
        table: payment
   partitions: NULL
         type: index_merge
possible_keys: idx_fk_customer_id,fk_payment_rental
          key: idx_fk_customer_id,fk_payment_rental
      key_len: 2,5
          ref: NULL
         rows: 826
     filtered: 100
        Extra: Using sort_union(idx_fk_customer_id,fk_payment_rental);
               Using where 1 row in set, 1 warning (0.0009 sec)

mysql> EXPLAIN FORMAT=TREE
        SELECT *
          FROM sakila.payment
         WHERE customer_id < 30
               OR rental_id < 10\G
```

```
*************************** 1. row ***************************
EXPLAIN: -> Filter: ((sakila.payment.customer_id < 30) or (sakila.payment.
rental_id < 10))  (cost=1040.52 rows=826)
    -> Index range scan on payment using sort_union(idx_fk_customer_id,fk_
        payment_rental)  (cost=1040.52 rows=826)

1 row in set (0.0005 sec)
```

Notice the using sort_union(...) in the Extra column and for the index range scan in the tree-formatted output. This shows that the idx_fk_customer_id and fk_payment_rental indexes are used for the index merge.

Performance Considerations

It is difficult for the optimizer to know when an index merge is more optimal than just using a single index. It may seem at first that using indexes for more columns is always a win, but there is a significant overhead of index merges, so they are only useful when the right combination of index selectivity for the indexes exists. One of the more frequent causes of severe performance regression happens when an index merge is chosen due to out-of-date index statistics.

The first thing you should do if the optimizer chooses an index merge and the query performs poorly – for example, compared to how it usually performs – is to execute ANALYZE TABLE for the table where the index merge is used. This will usually improve the query plan. Otherwise, it may be necessary to change the optimizer configuration to decide whether index merges are used or not.

Configuration

The index merge feature is controlled using four optimizer switches, of which one controls the overall feature and the three others control each of the three algorithms. The options are

- **index_merge:** Whether to enable or disable index merges altogether.

- **index_merge_intersection:** Whether to enable the intersection algorithm.

- **index_merge_union:** Whether to enable the union algorithm.

- **index_merge_sort_union:** Whether to enable the sort-union algorithm.

All of the index merge optimizer switches are enabled by default.

Additionally, there are two optimizer hints: `INDEX_MERGE()` and `NO_INDEX_MERGE()`. Both hints take a table name as argument and optionally the indexes that should be considered or ignored. If you, for example, want to execute the query looking for payments with the `staff_id` set to 1 and the `customer_id` set to 75 without using index merges, you can do that using one of the following queries:

```
SELECT /*+ NO_INDEX_MERGE(payment) */
       *
  FROM sakila.payment
 WHERE staff_id = 1
       AND customer_id = 75;

SELECT /*+ NO_INDEX_MERGE(
           payment
           idx_fk_staff_id,idx_fk_customer_id) */
       *
  FROM sakila.payment
 WHERE staff_id = 1
       AND customer_id = 75;
```

Since an index merge is considered a special case of a range optimization, the `NO_RANGE_OPTIMIZATION()` optimizer hint also disables index merges. It can be confirmed with the `EXPLAIN` output that an index merge is no longer used as shown for the first query in Listing 17-7.

Listing 17-7. The EXPLAIN output when index merges are unselected

```
mysql> EXPLAIN
       SELECT /*+ NO_INDEX_MERGE(payment) */
              *
         FROM sakila.payment
        WHERE staff_id = 1
              AND customer_id = 75\G
*************************** 1. row ***************************
           id: 1
  select_type: SIMPLE
        table: payment
```

```
    partitions: NULL
          type: ref
 possible_keys: idx_fk_staff_id,idx_fk_customer_id
           key: idx_fk_customer_id
       key_len: 2
           ref: const
          rows: 41
      filtered: 50.0870361328125
         Extra: Using where
1 row in set, 1 warning (0.0010 sec)

mysql> EXPLAIN FORMAT=TREE
       SELECT /*+ NO_INDEX_MERGE(payment) */
              *
         FROM sakila.payment
        WHERE staff_id = 1
              AND customer_id = 75\G
*************************** 1. row ***************************
EXPLAIN: -> Filter: (sakila.payment.staff_id = 1)  (cost=26.98 rows=21)
    -> Index lookup on payment using idx_fk_customer_id (customer_
       id=75)  (cost=26.98 rows=41)

1 row in set (0.0006 sec)
```

Another optimization is the Multi-Range Read optimization.

Multi-Range Read (MRR)

The Multi-Range Read (MRR) optimization aims at reducing the amount of random I/O caused by range scans on secondary indexes. The optimization reads the index first, sorts the keys according to the row id (the clustered index for InnoDB), and then retrieves the rows in the order the rows are stored. The Multi-Range Read optimization can be used for range scans and equi-joins that use an index. It is not supported for secondary indexes on virtual generated columns.

The primary use case for the Multi-Range Read optimization with InnoDB is for disk-bound queries where there is no covering index. The effect of the optimization depends on how many rows are needed and the seek times of the storage. MySQL will try to estimate when the optimization is useful; however, the cost estimation is erroring on the side of being too pessimistic rather than too optimistic, so it may be necessary to provide information to help the optimizer make the right decision.

The Multi-Range Read optimization is controlled by two optimizer switches:

- **mrr:** Whether the optimizer is allowed to use the Multi-Range Read optimization. The default is ON.

- **mrr_cost_based:** Whether the decision to use the Multi-Range Read optimization is cost based. You can disable this option to always use the optimization when it is supported. The default is ON.

Alternatively, you can use the MRR() and NO_MRR() optimizer switches to enable and disable the Multi-Range Read optimization on a per table or index basis.

You can see from the query plan whether the Multi-Range Read optimization is used. When that is the case, the traditional EXPLAIN output specifies Using MRR in the Extra column, and the JSON output sets the using_MRR field to true. Listing 17-8 shows an example of the full EXPLAIN output in the traditional format when the Multi-Range Read optimization is used.

Listing 17-8. The EXPLAIN output for a query using Multi-Range Read

```
mysql> EXPLAIN
        SELECT /*+ MRR(city) */
                *
        FROM world.city
        WHERE CountryCode BETWEEN 'AUS' AND 'CHN'\G
*************************** 1. row ***************************
           id: 1
  select_type: SIMPLE
        table: city
   partitions: NULL
         type: range
possible_keys: CountryCode
          key: CountryCode
      key_len: 3
          ref: NULL
```

```
        rows: 812
    filtered: 100
       Extra: Using index condition; Using MRR
1 row in set, 1 warning (0.0006 sec)
```

It is necessary to explicitly request the use of the Multi-Range Read optimization using the MRR() optimizer hint or by disabling the mrr_cost_based optimizer switch as the estimated number of rows for the example query is too small to use the Multi-Range Read optimization with the cost-based optimization to choose it.

When the optimization is used, MySQL uses the random read buffer for storing the indexes. The size of the buffer is set with the read_rnd_buffer_size option.

A related optimization is the Batched Key Access optimization.

Batched Key Access (BKA)

The Batched Key Access (BKA) optimization combines a block nested loop and the Multi-Range Read optimization. This makes it possible to use the join buffer for indexed joins in a similar way as for non-indexed joins and use the Multi-Range Read optimization to reduce the amount of random I/O.

The most useful types of queries for the Batched Key Access are large disk-bound queries, but there is no definitive guide to determining when the optimization helps and when it causes worse performance. When the optimization works the best, it reduces the query execution time by a factor of 2–10. However, when it performs the worst, the query execution time can increase by a factor of 2–3.[5]

Because the Batched Key Access optimization primary benefits a relatively narrow range of queries and the performance may degrade for other queries, the optimization is disabled by default. The best way to enable the optimization is to use the BKA() optimizer hint in the queries where you have found the optimization to provide a gain.

If you want to enable the optimization using the optimizer_switch variable, you must enable the batched_key_access optimizer switch (disabled by default), disable the mrr_cost_based optimizer switch (enabled by default), and ensure the mrr optimizer switch is enabled (enabled by default). To enable Batched Key Access for the session, you can do that using the following query:

---

[5]http://oysteing.blogspot.com/2012/04/improved-dbt-3-results-with-mysql-565.html

```
SET SESSION
    optimizer_switch
        = 'mrr=on,mrr_cost_based=off,batched_key_access=on';
```

When the optimization has been enabled this way, you can also use the BKA() and NO_BKA() optimizer hints to influence whether the optimization should be used. When it is used, the Extra column in the traditional EXPLAIN output includes Using join buffer (Batched Key Access), and in the JSON output the using_join_buffer field is set to Batched Key Access. Listing 17-9 shows an example of the full EXPLAIN output when Batched Key Access is used.

Listing 17-9. The EXPLAIN output with Batched Key Access

```
mysql> EXPLAIN
         SELECT /*+ BKA(ci) */
                 co.Code, co.Name AS Country,
                 ci.Name AS City
            FROM world.country co
                 INNER JOIN world.city ci
                     ON ci.CountryCode = co.Code\G
*************************** 1. row ***************************
            id: 1
   select_type: SIMPLE
         table: co
    partitions: NULL
          type: ALL
 possible_keys: PRIMARY
           key: NULL
       key_len: NULL
           ref: NULL
          rows: 239
      filtered: 100
         Extra: NULL
*************************** 2. row ***************************
            id: 1
   select_type: SIMPLE
         table: ci
```

```
    partitions: NULL
          type: ref
possible_keys: CountryCode
           key: CountryCode
       key_len: 3
           ref: world.co.Code
          rows: 18
      filtered: 100
         Extra: Using join buffer (Batched Key Access)
2 rows in set, 1 warning (0.0007 sec)
```

In this example, the Batched Key Access is enabled using an optimizer hint for the join on the city (ci) table using the CountryCode index.

The size of the join buffer is configured with the join_buffer_size option. Because the Batched Key Access optimization primarily is used with large joins, the join buffer should usually be configured relatively large, typically 4 megabytes or larger. As a large join buffer is a poor choice for most queries, it is recommended only to increase the size for the queries that use the Batched Key Access optimization.

Other Optimizations

MySQL includes support for several other optimizations. These are used automatically by the optimizer when they benefit the query, and it is rarely necessary to disable the optimizations manually. It is still useful to have an idea of what the optimizations are though, so you can know what it means when you encounter them, for example, in EXPLAIN outputs and you know how to change the behavior when the optimizer on a rare occasion needs a push in the right direction.

This subsection will go through some of the remaining optimizations in alphabetical order with focus on those that can be configured. For each optimization, the optimizer switch, optimizer hints, and EXPLAIN output details for the traditional format (the Extra column) and the JSON format are included.

Condition Filtering

The condition filtering optimization is used when a table has two or more conditions associated with it and an index can be used for part of the condition. When condition filtering is enabled, the filtering effects of the remaining conditions are taken into consideration when estimating the overall filtering of the table.

The optimizer switch, hints, and EXPLAIN details are as follows:

- **Optimizer Switch:** condition_fanout_filter – enabled by default
- **Optimizer Hints:** None
- **EXPLAIN Output:** None

Derived Merge

The optimizer can merge a derived table, a view reference, and common table expressions into the query block they are part of. The alternative to the optimization is to materialize the table, view reference, or common table expression.

The optimizer switch, hints, and EXPLAIN details are as follows:

- **Optimizer Switch:** derived_merge – enabled by default.
- **Optimizer Hints:** MERGE(), NO_MERGE().
- **EXPLAIN Output:** The query plan reflects that the derived table has been merged.

Engine Condition Pushdown

This optimization pushes a condition down to the storage engine. It is currently only supported for the NDBCluster storage engine.

The optimizer switch, hints, and EXPLAIN details are as follows:

- **Optimizer Switch:** engine_condition_pushdown – enabled by default.
- **Optimizer Hints:** None.
- **EXPLAIN Output:** The warnings include information about the conditions that have been pushed down.

Index Condition Pushdown

MySQL can push down conditions that can all be determined by using the columns in a single index, but the index can only directly filter part of the conditions. This, for example, happens when you have a condition like `Name LIKE '%abc%'` and `Name` is part of a multicolumn index. The optimization is also used for range conditions on secondary indexes. For InnoDB, index condition pushdown is only supported for secondary indexes.

The optimizer switch, hints, and EXPLAIN details are as follows:

- **Optimizer Switch:** `index_condition_pushdown` – enabled by default.

- **Optimizer Hints:** `NO_ICP()`.

- **EXPLAIN Output:** The traditional format has `Using index condition` in the `Extra` column, and the JSON format sets the `index_condition` field with the index condition that is pushed.

Index Extensions

All secondary nonunique indexes in InnoDB have the primary key columns appended to the index. When the index extension optimization is enabled, MySQL will consider the primary key columns as part of the index.

The optimizer switch, hints, and EXPLAIN details are as follows:

- **Optimizer Switch:** `use_index_extensions` – enabled by default

- **Optimizer Hints:** None

- **EXPLAIN Output:** None

Index Visibility

When a table has an invisible index, by default the optimizer will not consider it when creating the query plan. If the index visibility optimizer switch is enabled, invisible indexes will be considered. This can, for example, be useful to test the effect of an index that has been added but not yet made visible.

The optimizer switch, hints, and EXPLAIN details are as follows:

- **Optimizer Switch:** `use_invisible_indexes` – disabled by default

- **Optimizer Hints:** None

- **EXPLAIN Output:** None

Loose Index Scan

In some cases, MySQL can use part of an index to improve the performance of a query that aggregates data or includes the DISTINCT clause. This requires that the columns used to group the data by form a left prefix of a multi-column index with additional columns that are not used for the grouping. When there is a GROUP BY clause, only the MIN() and MAX() aggregate functions are allowed.

The optimizer switch, hints, and EXPLAIN details are as follows:

- **Optimizer Switch:** None.

- **Optimizer Hints:** NO_RANGE_OPTIMIZATION() disables the loose index scan optimization as well as index merges and range scans.

- **EXPLAIN Output:** The traditional format has Using index for group-by in the Extra column. The JSON format sets the using_index_for_group_by field to true.

Range Access Method

The range optimization is a little different from the other optimizations as it is considered an access method. Instead of doing a full table or index scan, MySQL will only scan one or more parts of the table or index. The range access method is often used for filter conditions that involve the operators >, >=, <, =<, BETWEEN., IN(), IS NULL, LIKE, and similar.

The optimizer switch, hints, and EXPLAIN details are as follows:

- **Optimizer Switch:** None.

- **Optimizer Hints:** NO_RANGE_OPTIMIZATION() – this also disables the loose index scan and index merge optimizations. It does however not disable the skip scan optimization even though that also uses range access.

- **EXPLAIN Output:** The access method is set to range.

You can use the range_optimizer_max_mem_size option to limit the amount of memory used for the range access. The default is 8 MiB. If you set the value to 0, it means that an unlimited amount of memory can be used.

Semijoin

The semijoin optimization is used for IN and EXIST conditions. There are four supported strategies: materialization, duplicate weedout, first match, and loose scan (not to be confused with the loose index scan optimization). When subquery materialization is enabled, the semijoin optimization uses the materialization strategy when it is possible. For EXISTS, the semijoin optimization is only supported in MySQL 8.0.16 and later, and for NOT EXISTS (and similar – this is also called an antijoin), MySQL 8.0.17 or later is required.

The semijoin optimization can be controlled using the semijoin optimizer switch to enable or disable the optimization altogether. The SEMIJOIN() and NO_SEMIJOIN() optimizer hints can be used for a single query using one or more of MATERIALIZATION, DUPSWEEDOUT, FIRSTMATCH, and LOOSESCAN as arguments.

The materialization strategy is the same as the subquery materialization optimization. See that for details.

The duplicate weedout strategy executes the semijoin as if it is a normal join and removes the duplicates using a temporary table. The optimizer switch, hints, and EXPLAIN details are as follows:

- **Optimizer Switch:** duplicateweedout – enabled by default.

- **Optimizer Hints:** SEMIJOIN(DUPSWEEDOUT), NO_SEMIJOIN(DUPSWEEDOUT).

- **EXPLAIN Output:** The traditional format has Start temporary and End temporary in the Extra column for the tables involved. The JSON-formatted output uses a block named duplicates_removal.

The first match strategy returns the first match for each value rather than all values. The optimizer switch, hints, and EXPLAIN details are as follows:

- **Optimizer Switch:** firstmatch – enabled by default.

- **Optimizer Hints:** SEMIJOIN(FIRSTMATCH), NO_SEMIJOIN(FIRSTMATCH).

- **EXPLAIN Output:** The traditional format has FirstMatch(...) in the Extra column where the value between parentheses is the name of the reference table. The JSON format sets the value of the first_match field to the name of the reference table.

The loose scan strategy uses an index to choose a single value from each of the subquery's value groups. The optimizer switch, hints, and EXPLAIN details are as follows:

- **Optimizer Switch:** loosescan – enabled by default.

- **Optimizer Hints:** SEMIJOIN(LOOSESCAN), NO_SEMIJOIN(LOOSESCAN).

- **EXPLAIN Output:** The traditional format has LooseScan(m..n) in the Extra column where m and n indicate which parts of the index are used for the loose scan. The JSON format sets the loosescan field equal to true.

Skip Scan

The skip scan optimization is new in MySQL 8.0.13 and works similarly to the loose index scan. It is used when there is a range condition on the second column of a multicolumn index, but there is no condition on the first column. The skip scan optimization turns a full index scan into a series of range scans (one range scan for each value of the first column in the index).

The optimizer switch, hints, and EXPLAIN details are as follows:

- **Optimizer Switch:** skip_scan – enabled by default.

- **Optimizer Hints:** SKIP_SCAN(), NO_SKIP_SCAN().

- **EXPLAIN Output:** The traditional format has Using index for skip scan in the Extra column, and the JSON format sets the using_index_for_skip_scan field to true.

Subquery Materialization

The subquery materialization strategy stores the result of a subquery in an internal temporary table. When possible, the optimizer will add an auto-generated hash index on the temporary table which makes joining it to the rest of the query fast.

The optimizer switch, hints, and EXPLAIN details are as follows:

- **Optimizer Switch:** materialization – enabled by default.

- **Optimizer Hints:** SUBQUERY(MATERIALIZATION).

- **EXPLAIN Output:** The traditional format has MATERIALIZED as the select type. The JSON format creates a block named materialized_from_subquery.

When the `subquery_materialization_cost_based` optimizer switch is enabled (the default), the optimizer will use cost estimated to decide between the subquery materialization optimization and the `IN-to-EXIST` subquery transformation (rewriting an `IN` condition as `EXISTS`). When the switch is off, the optimizer always chooses subquery materialization.

As it has been evident in the last two sections, there are plenty of possibilities to configure the optimizer. The next section will look closer into that.

Configuring the Optimizer

There are several ways you can configure MySQL to influence the optimizer. You have already encountered some configuration options, the optimizer switches, and optimizer hints. This section will start out showing how you can configure the engine and server costs associated with different operations and then go through the configuration options with additional details about the optimizer switches. Finally, the optimizer hints will be discussed.

Engine Costs

The engine costs provide information about how expensive it is to read data. Since data can be fetched either from memory or disk and different storage engines can have different costs for reading data, it is not a case of one size fits all. For this reason, MySQL allows you to configure the cost for reading from memory and disk per storage engine.

You can use the `mysql.engine_cost` table to change the costs of reading data. The table has the following columns:

- **engine_name:** The storage engine the cost data is for. The value `default` is used to represent all storage engines that do not have specific data.

- **device_type:** Currently not in use and must have the value 0.

- **cost_name:** The name of the cost. Currently, there are two supported values: `io_block_read_cost` for disk-based reads and `memory_block_read_cost` for memory-based reads.

- **cost_value:** The cost of the read operations. A value of `NULL` (the default) means the value stored in the `default_value` column is used.

- **last_update:** When the row was last updated. The time is returned in the time zone set by the time_zone session variable.

- **comment:** An optional comment that you can provide to give context to why the cost was changed. The comment can be up to 1024 characters long.

- **default_value:** The default cost used for the operation. This is a read-only column. The default value is 1 for io_block_read_cost is and 0.25 for memory_block_read_cost.

The primary key consists of the engine_name, device_type, and cost_name columns. The engine costs are particularly useful for InnoDB as in MySQL 8, InnoDB can provide an estimate to the optimizer whether the data is in the buffer pool or it is necessary to read it from disk.

You can update the existing cost estimates using an UPDATE statement. If you want to insert estimates for a storage engine, you use the INSERT statement, and if you want to remove custom cost values, you use the DELETE statement. In either case, you must execute the FLUSH OPTIMIZER_COSTS statement for the changes to take effect for new connections (existing connections continue to use the old values). For example, if you want to add data specific for InnoDB assuming a host with slow disk I/O and very fast memory, you can use statements like

```
mysql> INSERT INTO mysql.engine_cost
              (engine_name, device_type, cost_name,
               cost_value, comment)
        VALUES ('InnoDB', 0, 'io_block_read_cost',
                2, 'InnoDB on non-local cloud storage'),
               ('InnoDB', 0, 'memory_block_read_cost',
                0.15, 'InnoDB with very fast memory');
Query OK, 2 rows affected (0.0887 sec)

Records: 2  Duplicates: 0  Warnings: 0

mysql> FLUSH OPTIMIZER_COSTS;
Query OK, 0 rows affected (0.0877 sec)
```

If you want to change the cost values, the recommendation is to roughly double or half the values and evaluate the effect. Since the engine costs are global, you should ensure you have a good monitoring baseline before the change and compare the query performance after the change to detect whether the change has the intended effect.

MySQL also has some more general server costs that can be used to affect various operations related to queries.

Server Costs

MySQL uses a cost-based approach to determine the optimal query plans. For this to work as good as possible, it must know how expensive the various types of operations are. The most important part for the calculation is that the relative costs are correct which fortunately helps. Yet, there can be differences from system to system how the relative costs are and how it affects the workload.

You can use the `mysql.server_cost` table to change the costs of several operations. The table has the following columns:

- **cost_name:** The name of the operation.

- **cost_value:** The cost of performing the operation. If the cost is set to NULL, then the default cost is used (the `default_value` column). The cost is provided as a floating point number.

- **last_update:** When the cost was last updated. The time is returned in the time zone set by the `time_zone` session variable.

- **comment:** An optional comment that you can provide to give context to why the cost was changed. The comment can be up to 1024 characters long.

- **default_value:** The default cost used for the operation. This is a read-only column.

There are currently six operations that can be configured in the `server_cost` table. These are

- **disk_temptable_create_cost:** The cost of creating internal temporary tables on disk. The lower the cost of `disk_temptable_ create_cost` and `disk_temptable_row_cost`, the more likely it is that the optimizer will choose a query plan that requires on-disk temporary tables. The default cost is 20.

- **disk_temptable_row_cost:** The cost of row operations for internal temporary tables created on disk. The default cost is 0.5.

- **key_compare_cost:** The cost of comparing record keys. If you have problems with query plans sorting by index using a file sort where a non-indexed based sort would be faster, you can increase the cost of these operations. The default cost is 0.05.

- **memory_temptable_create_cost:** The cost of creating internal temporary tables in memory. The lower the cost of memory_temptable_create_cost and memory_temptable_row_cost, the more likely it is that the optimizer chooses a query plan that requires in-memory internal temporary tables. The default cost is 1.

- **memory_temptable_row_cost:** The cost of row operations for internal temporary tables created in memory. The default cost is 0.1.

- **row_evaluate_cost:** The general cost of evaluating row conditions. The lower the cost, the more MySQL is inclined to examine many rows such as using a full table scan. The higher the cost, the more MySQL will try to reduce the number of examined rows and use more index lookups and range scans. The default cost is 0.1.

If you do want to change one of the server costs, then you need to use a regular UPDATE statement followed by FLUSH OPTIMIZER_COSTS. The changes will then affect new connections. For example, if you store on-disk internal temporary tables on a RAM disk (shared memory disk) and want to reduce the costs to reflect that

```
mysql> UPDATE mysql.server_cost
          SET cost_value = 1,
              Comment = 'Stored on memory disk'
       WHERE cost_name = 'disk_temptable_create_cost';
Query OK, 1 row affected (0.1051 sec)

Rows matched: 1  Changed: 1  Warnings: 0

mysql> UPDATE mysql.server_cost
          SET cost_value = 0.1,
              Comment = 'Stored on memory disk'
```

```
        WHERE cost_name = 'disk_temptable_row_cost';
Query OK, 1 row affected (0.1496 sec)

Rows matched: 1  Changed: 1  Warnings: 0

mysql> FLUSH OPTIMIZER_COSTS;
Query OK, 0 rows affected (0.1057 sec)
```

Changing the costs may not always end up affecting the query plan, because the optimizer may have little choice than to use a given query plan or the calculated costs are so different that changing the server costs to affect the query plan will have too great effect on other queries. Remember that the server costs are global for all connections, so you should only change the costs if there are systemic problems. If the issue only affects a few queries, it is better to use optimizer hints to affect the query plan.

Another option for affecting the query plans is the optimizer switches.

Optimizer Switches

The optimizer switches have been mentioned throughout this chapter. They are configured through the optimizer_switch option. The optimizer switches work somewhat different than other configuration options, so it is worth diving deeper into their use.

The optimizer_switch option is a composite option with all optimizer switches using the same option, but with the possibility to change individual switches without including the switches you do not want to change. You set the switch you want to change to on or off to enable or disable it. The optimizer switches can be changed either at the global scope which affects all new connections or at the session level. For example, if you want to disable the derived_merge optimizer switch for the current connection, you can use the following statement:

```
mysql> SET SESSION optimizer_switch = 'derived_merge=off';
Query OK, 0 rows affected (0.0003 sec)
```

If you want to change the value permanently, you can use SET PERSIST or SET PERSIST_ONLY in the same way:

```
mysql> SET PERSIST optimizer_switch = 'derived_merge=off';
Query OK, 0 rows affected (0.0431 sec)
```

The same principle applies if you prefer to store the value in the MySQL configuration file, for example:

```
[mysqld]
optimizer_switch = "derived_merge=off"
```

Table 17-3 lists the optimizer switches available as of MySQL 8.0.18 together with their default values and a brief summary of what the switch does. The optimizer switches are ordered in the order they appear in the optimizer_switch option.

Table 17-3. *The optimizer switches*

Optimizer Switch	Default Value	Description
index_merge	on	The overall switch controlling index merges.
index_merge_union	on	The union index merge strategy.
index_merge_sort_union	on	The sort-union index merge strategy.
index_merge_intersection	on	The intersection index merge strategy.
engine_condition_pushdown	on	Pushing down conditions to the NDBCluster storage engine.
index_condition_pushdown	on	Pushing down index conditions to the storage engine.
mrr	on	The Multi-Range Read optimization.
mrr_cost_based	on	Whether using the Multi-Range Read optimization should be based on cost estimates.
block_nested_loop	on	The block nested loop join algorithm. This together with the hash_join switch also controls whether hash joins can be used.
batched_key_access	off	The Batched Key Access optimization. It is also required that the mrr switch is enabled and the mrr_cost_based switch is disabled for Batched Key Access to be used.

(continued)

Table 17-3. (*continued*)

Optimizer Switch	Default Value	Description
materialization	on	Whether materialized subqueries can be used. This also affects whether the materialization semijoin optimization is available.
semijoin	on	The overall switch enabling or disabling the semijoin optimization.
loosescan	on	The semijoin loose scan strategy.
firstmatch	on	The semijoin first match strategy.
duplicateweedout	on	The semijoin duplicate weedout strategy.
subquery_ materialization_cost_ based	on	Whether using subquery materialization is based on cost estimates.
use_index_extensions	on	Whether the primary key columns that InnoDB adds to nonunique secondary indexes are used as part of the index.
condition_fanout_ filter	on	Whether conditions not handled by the access method are included in the filtering estimate.
derived_merge	on	The derived merge optimization.
use_invisible_indexes	off	Whether the invisible indexes should be used.
skip_scan	on	The skip scan optimization.
hash_join	on	The hash join algorithm. For hash joins to be enabled, the block_nested_loop switch must also be enabled.

The various optimizations, strategies, and algorithms are described in more detail earlier in this chapter.

The `optimizer_switch` option is great if you want to change the setting globally or for the duration of a session; however, in many cases, you only need to change an optimizer switch or a setting for a single query. In that case, optimizer hints are a better option.

Optimizer Hints

The optimizer hints feature was introduced in MySQL 5.7 and extended in MySQL 8. It allows you to provide information to the optimizer, so you can influence how the query plan ends up. Unlike for the `optimizer_switch` option that either switches an option on or off, the optimizer hint equivalents can be set per query block, table, or index. Additionally, there is support for changing the value of configuration options for the duration of the query. This is a powerful way to improve the performance of a query when the optimizer cannot quite get the optimal query plan on its own or you need the query to execute, for example, with a larger value than the global default for some option.

Optimizer hints are set using a special comment syntax right after the `SELECT`, `INSERT`, `REPLACE`, `UPDATE`, or `DELETE` clause. The syntax uses the inline comments with a + immediately after the start of the comment, for example:

```
SELECT /*+ MAX_EXECUTION_TIME(2000) */
       id, Name, District
  FROM world.city
 WHERE CountryCode = 'AUS';
```

This example sets the maximum execution time for the query to 2000 milliseconds.

Table 17-4 lists the optimizer hints available as of MySQL 8.0.18 including the scopes supported for each hint and a brief description. For many of the hints, there are two versions, one for enabling the feature and the other for disabling it; these are listed together. The hints are listed alphabetically according to the hint that enables the feature except for `NO_ICP` and `NO_RANGE_OPTIMIZATION` hints which have no corresponding hint to enable the feature.

Table 17-4. *Optimizer hints*

Hint	Scope	Description
BKA NO_BKA	Query block Table	The Batched Key Access optimization.
BNL NO_BNL	Query block Table	The block nested loop join algorithm.
HASH_JOIN NO_HASH_JOIN	Query block Table	The hash join algorithm.
INDEX_MERGE NO_INDEX_MERGE	Table Index	The index merge optimization.
JOIN_FIXED_ORDER	Query block	Forces all joins in the query block to be executed in the order they are listed in the query. This is the same as using SELECT STRAIGHT_JOIN.
JOIN_ORDER	Query block	Forces two or more tables to be joined in a specific order. The optimizer is free to change the join order of the tables not listed.
JOIN_PREFIX	Query block	Forces the specified tables to be the first tables of the join and join them in the order given.
JOIN_SUFFIX	Query block	Forces the specified tables to be the last tables of the join and join them in the order given.
MAX_EXECUTION_TIME	Global	Limits the query execution time for SELECT statements. The value is in milliseconds.
MERGE NO_MERGE	Table	The derived merge optimization.
MRR NO_MRR	Table Index	The Multi-Range Read optimization.
NO_ICP	Table Index	The Index Condition Pushdown optimization.

(*continued*)

Table 17-4. (*continued*)

Hint	Scope	Description
NO_RANGE_ OPTIMIZATION	Table Index	Do not use range access to tables and/or indexes. This also disables index merges and loose index scans. It is mostly useful if the query will cause many range scans and it is causing performance or resource problems.
QB_NAME	Query block	Sets the name of a query block. The name can be used to reference the query block in other optimizer hints.
RESOURCE_GROUP	Global	The resource group to use for the query. Resource groups are discussed in the next section.
SEMIJOIN NO_SEMIJOIN	Query block	The semijoin optimization.
SKIP_SCAN NO_SKIP_SCAN	Table Index	The skip scan optimization.
SET_VAR	Global	Sets the value of a configuration variable for the duration of the query.
SUBQUERY	Query block	Whether subqueries can use the materialization optimization or the IN-to-EXISTS transformation.

Several of these optimizer hints have been encountered earlier in the chapter when join algorithms and optimizations were discussed. The scope specifies which part of the query the hint applies to. The scopes include

- **Global:** The hint applies to the whole query.

- **Query Block:** The hint applies to a group of joins. For example, the top level of the query is a query block; a subquery is another query block. Hints that apply to a query block can in some cases also take the table names for a join to limit the hint to a specific join.

- **Table:** The hint applies to a specific table.

- **Index:** The hint applies to the use of a specific index.

When you specify a table, you need to use the name that the table is used as in the query. If you have specified an alias for a table, you need to use the alias rather than the table name which ensures that all tables in a query block can be uniquely identified.

Tip   It is beyond the scope of this book to go into detail with all the details of using optimizer hints. The list of hints also gets updated relatively frequently as new features are added. You are encouraged to read `https://dev.mysql.com/doc/refman/en/optimizer-hints.html` to see the current list of optimizer hints and all details regarding usage and possible conflicts.

The optimizer hints are specified in the same way as a function call with the arguments specified in parentheses. When an optimizer hint does not take any arguments, an empty set of parentheses is used. You can specify several optimizer hints for the same query in which case you use a space to separate them. If you specify several arguments other than a leading query block name, you must separate the arguments with a comma (but note that in some cases a space is used to combine two pieces of information into one argument, e.g., when specifying an index, then the table and index names are separated by a space).

For complex queries with multiple query blocks, it is useful to name the query blocks, so that you can specify the query block an optimizer hint should apply to. You use the QB_NAME() optimizer hint to set the name of a query block:

```
SELECT /*+ QB_NAME(payment) */
       rental_id
  FROM sakila.payment
 WHERE staff_id = 1 AND customer_id = 75;
```

You can then refer to the query block by adding an @ in front of the query block name when specifying a hint:

```
SELECT /*+ NO_INDEX_MERGE(@payment payment) */
       rental_id, rental_date, return_date
  FROM sakila.rental
 WHERE rental_id IN (
       SELECT /*+ QB_NAME(payment) */
              rental_id
```

```
      FROM sakila.payment
      WHERE staff_id = 1 AND customer_id = 75
   );
```

The example sets the name of the query block inside the IN condition to *payment*. This block name is then referenced at the top level to disable the index merge feature for the payment table in the payment query block. When you use the query block name in this way, all tables listed in the hint must be from the same query block. An alternative notation for specifying the query block is to add it after the table name, for example:

```
SELECT /*+ NO_INDEX_MERGE(payment@payment) */
      rental_id, rental_date, return_date
  FROM sakila.rental
 WHERE rental_id IN (
        SELECT /*+ QB_NAME(payment) */
              rental_id
          FROM sakila.payment
         WHERE staff_id = 1 AND customer_id = 75
      );
```

This does the same as in the previous example, but it has the advantage that you can use the one hint for tables in different query blocks.

A great use of optimizer hints is to change the value of a configuration variable for the duration of the query. This is particularly useful for options such as join_buffer_size and read_rnd_buffer_size that are best kept at a small global value, but where a larger value for some queries can improve the performance. You use the SET_VAR() optimizer hint with the argument being the variable assignment. In the reference manual, the variables that can be used with the SET_VAR() optimizer hint have "SET_VAR Hint Applies: Yes". For example, to set join_buffer_size to 1 MiB and optimizer_search_depth to 0 (this option will be explained shortly), you can use

```
SELECT /*+ SET_VAR(join_buffer_size = 1048576)
          SET_VAR(optimizer_search_depth = 0) */
      CountryCode, country.Name AS Country,
      city.Name AS City, city.District
```

```
FROM world.country IGNORE INDEX (Primary)
     INNER JOIN world.city IGNORE INDEX (CountryCode)
          ON city.CountryCode = country.Code
WHERE Continent = 'Asia';
```

There are a couple of things to note from the example. First, the SET_VAR() hint does not support setting two options in the same hint, so you need to specify the hint once for each option. Second, there is no support for expressions or units, so for the join_buffer_size it is necessary to provide the value directly in bytes.

There is one thing the optimizer hints cannot help you with. If you are not happy with the choice of index made by the optimizer, you will need to use index hints.

Index Hints

Index hints have been around in MySQL for a long time. You can use them to specify for each table which indexes the optimizer is allowed to use and which it should ignore. You have already encountered the IGNORE INDEX hint when disabling the indexes for the examples used for the block nested loop and hash join algorithms.

MySQL has support for three index hints:

- **IGNORE INDEX:** The optimizer is not allowed to use the named indexes at all.

- **USE INDEX:** The optimizer should use one of the named indexes if an index is used.

- **FORCE INDEX:** This is the same as USE INDEX except that a table scan should always be avoided if it is at all possible to use one of the named indexes.

When you use one of the index hints, you need to provide the names of the indexes that should be affected by the hint in a comma-separated list inside parentheses. The index hint is placed right after the table name. If you add an alias for the table, place the index hint after the alias. For example, to query all cities in Asia without using the primary key on the country table nor the CountryCode index of the city table, you can use the following query:

```
SELECT ci.CountryCode, co.Name AS Country,
       ci.Name AS City, ci.District
  FROM world.country co IGNORE INDEX (Primary)
       INNER JOIN world.city ci IGNORE INDEX (CountryCode)
           ON ci.CountryCode = co.Code
 WHERE co.Continent = 'Asia';
```

Notice how the primary key is called Primary. In the example, the index hints apply to all operations that can use indexes for the table. It is possible to limit the scope to either joins, sorting, or grouping by adding FOR JOIN, FOR ORDER BY, or FOR GROUP BY, for example:

```
SELECT *
  FROM world.city USE INDEX FOR ORDER BY (Primary)
 WHERE CountryCode = 'AUS'
 ORDER BY ID;
```

While it is in most cases best to limit the use of index hints so the optimizer is free to change the query plan as the indexes and data change, index hints are one of the most powerful tools available, and you should not shy away from using them when needed.

The last way to influence the optimizer is to use configuration options.

Configuration Options

There are a few configuration options that affect the optimizer beyond the optimizer_ switch option. These options control how exhaustive the optimizer searches for the optimal query plan and whether its steps should be traced using the optimizer trace feature. The optimizer trace feature will be deferred until Chapter 20 where it is discussed together with the EXPLAIN statement.

The two options that will be discussed here are

- optimizer_prune_level
- optimizer_search_depth

The optimizer_prune_level option can have a value of 0 or 1. The default is 1. It determines whether the optimizer will prune query plans to avoid doing an exhaustive search. A value of 1 enables pruning. Should you encounter a query where pruning prevents the optimizer finding a good enough query plan, `optimizer_prune_level` can be changed for the session. The global value should almost always be 1.

The `optimizer_search_depth` option determines how many tables (joins) should be included in the search for the optimal query plan. Allowed values are 0–62 with 62 being the default. Since the greatest number of tables that are allowed for one query block is 61, a value of 62 means an exhaustive search is made except for the search paths removed by the pruning. The value 0 means that MySQL picks the maximum search depth; currently that is the same as setting the value to 7.

If you have query blocks with many tables joined by inner joins, and it takes a long time to determine the query plan compared to the query execution time, you may want to set `optimizer_search_depth` to 0 or a value lower than 62. An alternative is to use the `JOIN_ORDER()`, `JOIN_PREFIX()`, and `JOIN_SUFFIX()` optimizer hints to lock the join order for part of the query.

The discussion thus far has been around the optimization process and the options the optimizer has. There is one more level to consider: which resource group should be used when the query is executing.

Resource Groups

The concept of resource groups is new in MySQL 8 and allows you to set rules for the resource usage a query or a group of queries can use. This can be a powerful way to improve the performance on high-concurrency systems and to allow you to prioritize some queries higher than others. This section covers how you can get information about the existing resource groups, managing resource groups, and how to use them.

Note   At the time of writing, resource groups are not supported for macOS or when using the commercial thread pool plugin. Additionally, thread priorities are ignored on Solaris and FreeBSD as well as on Linux when the `CAP_SYS_NICE` capability is not set. To see the latest restrictions and how to enable the `CAP_SYS_NICE` capability, see `https://dev.mysql.com/doc/refman/en/resource-groups.html#resource-group-restrictions`.

Retrieving Information About Resource Groups

Information about the existing resource groups can be found in the information_
schema.RESOURCE_GROUPS view which is a view on top of the data dictionary table where
the resource groups are stored. The view includes the following columns:

- **RESOURCE_GROUP_NAME:** The name of the resource group.

- **RESOURCE_GROUP_TYPE:** Whether the resource group is for SYSTEM or
  USER level threads. SYSTEM is used by system threads, and USER is used
  by user connections.

- **RESOURCE_GROUP_ENABLED:** Whether the resource group is enabled.

- **VCPU_IDS:** Which *virtual CPUs* the resource group is allowed to use.
  A virtual CPU takes into account physical CPU cores, hyperthreading,
  hardware threads, and so on.

- **THREAD_PRIORITY:** The thread priority for the threads using the
  resource group. The lower the value, the higher the priority.

Listing 17-10 shows the resource group information for the default resource groups
that come with the MySQL installation. The values for the VCPU_IDS column depend on
the number of virtual CPUs on your system.

Listing 17-10. The information for the default resource groups

```
mysql> SELECT *
         FROM information_schema.RESOURCE_GROUPS\G
*************************** 1. row ***************************
   RESOURCE_GROUP_NAME: USR_default
   RESOURCE_GROUP_TYPE: USER
RESOURCE_GROUP_ENABLED: 1
              VCPU_IDS: 0-7
       THREAD_PRIORITY: 0
```

```
*************************** 2. row ***************************
   RESOURCE_GROUP_NAME: SYS_default
   RESOURCE_GROUP_TYPE: SYSTEM
RESOURCE_GROUP_ENABLED: 1
              VCPU_IDS: 0-7
       THREAD_PRIORITY: 0
2 rows in set (0.0007 sec)
```

There are two resource groups by default: the USR_default group for user connections and the SYS_default for system threads. The two groups are configured the same and are allowed to use all CPUs. These two groups can neither be dropped nor modified. However, you can create your own resource groups.

Managing Resource Groups

You can create, alter, and drop resource groups as long as you do not try to modify or drop one of the default groups. This allows you to create resource groups that you can use to divide resources among your queries. It requires the RESOURCE_GROUP_ADMIN privilege to create, change, or delete resource groups.

The following statements are available to manage resource groups:

- **CREATE RESOURCE GROUP:** Creates a new resource group

- **ALTER RESOURCE GROUP:** Modifies an existing resource group

- **DROP RESOURCE GROUP:** Deletes a resource group

For all three statements, the group name must always be specified, and it is specified without any argument name (examples will follow shortly). Table 17-5 shows the arguments for the three statements. Where the values specify N or M-N, M, and N represents integers.

Table 17-5. *The arguments used when managing resource groups*

Option	Syntax	Values	Operations
Name		At most 64 characters	CREATE ALTER DROP
Type	TYPE = ...	SYSTEM USER	CREATE
CPUs	VCPU = ...	N or M-N in comma-separated list	CREATE ALTER
Priority	THREAD_PRIORITY	N	CREATE ALTER
Status		ENABLED DISABLED	CREATE ALTER
Force	FORCE		ALTER DROP

For the priority, the valid range of values depends on the group type. The SYSTEM group can have priorities between -20 and 0, and the USER type can have priorities between -20 and 19. The meaning of the priorities follows the principle of the nice feature in Linux meaning the lower the value for the priority, the higher the priority the thread will get. Thus, -20 is the highest priority, whereas 19 has lowest priority. On Microsoft Windows, there are five native priority levels available. Table 17-6 lists the mapping from the resource group priorities to the Microsoft Windows priorities.

Table 17-6. *Mapping from resource group priorities for Microsoft Windows*

Start Priority	End Priority	Microsoft Windows Priority Level
-20	-10	THREAD_PRIORITY_HIGHEST
-9	-1	THREAD_PRIORITY_ABOVE_NORMAL
0	0	THREAD_PRIORITY_NORMAL
1	10	THREAD_PRIORITY_BELOW_NORMAL
11	19	THREAD_PRIORITY_LOWEST

When you create a new resource group, you must set the name and type of the group. The rest of the arguments are optional. The default is to set VCPU to include all CPUs available on the host, set the priority to 0, and enable the group. An example of creating an enabled group named my_group for user connections that can use the CPUs with ids 2, 3, 6, and 7 is (this requires that the host has at least eight virtual CPUs) as follows:

```
CREATE RESOURCE GROUP my_group
   TYPE = USER
   VCPU = 2-3,6,7
THREAD_PRIORITY = 0
ENABLE;
```

The specification of the VCPU argument shows how you can either list CPUs one by one or use a range. The resource group name is treated as an identifier, so you only need to quote it with backticks under the same circumstances as for schema and table names.

The ALTER RESOURCE GROUP statement is similar to the CREATE RESOURCE GROUP statement, but you cannot change the group name or group type. For example, to change the CPUs and priority for the group named my_group

```
 ALTER RESOURCE GROUP my_group
   VCPU = 2-5
THREAD_PRIORITY = 10;
```

If you need to delete a resource group, you can use the DROP RESOURCE GROUP statement which just requires the group name, for example:

```
DROP RESOURCE GROUP my_group;
```

For the ALTER RESOURCE GROUP and DROP RESOURCE GROUP statements, there is an optional argument FORCE. This specifies how MySQL should handle cases when there are threads using the resource group. Table 17-7 summarizes the behavior.

Table 17-7. *The effect of using FORCE or leaving it out*

Forcing	ALTER	DROP
Not forcing	The change takes effect when all existing threads using the group have terminated. Until then, no new threads can use the resource group.	An error occurs if any threads are assigned to the group.
Forcing	Existing threads are moved to the default group based on the thread type.	Existing threads are moved to the default group based on the thread type.

Both when modifying and deleting a resource group, if you have the FORCE option, existing threads assigned to the group will be reassigned to the default group. This means the USR_default group for user connections and the SYS_default group for system threads. For ALTER RESOURCE GROUP, the FORCE option can only be used if the DISABLE option is also specified.

Now you are ready to assign resource groups to threads.

Assigning Resource Groups

There are two ways to set a resource group for a thread. You can explicitly set the resource group for a thread, or you can use an optimizer hint to set it for a single query. It requires the RESOURCE_GROUP_ADMIN or RESOURCE_GROUP_USER privilege to assign threads to resource groups irrespective of the method used.

First, recreate the my_group group (this time using just a single CPU to make it work on all systems):

```
CREATE RESOURCE GROUP my_group
  TYPE = USER
  VCPU = 0
THREAD_PRIORITY = 0
ENABLE;
```

Note   Connections using the X Protocol (the default for MySQL Shell) are currently not allowed to create, modify, or set resource groups except by setting the resource group for a single query using an optimizer hint.

You use the `SET RESOURCE GROUP` statement to assign a thread to a resource group. This works for both system and user threads. To assign the connection itself to a resource group, use the statement with the resource group name as the only argument, for example:

```
SET RESOURCE GROUP my_group;
```

If you want to change the resource group for one or more other threads, you add the FOR keyword at the end followed by a comma-separated list of the Performance Schema thread ids you want to assign to the group. For example, to assign the threads 47, 49, and 50 to my_group (the thread ids will obviously be different in your case throughout this example – replace with threads that exist on your system)

```
SET RESOURCE GROUP my_group FOR 47, 49, 50;
```

As an alternative, you can use the `RESOURCE_GROUP()` optimizer hint to assign as resource group to a thread for the duration of the query, for example:

```
SELECT /*+ RESOURCE_GROUP(my_group) */
       *
  FROM world.city
 WHERE CountryCode = 'USA';
```

The optimizer hint is in general the best way to use resource groups as it allows you to set it per query and it is supported when you use the X Protocol. It can also be used in combination with the MySQL rewrite plugin or a proxy such as ProxySQL that supports adding the optimizer hint comment to the query.

You can use the RESOURCE_GROUP column in the `performance_schema.threads` table to see which resource group each thread is using. For example, to see the resource group in use for the three threads that were changed earlier with the `SET RESOURCE GROUP FOR 47, 49, 50` statement

```
mysql> SELECT THREAD_ID, RESOURCE_GROUP
         FROM performance_schema.threads
         WHERE THREAD_ID IN (47, 49, 50);
+-----------+----------------+
| THREAD_ID | RESOURCE_GROUP |
+-----------+----------------+
|        47 | my_group       |
|        49 | my_group       |
|        50 | my_group       |
+-----------+----------------+
3 rows in set (0.0008 sec)
```

That leaves the question of how you should use resource groups.

Performance Considerations

The effect of using resource groups depends on several factors. The default is that all threads can execute on any CPU and with the same midrange priority which is the same behavior as in MySQL 5.7 and earlier. The main benefit from using different configurations for the resource groups comes when MySQL is starting to encounter resource contention.

It is impossible to give concrete advise on how to use resource groups the most optimal as it very much depends on a combination of hardware and query workload. The optimal use of resource groups can also change as new improvements are made to the MySQL code. This means that as always, you need to use monitoring to determine the effect of changing the resource groups and the use of them.

That said, there are some suggestions that can be made of how to use resource groups to improve the performance or user experience. These include but are not limited to

- Give different priorities to different connections. This can, for example, be to ensure a batch job does not affect queries related to the frontend application too much, or it can be to give different applications different priorities.

- Assign threads for different applications to different CPU sets to reduce the interference between them.

- Assign write threads and read threads to different CPU sets to set the maximum concurrence for the different tasks. This can, for example, be useful to limit the concurrency of the write threads if they are encountering resource contention.

- Give high priority to a thread that executes a transaction that takes many locks, so the transaction can complete as quickly as possible and release the locks again.

As a rule of thumb, the resource groups are useful, if there are not enough CPU resources to execute everything in parallel or the write concurrency becomes too high and limiting it by restricting which CPUs handle the write workload can be used to avoid the contention. For low-concurrency workloads, it is usually best to use the default resource groups.

Summary

This chapter has gone through how the optimizer works, the join algorithms and optimizations available to it, how to configure the optimizer, and resource groups.

MySQL uses a cost-based optimizer where the cost of each part of the query execution is estimated and the overall query plan is chosen to minimize the cost. As part of the optimization, the optimizer will rewrite the query using various transformations, the optimal join order is found, and other decisions are made such as which indexes that should be used.

MySQL has support for three join algorithms. The simplest – and the original – algorithm is the nested loop join which simply iterates over the rows in the outermost table, then has a nested loop for the next table, and so forth. The block nested loop is an extension where non-indexed joins can use the join buffer to reduce the number of table scans of the inner table. New in MySQL 8.0.18 is the hash join algorithm which is also used for joins not using an index and is very effective for the joins it supports – so effective that it for low-selectivity indexes can outperform indexed joins.

There is a range of other optimizations that can be used. Special focus was put to the index merge, Multi-Range Read, and Batched Key Access optimizations. The index merge optimization allows MySQL to use more than one index per table. The Multi-Range Read optimization is used to reduce the amount of random I/O caused by secondary index reads. The Batched Key Access optimization combines the block nested loop and the Multi-Range Read optimization.

There are several ways to change the configuration of MySQL to influence the optimizer. The `mysql.engine_cost` table stores cost information for reading from memory and disk. This can be set per storage engine. The `mysql.server_cost` contains base cost estimates for various operations such as using internal temporary tables and comparing records. The `optimizer_switch` configuration option is used to enable or disable various optimizer features such as block nested loop, Batched Key Access, and so on.

Two flexible options to influence the optimizer are to use optimizer hints and index hints. The optimizer hints can be used to enable or disable features as well as setting options for the query or even more fine-grained down to the index level. The index hints can be used to enable or disable indexes for a table. Optionally, the index hints can be limited to a specific operation such as sorting. Finally, the `optimizer_prune_level` and `optimizer_search_depth` options can be used to limit how much work the optimizer will do to find the optimal query plan.

The last feature that was covered is resource groups which has been added in MySQL 8. Resource groups can be used to specify which CPUs a thread is allowed to use and which priority the thread should execute with. This can be useful to prioritize some threads higher than others or to prevent resource contention.

The next chapter will look into how locking works in MySQL.

CHAPTER 18

Locking Theory and Monitoring

Together with the optimizer that was discussed in the previous chapter, locks are possibly the most complex topic of query optimization. When locks show their worst side, they can cause gray hairs for even the best expert on locks. However, do not despair. This chapter will introduce you to most of the knowledge of locks you will need – and possibly some more. After you have read this chapter, you should be able to start investigating locks and use that to gain further knowledge.

The chapter starts out discussing why locks are needed and the lock access levels. The largest section of the chapter then goes through the most commonly encountered locks in MySQL. The other half of the chapter discusses why lock requests may fail, how to reduce the impact of locks, and how to monitor locks.

Note   Most of the examples include the statements to reproduce the important parts of the outputs (some data will by nature differ from case to case). Since the interesting parts of locking often include more than one connection, the prompts for the queries have been set to indicate which connection to use for which queries when that is important. For example, `Connection 1>` means that the query should be executed by the first of your connections.

© Jesper Wisborg Krogh 2020
J. W. Krogh, *MySQL 8 Query Performance Tuning*, https://doi.org/10.1007/978-1-4842-5584-1_18

Why Are Locks Needed?

It can seem like a perfect world where locking in databases is not needed. The price will however be so high that only few use cases can use that database, and it is impossible for a general-purpose database such as MySQL. If you do not have locking, you cannot have any concurrency. Imagine that only one connection is ever allowed to the database (you can argue that itself is a lock and thus the system is not lock-free anyway) – that is not very useful for most applications.

Note   Often what is called a lock in MySQL is really a lock request which can be in a granted or pending state.

When you have several connections executing queries concurrently, you need some way to ensure that the connections do not step on each other's toes. That is where locks enter the picture. You can think of locks in the same way as traffic signals in road traffic that regulate access to the resources to avoid accidents. In a road intersection, it is necessary to ensure that two cars do not cross each other's path and collide. In a database, it is necessary to ensure two queries' access to the data does not conflict.

As there are different levels of controlling the access to an intersection – yielding, stop signs, and traffic lights – there are different lock types in a database.

Lock Access Levels

The lock access level determines which kind of access a given lock allows. It is also sometimes called the lock type, but since that can be confused with the lock granularity, the term lock access level is used here.

There are essentially two access levels: shared or exclusive. The access levels do what their names suggest. A shared lock allows other connections to also get a shared lock. This is the most permissive lock access level. An exclusive lock only allows that one connection to get the lock. A shared lock is also known as a read lock, and an exclusive lock is also known as a write lock.

MySQL also has a concept called intention locks which specify the intention of a transaction. An intention lock can be either shared or exclusive. Intention locks are discussed in more detail when implicit table locks are covered in the next section that goes through the main lock granularity levels in MySQL.

Lock Granularity

MySQL uses a range of different lock granularities (also called lock types) to control access to the data. By using different lock granularities, it makes it possible, to the greatest intent possible, to allow for concurrent access to the data. This section will go through the main granularity levels used by MySQL.

User-Level Locks

User-level locks are an explicit lock type the application can use to protect, for example, a workflow. They are not often used, but they can be useful for some complex tasks where you want to serialize access. All user locks are exclusive locks and are obtained using a name which can be up to 64 characters long.

You manipulate user-level locks with a set of functions:

- **GET_LOCK(name, timeout):** Obtains a lock by specifying the name of the lock. The second argument is a timeout in seconds; if the lock is not obtained within that time, the function returns 0. If the lock is obtained, the return value is 1. If the timeout is negative, the function will wait indefinitely for the lock to become available.

- **IS_FREE_LOCK(name):** Checks whether the named lock is available or not. The function returns 1 if the lock is available and 0 if it is not available.

- **IS_USED_LOCK(name):** This is the opposite of the IS_FREE_LOCK() function. The function returns the connection id of the connection holding the lock if the lock is in use (not available) and NULL if it is not in use (available).

- **RELEASE_ALL_LOCKS():** Releases all user-level locks held by the connection. The return value is the number of locks released.

- **RELEASE_LOCK(name):** Releases the lock with the provided name. The return value is 1 if the lock is released, 0 if the lock exists but is not owned by the connection, or NULL if the lock does not exist.

It is possible to obtain multiple locks by invoking GET_LOCK() multiple times. If you do that, be careful to ensure locks are obtained in the same order by all users as otherwise a deadlock can occur. If a deadlock occurs, an ER_USER_LOCK_DEADLOCK error (error code 3058) is returned. An example of this is shown in Listing 18-1.

Listing 18-1. A deadlock for user-level locks

```
-- Connection 1
Connection 1> SELECT GET_LOCK('my_lock_1', -1);
+---------------------------+
| GET_LOCK('my_lock_1', -1) |
+---------------------------+
|                         1 |
+---------------------------+
1 row in set (0.0100 sec)

-- Connection 2
Connection 2> SELECT GET_LOCK('my_lock_2', -1);
+---------------------------+
| GET_LOCK('my_lock_2', -1) |
+---------------------------+
|                         1 |
+---------------------------+
1 row in set (0.0006 sec)

Connection 2> SELECT GET_LOCK('my_lock_1', -1);

-- Connection 1
Connection 1> SELECT GET_LOCK('my_lock_2', -1);
ERROR: 3058: Deadlock found when trying to get user-level lock; try rolling
back transaction/releasing locks and restarting lock acquisition.
```

When Connection 2 attempts to get the my_lock_1 lock, the statement will block until Connection 1 attempts to get the my_lock_2 lock triggering the deadlock. If you obtain multiple locks, you should be prepared to handle deadlocks. Note that for user-level locks, a deadlock does not trigger a rollback of the transaction.

The granted and pending user-level locks can be found in the performance_schema. metadata_locks table with the OBJECT_TYPE column set to USER LEVEL LOCK as shown in Listing 18-2. The locks listed assume you left the system as it was at the time the

deadlock in Listing 18-1 was triggered. Note that some values such as OBJECT_INSTANCE_
BEGIN will be different for you.

Listing 18-2. Listing user-level locks

```
mysql> SELECT *
         FROM performance_schema.metadata_locks
        WHERE OBJECT_TYPE = 'USER LEVEL LOCK'\G
*************************** 1. row ***************************
          OBJECT_TYPE: USER LEVEL LOCK
        OBJECT_SCHEMA: NULL
          OBJECT_NAME: my_lock_1
          COLUMN_NAME: NULL
OBJECT_INSTANCE_BEGIN: 2600542870816
            LOCK_TYPE: EXCLUSIVE
        LOCK_DURATION: EXPLICIT
          LOCK_STATUS: GRANTED
               SOURCE: item_func.cc:4840
      OWNER_THREAD_ID: 76
       OWNER_EVENT_ID: 33
*************************** 2. row ***************************
          OBJECT_TYPE: USER LEVEL LOCK
        OBJECT_SCHEMA: NULL
          OBJECT_NAME: my_lock_2
          COLUMN_NAME: NULL
OBJECT_INSTANCE_BEGIN: 2600542868896
            LOCK_TYPE: EXCLUSIVE
        LOCK_DURATION: EXPLICIT
          LOCK_STATUS: GRANTED
               SOURCE: item_func.cc:4840
      OWNER_THREAD_ID: 62
       OWNER_EVENT_ID: 25
*************************** 3. row ***************************
          OBJECT_TYPE: USER LEVEL LOCK
        OBJECT_SCHEMA: NULL
          OBJECT_NAME: my_lock_1
          COLUMN_NAME: NULL
```

```
OBJECT_INSTANCE_BEGIN: 2600542870336
            LOCK_TYPE: EXCLUSIVE
        LOCK_DURATION: EXPLICIT
          LOCK_STATUS: PENDING
               SOURCE: item_func.cc:4840
      OWNER_THREAD_ID: 62
       OWNER_EVENT_ID: 26
3 rows in set (0.0086 sec)
```

The OBJECT_TYPE for user-level locks is USER LEVEL LOCK, and the lock duration is EXPLICIT as it is up to the user or application to release the lock again. In row 1, the connection with Performance Schema thread id 76 has been granted the my_lock_1 lock, and in row 3 thread id 62 is waiting (pending) for it to be granted. Thread id 62 also has a granted lock which is included in row 2.

The next level of locks involves non-data table-level locks. The first of these that will be discussed is the flush lock.

Flush Locks

A flush lock will be familiar to most who have been involved in taking backups. It is taken when you use the FLUSH TABLES statement and last for the duration of the statement unless you add WITH READ LOCK in which case a shared (read) lock is held until the lock is explicitly released. An implicit table flush is also triggered at the end of the ANALYZE TABLE statement. The flush lock is a table-level lock. The read lock taken with FLUSH TABLES WITH READ LOCK is discussed later under explicit locks.

A common cause of lock issues for the flush lock is long-running queries. A FLUSH TABLES statement cannot flush a table as long as there is a query that has the table open. This means that if you execute a FLUSH TABLES statement while there is a long-running query using one or more of the tables being flushed, then the FLUSH TABLES statement will block all other statements needing any of those tables until the lock situation has been resolved.

Flush locks are subject to the lock_wait_timeout setting. If it takes more than lock_wait_timeout seconds to obtain the lock, MySQL will abandon the lock. The same applies if the FLUSH TABLES statement is killed. However, due to the internals of MySQL, a lower-level lock called the table definition cache (TDC) version lock cannot always be released until the long-running query completes.[1] That means that the only way to be sure the lock problem is resolved is to kill the long-running query, but be aware that if the query has changed many rows, it may take a long time to roll back the query.

When there is lock contention around the flush lock, both the FLUSH TABLES statement and the queries started subsequently will have the state set to "Waiting for table flush." Listing 18-3 shows an example of this involving three queries. To reproduce the scenario yourself, start out executing the three queries with the prompt set to Connection N> with N being 1, 2, or 3 representing three different connections. The query against sys.session is done in a fourth connection. All queries must be executed before the first completes (takes three minutes).

Listing 18-3. Example of waiting for a flush lock

```
-- Connection 1
Connection 1> SELECT *, SLEEP(180) FROM world.city WHERE ID = 130;

-- Connection 2
Connection 2> FLUSH TABLES world.city;

-- Connection 3
Connection 3> SELECT * FROM world.city WHERE ID = 201;

-- Connection 4
Connection 4> SELECT thd_id, conn_id, state,
                     current_statement
                FROM sys.session
               WHERE current_statement IS NOT NULL
                 AND thd_id <> PS_CURRENT_THREAD_ID()\G
*********************** 1. row ***********************
          thd_id: 61
         conn_id: 21
           state: User sleep
current_statement: SELECT *, SLEEP(180) FROM world.city WHERE ID = 130
```

---

[1]https://bugs.mysql.com/bug.php?id=44884

```
*************************** 2. row **************************
           thd_id: 62
          conn_id: 22
            state: Waiting for table flush
current_statement: FLUSH TABLES world.city
*************************** 3. row **************************
           thd_id: 64
          conn_id: 23
            state: Waiting for table flush
current_statement: SELECT * FROM world.city WHERE ID = 201
3 rows in set (0.0598 sec)
```

The example uses the sys.session view; similar results can be obtained using performance_schema.threads and SHOW PROCESSLIST. In order to reduce the output to only include the queries of relevance for the flush lock discussion, the current thread and threads without ongoing queries are filtered out.

The connection with conn_id = 21 is executing a slow query that uses the world.city table (a SLEEP(180) was used to ensure it took a long time). In the meantime, conn_id = 22 executed a FLUSH TABLES statement for the world.city table. Because the first query still has the table open (it is released once the query completes), the FLUSH TABLES statement ends up waiting for the table flush lock. Finally, conn_id = 23 attempts to query the table and thus must wait for the FLUSH TABLES statement.

Another non-data table lock is a metadata lock.

Metadata Locks

Metadata locks are one of the newer lock types in MySQL. They were introduced in MySQL 5.5, and their purpose is to protect the schema, so it does not get changed while queries or transactions rely on the schema to be unchanged. Metadata locks work at the table level, but they should be considered as an independent lock type to table locks as they do not protect the data in the tables.

SELECT statements and DML queries take a shared metadata lock, whereas DDL statements take an exclusive lock. A connection takes a metadata lock on a table when the table is first used and keeps the lock until the end of the transaction. While the metadata lock is held, no other connection is allowed to change the schema definition of the table. However, other connections that execute SELECT statements and DML statements are not restricted. Usually the biggest gotcha with respect to metadata locks is idle transactions preventing DDL statements from starting their work.

If you encounter a conflict around a metadata lock, you will see the query state in the process list set to "Waiting for table metadata lock." An example of this including queries to set up is shown in Listing 18-4.

Listing 18-4. Example of waiting for table metadata lock

```
-- Connection 1
Connection 1> SELECT CONNECTION_ID();
+-----------------+
| CONNECTION_ID() |
+-----------------+
|              21 |
+-----------------+
1 row in set (0.0003 sec)

Connection 1> START TRANSACTION;
Query OK, 0 rows affected (0.0003 sec)

Connection 1> SELECT * FROM world.city WHERE ID = 130\G
*************************** 1. row ***************************
         ID: 130
       Name: Sydney
CountryCode: AUS
   District: New South Wales
 Population: 3276207
1 row in set (0.0005 sec)

-- Connection 2
Connection 2> SELECT CONNECTION_ID();
+-----------------+
| CONNECTION_ID() |
+-----------------+
|              22 |
+-----------------+
1 row in set (0.0003 sec)

Connection 2> OPTIMIZE TABLE world.city;
```

```
-- Connection 3
Connection 3> SELECT thd_id, conn_id, state,
                     current_statement,
                     last_statement
                FROM sys.session
               WHERE conn_id IN (21, 22)\G
*************************** 1. row ***************************
           thd_id: 61
          conn_id: 21
            state: NULL
current_statement: SELECT * FROM world.city WHERE ID = 130
   last_statement: SELECT * FROM world.city WHERE ID = 130
*************************** 2. row ***************************
           thd_id: 62
          conn_id: 22
            state: Waiting for table metadata lock
current_statement: OPTIMIZE TABLE world.city
   last_statement: NULL
2 rows in set (0.0549 sec)
```

In this example, the connection with conn_id = 21 has an ongoing transaction and in the previous statement queried the world.city table (the current statement in this case is the same as it is not cleared until the next statement is executed). While the transaction is still active, conn_id = 22 has executed an OPTIMIZE TABLE statement which is now waiting for the metadata lock. (Yes, OPTIMIZE TABLE does not change the schema definition, but it as a DDL statement is still affected by the metadata lock.)

It is convenient when it is the current or last statement that is the cause of the metadata lock. In more general cases, you can use the performance_schema.metadata_locks table with the OBJECT_TYPE column set to TABLE to find granted and pending metadata locks. Listing 18-5 shows an example of granted and pending metadata locks using the same setup as in the previous example. Chapter 22 goes into more detail about investigating metadata locks.

Listing 18-5. Example of metadata locks

```
-- Connection 3
Connection 3> SELECT *
                FROM performance_schema.metadata_locks
               WHERE OBJECT_SCHEMA = 'world'
                 AND OBJECT_NAME = 'city'\G
*************************** 1. row ***************************
          OBJECT_TYPE: TABLE
        OBJECT_SCHEMA: world
          OBJECT_NAME: city
          COLUMN_NAME: NULL
OBJECT_INSTANCE_BEGIN: 2195760373456
            LOCK_TYPE: SHARED_READ
        LOCK_DURATION: TRANSACTION
          LOCK_STATUS: GRANTED
               SOURCE: sql_parse.cc:6014
      OWNER_THREAD_ID: 61
       OWNER_EVENT_ID: 53
*************************** 2. row ***************************
          OBJECT_TYPE: TABLE
        OBJECT_SCHEMA: world
          OBJECT_NAME: city
          COLUMN_NAME: NULL
OBJECT_INSTANCE_BEGIN: 2194784109632
            LOCK_TYPE: SHARED_NO_READ_WRITE
        LOCK_DURATION: TRANSACTION
          LOCK_STATUS: PENDING
               SOURCE: sql_parse.cc:6014
      OWNER_THREAD_ID: 62
       OWNER_EVENT_ID: 26
2 rows in set (0.0007 sec)

-- Connection 1
Connection 1> ROLLBACK;
Query OK, 0 rows affected (0.0003 sec)
```

In the example, thread id 61 (the same as conn_id = 22 from the sys.session output) owns a shared read lock on the world.city table due to an ongoing transaction, and thread id 62 is waiting for a lock as it is trying to execute a DDL statement on the table.

A special case of metadata locks are locks taken explicitly with the LOCK TABLES statement.

Explicit Table Locks

Explicit table locks are taken with the LOCK TABLES and the FLUSH TABLES WITH READ LOCK statements. With the LOCK TABLES statement, it is possible to take shared or exclusive locks; FLUSH TABLES WITH READ LOCK always takes a shared lock. The tables are locked, until they are explicitly released with the UNLOCK TABLES statement. When FLUSH TABLES WITH READ LOCK is executed without listing any tables, the global read lock (i.e., affecting all tables) is taken. While these locks also protect the data, they are considered as metadata locks in MySQL.

Explicit table locks, other than FLUSH TABLES WITH READ LOCK in connection with backups, are not often used with InnoDB as InnoDB's sophisticated lock features are in most cases superior to handling locks yourself. However, if you really need to lock the entire tables, explicit locks can be useful as they are very cheap for MySQL to check.

An example of a connection taking an explicit read lock on the world.country and world.countrylanguage tables and a write lock on the world.city table is

```
mysql> LOCK TABLES world.country READ,
                    world.countrylanguage READ,
                    world.city WRITE;
Query OK, 0 rows affected (0.0500 sec)
```

When you take explicit locks, you are only allowed to use the tables you have locked and in accordance with the requested locks. This means you will get an error if you take a read lock and attempt to write to the table (ER_TABLE_NOT_LOCKED_FOR_WRITE) or if you try to use a table you did not take a lock for (ER_TABLE_NOT_LOCKED), for example:

```
mysql> UPDATE world.country
          SET Population = Population + 1
        WHERE Code = 'AUS';
ERROR: 1099: Table 'country' was locked with a READ lock and can't be
updated
```

```
mysql> SELECT *
         FROM sakila.film
        WHERE film_id = 1;
ERROR: 1100: Table 'film' was not locked with LOCK TABLES
```

Since explicit locks are considered metadata locks, the symptoms and information in the `performance_schema.metadata_locks` table are the same as for implicit metadata locks.

Another table-level lock but handled implicitly is plainly called a table lock.

Implicit Table Locks

MySQL takes implicit table locks when a table is queried. Table locks do not play a large role for InnoDB tables except for flush, metadata, and explicit locks as InnoDB uses record locks to allow concurrent access to a table as long as the transactions do not modify the same rows (roughly speaking – as the next subsections show – there is more to it than that).

InnoDB does however work with the concept of intention locks at the table level. Since you are likely to encounter those when investigating lock issues, it is worth familiarizing yourself with them. As mentioned in the discussion of lock access levels, intention locks mark what the intention of the transaction is. If you use an explicit LOCK TABLES statement, the table will be locked directly with the access level you have requested.

For locks taken by transactions, first, an intention lock is taken, and then it may if needed be upgraded. To get a shared lock, the transaction first takes an intention shared lock and then the shared lock. Similarly, for an exclusive lock, an intention exclusive lock is first taken. Some examples of intention locks are as follows:

- A SELECT ... FOR SHARE statement takes an intention shared lock on the tables queried. The SELECT ... LOCK IN SHARE MODE syntax is a synonym.

- A SELECT ... FOR UPDATE statement takes an intention exclusive lock on the tables queried.

- A DML statement (not including SELECT) takes an intention exclusive lock on the modified tables. If a foreign key column is modified, an intention shared lock is taken on the parent table.

Two intention locks are always compatible with each other. This means that even if a transaction has an intention exclusive lock, it will not prevent another transaction to take an intention lock. It will however stop the other transaction from upgrading its intention lock to a full lock. Table 18-1 shows the compatibility between the lock types. Shared locks are denoted S and exclusive locks X. Intention locks are prefixed I, so IS is an intention shared lock and IX is an intention exclusive lock.

Table 18-1. *InnoDB lock compatibility*

	Exclusive (X)	Intention Exclusive (IX)	Shared (S)	Intention Shared (IS)
Exclusive (X)	X	X	X	X
Intention Exclusive (IX)	X	✓	X	✓
Shared (S)	X	X	✓	✓
Intention Shared (IS)	X	✓	✓	✓

In the table, a checkmark indicates that the two locks are compatible, whereas a cross mark indicates the two locks are conflicting with each other. The only conflicts of intention locks are the exclusive and shared locks. An exclusive lock conflicts with all other locks including both intention lock types. A shared lock conflicts only with an exclusive lock and an intention exclusive lock.

Why are the intention locks even necessary? They allow InnoDB to resolve the lock requests in order without blocking compatible operations. The details are beyond the scope of this discussion. The important thing is that you know that the intention locks exist, so when you see them you know where they come from.

The table-level locks can be found in the performance_schema.data_locks table with the LOCK_TYPE column set to TABLE. Listing 18-6 shows an example of an intention shared lock.

Listing 18-6. Example of an InnoDB intention shared lock

```
-- Connection 1
Connection 1> START TRANSACTION;
Query OK, 0 rows affected (0.0003 sec)
```

```
Connection 1> SELECT *
                FROM world.city
               WHERE ID = 130
                 FOR SHARE;
Query OK, 1 row affected (0.0010 sec)

-- Connection 2
Connection 2> SELECT *
                FROM performance_schema.data_locks
               WHERE LOCK_TYPE = 'TABLE'\G
*************************** 1. row ***************************
                ENGINE: INNODB
         ENGINE_LOCK_ID: 2195098223824:1720:2195068346872
  ENGINE_TRANSACTION_ID: 283670074934480
              THREAD_ID: 61
               EVENT_ID: 81
          OBJECT_SCHEMA: world
            OBJECT_NAME: city
         PARTITION_NAME: NULL
      SUBPARTITION_NAME: NULL
             INDEX_NAME: NULL
   OBJECT_INSTANCE_BEGIN: 2195068346872
              LOCK_TYPE: TABLE
              LOCK_MODE: IS
            LOCK_STATUS: GRANTED
              LOCK_DATA: NULL
1 row in set (0.0354 sec)

-- Connection 1
Connection 1> ROLLBACK;
Query OK, 0 rows affected (0.0003 sec)
```

This shows an intention shared lock on the world.city table. Notice that the ENGINE is set to INNODB and that LOCK_DATA is NULL. The values of the ENGINE_LOCK_ID, ENGINE_TRANSACTION_ID, and OBJECT_INSTANCE_BEGIN columns will be different if you execute the same query.

As mentioned, InnoDB's main access level protection is at the record level, so let's look at those.

501

Record Locks

Record locks are often called row locks; however, it is more than just locks on rows as it also includes index and gap locks. These are typically the locks that are meant when talking about InnoDB locks. They are fine-grained locks that aim at just locking the least amount of data while still ensuring the data integrity.

A record lock can be shared or exclusive and affect just the rows and indexes accessed by the transaction. The duration of exclusive locks is usually the transaction with an exception, for example, being delete-marked records used for uniqueness checks in INSERT INTO ... ON DUPLICATE KEY and REPLACE statements. For shared locks, the duration can depend on the transaction isolation level as discussed in "Transaction Isolation Levels" in the section "Reduce Locking Issues."

Record locks can be found using the performance_schema.data_locks table that was also used to find intention locks at the table level. Listing 18-7 shows an example of the locks from updating rows in the world.city table using the secondary index CountryCode.

Listing 18-7. Example of InnoDB record locks

```
-- Connection 1
Connection 1> START TRANSACTION;
Query OK, 0 rows affected (0.0003 sec)

Connection 1> UPDATE world.city
                 SET Population = Population + 1
               WHERE CountryCode = 'LUX';
Query OK, 1 row affected (0.0009 sec)

Rows matched: 1  Changed: 1  Warnings: 0

-- Connection 2
Connection 2> SELECT *
                FROM performance_schema.data_locks\G
*********************** 1. row ***********************
            ENGINE: INNODB
      ENGINE_LOCK_ID: 2195098223824:1720:2195068346872
ENGINE_TRANSACTION_ID: 117114
```

```
            THREAD_ID: 61
             EVENT_ID: 121
        OBJECT_SCHEMA: world
          OBJECT_NAME: city
       PARTITION_NAME: NULL
    SUBPARTITION_NAME: NULL
           INDEX_NAME: NULL
OBJECT_INSTANCE_BEGIN: 2195068346872
            LOCK_TYPE: TABLE
            LOCK_MODE: IX
          LOCK_STATUS: GRANTED
            LOCK_DATA: NULL
*************************** 2. row ***************************
               ENGINE: INNODB
       ENGINE_LOCK_ID: 2195098223824:507:30:1112:2195068344088
ENGINE_TRANSACTION_ID: 117114
            THREAD_ID: 61
             EVENT_ID: 121
        OBJECT_SCHEMA: world
          OBJECT_NAME: city
       PARTITION_NAME: NULL
    SUBPARTITION_NAME: NULL
           INDEX_NAME: CountryCode
OBJECT_INSTANCE_BEGIN: 2195068344088
            LOCK_TYPE: RECORD
            LOCK_MODE: X
          LOCK_STATUS: GRANTED
            LOCK_DATA: 'LUX', 2452
*************************** 3. row ***************************
               ENGINE: INNODB
       ENGINE_LOCK_ID: 2195098223824:507:20:113:2195068344432
ENGINE_TRANSACTION_ID: 117114
            THREAD_ID: 61
             EVENT_ID: 121
        OBJECT_SCHEMA: world
```

```
            OBJECT_NAME: city
         PARTITION_NAME: NULL
      SUBPARTITION_NAME: NULL
             INDEX_NAME: PRIMARY
   OBJECT_INSTANCE_BEGIN: 2195068344432
              LOCK_TYPE: RECORD
              LOCK_MODE: X,REC_NOT_GAP
            LOCK_STATUS: GRANTED
              LOCK_DATA: 2452
*************************** 4. row ***************************
                 ENGINE: INNODB
          ENGINE_LOCK_ID: 2195098223824:507:30:1113:2195068344776
   ENGINE_TRANSACTION_ID: 117114
              THREAD_ID: 61
               EVENT_ID: 121
          OBJECT_SCHEMA: world
            OBJECT_NAME: city
         PARTITION_NAME: NULL
      SUBPARTITION_NAME: NULL
             INDEX_NAME: CountryCode
   OBJECT_INSTANCE_BEGIN: 2195068344776
              LOCK_TYPE: RECORD
              LOCK_MODE: X,GAP
            LOCK_STATUS: GRANTED
              LOCK_DATA: 'LVA', 2434
4 rows in set (0.0005 sec)

-- Connection 1
Connection 1> ROLLBACK;
Query OK, 0 rows affected (0.0685 sec)
```

The first row is the intention exclusive table lock that has already been discussed. The second row is a next-key lock (more shortly) on the CountryCode index for the value ('LUX', 2452) where 'LUX' is the country code used in the WHERE clause and 2452 is the primary key id added to the nonunique secondary index. The city with ID = 2452 is the only city matching the WHERE clause, and the primary key record (the row itself) is shown in the third row of the output. The lock mode is X,REC_NOT_GAP which means it is an exclusive lock on the record but not on the gap.

What is a gap? An example is shown in the fourth row of the output. Gap locks are so important that the discussion of the gap lock is split out into its own.

Gap Locks, Next-Key Locks, and Predicate Locks

A gap lock protects the space between two records. This can be in the row through the clustered index or in a secondary index. Before the first record in an index page and after the last in the page, there are pseudo-records called the infimum record and supremum record, respectively. Gap locks are often the lock type causing the most confusion. Experience from studying lock issues is the best way to become familiar with them.

Consider the query from the previous example:

```
UPDATE world.city
   SET Population = Population + 1
 WHERE CountryCode = 'LUX';
```

This query changes the population of all cities with CountryCode = 'LUX'. What happens if a new city is inserted between the update and the commit of the transaction? If the UPDATE and INSERT statements commit in the same order they are executed, all is as such fine. However, if you commit the changes in the opposite order, then the result is inconsistent as it would be expected the inserted row would also have been updated.

This is where the gap lock comes into play. It guards the space where new records (including records moved from a different position) would be inserted, so it is not changed until the transaction holding the gap lock is completed. If you look at the last columns of the fourth row in the output from the example in Listing 18-7, you can see an example of a gap lock:

```
            INDEX_NAME: CountryCode
 OBJECT_INSTANCE_BEGIN: 2195068344776
             LOCK_TYPE: RECORD
             LOCK_MODE: X,GAP
           LOCK_STATUS: GRANTED
             LOCK_DATA: 'LVA', 2434
```

This is an exclusive gap lock on the CountryCode index for the value ('LVA', 2434). Since the query requested to update all rows with the CountryCode set to "LUX", the gap lock ensures that no new rows are inserted for the "LUX" country code. The country code "LVA" is the next value in the CountryCode index, so the gap between "LUX" and "LVA" is protected with an exclusive lock. On the other hand, it is still possible to insert new cities with CountryCode = 'LVA'. In some places this is referred to as a "gap before record" which makes it easier to understand how the gap lock works.

Gap locks are taken to a much less degree when you use the READ COMMITTED transaction isolation level rather than REPEATABLE READ or SERIALIZABLE. This is discussed further in "Transaction Isolation Levels" in the section "Reduce Locking Issues."

Related to gap locks are next-key locks and predicate locks. A next-key lock is the combination of a record lock and a gap lock on the gap before the record. This is actually the default lock type in InnoDB, and thus you will just see it as S and X in the lock outputs. In the example that has been discussed in this and the previous subsection, the lock on the CountryCode index for the value ('LUX', 2452) and the gap before it is an example of a next-key lock. The relevant parts of the output in Listing 18-7 from the performance_schema.data_locks table are

```
*************************** 2. row ***************************
        INDEX_NAME: CountryCode
         LOCK_TYPE: RECORD
         LOCK_MODE: X
       LOCK_STATUS: GRANTED
         LOCK_DATA: 'LUX', 2452
*************************** 3. row ***************************
        INDEX_NAME: PRIMARY
         LOCK_TYPE: RECORD
         LOCK_MODE: X,REC_NOT_GAP
       LOCK_STATUS: GRANTED
         LOCK_DATA: 2452
*************************** 4. row ***************************
        INDEX_NAME: CountryCode
         LOCK_TYPE: RECORD
         LOCK_MODE: X,GAP
       LOCK_STATUS: GRANTED
         LOCK_DATA: 'LVA', 2434
```

So to recapitulate, row 2 is the next-key lock, row 3 is the record lock on the primary key (the row), and row 4 is a gap lock between "LUX" and "LVA" (or a before-LVA gap lock).

A predicate lock is similar to a gap lock but applies to spatial indexes where an absolute ordering cannot be made and thus a gap lock does not make sense. Instead of a gap lock, for spatial indexes in the REPEATABLE READ and SERIALIZABLE transaction isolation levels, InnoDB creates a predicate lock on the minimum bounding rectangle (MBR) used for the query. This will allow consistent reads by preventing changes to the data within the minimum bounding rectangle.

One final lock type related to records that you should know is insert intention locks.

Insert Intention Locks

Remember that for table locks, InnoDB has intention locks for whether the transaction will use the table in a shared or exclusive manner. Similarly, InnoDB has insert intention locks at the record level. InnoDB uses these locks – as the name suggests – with INSERT statements to signal the intention to other transactions. As such, the lock is on a yet to be created record (so it is a gap lock) rather than on an existing record. The use of insert intention locks can help increase the concurrency that inserts can be performed at.

You are not very likely to see insert intention locks in lock outputs unless an INSERT statement is waiting for a lock to be granted. You can force a situation where this happens by creating a gap lock in another transaction that will prevent the INSERT statement from completing. The example in Listing 18-8 creates a gap lock in Connection 1 and then in Connection 2 attempts to insert a row which conflicts with the gap lock. Finally, in a third connection, the lock information is retrieved.

Listing 18-8. Example of an insert intention lock

```
-- Connection 1
Connection 1> START TRANSACTION;
Query OK, 0 rows affected (0.0004 sec)

Connection 1> SELECT *
                FROM world.city
               WHERE ID > 4079
                 FOR UPDATE;
Empty set (0.0009 sec)
```

```
-- Connection 2
Connection 2> SELECT PS_CURRENT_THREAD_ID();
+-----------------------+
| PS_CURRENT_THREAD_ID() |
+-----------------------+
|                    62 |
+-----------------------+
1 row in set (0.0003 sec)

Connection 2> START TRANSACTION;
Query OK, 0 rows affected (0.0003 sec)

Connection 2> INSERT INTO world.city
              VALUES (4080, 'Darwin', 'AUS',
                    'Northern Territory', 146000);

-- Connection 3
Connection 3> SELECT *
               FROM performance_schema.data_locks
               WHERE THREAD_ID = 62\G
*************************** 1. row ***************************
              ENGINE: INNODB
       ENGINE_LOCK_ID: 2195098220336:1720:2195068326968
ENGINE_TRANSACTION_ID: 117144
            THREAD_ID: 62
             EVENT_ID: 119
        OBJECT_SCHEMA: world
          OBJECT_NAME: city
       PARTITION_NAME: NULL
    SUBPARTITION_NAME: NULL
           INDEX_NAME: NULL
OBJECT_INSTANCE_BEGIN: 2195068326968
            LOCK_TYPE: TABLE
            LOCK_MODE: IX
          LOCK_STATUS: GRANTED
            LOCK_DATA: NULL
```

```
*************************** 2. row ***************************
            ENGINE: INNODB
     ENGINE_LOCK_ID: 2195098220336:507:29:1:2195068320072
ENGINE_TRANSACTION_ID: 117144
         THREAD_ID: 62
          EVENT_ID: 119
     OBJECT_SCHEMA: world
       OBJECT_NAME: city
    PARTITION_NAME: NULL
 SUBPARTITION_NAME: NULL
        INDEX_NAME: PRIMARY
OBJECT_INSTANCE_BEGIN: 2195068320072
         LOCK_TYPE: RECORD
         LOCK_MODE: X,INSERT_INTENTION
       LOCK_STATUS: WAITING
         LOCK_DATA: supremum pseudo-record
2 rows in set (0.0005 sec)

-- Connection 1
Connection 1> ROLLBACK;
Query OK, 0 rows affected (0.0004 sec)

-- Connection 2
Connection 2> ROLLBACK;
Query OK, 0 rows affected (0.0004 sec)
```

Connection 2 has the Performance Schema thread id 62, so in Connection 3, it is possible just to query for that thread and exclude the locks taken by Connection 1. Notice that for the RECORD lock, the lock mode includes INSERT_INTENTION – the insert intention lock. In this case, the data locked is the supremum pseudo-record, but that can also be the value of the primary key depending on the situation. If you recall the next-key lock discussion, then X means a next-key lock, but this is a special case as the lock is on the supremum pseudo-record, and it is not possible to lock that, so effectively it is just a gap lock on the gap before the supremum pseudo-record.

Another lock that you need to be aware of when inserting data is the auto-increment lock.

Auto-increment Locks

When you insert data into a table that has an auto-increment counter, it is necessary to protect the counter so two transactions are guaranteed to get unique values. If you use statement-based logging to the binary log, there are further restrictions as the auto-increment value is recreated for all rows except the first when the statement is replayed.

InnoDB supports three lock modes, so you can adjust the amount of locking according to your needs. You choose the lock mode with the innodb_autoinc_lock_mode option which takes the values 0, 1, and 2 with 2 being the default in MySQL 8. It requires a restart of MySQL to change the value. The meaning of the values is summarized in Table 18-2.

Table 18-2. *Supported values for the innodb_autoinc_lock_mode option*

Value	Mode	Description
0	Traditional	The locking behavior of MySQL 5.0 and earlier. The lock is held until the end of the statement, so values are assigned in repeatable and consecutive order.
1	Consecutive	For the INSERT statement where the number of rows is known at the start of the query, the required number of auto-increment values is assigned under a lightweight mutex, and the auto-increment lock is avoided. For statements where the number of rows is not known, the auto-increment lock is taken and held to the end of the statement. This was the default in MySQL 5.7 and earlier.
2	Interleaved	The auto-increment lock is never taken, and the auto-increment values for concurrent inserts may be interleaved. This mode is only safe when binary logging is disabled or binlog_format is set to ROW. It is the default value in MySQL 8.

The higher value of innodb_autoinc_lock_mode, the less locking. The price to pay for that is increased number of gaps in the sequence of auto-increment values and for innodb_autoinc_lock_mode = 2 the possibility of interleaved values. Unless you cannot use row-based binary logging or have special needs for consecutive auto-increment values, it is recommended to use the value of 2.

That concludes the discussion of user-level, metadata, and data-level locks. There are a couple other locks related to backups that you should know of.

Backup Locks

The backup lock is an instance-level lock; that is, it affects the system as a whole. It is a new lock introduced in MySQL 8. The backup lock prevents statements that can make a backup inconsistent while still allowing other statements to be executed concurrently with the backup. The statements that are blocked include

- Statements that create, rename, or remove files. This includes CREATE TABLE, CREATE TABLESPACE, RENAME TABLE, and DROP TABLE statements.

- Account management statements such as CREATE USER, ALTER USER, DROP USER, and GRANT.

- DDL statements that do not log their changes to the redo log. This, for example, includes adding an index.

A backup lock is created with the LOCK INSTANCE FOR BACKUP statement, and the lock is released with the UNLOCK INSTANCE statement. It requires the BACKUP_ADMIN privileges to execute LOCK INSTANCE FOR BACKUP. An example of obtaining the backup lock and releasing it again is

```
mysql> LOCK INSTANCE FOR BACKUP;
Query OK, 0 rows affected (0.00 sec)

mysql> UNLOCK INSTANCE;
Query OK, 0 rows affected (0.00 sec)
```

Note   At the time of writing, taking a backup lock and releasing it is not allowed when using the X Protocol (connecting through the port specified with mysqlx_port or the socket specified with mysqlx_socket). Attempting to do so returns an ER_PLUGGABLE_PROTOCOL_COMMAND_NOT_SUPPORTED error: ERROR: 3130: Command not supported by pluggable protocols.

Additionally, statements that conflict with the backup lock also take the backup lock. Since DDL statements sometimes consist of several steps, for example, rebuilding a table in a new file and renaming the file, the backup lock can be released between the steps to avoid blocking LOCK INSTANCE FOR BACKUP for longer than necessary.

Backup locks can be found in the performance_schema.metadata_locks table with the OBJECT_TYPE column set to BACKUP LOCK. Listing 18-9 shows an example of a query waiting for a backup lock held by LOCK INSTANCE FOR BACKUP.

Listing 18-9. Example of a conflict for the backup lock

```
-- Connection 1
Connection 1> LOCK INSTANCE FOR BACKUP;
Query OK, 0 rows affected (0.00 sec)

-- Connection 2
Connection 2> OPTIMIZE TABLE world.city;

-- Connection 3
Connection 3> SELECT *
                FROM performance_schema.metadata_locks
               WHERE OBJECT_TYPE = 'BACKUP LOCK'\G
*************************** 1. row ***************************
          OBJECT_TYPE: BACKUP LOCK
        OBJECT_SCHEMA: NULL
          OBJECT_NAME: NULL
          COLUMN_NAME: NULL
OBJECT_INSTANCE_BEGIN: 2520402231312
            LOCK_TYPE: SHARED
        LOCK_DURATION: EXPLICIT
          LOCK_STATUS: GRANTED
               SOURCE: sql_backup_lock.cc:101
      OWNER_THREAD_ID: 49
       OWNER_EVENT_ID: 8
*************************** 2. row ***************************
          OBJECT_TYPE: BACKUP LOCK
        OBJECT_SCHEMA: NULL
          OBJECT_NAME: NULL
          COLUMN_NAME: NULL
```

```
OBJECT_INSTANCE_BEGIN: 2520403183328
            LOCK_TYPE: INTENTION_EXCLUSIVE
        LOCK_DURATION: TRANSACTION
          LOCK_STATUS: PENDING
               SOURCE: sql_base.cc:5400
      OWNER_THREAD_ID: 60
       OWNER_EVENT_ID: 19
2 rows in set (0.0007 sec)

-- Connection 1
Connection 1> UNLOCK INSTANCE;
Query OK, 0 rows affected (0.00 sec)
```

In the example, the connection with thread id 49 owns the backup lock, whereas the connection with thread id 60 is waiting for it. Notice that LOCK INSTANCE FOR BACKUP holds a shared lock, whereas the DDL statement requests an intention exclusive lock.

Related to the backup lock is the log lock which has also been introduced to reduce locking during backups.

Log Locks

When you create a backup, you typically want to include information about the log positions the backup is consistent with. In MySQL 5.7 and earlier, you needed the global read lock while obtaining this information. In MySQL 8, the log lock was introduced to allow you to read information such as the executed global transaction identifiers (GTIDs), the binary log position, and the log sequence number (LSN) for InnoDB without taking a global read lock.

The log lock prevents operations that make changes to log-related information. In practice this means commits, FLUSH LOGS, and similar. The log lock is taken implicitly by querying the performance_schema.log_status table. It requires the BACKUP_ADMIN privilege to access the table. Listing 18-10 shows an example output of the log_ status table.

Listing 18-10. Example output of the `log_status` table

```
mysql> SELECT *
          FROM performance_schema.log_status\G
*************************** 1. row ***************************
       SERVER_UUID: 59e3f95b-e0d6-11e8-94e8-ace2d35785be
             LOCAL: {"gtid_executed": "59e3f95b-e0d6-11e8-94e8-
                    ace2d35785be:1-5343", "binary_log_file": "mysql-
                    bin.000033", "binary_log_position": 3874615}
       REPLICATION: {"channels": []}
   STORAGE_ENGINES: {"InnoDB": {"LSN": 7888992157, "LSN_checkpoint":
                    7888992157}}
1 row in set (0.0004 sec)
```

That concludes the review of the main lock types in MySQL. What happens when a query requests a lock, but it cannot be granted? Let's consider that.

Failure to Obtain Locks

The whole idea of locks is to restrict access to objects or records to avoid conflicting operations to execute concurrently. That means that sometimes a lock cannot be granted. What happens in that case? It depends on the lock requested and the circumstances. Metadata locks (including explicitly requested table locks) operate with a timeout. InnoDB record locks both support a timeout and explicit deadlock detection.

Note   Whether two locks are compatible with each other is very complex to determine. It becomes particularly interesting as the relationship is not symmetric, that is, a lock may be allowed in the presence of another lock, but not vice versa. For example, an insert intention lock must wait for a gap lock, but a gap lock does not have to wait for an insert intention lock. Another example (of lack of transitivity) is that a gap plus record lock must wait for a record-only lock, and an insert intention lock must wait for a gap plus record lock, but an insert intention lock does not need to wait for a record-only lock.

It is important to understand that failures to obtain locks are a fact of life when working with databases. In principle you can use very coarse-grained locks and avoid failed locks except for timeouts – this is what the MyISAM storage engine does with very poor write concurrency as a result. However, in practice to allow for high concurrency of write workloads, fine-grained locks are preferred which also introduces the possibility of deadlocks.

The conclusion is that you should always make your application prepared to retry getting a lock or fail gracefully. This applies whether it is an explicit or implicit lock.

Tip   Always be prepared to handle failures to obtain locks. Failing to get a lock is not a catastrophic error and should not normally be considered a bug. That said, as discussed in the section "Reducing Locking Issues," there are techniques to reduce lock contention that are worth having in mind when developing an application.

The rest of this chapter will discuss the specifics of table-level timeouts, record-level timeouts, and InnoDB deadlocks.

Metadata and Backup Lock Wait Timeouts

When you request a flush, metadata, or backup lock, the attempt to get the lock will time out after lock_wait_timeout seconds. The default timeout is 31536000 seconds (365 days). You can set the lock_wait_timeout option dynamically and both at the global and session scopes, which allows you to adjust the timeout to the specific needs for a given process.

When a timeout occurs, the statement fails with the error ER_LOCK_WAIT_TIMEOUT (error number 1205). For example:

```
mysql> LOCK TABLES world.city WRITE;
ERROR: 1205: Lock wait timeout exceeded; try restarting transaction
```

The recommended setting for the lock_wait_timeout option depends on the requirements of the application. It can be an advantage to use a small value to prevent the lock request to block other queries for a long time. This will typically require you to implement handling of a lock request failure, for example, by retrying the statement. A large value can on the other hand be useful to avoid having to retry the statement.

For the FLUSH TABLES statement, also remember that it interacts with the lower-level table definition cache (TDC) version lock which may mean that abandoning the statement does not allow subsequent queries from progressing. In that case, it can be better to have a high value for lock_wait_timeout to make it clearer what the lock relationship is.

InnoDB Lock Wait Timeouts

When a query requests a record-level lock in InnoDB, it is subject to a timeout similarly to the timeout for flush, metadata, and backup locks. Since record-level lock contention is more common than table-level lock contention, and record-level locks increase the potential for deadlocks, the timeout defaults to 50 seconds. It can be set using the innodb_lock_wait_timeout option which can be set both for the global and session scopes.

When a timeout occurs, the query fails with the ER_LOCK_WAIT_TIMEOUT error (error number 1205) just like for a table-level lock timeout. Listing 18-11 shows an example where an InnoDB lock wait timeout occurs.

Listing 18-11. Example of an InnoDB lock wait timeout

```
-- Connection 1
Connection 1> START TRANSACTION;
Query OK, 0 rows affected (0.0003 sec)

Connection 1> UPDATE world.city
                SET Population = Population + 1
              WHERE ID = 130;
Query OK, 1 row affected (0.0005 sec)

Rows matched: 1  Changed: 1  Warnings: 0

-- Connection 2
Connection 2> SET SESSION innodb_lock_wait_timeout = 3;
Query OK, 0 rows affected (0.0004 sec)

Connection 2> UPDATE world.city
                SET Population = Population + 1
              WHERE ID = 130;
ERROR: 1205: Lock wait timeout exceeded; try restarting transaction
```

```
-- Connection 1
Connection 1> ROLLBACK;
Query OK, 0 rows affected (0.0003 sec)
```

In this example, the lock wait timeout for Connection 2 is set to 3 seconds, so it is not necessary to wait the usual 50 seconds for the timeout to occur.

When the timeout occurs, the `innodb_rollback_on_timeout` option defines how much of the work done by the transaction is rolled back. When `innodb_rollback_on_timeout` is disabled (the default), only the statement that triggered the timeout is rolled back. When the option is enabled, the whole transaction is rolled back. The `innodb_rollback_on_timeout` option can only be configured at the global level, and it requires a restart to change the value.

Caution   It is very important that a lock wait timeout is handled as otherwise it may leave the transaction with locks that are not released. If that happens, other transactions may not be able to acquire the locks they require.

It is in general recommended to keep the timeout for InnoDB record-level locks low. Often it is best to lower the value from the default 50 seconds. The longer a query is allowed to wait for a lock, the larger the potential for other lock requests to be affected which can lead to other queries stalling as well. It also makes deadlocks more likely to occur. If you disable deadlock detection (discussed next), you should use a very small value for `innodb_lock_wait_timeout` such as one or two seconds as you will be using the timeout to detect deadlocks. Without deadlock detection, it is also recommended to enable the `innodb_rollback_on_timeout` option.

Deadlocks

Deadlocks sound like a very scary concept, but you should not let the name deter you. Just like lock wait timeout, deadlocks are a fact of life in the world of high-concurrency databases. What it really means is that there is a circular relationship between the lock requests. The only way to resolve the gridlock is to force one of the requests to abandon. In that sense, a deadlock is no different from a lock wait timeout. In fact, you can disable deadlock detection in which case, one of the locks will end up with a lock wait timeout instead.

So why are there deadlocks at all if they are not really needed? Since deadlocks occur when there is a circular relationship between the lock requests, it is possible for InnoDB to detect them as soon as the circle is completed. This allows InnoDB to tell the user immediately that a deadlock has occurred without having to wait for the lock wait timeout to happen. It is also useful to be told that a deadlock has occurred as it often provides opportunities to improve the data access in the application. You should thus consider deadlocks a friend rather than a foe. Figure 18-1 shows an example of two transactions querying a table which causes a deadlock.

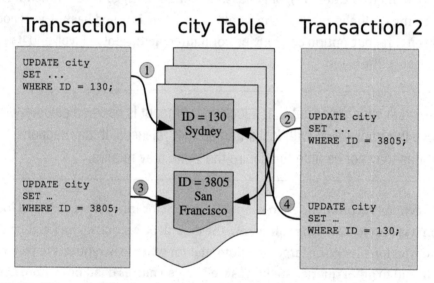

Figure 18-1. *Example of two transactions causing a deadlock*

In the example, transaction 1 first updates the row with ID = 130 and then the row with ID = 3805. In between, transaction 2 updates first the row with ID = 3805 and then the row with ID = 130. This means that by the time transaction 1 tries to update ID = 3805, transaction 2 already has a lock on the row. Transaction 2 can also not proceed as it cannot get a lock on ID = 130 because transaction 1 already holds that. This is a classic example of a simple deadlock. The circular lock relationship is also shown in Figure 18-2.

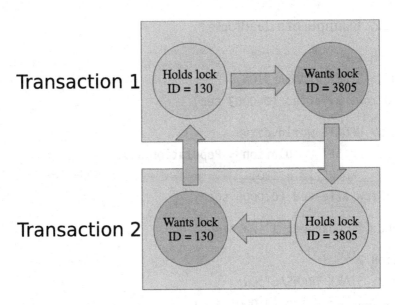

Figure 18-2. *The circular relationship of the locks causing the deadlock*

In this figure, it is clear which lock is held by transactions 1 and 2 and which locks are requested and how the conflict can never be resolved without intervention. That makes it qualify as a deadlock.

In the real world, deadlocks are often more complicated. In the example that has been discussed here, only primary key record locks have been involved. In general, often secondary keys, gap locks, and possible other lock types are also involved. There may also be more than two transactions involved. The principle, however, remains the same.

Note   A deadlock may even occur with as little as one query for each of two transactions. If one query reads the records in ascending order and the other on descending order, it is possible to get a deadlock.

When a deadlock occurs, InnoDB chooses the transaction that has "done the least work" to become a victim. You can check the trx_weight column in the information_schema.INNODB_TRX view to see the weight used by InnoDB (the more work done, the higher weight). In practice this means that the transaction that holds the fewest locks will be rolled back. When this occurs, the query in the transaction that is chosen as the victim fails with the error ER_LOCK_DEADLOCK returned (error code 1213), and the transaction is rolled back to release as many locks as possible. An example of a deadlock occurring is shown in Listing 18-12.

Listing 18-12. Example of a deadlock

```
-- Connection 1
Connection 1> START TRANSACTION;
Query OK, 0 rows affected (0.0003 sec)

Connection 1> UPDATE world.city
              SET Population = Population + 1
             WHERE ID = 130;
Query OK, 1 row affected (0.0006 sec)

Rows matched: 1  Changed: 1  Warnings: 0

-- Connection 2
Connection 2> START TRANSACTION;
Query OK, 0 rows affected (0.0003 sec)

Connection 2> UPDATE world.city
              SET Population = Population + 1
             WHERE ID = 3805;
Query OK, 1 row affected (0.0006 sec)

Rows matched: 1  Changed: 1  Warnings: 0

Connection 2> UPDATE world.city
              SET Population = Population + 1
             WHERE ID = 130;

-- Connection 1
Connection 1> UPDATE world.city
              SET Population = Population + 1
             WHERE ID = 3805;
ERROR: 1213: Deadlock found when trying to get lock; try restarting
             transaction

Connection 1> ROLLBACK;
Query OK, 0 rows affected (0.0438 sec)

-- Connection 2
Connection 2> ROLLBACK;
Query OK, 0 rows affected (0.0438 sec)
```

In most cases, the automatic deadlock detection is great to avoid queries stalling for longer than necessary. Deadlock detection is not for free though. For MySQL instances with a very high query concurrency, the cost of looking for deadlocks can become significant, and you are better off disabling the deadlock detection which is done by setting the innodb_deadlock_detect option to OFF. That said, in MySQL 8.0.18 and later, the deadlock detection has been moved to a dedicated background thread which improves the performance.

If you do disable deadlock detection, it is recommended to set innodb_lock_wait_timeout to a very low value such as one second to quickly detect lock contention. Additionally, enable the innodb_rollback_on_timeout option to ensure the locks are released.

Now that you have an understanding of how locks work and how lock requests can fail, you need to consider how you can reduce the impact of locking.

Reduce Locking Issues

It is important to have locks in mind when you write an application and design the schema for its data and access. The strategies to reduce locking include adding indexes, changing the transaction isolation level, and preemptive locking.

Tip   Do not be carried away in optimizing locks. If you only occasionally encounter lock wait timeouts and deadlocks, it is usually better to retry the query or transaction rather than spend time avoiding the issue. How frequent is too frequent depends on your workload, but several retries every hour will not be an issue for many applications.

Transaction Size and Age

An important strategy to reduce lock issues is to keep your transactions small and to avoid delays that keep the transactions open for longer than necessary. Among the most common causes of lock issues are transactions that modify a large number of rows or that are active for much longer than necessary.

The size of the transaction is the amount of work the transaction does, particularly the number of locks it takes, but the time the transaction takes to execute is also important. As some of the other topics in this discussion will address, you can partly reduce the impact through indexes and the transaction isolation level. However, it is also important to have the overall result in mind. If you need to modify many rows, ask yourself if you can split the work into smaller batches or it is required that everything is done in the same transaction. It may also be possible to split out some preparation work and do it outside the main transaction.

The duration of the transaction is also important. One common problem is connections using `autocommit = 0`. This starts a new transaction every time a query (including `SELECT`) is executed without an active transaction, and the transaction is not completed until an explicit `COMMIT` or `ROLLBACK` is executed (or the connection is closed). Some connectors disable auto-commit by default, so you may be using this mode without realizing it which can leave transactions open for hours by mistake.

Tip   Enable the `autocommit` option unless you have a specific reason to disable it. When you have auto-committing enabled, InnoDB can also for many `SELECT` queries detect it is a read-only transaction and reduce the overhead of the query.

Another pitfall is to start a transaction and perform slow operations in the application while the transaction is active. This can be data that is sent back to the user, interactive prompts, or file I/O. Make sure that you do these kinds of slow operations when you do not have an active transaction open in MySQL.

Indexes

Indexes reduce the amount of work performed to access a given row. That way indexes are a great tool to reduce locking as only records accessed while executing the query will be locked.

Consider a simple example where you query cities with the name Sydney in the `world.city` table:

```
START TRANSACTION;

SELECT *
  FROM world.city
 WHERE Name = 'Sydney'
   FOR SHARE;
```

The FOR SHARE option is used to force the query to take a shared lock on the records read. By default, there is no index on the Name column, so the query will perform a full table scan to find the rows needed in the result. Without an index, there are 4103 record locks (some are duplicates):

```
mysql> SELECT INDEX_NAME, LOCK_TYPE,
              LOCK_MODE, COUNT(*)
         FROM performance_schema.data_locks
        WHERE OBJECT_SCHEMA = 'world'
          AND OBJECT_NAME = 'city'
        GROUP BY INDEX_NAME, LOCK_TYPE, LOCK_MODE;
+------------+-----------+-----------+----------+
| INDEX_NAME | LOCK_TYPE | LOCK_MODE | COUNT(*) |
+------------+-----------+-----------+----------+
| NULL       | TABLE     | IS        |        1 |
| PRIMARY    | RECORD    | S         |     4103 |
+------------+-----------+-----------+----------+
2 rows in set (0.0210 sec)
```

If you add an index on the Name column, the lock count decreases to a total of three record locks:

```
mysql> SELECT INDEX_NAME, LOCK_TYPE,
              LOCK_MODE, COUNT(*)
         FROM performance_schema.data_locks
        WHERE OBJECT_SCHEMA = 'world'
          AND OBJECT_NAME = 'city'
        GROUP BY INDEX_NAME, LOCK_TYPE, LOCK_MODE;
```

```
+------------+-----------+----------------+----------+
| INDEX_NAME | LOCK_TYPE | LOCK_MODE      | COUNT(*) |
+------------+-----------+----------------+----------+
| NULL       | TABLE     | IS             |        1 |
| Name       | RECORD    | S              |        1 |
| PRIMARY    | RECORD    | S,REC_NOT_GAP  |        1 |
| Name       | RECORD    | S,GAP          |        1 |
+------------+-----------+----------------+----------+
4 rows in set (0.0005 sec)
```

On the flip side, more indexes provide more ways to access the same rows which potentially can increase the number of deadlocks.

Record Access Order

Ensure that you to as large degree as possible access the records in the same order for different transactions. In the deadlock example discussed earlier in this chapter, what led to the deadlock was that the two transactions accessed the rows in opposite order. If they had accessed the rows in the same order, there would have been no deadlock. This also applies when you access records in different tables.

Ensuring the same access order is by no means a trivial task. Different access orders may even happen when you perform joins and the optimizer decides on different join orders for two queries. If different join orders lead to excessive lock issues, you can consider using the optimizer hints described in Chapter 17 to tell the optimizer to change the join order, but you should of course also have the query performance in mind in such cases.

Transaction Isolation Levels

InnoDB supports several transaction isolation levels. Different isolation levels have different lock requirements: particularly REPEATABLE READ and SERIALIZABLE require more locks than READ COMMITTED.

The READ COMMITTED transaction isolation level can help on locking issues in two ways. Far less gap locks are taken, and rows that are accessed during a DML statement but not modified have their locks released again after the statement has completed. For REPEATABLE READ and SERIALIZABLE, locks are only released at the end of the transaction.

Note   It is often said that the READ COMMITTED transaction isolation level does not take gap locks. That is a myth and not correct. While far fewer gap locks are taken, there are still some that are required. This, for example, includes when InnoDB performs a page split as part of the update. (Page splits are discussed in Chapter 25.)

Consider an example where the population of the city named Sydney is changed using the CountryCode column to limit the query to one country. This can be done with the following query:

```
START TRANSACTION;

UPDATE world.city
   SET Population = 5000000
 WHERE Name = 'Sydney'
       AND CountryCode = 'AUS';
```

There is no index on the Name column, but there is one on CountryCode. So the update requires a scan of part of the CountryCode index. Listing 18-13 shows an example of executing the query in the REPEATABLE READ transaction isolation level.

Listing 18-13. The locks held in the REPEATABLE READ transaction isolation level

```
-- Connection 1
Connection 1> SET transaction_isolation = 'REPEATABLE-READ';
Query OK, 0 rows affected (0.0003 sec)

Connection 1> START TRANSACTION;
Query OK, 0 rows affected (0.0003 sec)

Connection 1> UPDATE world.city
                SET Population = 5000000
              WHERE Name = 'Sydney'
                AND CountryCode = 'AUS';
Query OK, 1 row affected (0.0005 sec)

Rows matched: 1  Changed: 1  Warnings: 0
```

```
-- Connection 2
Connection 2> SELECT INDEX_NAME, LOCK_TYPE,
                     LOCK_MODE, COUNT(*)
                FROM performance_schema.data_locks
               WHERE OBJECT_SCHEMA = 'world'
                 AND OBJECT_NAME = 'city'
               GROUP BY INDEX_NAME, LOCK_TYPE, LOCK_MODE;
+-------------+-----------+----------------+----------+
| INDEX_NAME  | LOCK_TYPE | LOCK_MODE      | COUNT(*) |
+-------------+-----------+----------------+----------+
| NULL        | TABLE     | IX             |        1 |
| CountryCode | RECORD    | X              |       14 |
| PRIMARY     | RECORD    | X,REC_NOT_GAP  |       14 |
| CountryCode | RECORD    | X,GAP          |        1 |
+-------------+-----------+----------------+----------+
4 rows in set (0.0007 sec)

Connection 1> ROLLBACK;
Query OK, 0 rows affected (0.0725 sec)
```

Fourteen record locks are taken on each of the CountryCode index and the primary key, and one gap lock is taken on the CountryCode index. Compare this to the locks held after executing the query in the READ COMMITTED transaction isolation level as shown in Listing 18-14.

Listing 18-14. The locks held in the READ-COMMITTED transaction isolation level

```
-- Connection 1
Connection 1> SET transaction_isolation = 'READ-COMMITTED';
Query OK, 0 rows affected (0.0003 sec)

Connection 1> START TRANSACTION;
Query OK, 0 rows affected (0.0003 sec)

Connection 1> UPDATE world.city
                 SET Population = 5000000
               WHERE Name = 'Sydney'
                 AND CountryCode = 'AUS';
```

```
Query OK, 1 row affected (0.0005 sec)

Rows matched: 1  Changed: 1  Warnings: 0

-- Connection 2
Connection 2> SELECT INDEX_NAME, LOCK_TYPE,
                     LOCK_MODE, COUNT(*)
                FROM performance_schema.data_locks
               WHERE OBJECT_SCHEMA = 'world'
                 AND OBJECT_NAME = 'city'
               GROUP BY INDEX_NAME, LOCK_TYPE, LOCK_MODE;
+-------------+-----------+----------------+----------+
| INDEX_NAME  | LOCK_TYPE | LOCK_MODE      | COUNT(*) |
+-------------+-----------+----------------+----------+
| NULL        | TABLE     | IX             |        1 |
| CountryCode | RECORD    | X,REC_NOT_GAP  |        1 |
| PRIMARY     | RECORD    | X,REC_NOT_GAP  |        1 |
+-------------+-----------+----------------+----------+
3 rows in set (0.0006 sec)

Connection 1> ROLLBACK;
Query OK, 0 rows affected (0.0816 sec)
```

Here the record locks are reduced to one lock on each of the CountryCode index and primary key. There are no gap locks.

It is not all workloads that can use the READ COMMITTED transaction isolation level. If you must have SELECT statements return the same result when executed multiple times in the same transaction or have different queries correspond to the same snapshot in time, you must use REPEATABLE READ or SERIALIZABLE. However, in many cases, it is an option to reduce the isolation level, and you can choose different isolation levels for different transactions. If you are migrating an application from Oracle DB, you are already using READ COMMITTED, and you can also use it in MySQL.

Preemptive Locking

The last strategy that will be discussed is preemptive locking. If you have a complex transaction executing several queries, it can in some cases be an advantage to execute a SELECT ... FOR UPDATE or SELECT ... FOR SHARE query to take locks on the records you know you will need later in the transaction. Another case where it can be useful is to ensure you access the rows in the same order for different tasks.

Preemptive locking is particularly effective to reduce the frequency of deadlocks. One drawback is that you will end up holding the locks for longer. Overall, preemptive locking is a strategy that should be used sparingly, but when used for the right cases, it can be powerful to prevent deadlocks.

The final topic of this chapter is to review how to monitor locks.

Monitoring Locks

There have already been several examples of querying information about the locks held. This section will review the sources already mentioned as well as introducing some extra ones. Chapter 22 will go further into this by showing examples of investigating lock issues. The monitoring options can be divided into four groups: the Performance Schema, the sys schema, status metrics, and InnoDB lock monitoring.

The Performance Schema

The Performance Schema contains the source of most of the lock information available except for deadlocks. Not only can you use the lock information in the Performance Schema directly; it is also used for two lock-related views in the sys schema.

The information is available through four tables:

- **data_locks:** This table contains details of table and lock records at the InnoDB level. It shows all locks currently held or are pending.

- **data_lock_waits:** Like the data_locks table, it shows locks related to InnoDB, but only those waiting to be granted with information on which threads is blocking the request.

- **metadata_locks:** This table contains information about user-level locks, metadata locks, and similar. To record information, the wait/lock/metadata/sql/mdl Performance Schema instrument must be enabled (it is enabled by default in MySQL 8). The OBJECT_TYPE column shows which kind of lock is held.

- **table_handles:** This table holds information about which table locks are currently in effect. The wait/lock/table/sql/handler Performance Schema instrument must be enabled for data to be recorded (this is the default). This table is less frequently used than the other tables.

The metadata_locks table is the most generic of the tables, and there is support for a wide range of locks ranging from the global read lock to low-level locks like for the access control list (ACL). Table 18-3 summarizes the possible values of the OBJECT_TYPE column in alphabetical order with a brief explanation of the locks each value represents.

Table 18-3. *Object types in the* performance_schema.metadata_locks *table*

Object Type	Description
ACL_CACHE	For the access control list (ACL) cache.
BACKUP_LOCK	For the backup lock.
CHECK_CONSTRAINT	For the names of CHECK constraints.
COLUMN_STATISTICS	For histograms and other column statistics.
COMMIT	For blocking commits. It is related to the global read lock.
EVENT	For stored events.
FOREIGN_KEY	For the foreign key names.
GLOBAL	For the global read lock (triggered by FLUSH TABLES WITH READ LOCK).
FUNCTION	For stored functions.
LOCKING_SERVICE	For locks acquired using the locking service interface.
PROCEDURE	For stored procedures.
RESOURCE_GROUPS	For the resource groups.

(continued)

Table 18-3. (*continued*)

Object Type	Description
SCHEMA	For schemas/databases. These are similar to the metadata locks for tables except they are for a schema.
SRID	For the spatial reference systems (SRIDs).
TABLE	For tables and views. This includes the metadata locks discussed in this chapter.
TABLESPACE	For tablespaces.
TRIGGER	For triggers (on tables).
USER_LEVEL_LOCK	For user-level locks.

The data in the Performance Schema tables is the raw lock data. Often when you investigate lock issues or monitor for lock issues, it is more interesting to determine if there are any lock waits. For that information, you need to use the sys schema.

The sys Schema

The sys schema has two views that take the information in the Performance Schema tables and return the lock pairs where one lock cannot be granted because of the other lock. Thus, they show where there are problems with lock waits. The two views are innodb_lock_waits and schema_table_lock_waits.

The innodb_lock_waits view uses the data_locks and data_lock_waits view in the Performance Schema to return all cases of lock waits for InnoDB record locks. It shows information such as what lock the connection is trying to obtain and which connections and queries are involved. The view also exists as x$innodb_lock_waits, if you need the information without formatting.

The schema_table_lock_waits view works in a similar way but uses the metadata_locks table to return lock waits related to schema objects. The information is also available unformatted in the x$schema_table_lock_waits view.

Chapter 22 includes examples of using both views to investigate lock issues.

Status Counters and InnoDB Metrics

There are several status counters and InnoDB metrics that provide information about locking. These are mostly used at the global (instance) level and can be useful to detect an overall increase in lock issues. A great way to monitor all of these metrics together is to use the sys.metrics view. Listing 18-15 shows an example of retrieving the metrics.

Listing 18-15. Lock metrics

```
mysql> SELECT Variable_name,
              Variable_value AS Value,
              Enabled
         FROM sys.metrics
        WHERE Variable_name LIKE 'innodb_row_lock%'
           OR Variable_name LIKE 'Table_locks%'
           OR Type = 'InnoDB Metrics - lock';
```

Variable_name	Value	Enabled
innodb_row_lock_current_waits	0	YES
innodb_row_lock_time	595876	YES
innodb_row_lock_time_avg	1683	YES
innodb_row_lock_time_max	51531	YES
innodb_row_lock_waits	354	YES
table_locks_immediate	4194	YES
table_locks_waited	0	YES
lock_deadlocks	1	YES
lock_rec_lock_created	0	NO
lock_rec_lock_removed	0	NO
lock_rec_lock_requests	0	NO
lock_rec_lock_waits	0	NO
lock_rec_locks	0	NO
lock_row_lock_current_waits	0	YES
lock_table_lock_created	0	NO
lock_table_lock_removed	0	NO

```
| lock_table_lock_waits          | 0      | NO       |
| lock_table_locks               | 0      | NO       |
| lock_timeouts                  | 1      | YES      |
+--------------------------------+--------+----------+
19 rows in set (0.0076 sec)
```

As you can see, not all of the metrics are enabled by default. Those that are not enabled can be enabled using the innodb_monitor_enable option as discussed in Chapter 7. The innodb_row_lock_%, lock_deadlocks, and lock_timeouts metrics are the most interesting. The row lock metrics show how many locks are currently waiting and statistics for the amount of time in milliseconds spent on waiting to acquire InnoDB record locks. The lock_deadlocks and lock_timeouts metrics show the number of deadlocks and lock wait timeouts that have been encountered, respectively.

InnoDB Lock Monitor and Deadlock Logging

InnoDB has for a long time had its own lock monitor with the lock information returned in the InnoDB monitor output. By default, the InnoDB monitor includes information about the latest deadlock as well as locks involved in lock waits. By enabling the innodb_status_output_locks option (disabled by default), all locks will be listed; this is similar to what you have in the Performance Schema data_locks table.

To demonstrate the deadlock and transaction information, you can create the deadlock from Listing 18-12 and create a new ongoing transaction that has updated a single row by primary key in the world.city table:

```
mysql> START TRANSACTION;
Query OK, 0 rows affected (0.0002 sec)

mysql> UPDATE world.city
          SET Population = Population + 1
        WHERE ID = 130;
Query OK, 1 row affected (0.0005 sec)

Rows matched: 1  Changed: 1  Warnings: 0
```

You generate the InnoDB lock monitor output using the SHOW ENGINE INNODB STATUS statement. Listing 18-16 shows an example of enabling all lock information and generating the monitor output. The complete InnoDB monitor output is also available from this book's GitHub repository in the file listing_18_16.txt.

Listing 18-16. The InnoDB monitor output

```
mysql> SET GLOBAL innodb_status_output_locks = ON;
Query OK, 0 rows affected (0.0022 sec)

mysql> SHOW ENGINE INNODB STATUS\G
*************************** 1. row ***************************
  Type: InnoDB
  Name:
Status:
=====================================
2019-11-04 17:04:48 0x6e88 INNODB MONITOR OUTPUT
=====================================
Per second averages calculated from the last 51 seconds
-----------------
BACKGROUND THREAD
-----------------
srv_master_thread loops: 170 srv_active, 0 srv_shutdown, 62448 srv_idle
srv_master_thread log flush and writes: 0
----------
SEMAPHORES
----------
OS WAIT ARRAY INFO: reservation count 138
OS WAIT ARRAY INFO: signal count 133
RW-shared spins 1, rounds 1, OS waits 0
RW-excl spins 109, rounds 1182, OS waits 34
RW-sx spins 24, rounds 591, OS waits 18
Spin rounds per wait: 1.00 RW-shared, 10.84 RW-excl, 24.63 RW-sx
```

```
-----------------------
LATEST DETECTED DEADLOCK
-----------------------
2019-11-03 19:41:43 0x4b78
*** (1) TRANSACTION:
TRANSACTION 5585, ACTIVE 10 sec starting index read
mysql tables in use 1, locked 1
LOCK WAIT 3 lock struct(s), heap size 1136, 2 row lock(s), undo log entries 1
MySQL thread id 37, OS thread handle 28296, query id 21071 localhost ::1
root updating
UPDATE world.city
                SET Population = Population + 1
              WHERE ID = 130

*** (1) HOLDS THE LOCK(S):
RECORD LOCKS space id 159 page no 28 n bits 248 index PRIMARY of table
`world`.`city` trx id 5585 lock_mode X locks rec but not gap
Record lock, heap no 26 PHYSICAL RECORD: n_fields 7; compact format; info
bits 0
 0: len 4; hex 80000edd; asc      ;;
 1: len 6; hex 0000000015d1; asc         ;;
 2: len 7; hex 01000000f51aa6; asc         ;;
 3: len 30; hex 53616e204672616e636973636f202020202020202020202020
           202020202020; asc San Francisco                ;
           (total 35 bytes);
 4: len 3; hex 555341; asc USA;;
 5: len 20; hex 43616c69666f726e6961202020202020202020; asc
California            ;;
 6: len 4; hex 800bda1e; asc      ;;

*** (1) WAITING FOR THIS LOCK TO BE GRANTED:
...
------------
TRANSACTIONS
------------
Trx id counter 5662
Purge done for trx's n:o < 5661 undo n:o < 0 state: running but idle
```

```
History list length 11
LIST OF TRANSACTIONS FOR EACH SESSION:
---TRANSACTION 284075292758256, not started
0 lock struct(s), heap size 1136, 0 row lock(s)
---TRANSACTION 284075292756560, not started
0 lock struct(s), heap size 1136, 0 row lock(s)
---TRANSACTION 284075292755712, not started
0 lock struct(s), heap size 1136, 0 row lock(s)
---TRANSACTION 5661, ACTIVE 60 sec
2 lock struct(s), heap size 1136, 1 row lock(s), undo log entries 1
MySQL thread id 40, OS thread handle 2044, query id 26453 localhost ::1
root
TABLE LOCK table `world`.`city` trx id 5661 lock mode IX
RECORD LOCKS space id 160 page no 7 n bits 248 index PRIMARY of table
`world`.`city` trx id 5661 lock_mode X locks rec but not gap
Record lock, heap no 41 PHYSICAL RECORD: n_fields 7; compact format; info
bits 0
 0: len 4; hex 80000082; asc       ;;
 1: len 6; hex 00000000161d; asc         ;;
 2: len 7; hex 01000001790a72; asc      y r;;
 3: len 30; hex 5379646e6579202020202020202020202020202020202020202020202020
            0; asc Sydney                        ; (total 35 bytes);
 4: len 3; hex 415553; asc AUS;;
 5: len 20; hex 4e657720536f7574682057616c65732020202020; asc New South
            Wales      ;;
 6: len 4; hex 8031fdb0; asc  1  ;;
...
```

Near the top is the section LATEST DETECTED DEADLOCK which includes details of the transactions and locks involved in the latest deadlock and when it occurred. If no deadlocks have occurred since the last restart of MySQL, this section is omitted. Chapter 22 will include an example of investigating a deadlock.

Note   The deadlock section in the InnoDB monitor output only includes information for deadlocks involving InnoDB record locks. For deadlocks involving user-level locks, there is no equivalent information.

A little further down the output, there is the section TRANSACTIONS which lists the InnoDB transactions. Do note that transactions that are not holding any locks (e.g., pure SELECT queries) are not included. In the example, there is an intention exclusive lock held on the world.city table and an exclusive lock on the row with the primary key equal to 130 (the 80000082 in the record lock information for the first field means the row with the value 0x82, which is the same as 130 in decimal notation).

Tip   Nowadays the lock information in the InnoDB monitor output is better obtained from the performance_schema.data_locks and performance_schema.data_lock_waits tables. The deadlock information is however still very useful.

You can request the monitor output to be dumped every 15 seconds to stderr. You enable the dumps by enabling the innodb_status_output option. Do note that the output is quite large, so be prepared for your error log to grow quickly if you enable it. The InnoDB monitor output can also easily end up hiding messages about more serious issues.

If you want to ensure you record all deadlocks, you can enable the innodb_print_all_deadlocks option. This causes deadlock information like that in the InnoDB monitor output to be printed to the error log every time a deadlock occurs. This can be useful, if you need to investigate deadlocks, but it is recommended only to enable it on demand to avoid the error log to become very large and potentially hide other problems.

Caution   Be careful if you enable regular outputs of the InnoDB monitor or information about all deadlocks. The information may easily hide important messages logged to the error log.

Summary

The topic of locks is large and complex. Hopefully this chapter has helped you get an overview of why locks are needed and the various kinds of locks.

The chapter started out asking why locks are needed. Without locks, it is not safe to have concurrent access to the schema and data. Metaphorically speaking, database locks work in the same way as traffic lights and stop signs work in the traffic. It regulates the access to the data, so transactions can be sure there will not be a collision with another transaction causing inconsistent results.

There are two access levels to the data: shared access also known a read access and exclusive access also known as write access. These access levels exist for various lock granularities ranging from a global read lock to record and gap locks. Additionally, InnoDB uses intention shared and intention exclusive locks at the table level.

It is important to work at reducing the number of locks the application needs and to reduce the impact of the locks required. The strategies to reduce lock issues essentially boil down to doing as little work as possible in a transaction by using indexes and splitting large transactions into smaller ones, and holding the locks for as short time as possible. It is also important to attempt to access the data in the same order for different tasks in the application; otherwise, unnecessary deadlocks may occur.

The final part of the chapter went through the lock monitoring options in the Performance Schema, the sys schema, status metrics, and the InnoDB monitor. Most of the monitoring is best done using the Performance Schema tables and the sys schema views. The exception is for deadlocks where the InnoDB monitor is still the best option.

This is the conclusion of Part IV. It is time to become more practical with query analysis starting with finding the queries that are candidate for optimization.

PART V

Query Analysis

Finding Candidate Queries for Optimization

When you encounter a performance problem, the first step is to determine what is causing it. There may be several causes for poor performance, so you should keep an open mind when looking for causes. The focus of this chapter is to find queries that may contribute to the poor performance or that may become a problem in the future when the load and amount of data increase. Still, as discussed in Chapter 1, you need to consider all aspects of your system, and often it may turn out to be a combination of factors that causes the problem.

This chapter goes through the various sources of query performance–related information. First, the Performance Schema will be discussed. The Performance Schema is the basis for many of the other features discussed in this chapter. Second, the views of the sys schema are covered as well as the statement performance analyzer feature. Third, it is shown how you can use MySQL Workbench as a way to get a graphical user interface for several of the reports discussed in the first two sections. Fourth, it is discussed how monitoring is important to find candidates for optimization. While the section uses MySQL Enterprise Monitor as the basis of the discussion, the principles apply to monitoring in general, so you are encouraged to read the section even if you use a different monitoring solution. Fifth and final is the slow query log which is the traditional tool for finding slow queries.

Note This chapter includes several examples with outputs. In general, your output for the same example will differ for values that include timings and other data that is not deterministic.

J. W. Krogh, *MySQL 8 Query Performance Tuning*, https://doi.org/10.1007/978-1-4842-5584-1_19

Queries that perform poorly due to lock contention will not be covered; instead, Chapter 22 goes into detail on how to investigate lock issues. Transactions are covered in Chapter 21.

The Performance Schema

The Performance Schema is a gold mine for information about the performance of your queries. This makes it the obvious place to start when discussing how to find queries that are candidates for optimization. You may likely end up using some of the methods that build on top of the Performance Schema, but you are still encouraged to get a good understanding of the underlying tables, so you know how to access the raw data and make your own custom reports.

This section will start out discussing how to get information about the statements and prepared statement, then table and file I/O are covered, and finally it is shown how to find out what are causing errors and which errors.

The Statement Event Tables

Using the Performance Schema tables based on statement events is the most straightforward way to look for queries that are candidates for optimization. These tables will allow you to get very detailed information about the queries that are executing on the instance. One important thing to note is that queries executed as prepared statements are not included in the statement tables.

There are several tables that include statement information. These are

- **events_statements_current:** The statements currently executing or for idle connections the latest executed query. When executing stored programs, there may be more than one row per connection.

- **events_statements_history:** The last statements for each connection. The number of statements per connection is capped at performance_schema_events_statements_history_size (defaults to 10). The statements for a connection are removed when the connection is closed.

- **events_statements_history_long:** The latest queries for the instance irrespective of which connection executed it. This table also includes statements from connections that have been closed. The consumer for this table is disabled by default. The number of rows is capped at `performance_schema_events_statements_history_long_size` (defaults to 10000).

- **events_statements_summary_by_digest:** The statement statistics grouped by the default schema and digest. This table is discussed in detail later.

- **events_statements_summary_by_account_by_event_name:** The statement statistics grouped by the account and event name. The event name shows what kind of statement is executed, for example, `statement/sql/select` for a `SELECT` statement executed directly (not executed through a stored program).

- **events_statements_summary_by_host_by_event_name:** The statement statistics grouped by the hostname of the account and the event name.

- **events_statements_summary_by_program:** The statement statistics grouped by the stored program (event, function, procedure, table, or trigger) that executed the statement. This is useful to find the stored programs that perform the most work.

- **events_statements_summary_by_thread_by_event_name:** The statement statistics grouped by thread and event name. Only threads currently connected are included.

- **events_statements_summary_by_user_by_event_name:** The statement statistics grouped by the username of the account and the event name.

- **events_statements_summary_global_by_event_name:** The statement statistics grouped by the event name.

- **events_statements_histogram_by_digest:** Histogram statistics grouped by the default schema and digest.

- **events_statements_histogram_global:** Histogram statistics where all queries are aggregated in one histogram.

- **threads:** Information about all threads in the instance, both background and foreground threads. You can use this table instead of the SHOW PROCESSLIST command. In addition to the process list information, there are columns showing whether the thread is instrumented, the operating system thread id, and more.

Other than the two histogram tables and the threads table, all of the listed tables have similar columns. The table most often used is events_statements_summary_by_digest, so it will be used as the base of the discussion. The events_statements_summary_by_digest table is essentially a report of all the queries that have been executed on the instance since the table was last reset (typically when restarting MySQL). The queries are grouped by their digest and the default schema used when executing them. The columns in the table are summarized in Table 19-1.

Table 19-1. *The columns in the* events_statements_summary_by_digest *table*

Column Name	Description
SCHEMA_NAME	The schema that was the default schema when executing the query. If no schema was the default, the value is NULL.
DIGEST	The digest of the normalized query. In MySQL 8, that is a sha256 hash.
DIGEST_TEXT	The normalized query.
COUNT_STAR	The number of times the query has been executed.
SUM_TIMER_WAIT	The total amount of time that has been spent executing the query. Note that the value flows over after a little more than 30 weeks of execution time.
MIN_TIMER_WAIT	The fastest the query has been executed.
AVG_TIMER_WAIT	The average execution time. This is the same as SUM_TIMER_WAIT/ COUNT_STAR unless SUM_TIMER_WAIT has overflown.
MAX_TIMER_WAIT	The slowest the query has been executed.
SUM_LOCK_TIME	The total amount of time that has been spent waiting for table locks.

(continued)

Table 19-1. (*continued*)

Column Name	Description
SUM_ERRORS	The total number of errors that have been encountered executing the query.
SUM_WARNINGS	The total number of warnings that have been encountered executing the query.
SUM_ROWS_AFFECTED	The total number of rows that have been modified by the query.
SUM_ROWS_SENT	The total number of rows that have been returned (sent) to the client.
SUM_ROWS_EXAMINED	The total number of rows that have been examined by the query.
SUM_CREATED_TMP_DISK_TABLES	The total number of on-disk internal temporary tables that have been created by the query.
SUM_CREATED_TMP_TABLES	The total number of internal temporary tables – whether created in memory or on disk – that have been created by the query.
SUM_SELECT_FULL_JOIN	The total number of joins that have performed full table scans as there is no index for the join condition or there is no join condition. This is the same that increments the Select_full_join status variable.
SUM_SELECT_FULL_RANGE_JOIN	The total number of joins that use a full range search. This is the same that increments the Select_full_range_join status variable.
SUM_SELECT_RANGE	The total number of times the query has used a range search. This is the same that increments the Select_range status variable.
SUM_SELECT_RANGE_CHECK	The total number of joins by the query where the join does not have an index that checks for the index usage after each row. This is the same that increments the Select_range_check status variable.
SUM_SELECT_SCAN	The total number of times the query has performed a full table scan on the first table in the join. This is the same that increments the Select_scan status variable.
SUM_SORT_MERGE_PASSES	The total number of sort merge passes that have been done to sort the result of the query. This is the same that increments the Sort_merge_passes status variable.

(*continued*)

Table 19-1. (*continued*)

Column Name	Description
SUM_SORT_RANGE	The total number of times a sort was done using ranges. This is the same that increments the Sort_range status variable.
SUM_SORT_ROWS	The total number of rows sorted. This is the same that increments the Sort_rows status variable.
SUM_SORT_SCAN	The total number of times a sort was done by scanning the table. This is the same that increments the Sort_scan status variable.
SUM_NO_INDEX_USED	The total number of times no index was used to execute the query.
SUM_NO_GOOD_INDEX_ USED	The total number of times no good index was used. This means that the Extra column in the EXPLAIN output includes "Range checked for each record."
FIRST_SEEN	When the query was first seen. When the table is truncated, the first seen value is also reset.
LAST_SEEN	When the query was seen the last time.
QUANTILE_95	The 95th percentile of the query latency. That is, 95% of the queries complete in the time given or in less time.
QUANTILE_99	The 99th percentile of the query latency.
QUANTILE_999	The 99.9th percentile of the query latency.
QUERY_SAMPLE_TEXT	An example of a query before it is normalized. You can use this to get the query execution plan for the query.
QUERY_SAMPLE_SEEN	When the example query was seen.
QUERY_SAMPLE_ TIMER_WAIT	How long the example query took to execute.

There is a unique index on (SCHEMA_NAME, DIGEST) which is used to group the data. There can be up to performance_schema_digests_size (dynamically sized, but usually defaults to 10000) rows in the table. When the last row is inserted, the schema and digest are both set to NULL, and that row is used as a catch-all row. Each time the catch-all row is used, the Performance_schema_digest_lost status variable is incremented. The information that is aggregated in this table is also available for individual queries

using the events_statements_current, events_statements_history, and events_
statements_history_long tables.

Tip   Since the data is grouped by SCHEMA_NAME, DIGEST, you get most out of the events_statements_summary_by_digest table, when the application is consistent about setting the default schema (e.g., \use world or the --schema command-line option in MySQL Shell or equivalent in the client/connector you use). Either always set it or never set it. In the same way, if you sometimes include the schema name when referencing tables and sometimes do not, then otherwise identical queries will be counted as two different digests.

Two groups of columns need a little more explanation, the quantile columns and the query sample columns. The values of the quantile columns are determined based on histogram statistics for the digests. Basically, if you take the events_statements_histogram_by_digest table for a given digest and default schema and go to the bucket with 95% of the query executions, then that bucket is used to determine the 95th percentile. The histogram tables will be discussed shortly.

For the sample query information, the sample query is replaced if at least one of three conditions is fulfilled:

- It is the first time the digest is encountered for the given default schema.

- A new occurrence of the digest and schema has a higher value for TIMER_WAIT than the query currently used as the sample query (i.e., it was slower).

- If the value of the performance_schema_max_digest_sample_age option is greater than 0 and the current sample query is older than performance_schema_max_digest_sample_age seconds.

The value of performance_schema_max_digest_sample_age defaults to 60 seconds, which works well if you monitor the events_statements_summary_by_digest table every minute. That way, the monitoring Agent will be able to pick up the slowest query in each one-minute interval and get a complete history of the slowest queries. If your monitoring interval is greater, consider increasing the value of performance_schema_max_digest_sample_age.

As you can see from the list of columns, there are ample opportunities to query for statements meeting some requirements. The trick is to query for the things that are important. What qualifies as important depends on the situation, so it is not possible to give specific queries that will apply to all situations. For example, if you know from your monitoring that there are problems with a large number of internal temporary tables using memory or disk, then the SUM_CREATED_TMP_DISK_TABLES and SUM_CREATED_TMP_TABLES columns are good candidates for filtering.

Some conditions are of general interest. Examples of some conditions that may warrant further investigation include

- A large amount of examined rows compared to the number of rows sent back to the client or that are modified. This may suggest poor index usage.

- The sum of no index used or no good index used is high. This may suggest that the query can benefit from new indexes or rewriting the query.

- The number of full joins is high. This suggests that either an index is needed or there is a join condition missing.

- The number of range checks is high. This may suggest that you need to change the indexes on the tables in the query.

- If the quantile latencies are showing a severe degradation when going toward higher quantiles, it may suggest you at times have problems resolving the queries in a timely fashion. This may be due to the instance in general being overloaded, lock issues, some conditions triggering poor query plans, or other reasons.

- The number of internal temporary tables created in disk is high. This may suggest that you need to consider which indexes are used for sorting and grouping, the amount of memory allowed to internal temporary tables, or other changes that can prevent writing the internal temporary table to disk or create internal temporary tables in the first place.

- The number of sort merges is high. This may suggest this query can benefit from a larger sort buffer.

- The number of executions is large. This does not suggest any problems with the query, but the more often a query is executed, the more impact improvements of the query have. In some cases, a high execute count may also be caused by unnecessary executions of the query.

- The number of errors or warnings is high. While this may not impact the performance, it suggests something is wrong. Do note that some queries always generate a warning, for example, EXPLAIN as it uses warnings to return additional information.

Caution   Be careful increasing the value of `sort_buffer_size` if you are still using MySQL 5.7 as it can decrease performance even if it reduces the number of sort merges. In MySQL 8, the sort buffer has been improved, and the performance degradation of a larger buffer is much less. Still, do not increase the size more than you need.

You should be aware that just because a query meets one of these conditions does not mean there is anything to change. As an example, consider a query that aggregates data from a table. That query may examine large parts of the table but only returns a few rows. It may even require a full table scan where there is no meaningful index that can help. The query will perform badly from the point of view of the ratio between the number of examined rows and the number of sent rows, and maybe the no index counter is incrementing. Yet, the query may very well do the minimum amount of work required to return the required result. If you determine the query is a performance problem, you will need to find a different solution than adding indexes; for example, you may be able to execute the query during non-peak periods and cache the result, or you may have a separate instance where queries like this are executed.

Listing 19-1 shows an example of finding the combination of default schema and statement digest that have been executed the most times since the events_statements_summary_by_digest table was last reset.

Listing 19-1. Using the events_statements_summary_by_digest table

```
mysql> SELECT *
       FROM performance_schema.events_statements_summary_by_digest
       ORDER BY COUNT_STAR DESC
       LIMIT 1\G
*************************** 1. row ***************************
                 SCHEMA_NAME: world
                      DIGEST: b49cb8f3db720a96fb29da86437bd7809ef304
                              63fac88e85ed4f851f96dcaa30
                 DIGEST_TEXT: SELECT * FROM `city` WHERE NAME = ?
                  COUNT_STAR: 102349
              SUM_TIMER_WAIT: 138758688272512
              MIN_TIMER_WAIT: 1098756736
              AVG_TIMER_WAIT: 1355485824
              MAX_TIMER_WAIT: 19321416576
               SUM_LOCK_TIME: 5125624000000
                  SUM_ERRORS: 0
                SUM_WARNINGS: 0
           SUM_ROWS_AFFECTED: 0
               SUM_ROWS_SENT: 132349
           SUM_ROWS_EXAMINED: 417481571
 SUM_CREATED_TMP_DISK_TABLES: 0
      SUM_CREATED_TMP_TABLES: 0
        SUM_SELECT_FULL_JOIN: 0
  SUM_SELECT_FULL_RANGE_JOIN: 0
            SUM_SELECT_RANGE: 0
      SUM_SELECT_RANGE_CHECK: 0
             SUM_SELECT_SCAN: 102349
        SUM_SORT_MERGE_PASSES: 0
              SUM_SORT_RANGE: 0
               SUM_SORT_ROWS: 0
               SUM_SORT_SCAN: 0
           SUM_NO_INDEX_USED: 102349
      SUM_NO_GOOD_INDEX_USED: 0
```

```
          FIRST_SEEN: 2019-06-22 10:25:18.260657
           LAST_SEEN: 2019-06-22 10:30:12.225425
        QUANTILE_95: 2089296130
        QUANTILE_99: 2884031503
       QUANTILE_999: 3630780547
   QUERY_SAMPLE_TEXT: SELECT * FROM city WHERE Name = 'San José'
   QUERY_SAMPLE_SEEN: 2019-06-22 10:29:56.81501
QUERY_SAMPLE_TIMER_WAIT: 19321416576
1 row in set (0.0019 sec)
```

The output shows that querying the `city` table in the `world` schema by name is the most executed query. You should compare the value `COUNT_STAR` to other queries to understand how often this query is executed compared to other queries. In this example, you can see that the query on average returns 1.3 rows per execution but examines 4079 rows. That means the query examines more than 3000 rows for each row returned. Since this is an often-executed query, that suggests that an index is needed on the `Name` column that is used for filtering. The bottom of the output shows an actual example of the query that you can use with `EXPLAIN` as described in the next chapter to analyze the query execution plan.

As mentioned, MySQL also maintains histogram statistics for the statements. There are two histogram tables available: `events_statements_histogram_by_digest` and `events_statements_histogram_global`. The difference between the two is that the former has the histogram information grouped by default schema and digest, whereas the latter contains information for all queries grouped together. The histogram information can be useful to determine the distribution of query latencies, similar to what has been discussed for the quantile columns in the `events_statements_summary_by_digest` table but more fine-grained. The tables are managed automatically.

As mentioned, prepared statements are not included in the statement event tables. Instead, you need to use the `prepared_statements_instances` table.

Prepared Statements Summary

Prepared statements can be useful to speed up execution of queries that are reused within a connection. For example, if you have an application that keeps using the same connection(s), then you can prepare the statements the application uses and then execute the prepared statement when it is needed.

Prepared statements use placeholders, so you only need to submit the template of the query when you prepare it. That way you can submit different parameters for each execution. When used in that way, prepared statements serve as a catalogue of statements that the application can use with the parameters needed for a given execution.

Listing 19-2 shows a simple example of using prepared statements through the SQL interface. In applications, you will typically be using a connector that handles prepared statements in a more transparent manner. For example, for MySQL Connector/Python, you tell that you want to use prepared statements, and the connector will automatically prepare the statement for you the first time you execute it. The underlying principle is the same though.

Listing 19-2. Example of using prepared statements

```
mysql> SET @sql = 'SELECT * FROM world.city WHERE ID = ?';
Query OK, 0 rows affected (0.0002 sec)

mysql> PREPARE stmt FROM @sql;
Query OK, 0 rows affected (0.0080 sec)

Statement prepared

mysql> SET @val = 130;
Query OK, 0 rows affected (0.0003 sec)

mysql> EXECUTE stmt USING @val\G
*************************** 1. row ***************************
         ID: 130
       Name: Sydney
CountryCode: AUS
   District: New South Wales
 Population: 3276207
1 row in set (0.0023 sec)

mysql> SET @val = 3805;
Query OK, 0 rows affected (0.0003 sec)

mysql> EXECUTE stmt USING @val\G
```

```
*************************** 1. row ***************************
         ID: 3805
       Name: San Francisco
CountryCode: USA
   District: California
 Population: 776733
1 row in set (0.0004 sec)

mysql> DEALLOCATE PREPARE stmt;
Query OK, 0 rows affected (0.0003 sec)
```

The SQL interface uses user variables to pass the statement and values to
MySQL. The first step is to prepare the statement; then it can be used as many times as
needed passing the parameters required for the query. Finally, the prepared statement is
deallocated.

When you want to investigate the performance of prepared statements, you can use
the prepared_statements_instances table. The information is similar to what is in the
events_statements_summary_by_digest table. Listing 19-3 shows an example output
for the prepared statement that was used in Listing 19-2.

Listing 19-3. Using the prepared_statements_instances table

```
mysql> SELECT *
         FROM performance_schema.prepared_statements_instances\G
*************************** 1. row ***************************
    OBJECT_INSTANCE_BEGIN: 1999818114352
             STATEMENT_ID: 1
           STATEMENT_NAME: stmt
                 SQL_TEXT: SELECT * FROM world.city WHERE ID = ?
          OWNER_THREAD_ID: 87543
           OWNER_EVENT_ID: 20012
         OWNER_OBJECT_TYPE: NULL
       OWNER_OBJECT_SCHEMA: NULL
         OWNER_OBJECT_NAME: NULL
             TIMER_PREPARE: 369412736
           COUNT_REPREPARE: 0
             COUNT_EXECUTE: 2
```

```
        SUM_TIMER_EXECUTE: 521116288
        MIN_TIMER_EXECUTE: 247612288
        AVG_TIMER_EXECUTE: 260375808
        MAX_TIMER_EXECUTE: 273504000
           SUM_LOCK_TIME: 163000000
              SUM_ERRORS: 0
            SUM_WARNINGS: 0
        SUM_ROWS_AFFECTED: 0
           SUM_ROWS_SENT: 2
       SUM_ROWS_EXAMINED: 2
 SUM_CREATED_TMP_DISK_TABLES: 0
      SUM_CREATED_TMP_TABLES: 0
        SUM_SELECT_FULL_JOIN: 0
   SUM_SELECT_FULL_RANGE_JOIN: 0
            SUM_SELECT_RANGE: 0
      SUM_SELECT_RANGE_CHECK: 0
             SUM_SELECT_SCAN: 0
       SUM_SORT_MERGE_PASSES: 0
              SUM_SORT_RANGE: 0
               SUM_SORT_ROWS: 0
               SUM_SORT_SCAN: 0
           SUM_NO_INDEX_USED: 0
      SUM_NO_GOOD_INDEX_USED: 0
1 row in set (0.0008 sec)
```

The main differences from the events statements tables are that there are no quantile statistics and query example and the primary key is the OBJECT_INSTANCE_BEGIN – that is, the memory address of the prepared statement instead of a unique key on the default schema and digest. In fact, the default schema and digest are not even mentioned in the prepared_statements_instances table.

As it is hinted by the primary key being the memory address of the prepared statement, the prepared statement statistics are only maintained while the prepared statement exists. So, when the statement is deallocated either explicitly or implicitly because the connection is closed, the statistics are cleared.

That ends the discussion of statement statistics. There are also higher-level statistics such as the table I/O summaries.

Table I/O Summaries

The table I/O information in the Performance Schema is often misunderstood. The I/O that is referred to for the table I/O summaries is a general concept of input-output related to the table. Thus, it does not refer to disk I/O. Rather, it is a general measure of how busy the table is. That said, the more disk I/O there is for a table, the more time will also be spent on table I/O.

There are two Performance Schema tables that include latency statistics for the table I/O:

- **table_io_waits_summary_by_table:** The aggregate information for the table with details of read, write, fetch, insert, and update I/O.

- **table_io_waits_summary_by_index_usage:** The same information as for the table_io_waits_summary_by_table table except the statistics are per index or lack thereof.

These tables allow you to get a detailed view of how the tables are used and how much time is used on various operations. There are seven groups of activities for which there are both the sum, minimum, average, and maximum latencies and the number of operations. Table 19-2 shows the groups based on their column names.

Table 19-2. *The groups of latencies for table and index I/O statistics*

Group	Columns	Descriptions
Overall	COUNT_STAR SUM_TIMER_WAIT MIN_TIMER_WAIT AVG_TIMER_WAIT MAX_TIMER_WAIT	The statistics for the whole table or index.
Reads	COUNT_READ SUM_TIMER_READ MIN_TIMER_READ AVG_TIMER_READ MAX_TIMER_READ	The aggregate statistics for all read operations. Currently there is only one read operation, fetch, so the read statistics will be the same as the fetch statistics.

(continued)

Table 19-2. (*continued*)

Group	Columns	Descriptions
Writes	COUNT_WRITE SUM_TIMER_WRITE MIN_TIMER_WRITE AVG_TIMER_WRITE MAX_TIMER_WRITE	The aggregate statistics for all write operations. The write operations are inserts, updates, and deletes.
Fetches	COUNT_FETCH SUM_TIMER_FETCH MIN_TIMER_FETCH AVG_TIMER_FETCH MAX_TIMER_FETCH	The statistics for fetching records. The reason this is not called "select" is that records may be fetched for other purposes than for SELECT statements.
Inserts	COUNT_INSERT SUM_TIMER_INSERT MIN_TIMER_INSERT AVG_TIMER_INSERT MAX_TIMER_INSERT	The statistics for inserting records.
Updates	COUNT_UPDATE SUM_TIMER_UPDATE MIN_TIMER_UPDATE AVG_TIMER_UPDATE MAX_TIMER_UPDATE	The statistics for updating records.
Deletes	COUNT_DELETE SUM_TIMER_DELETE MIN_TIMER_DELETE AVG_TIMER_DELETE MAX_TIMER_DELETE	The statistics for deleting records.

An example of the information for these columns in the `table_io_waits_summary_` `by_table` table can be seen in Listing 19-4 for the `world.city` table.

Listing 19-4. Example of using the `table_io_waits_summary_by_table` table

```
mysql> SELECT *
         FROM performance_schema.table_io_waits_summary_by_table
        WHERE OBJECT_SCHEMA = 'world'
          AND OBJECT_NAME = 'city'\G
*************************** 1. row ***************************
      OBJECT_TYPE: TABLE
    OBJECT_SCHEMA: world
      OBJECT_NAME: city
       COUNT_STAR: 418058733
   SUM_TIMER_WAIT: 125987200409940
   MIN_TIMER_WAIT: 1082952
   AVG_TIMER_WAIT: 301176
   MAX_TIMER_WAIT: 43045491156
       COUNT_READ: 417770654
   SUM_TIMER_READ: 122703207563448
   MIN_TIMER_READ: 1082952
   AVG_TIMER_READ: 293700
   MAX_TIMER_READ: 19644079288
      COUNT_WRITE: 288079
  SUM_TIMER_WRITE: 3283992846492
  MIN_TIMER_WRITE: 1937352
  AVG_TIMER_WRITE: 11399476
  MAX_TIMER_WRITE: 43045491156
      COUNT_FETCH: 417770654
  SUM_TIMER_FETCH: 122703207563448
  MIN_TIMER_FETCH: 1082952
  AVG_TIMER_FETCH: 293700
  MAX_TIMER_FETCH: 19644079288
     COUNT_INSERT: 4079
 SUM_TIMER_INSERT: 209027413892
 MIN_TIMER_INSERT: 10467468
 AVG_TIMER_INSERT: 51244420
```

```
MAX_TIMER_INSERT: 31759300408
    COUNT_UPDATE: 284000
SUM_TIMER_UPDATE: 3074965432600
MIN_TIMER_UPDATE: 1937352
AVG_TIMER_UPDATE: 10827028
MAX_TIMER_UPDATE: 43045491156
    COUNT_DELETE: 0
SUM_TIMER_DELETE: 0
MIN_TIMER_DELETE: 0
AVG_TIMER_DELETE: 0
MAX_TIMER_DELETE: 0
1 row in set (0.0015 sec)
```

In this output, there is a broad usage of the table except rows have not been deleted. It can also be seen that most of the time is spent on reading data (122703207563448 picoseconds out of a total of 125987200409940 picoseconds – or 97%).

Listing 19-5 shows the output for the same table but using the table_io_waits_summary_by_index_usage table. The usage columns are the same as for the table_io_waits_summary_by_table table and have mostly been omitted in the example to focus on the differences between the two tables. If you have any extra indexes from previous examples, you will have more rows returned.

Listing 19-5. Example of using the table_io_waits_summary_by_index_usage table

```
mysql> SELECT OBJECT_TYPE, OBJECT_SCHEMA,
              OBJECT_NAME, INDEX_NAME,
              COUNT_STAR
         FROM performance_schema.table_io_waits_summary_by_index_usage
        WHERE OBJECT_SCHEMA = 'world'
          AND OBJECT_NAME = 'city'\G
*************************** 1. row ***************************
  OBJECT_TYPE: TABLE
OBJECT_SCHEMA: world
  OBJECT_NAME: city
   INDEX_NAME: PRIMARY
   COUNT_STAR: 20004
```

```
*************************** 2. row ***************************
  OBJECT_TYPE: TABLE
OBJECT_SCHEMA: world
  OBJECT_NAME: city
   INDEX_NAME: CountryCode
   COUNT_STAR: 549000
*************************** 3. row ***************************
  OBJECT_TYPE: TABLE
OBJECT_SCHEMA: world
  OBJECT_NAME: city
   INDEX_NAME: NULL
   COUNT_STAR: 417489729
3 rows in set (0.0017 sec)
```

Consider the three values of COUNT_STAR. If you sum those, 20004 + 549000 + 417489729 = 418058733, you get the same value as COUNT_STAR in the table_io_waits_ summary_by_table table. This example shows the same data but split out across the two indexes on the city table as well as the NULL index, which means that no index was used. This makes the table_io_waits_summary_by_index_usage table very useful to estimate the usefulness of the indexes and whether table scans are executed for the table.

It is useful to take a minute to consider when the fetch, insert, update, and delete counters increase and for which indexes. Consider the world.city table which has a primary key in the ID column and a secondary index on the CountryCode column. This means you can set up three types of filters depending on the index that is used or lack thereof:

- **By Primary Key:** Using the primary key to locate the rows, for example, WHERE ID = 130

- **By Secondary Index:** Using the CountryCode index to locate the rows, for example, WHERE CountryCode = 'AUS'

- **By No Index:** Using a full table scan to locate the rows, for example, WHERE Name = 'Sydney'

Table 19-3 shows the matrix of using each of the three example WHERE clauses with a SELECT, UPDATE, or DELETE statement as well as executing an INSERT statement. The INSERT statement does not have a WHERE clause, so it is a little different. For each affected index, the number of reads and writes is listed. The *Rows* column shows the number of rows returned or affected for each statement.

Table 19-3. *The effect of various queries on the table I/O counters*

Query/Index	Rows	Reads	Writes
SELECT by primary key PRIMARY	1	FETCH: 1	
SELECT by secondary index CountryCode	14	FETCH: 14	
SELECT by no index NULL	1	FETCH: 4079	
UPDATE by primary key PRIMARY	1	FETCH: 1	UPDATE: 1
UPDATE by secondary index CountryCode	14	FETCH: 15	UPDATE: 14
UPDATE by no index PRIMARY NULL	1	FETCH: 4080	UPDATE: 1
DELETE by primary key PRIMARY	1	FETCH: 1	DELETE: 1
DELETE by secondary index CountryCode	14	FETCH: 15	DELETE: 14
DELETE by no index PRIMARY NULL	1	FETCH: 4080	DELETE: 1
INSERT NULL	1		INSERT: 1

A key takeaway from the table is that for UPDATE and DELETE statements, there are still reads even though they are write statements. The reason is that the rows still must be located before they can be changed. Another observation is that when using the secondary index or no index for updating or deleting rows, then one more record is read than matches the condition. Finally, inserting a row counts as a non-index operation.

WHAT TO MAKE OF THE I/O LATENCIES?

When you see a monitoring graph showing a spike in I/O latencies – whether it is table or file I/O – it can be tempting to make the conclusion that there is a problem. Before you do that, take a step back and consider what the data means.

An increase in I/O latencies measured from the Performance Schema is neither a good nor a bad thing. It is a fact. It means that something was doing I/O, and if there is a spike it means there was more I/O during that period than usual, but otherwise you cannot make conclusions from the event on its own.

A more useful way to use this data is in case a problem is reported. This can be that the system administrator reports the disks are 100% utilized or that end users report the system is slow. Then, you can go and look at what happened. If the disk I/O was unusually high at that point in time, then that is likely related, and you can continue your investigation from there. If the I/O is on the other hand normal, then the high utilization is likely caused by another process than MySQL, or a disk in the disk array is being rebuilt, or similar.

Using the information in the `table_io_waits_summary_by_table` and `table_io_waits_summary_by_index_usage` tables, you can determine which tables are the most used for the various workloads. For example, if you have one table that is particularly busy with writes, you may want to consider moving its tablespace to a faster disk. Before taking such as a decision, you should also consider the actual file I/O.

File I/O

Unlike the table I/O that has just been discussed, the file I/O statistics are for the actual disk I/O involved with the various files that MySQL uses. This is a good supplement to the table I/O information.

There are three Performance Schema tables you can use to get information about the file I/O for the MySQL instance:

- **events_waits_summary_global_by_event_name:** This is a summary table grouped by the event names. By querying event names starting with `wait/io/file/`, you can get I/O statistics grouped by the type of I/O. For example, I/O caused by reading and writing the binary log files uses a single event (`wait/io/file/sql/binlog`). Note that events set to `wait/io/table/sql/handler` correspond to the table I/O that has just been discussed; including the table I/O allows you to easily compare the time spent on file I/O with the time spent on table I/O.

- **file_summary_by_event_name:** This is similar to the `events_waits_summary_global_by_event_name` table but just including file I/O and with the events split into reads, writes, and miscellaneous.

- **file_summary_by_instance:** This is a summary table grouped by the actual files and with the events divided into reads, writes, and miscellaneous. For example, for the binary logs, there is one row per binary log file.

All three tables are useful, and you need to choose between them depending on what information you are looking for. For example, if you want aggregates for the types of files, the `events_waits_summary_global_by_event_name` and `file_summary_by_event_name` tables are the better choice, whereas investigating the I/O for individual files, the `file_summary_by_instance` table is more useful.

The `file_summary_by_event_name` and `file_summary_by_instance` tables split the events into reads, writes, and miscellaneous. Reads and writes are straightforward to understand. The miscellaneous I/O is everything that is not reads or writes. That includes but is not limited to creating, opening, closing, deleting, flushing, and getting metadata for the files. None of the miscellaneous operations involves transferring data, so there are no miscellaneous byte counters.

Listing 19-6 shows an example of the data available in the `events_waits_summary_global_by_event_name` table. The query finds the event with the most overall time spent on I/O.

Listing 19-6. The file I/O event spending the most time overall

```
mysql> SELECT *
       FROM performance_schema.events_waits_summary_global_by_event_name
       WHERE EVENT_NAME LIKE 'wait/io/file/%'
       ORDER BY SUM_TIMER_WAIT DESC
       LIMIT 1\G
*************************** 1. row ***************************
    EVENT_NAME: wait/io/file/innodb/innodb_log_file
    COUNT_STAR: 58175
```

```
SUM_TIMER_WAIT: 20199487047180
MIN_TIMER_WAIT: 5341780
AVG_TIMER_WAIT: 347219260
MAX_TIMER_WAIT: 18754862132
1 row in set (0.0031 sec)
```

This shows that for this instance, the most active event is for the InnoDB redo log files. That is a quite typical result. Each of the events has a corresponding instrument. By default, all of the file wait I/O events are enabled. One particularly interesting event is wait/io/file/innodb/innodb_data_file which is for the I/O on InnoDB tablespace files.

One disadvantage of the events_waits_summary_global_by_event_name table is all the time spent doing I/O is aggregated into a total counter instead of into reads and writes. There are also only timings available. If you use the file_summary_by_event_name table, you can get much more details.

Listing 19-7 shows an example of the file_summary_by_event_name table for the InnoDB redo log I/O event that was found in the previous example.

Listing 19-7. The I/O statistics for the InnoDB redo log

```
mysql> SELECT *
        FROM performance_schema.file_summary_by_event_name
       WHERE EVENT_NAME =
               'wait/io/file/innodb/innodb_log_file'\G
*************************** 1. row ***************************
          EVENT_NAME: wait/io/file/innodb/innodb_log_file
          COUNT_STAR: 58175
      SUM_TIMER_WAIT: 20199487047180
      MIN_TIMER_WAIT: 5341780
      AVG_TIMER_WAIT: 347219260
      MAX_TIMER_WAIT: 18754862132
          COUNT_READ: 8
      SUM_TIMER_READ: 778174704
      MIN_TIMER_READ: 5341780
      AVG_TIMER_READ: 97271660
      MAX_TIMER_READ: 409998080
```

```
   SUM_NUMBER_OF_BYTES_READ: 70656
               COUNT_WRITE: 33672
           SUM_TIMER_WRITE: 870804229376
           MIN_TIMER_WRITE: 7867956
           AVG_TIMER_WRITE: 25861264
           MAX_TIMER_WRITE: 14021439496
  SUM_NUMBER_OF_BYTES_WRITE: 61617664
                COUNT_MISC: 24495
            SUM_TIMER_MISC: 19327904643100
            MIN_TIMER_MISC: 12479224
            AVG_TIMER_MISC: 789054776
            MAX_TIMER_MISC: 18754862132
1 row in set (0.0005 sec)
```

Notice how the SUM_TIMER_WAIT and the other columns with the overall aggregates have the same values as when querying the events_waits_summary_global_by_event_name table. (Since I/O often happens in the background, this will not always be the case even if you do not execute queries in between comparing the two tables.) With the I/O split into reads, writes, and miscellaneous, you can get a better understanding of the I/O workload on your instance.

If you want the statistics for an individual file, you need to use the file_summary_by_instance table. Listing 19-8 shows an example for the tablespace file for the world.city table on Microsoft Windows. Note that there are four backslashes to represent one backslash in the path.

Listing 19-8. The file I/O for the world.city tablespace file

```
mysql> SELECT *
         FROM performance_schema.file_summary_by_instance
        WHERE FILE_NAME LIKE '%\\\\world\\\\city.ibd'\G
*************************** 1. row ***************************
                FILE_NAME: C:\ProgramData\MySQL\MySQL Server 8.0\Data\
                           world\city.ibd
               EVENT_NAME: wait/io/file/innodb/innodb_data_file
    OBJECT_INSTANCE_BEGIN: 1999746796608
               COUNT_STAR: 380
           SUM_TIMER_WAIT: 325377148780
```

```
              MIN_TIMER_WAIT: 12277372
              AVG_TIMER_WAIT: 856255472
              MAX_TIMER_WAIT: 10778110040
                  COUNT_READ: 147
              SUM_TIMER_READ: 144057058960
              MIN_TIMER_READ: 85527220
              AVG_TIMER_READ: 979979712
              MAX_TIMER_READ: 7624205292
   SUM_NUMBER_OF_BYTES_READ: 2408448
                 COUNT_WRITE: 125
             SUM_TIMER_WRITE: 21938183516
             MIN_TIMER_WRITE: 12277372
             AVG_TIMER_WRITE: 175505152
             MAX_TIMER_WRITE: 5113313440
  SUM_NUMBER_OF_BYTES_WRITE: 2146304
                  COUNT_MISC: 108
              SUM_TIMER_MISC: 159381906304
              MIN_TIMER_MISC: 160612960
              AVG_TIMER_MISC: 1475758128
              MAX_TIMER_MISC: 10778110040
1 row in set (0.0007 sec)
```

You can see that the event name is indicating it is an InnoDB tablespace file and the I/O is split out as reads, writes, and miscellaneous. For reads and writes, the total number of bytes is also included.

The last group of Performance Schema tables to consider are the error summary tables.

The Error Summary Tables

While errors are not directly related to query tuning, an error does suggest something is going wrong. A query resulting in an error will still be using resources, but when the error occurs, it will be all in vain. So indirectly errors affect the query performance by adding unnecessary load to the system. There are also errors that are more directly related to the performance such as errors caused by failure to obtain locks.

There are five tables in the Performance Schema grouping the errors encountered by different groupings. The tables are

- events_errors_summary_by_account_by_error

- events_errors_summary_by_host_by_error

- events_errors_summary_by_thread_by_error

- events_errors_summary_by_user_by_error

- events_errors_summary_global_by_error

The table names are self-explanatory. You can use the tables to determine who are executing the queries triggering the errors and combine that with the statement event tables, for example, events_statements_summary_by_digest, to get a picture of both who triggers errors and which statements the errors are for. Listing 19-9 shows an example of querying how many times a deadlock has occurred grouped by the account.

Listing 19-9. Using the events_errors_summary_by_account_by_error table

```
mysql> SELECT *
         FROM performance_schema.events_errors_summary_by_account_by_error
        WHERE ERROR_NAME = 'ER_LOCK_DEADLOCK'\G
*************************** 1. row ***************************
            USER: NULL
            HOST: NULL
    ERROR_NUMBER: 1213
      ERROR_NAME: ER_LOCK_DEADLOCK
       SQL_STATE: 40001
 SUM_ERROR_RAISED: 0
SUM_ERROR_HANDLED: 0
      FIRST_SEEN: NULL
       LAST_SEEN: NULL
*************************** 2. row ***************************
            USER: root
            HOST: localhost
    ERROR_NUMBER: 1213
      ERROR_NAME: ER_LOCK_DEADLOCK
       SQL_STATE: 40001
```

```
SUM_ERROR_RAISED: 2
SUM_ERROR_HANDLED: 0
      FIRST_SEEN: 2019-06-16 10:58:05
       LAST_SEEN: 2019-06-16 11:07:29
2 rows in set (0.0105 sec)
```

This shows that there have been two deadlocks raised for the root@localhost account, but neither was handled. The first row where the user and host are NULL represents background threads.

Tip   You can get the error numbers and names and SQL states from the MySQL reference manual at https://dev.mysql.com/doc/refman/en/server-error-reference.html.

That concludes the discussion of the Performance Schema. If you feel the Performance Schema tables can be overwhelming, it is a good idea to try to use them and, for example, execute some queries on an otherwise idle test system, so you know what to expect. Another option is to use the sys schema which makes it easier to get started with reports based on the Performance Schema.

The sys Schema

One of the main objectives of the sys schema is to make it simpler to create reports based on the Performance Schema. This includes reports that can be used to find candidates for optimization. All of the reports discussed in this section can be generated equally well querying the Performance Schema tables directly; however, the sys schema provides reports that are ready to use optionally with formatting making it easier for humans to read the data.

The reports discussed in this section are created as views using the Performance Schema tables, of which most were covered earlier in this chapter. The views are divided into categories based on whether they can be used to find statements or what uses I/O. The final part of the section will show how you can use the statement_performance_analyzer() procedure to find statements executed during a monitoring window.

Statement Views

The statement views make it simple to query statements grouped by host or user and to find statements matching some condition such as it uses a full table scan. Unless noted otherwise, the views use the events_statements_summary_by_digest Performance Schema table. The views available are listed in Table 19-4.

Table 19-4. *The statement views*

View	Description
host_summary_by_statement_latency	This view uses the events_statements_summary_by_host_by_event_name table to return one row per hostname plus one for the background threads. Each row includes high-level statistics for the statements such as total latency, rows sent, and so on. The rows are ordered by the total latency in descending order.
host_summary_by_statement_type	This view uses the same Performance Schema table as the host_summary_by_statement_latency view, but in addition to the hostname, it also includes the statement type. The rows are first ordered by the hostname in ascending order and then the total latency in descending order.
innodb_lock_waits	This view shows ongoing InnoDB row lock waits. It uses the data_locks and data_lock_waits tables. The view is used in Chapter 22 to investigate lock issues.
schema_table_lock_waits	This view shows ongoing metadata and user lock waits. It uses the metadata_locks table. The view is used in Chapter 22 to investigate lock issues.
session	This view returns an advanced process list based on the threads and events_statements_current tables with some additional information from other Performance Schema tables. The view includes the current statement for active connections and the last executed statement for idle connections. The rows are returned in descending order according to the process list time and the duration of the previous statement. The session view is particularly useful to understand what is happening right now.

(continued)

Table 19-4. (*continued*)

View	Description
statement_analysis	This view is a formatted version of the events_statements_ summary_by_digest table ordered by the total latency in descending order.
statements_with_ errors_or_warnings	This view returns the statements that cause errors or warnings. The rows are ordered in descending order by the number of errors and then number of warnings.
statements_with_ full_table_scans	This view returns the statements that include a full table scan. The rows are first ordered by the percentage of times no index is used and then by the total latency, both in descending order.
statements_with_ runtimes_in_95th_ percentile	This view returns the statements that are in the 95th percentile of all queries in the events_statements_summary_by_digest table. The rows are ordered by the average latency in descending order.
statements_with_ sorting	This view returns the statements that sort the rows in its result. The rows are ordered by the total latency in descending order.
statements_with_ temp_tables	This view returns the statements that use internal temporary tables. The rows are ordered in descending order by the number of internal temporary tables on disk and internal temporary tables in memory.
user_summary_by_ statement_latency	This view is like the host_summary_by_statement_latency view, except it groups by the username instead. The view is based on the events_statements_summary_by_user_by_event_name table.
user_summary_by_ statement_type	This view is the same as the user_summary_by_statement_ latency view except is also includes the statement type.

The main differences between querying the views and using the underlying Performance Schema tables directly are that you do not need to add filters and the data is formatted to make it easier for humans to read. This makes it easy to use the sys schema views as ad hoc reports when investigating a performance issue.

Tip   Remember that the views are also available with x$ prefixed, for example, x$statement_analysis. The views with x$ prefixed do not add the formatting making them better if you want to add additional filters on the formatted columns, change the ordering, or similar.

An example of using the views can be seen in Listing 19-10 where the statement_analysis view is used to find the statement that overall has used the most time since the Performance Schema table was last reset.

Listing 19-10. Finding the query using the most time executing

```
mysql> SELECT *
       FROM sys.statement_analysis
       LIMIT 1\G
*************************** 1. row ***************************
            query: UPDATE `world` . `city` SET `Population` = ?
                   WHERE `ID` = ?
               db: world
        full_scan:
       exec_count: 3744
        err_count: 3
       warn_count: 0
    total_latency: 9.70 m
      max_latency: 51.53 s
      avg_latency: 155.46 ms
     lock_latency: 599.31 ms
        rows_sent: 0
    rows_sent_avg: 0
    rows_examined: 3741
rows_examined_avg: 1
    rows_affected: 3741
```

```
 rows_affected_avg: 1
         tmp_tables: 0
    tmp_disk_tables: 0
        rows_sorted: 0
  sort_merge_passes: 0
             digest: 8f3799ba6b1f47fc2d76f018eaafb6ef8a9d743a7dbe5e558
                     e37371408a1ad5e
         first_seen: 2019-06-15 17:30:13.674383
          last_seen: 2019-06-15 17:52:42.881701
1 row in set (0.0028 sec)
```

The view is already ordered by the total latency in descending order, so it is not necessary to add any ordering to the query. If you recall the example using the events_statements_summary_by_digest Performance Schema table earlier in this chapter, the information returned is similar, but the latencies are easier to read as the values in picoseconds have been converted to values between 0 and 1000 with a unit. The digest is also included, so you can use that to find more information about the statement if needed.

The other views also include useful information. It is left as an exercise for the reader to query the views on your systems and explore the results.

Table I/O Views

The sys schema views for table I/O can be used to find information about the usage of tables and indexes. This includes finding indexes that are not used and tables where full table scans are executed.

The views that base their information on the table I/O all have schema_ as the prefix for the name. The views include those summarized in Table 19-5.

Table 19-5. *Table I/O views*

View	Description
schema_index_ statistics	This view includes all the rows of the table_io_waits_summary_by_ index_usage table where the index name is not NULL. The rows are ordered by the total latency in descending order. The view shows you how much each index is used for selecting, inserting, updating, and deleting data.
schema_table_ statistics	This view combines data from the table_io_waits_summary_by_ table and file_summary_by_instance tables to return both the table I/O and the file I/O related to the table. The file I/O statistics are only included for tables in their own tablespace. The rows are ordered by the total table I/O latency in descending order.
schema_table_ statistics_with_ buffer	This view is the same as the schema_table_statistics view except that is also includes buffer pool usage information from the innodb_ buffer_page Information Schema table. Be aware that querying the innodb_buffer_page table can have a significant overhead and is best used on test systems.
schema_tables_ with_full_table_ scans	This view queries the table_io_waits_summary_by_index_usage table for rows where the index name is NULL – that is, where an index was not used – and includes the rows where the read count is greater than 0. These are the tables where there are rows that are read without using an index – that is, through a full table scan. The rows are ordered by the total number of rows read in descending order.
schema_unused_ indexes	This view also uses the table_io_waits_summary_by_index_usage table but includes rows where no rows have been read for an index, and that index is not a primary key or a unique index. Tables in the mysql schema are excluded as you should not change the definition of any of those. The tables are ordered alphabetically according to the schema and table names.

Usually these views are used in combination of other views and tables. For example, you may detect that the CPU usage is very high. A typical cause of high CPU usage is large table scans, so you may look at the `schema_tables_with_full_table_scans` view and find that one or more tables are returning a large number of rows through table scans. Then go on to query the `statements_with_full_table_scans` view to find statements using that table without using indexes.

As mentioned, the `schema_table_statistics` view combines table I/O statistics and file I/O statistics. There are also views that purely look at the file I/O.

File I/O Views

The views to explore the file I/O usage follow the same pattern as the statement views that were grouped by the hostname or username. The views are best used to determine what is causing the I/O once you have determined that the disk I/O is a bottleneck. You can then work backward to find the tables involved. From there you may determine you can optimize queries using the tables or that you need to increase the I/O capacity.

The file I/O includes the views in Table 19-6.

Table 19-6. *File I/O views*

View	Description
host_summary_by_file_io	This view uses the events_waits_summary_by_host_by_event_name table and groups the file I/O wait events by the account hostname. The rows are ordered by the total latency in descending order.
host_summary_by_file_io_type	This view is the same as the host_summary_by_file_io view except that it also includes the event name for the file I/O. The rows are ordered by the hostname and then in descending order the total latency.
io_by_thread_by_latency	This view uses the events_waits_summary_by_thread_by_event_name table to return the file I/O statistics grouped by the thread with the rows ordered by the total latency in descending order. The threads include the background threads which are the ones causing a large part of the write I/O.

(continued)

Table 19-6. (*continued*)

View	Description
io_global_by_file_by_bytes	This view uses the file_summary_by_instance table to return the number of read and write operations and the amount of I/O in bytes for each file. The rows are ordered by the total amount of read plus write I/O in bytes in descending order.
io_global_by_file_by_latency	This view is the same as the io_global_by_file_by_bytes view except it reports the I/O latencies.
io_global_by_wait_by_bytes	This view is similar to the io_global_by_file_by_bytes view except it groups by the I/O event names instead of filenames and it uses the file_summary_by_event_name table.
io_global_by_wait_by_latency	This view is the same as the io_global_by_wait_by_bytes view except it reports the I/O latencies.
user_summary_by_file_io	This view is the same as the host_summary_by_file_io view except it uses the events_waits_summary_by_user_by_event_name table and groups by the username instead of hostname.
user_summary_by_file_io_type	This view is the same as the user_summary_by_file_io view except that it also includes the event name for the file I/O. The rows are ordered by the username and then in descending order the total latency.

The views are straightforward to use, yet it is still worth taking a look at a couple of examples to show some specifics relating to them. Listing 19-11 shows an example of the io_by_thread_by_latency view for a background and a foreground thread. The thread ids are chosen based on the threads available on the test system.

Listing 19-11. Example of using the io_by_thread_by_latency view

```
mysql> SELECT *
         FROM sys.io_by_thread_by_latency
        WHERE THREAD_ID IN (19, 87543)\G
*********************** 1. row ***************************
          user: log_flusher_thread
         total: 24489
```

```
   total_latency: 19.33 s
     min_latency: 56.39 us
     avg_latency: 789.23 us
     max_latency: 18.75 ms
       thread_id: 19
  processlist_id: NULL
*************************** 2. row ***************************
            user: root@localhost
           total: 40683
   total_latency: 15.48 s
     min_latency: 5.27 us
     avg_latency: 353.57 us
     max_latency: 262.23 ms
       thread_id: 87543
  processlist_id: 87542
2 rows in set (0.0066 sec)
```

The main thing to notice in the example is the username. In row 1, there is an example of a background thread in which case the last part (using / as a delimiter) of the thread name is used as the username. In row 2, it is a foreground thread, and the user is the username and hostname for the account with an @ between them. The rows also include information about the Performance Schema thread id and the process list id (connection id), so you can use those to find more information about the threads.

The other example is shown in Listing 19-12 and is for the io_global_by_file_by_ bytes view.

Listing 19-12. Example of using the io_global_by_file_by_bytes view

```
mysql> SELECT *
         FROM sys.io_global_by_file_by_bytes
        LIMIT 1\G
*************************** 1. row ***************************
            file: @@datadir\undo_001
      count_read: 15889
      total_read: 248.31 MiB
        avg_read: 16.00 KiB
```

```
    count_write: 15149
  total_written: 236.70 MiB
      avg_write: 16.00 KiB
          total: 485.02 MiB
      write_pct: 48.80
1 row in set (0.0028 sec)
```

Notice here how the path to the filename is using @@datadir. This is part of the formatting the sys schema uses to make it easier to understand at a glance where the files are located. The data amounts are also scaled.

The sys schema views that have been discussed thus far all report the statistics recorded since the corresponding Performance Schema tables were last reset. Often performance issues only show up intermittently in which case you want to determine what is going on during that period. That is where you need the statement performance analyzer.

Statement Performance Analyzer

The statement performance analyzer allows you to take two snapshots of the events_statements_summary_by_digest table and use the delta between the two snapshots with a view that usually uses the events_statements_summary_by_digest table directly. This is useful, for example, to determine which queries are executing during a period of peak load.

The snapshots are created and the analysis performed using the statement_performance_analyzer() procedure. It takes three arguments as shown in Table 19-7.

Table 19-7. *The arguments for the* `statement_performance_analyzer()` *procedure*

Argument	Valid Values	Description
action	Snapshot Overall Delta create_tmp create_table save cleanup	The action you want the procedure to perform. The actions will be discussed in more detail shortly.
table	<schema>.<table>	This parameter is used for actions requiring a table name. The format must be `schema.table` or the table name on its own. In either case, do not use backticks. A dot is not allowed in the schema or table name.
views	with_runtimes_in_95th_ percentile analysis with_errors_or_warnings with_full_table_scans with_sorting with_temp_tables custom	The view names to generate the report with. It is allowed to specify more than one view. All views but the custom view are using one of the statement views in the `sys` schema. For a custom view, the view name of the custom view is specified using the `statement_performance_analyzer.view` sys schema configuration option.

The action specifies what you want the procedure to do. The different actions are used at different stages of the workflow of generating a statement performance report. The supported actions are listed in Table 19-8.

Table 19-8. *The actions for the* `statement_performance_analyzer()` *procedure*

Action	Description
snapshot	This creates a snapshot of the `events_statements_summary_by_digest` table unless the `table` argument is given in which case the content of the provided table is used as the snapshot. The snapshot is stored in a temporary table called `tmp_digests` in the `sys` schema.
overall	This creates a report based on the content in the table provided with the `table` argument. If you set the table argument to `NOW()`, the current content of the summary by digest table is used to create a new snapshot. If you set the table argument to `NULL`, the current snapshot will be used.
delta	This creates a report based on the difference between two snapshots using the table provided with the `table` argument and the existing snapshot. This action creates the `sys.tmp_digests_delta` temporary table. An example of this action will be shown later in this section.
create_table	Creates a regular user table with the name given by the `table` argument. The table can be used to store a snapshot using the `save` action.
create_tmp	Creates a temporary table with the name given by the `table` argument. This table can be used to store a snapshot using the `save` action.
save	Saves the existing snapshot to the table specified by the `table` argument.
cleanup	Removes the temporary tables that have been used for snapshots and delta calculations. Tables created with the `create_table` and `create_tmp` actions are not deleted.

The procedure is particularly useful to create two snapshots and calculate the delta between them. The workflow to perform a delta analysis is as follows:

1. Create a temporary table to store the initial snapshot. This is done by using the `create_tmp` action.

2. Create the initial snapshot using the `snapshot` action.

3. Save the initial snapshot to the temporary table from step 1 by using the `save` action.

4. Wait for the duration that data should be collected.

5. Create a new snapshot using the `snapshot` action.

6. Use the `delta` action with one or more views to generate the report.

7. Clean up using the `cleanup` action.

It can be useful to try the procedure in a controlled environment where you know which queries have been executed. That way you know what to expect in the generated output. The example will use a schema called `monitor` to store the initial snapshot:

```
mysql> CREATE SCHEMA monitor;
```

You will need to execute some queries while the monitoring is ongoing in a second connection. You are encouraged to try some of your own queries. If you want to reproduce the output in the example, you can use MySQL Shell and start out (before starting the monitoring) changing the language mode to Python and set the default schema to `world`:

```
\py
\use world
```

The Python code that will execute the nine queries for the example is shown in Listing 19-13. You can execute the code in MySQL Shell. The code is also available from the file `listing_19_13.py` in this book's GitHub repository.

Listing 19-13. Python code for example queries for statement analysis

```
queries = [
    ("SELECT * FROM `city` WHERE `ID` = ?", [130, 3805]),
    ("SELECT * FROM `city` WHERE `CountryCode` = ?", ['AUS', 'CHN', 'IND']),
    ("SELECT * FROM `country` WHERE CODE = ?", ['DEU', 'GBR', 'BRA', 'USA']),
]

for query in queries:
    sql = query[0]
    parameters = query[1]
    for param in parameters:
        result = session.run_sql(sql, (param,))
```

The queries with placeholders are defined as a list of tuples with values to use for that query as the second element in the tuple. That allows you to quickly add more queries and values if you want to execute more queries. The queries are executed in a double loop over the queries and parameters. When you paste the code into MySQL Shell, finish it off with two new lines to tell MySQL Shell that the multiline code block is complete.

Listing 19-14 shows the example of creating a report with approximately one minute between the two snapshots. The example uses the analysis view which is based on sys. statement_analysis for the report. Since the limitations of the pages in this book do not allow the report to be shown very well, the full output of the steps and the report can be found in this book's GitHub repository in the file listing_19_14_statement_analysis. txt. The order of the queries in the report may be different as it depends on how long it takes to execute the queries, and the statistics will be different.

Listing 19-14. Using the statement_performance_analyzer() procedure

```
mysql> CALL sys.ps_setup_disable_thread(CONNECTION_ID());
+--------------------+
| summary            |
+--------------------+
| Disabled 1 thread  |
+--------------------+
1 row in set (0.0012 sec)

Query OK, 0 rows affected (0.0012 sec)

mysql> CALL sys.statement_performance_analyzer(
                'create_tmp', 'monitor._tmp_ini', NULL);
Query OK, 0 rows affected (0.0028 sec)

mysql> CALL sys.statement_performance_analyzer(
                'snapshot', NULL, NULL);
Query OK, 0 rows affected (0.0065 sec)

mysql> CALL sys.statement_performance_analyzer(
                'save', 'monitor._tmp_ini', NULL);
Query OK, 0 rows affected (0.0017 sec)

-- Execute your queries or the Python code in Listing 19-13
-- in a second connection while the SLEEP(60) is executing.
```

```
mysql> DO SLEEP(60);
Query OK, 0 rows affected (1 min 0.0064 sec)

mysql> CALL sys.statement_performance_analyzer(
           'snapshot', NULL, NULL);
Query OK, 0 rows affected (0.0041 sec)

mysql> CALL sys.statement_performance_analyzer(
           'delta', 'monitor._tmp_ini',
           'analysis');
+-----------------------------------------+
| Next Output                             |
+-----------------------------------------+
| Top 100 Queries Ordered by Total Latency |
+-----------------------------------------+
1 row in set (0.0049 sec)

+------------------------------------------------+-------+...
| query                                          | db    |...
+------------------------------------------------+-------+...
| SELECT * FROM `city` WHERE `CountryCode` = ?   | world |...
| SELECT * FROM `country` WHERE CODE = ?         | world |...
| SELECT * FROM `city` WHERE `ID` = ?            | world |...
+------------------------------------------------+-------+...
3 rows in set (0.0049 sec)

Query OK, 0 rows affected (0.0049 sec)

mysql> CALL sys.statement_performance_analyzer(
           'cleanup', NULL, NULL);
Query OK, 0 rows affected (0.0018 sec)

mysql> DROP TEMPORARY TABLE monitor._tmp_ini;
Query OK, 0 rows affected (0.0007 sec)

mysql> CALL sys.ps_setup_enable_thread(CONNECTION_ID());
```

```
+------------------+
| summary          |
+------------------+
| Enabled 1 thread |
+------------------+
1 row in set (0.0015 sec)

Query OK, 0 rows affected (0.0015 sec)
```

The use of the ps_setup_disable_thread() and ps_setup_enable_thread() procedures at the start and end of the example is there to disable Performance Schema instrumentation of the thread doing the analysis and then enable instrumentation when the analysis is done. By disabling instrumentation, the queries executed by the analysis are not included in the report. This is not so important on a busy system, but it is very useful when testing with just a few queries.

For the analysis itself, a temporary table is created so a snapshot can be created and saved to it. After that, data is collected for a minute, then a new snapshot is created, and the report is generated. The final steps clean up the temporary tables used for the analysis. Notice that the temporary table monitor._tmp_ini was not cleaned up by the cleanup action as that was explicitly created by the create_tmp action.

The report output shows that three statements were executed during the monitoring period. In a real-world case, there would usually be more, and the report is by default limited to the top 100 queries. You can configure how many queries that can be included in the report as well as a couple of other settings. This is done using the sys schema configuration mechanism with support for the following settings:

- **debug:** When the option is set to ON, debugging output is produced. The default is OFF.

- **statement_performance_analyzer.limit:** The maximum number of statements to include in the report. The default is 100.

- **statement_performance_analyzer.view:** The view to use with the custom view.

Tip   The sys schema options can either be set in the sys.sys_config table or as user variables by prepending @sys. to the option name. For example, debug becomes @sys.debug.

Thus far, it has been assumed the sys schema views are used directly by executing queries explicitly against them. That is not the only way you can use them though; the views are also available through MySQL Workbench.

MySQL Workbench

MySQL Workbench is great if you prefer to work using a graphical user interface rather than a command-line interface. Not only does MySQL Workbench allow you to execute your own queries; it also comes with several features to help you manage and monitor your instance. For the purpose of this discussion, it is primarily the *performance reports* and the *client connections* report that are of interest.

Both reports are accessed through the navigator to the left in the MySQL Workbench window. The navigator is available once you are connected to MySQL. Figure 19-1 highlights the reports.

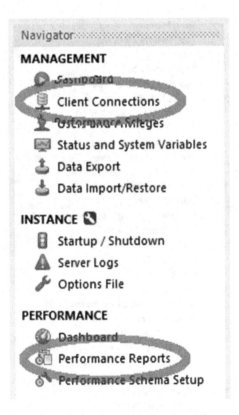

Figure 19-1. *Accessing the client connections and performance reports*

The rest of the section will discuss the two types of reports in more detail.

Performance Reports

The performance reports in MySQL Workbench are a great way to investigate what is happening in the instance. As the performance reports are based on the sys schema views, the information available will be the same as was discussed when going through the sys schema views.

You get to the performance reports by connecting to the instance you want to investigate and choosing *Performance Reports* from the *PERFORMANCE* section of the navigator. You have access to most of the reports that can also be made directly using the sys schema. Figure 19-2 shows how you can select the report you are interested in.

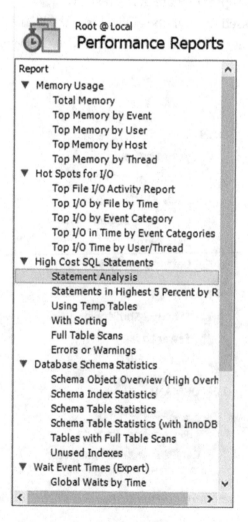

Figure 19-2. *Choosing a performance report*

An example of a report is shown in Figure 19-3 where the statement statistics report has been executed. That is the same report as you get using the `sys.statement_analysis` view. An example of the report with all columns present can be seen in the file `figure_19_3_performance_report.png` in this book's GitHub repository.

Statement Analysis

Lists statements with various aggregated statistics

Query	Full Table S...	Executed (#)	Errors (#)	Warnings (#)	Total Time (.
UPDATE `world` . `city` SET `Population` = ? WHER...		3744	3	0	582056916.
SELECT * FROM `city` WHERE NAME = ?	*	102349	0	0	138758688.
DO `SLEEP` (?)		1	0	0	60005489.
SELECT (`cat` . `name` COLLATE `utf8_tolower_ci`...	*	44070	0	0	49955606.(
UPDATE `world` . `city` SET `Population` = `Populati...		10000	0	0	32961839.(
SHOW GLOBAL VARIABLES	*	6248	0	0	21859065.
SET SESSION `sql_mode` = ? , SESSION `wait_timeo...		124099	0	124099	21345764.
UPDATE `city` SET `Population` = `Population` * ?...		3	0	0	15902598.
SHOW GLOBAL VARIABLES LIKE ?	*	4163	0	0	14220974.
SET `character_set_results` = ?		124099	0	0	13919508.
SET `autocommit` = ?		124791	0	0	13237521.
SHOW WARNINGS		124099	0	0	12784969.
UPDATE `world` . `city` SET `Population` = `Populati...		1190	0	0	7423772.
SHOW VARIABLES LIKE ?	*	2106	0	0	6732233.
SELECT `ROUND` (SUM (`sum_timer_wait`) / ?) `t...	*	2091	0	0	5143966.
SHOW GLOBAL STATUS	*	4165	0	0	4970374.
SELECT `digest` AS `digest` , SCHEMA_NAME AS `sc...	*	2077	0	0	4706200.:
SHOW BINARY LOGS	*	2106	0	0	3846203.(
SELECT `substring_index` (`performance_schema`	*	2091	0	0	2858649.'
UPDATE `country` SET `Population` = `Population` *...		2	0	0	2512154.(
SELECT `conn_conf` . `channel_name` AS ? , `conn_...	*	4162	0	0	2336868.
SELECT `plugin_name` FROM `information_schema`	*	2501	0	0	1960398.:
SELECT COUNT (*) AS `num_long_running` , @@`lo...	*	2092	0	0	1734821.

Export...   Copy Selected   Copy Query   Refresh

***Figure 19-3.** The statement statistics performance report*

One advantage of the performance reports is that they use the unformatted view definitions, so you can change the ordering using the GUI. You change the ordering by clicking the column header for the column you want to order by. The order toggles between ascending and descending order each time you click the column header.

At the bottom of the report, there are buttons to help you use the report. The *Export...* button allows you to save the result of the report as a CSV file. The *Copy Selected* button copies the header and the selected rows into memory in the CSV format. The *Copy Query* button copies the query used for the report. This allows you to edit the query and manually execute it. For the report in Figure 19-3, the query returned is `select * from sys.`x$statement_analysis``. The final button is the *Refresh* button to the right which executes the report again.

There is no performance report based on the sys.session view. Instead you need to use the client connections report.

Client Connections Report

If you want to get a list of the connections currently connected to the instance, you need to use the client connections report. It does not include quite as much information as the sys.session view, but it does include the most essential data. The report is based on the threads table in the Performance Schema, and additionally, the program name is included if possible.

Figure 19-4 shows an example of the leftmost columns of the report. To see the full list of columns, check the file figure_19_4_client_connections.png in the book's GitHub repository.

Root @ Local
Client Connections

Threads Connected: 9		Threads Running: 2		Threads Created: 9		Threads Cached: 2		Rejected (over limit): 0		
Total Connections: 125892		Connection Limit: 151		Aborted Clients: 0		Aborted Connections: 0		Errors: 0		

Id	User	Host	DB	Command	Time	State	Threa...	Type	Name	Paren...	Instrumented	Info
4	event_sched...	None	None	Sleep	0	Waiting on e...	44	FOREGROUND	thread/sql/e...	1	YES	NULL
6	None	None	None	Daemon	666439	Suspending	45	FOREGROUND	thread/sql/c...	1	YES	NULL
13	root	localhost	mysql	Sleep	26	None	52	FOREGROUND	thread/sql/o...	0	YES	NULL
122...	root	localhost	performance_sc...	Sleep	11	None	122988	FOREGROUND	thread/mysq...	0	NO	NULL
87542	root	localhost	world	Sleep	56024	None	87543	FOREGROUND	thread/mysq...	0	YES	NULL
124...	root	localhost	employees	Sleep	10	None	124112	FOREGROUND	thread/sql/o...	0	YES	NULL
124...	root	localhost	employees	Sleep	10	None	124114	FOREGROUND	thread/sql/o...	0	YES	NULL
124...	root	localhost	None	Query	0	Sending data	124159	FOREGROUND	thread/sql/o...	0	YES	SELECT t.
124...	root	localhost	None	Sleep	0	None	124160	FOREGROUND	thread/sql/o...	0	YES	NULL
125...	root	localhost	mysql	Sleep	36	None	125899	FOREGROUND	thread/sql/o...	0	YES	NULL
125...	root	localhost	mysql	Sleep	37	None	125900	FOREGROUND	thread/sql/o...	0	YES	NULL

Figure 19-4.   *The client connections report*

If you already have the client connections report or one of the performance reports open, you can reuse the connection to fetch the client connections report. That can be useful if all connections have been used up and you need to get a report of what the connections are doing. The client connections report also allows you to kill queries or connections by selecting the query and using one of the kill buttons to the lower right of the report.

While MySQL Workbench is very useful for investigating performance issues, it is primarily targeted at ad hoc investigations. For proper monitoring, you need a full monitoring solution.

MySQL Enterprise Monitor

There is not really anything replacing a full-featured monitoring solution when you need to investigate performance issues whether you are reacting to user complaints or are proactive looking to make improvements. This section will base the discussion on MySQL Enterprise Monitor (MEM). Other monitoring solutions may provide similar features.

There are three features that will be discussed in this section. The first is the Query Analyzer, then timeseries graphs, and finally ad hoc reports such as the processes and lock waits reports. You should use the various metrics in combination when you investigate an issue. For example, if you have a report of high disk I/O usage, then find the timeseries graphs showing disk I/O and determine how and when the I/O has developed. You can then use the Query Analyzer to investigate which queries were executed during this period. If the issue is still ongoing, a report like the processes report or one of the other ad hoc reports can be used to see what is going on.

The Query Analyzer

The Query Analyzer in MySQL Enterprise Monitor is one of the most important places to look when you need to investigate performance issues. MySQL Enterprise Monitor uses the events_statements_summary_by_digest table in the Performance Schema to regularly collect which queries have been executed. It then compares successive outputs to determine the statistics since the previous data collection. This is similar to what you saw in the example using the statement performance analyzer in the sys schema, just that this is happening automatically and is integrated together with the rest of the collected data.

You get to the Query Analyzer by choosing the *Queries* option in the left-hand menu as shown in Figure 19-5.

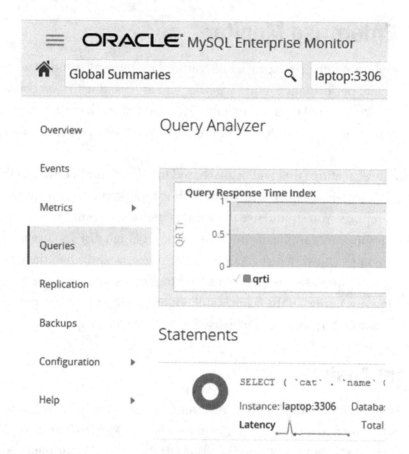

Figure 19-5.   *Accessing the Query Analyzer*

Once you open the Query Analyzer, it will default to open with the Query Response Time index (QRTi) graph at the top and a list of queries below. The default time frame is the past hour. You can choose to display another graph or change the number of graphs. The default graph with the Query Response Time index is worth some consideration.

The Query Response Time index is a measure of how well a single query or a group of queries perform. It is calculated using the Apdex (Application Performance Index) formula.[1] The shape next to the query information consisting of two concentric circles (donut shaped) is colored according to how well the query performs with the colors green, yellow, and red indicating the percentage of time the query performs according to the optimum, acceptable, and unacceptable criteria:

---

[1] https://en.wikipedia.org/wiki/Apdex

- **Optimum:** When the query executes in less time than the threshold set to define optimal performance. The default threshold is 100 ms. The threshold can be configured. Green is used for the optimal time frame.

- **Acceptable:** When the query executes in more time than the threshold for the optimal time frame but less than four times the threshold. This frame uses yellow.

- **Unacceptable:** When the query is slower than four times the threshold for the optimal threshold. This frame uses red.

The Query Response Time index is not a perfect measure of how well the instance is performing, but for systems where the various queries are expected to have response times around the same interval, it does provide a good indication of how well the system or query performs at different times. If you have a mix of very fast OLTP queries and slow OLAP queries, it is not so good a measure of the performance.

If you spot something interesting in the graph, you can select that period and use that as the new time frame for filtering the queries. There is also the *Configuration View* button to the upper right of the graph that can be used to set the time frames for the graphs and queries, which graphs to show, filters for the queries, and so on.

The query list is what you need to use to look at actual queries. An example for a query is shown in Figure 19-6.

Figure 19-6. Overview of a query in the Query Analyzer

The information is high level and is meant to help you narrow down which candidate queries to look closer at for a given period. In the example, you can see that there have been almost 160,000 executions of the query to find cities by name. The first question you should ask is whether that is a reasonable amount of times to execute this query. It may be expected, but a high execution count may also be a sign of a runway process that keeps executing the same query over and over or that you need to implement caching for the query. You can also see from the green donut that all executions are in the optimal time frame with respect to the Query Response Time index.

The icon in the upper-right corner of the query area, just to the left of the three vertical dots, shows that MySQL Enterprise Monitor has flagged this query. To get the meaning of the icon, hover over the icon. The icon in this example means that the query is doing full table scans. Thus, even though the Query Response Time index looks good for the query, it is worth looking closer at the query. Whether it is acceptable that a full table scan is done depends on several factors such as the number of rows in the table and how often the query is executed. You can also see that the query latency graph shows an increase in latency at the right end of the graph suggesting the performance is degrading.

If you want to investigate a query in more detail, click the three vertical dots in the upper-right corner of the query area which allows you to go to the details screen for the query. Figure 19-7 shows an example of the query details. The full-sized screenshot is available in the file `figure_19_7_mem_query_details.png` from the book's GitHub repository.

Figure 19-7. *Query details from the Query Analyzer*

The details include the metrics that are available from the Performance Schema digest summary. Here you can see that there are indeed much more rows examined than returned, so it is worth investigating further whether an index is required. The graphs give an idea of the development of the query execution over time.

At the bottom are examples of actual query execution latencies. In this case there are two executions included. The first is the red circle in the left of the graph. The second is the blue-greenish mark at the lower right. The color symbolized the Query Response Time index for each execution. This graph is only available if the `events_statements_history_long` consumer is enabled.

The Query Analyzer is great for investigating queries, but to get a higher-level summary of the activity, you need to use the timeseries graphs.

Timeseries Graphs

Timeseries graphs are what is often thought of when talking about a monitoring system. They are important to understand the overall load on the system and to spot changes over time. However, they are often not very good at finding the root cause of an issue. For that you need to analyze the queries or generate ad hoc reports to see the issue happening.

When you look at timeseries graphs, you need to consider a few things; otherwise, you may end up drawing the wrong conclusions and declare an emergency when there are no problems. First, you need to know what the metric in the graph means, like the discussion earlier in the chapter of what the I/O latencies mean. Second, remember that a change in the metric does not on its own mean there is a problem. It just means that the activity changed. If you start to execute more queries, because you enter the peak period of the day or year, it is only natural that the database activity increases and vice versa when you go to a quiet period. Similarly, if you implement a new feature such as adding an element to the start screen of the application, that is also expected to increase the amount of work performed. Third, be careful not just to consider a single graph. If you look at monitoring data without taking the other data into consideration, it is easy to make the wrong conclusions.

If you look at Figure 19-8, there is an example of several timeseries graphs for a period where the utilization of the database and system changes.

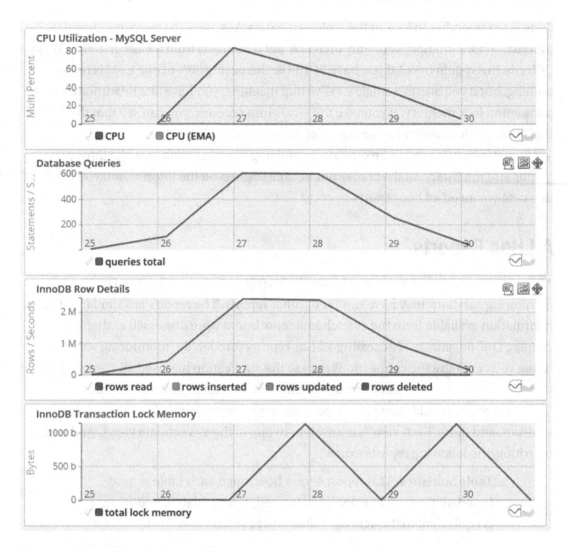

Figure 19-8. *Timeseries graphs*

If you look at the graphs, you can see the CPU utilization in the topmost graph suddenly increases and peaks at more than 80%. Why did that happen and is it a bad thing? The database queries graph shows that the number of statements per second increases at the same time and so does the number of rows read in the InnoDB row details graph. So the CPU usage is most likely caused by increased query activity. From there, you can go to the Query Analyzer and investigate which queries are running.

A couple of other points can be taken away from the graphs. If you look at the x-axis, the graph only covers six minutes of data. Be careful not to draw conclusions based on a very short time frame as that may not represent the true state of the system. The other thing is to remember to look at the scale of the data. Yes, the CPU usage and InnoDB transaction lock memory suddenly increase, but it happens from a base of 0. How many CPUs do the system have? If you have 96 CPUs, then using 80% of one CPU is really nothing, but if you are on a single CPU virtual machine, you have less headroom. For the transaction lock memory, if you take the y-axis into account, you can see that the "spike" is just 1 KiB of lock memory – so not something to worry about.

Sometimes you need to investigate an ongoing issue in which case the timeseries graphs and the Query Analyzer may not be able to give you the information you need. In that case you need ad hoc reports.

Ad Hoc Reports

There are several ad hoc reports available in MySQL Enterprise Monitor. Other monitoring solutions may have similar or other reports. The reports are similar to the information available from the sys schema reports that were discussed earlier in the chapter. One advantage of accessing ad hoc reports through the monitoring solution is that you can reuse the connections in case the application has used all connections available, and it provides a graphical user interface to manipulate the reports.

The reports include the ability to get a list of processes, lock information, schema statistics, and more. Each view is equivalent to one of the sys schema views. At the time of writing, the following reports exist:

- **Table Statistics:** This report shows how much each table is used based on the total latency, rows fetched, rows updated, and so on. It is equivalent to the schema_table_statistics view.

- **User Statistics:** This report shows the activity for each username. It is equivalent to the user_summary view.

- **Memory Usage:** This report shows the memory usage per memory type. It is equivalent to the memory_global_by_current_bytes view.

- **Database File I/O:** This report shows the disk I/O usage. There are three options for the report: to group by file which is equivalent to the io_global_by_file_by_latency view, to group by the wait (I/O) type which is equivalent to the io_global_by_wait_by_latency view, and to group by thread which is equivalent to the io_by_thread_by_latency view. Grouping by the wait type adds the I/O-related timeseries graphs.

- **InnoDB Buffer Pool:** This report shows what data is stored in the InnoDB buffer pool. It is based on the innodb_buffer_page Information Schema table. Since there can be a significant overhead querying the information for this report, it is recommended only to use the report on test systems.

- **Processes:** This report shows the foreground and background threads that are currently present in MySQL. It uses the sys. processlist view which is the same as the session view except that it also includes background threads.

- **Lock Waits:** This report has two options. You can either get a report for the InnoDB lock waits (the innodb_lock_waits view) or metadata locks (the schema_table_lock_waits view).

The principle of using the reports is the same, so only two examples will be shown. The first is in Figure 19-9 where an InnoDB lock wait situation is shown in the lock waits report.

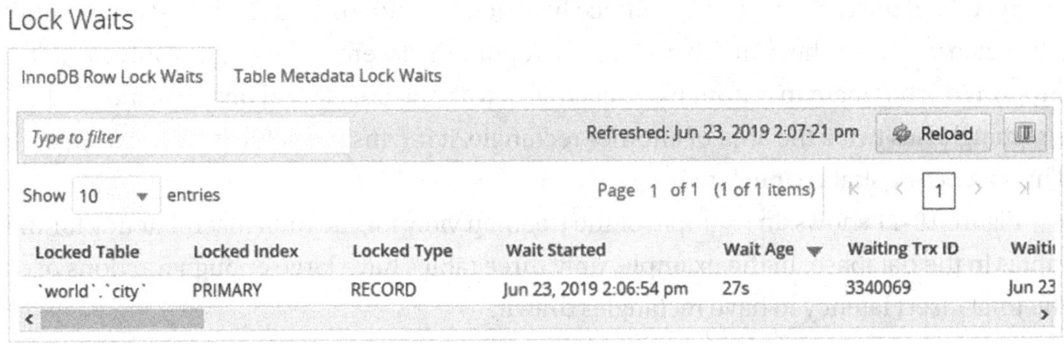

Figure 19-9. *The InnoDB row lock waits report*

The report shows the rows in a paginated mode, and you can change the ordering by clicking the column headers. Changing the ordering does not reload the data. If you need to reload the data, use the *Reload* button at the top of the screenshot.

You can also manipulate the columns available in the report. In the upper-right corner, there is a button to select which columns you want to be visible in the report. The screenshot in Figure 19-10 shows an example of how you can choose which columns to display.

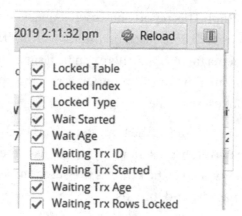

Figure 19-10. Choosing which columns to include in the report

When you toggle whether the columns are included or not, the report updates immediately without reloading the report. That means that for intermittent issues such as lock waits, you can manipulate the report without losing the data you are looking at. The same is the case if you change the ordering of the columns by dragging the column headers around.

Several of the reports have the choice between a standard column-based output and a treemap view. For the InnoDB buffer pool report, the treemap view is the only format supported. The treemap output uses rectangles with the area based on the value, so if a rectangle has twice the area of another rectangle, it means the value is twice as large. This can help visualize the data.

Figure 19-11 shows an example of the treemap view for the total insert latency for the tables in the database. In the example, only three tables have large enough fractions of the total insert latency to have rectangles drawn.

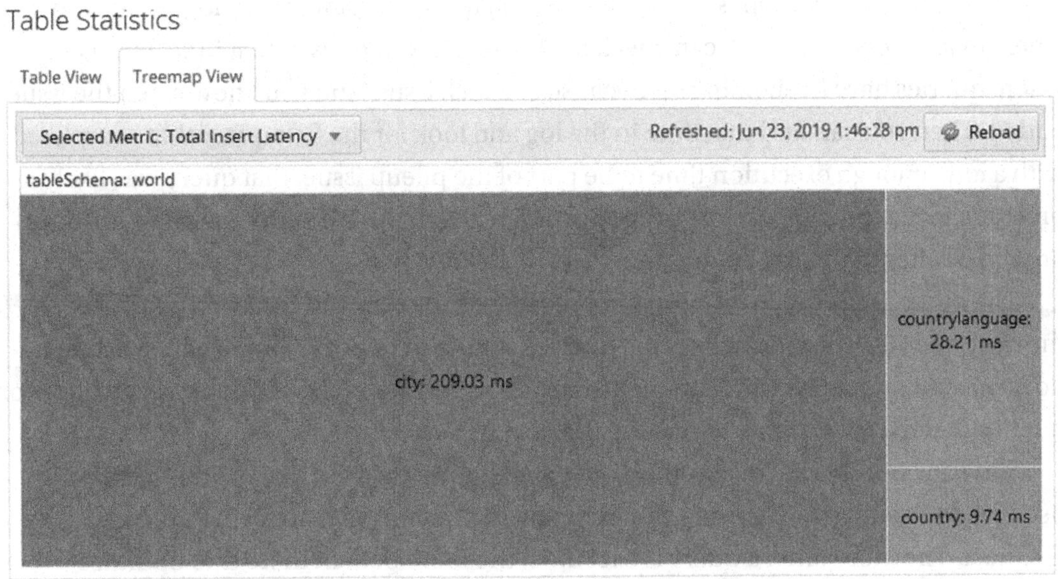

Table Statistics

| Table View | Treemap View |

Selected Metric: Total Insert Latency ▼   Refreshed: Jun 23, 2019 1:46:28 pm   🔄 Reload

tableSchema: world

Figure 19-11. *The treemap view of the total insert latency*

When you look at the treemap view, you can immediately see that the amount of time spent on inserting data into the city table is much larger than for the other tables.

The ad hoc queries all deal with the state as it is at the time the report is executed. The Query Analyzer and timeseries graphs on the other hand work with what happened in the past. Another tool that shows what happened in the past is the slow query log.

The Slow Query Log

The slow query log is a trusty old tool for finding poorly performing queries and to investigate past problems in MySQL. It may seem unnecessary today where the Performance Schema has so many options to query statements that are slow, do not use indexes, or fulfill other criteria. However, the slow query log has one main advantage that it is persisted, so you can go back and use it even after MySQL has been restarted.

Tip   The slow query log is not enabled by default. You can enable and disable it using the slow_query_log option. The log can also be enabled and disabled dynamically without restarting MySQL.

There are two basic types of modes in which to use the slow query log. If you know when an issue occurred, you can check the log for slow queries at that time. One case is where queries have been piling up because of a lock issue, and you know when the issue ended. Then you can find that time in the log and look for the first query that completed with a long enough execution time to be part of the pileup issue; that query was likely the one causing the pileup possible in connection with some of the other queries finishing around or after that point in time.

The other usage mode is to use the mysqldumpslow utility to create an aggregate of the slow queries. This normalizes the queries similar to how the Performance Schema does, so similar queries will have their statistics aggregated. This mode is great to look for queries that may contribute to making the system busy.

You can choose what to sort the aggregated queries by with the -s option. You can use the total count (the c sorting value) to find the queries that are being executed the most. The more often a query is executed, the more benefit there is to optimize the query. You can use the total execution time (t) in a similar manner. If users are complaining about slow response times, the average execution time (at) is useful for sorting. If you suspect some queries return too many rows because they are missing filter conditions, you can sort the queries according to the number of rows they return (r for total rows, ar for average rows). Often it can be useful to combine the sorting option with the -r option to reverse the order and the -t to only include the first N queries. That way it is easier to focus on the queries causing the biggest impact.

You also need to remember that by default the slow query log does not log all queries, so you do not get the same insight into the workload as with the Performance Schema. You need to adjust the threshold for considering a query slow by changing the long_query_time configuration option. The option can be changed for a session, so if you have significant variations in expected execution time, you can set the global value to match the majority of queries and change per session for the connection executing queries that deviate from the normal. If you need to investigate issues that involve DDL statements, you need to make sure you enable the log_slow_admin_statements option.

Caution   The slow query log has a larger overhead than the Performance Schema. When just logging a few slow queries, the overhead is usually negligible, but it can be significant if you log many queries. Do not log all queries by setting long_query_time to 0 except on a test system or for a short period of time.

You analyze the `mysqldumpslow` reports in much the same way as the Performance Schema and `sys` schema, so it will be left as an exercise for the reader to generate reports from your systems and use them to find candidate queries for further optimization.

Summary

This chapter has explored the sources available to find queries that are candidates to be optimized. It was also discussed how to look for resource utilization that can be used to know at what times there are workloads that push the system most toward its limit. It is the queries running at that time that are the most important to focus on, though you should keep your eyes open for queries in general that do more work than they should.

The discussion started out going through the Performance Schema and considered which information is available and how to use it. Particularly the `events_statements_summary_by_digest` table is a gold mine when looking for queries that may have performance issues. You should however not restrict yourself to just looking at queries. You should also take table and file I/O into consideration as well as whether queries cause errors. These errors may include lock wait timeouts and deadlocks.

The `sys` schema provides a range of ready-made reports that you can use to find information. These reports are based on the Performance Schema, but they include filters, sorting, and formatting that make the reports easy to use, particularly as ad hoc reports when investigating an issue. It was also shown how the statement performance analyzer can be used to create a report of the queries running during a period of interest.

MySQL Workbench provides both performance reports based on the `sys` schema views and a client connections report based on the `threads` table in the Performance Schema. These features allow you to make ad hoc reports through a graphical user interface which makes it easy to change the ordering of the data and to navigate the reports.

Monitoring is one of the most important tools available to maintain a good health of your system and investigate performance problems. MySQL Enterprise Monitor was used as the base of the monitoring discussion. Particularly the Query Analyzer feature is very useful to determine which queries impact the system the most, but it should be used in conjunction with the timeseries graphs to understand the overall state of the system. You can also create ad hoc queries that can be used, for example, to investigate ongoing issues.

Finally, you should not forget the slow query log that has the advantage over the Performance Schema statement tables that it persists the recording of the slow queries. This makes it possible to investigate issues that happened before a restart. The slow query log also records the time when a query completed which is useful when a user reports that at some time the system was slow.

What do you do when you have found a query that you want to investigate further? The first step is to analyze it which will be discussed in the next chapter.

Analyzing Queries

In the previous chapter, you learned how to find queries that are candidates for optimization. It is now time to take the next step – analyzing the queries to determine why they do not perform as expected. The main tool during the analysis is the EXPLAIN statement which shows the query plan the optimizer will use. Related is the optimizer trace that can be used to investigate why the optimizer ended up with the query plan. Another possibility is to use the statement and stage information in the Performance Schema to see where a stored procedure or a query spends the most time. These three topics will be discussed in this chapter.

The discussion of the EXPLAIN statement is by far the largest part of this chapter and has been split into four sections:

- **EXPLAIN Usage:** The basic usage of the EXPLAIN statement.

- **EXPLAIN Formats:** The details specific to each of the formats that the query plan can be viewed in. This includes both formats explicitly chosen with the EXPLAIN statement and *Visual Explain* used by MySQL Workbench.

- **EXPLAIN Output:** A discussion of the information available in the query plans.

- **EXPLAIN Examples:** Some examples of using the EXPLAIN statement with a discussion of the data returned.

EXPLAIN Usage

The EXPLAIN statement returns an overview of the query plan the MySQL optimizer will use for a given query. It is at the same time very simple and one of the more complex tools in query tuning. It is simple, because you just need to add the EXPLAIN command before the query you want to investigate, and complex because understanding the

601

© Jesper Wisborg Krogh 2020
J. W. Krogh, *MySQL 8 Query Performance Tuning*, https://doi.org/10.1007/978-1-4842-5584-1_20

information requires some understanding of how MySQL and its optimizer work. You can use EXPLAIN both with a query you explicitly specify and with a query currently being executed by another connection. This section goes through the basic usage of the EXPLAIN statement.

Usage for Explicit Queries

You generate the query plan for a query by adding EXPLAIN in front of the query, optionally adding the FORMAT option to specify whether you want the result returned in a traditional table format, using the JSON format, or in a tree-style format. There is support for SELECT, DELETE, INSERT, REPLACE, and UPDATE statements. The query is not executed (but see the next subsection about EXPLAIN ANALYZE for an exception), so it is safe to obtain the query plan.

If you need to analyze composite queries such as stored procedures and stored functions, you will need first to split the execution out into individual queries and then use EXPLAIN for each of the queries that should be analyzed. One method to determine the individual queries in a stored program is to use the Performance Schema. An example of achieving this will be shown later in this chapter.

The simplest use of EXPLAIN is just to specify EXPLAIN with the query that you want to analyze:

```
mysql> EXPLAIN <query>;
```

In the example, <query> is the query you want to analyze. Using the EXPLAIN statement without the FORMAT option returns the result in the traditional table format. If you want to specify the format, you can do so by adding FORMAT=TRADITIONAL|JSON|TREE:

```
mysql> EXPLAIN FORMAT=TRADITIONAL <query>
```

```
mysql> EXPLAIN FORMAT=JSON <query>
```

```
mysql> EXPLAIN FORMAT=TREE <query>
```

Which format that is the preferred depends on your needs. The traditional format is easier to use when you need an overview of the query plan, the indexes used, and other basic information about the query plan. The JSON format provides more details and is easier for an application to use. For example, Visual Explain in MySQL Workbench uses the JSON-formatted output.

The tree format is the newest format and supported in MySQL 8.0.16 and later. It requires the query to be executed using the Volcano iterator executor which at the time of writing is not supported for all queries. A special use of the tree format is for the EXPLAIN ANALYZE statement.

EXPLAIN ANALYZE

The EXPLAIN ANALYZE statement[1] is new as of MySQL 8.0.18 and is an extension of the standard EXPLAIN statement using the tree format. The key difference is that EXPLAIN ANALYZE actually executes the query and, while executing it, statistics for the execution are collected. While the statement is executed, the output from the query is suppressed so only the query plan and statistics are returned. Like for the tree output format, it is required that the Volcano iterator executor is used.

Note   At the time of writing, the requirement on the Volcano iterator executor limits the queries you can use EXPLAIN ANALYZE with to a subset of SELECT statements. It is expected that the range of supported queries will increase over time.

The usage of EXPLAIN ANALYZE is very similar to what you have already seen for the EXPLAIN statement:

```
mysql> EXPLAIN ANALYZE <query>
```

The output of EXPLAIN ANALYZE will be discussed together with the tree format output later in this chapter.

By nature, EXPLAIN ANALYZE only works with an explicit query as it is required to monitor the query from start to finish. The plain EXPLAIN statement on the other hand can also be used for ongoing queries.

---

[1]https://dev.mysql.com/doc/refman/en/explain.html#explain-analyze

Usage for Connections

Imagine you are investigating an issue with poor performance and you notice there is a query that has been running for several hours. You know this is not supposed to happen, so you want to analyze why the query is so slow. One option is to copy the query and execute EXPLAIN for it. However, this may not provide the information you need as the index statistics may have changed since the slow query started, and thus analyzing the query now does not show the actual query plan causing the slow performance.

A better solution is to request the actual query plan used for the slow query. You can get that using the EXPLAIN FOR CONNECTION variant of the EXPLAIN statement. If you want to try it, you need a long-running query, for example:

```
SELECT * FROM world.city WHERE id = 130 + SLEEP(0.1);
```

This will take around 420 seconds (0.1 second per row in the world.city table).

You will need the connection id of the query you want to investigate and pass this as an argument to EXPLAIN. You can get the connection id from the process list information. For example, if you use the sys.session view, the connection id can be found in the conn_id column:

```
mysql> SELECT conn_id, current_statement,
             statement_latency
       FROM sys.session
      WHERE command = 'Query'
      ORDER BY time
       DESC LIMIT 1\G
*************************** 1. row ***************************
          conn_id: 8
current_statement: SELECT * FROM world.city WHERE id = 130 + SLEEP(0.1)
statement_latency: 4.22 m
1 row in set (0.0551 sec)
```

In order to keep the output simple, it has been limited to the connection of interest for this example. The connection id for the query is 8. You can use this to get the execution plan for the query as follows:

```
mysql> EXPLAIN FOR CONNECTION 8\G
*************************** 1. row ***************************
           id: 1
  select_type: SIMPLE
        table: city
   partitions: NULL
         type: ALL
possible_keys: NULL
          key: NULL
      key_len: NULL
          ref: NULL
         rows: 4188
     filtered: 100
        Extra: Using where
1 row in set (0.0004 sec)
```

You can optionally add which format you want in the same way as when you explicitly specify a query. The filtered column may show 100.00 if you are using a different client than MySQL Shell. Before discussing what the output means, it is worth familiarizing yourself with the output formats.

EXPLAIN Formats

You can choose between several formats when you need to examine the query plans. Which one you choose mostly depends on your preferences. That said, the JSON format does include more information than the traditional and tree formats. If you prefer a visual representation of the query plan, Visual Explain from MySQL Workbench is a great option.

This section will discuss each format and show the output for the query plan of the following query:

```
SELECT ci.ID, ci.Name, ci.District,
       co.Name AS Country, ci.Population
  FROM world.city ci
       INNER JOIN
```

```
        (SELECT Code, Name
           FROM world.country
          WHERE Continent = 'Europe'
          ORDER BY SurfaceArea
          LIMIT 10
        ) co ON co.Code = ci.CountryCode
 ORDER BY ci.Population DESC
 LIMIT 5;
```

The query finds the five largest cities across the ten smallest countries by area in Europe and orders them by the city population in descending order. The reason for choosing this query is that it shows how the various output formats represent subqueries, ordering, and limits. The information returned by the EXPLAIN statements will not be discussed in this section; that is deferred to the "EXPLAIN Examples" section.

Note   The output of EXPLAIN statements depends on the settings of the optimizer switches, the index statistics, and the values in the mysql.engine_ cost and mysql.server_cost tables, so you may not see the same as in the examples. The example outputs have been used with the default values and a freshly loaded world sample database with ANALYZE TABLE executed for the tables after the load has completed, and they have been created in MySQL Shell where warnings are fetched automatically by default (but the warnings are only included in the output when they are discussed). If you are not using MySQL Shell, you will have to execute SHOW WARNINGS to retrieve the warnings.

The query plan outputs are quite verbose. To make it easier to compare the outputs, the examples in this section have been combined with the result of the query into the file explain_formats.txt in this book's GitHub repository. For the tree output format (including for EXPLAIN ANALYZE), an extra new line has been added between the column name and the query plan to get the tree hierarchy displaying clearer:

```
*********************** 1. row ***************************
EXPLAIN:
-> Limit: 5 row(s)
   -> Sort: <temporary>.Population DESC, limit input to 5 row(s) per chunk
```

Instead of:

```
*************************** 1. row ***************************
EXPLAIN: -> Limit: 5 row(s)
    -> Sort: <temporary>.Population DESC, limit input to 5 row(s) per chunk
```

This convention is used throughout the chapter.

Traditional Format

When you execute the EXPLAIN command without the FORMAT argument or with the format set to TRADITIONAL, the output is returned as a table as if you had queried a normal table. This is useful when you want an overview of the query plan and it is a human database administrator or developer who examines the output.

Tip   The table output can be quite wide particularly if there are many partitions, several possible indexes that can be used, or several pieces of extra information. You can request to get the output in a vertical format by using the --vertical option when you invoke the mysql command-line client, or you can use \G to terminate the query.

There are 12 columns in the output. If a field does not have any value, NULL is used. The meaning of each column will be discussed in the next section. Listing 20-1 shows the traditional output for the example query.

Listing 20-1. Example of the traditional EXPLAIN output

```
mysql> EXPLAIN FORMAT=TRADITIONAL
        SELECT ci.ID, ci.Name, ci.District,
            co.Name AS Country, ci.Population
        FROM world.city ci
            INNER JOIN
              (SELECT Code, Name
                FROM world.country
                WHERE Continent = 'Europe'
                ORDER BY SurfaceArea
```

```
                LIMIT 10
            ) co ON co.Code = ci.CountryCode
        ORDER BY ci.Population DESC
        LIMIT 5\G
*************************** 1. row ***************************
           id: 1
  select_type: PRIMARY
        table: <derived2>
   partitions: NULL
         type: ALL
possible_keys: NULL
          key: NULL
      key_len: NULL
          ref: NULL
         rows: 10
     filtered: 100
        Extra: Using temporary; Using filesort
*************************** 2. row ***************************
           id: 1
  select_type: PRIMARY
        table: ci
   partitions: NULL
         type: ref
possible_keys: CountryCode
          key: CountryCode
      key_len: 3
          ref: co.Code
         rows: 18
     filtered: 100
        Extra: NULL
*************************** 3. row ***************************
           id: 2
  select_type: DERIVED
        table: country
   partitions: NULL
         type: ALL
```

```
   possible_keys: NULL
             key: NULL
         key_len: NULL
             ref: NULL
            rows: 239
        filtered: 14.285715103149414
           Extra: Using where; Using filesort
3 rows in set, 1 warning (0.0089 sec)
Note (code 1003): /* select#1 */ select `world`.`ci`.`ID` AS
`ID`,`world`.`ci`.`Name` AS `Name`,`world`.`ci`.`District` AS
`District`,`co`.`Name` AS `Country`,`world`.`ci`.`Population` AS
`Population` from `world`.`city` `ci` join (/* select#2 */ select
`world`.`country`.`Code` AS `Code`,`world`.`country`.`Name` AS
`Name` from `world`.`country` where (`world`.`country`.`Continent`
= 'Europe') order by `world`.`country`.`SurfaceArea` limit 10)
`co` where (`world`.`ci`.`CountryCode` = `co`.`Code`) order by
`world`.`ci`.`Population` desc limit 5
```

Notice how the first table is called <derived 2>. This is for the subquery on the country table, and the number 2 refers to the value of the id column where the subquery is executed. The Extra column contains information such as whether the query uses a temporary table and a file sort. At the end of the output is the query after the optimizer has rewritten it. In many cases there are not many changes, but in some cases the optimizer may be able to make significant changes to the query. In the rewritten query, notice how a comment, for example, /* select#1 */, is used to show which id value is used for that part of the query. There may be other hints in the rewritten query to tell how the query is executed. The rewritten query is returned as a note by SHOW WARNINGS (by default, executed implicitly by MySQL Shell).

The output can seem overwhelming, and it can be hard to understand how the information can be used to analyze queries. Once the other output formats, the detailed information for the select types and join types, and the extra information have been discussed, there will be some examples where the EXPLAIN information will be used.

What do you do if you want to analyze the query plan programmatically? You can handle the EXPLAIN output like that of a normal SELECT query – or you can request the information in the JSON format which includes some additional information.

JSON Format

Since MySQL 5.6, it has been possible to request the EXPLAIN output using the JSON format. One advantage of the JSON format over the traditional table format is that the added flexibility of the JSON format has been used to group the information in a more logical way.

The basic concept in the JSON output is a *query block*. The query block defines a part of the query and may in turn include query blocks of its own. This allows MySQL to specify the details of the query execution to the query block they belong. This is also visible from the output of the example query that is shown in Listing 20-2.

Listing 20-2. Example of the JSON EXPLAIN output

```
mysql> EXPLAIN FORMAT=JSON
       SELECT ci.ID, ci.Name, ci.District,
              co.Name AS Country, ci.Population
         FROM world.city ci
              INNER JOIN
                (SELECT Code, Name
                   FROM world.country
                  WHERE Continent = 'Europe'
                  ORDER BY SurfaceArea
                  LIMIT 10
                ) co ON co.Code = ci.CountryCode
       ORDER BY ci.Population DESC
       LIMIT 5\G
*************************** 1. row ***************************
EXPLAIN: {
  "query_block": {
    "select_id": 1,
    "cost_info": {
      "query_cost": "247.32"
    },
    "ordering_operation": {
      "using_temporary_table": true,
      "using_filesort": true,
```

```
"cost_info": {
  "sort_cost": "180.52"
},
"nested_loop": [
  {
    "table": {
      "table_name": "co",
      "access_type": "ALL",
      "rows_examined_per_scan": 10,
      "rows_produced_per_join": 10,
      "filtered": "100.00",
      "cost_info": {
        "read_cost": "2.63",
        "eval_cost": "1.00",
        "prefix_cost": "3.63",
        "data_read_per_join": "640"
      },
      "used_columns": [
        "Code",
        "Name"
      ],
      "materialized_from_subquery": {
        "using_temporary_table": true,
        "dependent": false,
        "cacheable": true,
        "query_block": {
          "select_id": 2,
          "cost_info": {
            "query_cost": "25.40"
          },
          "ordering_operation": {
            "using_filesort": true,
            "table": {
              "table_name": "country",
              "access_type": "ALL",
```

```
                    "rows_examined_per_scan": 239,
                    "rows_produced_per_join": 34,
                    "filtered": "14.29",
                    "cost_info": {
                      "read_cost": "21.99",
                      "eval_cost": "3.41",
                      "prefix_cost": "25.40",
                      "data_read_per_join": "8K"
                    },
                    "used_columns": [
                      "Code",
                      "Name",
                      "Continent",
                      "SurfaceArea"
                    ],
                    "attached_condition": "(`world`.`country`.`Continent` =
                    'Europe')"
                  }
                }
              }
            }
          }
        },
        {
          "table": {
            "table_name": "ci",
            "access_type": "ref",
            "possible_keys": [
              "CountryCode"
            ],
            "key": "CountryCode",
            "used_key_parts": [
              "CountryCode"
            ],
```

```
              "key_length": "3",
              "ref": [
                "co.Code"
              ],
              "rows_examined_per_scan": 18,
              "rows_produced_per_join": 180,
              "filtered": "100.00",
              "cost_info": {
                "read_cost": "45.13",
                "eval_cost": "18.05",
                "prefix_cost": "66.81",
                "data_read_per_join": "12K"
              },
              "used_columns": [
                "ID",
                "Name",
                "CountryCode",
                "District",
                "Population"
              ]
            }
          }
        ]
      }
    }
  }
}
1 row in set, 1 warning (0.0061 sec)
```

As you can see, the output is quite verbose, but the structure makes it relatively easy to see what information belongs together and how parts of the query relate to each other. In this example, there is a nested loop that includes two tables (co and ci). The co table itself includes a new query block that is a materialized subquery using the country table.

The JSON format also includes additional information such as the estimated cost of each part in the cost_info elements. The cost information can be used to see where the optimizer thinks the most expensive parts of the query are. If you, for example, see that the cost of a part of a query is very high, but your knowledge of the data means that you know that it should be cheap, it can suggest that the index statistics are not up to date or a histogram is needed.

The biggest issue of using the JSON-formatted output is that there is so much information and so many lines of output. A very convenient way to get around that is to use the Visual Explain feature in MySQL Workbench which is covered after discussing the tree-formatted output.

Tree Format

The tree format focuses on describing how the query is executed in terms of the relationship between the parts of the query and the order the parts are executed. In that sense, it may sound similar to the JSON output; however, the tree format is simpler to read, and there are not as many details. The tree format was introduced as an experimental feature in MySQL 8.0.16 and relies on the Volcano iterator executor. Starting with MySQL 8.0.18, the tree format is also used for the EXPLAIN ANALYZER feature.

Listing 20-3 shows the output using the tree format for the example query. This output is the non-analyze version. An example of the output of EXPLAIN ANALYZE will be shown shortly for the same query, so you can see the difference.

Listing 20-3. Example of the tree EXPLAIN output

```
mysql> EXPLAIN FORMAT=TREE
       SELECT ci.ID, ci.Name, ci.District,
              co.Name AS Country, ci.Population
         FROM world.city ci
              INNER JOIN
                (SELECT Code, Name
                   FROM world.country
                  WHERE Continent = 'Europe'
                  ORDER BY SurfaceArea
                  LIMIT 10
                ) co ON co.Code = ci.CountryCode
        ORDER BY ci.Population DESC
        LIMIT 5\G
```

```
*************************** 1. row ***************************
EXPLAIN:
-> Limit: 5 row(s)
    -> Sort: <temporary>.Population DESC, limit input to 5 row(s) per chunk
        -> Stream results
            -> Nested loop inner join
                -> Table scan on co
                    -> Materialize
                        -> Limit: 10 row(s)
                            -> Sort: country.SurfaceArea, limit input to 10
                               row(s) per chunk  (cost=25.40 rows=239)
                                -> Filter: (country.Continent = 'Europe')
                                    -> Table scan on country
                -> Index lookup on ci using CountryCode
                   (CountryCode=co.`Code`)  (cost=4.69 rows=18)
```

The output gives a good overview of how the query is executed. It can be easier to understand the execution by reading the output to some extent from the inside and out. For the nested loop, you have two tables, of which the first is a table scan on co (the indentation has been reduced):

```
-> Table scan on co
  -> Materialize
    -> Limit: 10 row(s)
      -> Sort: country.SurfaceArea, limit input to 10 row(s) per
              chunk  (cost=25.40 rows=239)
        -> Filter: (country.Continent = 'Europe')
          -> Table scan on country
```

Here you can see how the co table is a materialized subquery created by first doing a table scan on the country table, then applying a filter for the continent, then sorting based on the surface area, and then limiting the result to ten rows.

The second part of the nested loop is simpler as it just consists of an index lookup on the ci table (the city table) using the CountryCode index:

```
-> Index lookup on ci using CountryCode (CountryCode=co.`Code`)  (cost=4.69
rows=18)
```

When the nested loop has been resolved using an inner join, the result is streamed (i.e., not materialized) to the sorting, and the first five rows are returned:

```
-> Limit: 5 row(s)
    -> Sort: <temporary>.Population DESC, limit input to 5 row(s) per chunk
        -> Stream results
            -> Nested loop inner join
```

While this does not give quite as detailed a picture as the JSON output, it still includes a lot of information about the query plan. This includes the estimated cost and estimated number of rows for each of the tables. For example, from the sorting step on the countries' surface area

```
(cost=25.40 rows=239)
```

A good question is how that relates to the actual cost of querying the table. You can use the EXPLAIN ANALYZE statement for this. Listing 20-4 shows an example of the output generated for the example query.

Listing 20-4. Example of the EXPLAIN ANALYZE output

```
mysql> EXPLAIN ANALYZE
       SELECT ci.ID, ci.Name, ci.District,
              co.Name AS Country, ci.Population
         FROM world.city ci
              INNER JOIN
                (SELECT Code, Name
                   FROM world.country
                  WHERE Continent = 'Europe'
                  ORDER BY SurfaceArea
                  LIMIT 10
                ) co ON co.Code = ci.CountryCode
        ORDER BY ci.Population DESC
        LIMIT 5\G
*************************** 1. row ***************************
EXPLAIN: -> Limit: 5 row(s)  (actual time=34.492..34.494 rows=5 loops=1)
    -> Sort: <temporary>.Population DESC, limit input to 5 row(s) per
       chunk  (actual time=34.491..34.492 rows=5 loops=1)
        -> Stream results  (actual time=34.371..34.471 rows=15 loops=1)
```

```
   -> Nested loop inner join  (actual time=34.370..34.466 rows=15
      loops=1)
      -> Table scan on co  (actual time=0.001..0.003 rows=10
         loops=1)
         -> Materialize  (actual time=34.327..34.330 rows=10
            loops=1)
            -> Limit: 10 row(s)  (actual time=34.297..34.301
               rows=10 loops=1)
               -> Sort: country.SurfaceArea, limit input to
                  10 row(s) per chunk  (cost=25.40 rows=239)
                  (actual time=34.297..34.298 rows=10 loops=1)
                  -> Filter: (world.country.Continent =
                     'Europe')  (actual time=0.063..0.201
                     rows=46 loops=1)
                     -> Table scan on country  (actual
                        time=0.057..0.166 rows=239 loops=1)
      -> Index lookup on ci using CountryCode
         (CountryCode=co.`Code`)  (cost=4.69 rows=18) (actual
         time=0.012..0.013 rows=2 loops=10)

1 row in set (0.0353 sec)
```

This is the same tree output as for FORMAT=TREE except that for each step, there is information about the performance. If you look at the line for the ci table, you can see there are two timings, the number of rows and the number of loops (reformatted to improve the readability):

```
-> Index lookup on ci using CountryCode
   (CountryCode=co.`Code`)
   (cost=4.69 rows=18)
   (actual time=0.012..0.013 rows=2 loops=10)
```

Here the estimated cost was 4.69 for an expected 18 rows (per loop). The actual statistics show that the first row was read after 0.012 millisecond and all rows were read after 0.013 millisecond. There were ten loops (one for each of the ten countries), each fetching an average of two rows for a total of 20 rows. So, in this case, the estimate was not very accurate (because the query exclusively picks small countries).

Note   The row count for EXPLAIN ANALYZE is the average per loop rounded to an integer. With rows=2 and loops=10, this means the total number of rows read is between 15 and 24. In this specific example, using the table_io_waits_ summary_by_table table in the Performance Schema shows that 15 rows are read.

If you have queries that use the hash joins in MySQL 8.0.18 and later, you will need to use the tree-formatted output to confirm when the hash join algorithm is used. For example, if the city table is joined with the country table using a hash join

```
mysql> EXPLAIN FORMAT=TREE
       SELECT CountryCode, country.Name AS Country,
              city.Name AS City, city.District
         FROM world.country IGNORE INDEX (Primary)
              INNER JOIN world.city IGNORE INDEX (CountryCode)
                    ON city.CountryCode = country.Code\G
*************************** 1. row ***************************
EXPLAIN:
-> Inner hash join (world.city.CountryCode = world.
country.`Code`)  (cost=100125.16 rows=4314)
    -> Table scan on city  (cost=0.04 rows=4188)
    -> Hash
        -> Table scan on country  (cost=25.40 rows=239)

1 row in set (0.0005 sec)
```

Notice how the join is an Inner hash join and that the table scan on the country table is given as using a hash.

Thus far, all the examples have used text-based outputs. Particularly the JSON-formatted output could be difficult to use to get an overview of the query plan. For that Visual Explain is a better option.

Visual Explain

The Visual Explain feature is part of MySQL Workbench and works by converting the JSON-formatted query plan into a graphical representation. You have already used Visual Explain back in Chapter 16 when you investigated the effect of adding a histogram to the sakila.film table.

You get the Visual Explain diagram by clicking the icon with the magnifying glass in front of the lightning symbol as shown in Figure 20-1.

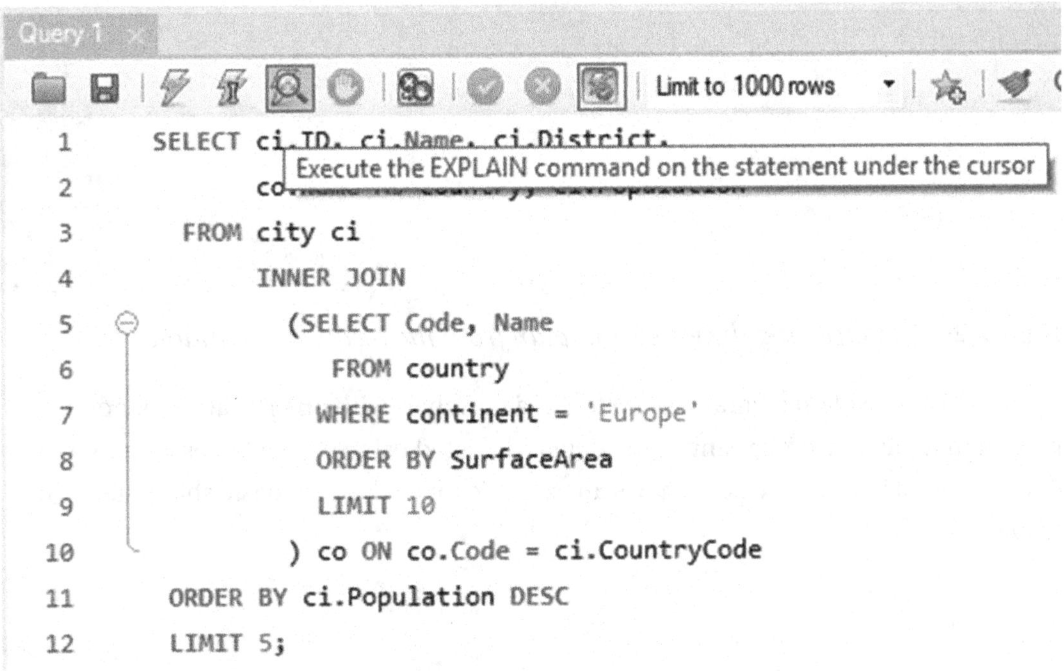

Figure 20-1. *Obtaining the Visual Explain diagram for a query*

This is a particularly useful way to generate the query plan, if the query takes a long time to execute or the query modifies the data. If you already have executed the query, you can alternatively click the *Execution Plan* icon to the right of the result grid as it is shown in Figure 20-2.

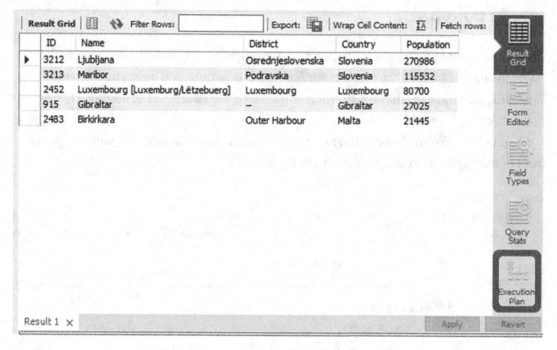

Figure 20-2. *Retrieving the execution plan from the result grid window*

The Visual Explain diagram is created as a flowchart with one rectangle per query block and table. The processing of the data is depicted using other shapes such as a diamond for a join. Figure 20-3 shows an example for each of the basic shapes used in Visual Explain.

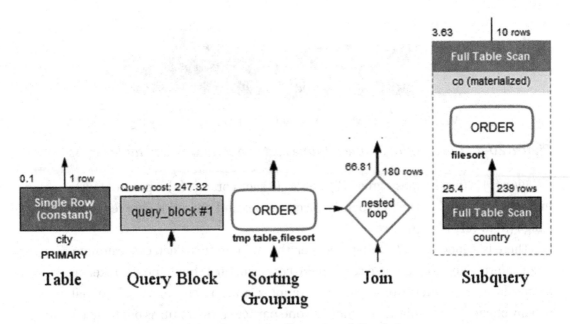

Figure 20-3. *Examples of the shapes used in Visual Explain*

In the figure, a query block is gray, while the two examples of a table (the single row lookup and full table scan in the subquery) are blue and red, respectively. The gray blocks are also used, for example, in case of unions. The text below a table box shows the table name or alias in standard text and the index name in bold text. The rectangles with rounded corners depict operations on the rows such as sorting, grouping, distinct operations, and so on.

The number to the top left is the relative cost for that table, operation, or query block. The number to the top right of tables and joins is the number of rows estimated to be carried forward. The color of the operations is used to show how expensive it is to apply the operation. Tables also use colors based on the table access type, primarily to group similar access types and secondarily to indicate the cost of the access type. The relationship between the color and cost using the cost estimated from Visual Explain can be seen in Figure 20-4.

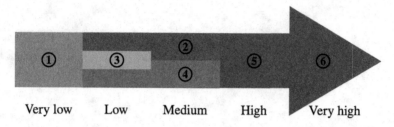

Figure 20-4. *Color codes for the relative cost of operations and table access*

Blue (1) is the cheapest; green (2), yellow (3), and orange (4) represent low to medium costs; and the most expensive access types and operations are red symbolizing a high (5) to very high (6) cost.

There is a good deal of overlap between the color groups. Each cost estimate is considering an "average" use case, so the cost estimates should not be taken as an absolute truth. Query optimization is complex, and sometimes a method that is usually cheaper than another method for one particular query turns out to give better performance.

Note   The author of this book once decided to improve a query that had a query plan which looked terrible: internal temporary tables, file sorting, poor access methods, and so on. After a long time rewriting the query and verifying whether the tables had the correct indexes, the query plan looked beautiful – but it turned out the query performed worse than the original. The lesson: Always test the query performance after optimization and do not rely on whether the cost of the access methods and operations has improved on paper.

For the tables, the cost is associated with the access type, which is the value of the type column in the traditional EXPLAIN output and access_type field in the JSON-formatted output. Figure 20-5 shows how Visual Explain represents the 12 access types that currently exist. The explanation of the access types is deferred until the next section.

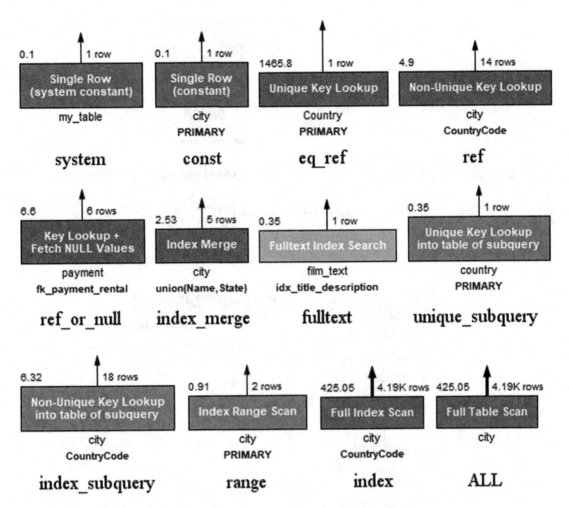

Figure 20-5. *The access types as displayed in Visual Explain*

Additionally, Visual Explain has an "unknown" access type colored black in case it comes across an access type that is not known. The access types are ordered from left to right and then top to bottom according to their color and approximate cost.

Figure 20-6 puts all of this together to display the query plan for the example query that has been used throughout this section.

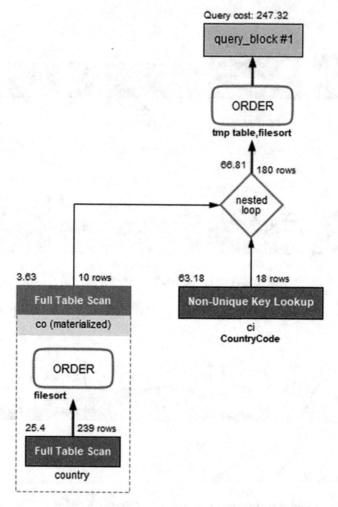

Figure 20-6. *The Visual Explain diagram for the example query*

You read the diagram from the bottom left to the right and then up. So the diagram shows that the subquery with a full table scan on the country table is performed first and then another full table scan on the materialized co table with the rows joined on the ci (city) table using a nonunique index lookup. Finally, the result is sorted using a temporary table and a file sort.

If you want more details than the diagram shows initially, you can hover over the part of the query plan you want to know more about. Figure 20-7 shows an example of the details included for the ci table.

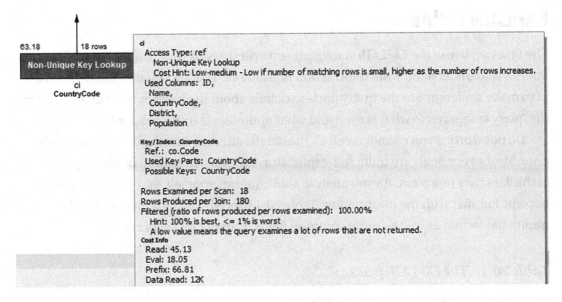

Figure 20-7. *Details for the* ci *table in Visual Explain*

Not only does the pop-up frame show the remaining details that also are available in the JSON output, there are also hints to help understand what the data means. All of this means that Visual Explain is a great way to get started analyzing queries through their query plans. As you gain experience, you may prefer using the text-based outputs, particularly if you prefer to work from a shell, but do not dismiss Visual Explain because you think it is better to use the text-based output format. Even for experts, Visual Explain is a great tool for understanding how queries are executed.

Hopefully, discussing the output formats has given you an idea of what information EXPLAIN can give you. Yet, to fully understand it and take advantage of it, it is necessary to dive deeper into the meaning of the information.

EXPLAIN Output

There is a lot of information available in the explain outputs, so it is worth delving into what this information means. This section starts out with an overview of the fields included in the traditional and JSON-formatted outputs; then the select types and access types and the extra information will be covered in more detail.

EXPLAIN Fields

The first step to use the EXPLAIN statement constructively in your work to improve your queries is to understand what information is available. The information ranges from an id to make a reference to the query parts to details about the indexes that can be used for the query compared to what is used and what optimizer features are applied.

Do not worry if you cannot recall all the details after reading the definitions the first time. Most of the fields are quite self-explanatory, so you can make a qualified guess at the data they represent. As you analyze some queries yourself, you will also quickly become familiar with the information. Table 20-1 lists all the fields included in the traditional format as well as some common fields from the JSON format.

Table 20-1. *The EXPLAIN fields*

Traditional	JSON	Description
id	select_id	A numeric identifier that shows which part of the query the table or subquery is part of. The top-level tables have id = 1, the first subquery has id = 2, and so forth. In case of a union, the id will be NULL with the table value set to <unionM,N> (see also the table column) for the row that represents the aggregation of the union result.
select_ type		This shows how the table will be included in the overall statement. The known select types will be discussed later in the "Select Types" section. For the JSON format, the select type is implied by the structure of the JSON document and from fields such as dependent and cacheable.
	dependent	Whether it is a dependent subquery, that is, it depends on the outer parts of the query.
	cacheable	Whether the result of the subquery can be cached or it must be reevaluated for each row in the outer query.

(continued)

Table 20-1. (*continued*)

Traditional	JSON	Description
table	table_name	The name of the table or subquery. If an alias has been specified, it is the alias that is used. This ensures that each table name is unique for a given value of the id column. Special cases include unions, derived tables, and materialized subqueries where the table name is <unionM,N>, <derivedN>, and <subqueryN>, respectively, where N and M refer to the ids of earlier parts of the query plan.
partitions	partitions	The partitions that will be included for the query. You can use this to determine whether partition pruning is applied as expected.
type	access_type	How the data is accessed. This shows how the optimizer has decided to limit the number of rows that are examined in the table. The types will be discussed in the "Access Types" section.
possible_keys	possible_keys	A list of the indexes that are candidates to be used for the table. A key name using the schema <auto_key0> means an auto-generated index is available.
key	key	The index(es) chosen for the table. A key name using the schema <auto_key0> means an auto-generated index is used.
key_len	key_length	The number of bytes that are used of the index. For indexes that consist of multiple columns, the optimizer may only be able to use a subset of the columns. In that case, the key length can be used to determine how much of the index is useful for this query. If the column in the index supports NULL values, 1 byte is added to the length compared to the case of a NOT NULL column.
	used_key_parts	The columns in the index that are used.
ref	ref	What the filtering is performed against. This can, for example, be a constant for a condition like <table>.<column> = 'abc' or a name of a column in another table in case of a join.

(*continued*)

Table 20-1. (*continued*)

Traditional	JSON	Description
rows	rows_ examined_ per_scan	An estimate of the number of rows that is the result of including the table. For a table that is joined to an earlier table, it is the number of rows estimated to be found per join. A special case is when the reference is the primary key or a unique key on the table, in which case the row estimate is exactly 1.
	rows_ produced_ per_join	The estimated number of rows resulting from the join. Effectively the number of loops expected multiplied with rows_examined_ per_scan and the percentage of rows filtered.
filtered	filtered	This is an estimate of how many of the examined rows will be included. The value is in percent, so that for a value of 100.00 all examined rows will be returned. A value of 100.00 is the optimal, and the worst value is 0. Note: The rounding of the value in the traditional format depends on the client you use. MySQL Shell will, for example, return 100 where the mysql command-line client returns 100.00.
	cost_info	A JSON object with the breakdown of the cost of the query part.
Extra		Additional information about the decisions of the optimizer. This can include information about the sorting algorithm used, whether a covering index is used, and so on. The most common of the supported values will be discussed in the section "Extra Information."
	message	Information that is in the Extra column for the traditional output that does not have a dedicated field in the JSON output. An example is Impossible WHERE.
	using_ filesort	Whether a file sort is used.
	using_index	Whether a covering index is used.

(*continued*)

Table 20-1. (*continued*)

Traditional	JSON	Description
	using_ temporary_ table	Whether an operation such as a subquery or sorting requires an internal temporary table.
	attached_ condition	The WHERE clause associated with the part of the query.
	used_ columns	The columns required from the table. This is useful to see if you are close to be able to use a covering index.

Some of the information appears at first to be missing in the JSON format as the field only exists for the traditional format. That is not the case; instead the information is available using other means, for example, several of the messages in Extra have their own field in the JSON format. Other Extra messages use the message field. Some of the fields that are not included in the table for the JSON output will be mentioned when discussing the information in the Extra column later in this section.

In general, Boolean fields in the JSON-formatted output are omitted, if the value is false; one exception is for cacheable as a non-cacheable subquery or union indicates a higher cost compared to the cacheable cases.

For the JSON output, there are also fields used to group information for an operation. The operations range from accessing a table to complex operations that group several operations. Some of the common operations with examples of what triggers them are

- **table:** Access a table. This is the lowest level of the operations.

- **query_block:** The highest-level concept with one query block corresponding to an id for the traditional format. All queries have at least one query block.

- **nested_loop:** A join operation.

- **grouping_operation:** The operation, for example, resulting from a GROUP BY clause.

- **ordering_operation:** The operation, for example, resulting for an ORDER BY clause.

- **duplicates_removal:** The operation, for example, resulting when using the DISTINCT keyword.

- **windowing:** The operation resulting from using window functions.

- **materialized_from_subquery:** Execute a subquery and materialize the result.

- **attached_subqueries:** A subquery that is attached to the rest of the query. This, for example, happens with clauses such as IN (SELECT ...) for the subquery inside the IN clause.

- **union_result:** For queries using UNION to combine the result of two or more queries. Inside the union_result block, there is a query_specifications block with the definition of each query in the union.

The fields in Table 20-1 and the list of complex operations are not comprehensive for the JSON format, but it should give you a good idea of the information available. In general, the field names carry information in themselves, and combining with the context where they occur is usually enough to understand the meaning of the field. The values of some of the fields deserve some more attention though – starting with the select types.

Select Types

The select type shows what kind of query block each part of the query is. A part of a query can in this context include several tables. For example, if you have a simple query joining a list of tables but not using constructs such as subqueries, then all tables will be in the same (and only) part of the query. Each part of the query gets each own id (select_id in the JSON output).

There are several select types. For most of them, there is no direct field in the JSON output; however, it is possible to derive the select type from the structure and some of the other fields. Table 20-2 shows the currently existing select types with hints how to derive the type from the JSON output. In the table, the value of the *Select Type* column is the value used for the select_type column in the traditional output format.

Table 20-2. *EXPLAIN select types*

Select Type	JSON	Description
SIMPLE		For SELECT queries not using derived tables, subqueries, unions, or similar.
PRIMARY		For queries using subqueries or unions, the primary part is the outermost part.
INSERT		For INSERT statements.
DELETE		For DELETE statements.
UPDATE		For UPDATE statements.
REPLACE		For REPLACE statements.
UNION		For union statements, the second or later SELECT statement.
DEPENDENT UNION	dependent=true	For union statements, the second or later SELECT statement where it depends on an outer query.
UNION RESULT	union_result	The part of the query that aggregates the results from the union SELECT statements.
SUBQUERY		For SELECT statements in subqueries.
DEPENDENT SUBQUERY	dependent=true	For dependent subqueries, the first SELECT statement.
DERIVED		A derived table – a table created through a query but otherwise behaves like a normal table.
DEPENDENT DERIVED	dependent=true	A derived table dependent on another table.
MATERIALIZED	materialized_ from_subquery	A materialized subquery.
UNCACHEABLE SUBQUERY	cacheable=false	A subquery where the result must be evaluated for each row in the outer query.
UNCACHEABLE UNION	cacheable=false	For a union statement, a second or later SELECT statement that is part of an uncacheable subquery.

Some of the select types can be taken just as information to make it easier to understand which part of the query you are looking at. This, for example, includes PRIMARY and UNION. However, some of the select types indicate that it is an expensive part of the query. This particularly applies to the uncacheable types. Dependent types also mean that the optimizer has less flexibility when deciding where in the execution plan to add the table. If you have slow queries and you see uncacheable or dependent parts, it can be worth looking into whether you can rewrite those parts or split the query into two.

Another important piece of information is how the tables are accessed.

Access Types

The table access types were already encountered when Visual Explain was discussed. They show whether a query accesses the table using an index, scan, and similar. Since the cost associated with each access type varies greatly, it is also one of the important values to look for in the EXPLAIN output to determine which parts of the query to work on to improve the performance.

The rest of this subsection summarizes the access types in MySQL. The headings are the values used in the type column in the traditional format. For each access type, there is an example that uses that access type.

system

The system access type is used with tables that have exactly one row. This means the table can be treated as a constant. The Visual Explain cost, message, and color are as follows:

- **Cost: Very low**

- **Message:** Single Row (system constant)

- **Color:** Blue

An example of a query using the system access type is

```
SELECT *
  FROM (SELECT 1) my_table
```

The system access type is a special case of the const access type.

const

At most one row is matched for the table, for example, when there is a filter on a single value of the primary key or a unique index. The Visual Explain cost, message, and color are as follows:

- **Cost:** Very low
- **Message:** Single Row (constant)
- **Color:** Blue

An example of a query using the const access type is

```
SELECT *
  FROM world.city
 WHERE ID = 130;
```

eq_ref

The table is the right-hand table in a join where the condition on the table is on a primary key or not null unique index. The Visual Explain cost, message, and color are as follows:

- **Cost:** Low
- **Message:** Unique Key Lookup
- **Color:** Green

An example of a query using the eq_ref access type is

```
SELECT *
  FROM world.city
       STRAIGHT_JOIN world.country
            ON CountryCode = Code;
```

The eq_ref access type is a specialized case of the ref access type where only one row can be returned per lookup.

ref

The table is filtered by a nonunique secondary index. The Visual Explain cost, message, and color are as follows:

- **Cost:** Low to medium
- **Message:** Non-Unique Key Lookup
- **Color:** Green

An example of a query using the ref access type is

```
SELECT *
  FROM world.city
 WHERE CountryCode = 'AUS';
```

ref_or_null

The same as ref but the filtered column may also be NULL. The Visual Explain cost, message, and color are as follows:

- **Cost:** Low to medium
- **Message:** Key Lookup + Fetch NULL Values
- **Color:** Green

An example of a query using the ref_or_null access type is

```
SELECT *
  FROM sakila.payment
 WHERE rental_id = 1
       OR rental_id IS NULL;
```

index_merge

The optimizer chooses a combination of two or more indexes to resolve a filter that includes an OR or AND between columns in different indexes. The Visual Explain cost, message, and color are as follows:

- **Cost:** Medium

- **Message:** Index Merge

- **Color:** Green

An example of a query using the `index_merge` access type is

```
SELECT *
  FROM sakila.payment
 WHERE rental_id = 1
       OR customer_id = 5;
```

While the cost is listed as medium, one of the more common severe performance issues is a query usually using a single index or doing a full table scan and the index statistics becoming inaccurate, so the optimizer chooses an index merge. If you have a poorly performing query using an index merge, try to tell the optimizer to ignore the index merge optimization or the used indexes and see if that helps or analyze the table to update the index statistics. Alternatively, the query can be rewritten to a union of two queries, with each query using a part of the filter. An example of this will be shown in Chapter 24.

fulltext

The optimizer chooses a full text index to filter the table. The Visual Explain cost, message, and color are as follows:

- **Cost:** Low

- **Message:** Fulltext Index Search

- **Color:** Yellow

An example of a query using the `fulltext` access type is:

```
SELECT *
  FROM sakila.film_text
 WHERE MATCH(title, description)
       AGAINST ('Circus' IN BOOLEAN MODE);
```

unique_subquery

For a subquery inside an IN operator where the subquery returns the value of a primary key or unique index. In MySQL 8 these queries are usually rewritten by the optimizer, so unique_subquery requires disabling the materialization and semijoin optimizer switches. The Visual Explain cost, message, and color are as follows:

- **Cost:** Low

- **Message:** Unique Key Lookup into table of subquery

- **Color:** Orange

An example of a query using the unique_subquery access type is

```
SET optimizer_switch = 'materialization=off,semijoin=off';

SELECT *
  FROM world.city
 WHERE CountryCode IN (
         SELECT Code
           FROM world.country
          WHERE Continent = 'Oceania');

SET optimizer_switch = 'materialization=on,semijoin=on';
```

The unique_subquery access method is a special case of the index_subquery method for the case where a primary or unique index is used.

index_subquery

For a subquery inside an IN operator where the subquery returns the value of a secondary nonunique index. In MySQL 8 these queries are usually rewritten by the optimizer, so unique_subquery requires disabling the materialization and semijoin optimizer switches. The Visual Explain cost, message, and color are as follows:

- **Cost:** Low

- **Message:** Nonunique Key Lookup into table of subquery

- **Color:** Orange

An example of a query using the `index_subquery` access type is

```
SET optimizer_switch = 'materialization=off,semijoin=off';

SELECT *
  FROM world.country
 WHERE Code IN (
          SELECT CountryCode
            FROM world.city
           WHERE Name = 'Sydney');

SET optimizer_switch = 'materialization=on,semijoin=on';
```

range

The range access type is used when an index is used to look up several values either in sequence or in groups. It is used both for explicit ranges like `ID BETWEEN 1 AND 10`, for `IN` clauses, or where several conditions on the same column are separated by `OR`. The Visual Explain cost, message, and color are as follows:

- **Cost:** Medium
- **Message:** Index Range Scan
- **Color:** Orange

An example of a query using the `range` access type is

```
SELECT *
  FROM world.city
 WHERE ID IN (130, 3805);
```

The cost of using range access largely depends on how many rows are included in the range. In one extreme, the range scan only matches a single row using the primary key, so the cost is very low. In the other extreme, the range scan includes a large part of the table using a secondary index in which case it can end up being cheaper to perform a full table scan.

The `range` access type is related to the `index` access type with the difference being whether partial or a full scan is required.

index

The optimizer has chosen to perform a full index scan. This may be chosen in combination of using a covering index. The Visual Explain cost, message, and color are as follows:

- **Cost:** High

- **Message:** Full Index Scan

- **Color:** Red

An example of a query using the index access type is

```
SELECT ID, CountryCode
  FROM world.city;
```

Since an index scan requires a second lookup using the primary key, it can become very expensive unless the index is a covering index for the query, to the extent that it ends up being cheaper to perform a full table scan.

ALL

The most basic access type is to scan all rows for the table. It is also the most expensive access type, and for this reason the type is written in all uppercase. The Visual Explain cost, message, and color are as follows:

- **Cost:** Very high

- **Message:** Full Table Scan

- **Color:** Red

An example of a query using the ALL access type is

```
SELECT *
  FROM world.city;
```

If you see a table other than the first table using a full table scan, it is usually a red flag that indicates that either there is a missing condition on the table or there are no indexes that can be used. Whether ALL is a reasonable access type for the first table depends on how much of the table you need for the query; the larger the part of the table is required, the more reasonable a full table scan is.

Note   While a full table scan is considered the most expensive access type, it is together with primary key lookups the cheapest per row. So, if you genuinely need to access most or all of the table, a full table scan is the most effective way to read the rows.

That concludes the discussion of the access types for now. The access types will be referenced again when looking at EXPLAIN examples later in this chapter as well as later in the book when looking at optimizing queries, for example, in Chapter 24. In the meantime, let's look at the information in the Extra column.

Extra Information

The Extra column in the traditional output format is a catch-all bin for information that does not have its own column. When the JSON format was introduced, there was no reason to keep it as it was easy to introduce additional fields and it is not necessary to include all fields for every output. For that reason, the JSON format does not have an Extra field but instead has a range of fields. A few leftover messages have been left for a generic message field.

Note   The information available in the Extra column is in some cases storage engine dependent or only used in rare cases. This discussion will only cover the most commonly encountered messages. For a full list of messages, refer to the MySQL reference manual at https://dev.mysql.com/doc/refman/en/explain-output.html#explain-extra-information.

Some of the more commonly occurring messages include

- **Using index:** When a covering index is used. For the JSON format, the using_index field is set to true.

- **Using index condition:** When an index is used to test whether it is necessary to read the full row. This is, for example, used when there is a range condition on an indexed column. For the JSON format, the index_condition field is set with the filter condition.

- **Using where:** When a WHERE clause is applied to the table without using an index. This may be an indication that the indexes on the table are not optimal. In the JSON format, the `attached_condition` field is set with the filter condition.

- **Using index for group-by:** When a loose index scan is used to resolve GROUP BY or DISTINCT. In the JSON format, the `using_index_for_group_by` field is set to `true`.

- **Using join buffer (Block Nested Loop):** This means that a join is made where no index can be used, so the join buffer is used instead. Tables with this message are candidates to have an index added. For the JSON format, the `using_join_buffer` field is set to `Block Nested Loop`. One thing to be aware of is that when a hash join is used, then the traditional and JSON-formatted outputs will still show that a block nested loop is used. To see whether it is an actual block nested loop join or a hash join, you need to use the tree-formatted output.

- **Using join buffer (Batched Key Access):** This means that a join is using the Batched Key Access (BKA) optimization. To enable the Batched Key Access optimization, you must enable the `mrr` (defaults to on) and `batch_key_access` (defaults to off) and disable the `mrr_cost_based` (defaults to on) optimizer switches. The optimization requires an index for the join, so unlike using the join buffer for a block nested loop, using the Batched Key Access algorithm is not a sign of expensive access to the table. For the JSON format, the `using_join_buffer` field is set to `Batched Key Access`.

- **Using MRR:** The Multi-Range Read (MRR) optimization is used. This is sometimes used to reduce the amount of random I/O for range conditions on secondary indexes where the full row is needed. The optimization is controlled by the `mrr` and `mrr_cost_based` optimizer switches (both are enabled by default). For the JSON format, the `using_MRR` field is set to `true`.

- **Using filesort:** MySQL uses an extra pass to determine how to retrieve the rows in the correct order. This, for example, happens with sorting by a secondary index; and the index is not a covering index. For the JSON format, the `using_filesort` field is set to `true`.

- **Using temporary:** An internal temporary table is used to store the result of a subquery, for sorting, or for grouping. For sorting and grouping, the use of an internal temporary table can sometimes be avoided by adding an index or rewriting the query. For the JSON format, the using_temporary_table field is set to true.

- **sort_union(...), Using union(...), Using intersect(...):** These three messages are used with index merges to say how the index merge is performed. For either message, information about the indexes involved in the index merge is included inside the parentheses. For the JSON format, the key field specifies the method and indexes used.

- **Recursive:** The table is part of a recursive common table expression (CTE). For the JSON format, the recursive field is set to true.

- **Range checked for each record (index map: 0x1):** This happens when you have a join where there is a condition on an indexed column of the second table that depends on the value of a column from the first table, for example, with an index on t2.val2: SELECT * FROM t1 INNER JOIN t2 WHERE t2.val2 < t1.val1; This is what triggers the NO_GOOD_INDEX_USED counter in the Performance Schema statement event tables to increment. The index map is a bitmask that indicates which indexes are candidates for the range check. The index numbers are 1-based as shown by SHOW INDEXES. When you write out the bitmask, the index numbers with the bit set are the candidates. For the JSON format, the range_checked_for_each_record field is set to the index map.

- **Impossible WHERE:** When there is a filter that cannot possibly be true, for example, WHERE 1 = 0. This also applies if the value in the filter is outside the range supported by the data type, for example, WHERE ID = 300 for a tinyint data type. For the JSON format, the message is added to the message field.

- **Impossible WHERE noticed after reading const tables:** The same as Impossible WHERE except it applies after resolving the tables using the system or const access method. An example is SELECT * FROM (SELECT 1 AS ID) a INNER JOIN city USING (ID) WHERE a.id = 130; For the JSON format, the message is added to the message field.

- **Impossible HAVING:** The same as Impossible WHERE except it applies to a HAVING clause. For the JSON format, the message is added to the message field.

- **Using index for skip scan:** When the optimizer chooses to use multiple range scans similar to a loose index scan. It can, for example, be used for a covering index where the first column of the index is not used for the filter condition. This method is available in MySQL 8.0.13 and later. For the JSON format, the using_index_for_skip_scan field is set to true.

- **Select tables optimized away:** This message means that MySQL was able to remove the table from the query because only a single row will result, and that row can be generated from a deterministic set of rows. It usually occurs when only the minimum and/or maximum values of an index are required from the table. For the JSON format, the message is added to the message field.

- **No tables used:** For subqueries that do not involve any tables, for example, SELECT 1 FROM dual; For the JSON format, the message is added to the message field.

- **no matching row in const table:** For a table where the system or const access type is possible but there are no rows matching the condition. For the JSON format, the message is added to the message field.

Tip At the time of writing, you need to use the tree-formatted output to see if a join that does not use indexes is using the hash join algorithm.

That concludes the discussion about the meaning of the output of the EXPLAIN statement. All there is left is to start using it to examine the query plans.

EXPLAIN Examples

To finish off the discussion of query plans, it is worth going through a few examples to get a better feeling of how you can put all of it together. The examples here are meant as an introduction. Further examples will occur in the remainder of the book, particularly Chapter 24.

Single Table, Table Scan

As the first example, consider a query on the city table in the world sample database with a condition on the non-indexed column Name. Since there is no index that can be used, it will require a full table scan to evaluate the query. An example of a query matching these requirements is

```
SELECT *
  FROM world.city
 WHERE Name = 'London';
```

Listing 20-5 shows the traditional EXPLAIN output for the query.

Listing 20-5. The EXPLAIN output for a single table with a table scan

```
mysql> EXPLAIN
        SELECT *
          FROM world.city
         WHERE Name = 'London'\G
*************************** 1. row ***************************
           id: 1
  select_type: SIMPLE
        table: city
   partitions: NULL
         type: ALL
possible_keys: NULL
          key: NULL
      key_len: NULL
          ref: NULL
         rows: 4188
```

```
     filtered: 10
        Extra: Using where
1 row in set, 1 warning (0.0007 sec)
```

The output has the access type set to ALL which is also what would be expected since there are no conditions on columns with indexes. It is estimated that 4188 rows will be examined (the actual number is 4079) and for each row a condition from the WHERE clause will be applied. It is expected that 10% of the rows examined will match the WHERE clause (note that depending on the client used, the output for the filtered column may say 10 or 10.00). Recall from the optimizer discussion in Chapter 17 that the optimizer uses default values to estimate the filtering effect of various conditions, so you cannot use the filtering value directly to estimate whether an index is useful.

The corresponding Visual Explain diagram can be seen in Figure 20-8.

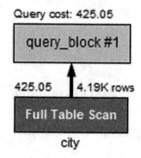

Figure 20-8. *Visual Explain diagram for a single table with a table scan*

The full table scan is shown by a red *Full Table Scan* box, and it can be seen that the cost is estimated to be 425.05.

This query just returns two rows (the table has a London in England and one in Ontario, Canada). What happens if all cities in a single country are requested instead?

Single Table, Index Access

The second example is similar to the first except the filter condition is changed to use the CountryCode column which has a secondary nonunique index. This should make it cheaper to access matching rows. For this example, all German cities will be retrieved:

```
SELECT *
  FROM world.city
 WHERE CountryCode = 'DEU';
```

Listing 20-6 shows the traditional EXPLAIN output for the query.

Listing 20-6. The EXPLAIN output for a single table with index lookups

```
mysql> EXPLAIN
        SELECT *
          FROM world.city
         WHERE CountryCode = 'DEU'\G
*************************** 1. row ***************************
           id: 1
  select_type: SIMPLE
        table: city
   partitions: NULL
         type: ref
possible_keys: CountryCode
          key: CountryCode
      key_len: 3
          ref: const
         rows: 93
     filtered: 100
        Extra: NULL
1 row in set, 1 warning (0.0008 sec)
```

This time the possible_keys column shows that the CountryCode index can be used for the query, and the key column shows that the index is used. The access type is ref to reflect that a nonunique index is used for the table access. It is estimated that 93 rows will be accessed, which is exact as the optimizer asks InnoDB how many rows will match. The filtered column shows that the index does a perfect job of filtering the table. The corresponding Visual Explain diagram is shown in Figure 20-9.

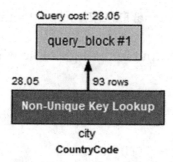

Figure 20-9. *Visual Explain diagram for a single table with index lookup*

Despite returning more than 45 times as many rows as the first example, the cost is only estimated as 28.05 or less than one-tenth of the cost of a full table scan.

What happens if only the ID and CountryCode columns are used?

Two Tables and a Covering Index

If there is an index that includes all columns required from the table, then it is called a covering index. MySQL will use this to avoid retrieving the whole row. Since the CountryCode index of the city table is a nonunique index, it also includes the ID column as it is the primary key. To make the query a little more realistic, the query will also include the country table and filter the countries included based on the continent. An example of such a query is

```
SELECT ci.ID
  FROM world.country co
       INNER JOIN world.city ci
         ON ci.CountryCode = co.Code
 WHERE co.Continent = 'Asia';
```

Listing 20-7 shows the traditional EXPLAIN output for the query.

Listing 20-7. The EXPLAIN output for a simple join between two tables

```
mysql> EXPLAIN
        SELECT ci.ID
          FROM world.country co
               INNER JOIN world.city ci
```

```
          ON ci.CountryCode = co.Code
      WHERE co.Continent = 'Asia'\G
*************************** 1. row ***************************
           id: 1
  select_type: SIMPLE
        table: co
   partitions: NULL
         type: ALL
possible_keys: PRIMARY
          key: NULL
      key_len: NULL
          ref: NULL
         rows: 239
     filtered: 14.285715103149414
        Extra: Using where
*************************** 2. row ***************************
           id: 1
  select_type: SIMPLE
        table: ci
   partitions: NULL
         type: ref
possible_keys: CountryCode
          key: CountryCode
      key_len: 3
          ref: world.co.Code
         rows: 18
     filtered: 100
        Extra: Using index
```

The query plan shows that the optimizer has chosen to start with a full table scan on the co (country) table and to use the CountryCode index for the join on the ci (city) table. What is special here is that the Extra column includes Using index. So it is not necessary to read the full row of the city table. Notice also that the key length is 3 (bytes) which is the width of the CountryCode column. The corresponding Visual Explain diagram can be seen in Figure 20-10.

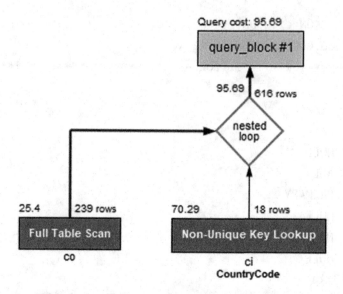

Figure 20-10. *Visual Explain diagram for a simple join between two tables*

The key_len field does not include the primary key part of the index even though it is used. It is however useful to see how much of a multicolumn index is used.

Multicolumn Index

The countrylanguage table has a primary key that includes the CountryCode and Language columns. Imagine you want to find all languages spoken in a single country; in that case you need to filter on CountryCode but not on Language. The index can still be used to perform the filtering, and you can use the key_len field of the EXPLAIN output to see how much of the index is used. A query that can be used to find all languages spoken in China is

```
SELECT *
  FROM world.countrylanguage
 WHERE CountryCode = 'CHN';
```

Listing 20-8 shows the traditional EXPLAIN output for the query.

Listing 20-8. The EXPLAIN output using part of a multicolumn index

```
mysql> EXPLAIN
         SELECT *
           FROM world.countrylanguage
          WHERE CountryCode = 'CHN'\G
*************************** 1. row ***************************
           id: 1
  select_type: SIMPLE
        table: countrylanguage
   partitions: NULL
         type: ref
possible_keys: PRIMARY,CountryCode
          key: PRIMARY
      key_len: 3
          ref: const
         rows: 12
     filtered: 100
        Extra: NULL
```

The total width of the primary key is 3 bytes from the CountryLanguage column and 30 bytes from the Language column. Since the key_len column shows that only 3 bytes is used, it can be concluded only the CountryLanguage part of the index is used for filtering (the used part of the index is always the leftmost part). In Visual Explain you need to hover over the table in question to get the extended information as shown in Figure 20-11.

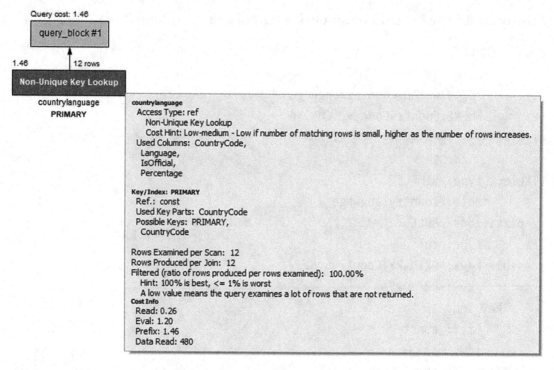

Figure 20-11. *Visual Explain diagram for using part of a multicolumn index*

In the figure, look for the *Used Key Parts* label under *Key/Index: PRIMARY*. This directly shows that only the CountryCode column of the index is used.

As a final example, let's return to the query that was used as an example when going through the EXPLAIN formats.

Two Tables with Subquery and Sorting

The example query that has been used extensively earlier in the chapter will be used to round off the discussion about EXPLAIN. The query uses a mix of various features, so it triggers several parts of the information that has been discussed. It is also an example of a query with multiple query blocks. As a reminder, the query is repeated here.

The output of the traditional EXPLAIN format is repeated in Listing 20-9.

Listing 20-9. The EXPLAIN output when joining a subquery and a table

```
mysql> EXPLAIN
        SELECT ci.ID, ci.Name, ci.District,
                co.Name AS Country, ci.Population
          FROM world.city ci
              INNER JOIN
                (SELECT Code, Name
                   FROM world.country
                  WHERE Continent = 'Europe'
                  ORDER BY SurfaceArea
                  LIMIT 10
                ) co ON co.Code = ci.CountryCode
        ORDER BY ci.Population DESC
        LIMIT 5\G
*************************** 1. row ***************************
           id: 1
  select_type: PRIMARY
        table: <derived2>
   partitions: NULL
         type: ALL
possible_keys: NULL
          key: NULL
      key_len: NULL
          ref: NULL
         rows: 10
     filtered: 100
        Extra: Using temporary; Using filesort
*************************** 2. row ***************************
           id: 1
  select_type: PRIMARY
        table: ci
   partitions: NULL
         type: ref
possible_keys: CountryCode
          key: CountryCode
```

```
        key_len: 3
            ref: co.Code
           rows: 18
       filtered: 100
          Extra: NULL
*********************** 3. row **************************
             id: 2
    select_type: DERIVED
          table: country
     partitions: NULL
           type: ALL
  possible_keys: NULL
            key: NULL
        key_len: NULL
            ref: NULL
           rows: 239
       filtered: 14.285715103149414
          Extra: Using where; Using filesort
```

The Visual Explain diagram for the query is repeated in Figure 20-12. Before proceeding to read the analysis of the output, you are encouraged to study it on your own.

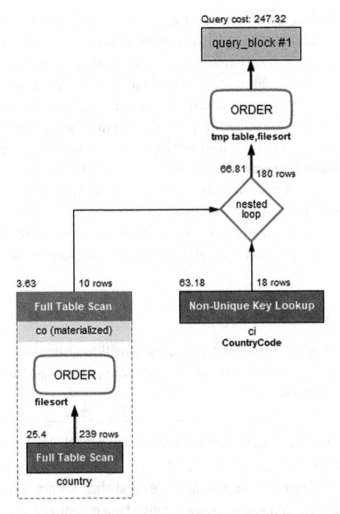

Figure 20-12. *Visual Explain diagram for joining a subquery and a table*

The query plan starts out with the subquery that uses the country table to find the ten smallest countries by area. The subquery is given the table label <derived2>, so you will need to find the row (could be several rows for other queries) with id = 2 which is row 3 in this case. Row 3 has the select type set to DERIVED, so it is a derived table; that is a table created through a query but otherwise behaves like a normal table. The derived table is generated using a full table scan (type = ALL) with a WHERE clause applied to each row, followed by a file sort. The resulting derived table is materialized (visible from Visual Explain) and called co.

Once the derived table has been constructed, it is used as the first table for the join with the ci (city) table. You can see that from the ordering of the rows with <derived2> in row 1 and ci in row 2. For each row in the derived table, it is estimated that 18 rows will be examined in the ci table using the CountryCode index. The CountryCode index is a nonunique index which can be seen from the label for the table box in Visual Explain, and the type column has the value ref. It is estimated that the join will return 180 rows which comes from the ten rows in the derived table multiplied with the estimate of 18 rows per index lookup in the ci table.

Finally, the result is sorted using an internal temporary table and a file sort. The total cost of the query is estimated to be 247.32.

Thus far, the discussion has been on what the query plan ended up being. If you want to know how the optimizer got there, you will need to examine the optimizer trace.

Optimizer Trace

The optimizer trace is not needed very often, but sometimes when you encounter an unexpected query plan, it can be useful to see how the optimizer got there. That is what the optimizer trace shows.

Tip   Most often when a query plan is not what you expect, it is because of a missing or wrong WHERE clause, a missing or wrong join condition, or some other kind of error in the query or because the index statistics are not correct. Check these things before diving into the gory details of the optimizer's decision process.

The optimizer trace is enabled by setting the optimizer_trace option to 1. This makes the optimizer record the trace information for the subsequent queries (until optimizer_trace is disabled again), and the information is made available through the information_schema.OPTIMIZER_TRACE table. The maximum number of traces that are retained is configured with the optimizer_trace_limit option (defaults to 1).

You can choose between executing the query you need the optimizer trace for and using EXPLAIN to get the query plan. The latter is very useful as it gives you both the query plan and the optimizer trace. A typical workflow to get the optimizer trace for a query is as follows:

1. Enable the `optimizer_trace` option for the session.

2. Execute EXPLAIN for the query you want to investigate.

3. Disable the `optimizer_trace` option again.

4. Retrieve the optimizer trace from the `information_schema.OPTIMIZER_TRACE` table.

The `information_schema.OPTIMIZER_TRACE` table includes four columns:

- **QUERY:** The original query.

- **TRACE:** A JSON document with the trace information. There will be more about the trace shortly.

- **MISSING_BYTES_BEYOND_MAX_MEM_SIZE:** The size (in bytes) of the recorded trace is limited to the value of the `optimizer_trace_max_mem_size` option (defaults to 1 MiB in MySQL 8). This column shows how much more memory is required to record the full trace. If the value is greater than 0, increase the `optimizer_trace_max_mem_size` option with that amount.

- **INSUFFICIENT_PRIVILEGES:** Whether you were missing privileges to generate the optimizer trace.

The table is created as a temporary table, so the traces are unique to the session.

Listing 20-10 shows an example of obtaining the optimizer trace for a query (the same as was used as the recurring example query in the previous sections). The optimizer trace output has been truncated here as it is more than 15000 characters and almost 500 lines long. Similarly, the output of the EXPLAIN statement has been omitted as it is the same as previously shown and it is not important for this discussion. The full output is included in the file `listing_20_10.txt` and the trace itself in `listing_20_10.json` in this book's GitHub repository.

Listing 20-10. Obtaining the optimizer trace for a query

```
mysql> SET SESSION optimizer_trace = 1;
Query OK, 0 rows affected (0.0003 sec)

mysql> EXPLAIN
       SELECT ci.ID, ci.Name, ci.District,
              co.Name AS Country, ci.Population
```

```
            FROM world.city ci
                INNER JOIN
                  (SELECT Code, Name
                    FROM world.country
                    WHERE Continent = 'Europe'
                    ORDER BY SurfaceArea
                    LIMIT 10
                  ) co ON co.Code = ci.CountryCode
        ORDER BY ci.Population DESC
        LIMIT 5\G
...

mysql> SET SESSION optimizer_trace = 0;
Query OK, 0 rows affected (0.0002 sec)

mysql> SELECT * FROM information_schema.OPTIMIZER_TRACE\G
*************************** 1. row ***************************
                        QUERY: EXPLAIN
SELECT ci.ID, ci.Name, ci.District,
       co.Name AS Country, ci.Population
  FROM world.city ci
        INNER JOIN
          (SELECT Code, Name
            FROM world.country
            WHERE Continent = 'Europe'
            ORDER BY SurfaceArea
            LIMIT 10
          ) co ON co.Code = ci.CountryCode
 ORDER BY ci.Population DESC
 LIMIT 5
                        TRACE: {
...
}
MISSING_BYTES_BEYOND_MAX_MEM_SIZE: 0
            INSUFFICIENT_PRIVILEGES: 0
1 row in set (0.0436 sec)
```

The trace is the most interesting in the result. While there is a lot of information available, fortunately it is largely self-explanatory, and if you have familiarized yourself with the JSON-formatted EXPLAIN outputs, there are some similarities. Much of the information is regarding the cost estimates for the various parts of executing the query. Where there are multiple possible options, the optimizer calculates the cost for each choice and chooses the cheapest option. One such example from this trace is for accessing the ci (city) table. This can be done either through the CountryCode index or a table scan. The part of the trace for this decision is shown in Listing 20-11 (the indentation has been reduced).

Listing 20-11. The optimizer trace for choosing the access type for the ci table

```
"table": "`city` `ci`",
"best_access_path": {
  "considered_access_paths": [
    {
      "access_type": "ref",
      "index": "CountryCode",
      "rows": 18.052,
      "cost": 63.181,
      "chosen": true
    },
    {
      "rows_to_scan": 4188,
      "filtering_effect": [
      ],
      "final_filtering_effect": 1,
      "access_type": "scan",
      "using_join_cache": true,
      "buffers_needed": 1,
      "resulting_rows": 4188,
      "cost": 4194.3,
      "chosen": false
    }
  ]
},
```

This shows that it is estimated that on average a little more than 18 rows will be examined when using the CountryCode index ("access_type": "ref") with a cost of 63.181. For the full table scan ("access_type": "scan"), it is expected that it will be necessary to examine 4188 rows with a total cost of 4194.3. The "chosen" element shows that the ref access type has been chosen.

While it is rarely necessary to delve into the details of how the optimizer arrived at the query plan, it can be useful to learn about how the optimizer works. Occasionally, it can also be useful to see the estimated cost of other options for the query plan to understand why they are not chosen.

Tip   If you are interested in learning more about using the optimizer traces, you can read more in the MySQL internals manual at `https://dev.mysql.com/doc/internals/en/optimizer-tracing.html`.

Thus far, the whole discussion – except for EXPLAIN ANALYZE – has been about analyzing the query at the stage before it is executed. If you want to examine the actual performance, EXPLAIN ANALYZE is usually the best option. Another option is to use the Performance Schema.

Performance Schema Events Analysis

The Performance Schema allows you to analyze how much time is spent on each of the events that are instrumented. You can use that to analyze where time is spent when a query is executed. This section will examine how you can use the Performance Schema to analyze a stored procedure to see which of the statements in the procedure take the longest and how to use the stage events to analyze a single query. At the end of the section, it will be shown how you can use the sys.ps_trace_thread() procedure to create a diagram of work done by a thread and how you can use the ps_trace_statement_digest() to collect statistics for statements with a given digest.

Examining a Stored Procedure

It can be challenging to examine the work done by a stored procedure as you cannot use EXPLAIN directly on the procedure and it may not be obvious which queries will be executed by the procedure. Instead you can use the Performance Schema. It records each statement executed and maintains the history in the events_statements_history table.

Unless you need to store more than the last ten queries per thread, you do not need to do anything to start the analysis. If the procedure generates more than ten statement events, you will need to either increase the value of the performance_schema_events_ statements_history_size option (requires a restart), use the events_statements_ history_long table, or use the sys.ps_trace_thread() procedure as explained later. The remaining part of this discussion assumes you can use the events_statements_ history table.

As an example of examining the queries executed by a stored procedure, consider the procedure in Listing 20-12. The procedure is also available in the file listing_20_12. sql which can be sourced into any schema.

Listing 20-12. An example procedure

```
CREATE SCHEMA IF NOT EXISTS chapter_20;

DELIMITER $$

CREATE PROCEDURE chapter_20.testproc()
    SQL SECURITY INVOKER
    NOT DETERMINISTIC
    MODIFIES SQL DATA
BEGIN
    DECLARE v_iter, v_id int unsigned DEFAULT 0;
    DECLARE v_name char(35) CHARSET latin1;

    SET v_id = CEIL(RAND()*4079);
    SELECT Name
      INTO v_name
      FROM world.city
     WHERE ID = v_id;
```

```
    SELECT *
      FROM world.city
     WHERE Name = v_name;
END$$

DELIMITER ;
```

The procedure executes three queries. The first query sets the v_id variable to an integer between 1 and 4079 (the available ID values in the world.city table). The second query fetches the name for the city with that id. The third query finds all cities with the same name as was found in the second query.

If you invoke this procedure in a connection, you can then subsequently analyze the queries triggered by the procedure and the performance of those queries. For example:

```
mysql> SELECT PS_CURRENT_THREAD_ID();
+------------------------+
| PS_CURRENT_THREAD_ID() |
+------------------------+
|                     83 |
+------------------------+
1 row in set (0.00 sec)

mysql> CALL chapter_20.testproc();
+------+--------+-------------+----------+------------+
| ID   | Name   | CountryCode | District | Population |
+------+--------+-------------+----------+------------+
| 2853 | Jhelum | PAK         | Punjab   |     145800 |
+------+--------+-------------+----------+------------+
1 row in set (0.0019 sec)
Query OK, 0 rows affected (0.0019 sec)
```

The output of the procedure is random, so will differ for each execution. You can then use the thread id found with the PS_CURRENT_THREAD_ID() function (use sys.ps_thread_id(NULL) in MySQL 8.0.15 and earlier) to determine which queries were executed.

Listing 20-13 shows how this analysis can be done. You must do this analysis in a different connection, change THREAD_ID = 83 to use the thread id you found, and change NESTING_EVENT_ID = 64 in the second query to use the event id from the first query. Some of the details have been removed from the output to focus on the values of most interest.

Listing 20-13. Analyzing the queries executed by a stored procedure

```
mysql> SELECT *
         FROM performance_schema.events_statements_history
        WHERE THREAD_ID = 83
          AND EVENT_NAME = 'statement/sql/call_procedure'
        ORDER BY EVENT_ID DESC
        LIMIT 1\G
*************************** 1. row ***************************
        THREAD_ID: 83
         EVENT_ID: 64
     END_EVENT_ID: 72
       EVENT_NAME: statement/sql/call_procedure
           SOURCE: init_net_server_extension.cc:95
      TIMER_START: 533823963611947008
        TIMER_END: 533823965937460352
       TIMER_WAIT: 2325513344
        LOCK_TIME: 129000000
         SQL_TEXT: CALL testproc()
           DIGEST: 72fd8466a0e05fe215308832173a3be50e7edad960
                   408c70078ef94f8ffb52b2
      DIGEST_TEXT: CALL `testproc` ( )
...
1 row in set (0.0008 sec)

mysql> SELECT *
         FROM performance_schema.events_statements_history
        WHERE THREAD_ID = 83
          AND NESTING_EVENT_ID = 64
        ORDER BY EVENT_ID\G
*************************** 1. row ***************************
        THREAD_ID: 83
         EVENT_ID: 65
     END_EVENT_ID: 65
       EVENT_NAME: statement/sp/set
...
```

```
*************************** 2. row ***************************
          THREAD_ID: 83
           EVENT_ID: 66
       END_EVENT_ID: 66
         EVENT_NAME: statement/sp/set
...
*************************** 3. row ***************************
          THREAD_ID: 83
           EVENT_ID: 67
       END_EVENT_ID: 67
         EVENT_NAME: statement/sp/set
...
*************************** 4. row ***************************
          THREAD_ID: 83
           EVENT_ID: 68
       END_EVENT_ID: 68
         EVENT_NAME: statement/sp/set
...
*************************** 5. row ***************************
          THREAD_ID: 83
           EVENT_ID: 69
       END_EVENT_ID: 70
         EVENT_NAME: statement/sp/stmt
             SOURCE: sp_head.cc:2166
        TIMER_START: 533823963993029248
          TIMER_END: 533823964065598976
         TIMER_WAIT: 72569728
         LOCK_TIME: 0
           SQL_TEXT: SELECT Name
    INTO v_name
    FROM world.city
   WHERE ID = v_id
             DIGEST: NULL
        DIGEST_TEXT: NULL
     CURRENT_SCHEMA: db1
```

```
            OBJECT_TYPE: PROCEDURE
          OBJECT_SCHEMA: db1
            OBJECT_NAME: testproc
  OBJECT_INSTANCE_BEGIN: NULL
            MYSQL_ERRNO: 0
       RETURNED_SQLSTATE: 00000
           MESSAGE_TEXT: NULL
                 ERRORS: 0
               WARNINGS: 0
          ROWS_AFFECTED: 1
              ROWS_SENT: 0
          ROWS_EXAMINED: 1
CREATED_TMP_DISK_TABLES: 0
     CREATED_TMP_TABLES: 0
       SELECT_FULL_JOIN: 0
 SELECT_FULL_RANGE_JOIN: 0
           SELECT_RANGE: 0
     SELECT_RANGE_CHECK: 0
            SELECT_SCAN: 0
      SORT_MERGE_PASSES: 0
             SORT_RANGE: 0
              SORT_ROWS: 0
              SORT_SCAN: 0
          NO_INDEX_USED: 0
     NO_GOOD_INDEX_USED: 0
       NESTING_EVENT_ID: 64
     NESTING_EVENT_TYPE: STATEMENT
    NESTING_EVENT_LEVEL: 1
           STATEMENT_ID: 25241
*************************** 6. row ***************************
              THREAD_ID: 83
               EVENT_ID: 71
           END_EVENT_ID: 72
             EVENT_NAME: statement/sp/stmt
                 SOURCE: sp_head.cc:2166
```

```
              TIMER_START: 533823964067422336
                TIMER_END: 533823965880571520
               TIMER_WAIT: 1813149184
               LOCK_TIME: 0
                 SQL_TEXT: SELECT *
      FROM world.city
     WHERE Name = v_name
                   DIGEST: NULL
              DIGEST_TEXT: NULL
           CURRENT_SCHEMA: db1
              OBJECT_TYPE: PROCEDURE
            OBJECT_SCHEMA: db1
              OBJECT_NAME: testproc
    OBJECT_INSTANCE_BEGIN: NULL
              MYSQL_ERRNO: 0
         RETURNED_SQLSTATE: NULL
             MESSAGE_TEXT: NULL
                   ERRORS: 0
                 WARNINGS: 0
            ROWS_AFFECTED: 0
                ROWS_SENT: 1
            ROWS_EXAMINED: 4080
  CREATED_TMP_DISK_TABLES: 0
       CREATED_TMP_TABLES: 0
         SELECT_FULL_JOIN: 0
   SELECT_FULL_RANGE_JOIN: 0
             SELECT_RANGE: 0
       SELECT_RANGE_CHECK: 0
              SELECT_SCAN: 1
        SORT_MERGE_PASSES: 0
               SORT_RANGE: 0
                SORT_ROWS: 0
                SORT_SCAN: 0
            NO_INDEX_USED: 1
       NO_GOOD_INDEX_USED: 0
```

```
     NESTING_EVENT_ID: 64
   NESTING_EVENT_TYPE: STATEMENT
  NESTING_EVENT_LEVEL: 1
         STATEMENT_ID: 25242
6 rows in set (0.0008 sec)
```

The analysis consists of two queries. The first determines the overall information for the procedure which is done by querying for the latest occurrence (sorting by EVENT_ID) of the statement/sql/call_procedure event which is the event for calling a procedure.

The second query asks for the events for the same thread that has the event id of the statement/sql/call_procedure event as the nesting event id. These are the statements executed by the procedure. By ordering by EVENT_ID, the statements are returned in the order they are executed.

The query result of the second query shows that the procedure starts out with four SET statements. Some of these are expected, but there are also some that are triggered by implicitly setting variables. The last two rows are the most interesting for this discussion as they show that two queries were executed. First, the city table is queried by its ID column (the primary key). As expected, it examines one row. Because the result is saved in the v_name variable, the ROWS_AFFECTED counter is incremented instead of ROWS_SENT.

The second query does not perform as well. It also queries the city table but by name where there is no index. This results in 4080 rows being examined to return a single row. The NO_INDEX_USED column is set to 1 to reflect that a full table scan was performed.

One disadvantage of using this approach to examine stored procedures is that – as you can see – it can quickly use all ten rows in the history table. One alternative is to enable the events_statements_history_long consumer and test the procedure on an otherwise idle test system or disable history logging for the other connections. This allows you to analyze procedures executing up to 10000 statement events. An alternative is to use the sys.ps_trace_thread() procedure which also uses the long history but supports polling while the procedure is executing, so it can collect the events even if the table is not large enough to hold all events for the duration of the procedure.

This example has been using the statement events to analyze the performance. Sometimes you need to know what happens at a finer-grained level in which case you need to start looking at the stage events.

Analyzing Stage Events

If you need to get finer-grained details of where a query spends time, the first step is to look at the stage events. Optionally, you can also include wait events. Since the step to work with wait events is essentially the same as for stage events, it is left as an exercise for the reader to analyze the wait events for a query.

Caution   The finer-grained the events you examine, the more overhead they will have. Thus, be careful enabling stage and wait events on production systems. Some wait events, particularly related to mutexes, may also impact the query enough that they affect the conclusions of the analysis. Using wait events to analyze a query is usually something only performance architects and developers working with the MySQL source code need to do.

The number of stage events generated is much larger than the number of statement events. This means that in order to avoid the stage events disappearing from the history table, it is recommended to perform the analysis on an idle test system and to use the events_stages_history_long table. This table is disabled by default; to enable it, enable the corresponding consumer:

```
mysql> UPDATE performance_schema.setup_consumers
          SET ENABLED = 'YES'
        WHERE NAME IN ('events_stages_current',
                       'events_stages_history_long');
Query OK, 2 rows affected (0.0008 sec)

Rows matched: 2  Changed: 2  Warnings: 0
```

The events_stages_history_long consumer depends on the events_stages_current consumer, so you will need to enable both. By default, only stage events related to progress information are enabled. For a general analysis, you will want to enable all of the stage events:

```
mysql> UPDATE performance_schema.setup_instruments
          SET ENABLED = 'YES',
              TIMED = 'YES'
```

```
      WHERE NAME LIKE 'stage/%';
Query OK, 125 rows affected (0.0011 sec)

Rows matched: 125  Changed: 109  Warnings: 0
```

At this point, the analysis can proceed in much the same way as it was done when analyzing the stored procedure. For example, consider the following query being executed by the connection with the Performance Schema thread id equal to 83:

```
SELECT *
  FROM world.city
 WHERE Name = 'Sydney';
```

Assuming this is the last executed query, you can get the amount of time spent in each stage as shown in Listing 20-14. You need to execute this is a separate connection and change SET @thread_id = 83 to use the thread id for your connection. Other than the timings obviously being different, then the list of stages your query goes through may also differ.

Listing 20-14. Finding the stages for the last statement of a connection

```
mysql> SET @thread_id = 83;
Query OK, 0 rows affected (0.0004 sec)

mysql> SELECT EVENT_ID,
              SUBSTRING_INDEX(EVENT_NAME, '/', -1) AS Event,
              FORMAT_PICO_TIME(TIMER_WAIT) AS Latency
         FROM performance_schema.events_stages_history_long
        WHERE THREAD_ID = @thread_id
              AND NESTING_EVENT_ID = (
                  SELECT EVENT_ID
                    FROM performance_schema.events_statements_history
                   WHERE THREAD_ID = @thread_id
                   ORDER BY EVENT_ID DESC
                   LIMIT 1);
```

```
+-----------+-------------------------------------+-----------+
| EVENT_ID  | Event                               | Latency   |
+-----------+-------------------------------------+-----------+
|      7193 | Executing hook on transaction begin. | 200.00 ns |
|      7194 | cleaning up                         | 4.10 us   |
|      7195 | checking permissions                | 2.60 us   |
|      7196 | Opening tables                      | 41.50 us  |
|      7197 | init                                | 3.10 us   |
|      7198 | System lock                         | 6.50 us   |
|      7200 | optimizing                          | 5.30 us   |
|      7201 | statistics                          | 15.00 us  |
|      7202 | preparing                           | 12.10 us  |
|      7203 | executing                           | 1.18 ms   |
|      7204 | end                                 | 800.00 ns |
|      7205 | query end                           | 500.00 ns |
|      7206 | waiting for handler commit          | 6.70 us   |
|      7207 | closing tables                      | 3.30 us   |
|      7208 | freeing items                       | 70.30 us  |
|      7209 | cleaning up                         | 300.00 ns |
+-----------+-------------------------------------+-----------+
16 rows in set (0.0044 sec)
```

The event id, the stage name (removing the two first parts of the full event name for brevity), and the latency formatted with the FORMAT_PICO_TIME() function (use the sys. format_time() function in MySQL 8.0.15 and earlier) are selected from the events_ stages_history_long table. The WHERE clause filters on the thread id of the connection that executed the query and by the nesting event id. The nesting event id is set to the event id of the latest executed statement for the connection with thread id equal to 83. The result shows that the slowest part of the query is Sending data which is the stage where the storage engine finds and sends the rows.

The main issue analyzing queries this way is that you are either limited by the ten events per thread saved by default or you risk the events being expunged from the long history table before you are done examining it. The sys.ps_trace_thread() procedure was created to help with that problem.

Analysis with the sys.ps_trace_thread() Procedure

When you need to analyze a complex query or a stored program executing more than a few statements, you can benefit from using a tool that automatically collects the information as the execution progresses. An option to do this from the sys schema is the ps_trace_thread() procedure.

The procedure loops for a period of time polling the long history tables for new transactions, statements, stages, and wait events. Optionally, the procedure can also set up the Performance Schema to include all events and enable the consumers to record the events. However, since it is usually too much to include all events, it is recommended to set up the Performance Schema yourself to instrument and consume the events that are of interest for your analysis.

Another optional feature is to reset the Performance Schema tables at the start of the monitoring. This can be great if it is acceptable to remove the content of the long history tables.

When you call the procedure, you must provide the following arguments:

- **Thread ID:** The Performance Schema thread id that you want to monitor.

- **Out File:** A file to write the result to. The result is created using the dot graph description language.[2] This requires that the secure_file_priv option has been set to allow writing files to the target directory and the file does not exist and the user executing the procedure has the FILE privilege.

- **Max Runtime:** The maximum time to monitor in seconds. There is support for specifying the value with 1/100 of a second precision. If the value is set to NULL, the runtime is set to 60 seconds.

- **Poll Interval:** The interval between polling the history tables. The value can be set with the precision of 1/100 of a second. If the value is set to NULL, then the polling interval will be set to one second.

- **Refresh:** A Boolean whether to reset the Performance Schema tables used for the analysis.

---

[2]https://en.wikipedia.org/wiki/DOT_%28graph_description_language%29 and
www.graphviz.org/doc/info/lang.html

- **Auto Setup:** A Boolean whether to enable all instruments and consumers that can be used by the procedure. When enabled, the current settings are restored when the procedure completes.

- **Debug:** A Boolean whether to include additional information such as where in the source code the event is triggered. This is mostly useful when including wait events.

An example of using the ps_trace_thread() procedure can be seen in Listing 20-15. While the procedure is executing, the testproc() procedure from earlier is called from the thread that is being monitored. The example assumes you start out with the default Performance Schema settings.

Listing 20-15. Using the ps_trace_thread() procedure

```
Connection 1> UPDATE performance_schema.setup_consumers
              SET ENABLED = 'YES'
            WHERE NAME = 'events_statements_history_long';
Query OK, 1 row affected (0.0074 sec)

Rows matched: 1  Changed: 1  Warnings: 0

-- Find the Performance Schema thread id for the
-- thread that will be monitored.
Connection 2> SELECT PS_CURRENT_THREAD_ID();
+------------------+
| PS_THREAD_ID(9)  |
+------------------+
|               32 |
+------------------+
1 row in set (0.0016 sec)

-- Replace the first argument with the thread id
-- just found.
--
-- Once the procedure returns
-- "Data collection starting for THREAD_ID = 32"
-- (replace 32 with your thread id) invoke the
-- chapter_20.testproc() chapter from connection 2.
```

```
-- The example is set to poll for 10 seconds. If you
-- need more time, change the third argument to the
-- number of seconds you need.
Connection 1> CALL sys.ps_trace_thread(
                32,
                '/mysql/files/thread_32.gv',
                10, 0.1, False, False, False);
```

```
+--------------------+
| summary            |
+--------------------+
| Disabled 1 thread  |
+--------------------+
1 row in set (0.0316 sec)
```

```
+-----------------------------------------------+
| summary                                       |
+-----------------------------------------------+
| Data collection starting for THREAD_ID = 32   |
+-----------------------------------------------+
1 row in set (0.0316 sec)
```

```
-- Here, sys.ps_trace_id() blocks - execute the
-- query you want to trace. The output is random.
Connection 2> CALL chapter_20.testproc();
```

```
+------+--------+-------------+----------+------------+
| ID   | Name   | CountryCode | District | Population |
+------+--------+-------------+----------+------------+
| 3607 | Rjazan | RUS         | Rjazan   |     529900 |
+------+--------+-------------+----------+------------+
1 row in set (0.0023 sec)
```

```
Query OK, 0 rows affected (0.0023 sec)
```

```
-- Back in connection 1, wait for the sys.ps_trace_id()
-- procedure to complete.
```

```
+----------------------------------------------------+
| summary                                            |
+----------------------------------------------------+
| Stack trace written to /mysql/files/thread_32.gv   |
+----------------------------------------------------+
1 row in set (0.0316 sec)
+--------------------------------------------------------------+
| summary                                                      |
+--------------------------------------------------------------+
| dot -Tpdf -o /tmp/stack_32.pdf /mysql/files/thread_32.gv     |
+--------------------------------------------------------------+
1 row in set (0.0316 sec)
+--------------------------------------------------------------+
| summary                                                      |
+--------------------------------------------------------------+
| dot -Tpng -o /tmp/stack_32.png /mysql/files/thread_32.gv     |
+--------------------------------------------------------------+
1 row in set (0.0316 sec)
+-------------------+
| summary           |
+-------------------+
| Enabled 1 thread  |
+-------------------+
1 row in set (0.0316 sec)
Query OK, 0 rows affected (0.0316 sec)
```

In this example, only the events_statements_history_long consumer is enabled. This will allow to record all the statement events that result for calling the testproc() procedure as it was done manually earlier. The thread id that will be monitored is obtained using the PS_CURRENT_THREAD_ID() function (in MySQL 8.0.15 and earlier, use sys.ps_thread_id(NULL)).

The ps_trace_thread() procedure is invoked for thread id 32 with the output written to /mysql/files/thread_32.gv. The procedure polls every 0.1 second for 10 seconds, and all the optional features are disabled.

You will need a program that understands the dot format to convert it into an image. One option is the *Graphviz* toolset which is available from several Linux distributions

through the package repository. It can also be downloaded from the project's
homepage, www.graphviz.org/, for Linux, Microsoft Windows, and macOS, Solaris, and
FreeBSD. The output of the procedure shows examples of how to convert the file with the
dot graph definition to either a PDF or PNG file. Figure 20-13 shows the generated graph
for the CALL testproc() statement.

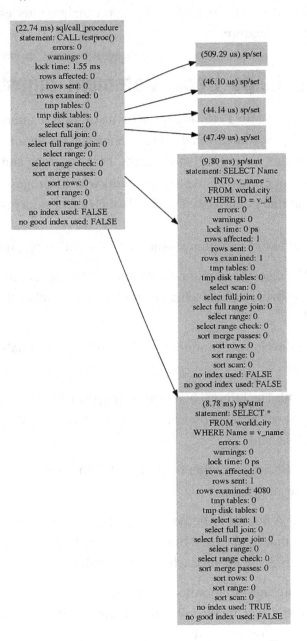

Figure 20-13. *The statement graph for the* CALL testproc() *statement*

The statement graph includes the same information as when the procedure was analyzed manually. For a procedure as simple as testproc(), the advantage of generating the graph is limited, but for more complex procedures or for analyzing queries with lower-level events enabled, it can be a good way to visualize the flow of the execution.

Another sys schema procedure that can help you analyze queries is the ps_trace_statement_digest() procedure.

Analysis with the ps_trace_statement_digest() Procedure

As a final example of using the Performance Schema to analyze queries, the ps_trace_statement_digest() procedure from the sys schema will be demonstrated. It takes a digest and then monitors the events_statements_history_long and events_stages_history_long tables for events related to statements with that digest. The result of the analysis includes summary data as well as details such as the query plan for the longest-running query.

The procedure takes five arguments which are all mandatory. The arguments are

- **Digest:** The digest to monitor. Statements will be monitored irrespective of the default schema if their digest matches the one provided.

- **Runtime:** How long to monitor for in seconds. No decimals are allowed.

- **Poll Interval:** The interval between polling the history tables. The value can be set with the precision of 1/100 of a second and must be less than 1 second.

- **Refresh:** A Boolean whether to reset the Performance Schema tables used for the analysis.

- **Auto Setup:** A Boolean whether to enable all instruments and consumers that can be used by the procedure. When enabled, the current settings are restored when the procedure completes.

As an example, you can start monitoring with the sys.ps_trace_statement_digest() procedure and execute the following queries while the monitoring is ongoing (the example of the monitoring follows):

```
SELECT * FROM world.city WHERE CountryCode = 'AUS';
SELECT * FROM world.city WHERE CountryCode = 'USA';
SELECT * FROM world.city WHERE CountryCode = 'CHN';
SELECT * FROM world.city WHERE CountryCode = 'ZAF';
SELECT * FROM world.city WHERE CountryCode = 'BRA';
SELECT * FROM world.city WHERE CountryCode = 'GBR';
SELECT * FROM world.city WHERE CountryCode = 'FRA';
SELECT * FROM world.city WHERE CountryCode = 'IND';
SELECT * FROM world.city WHERE CountryCode = 'DEU';
SELECT * FROM world.city WHERE CountryCode = 'SWE';
SELECT * FROM world.city WHERE CountryCode = 'LUX';
SELECT * FROM world.city WHERE CountryCode = 'NZL';
SELECT * FROM world.city WHERE CountryCode = 'KOR';
```

It may vary from execution to execution which of these queries is the slowest.

Listing 20-16 shows an example of using the procedure to monitor for a query selecting all cities in a given country. In the example, the digest is found using the STATEMENT_DIGEST() function, but you may also have found it through monitoring based on the events_statements_summary_by_digest table. It will be left to the procedure to enable the instruments and consumers needed, and the monitored tables will be reset to avoid including occurrences of the statement executed before the monitoring starts. The polling frequency is set to poll every 0.5 second. To reduce the width of the output, the stage event names have had the stage/sql/ prefix removed, and the dashed lines for the EXPLAIN output have been made shorter. The unmodified output can be found in the file listing_20_16.txt in this book's GitHub repository.

Listing 20-16. Using the ps_trace_statement_digest() procedure

```
mysql> SET @digest = STATEMENT_DIGEST('SELECT * FROM world.city WHERE
CountryCode = ''AUS''');
Query OK, 0 rows affected (0.0004 sec)

-- Execute your queries once the procedure has started.
mysql> CALL sys.ps_trace_statement_digest(@digest, 60, 0.5, TRUE, TRUE);
```

```
+--------------------+
| summary            |
+--------------------+
| Disabled 1 thread  |
+--------------------+
1 row in set (1 min 0.0861 sec)

+--------------------+
| SUMMARY STATISTICS |
+--------------------+
| SUMMARY STATISTICS |
+--------------------+
1 row in set (1 min 0.0861 sec)

+------------+-----------+-----------+-----------+----------------+--------
------+------------+------------+
| executions | exec_time | lock_time | rows_sent | rows_affected | rows_
examined | tmp_tables | full_scans |
+------------+-----------+-----------+-----------+----------------+--------
------+------------+------------+
|         13 | 7.29 ms   | 1.19 ms   |      1720 |             0 |
1720 |         0 |         0 |
+------------+-----------+-----------+-----------+----------------+--------
------+------------+------------+
1 row in set (1 min 0.0861 sec)

+------------------------------------+-------+-----------+
| event_name                         | count | latency   |
+------------------------------------+-------+-----------+
| Sending data                       |    13 | 2.99 ms   |
| freeing items                      |    13 | 2.02 ms   |
| statistics                         |    13 | 675.37 us |
| Opening tables                     |    13 | 401.50 us |
| preparing                          |    13 | 100.28 us |
| optimizing                         |    13 | 66.37 us  |
| waiting for handler commit         |    13 | 64.18 us  |
| closing tables                     |    13 | 54.70 us  |
```

```
| System lock                         |    13 | 54.34 us |
| cleaning up                         |    26 | 45.22 us |
| init                                |    13 | 29.54 us |
| checking permissions                |    13 | 23.34 us |
| end                                 |    13 | 10.21 us |
| query end                           |    13 | 8.02 us  |
| executing                           |    13 | 4.01 us  |
| Executing hook on transaction begin. |   13 | 3.65 us  |
+-------------------------------------+-------+----------+
16 rows in set (1 min 0.0861 sec)

+---------------------------+
| LONGEST RUNNING STATEMENT |
+---------------------------+
| LONGEST RUNNING STATEMENT |
+---------------------------+
1 row in set (1 min 0.0861 sec)

+-----------+-----------+-----------+-----------+---------------+----------
-----+------------+-----------+
| thread_id | exec_time | lock_time | rows_sent | rows_affected | rows_
examined | tmp_tables | full_scan |
+-----------+-----------+-----------+-----------+---------------+----------
-----+------------+-----------+
|        32 | 1.09 ms   | 79.00 us  |       274 |             0
     274 |         0 |         0 |
+-----------+-----------+-----------+-----------+---------------+----------
-----+------------+-----------+
1 row in set (1 min 0.0861 sec)

+-------------------------------------------------------+
| sql_text                                              |
+-------------------------------------------------------+
| SELECT * FROM world.city WHERE CountryCode = 'USA'   |
+-------------------------------------------------------+
1 row in set (59.91 sec)
```

```
+----------------------------------------+------------+
| event_name                             | latency    |
+----------------------------------------+------------+
| Executing hook on transaction begin.   | 364.67 ns  |
| cleaning up                            | 3.28 us    |
| checking permissions                   | 1.46 us    |
| Opening tables                         | 27.72 us   |
| init                                   | 2.19 us    |
| System lock                            | 4.01 us    |
| optimizing                             | 5.11 us    |
| statistics                             | 46.68 us   |
| preparing                              | 7.66 us    |
| executing                              | 364.67 ns  |
| Sending data                           | 528.41 us  |
| end                                    | 729.34 ns  |
| query end                              | 729.34 ns  |
| waiting for handler commit             | 4.38 us    |
| closing tables                         | 16.77 us   |
| freeing items                          | 391.29 us  |
| cleaning up                            | 364.67 ns  |
+----------------------------------------+------------+
17 rows in set (1 min 0.0861 sec)

+--------------------------------------------------+
| EXPLAIN                                          |
+--------------------------------------------------+
| {
  "query_block": {
    "select_id": 1,
    "cost_info": {
      "query_cost": "46.15"
    },
    "table": {
      "table_name": "city",
      "access_type": "ref",
      "possible_keys": [
```

```
      "CountryCode"
    ],
    "key": "CountryCode",
    "used_key_parts": [
      "CountryCode"
    ],
    "key_length": "3",
    "ref": [
      "const"
    ],
    "rows_examined_per_scan": 274,
    "rows_produced_per_join": 274,
    "filtered": "100.00",
    "cost_info": {
      "read_cost": "18.75",
      "eval_cost": "27.40",
      "prefix_cost": "46.15",
      "data_read_per_join": "19K"
    },
    "used_columns": [
      "ID",
      "Name",
      "CountryCode",
      "District",
      "Population"
    ]
  }
 }
} |
+---------------------------------------------------+
1 row in set (1 min 0.0861 sec)
```

```
+------------------+
| summary          |
+------------------+
| Enabled 1 thread |
+------------------+
1 row in set (1 min 0.0861 sec)

Query OK, 0 rows affected (1 min 0.0861 sec)
```

The output starts out with the summary for all the queries found during the analysis. A total of 13 executions were detected using a total of 7.29 milliseconds. The overall summary also includes the aggregates for the time spent for various stages. The next part of the output are the details for the slowest of the 13 executions. The output concludes with the JSON-formatted query plan for the slowest of the queries.

There is a limitation you should be aware of for generating the query plan. The EXPLAIN statement will be executed with the default schema set to the same as where the procedure executed. That means that if the query is executed in a different schema and it does not use a fully qualified table name (i.e., including the schema name), then the EXPLAIN statement will fail, and the procedure does not output the query plan.

Summary

This chapter has covered how you can analyze queries that you believe may need optimization. The bulk of the chapter focused on the EXPLAIN statement that is the main tool for analyzing queries. The remainder of the chapter went through optimizer traces and how to use the Performance Schema to analyze queries.

The EXPLAIN statement supports several different formats that help you get the query plan in the format that works best for you. The traditional format uses a standard table output, the JSON format returns a detailed JSON document, and the tree format shows a relatively simple tree of the execution. The tree format is only supported in MySQL 8.0.16 and later and requires that the Volcano iterator executor is used to execute the query. The JSON format is what the Visual Explain feature in MySQL Workbench uses to create diagrams of the query plan.

There is a vast amount of information available about the query plan in the EXPLAIN outputs. The fields of the traditional format as well as the most commonly encountered fields of JSON were discussed. This included discussing the select types and access types and the extra information in detail. Finally, a series of examples were used to show how this information can be used.

The optimizer traces can be used to get information on how the optimizer ended up with the query plan that the EXPLAIN statement returned. It is usually not necessary to use the optimizer traces for end users, but they can be useful to learn more about the optimizer and the decision process that leads to the query plans.

The final part of the chapter showed how you can use the Performance Schema events to determine what is taking the time for a statement. It was first shown how you can break a stored procedure into individual statements and then how a statement can be broken into stages. Finally the ps_trace_thread() procedure was used to automate the analysis and create a graph of the events, and the ps_trace_statement_digest() procedure was used to collect statistics for a given statement digest.

This chapter analyzed queries. It is sometimes necessary to take the whole transaction into account. The next chapter will show how you can analyze transactions.

CHAPTER 21

Transactions

Transactions are the big brother of statements. They group multiple changes together whether in a single statement or several statements, so they are applied or abandoned as a single unit. Mostly transactions are not much more than an afterthought and just considered when it is necessary to apply several statements together. That is a bad way to consider transactions. They are very important to ensure data integrity, and when used wrong, they can cause severe performance issues.

This chapter starts out discussing why you need to take transactions seriously from a performance point of view by reviewing the impacts of transactions on locks and performance. The rest of the chapter focuses on analyzing transactions, first by using the INNODB_TRX table in the Information Schema, then the InnoDB monitor, the InnoDB metrics, and finally the Performance Schema.

Impact of Transactions

Transactions may seem as an innocent concept if you think of them as containers used to group queries. However, it is important to understand that since transactions provide atomicity for groups of queries, the longer a transaction is active, the longer resources associated with the queries are held, and the more work done in a transaction, the more resources are required. What resources are used by queries that remain in use until the transaction has been committed? The main two are locks and undo logs.

Tip InnoDB supports read-only transactions which have a lower overhead than read-write transactions. For auto-committing single-statement transactions, InnoDB will try to determine if the statement is read-only automatically. For multi-statement transactions, you can specify explicitly that it is a read-only transaction, when you start it: `START TRANSACTION READ ONLY;`

© Jesper Wisborg Krogh 2020
J. W. Krogh, *MySQL 8 Query Performance Tuning*, https://doi.org/10.1007/978-1-4842-5584-1_21

Locks

When the query executes, it takes locks, and when you use the default transaction isolation level – REPEATABLE READ – all locks are kept until the transaction is committed. When you use the READ COMMITTED transaction isolation level, some locks may be released, but at least those involving the changed records are kept. Locks themselves are a resource, but it also requires memory to store the information about the locks. You may not think much of this for a normal workload, but huge transactions can end up using so much memory that the transaction fails with the ER_LOCK_TABLE_FULL error:

```
ERROR: 1206: The total number of locks exceeds the lock table size
```

As it can be seen from the warning message logged to the error log (more shortly), the memory required for the locks is taken from the buffer pool. Thus, the more locks you hold and the longer they are held, the less memory is available for caching data and indexes.

Caution   Having a transaction aborted because it has used all the lock memory is a quadruple whammy. First, it would have taken a while to update enough rows to use enough lock memory to trigger the error. That work has been wasted. Second, because of the number of changes required, it is likely going to take a very long time to roll back the transaction. Third, while the lock memory is used, InnoDB is effectively in read-only mode (some small transactions may be possible), and the lock memory is not released until the rollback has completed. Fourth, there is very little space left in the buffer pool to cache data and indexes.

The error is preceded by a warning in the error log saying that more than 67% of the buffer pool is used for locks or the adaptive hash index:

```
2019-07-06T03:23:04.345256Z 10 [Warning] [MY-011958] [InnoDB] Over 67
percent of the buffer pool is occupied by lock heaps or the adaptive hash
index! Check that your transactions do not set too many row locks. Your
buffer pool size is 7 MB. Maybe you should make the buffer pool bigger?.
Starting the InnoDB Monitor to print diagnostics, including lock heap and
hash index sizes.
```

The warning is followed by regular repeating outputs of the InnoDB monitor, so you can determine which transactions are the culprits. The InnoDB monitor output for transactions will be discussed in the "InnoDB Monitor" section.

One lock type that is often neglected when it comes to transactions is the metadata lock. When a statement queries a table, a shared metadata lock is taken, and that metadata lock is held until the end of the transaction. While there is a metadata lock on a table, no connections can execute any DDL statements – including OPTIMIZE TABLE – against the table. If a DDL statement is blocked by a long-running transaction, it will in turn block all new queries from using that table. Chapter 22 will show an example of investigating such an issue including using some of the methods from this chapter.

The locks are held while the transaction is active. The transaction can however still have an impact even after it has completed through the undo logs.

Undo Logs

The changes that have been made during the transaction must also be stored as they are required, if you choose to roll back the transaction. This is easy to understand. More surprising is that even a transaction that has made no changes also can make undo information from other transactions stay around. This happens when the transaction requires a read view (a consistent snapshot), which is the case for the duration of the transaction when using the REPEATABLE READ transaction isolation level. The read view means that the transaction will return the row data that corresponds to the time when the transaction was started no matter whether other transactions change the data. In order to be able to deliver that, it is necessary to keep the old values of the rows that change during the lifetime of the transaction. Long-running transactions with a read view are the most common reason for ending up with huge undo logs, which in MySQL 5.7 and earlier could mean the ibdata1 file ended up being large. (In MySQL 8, the undo logs are always stored in separate undo tablespaces that can be truncated.)

Tip   The READ COMMITTED transaction isolation level is much less prone to large undo logs as the read views are only maintained for the duration of a query.

The size of the active part of the undo log is measured in the *history list length*. The history list length is the number of transactions committed where the undo log has not yet been purged. This means that you cannot use the history list length to get a measure of the total amount of row changes. What it does tell you is how many units of old rows (one unit per transaction) there is in the linked list of changes that must be taken into consideration when you execute a query. The longer this linked list is, the more expensive it becomes to find the correct version of each row. In the end, if you have a large history list, it can severely impact the performance of all queries.

Note   The issue with the history list length is one of the biggest issues creating backups of large databases using logical backup tools such as `mysqlpump` and `mysqldump` using a single transaction to get a consistent backup. The backup can cause the history list length to become very large if there are many transactions committed during the backup.

What constitutes a large history list length? There are no firm rules about that – just that the smaller, the better. Typically, performance issues start to show up when the list is some thousand to a million transactions long, but the point where it becomes a bottleneck depends on the transactions committed in the undo logs and the workload while the history list length is large.

InnoDB automatically purges the history list in the background when the oldest parts are no longer needed. There are two options to control the purge as well as two to influence what happens, when the purge cannot be done. The options are

- **innodb_purge_batch_size:** The number of undo log pages that are purged per batch. The batch is divided among the purge threads. This option is not intended to be changed on production systems. The default is 300 with valid values between 1 and 5000.

- **innodb_purge_threads:** The number of purge threads to use in parallel. A higher parallelism can be useful if the data changes span many tables. On the other hand, if all changes are concentrated on few tables, a low value is preferred. Changing the number of purge threads requires a restart of MySQL. The default is 4 with valid values between 1 and 32.

- **innodb_max_purge_lag:** When the history list length is longer than the value of innodb_max_purge_lag, a delay is added to operations changing data to reduce the rate the history list is growing at the expense of higher statement latencies. The default value is 0 which means that a delay will never be added. Valid values are 0–4294967295.

- **innodb_max_purge_lag_delay:** The maximum delay that can be added to DML queries when the history list length is larger than innodb_max_purge_lag.

It is usually not necessary to change any of these settings; however, in special circumstances, it can be useful. If the purge threads cannot keep up, you can try to change the number of purge threads based on the number of tables that get modified; the more tables that are modified, the more purge threads are useful. When you change the number of purge threads, it is important to monitor the effect starting with a baseline before the change, so you can see whether the change makes an improvement.

The maximum purge lag options can be used to slow down DML statements modifying data. It is mostly useful when writes are limited to specific connections and delays do not cause additional write threads to be created in order to maintain the same throughput.

How do you monitor how old the transactions are, how much memory is used for locks, and how long the history list is? You can use the Information Schema, the InnoDB monitor, and the Performance Schema to get this information.

INNODB_TRX

The INNODB_TRX table in the Information Schema is the most dedicated source of information about InnoDB transactions. It includes information such as when the transaction started, how many rows have been modified, and how many locks are held. The INNODB_TRX table is also used by the sys.innodb_lock_waits view to provide some information about the transactions involved in lock wait issues. Table 21-1 summarizes the columns in the table.

Table 21-1. *The columns in the* `information_schema.INNODB_TRX` *table*

Column/Data Type	Description
trx_id varchar(18)	The transaction id. This can be useful when referring to the transaction or comparing with the output of the InnoDB monitor. Otherwise, the id should be treated purely internal and not be given any significance. The id is only assigned to transactions that have modified data or locked rows; a transaction that only has executed read-only SELECT statements will have a dummy id like 421124985258256 which will change if the transaction starts to modify or lock records.
trx_state varchar(13)	The state of the transaction. This can be one of RUNNING, LOCK WAIT, ROLLING BACK, and COMMITTING.
trx_started datetime	When the transaction was started using the system time zone.
trx_requested_ lock_id varchar(105)	When the trx_state is LOCK WAIT, this column shows the id of the lock that the transaction is waiting for.
trx_wait_started datetime	When the trx_state is LOCK WAIT, this column shows when the lock wait started using the system time zone.
trx_weight bigint unsigned	A measure of how much work has been done by the transaction in terms of rows modified and locks held. This is the weight that is used to determine which transaction is rolled back in case of a deadlock. The higher the weight, the more work has been done.
trx_mysql_ thread_id bigint unsigned	The connection id (the same as the PROCESSLIST_ID column in the Performance Schema threads table) of the connection executing the transaction.
trx_query varchar(1024)	The query currently executed by the transaction. If the transaction is idle, the query is NULL.

(continued)

Table 21-1. (*continued*)

Column/Data Type	Description
trx_operation_ state varchar(64)	The current operation performed by the transaction. This may be NULL even when a query is executing.
trx_tables_ in_use bigint unsigned	The number of tables the transaction has used.
trx_tables_ locked bigint unsigned	The number of tables the transaction holds row locks in.
trx_lock_structs bigint unsigned	The number of lock structures created by the transaction.
trx_lock_memory_ bytes bigint unsigned	The amount of memory in bytes used by the locks held by the transaction.
trx_rows_locked bigint unsigned	The number of record locks held by the transaction. While called row locks, it also includes index locks.
trx_rows_ modified bigint unsigned	The number of rows modified by the transaction.
trx_concurrency_ tickets bigint unsigned	When innodb_thread_concurrency is not 0, a transaction is assigned innodb_concurrency_tickets tickets that it can use before it must allow another transaction to perform work. One ticket corresponds to accessing one row. This column shows how many tickets are left.
trx_isolation_ level varchar(16)	The transaction isolation level used for the transaction.

(*continued*)

Table 21-1. (*continued*)

Column/Data Type	Description
trx_unique_ checks int	Whether the unique_checks variable is enabled for the connection.
trx_foreign_key_ checks int	Whether the foreign_key_checks variable is enabled for the connection.
trx_last_ foreign_ key_error varchar(256)	The error message of the last (if any) foreign key error encountered by the transaction.
trx_adaptive_ hash_latched int	Whether the transaction has locked a part of the adaptive hash index. There is a total of innodb_adaptive_hash_index_parts parts. This column is effectively a Boolean value.
trx_adaptive_ hash_timeout bigint unsigned	Whether to keep the lock on the adaptive hash index across multiple queries. If there is only one part for the adaptive hash index and there is no contention, then the timeout counts down, and the lock is released when the timeout reaches 0. When there is contention or there are multiple parts, the lock is always released after each query, and the timeout value is 0.
trx_is_read_only int	Whether the transaction is a read-only transaction. A transaction can be read-only either by declaring it explicitly or for single-statement transactions with autocommit enabled where InnoDB can detect that the query will only read data.
trx_autocommit_ non_locking int	When the transaction is a single-statement non-locking SELECT and the autocommit option is enabled, this column is set to 1. When both this column and trx_is_read_only are 1, InnoDB can optimize the transaction to reduce the overhead.

The information available from the INNODB_TRX table makes it possible to determine which transactions have the greatest impact. Listing 21-1 shows an example of the information returned for two transactions.

Listing 21-1. Example output of the INNODB_TRX table

```
mysql> SELECT *
          FROM information_schema.INNODB_TRX\G
*************************** 1. row ***************************
                    trx_id: 5897
                 trx_state: RUNNING
               trx_started: 2019-07-06 11:11:12
     trx_requested_lock_id: NULL
           trx_wait_started: NULL
                trx_weight: 4552416
        trx_mysql_thread_id: 10
                 trx_query: UPDATE db1.t1 SET val1 = 4
      trx_operation_state: updating or deleting
         trx_tables_in_use: 1
         trx_tables_locked: 1
          trx_lock_structs: 7919
     trx_lock_memory_bytes: 1417424
            trx_rows_locked: 4552415
          trx_rows_modified: 4544497
    trx_concurrency_tickets: 0
        trx_isolation_level: REPEATABLE READ
          trx_unique_checks: 1
     trx_foreign_key_checks: 1
  trx_last_foreign_key_error: NULL
  trx_adaptive_hash_latched: 0
  trx_adaptive_hash_timeout: 0
          trx_is_read_only: 0
  trx_autocommit_non_locking: 0
```

```
*************************** 2. row ***************************
                  trx_id: 421624759431440
               trx_state: RUNNING
             trx_started: 2019-07-06 11:46:55
   trx_requested_lock_id: NULL
         trx_wait_started: NULL
               trx_weight: 0
      trx_mysql_thread_id: 8
                trx_query: SELECT COUNT(*) FROM db1.t1
      trx_operation_state: counting records
        trx_tables_in_use: 1
        trx_tables_locked: 0
         trx_lock_structs: 0
    trx_lock_memory_bytes: 1136
          trx_rows_locked: 0
        trx_rows_modified: 0
   trx_concurrency_tickets: 0
       trx_isolation_level: REPEATABLE READ
        trx_unique_checks: 1
    trx_foreign_key_checks: 1
trx_last_foreign_key_error: NULL
 trx_adaptive_hash_latched: 0
 trx_adaptive_hash_timeout: 0
           trx_is_read_only: 1
trx_autocommit_non_locking: 1
2 rows in set (0.0023 sec)
```

The first row shows an example of a transaction that modifies data. At the time the information is retrieved, 4,544,497 rows have been modified, and there are a little more record locks. You can also see that the transaction is still actively executing a query (an UPDATE statement).

The second row is an example of a SELECT statement executed with autocommit enabled. Since auto-committing is enabled, there can only be one statement in the transaction (an explicit START TRANSACTION disables auto-committing). The trx_query column shows it is a SELECT COUNT(*) query without any lock clauses, so it is a read-only statement. This means that InnoDB can skip some things such as preparing to hold lock and undo information for the transaction which reduces the overhead of the transaction. The `trx_autocommit_non_locking` column is set to 1 to reflect that.

Which transactions you should be worried about depends on the expected workload on your system. If you have an OLAP workload, it is expected that there will be relatively long-running SELECT queries. For a pure OLTP workload, any transaction running for more than a few seconds and modifying more than a handful of rows may be a sign of problems. For example, to find transactions that are older than one minute, you can use the following query:

```
SELECT *
  FROM information_schema.INNODB_TRX
 WHERE trx_started < NOW() - INTERVAL 1 MINUTE;
```

Related to the INNODB_TRX table is the transaction list in the InnoDB monitor.

InnoDB Monitor

The InnoDB monitor is a kind of Swiss army knife of InnoDB information and also includes information about transactions. The TRANSACTIONS section in the output from the InnoDB monitor is dedicated to transactional information. This information does not only include a list of transactions but also the history list length. Listing 21-2 shows an excerpt of the InnoDB monitor with example of the transaction section taken just after the previous output from the INNODB_TRX table.

Listing 21-2. Transaction information from the InnoDB monitor

```
mysql> SHOW ENGINE INNODB STATUS\G
*************************** 1. row ***************************
  Type: InnoDB
  Name:
Status:
=====================================
2019-07-06 11:46:58 0x7f7728f69700 INNODB MONITOR OUTPUT
=====================================
```

```
Per second averages calculated from the last 6 seconds
...
------------
TRANSACTIONS
------------
Trx id counter 5898
Purge done for trx's n:o < 5894 undo n:o < 0 state: running but idle
History list length 3
LIST OF TRANSACTIONS FOR EACH SESSION:
---TRANSACTION 421624759429712, not started
0 lock struct(s), heap size 1136, 0 row lock(s)
---TRANSACTION 421624759428848, not started
0 lock struct(s), heap size 1136, 0 row lock(s)
---TRANSACTION 5897, ACTIVE 2146 sec updating or deleting
mysql tables in use 1, locked 1
7923 lock struct(s), heap size 1417424, 4554508 row lock(s), undo log
entries 4546586
MySQL thread id 10, OS thread handle 140149617817344, query id 25 localhost
127.0.0.1 root updating
UPDATE db1.t1 SET val1 = 4
```

The top of the TRANSACTIONS section shows the current value of the transaction id counter followed by information of what has been purged from the undo logs. It shows that the undo logs for transaction ids less than 5894 have been purged. The further this purge is behind, the larger the history list length (in the third line of the section) is. Reading the history list length from the InnoDB monitor output is the traditional way to get the length of the history list. In the next section, it will be shown how to get the value in a better way when used for monitoring purposes.

The rest of the section is a list of transactions. Notice that while the output is generated with the same two active transactions as were found in INNODB_TRX, the transaction list only includes one active transaction (the one for the UPDATE statement). In MySQL 5.7 and later, read-only non-locking transactions are not included in the InnoDB monitor transaction list. For this reason, it is better to use the INNODB_TRX table, if you need to include all active transactions.

As mentioned, there is an alternative way to get the history list length. You need to use the InnoDB metrics for this.

INNODB_METRICS and sys.metrics

The InnoDB monitor report is useful for a database administrator to get an overview of what is going on in InnoDB, but for monitoring it is not as useful as it requires parsing to get out the data in a way monitoring can use it. You saw earlier in the chapter how the information about the transactions can be obtained from the information_schema. INNODB_TRX table, but how about metrics such as the history list length?

The InnoDB metric system includes several metrics that show information about the transactions in the information_schema.INNODB_METRICS view. These metrics are all located in the transaction subsystem. Listing 21-3 shows a list of the transaction metrics, whether they are enabled by default, and a brief comment explaining what the metric measures.

Listing 21-3. InnoDB metrics related to transactions

```
mysql> SELECT NAME, COUNT, STATUS, COMMENT
         FROM information_schema.INNODB_METRICS
         WHERE SUBSYSTEM = 'transaction'\G
*************************** 1. row ***************************
   NAME: trx_rw_commits
  COUNT: 0
 STATUS: disabled
COMMENT: Number of read-write transactions  committed
*************************** 2. row ***************************
   NAME: trx_ro_commits
  COUNT: 0
 STATUS: disabled
COMMENT: Number of read-only transactions committed
*************************** 3. row ***************************
   NAME: trx_nl_ro_commits
  COUNT: 0
 STATUS: disabled
COMMENT: Number of non-locking auto-commit read-only transactions committed
*************************** 4. row ***************************
   NAME: trx_commits_insert_update
  COUNT: 0
 STATUS: disabled
COMMENT: Number of transactions committed with inserts and updates
```

```
*************************** 5. row ***************************
   NAME: trx_rollbacks
  COUNT: 0
 STATUS: disabled
COMMENT: Number of transactions rolled back
*************************** 6. row ***************************
   NAME: trx_rollbacks_savepoint
  COUNT: 0
 STATUS: disabled
COMMENT: Number of transactions rolled back to savepoint
*************************** 7. row ***************************
   NAME: trx_rollback_active
  COUNT: 0
 STATUS: disabled
COMMENT: Number of resurrected active transactions rolled back
*************************** 8. row ***************************
   NAME: trx_active_transactions
  COUNT: 0
 STATUS: disabled
COMMENT: Number of active transactions
*************************** 9. row ***************************
   NAME: trx_on_log_no_waits
  COUNT: 0
 STATUS: disabled
COMMENT: Waits for redo during transaction commits
*************************** 10. row ***************************
   NAME: trx_on_log_waits
  COUNT: 0
 STATUS: disabled
COMMENT: Waits for redo during transaction commits
*************************** 11. row ***************************
   NAME: trx_on_log_wait_loops
  COUNT: 0
 STATUS: disabled
COMMENT: Waits for redo during transaction commits
```

```
*************************** 12. row ***************************
   NAME: trx_rseg_history_len
  COUNT: 45
 STATUS: enabled
COMMENT: Length of the TRX_RSEG_HISTORY list
*************************** 13. row ***************************
   NAME: trx_undo_slots_used
  COUNT: 0
 STATUS: disabled
COMMENT: Number of undo slots used
*************************** 14. row ***************************
   NAME: trx_undo_slots_cached
  COUNT: 0
 STATUS: disabled
COMMENT: Number of undo slots cached
*************************** 15. row ***************************
   NAME: trx_rseg_current_size
  COUNT: 0
 STATUS: disabled
COMMENT: Current rollback segment size in pages
15 rows in set (0.0403 sec)
```

The most important of these metrics is trx_rseg_history_len which is the history list length. This is also the only metric that is enabled by default. The metrics related to commits and rollbacks can be used to determine how many read-write, read-only, and non-locking read-only transactions you have and how often they are committed and rolled back. Many rollbacks suggest there is a problem. If you suspect the redo log is a bottleneck, the trx_on_log_% metrics can be used to get a measure of how much transactions are waiting for the redo log during transaction commits.

Tip   You enable InnoDB metrics with the innodb_monitor_enable option and disable them with innodb_monitor_disable. This can be done dynamically.

An alternative and convenient way to query the InnoDB metrics is to use the sys. metrics view which also includes the global status variables. Listing 21-4 shows an example of using the sys.metrics view to obtain the current values and whether the metric is enabled.

Listing 21-4. Using the sys.metrics view to get the transaction metrics

```
mysql> SELECT Variable_name AS Name,
              Variable_value AS Value,
              Enabled
         FROM sys.metrics
        WHERE Type = 'InnoDB Metrics - transaction';
+---------------------------+-------+---------+
| Name                      | Value | Enabled |
+---------------------------+-------+---------+
| trx_active_transactions   | 0     | NO      |
| trx_commits_insert_update | 0     | NO      |
| trx_nl_ro_commits         | 0     | NO      |
| trx_on_log_no_waits       | 0     | NO      |
| trx_on_log_wait_loops     | 0     | NO      |
| trx_on_log_waits          | 0     | NO      |
| trx_ro_commits            | 0     | NO      |
| trx_rollback_active       | 0     | NO      |
| trx_rollbacks             | 0     | NO      |
| trx_rollbacks_savepoint   | 0     | NO      |
| trx_rseg_current_size     | 0     | NO      |
| trx_rseg_history_len      | 45    | YES     |
| trx_rw_commits            | 0     | NO      |
| trx_undo_slots_cached     | 0     | NO      |
| trx_undo_slots_used       | 0     | NO      |
+---------------------------+-------+---------+
15 rows in set (0.0152 sec)
```

This shows that the history list length is 45 which is a good low value, so there is next to none overhead from the undo logs. The rest of the metrics are disabled.

Thus far, the discussion of transaction information has been about aggregate statistics either for all transactions or individual transactions. If you want to go deeper into what work a transaction has done, you need to use the Performance Schema.

Performance Schema Transactions

The Performance Schema supports transaction monitoring in MySQL 5.7 and later, and it is enabled by default in MySQL 8. There are not many transaction details other than related to XA transactions and savepoints available in the Performance Schema that cannot be obtained from the INNODB_TRX table in the Information Schema. However, the Performance Schema transaction events have the advantage that you can combine them with other event types such as statements to get information about the work done by a transaction. This is the main focus of this section. Additionally, the Performance Schema offers summary tables with aggregate statistics.

Transaction Events and Their Statements

The main tables for investigating transactions in the Performance Schema are the transaction event tables. There are three tables for recording current or recent transactions: events_transactions_current, events_transactions_history, and events_transactions_history_long. They have the columns as summarized in Table 21-2.

Table 21-2. *The columns of the non-summary transaction event tables*

Column/Data Type	Description
THREAD_ID bigint unsigned	The Performance Schema thread id of the connection executing the transaction.
EVENT_ID bigint unsigned	The event id for the event. You can use the event id to order the events for a thread or as a foreign key together with the thread id between event tables.
END_EVENT_ID bigint unsigned	The event id when the transaction completed. If the event id is NULL, the transaction is still ongoing.

(continued)

Table 21-2 (*continued*)

Column/Data Type	Description
EVENT_NAME varchar(128)	The transaction event name. Currently this column always has the value `transaction`.
STATE enum	The state of the transaction. Possible values are `ACTIVE`, `COMMITTED`, and `ROLLED BACK`.
TRX_ID bigint unsigned	This is currently unused and will always be NULL.
GTID varchar(64)	The GTID for the transaction. When the GTID is automatically determined (the usual), `AUTOMATIC` is returned. This is the same as the `gtid_next` variable for the connection executing the transaction.
XID_FORMAT_ID int	For XA transactions, the format id.
XID_GTRID varchar(130)	For XA transactions, the gtrid value.
XID_BQUAL varchar(130)	For XA transactions, the bqual value.
XA_STATE varchar(64)	For a XA transaction, the state of the transaction. This can be `ACTIVE`, `IDLE`, `PREPARED`, `ROLLED BACK`, or `COMMITTED`.
SOURCE varchar(64)	The source code file and line number where the event was recorded.
TIMER_START bigint unsigned	The time in picoseconds when the event started.
TIMER_END bigint unsigned	The time in picoseconds when the event completed. If the transaction has not completed yet, the value corresponds to the current time.

(*continued*)

Table 21-2 (*continued*)

Column/Data Type	Description
TIMER_WAIT bigint unsigned	The total time in picoseconds it took to execute the event. If the event has not completed yet, the value corresponds to how long the transaction has been active.
ACCESS_MODE enum	Whether the transaction is in read-only (READ ONLY) or in read-write (READ WRITE) mode.
ISOLATION_LEVEL varchar(64)	The transaction isolation level for the transaction.
AUTOCOMMIT enum	Whether the transaction is auto-committing based on the autocommit option and whether an explicit transaction has been started. Possible values are NO and YES.
NUMBER_OF_SAVEPOINTS bigint unsigned	The number of savepoints created in the transaction.
NUMBER_OF_ROLLBACK_TO_SAVEPOINT bigint unsigned	The number of times the transaction has rolled back to a savepoint.
NUMBER_OF_RELEASE_SAVEPOINT bigint unsigned	The number of times the transaction has released a savepoint.
OBJECT_INSTANCE_BEGIN bigint unsigned	This field is currently unused and always set to NULL.
NESTING_EVENT_ID bigint unsigned	The event id of the event that triggered the transaction.
NESTING_EVENT_TYPE enum	The event type of the event that triggered the transaction.

If you are working with XA transactions, the transaction event tables are great when you need to recover a transaction as the format id, gtrid, and bqual values are directly available from the tables, unlike for the XA RECOVER statement where you have to parse the output. In the same way, if you work with savepoints, you can get statistics on the savepoint usage. Otherwise, the information is very similar to what is available in the INNODB_TRX table.

For an example of using the events_transactions_current table, you can start two transactions. The first transaction is a normal transaction that updates the population of several cities:

```
START TRANSACTION;
UPDATE world.city SET Population = 5200000 WHERE ID = 130;
UPDATE world.city SET Population = 4900000 WHERE ID = 131;
UPDATE world.city SET Population = 2400000 WHERE ID = 132;
UPDATE world.city SET Population = 2000000 WHERE ID = 133;
```

The second transaction is an XA transaction:

```
XA START 'abc', 'def', 1;
UPDATE world.city SET Population = 900000 WHERE ID = 3805;
```

Listing 21-5 shows an example output of the events_transactions_current table listing the currently active transactions.

Listing 21-5. Using the events_transactions_current table

```
mysql> SELECT *
         FROM performance_schema.events_transactions_current
       WHERE STATE = 'ACTIVE'\G
*************************** 1. row ***************************
           THREAD_ID: 54
            EVENT_ID: 39
        END_EVENT_ID: NULL
          EVENT_NAME: transaction
               STATE: ACTIVE
              TRX_ID: NULL
                GTID: AUTOMATIC
       XID_FORMAT_ID: NULL
           XID_GTRID: NULL
           XID_BQUAL: NULL
            XA_STATE: NULL
              SOURCE: transaction.cc:219
         TIMER_START: 488967975158077184
           TIMER_END: 489085567376530432
          TIMER_WAIT: 117592218453248
```

```
               ACCESS_MODE: READ WRITE
            ISOLATION_LEVEL: REPEATABLE READ
                 AUTOCOMMIT: NO
         NUMBER_OF_SAVEPOINTS: 0
NUMBER_OF_ROLLBACK_TO_SAVEPOINT: 0
    NUMBER_OF_RELEASE_SAVEPOINT: 0
          OBJECT_INSTANCE_BEGIN: NULL
            NESTING_EVENT_ID: 38
          NESTING_EVENT_TYPE: STATEMENT
*************************** 2. row ***************************
                  THREAD_ID: 57
                   EVENT_ID: 10
               END_EVENT_ID: NULL
                 EVENT_NAME: transaction
                      STATE: ACTIVE
                     TRX_ID: NULL
                       GTID: AUTOMATIC
               XID_FORMAT_ID: 1
                  XID_GTRID: abc
                  XID_BQUAL: def
                   XA_STATE: ACTIVE
                     SOURCE: transaction.cc:219
                TIMER_START: 488977176010232448
                  TIMER_END: 489085567391481984
                 TIMER_WAIT: 108391381249536
               ACCESS_MODE: READ WRITE
            ISOLATION_LEVEL: REPEATABLE READ
                 AUTOCOMMIT: NO
         NUMBER_OF_SAVEPOINTS: 0
NUMBER_OF_ROLLBACK_TO_SAVEPOINT: 0
    NUMBER_OF_RELEASE_SAVEPOINT: 0
          OBJECT_INSTANCE_BEGIN: NULL
            NESTING_EVENT_ID: 9
          NESTING_EVENT_TYPE: STATEMENT
2 rows in set (0.0007 sec)
```

The transaction in row 1 is a regular transaction, whereas the transaction in row 2 is an XA transaction. Both transactions were started by a statement which can be seen from the nesting event type. If you want to find the statement that triggered the transaction, you can use that to query the events_statements_history table like

```
mysql> SELECT SQL_TEXT
         FROM performance_schema.events_statements_history
        WHERE THREAD_ID = 54
          AND EVENT_ID = 38\G
*************************** 1. row ***************************
SQL_TEXT: START TRANSACTION
1 row in set (0.0009 sec)
```

This shows that the transaction executed by THREAD_ID = 54 was started using a START TRANSACTION statement. Since the events_statements_history table only includes the last ten statements for the connection, it is not guaranteed that the statement that started the transaction is still in the history table. If you are looking at a single-statement transaction or the first statement (while it is still executing) when autocommit is disabled, you will need to query the events_statements_current table instead.

The relationship between transactions and statements also goes the other way. Given a transaction event id and the thread id, you can query the last ten statements executed for that transaction using the statement event history and current tables. Listing 21-6 shows an example for THREAD_ID = 54 and transaction EVENT_ID = 39 (from row 1 of Listing 21-5) where both the statement starting the transaction and subsequent statements are included.

Listing 21-6. Finding the last ten statements executed in a transaction

```
mysql> SET @thread_id = 54,
           @event_id = 39,
           @nesting_event_id = 38;

mysql> SELECT EVENT_ID, SQL_TEXT,
              FORMAT_PICO_TIME(TIMER_WAIT) AS Latency,
              IF(END_EVENT_ID IS NULL, 'YES', 'NO') AS IsCurrent
```

```
         FROM ((SELECT EVENT_ID, END_EVENT_ID,
                       TIMER_WAIT,
                       SQL_TEXT, NESTING_EVENT_ID,
                       NESTING_EVENT_TYPE
                  FROM performance_schema.events_statements_current
                 WHERE THREAD_ID = @thread_id
               ) UNION (
                SELECT EVENT_ID, END_EVENT_ID,
                       TIMER_WAIT,
                       SQL_TEXT, NESTING_EVENT_ID,
                       NESTING_EVENT_TYPE
                  FROM performance_schema.events_statements_history
                 WHERE THREAD_ID = @thread_id
               )
             ) events
        WHERE (NESTING_EVENT_TYPE = 'TRANSACTION'
               AND NESTING_EVENT_ID = @event_id)
              OR EVENT_ID = @nesting_event_id
        ORDER BY EVENT_ID DESC\G
*************************** 1. row ***************************
  EVENT_ID: 43
  SQL_TEXT: UPDATE city SET Population = 2000000 WHERE ID = 133
   Latency: 291.01 us
 IsCurrent: NO
*************************** 2. row ***************************
  EVENT_ID: 42
  SQL_TEXT: UPDATE city SET Population = 2400000 WHERE ID = 132
   Latency: 367.59 us
 IsCurrent: NO
*************************** 3. row ***************************
  EVENT_ID: 41
  SQL_TEXT: UPDATE city SET Population = 4900000 WHERE ID = 131
   Latency: 361.03 us
 IsCurrent: NO
```

```
*************************** 4. row ***************************
 EVENT_ID: 40
 SQL_TEXT: UPDATE city SET Population = 5200000 WHERE ID = 130
  Latency: 399.32 us
IsCurrent: NO
*************************** 5. row ***************************
 EVENT_ID: 38
 SQL_TEXT: START TRANSACTION
  Latency: 97.37 us
IsCurrent: NO
9 rows in set (0.0012 sec)
```

The subquery (a derived table) finds all statement events for the thread from the events_statements_current and events_statements_history tables. It is necessary to include the current events as there may be an ongoing statement for the transaction. The statements are filtered by either being a child of the transaction or the nesting event for the transaction (EVENT_ID = 38). This will include all statements beginning with the one starting the transactions. There will be up to 11 statements if there is an ongoing statement and otherwise up to ten.

The END_EVENT_ID is used to determine whether the statement is currently executing, and the statements are ordered in reverse using the EVENT_ID, so the most recent statement is in row 1 and the oldest (the START TRANSACTION statement) in row 5.

This type of query is not only useful to investigate transactions still executing queries. It can also be very useful when you encounter an idle transaction and you want to know what the transaction did before it was left abandoned. Another related way to look for active transactions is to use the sys.session view which uses the events_ transactions_current table to include information about the transactional state for each connection. Listing 21-7 shows an example of querying for active transactions excluding the row for the connection executing the query.

Listing 21-7. Finding active transactions with sys.session

```
mysql> SELECT *
         FROM sys.session
        WHERE trx_state = 'ACTIVE'
              AND conn_id <> CONNECTION_ID()\G
```

```
*************************** 1. row ***************************
                 thd_id: 54
                conn_id: 16
                   user: mysqlx/worker
                     db: world
                command: Sleep
                  state: NULL
                   time: 690
      current_statement: UPDATE world.city SET Population = 2000000 WHERE ID = 133
      statement_latency: NULL
               progress: NULL
           lock_latency: 281.76 ms
          rows_examined: 341
              rows_sent: 341
          rows_affected: 0
             tmp_tables: 0
        tmp_disk_tables: 0
              full_scan: NO
         last_statement: UPDATE world.city SET Population = 2000000 WHERE ID = 133
 last_statement_latency: 391.80 ms
         current_memory: 2.35 MiB
              last_wait: NULL
      last_wait_latency: NULL
                 source: NULL
            trx_latency: 11.49 m
              trx_state: ACTIVE
         trx_autocommit: NO
                    pid: 23376
           program_name: mysqlsh
*************************** 2. row ***************************
                 thd_id: 57
                conn_id: 18
                   user: mysqlx/worker
                     db: world
                command: Sleep
                  state: NULL
```

```
                 time: 598
    current_statement: UPDATE world.city SET Population = 900000 WHERE ID = 3805
    statement_latency: NULL
             progress: NULL
         lock_latency: 104.00 us
        rows_examined: 1
            rows_sent: 0
        rows_affected: 1
           tmp_tables: 0
      tmp_disk_tables: 0
            full_scan: NO
       last_statement: UPDATE world.city SET Population = 900000 WHERE ID = 3805
last_statement_latency: 40.21 ms
       current_memory: 344.76 KiB
            last_wait: NULL
     last_wait_latency: NULL
               source: NULL
          trx_latency: 11.32 m
            trx_state: ACTIVE
       trx_autocommit: NO
                  pid: 25836
         program_name: mysqlsh
2 rows in set (0.0781 sec)
```

This shows that the transaction in the first row has been active for more than 11 minutes and it is 690 seconds (11.5 minutes) since the last query was executed (your values will differ). The last_statement can be used to determine the last query executed by the connection. This is an example of an abandoned transaction which prevents InnoDB from purging its undo logs. The most common causes of abandoned transactions are a database administrator starting a transaction interactively and getting distracted or that autocommit is disabled and it is not realized a transaction was started.

Caution   If you disable autocommit, be careful always to commit or roll back at the end of the work. Some connectors disable autocommit by default, so be aware that your application may not be using the server default.

You can roll the transactions back to avoid changing any data. For the first (normal) transaction:

```
mysql> ROLLBACK;
Query OK, 0 rows affected (0.0841 sec)
```

And for the XA transaction:

```
mysql> XA END 'abc', 'def', 1;
Query OK, 0 rows affected (0.0003 sec)

mysql> XA ROLLBACK 'abc', 'def', 1;
Query OK, 0 rows affected (0.0759 sec)
```

Another way the Performance Schema tables are useful for analyzing transactions is to use the summary tables to obtain aggregate data.

Transaction Summary Tables

In the same way as there are statement summary tables that can be used to get reports of the statements that are executed, there are transaction summary tables that can be used to analyze the use of transactions. While they are not quite as useful as their statement counterparts, they do offer insight into which connections and accounts that use transactions in different ways.

There are five transaction summary tables grouping the data globally or by account, host, thread, or user. All of the summaries also group by the event name, but as there currently only is one transaction event (transaction), it is a nil operation. The tables are

- **events_transactions_summary_global_by_event_name:** All transactions aggregated. There is only a single row in this table.

- **events_transactions_summary_by_account_by_event_name:** The transactions grouped by username and hostname.

- **events_transactions_summary_by_host_by_event_name:** The transactions grouped by hostname of the account.

- **events_transactions_summary_by_thread_by_event_name:** The transactions grouped by thread. Only currently existing threads are included.

- **events_transactions_summary_by_user_by_event_name:** The events grouped by the username part of the account.

Each table includes the columns that the transaction statistics are grouped by and three groups of columns: total, for read-write transactions, and for read-only transactions. For each of these three groups of columns, there is the total number of transactions as well as the total, minimum, average, and maximum latencies. Listing 21-8 shows an example of the data from the events_transactions_summary_global_by_ event_name table.

Listing 21-8. The events_transactions_summary_global_by_event_name table

```
mysql> SELECT *
        FROM performance_schema.events_transactions_summary_global_by_
        event_name\G
*************************** 1. row ***************************
          EVENT_NAME: transaction
          COUNT_STAR: 1274
      SUM_TIMER_WAIT: 13091950115512576
      MIN_TIMER_WAIT: 7293440
      AVG_TIMER_WAIT: 10276255661056
      MAX_TIMER_WAIT: 11777025727144832
    COUNT_READ_WRITE: 1273
SUM_TIMER_READ_WRITE: 13078918924805888
MIN_TIMER_READ_WRITE: 7293440
AVG_TIMER_READ_WRITE: 10274091697408
MAX_TIMER_READ_WRITE: 11777025727144832
     COUNT_READ_ONLY: 1
 SUM_TIMER_READ_ONLY: 13031190706688
 MIN_TIMER_READ_ONLY: 13031190706688
 AVG_TIMER_READ_ONLY: 13031190706688
 MAX_TIMER_READ_ONLY: 13031190706688
1 row in set (0.0005 sec)
```

It may surprise you when you study the output how many transactions there are, particularly read-write transactions. Remember that when querying an InnoDB table, everything is a transaction even if you have not explicitly specified one. So even a simple SELECT statement querying a single row counts as a transaction. Regarding the distribution between read-write and read-only transactions, then the Performance Schema only considers a transaction read-only if you explicitly started it as such:

```
START TRANSACTION READ ONLY;
```

When InnoDB determines that an auto-committing single-statement transaction can be treated as a read-only transaction, that is still counting toward the read-write statistics in the Performance Schema.

Summary

Transactions are an important concept in databases. They help ensure that you can apply changes to several rows as a unit and that you can choose whether to apply the changes or roll them back.

This chapter started out discussing why it is important to be aware of how transactions are being used. While they as such can be considered a container for changes, locks are held until the transaction is committed or rolled back, and they can block the undo logs from being purged. Both locks and large undo logs can affect the performance of queries even if they are not executed in one of the transactions causing the high number of locks or large number of undo logs. Locks use memory, which is taken from the buffer pool, so there is less memory available for caching data and indexes. A large amount of undo logs as measured by the history list length means that more row versions must be considered when InnoDB executes statements.

The rest of the chapter went into how you can analyze ongoing and past transactions. The INNODB_TRX table in the Information Schema is the best source of information for ongoing transactions. The InnoDB monitor and the InnoDB metrics supplement this. For XA transactions and transactions using savepoints or when you need to investigate which statements are executed as part of the transaction, you need to use the Performance Schema transaction event tables. The Performance Schema also includes summary tables that you can use to get more information on who spends time on read-write and read-only transactions.

Locks have played a significant role in the discussion of transactions. The next chapter will show how you can analyze a series of lock issues.

CHAPTER 22

Diagnosing Lock Contention

In Chapter 18, you were introduced to the world of locks in MySQL. If you have not read Chapter 18 yet, you are strongly encouraged to do so now as this chapter is closely related. You may even want to refresh your memory if it is a while since you read it. Lock issues is one of the common causes of performance issues, and the impact can be severe. In the worst cases, queries can fail, and connections pile up so no new connections can be made. Therefore, it is important to know how to investigate lock issues and remediate the problems.

This chapter will discuss four categories of lock issues:

- Flush locks

- Metadata and schema locks

- Record-level locks including gap locks

- Deadlocks

Each category of locks uses different techniques to determine what is the cause of the lock contention. When you read the examples, you should have in mind that similar techniques can be used to investigate lock issues that do not 100% match the example.

For each lock category, the discussion has been split into six parts:

- **The Symptoms:** This describes how you identify that you are encountering this kind of lock issue.

- **The Cause:** The underlying reason you encounter this kind of lock issues. This is related to the general discussion of the locks in Chapter 18.

J. W. Krogh, *MySQL 8 Query Performance Tuning*, https://doi.org/10.1007/978-1-4842-5584-1_22

- **The Setup:** This includes the steps to set up the lock issue, if you want to try it yourself. As lock contention requires multiple connections, the prompt, for example, `Connection 1>`, is used to tell which connection should be used for which statements. If you want to follow the investigation with no more information than you would have in a real-world case, you can skip this section and go back and review it after getting through the investigation.

- **The Investigation:** The details of the investigation. This draws on the "Monitoring Locks" section of Chapter 18.

- **The Solution:** How you resolve the immediate lock problem, so you minimize the outage caused by it.

- **The Prevention:** A discussion of how to reduce the chance of encountering the issue. This is closely related to the section "Reduce Locking Issues" in Chapter 18.

Enough talk, the first lock category that will be discussed is flush locks.

Flush Locks

One of the common lock issues encountered in MySQL is the flush lock. When this issue happens, users will typically complain that queries are not returning, and monitoring may show that queries are piling up and eventually MySQL will run out of connections. Issues around the flush lock can also sometimes be one of the most difficult lock issues to investigate.

The Symptoms

The main symptom of a flush lock issue is that the database comes to a grinding halt where all new queries using some or all tables end up waiting for the flush lock. The telltale signs to look for include the following:

- The query state of new queries is "Waiting for table flush." This may occur for all new queries or only for queries accessing specific tables.

- More and more connections are created.

- Eventually, new connections fail as MySQL is out of connection. The error received for new connections is ER_CON_COUNT_ERROR: "ERROR 1040 (HY000): Too many connections" when using the classic MySQL protocol (by default port 3306) or "MySQL Error 5011: Could not open session" when using the X Protocol (by default port 33060).

- There is at least one query that has been running later than the oldest request for a flush lock.

- There may be a FLUSH TABLES statement in the process list, but this is not always the case.

- When the FLUSH TABLES statement has waited for lock_wait_ timeout, an ER_LOCK_WAIT_TIMEOUT error occurs: ERROR: 1205: Lock wait timeout exceeded; try restarting transaction. Since the default value for lock_wait_timeout is 365 days, this is only likely to occur if the timeout has been reduced.

- If you connect with the mysql command-line client with a default schema set, the connection may seem to hang before you get to the prompt. The same can happen if you change the default schema with a connection open.

Tip   The issue that the mysql command-line client is blocking does not occur if you start the client with the -A option which disables collecting the auto-completion information. A better solution is to use MySQL Shell that fetches the auto-completion information in a way that does not block due to the flush lock.

If you see these symptoms, it is time to understand what is causing the lock issue.

The Cause

When a connection requests a table to be flushed, it requires all references to the table to be closed which means no active queries can be using the table. So, when a flush request arrives, it must wait for all queries using the tables that are to be flushed to finish. Note that unless you explicitly specify which tables to flush, it is just the query and not the entire transaction that must finish. Obviously, the case where all tables are flushed, for example, due to FLUSH TABLES WITH READ LOCK, is the most severe as it means all active queries must finish before the flush statement can proceed.

When the wait for the flush lock becomes a problem, it means that there are one or more queries preventing the FLUSH TABLES statement from obtaining the flush lock. Since the FLUSH TABLES statement requires an exclusive lock, it in turn stops subsequent queries from acquiring the shared lock they need.

This issue is often seen in connection with backups where the backup process needs to flush all tables and get a read lock in order to create a consistent backup.

A special case can occur when the FLUSH TABLES statement has timed out or has been killed, but the subsequent queries are not proceeding. When that happens, it is because the low-level table definition cache (TDC) version lock is not released. This is a case that can cause confusion as it is not obvious why the subsequent queries are still waiting for the table flush.

The Setup

The lock situation that will be investigated involves three connections (not including the connection used for the investigation). The first connection executes a slow query, the second flushes all tables with a read lock, and the last connection executes a quick query. The statements are

```
Connection 1> SELECT city.*, SLEEP(180) FROM world.city WHERE ID = 130;

Connection 2> FLUSH TABLES WITH READ LOCK;

Connection 3> SELECT * FROM world.city WHERE ID = 3805;
```

The use of SLEEP(180) in the first query means you have three minutes (180 seconds) to execute the two other queries and perform the investigation. If you want longer time, you can increase the duration of the sleep. You are now ready to start the investigation.

The Investigation

The investigation of flush locks requires you to look at the list of queries running on the instance. Unlike other lock contentions, there are no Performance Schema tables or InnoDB monitor report that can be used to query for the blocking query directly.

Listing 22-1 shows an example of the output using the sys.session view. Similar results will be produced using the alternative ways to get a list of queries. The thread and connection ids as well as the statement latencies will vary.

Listing 22-1. Investigating flush lock contention using `sys.session`

```
mysql> SELECT thd_id, conn_id, state,
              current_statement,
              statement_latency
         FROM sys.session
        WHERE command = 'Query'\G
*************************** 1. row ***************************
           thd_id: 30
          conn_id: 9
            state: User sleep
current_statement: SELECT city.*, SLEEP(180) FROM city WHERE ID = 130
statement_latency: 49.97 s
*************************** 2. row ***************************
           thd_id: 53
          conn_id: 14
            state: Waiting for table flush
current_statement: FLUSH TABLES WITH READ LOCK
statement_latency: 44.48 s
*************************** 3. row ***************************
           thd_id: 51
          conn_id: 13
            state: Waiting for table flush
current_statement: SELECT * FROM world.city WHERE ID = 3805
statement_latency: 41.93 s
*************************** 4. row ***************************
           thd_id: 29
          conn_id: 8
            state: NULL
current_statement: SELECT thd_id, conn_id, state, ... ession WHERE command
= 'Query'
statement_latency: 56.13 ms
4 rows in set (0.0644 sec)
```

There are four queries in the output. The sys.session and sys.processlist views by default sort the queries according to the execution time in descending order. This makes it easy to investigate issues like contention around the flush lock where the query time is the primary thing to consider when looking for the cause.

You start out looking for the FLUSH TABLES statement (the case where there is no FLUSH TABLES statement will be discussed shortly). In this case, that is thd_id = 53 (the second row). Notice that the state of the FLUSH statement is "Waiting for table flush." You then look for queries that have been running for a longer time. In this case, there is only one query: the one with thd_id = 30. This is the query that blocks the FLUSH TABLES WITH READ LOCK from completing. In general, there may be more than one query.

The two remaining queries are a query being blocked by the FLUSH TABLES WITH READ LOCK and the query to obtain the output. Together, the three first queries form a typical example of a long-running query blocking a FLUSH TABLES statement which in turn blocks other queries.

You can also get the process list from MySQL Workbench and in some cases also from your monitoring solution. Figure 22-1 shows how to get the process list from MySQL Workbench.

Root @ Local
Client Connections

| **Threads Connected:** 11 | **Threads Running:** 5 | **Threads Created:** 8 | **Threads Cached:** 1 |
| **Total Connections:** 680 | **Connection Limit:** 151 | **Aborted Clients:** 0 | **Aborted Connections:** 0 |

Id	User	Host	DB	Command	Time ▼	State	Threa...
6	None	None	None	Daemon	3989	Suspending	44
9	root	localhost	world	Query	52	User sleep	30
14	root	localhost	world	Query	47	Waiting for t..	53
13	root	localhost	world	Query	44	Waiting for t..	51
405	root	localhost	None	Query	0	Sending data	444

Figure 22-1. *Showing the client connections in MySQL Workbench*

To get the process list report in MySQL Workbench, choose the *Client Connections* item under *Management* in the navigator pane to the left of the screen. You cannot choose which columns to include, and to make the text readable, only part of the report is included in the screenshot. The *Id* column corresponds to conn_id in the sys.session output, and *Thread* (the rightmost column) corresponds to thd_id. The full screenshot is included in this book's GitHub repository as figure_22_1_workbench_flush_lock.png.

Figure 22-2 shows an example of the *Processes* report from MySQL Enterprise Monitor (MEM) for the same lock situation.

Processes

MySQL Processes				

Query			Refreshed: Jun 15, 2019 10:54:53 am	Reload

Show 10 ▾ entries   Page 1 of 6 (1-51 of 51 items)   K < 1 2 3 4 5 6 > Я

Connection ID	Command	State	Statement Latency ▾	Current Statement
9	Query	User sleep	56.51 s	SELECT *, SLEEP(60) FRC
14	Query	Waiting for table flush	51.02 s	FLUSH TABLES WITH READ
13	Query	Waiting for table flush	48.48 s	SELECT * FROM world.cit
140	Query	Creating sort index	45.01 ms	SELECT `thd_id` as `thr

Figure 22-2. *The Processes report in MEM for a flush lock investigation*

The *Processes* report is found under the *Metrics* menu item for individual instances. You can choose which column you want to include in the output. An example of the report with more details can be found in the book's GitHub repository as figure_22_2_mem_flush_lock.png.

An advantage of reports like the ones in MySQL Workbench and MySQL Enterprise Monitor is that they use existing connections to create the report. In cases where the lock issue causes all connections to be used, then it can be invaluable to be able to get the list of queries using a monitoring solution.

As mentioned, the FLUSH TABLES statement may not always be present in the list of queries. The reason there still are queries waiting for flush tables is the low-level TDC version lock. The principles of the investigation remain the same, but it can seem confusing. Listing 22-2 shows such an example using the same setup but killing the connection executing the flush statement before the investigation (Ctrl+C can be used in MySQL Shell in the connection executing FLUSH TABLES WITH READ LOCK).

Listing 22-2. Flush lock contention without a FLUSH TABLES statement

```
mysql> SELECT thd_id, conn_id, state,
              current_statement,
              statement_latency
         FROM sys.session
        WHERE command = 'Query'\G
*************************** 1. row ***************************
           thd_id: 30
          conn_id: 9
            state: User sleep
current_statement: SELECT *, SLEEP(180) FROM city WHERE ID = 130
statement_latency: 24.16 s
*************************** 2. row ***************************
           thd_id: 51
          conn_id: 13
            state: Waiting for table flush
current_statement: SELECT * FROM world.city WHERE ID = 3805
statement_latency: 20.20 s
*************************** 3. row ***************************
           thd_id: 29
          conn_id: 8
            state: NULL
current_statement: SELECT thd_id, conn_id, state, ... ession WHERE command
= 'Query'
statement_latency: 47.02 ms
3 rows in set (0.0548 sec)
```

This situation is identical to the previous except the FLUSH TABLES statement is gone. In this case, find the query that has been waiting the longest with the state "Waiting for table flush." Queries that have been running longer than this query has been waiting are the ones preventing the TDC version lock being released. In this case, that means thd_id = 30 is the blocking query.

Once you have identified the issue and the principal queries involved, you need to decide what to do about the issue.

The Solution

There are two levels of solving the issue. First of all, you need to resolve the immediate problem of queries not executing. Second, you need to work at avoiding the issue in the future. This subsection will discuss the immediate solution, and the next will consider how to reduce the chance of the issue occurring.

To resolve the immediate issue, you have the option of waiting for the queries to complete or starting to kill queries. If you can redirect the application to use another instance while the flush lock contention is ongoing, you may be able to let the situation resolve itself by letting the long-running queries complete. If there are data changing queries among those running or waiting, you do in that case need to consider whether it will leave the system in a consistent state after all queries have completed. One option may be to continue in read-only mode with the read queries executed on a different instance.

If you decide to kill queries, you can try to kill the FLUSH TABLES statement. If that works, it is the simplest solution. However, as discussed that will not always help, and in that case the only solution is to kill the queries that were preventing the FLUSH TABLES statement from completing. If the long-running queries look like runaway queries and the application/client that executed them anyway is not waiting for them any longer, you may want to kill them without trying to kill the FLUSH TABLES statement first.

One important consideration when looking to kill a query is how much data has been changed. For a pure SELECT query (not involving stored routines), that is always nothing, and from the perspective of work done, it is safe to kill it. For INSERT, UPDATE, DELETE, and similar queries, however, the changed data must be rolled back if the query is killed. It will usually take longer to roll back changes than making them in the first place, so be prepared to wait a long time for the rollback if there are many changes. You can use the information_schema.INNODB_TRX table to estimate the amount of work done by looking at the trx_rows_modified column. If there is a lot of work to roll back, it is usually better to let the query complete.

Caution   When a DML statement is killed, the work it has done must be rolled back. The rollback will usually take longer than creating the change, sometimes much longer. You need to factor that in, if you consider killing a long-running DML statement.

Of course, optimally you prevent the issue from happening at all.

The Prevention

The flush lock contention happens because of the combination of a long-running query and a FLUSH TABLES statement. So, to prevent the issue, you need to look at what you can do to avoid these two conditions to be present at the same time.

Finding, analyzing, and handling long-running queries are discussed in other chapters throughout the book. One option of particular interest is to set a timeout for the query. This is supported for SELECT statements using the max_execution_time system variable and the MAX_EXECUTION_TIME(N) optimizer hint and is a great way to protect against runaway queries. Some connectors also have support for timing out queries.

Tip   To avoid long-running SELECT queries, you can configure the max_execution_time option or set the MAX_EXECUTION_TIME(N) optimizer hint. This will make the SELECT statement time out after the specified period and help prevent issues like flush lock waits.

Some long-running queries cannot be prevented. It may be a reporting job, building a cache table, or another task that must access a lot of data. In that case, the best you can do is to try to avoid them running while it is also necessary to flush the tables. One option is to schedule the long-running queries to run at different times than when it is necessary to flush tables. Another option is to have the long-running queries run on a different instance than the jobs that require flushing tables.

A common task that requires flushing the tables is taking a backup. In MySQL 8, you can avoid that issue by using the backup and log locks. For example, MySQL Enterprise Backup (MEB) does this in version 8.0.16 and later, so InnoDB tables are never flushed. Alternatively, you can perform the backup at a period with low usage, so the potential for conflicts is lower, or you can even do the backup while the system is in read-only mode and avoid the FLUSH TABLES WITH READ LOCK altogether.

Another lock type that often causes confusion is the metadata lock.

Metadata and Schema Locks

In MySQL 5.7 and earlier, metadata locks were often a source of confusion. The problem is that it is not obvious who holds the metadata lock. In MySQL 5.7, instrumentation of the metadata locks was added to the Performance Schema, and in MySQL 8.0 it is enabled by default. With the instrumentation enabled, it becomes easy to determine who is blocking the connection trying to obtain the lock.

The Symptoms

The symptoms of metadata lock contention are similar to those of flush lock contention. In a typical situation, there will be a long-running query or transaction, a DDL statement waiting for the metadata lock, and possible queries pilling up. The symptoms to look out for are as follows:

- A DDL statement and possible other queries are stuck in the state "Waiting for table metadata lock."

- Queries may be pilling up. The queries that are waiting all use the same table. (There may potentially be more than one group of queries waiting if there are DDL statements for multiple tables waiting for the metadata lock.)

- When the DDL statement has waited for lock_wait_timeout, an ER_LOCK_WAIT_TIMEOUT error occurs: ERROR: 1205: Lock wait timeout exceeded; try restarting transaction. Since the default value for lock_wait_timeout is 365 days, this is only likely to occur if the timeout has been reduced.

- There is a long-running query or a long-running transaction. In the latter case, the transaction may be idle or executing a query that does not use the table that the DDL statement acts on.

What makes the situation potentially confusing is the last point: there may not be any long-running queries that are the clear candidates for causing the lock issue. So what is the cause of the metadata lock contention?

The Cause

Remember that the metadata locks exist to protect the schema definition (as well as being used with explicit locks). The schema protection will exist for as long as a transaction is active, so when a transaction queries a table, the metadata lock will last until the end of the transaction. Therefore, you may not see any long-running queries. In fact, the transaction holding the metadata lock may not be doing anything at all.

In short, the metadata lock exists as one or more connections may rely on the schema for a given table not changing, or they have explicitly locked the table either using the LOCK TABLES or FLUSH TABLES WITH READ LOCK statement.

The Setup

The example investigation of metadata locks uses three connections like in the previous example. The first connection is in the middle of a transaction, the second connection tries to add an index to the table used by the transaction, and the third connection attempts to execute a query against the same table. The queries are

```
Connection 1> START TRANSACTION;
Query OK, 0 rows affected (0.0003 sec)

Connection 1> SELECT * FROM world.city WHERE ID = 3805\G
*************************** 1. row ***************************
        ID: 3805
      Name: San Francisco
CountryCode: USA
  District: California
Population: 776733
1 row in set (0.0006 sec)

Connection 1> SELECT Code, Name FROM world.country WHERE Code = 'USA'\G
*************************** 1. row ***************************
Code: USA
Name: United States
1 row in set (0.0020 sec)

Connection 2> ALTER TABLE world.city ADD INDEX (Name);

Connection 3> SELECT * FROM world.city WHERE ID = 130;
```

At this point, you can start the investigation. The situation will not resolve itself (unless you have a low value for lock_wait_timeout or you are prepared to wait a year), so you have all the time you want. When you want to resolve the block, you can start terminating the ALTER TABLE statement in Connection 2 to avoid modifying the world. city table. Then commit or roll back the transaction in Connection 1.

The Investigation

If you have the wait/lock/metadata/sql/mdl Performance Schema instrument enabled (the default in MySQL 8), it is straightforward to investigate metadata lock issues. You can use the metadata_locks table in the Performance Schema to list the granted and pending locks. However, a simpler way to get a summary of the lock situation is to use the schema_table_lock_waits view in the sys schema.

As an example, consider the metadata lock wait issue that can be seen in Listing 22-3 where three connections are involved. The WHERE clause has been chosen to just include the rows of interest for this investigation.

Listing 22-3. A metadata lock wait issue

```
mysql> SELECT thd_id, conn_id, state,
              current_statement,
              statement_latency
         FROM sys.session
        WHERE command = 'Query' OR trx_state = 'ACTIVE'\G
*************************** 1. row ***************************
           thd_id: 30
          conn_id: 9
            state: NULL
current_statement: SELECT Code, Name FROM world.country WHERE Code = 'USA'
statement_latency: NULL
*************************** 2. row ***************************
           thd_id: 7130
          conn_id: 7090
            state: Waiting for table metadata lock
current_statement: ALTER TABLE world.city ADD INDEX (Name)
statement_latency: 19.92 m
```

```
*************************** 3. row ***************************
          thd_id: 51
         conn_id: 13
           state: Waiting for table metadata lock
current_statement: SELECT * FROM world.city WHERE ID = 130
statement_latency: 19.78 m
*************************** 4. row ***************************
          thd_id: 107
         conn_id: 46
           state: NULL
current_statement: SELECT thd_id, conn_id, state, ... Query' OR trx_state =
'ACTIVE'
statement_latency: 56.77 ms
3 rows in set (0.0629 sec)
```

Two connections are waiting for a metadata lock (on the world.city table). There
is a third connection included (conn_id = 9) which is idle which can be seen from the
NULL for the statement latency (in some versions earlier than 8.0.18, you may also see
that the current statement is NULL). In this case, the list of queries is limited to those with
an active query or an active transaction, but usually you will start out with a full process
list. However, to make it easy to focus on the important parts, the output is filtered.

Once you know there is a metadata lock issue, you can use the sys.schema_table_
lock_waits view to get information about the lock contention. Listing 22-4 shows an
example of the output corresponding to the just discussed process list.

Listing 22-4. Finding metadata lock contention

```
mysql> SELECT *
          FROM sys.schema_table_lock_waits\G
*************************** 1. row ***************************
            object_schema: world
              object_name: city
         waiting_thread_id: 7130
                waiting_pid: 7090
            waiting_account: root@localhost
          waiting_lock_type: EXCLUSIVE
      waiting_lock_duration: TRANSACTION
```

```
          waiting_query: ALTER TABLE world.city ADD INDEX (Name)
     waiting_query_secs: 1219
waiting_query_rows_affected: 0
waiting_query_rows_examined: 0
      blocking_thread_id: 7130
           blocking_pid: 7090
       blocking_account: root@localhost
     blocking_lock_type: SHARED_UPGRADABLE
 blocking_lock_duration: TRANSACTION
 sql_kill_blocking_query: KILL QUERY 7090
sql_kill_blocking_connection: KILL 7090
*************************** 2. row ***************************
          object_schema: world
            object_name: city
       waiting_thread_id: 51
            waiting_pid: 13
        waiting_account: root@localhost
      waiting_lock_type: SHARED_READ
  waiting_lock_duration: TRANSACTION
          waiting_query: SELECT * FROM world.city WHERE ID = 130
     waiting_query_secs: 1210
waiting_query_rows_affected: 0
waiting_query_rows_examined: 0
      blocking_thread_id: 7130
           blocking_pid: 7090
       blocking_account: root@localhost
     blocking_lock_type: SHARED_UPGRADABLE
 blocking_lock_duration: TRANSACTION
 sql_kill_blocking_query: KILL QUERY 7090
sql_kill_blocking_connection: KILL 7090
*************************** 3. row ***************************
          object_schema: world
            object_name: city
       waiting_thread_id: 7130
            waiting_pid: 7090
```

```
              waiting_account: root@localhost
            waiting_lock_type: EXCLUSIVE
        waiting_lock_duration: TRANSACTION
                waiting_query: ALTER TABLE world.city ADD INDEX (Name)
           waiting_query_secs: 1219
   waiting_query_rows_affected: 0
   waiting_query_rows_examined: 0
            blocking_thread_id: 30
                  blocking_pid: 9
             blocking_account: root@localhost
            blocking_lock_type: SHARED_READ
        blocking_lock_duration: TRANSACTION
        sql_kill_blocking_query: KILL QUERY 9
   sql_kill_blocking_connection: KILL 9
*************************** 4. row ***************************
                 object_schema: world
                   object_name: city
             waiting_thread_id: 51
                   waiting_pid: 13
              waiting_account: root@localhost
            waiting_lock_type: SHARED_READ
        waiting_lock_duration: TRANSACTION
                waiting_query: SELECT * FROM world.city WHERE ID = 130
           waiting_query_secs: 1210
   waiting_query_rows_affected: 0
   waiting_query_rows_examined: 0
            blocking_thread_id: 30
                  blocking_pid: 9
             blocking_account: root@localhost
            blocking_lock_type: SHARED_READ
        blocking_lock_duration: TRANSACTION
        sql_kill_blocking_query: KILL QUERY 9
   sql_kill_blocking_connection: KILL 9
4 rows in set (0.0024 sec)
```

The output shows that there are four cases of queries waiting and blocking. This may be surprising, but it happens because there are several locks involved and there is a chain of waits. Each row is a pair of a waiting and blocking connection. The output uses "pid" for the process list id which is the same as the connection id used in earlier outputs. The information includes what the lock is on, details about the waiting connection, details about the blocking connection, and two queries that can be used to kill the blocking query or connection.

The first row shows process list id 7090 waiting on itself. That sounds like a deadlock, but it is not. The reason is that the ALTER TABLE first took a shared lock that can be upgraded and then tried to get the exclusive lock which is waiting. Because there is no explicit information on which existing lock is actually blocking the new lock, this information ends up being included.

The second row shows that the SELECT statement is waiting for process list id 7090 which is the ALTER TABLE. This is the reason that connections can start to pile up as the DDL statement requires an exclusive lock, so it will block requests for shared locks.

The third and fourth rows are where the underlying issue for the lock contention is revealed. Process list id 9 is blocking for both of the other connections which shows that this is the main culprit that is blocking the DDL statement. So, when you are investigating an issue like this, look for a connection waiting for an exclusive metadata lock that is blocked by another connection. If there is a large number of rows in the output, you can also look for the connection causing the most blocks and use that as a starting point. Listing 22-5 shows an example of how you can do this.

Listing 22-5. Looking for the connection causing the metadata lock block

```
mysql> SELECT *
         FROM sys.schema_table_lock_waits
        WHERE waiting_lock_type = 'EXCLUSIVE'
          AND waiting_pid <> blocking_pid\G
*************************** 1. row ***************************
         object_schema: world
           object_name: city
      waiting_thread_id: 7130
            waiting_pid: 7090
        waiting_account: root@localhost
      waiting_lock_type: EXCLUSIVE
```

```
          waiting_lock_duration: TRANSACTION
                   waiting_query: ALTER TABLE world.city ADD INDEX (Name)
              waiting_query_secs: 4906
      waiting_query_rows_affected: 0
      waiting_query_rows_examined: 0
              blocking_thread_id: 30
                    blocking_pid: 9
                blocking_account: root@localhost
              blocking_lock_type: SHARED_READ
          blocking_lock_duration: TRANSACTION
          sql_kill_blocking_query: KILL QUERY 9
    sql_kill_blocking_connection: KILL 9
1 row in set (0.0056 sec)

mysql> SELECT blocking_pid, COUNT(*)
         FROM sys.schema_table_lock_waits
        WHERE waiting_pid <> blocking_pid
        GROUP BY blocking_pid
        ORDER BY COUNT(*) DESC;
+--------------+----------+
| blocking_pid | COUNT(*) |
+--------------+----------+
|            9 |        2 |
|         7090 |        1 |
+--------------+----------+
2 rows in set (0.0028 sec)
```

The first query looks for a wait for an exclusive metadata lock where the blocking process list id is not itself. In this case, that immediately gives the main block contention. The second query determines the number of blocking queries triggered by each process list id. It may not be as simple as shown in this example, but using queries as shown here will help narrow down where the lock contention is.

Once you have determined where the lock contention originates, you need to determine what the transaction is doing. In this case, the root of the lock contention is Connection 9. Going back to the process list output, you can see that it is not doing anything in this case:

```
*************************** 1. row ***************************
            thd_id: 30
           conn_id: 9
             state: NULL
 current_statement: SELECT Code, Name FROM world.country WHERE Code = 'USA'
 statement_latency: NULL
```

What did this connection do to take the metadata lock? The fact that there is no current statement that involves the world.city table suggests the connection has an active transaction open. In this case, the transaction is idle (as seen by statement_latency = NULL), but it could also be that there was a query executing that is unrelated to the metadata lock on the world.city table. In either case, you need to determine what the transaction was doing prior to the current state. You can use the Performance Schema and Information Schema for this. Listing 22-6 shows an example of investigating the status and recent history of a transaction.

Listing 22-6. Investigating a transaction

```
mysql> SELECT *
         FROM information_schema.INNODB_TRX
        WHERE trx_mysql_thread_id = 9\G
*************************** 1. row ***************************
                    trx_id: 283529000061592
                 trx_state: RUNNING
               trx_started: 2019-06-15 13:22:29
     trx_requested_lock_id: NULL
           trx_wait_started: NULL
                trx_weight: 0
        trx_mysql_thread_id: 9
                 trx_query: NULL
       trx_operation_state: NULL
         trx_tables_in_use: 0
          trx_tables_locked: 0
           trx_lock_structs: 0
     trx_lock_memory_bytes: 1136
            trx_rows_locked: 0
          trx_rows_modified: 0
```

```
  trx_concurrency_tickets: 0
      trx_isolation_level: REPEATABLE READ
        trx_unique_checks: 1
   trx_foreign_key_checks: 1
trx_last_foreign_key_error: NULL
 trx_adaptive_hash_latched: 0
 trx_adaptive_hash_timeout: 0
          trx_is_read_only: 0
trx_autocommit_non_locking: 0
1 row in set (0.0006 sec)

mysql> SELECT *
         FROM performance_schema.events_transactions_current
        WHERE THREAD_ID = 30\G
*************************** 1. row ***************************
                    THREAD_ID: 30
                     EVENT_ID: 113
                 END_EVENT_ID: NULL
                   EVENT_NAME: transaction
                        STATE: ACTIVE
                       TRX_ID: NULL
                         GTID: AUTOMATIC
                XID_FORMAT_ID: NULL
                    XID_GTRID: NULL
                    XID_BQUAL: NULL
                     XA_STATE: NULL
                       SOURCE: transaction.cc:219
                  TIMER_START: 12849615560172160
                    TIMER_END: 18599491723543808
                   TIMER_WAIT: 5749876163371648
                  ACCESS_MODE: READ WRITE
              ISOLATION_LEVEL: REPEATABLE READ
                   AUTOCOMMIT: NO
          NUMBER_OF_SAVEPOINTS: 0
NUMBER_OF_ROLLBACK_TO_SAVEPOINT: 0
    NUMBER_OF_RELEASE_SAVEPOINT: 0
```

```
        OBJECT_INSTANCE_BEGIN: NULL
            NESTING_EVENT_ID: 112
          NESTING_EVENT_TYPE: STATEMENT
1 row in set (0.0008 sec)

mysql> SELECT EVENT_ID, CURRENT_SCHEMA,
              SQL_TEXT
         FROM performance_schema.events_statements_history
        WHERE THREAD_ID = 30
          AND NESTING_EVENT_ID = 113
          AND NESTING_EVENT_TYPE = 'TRANSACTION'\G
*************************** 1. row ***************************
    EVENT_ID: 114
CURRENT_SCHEMA: world
    SQL_TEXT: SELECT * FROM world.city WHERE ID = 3805
*************************** 2. row ***************************
    EVENT_ID: 115
CURRENT_SCHEMA: world
    SQL_TEXT: SELECT * FROM world.country WHERE Code = 'USA'
2 rows in set (0.0036 sec)

mysql> SELECT ATTR_NAME, ATTR_VALUE
         FROM performance_schema.session_connect_attrs
        WHERE PROCESSLIST_ID = 9;
+-----------------+------------+
| ATTR_NAME       | ATTR_VALUE |
+-----------------+------------+
| _pid            | 23256      |
| program_name    | mysqlsh    |
| _client_name    | libmysql   |
| _thread         | 20164      |
| _client_version | 8.0.18     |
| _os             | Win64      |
| _platform       | x86_64     |
+-----------------+------------+
7 rows in set (0.0006 sec)
```

The first query uses the INNODB_TRX table in the Information Schema. It, for example, shows when the transaction was started, so you can determine how long it has been active. The trx_rows_modified column is also useful to know how much data has been changed by the transaction in case it is decided to roll back the transaction. Note that what InnoDB calls the MySQL thread id (the trx_mysql_thread_id column) is actually the connection id.

The second query uses the events_transactions_current table from the Performance Schema to get more transaction information. You can use the TIMER_WAIT column to determine the age of the transaction. The value is in picoseconds, so it can be easier to understand what the value is by using the FORMAT_PICO_TIME() function:

```
mysql> SELECT FORMAT_PICO_TIME(5749876163371648) AS Age;
+---------+
| Age     |
+---------+
| 1.60 h  |
+---------+
1 row in set (0.0003 sec)
```

If you are using MySQL 8.0.15 or earlier, use the sys.format_time() function instead.

The third query uses the events_statements_history table to find the previous queries executed in the transaction. The NESTING_EVENT_ID column is set to the value of the EVENT_ID from the output of the events_transactions_current table, and the NESTING_EVENT_TYPE column is set to match a transaction. This ensures that only events that are children of the ongoing transaction are returned. The result is ordered by the EVENT_ID (of the statement) to get the statements in the order they were executed. By default, the events_statements_history table will include at most the ten latest queries for the connection.

In this example, the investigation shows that the transaction has executed two queries: one selecting from the world.city table and one selecting from the world.country table. It is the first of these queries causing the metadata lock contention.

The fourth query uses the session_connect_attrs table to find the attributes submitted by the connection. Not all clients and connectors submit attributes, or they may be disabled, so this information is not always available. When the attributes are available, they can be useful to find out where the offending transaction is executed from. In this example, you can see the connection is from MySQL Shell (mysqlsh). This can be useful if you want to commit an idle transaction.

The Solution

For a metadata lock contention, you essentially have two options to resolve the issue: make the blocking transaction complete or kill the DDL statement. To complete the blocking transaction, you will need to either commit it or roll it back. If you kill the connection, it triggers a rollback of the transaction, so you need to take into consideration how much work will need to be rolled back. In order to commit the transaction, you must find where the connection is executed and commit it that way. You cannot commit a transaction owned by a different connection.

Killing the DDL statement will allow the other queries to proceed, but it does not solve the issue in the long term if the lock is held by an abandoned but still active transaction. For cases where there is an abandoned transaction holding the metadata lock, it can however be an option to kill both the DDL statement and the connection with the abandoned transaction. That way you avoid the DDL statement to continue blocking subsequent queries while the transaction rolls back. Then when the rollback has completed, you can retry the DDL statement.

The Prevention

The key to avoiding metadata lock contention is to avoid a long-running transaction at the same time as you need to execute DDL statements for the tables used by the transaction. You can, for example, execute DDL statements at times when you know there are no long-running transactions. You can also set the lock_wait_timeout option to a low value which makes the DDL statement abandon after lock_wait_timeout seconds. While that does not avoid the lock problem, it mitigates the issue by avoiding the DDL statement stopping other queries from executing. You can then find the root cause without the stress of having a large part of the application not working.

You can also aim at reducing how long transactions are active. One option is to split a large transaction into several smaller transactions, if it is not required that all operations are performed as an atomic unit. You should also make sure that the transaction is not kept open for unnecessarily long time by making sure you are not doing interactive work, file I/O, transferring data to the end user, and so on while the transaction is active.

One common cause of a long-running transaction is that the application or client does not commit or roll back the transaction at all. This is particularly likely to happen with the autocommit option disabled. When autocommit is disabled, any query – even a plain read-only SELECT statement – will start a new transaction when there is not already an active transaction. This means that an innocent-looking query may start a transaction, and if the developer is not aware that `autocommit` is disabled, then the developer may not think about explicitly ending the transaction. The `autocommit` setting is enabled by default in MySQL Server, but some connectors disable it by default.

That concludes the discussion about investigating metadata locks. The next level of locks to look at are the record locks.

Record-Level Locks

Record lock contention is the most frequently encountered, but usually also the least intrusive as the default lock wait timeout is just 50 seconds, so there is not the same potential for queries pilling up. That said, there are cases – as will be shown – where record locks can cause MySQL to come to a grinding halt. This section will look into investigating InnoDB record lock issues in general and in more detail lock wait timeout issues. Investigating the specifics of deadlocks is deferred until the next section.

The Symptoms

The symptoms of InnoDB record lock contention are often very subtle and not easily recognizable. In severe cases, you will get a lock wait timeout or a deadlock error, but in many cases, there may be no direct symptoms. Rather the symptom is that queries are slower than normal. This may range from being a fraction of a second slower to being many seconds slower.

For cases where there is a lock wait timeout, you will see an `ER_LOCK_WAIT_TIMEOUT` error like the one in the following example:

```
ERROR: 1205: Lock wait timeout exceeded; try restarting transaction
```

When the queries are slower than they would be without lock contention, the most likely way to detect the issue is through monitoring, either using something similar to the Query Analyzer in MySQL Enterprise Monitor or detecting lock contention using the `sys.innodb_lock_waits` view. Figure 22-3 shows an example of a query in the Query Analyzer. The `sys` schema view will be used when discussing the investigation of record lock contention. The figure is also available in full size in this book's GitHub repository as `figure_22_3_quan.png`.

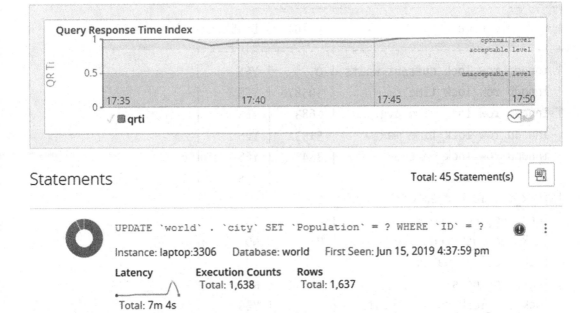

Figure 22-3. *Example of a lock contention detected in the Query Analyzer*

In the figure, notice how the latency graph for the query increases toward the end of the period and then suddenly drops again. There is also a red icon to the right of the normalized query – that icon means the query has returned errors. In this case the error is a lock wait timeout, but that cannot be seen from the figure. The donut-shaped chart to the left of the normalized query also shows a red area indicating the Query Response Time index for the query at times is considered poor. The large graph at the top shows a small dip showing there were enough issues in the instance to cause a general degradation of the performance of the instance.

There are also several instance-level metrics that show how much locking is occurring for the instance. These can be very useful to monitor the general lock contention over time. Listing 22-7 shows the available metrics using the sys.metrics view.

Listing 22-7. InnoDB lock metrics

```
mysql> SELECT Variable_name,
              Variable_value AS Value,
              Enabled
         FROM sys.metrics
        WHERE Variable_name LIKE 'innodb_row_lock%'
           OR Type = 'InnoDB Metrics - lock';
```

```
+-------------------------------+---------+----------+
| Variable_name                 | Value   | Enabled  |
+-------------------------------+---------+----------+
| innodb_row_lock_current_waits | 0       | YES      |
| innodb_row_lock_time          | 595876  | YES      |
| innodb_row_lock_time_avg      | 1683    | YES      |
| innodb_row_lock_time_max      | 51531   | YES      |
| innodb_row_lock_waits         | 354     | YES      |
| lock_deadlocks                | 0       | YES      |
| lock_rec_lock_created         | 0       | NO       |
| lock_rec_lock_removed         | 0       | NO       |
| lock_rec_lock_requests        | 0       | NO       |
| lock_rec_lock_waits           | 0       | NO       |
| lock_rec_locks                | 0       | NO       |
| lock_row_lock_current_waits   | 0       | YES      |
| lock_table_lock_created       | 0       | NO       |
| lock_table_lock_removed       | 0       | NO       |
| lock_table_lock_waits         | 0       | NO       |
| lock_table_locks              | 0       | NO       |
| lock_timeouts                 | 1       | YES      |
+-------------------------------+---------+----------+
17 rows in set (0.0203 sec)
```

For this discussion, the innodb_row_lock_% and lock_timeouts metrics are the most interesting. The three time variables are in milliseconds. It can be seen there has been a single lock wait timeout which on its own is not necessarily a cause for concern. You can also see there have been 354 cases when a lock could not be granted immediately (innodb_row_lock_waits) and there have been waits up to more than 51 seconds (innodb_row_lock_time_max). When the general level of lock contention increases, you will see these metrics increase as well.

Even better than monitoring the metrics manually, ensure your monitoring solution record the metrics and can plot them over time in timeseries graphs. Figure 22-4 shows an example of the metrics plotted for the same incident that was found in Figure 22-3.

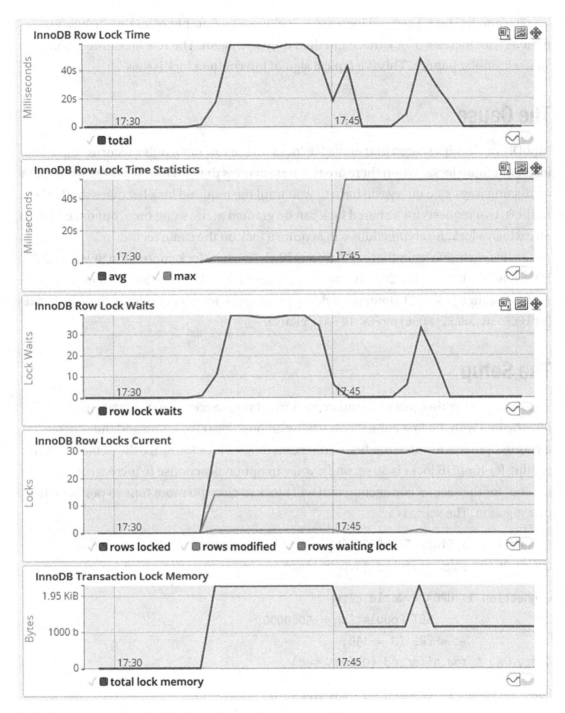

Figure 22-4. *Timeseries graphs for InnoDB row lock metrics*

The graphs show a general increase in locking. The number of lock waits has two periods with increased lock waits and then drops off again. The row lock time graph shows a similar pattern. This is a typical sign of intermittent lock issues.

The Cause

InnoDB works with shared and exclusive locks on the row data, index records, gaps, and insert intention locks. When there are two transactions that attempt to access the data in conflicting ways, one query will have to wait until the required lock becomes available. In short, two requests for a shared lock can be granted at the same time, but once there is an exclusive lock, no connections can acquire a lock on the same record.

As it is exclusive locks that are the most likely to cause lock contention, it is usually DML queries that change data that are the cause of InnoDB record lock contention. Another source is SELECT statements doing preemptive locking by adding the FOR SHARE (or LOCK IN SHARE MODE) or FOR UPDATE clause.

The Setup

This example requires just two connections to set up the scenario that is being investigated with the first connection having an ongoing transaction and the second trying to update a row that the first connection holds a lock for. Since the default timeout waiting for InnoDB locks is 50 seconds, you can optionally choose to increase this timeout for the second connection that will block to give you more time to perform the investigation. The setup is

```
Connection 1> START TRANSACTION;
Query OK, 0 rows affected (0.0002 sec)

Connection 1> UPDATE world.city
              SET Population = 5000000
            WHERE ID = 130;
Query OK, 1 row affected (0.0005 sec)

Rows matched: 1  Changed: 1  Warnings: 0

Connection 2> SET SESSION innodb_lock_wait_timeout = 300;
Query OK, 0 rows affected (0.0003 sec)
```

```
Connection 2> START TRANSACTION;
Query OK, 0 rows affected (0.0003 sec)

Connection 2> UPDATE world.city SET Population = Population * 1.10 WHERE
CountryCode = 'AUS';
```

In this example the lock wait timeout for Connection 2 is set to 300 seconds. The START TRANSACTION for Connection 2 is not required but allows you to roll both transactions back when you are done to avoid making changes to the data.

The Investigation

The investigation of record locks is very similar to investigating metadata locks. You can query the data_locks and data_lock_waits tables in the Performance Schema which will show the raw lock data and pending locks, respectively. There is also the sys. innodb_lock_waits view which queries the two tables to find pairs of locks with one being blocked by the other.

Note   The data_locks and data_lock_waits tables are new in MySQL 8. In MySQL 5.7 and earlier, there were two similar tables in the Information Schema named INNODB_LOCKS and INNODB_LOCK_WAITS. An advantage of using the innodb_lock_waits view is that it works the same (but with some extra information in MySQL 8) across the MySQL versions.

In most cases, it is easiest to start the investigation using the innodb_lock_waits view and only dive into the Performance Schema tables as needed. Listing 22-8 shows an example of the output from innodb_lock_waits for a lock wait situation.

Listing 22-8.   Retrieving lock information from the innodb_lock_waits view

```
mysql> SELECT * FROM sys.innodb_lock_waits\G
*************************** 1. row ***************************
            wait_started: 2019-06-15 18:37:42
                wait_age: 00:00:02
           wait_age_secs: 2
            locked_table: `world`.`city`
```

```
        locked_table_schema: world
          locked_table_name: city
     locked_table_partition: NULL
  locked_table_subpartition: NULL
               locked_index: PRIMARY
                locked_type: RECORD
             waiting_trx_id: 3317978
        waiting_trx_started: 2019-06-15 18:37:42
            waiting_trx_age: 00:00:02
     waiting_trx_rows_locked: 2
   waiting_trx_rows_modified: 0
               waiting_pid: 4172
             waiting_query: UPDATE city SET Population = P ... 1.10 WHERE
CountryCode = 'AUS'
           waiting_lock_id: 1999758099664:525:6:131:1999728339632
         waiting_lock_mode: X,REC_NOT_GAP
            blocking_trx_id: 3317977
               blocking_pid: 9
             blocking_query: NULL
          blocking_lock_id: 1999758097920:525:6:131:1999728329336
        blocking_lock_mode: X,REC_NOT_GAP
        blocking_trx_started: 2019-06-15 18:37:40
           blocking_trx_age: 00:00:04
    blocking_trx_rows_locked: 1
  blocking_trx_rows_modified: 1
     sql_kill_blocking_query: KILL QUERY 9
sql_kill_blocking_connection: KILL 9
1 row in set (0.0145 sec)
```

The columns in the output can be divided into five sections based on the prefix of the column name. The groups are

- **wait_:** These columns show some general information around the age of the lock wait.

- **locked_:** These columns show what is locked ranging from the schema to the index as well as the lock type.

- **waiting_:** These columns show details of the transaction that is waiting for the lock to be granted including the query and the lock mode requested.

- **blocking_:** These columns show details of the transaction that is blocking the lock request. Note that in the example, the blocking query is NULL. This means the transaction is idle at the time the output was generated. Even when there is a blocking query listed, the query may not have anything to do with the lock that there is contention for – other than the query is executed by the same transaction that holds the lock.

- **sql_kill_:** These two columns provide the KILL queries that can be used to kill the blocking query or connection.

Note   The column blocking_query is the query currently executed (if any) for the blocking transaction. It does not mean that the query itself is necessarily causing the lock request to block.

The case where the blocking_query column is NULL is a common situation. It means that the blocking transaction is currently not executing a query. This may be because it is between two queries. If this period is an extended period, it suggests the application is doing work that ideally should be done outside the transaction. More commonly, the transaction is not executing a query because it has been forgotten about, either in an interactive session where the human has forgotten to end the transaction or an application flow that does not ensure transactions are committed or rolled back.

The Solution

The solution depends on the extent of the lock waits. If it is a few queries having short lock waits, it may very well be acceptable to just let the affected queries wait for the lock to become available. Remember locks are there to ensure the integrity of the data, so locks are not inherently a problem. Locks are only a problem when they cause a significant impact on the performance or cause queries to fail to an extent where it is not feasible to retry them.

If the lock situation lasts for an extended period – particularly if the blocking transaction has been abandoned – you can consider killing the blocking transaction. As always you need to consider that the rollback may take a significant amount of time if the blocking transaction has performed a large amount of work.

For queries that fail because of a lock wait timeout error, the application should retry them. Remember that by default a lock wait timeout only rolls back the query that was executing when the timeout occurred. The rest of the transaction is left as it were before the query. A failure to handle the timeout may thus leave an unfinished transaction with its own locks that can cause further lock issues. Whether just the query or the whole transaction will be rolled back is controlled by the `innodb_rollback_on_timeout` option.

Caution   It is very important that a lock wait timeout is handled as otherwise it may leave the transaction with locks that are not released. If that happens, other transactions may not be able to acquire the locks they require.

The Prevention

Preventing significant record-level lock contention largely follows the guidelines that were discussed in the section "Reduce Locking Issues" in Chapter 18. To recapitulate the discussion, the way to reduce lock wait contention is largely about reducing the size and duration of transactions, using indexes to reduce the number of records accessed, and possibly switching the transaction isolation level to READ COMMITTED to release locks earlier and reduce the number of gap locks.

Deadlocks

One of the lock issues causing the most concerns for database administrators are deadlocks. This is partly because of the name and partly because they unlike the other lock issues discussed always cause an error. However, there is as such nothing specially worrying about deadlocks compared to other locking issues. On the contrary, that they cause an error means that you know about them sooner and the lock issue resolves itself.

The Symptoms

The symptoms are straightforward. The victim of a deadlock receives an error, and the lock_deadlocks InnoDB metric increments. The error that will be returned to the transaction that InnoDB chooses as the victim is ER_LOCK_DEADLOCK:

```
ERROR: 1213: Deadlock found when trying to get lock; try restarting
transaction
```

The lock_deadlocks metric is very useful to keep an eye on how often deadlocks occur. A convenient way to track the value of lock_deadlocks is to use the sys.metrics view:

```
mysql> SELECT *
         FROM sys.metrics
        WHERE Variable_name = 'lock_deadlocks'\G
*************************** 1. row ***************************
 Variable_name: lock_deadlocks
Variable_value: 42
          Type: InnoDB Metrics - lock
       Enabled: YES
1 row in set (0.0087 sec)
```

You can also check the LATEST DETECTED DEADLOCK section in the output of the InnoDB monitor, for example, by executing SHOW ENGINE INNODB STATUS. This will show when the last deadlock last occurred, and thus you can use that to judge how frequently deadlocks occur. If you have the innodb_print_all_deadlocks option enabled, the error lock will have many outputs of deadlock information. The details of the InnoDB monitor output for deadlocks will be covered in "The Investigation" after the cause of deadlocks and the setup have been discussed.

The Cause

Deadlocks are caused by locks being obtained in different orders for two or more transactions. Each transaction ends up holding a lock that the other transaction needs. This lock may be a record lock, gap lock, predicate lock, or insert intention lock. Figure 22-5 shows an example of a circular dependency that triggers a deadlock.

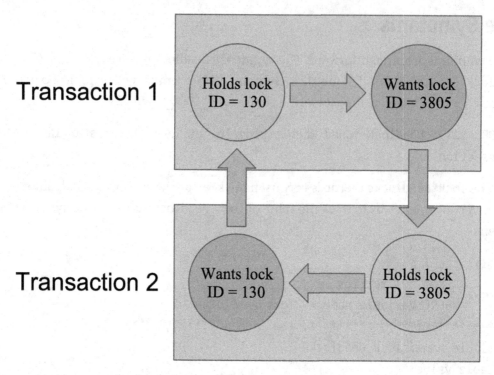

Figure 22-5. *A circular lock dependency triggering a deadlock*

The deadlock shown in the figure is due to two record locks on the primary keys of a table. That is one of the simplest deadlocks that can occur. As shown when investigating a deadlock, the circle can be more complex than this.

The Setup

This example uses two connections as the previous example, but this time both make changes before Connection 1 ends up blocking until Connection 2 rolls back its changes with an error. Connection 1 updates the population of Australia and its cities with 10%, whereas Connection 2 updates the Australian population with that of the city of Darwin and adds the city. The statements are

```
Connection 1> START TRANSACTION;
Query OK, 0 rows affected (0.0001 sec)

Connection 1> UPDATE world.city SET Population = Population * 1.10 WHERE
                                                  CountryCode = 'AUS';
Query OK, 14 rows affected (0.0010 sec)

Rows matched: 14  Changed: 14  Warnings: 0
```

```
Connection 2> START TRANSACTION;
Query OK, 0 rows affected (0.0003 sec)

Connection 2> UPDATE world.country SET Population = Population + 146000
WHERE Code = 'AUS';
Query OK, 1 row affected (0.0317 sec)

Rows matched: 1  Changed: 1  Warnings: 0

-- Blocks
Connection 1> UPDATE world.country SET Population = Population * 1.1 WHERE
Code = 'AUS';

Connection 2> INSERT INTO world.city VALUES (4080, 'Darwin', 'AUS',
'Northern Territory', 146000);
ERROR: 1213: Deadlock found when trying to get lock; try restarting transaction

Connection 2> ROLLBACK;
Query OK, 0 rows affected (0.0003 sec)

Connection 1> ROLLBACK;
Query OK, 0 rows affected (0.3301 sec)
```

The key is that the two transactions both update the city and country tables but in opposite order. The setup completes by explicitly rolling back both transactions to ensure the tables are left without changes.

The Investigation

The main tool to analyze deadlocks is the section with information about the latest detected deadlock in the InnoDB monitor output. If you have the innodb_print_all_deadlocks option enabled (OFF by default), you may also have the deadlock information from the error log; however, the information is the same, so it does not change the analysis.

The deadlock information contains four parts describing the deadlock and the result. The parts are

- When the deadlock occurred.

- Information for the first of the transactions involved in the deadlock.

- Information for the second of the transactions involved in the deadlock.

- Which of the transactions that was rolled back. This information is not included in the error log when `innodb_print_all_deadlocks` is enabled.

The numbering of the two transactions is arbitrary, and the main purpose is to be able to refer to one transaction or the other. The two parts with transaction information are the most important ones. They include how long the transaction was active, some statistics about the size of the transactions in terms of locks taken and undo log entries and similar, the query that was blocking waiting for a lock, and information about the locks involved in the deadlock.

The lock information is not as easy to interpret as when you use the `data_locks` and `data_lock_waits` tables and the `sys.innodb_lock_waits` view. However, it is not too difficult once you have tried to perform the analysis a few times.

Tip   Create some deadlocks on purpose in a test system and study the resulting deadlock information. Then work your way through the information to determine why the deadlock occurred. Since you know the queries, it is easier to interpret the lock data.

For this deadlock investigation, consider the deadlock section from the InnoDB monitor that is shown in Listing 22-9. The listing is rather long and the lines wide, so the information is also available in this book's GitHub repository as `listing_22_9_deadlock.txt`, so you can open the output in a text editor of your choice.

Listing 22-9. Example of a detected deadlock

```
mysql> SHOW ENGINE INNODB STATUS\G
...
------------------------
LATEST DETECTED DEADLOCK
------------------------
2019-11-06 18:29:07 0x4b78
*** (1) TRANSACTION:
TRANSACTION 6260, ACTIVE 62 sec starting index read
```

mysql tables in use 1, locked 1
LOCK WAIT 6 lock struct(s), heap size 1136, 30 row lock(s), undo log
entries 14
MySQL thread id 61, OS thread handle 22592, query id 39059 localhost ::1
root updating
UPDATE world.country SET Population = Population * 1.1 WHERE Code = 'AUS'

*** (1) HOLDS THE LOCK(S):
RECORD LOCKS space id 160 page no 14 n bits 1368 index CountryCode of table
`world`.`city` trx id 6260 lock_mode X locks gap before rec
Record lock, heap no 652 PHYSICAL RECORD: n_fields 2; compact format; info
bits 0
 0: len 3; hex 415554; asc AUT;;
 1: len 4; hex 800005f3; asc   ;;

*** (1) WAITING FOR THIS LOCK TO BE GRANTED:
RECORD LOCKS space id 161 page no 5 n bits 128 index PRIMARY of table
`world`.`country` trx id 6260 lock_mode X locks rec but not gap waiting
Record lock, heap no 16 PHYSICAL RECORD: n_fields 17; compact format; info
bits 0
 0: len 3; hex 415553; asc AUS;;
 1: len 6; hex 000000001875; asc   u;;
 2: len 7; hex 0200000122066e; asc   " n;;
 3: len 30; hex 4175737472616c696120202020202020202020202020202020202020;
    asc Australia   ; (total 52 bytes);
 4: len 1; hex 05; asc ;;
 5: len 26; hex 4175737472616c696120616e64204e6577205a65616c616e6420; asc
    Australia and New Zealand ;;
 6: len 4; hex 483eec4a; asc H> J;;
 7: len 2; hex 876d; asc m;;
 8: len 4; hex 812267c0; asc "g ;;
 9: len 4; hex 9a999f42; asc   B;;
 10: len 4; hex c079ab48; asc y H;;
 11: len 4; hex e0d9bf48; asc   H;;
 12: len 30; hex 4175737472616c696120202020202020202020202020202020202020;
    asc Australia   ; (total 45 bytes);

13: len 30; hex 436f6e737469747574696f6e616c204d6f6e61726368792c204665646572; asc Constitutional Monarchy, Feder; (total 45 bytes);

14: len 30; hex 456c697361626574682049492020202020202020202020202020202020202020; asc Elisabeth II   ; (total 60 bytes);

15: len 4; hex 80000087; asc   ;;

16: len 2; hex 4155; asc AU;;

*** (2) TRANSACTION:
TRANSACTION 6261, ACTIVE 37 sec inserting
mysql tables in use 1, locked 1
LOCK WAIT 4 lock struct(s), heap size 1136, 2 row lock(s), undo log entries 2
MySQL thread id 62, OS thread handle 2044, query id 39060 localhost ::1
root update
INSERT INTO world.city VALUES (4080, 'Darwin', 'AUS', 'Northern Territory', 146000)

*** (2) HOLDS THE LOCK(S):
RECORD LOCKS space id 161 page no 5 n bits 128 index PRIMARY of table
`world`.`country` trx id 6261 lock_mode X locks rec but not gap
Record lock, heap no 16 PHYSICAL RECORD: n_fields 17; compact format; info bits 0

 0: len 3; hex 415553; asc AUS;;

 1: len 6; hex 000000001875; asc   u;;

 2: len 7; hex 0200000122066e; asc   " n;;

 3: len 30; hex 4175737472616c69612020202020202020202020202020202020202020202020; asc Australia   ; (total 52 bytes);

 4: len 1; hex 05; asc ;;

 5: len 26; hex 4175737472616c696120616e64204e6577205a65616c616e6420; asc Australia and New Zealand ;;

 6: len 4; hex 483eec4a; asc H> J;;

 7: len 2; hex 876d; asc m;;

 8: len 4; hex 812267c0; asc "g ;;

 9: len 4; hex 9a999f42; asc   B;;

 10: len 4; hex c079ab48; asc y H;;

 11: len 4; hex e0d9bf48; asc   H;;

 12: len 30; hex 4175737472616c69612020202020202020202020202020202020202020202020; asc Australia   ; (total 45 bytes);

 13: len 30; hex 436f6e737469747574696f6e616c204d6f6e61726368792c204665646572; asc Constitutional Monarchy, Feder; (total 45 bytes);

14: len 30; hex 456c6973616265746820494920202020202020202020202020202020202020;
   asc Elisabeth II   ; (total 60 bytes);
15: len 4; hex 80000087; asc   ;;
16: len 2; hex 4155; asc AU;;

*** (2) WAITING FOR THIS LOCK TO BE GRANTED:
RECORD LOCKS space id 160 page no 14 n bits 1368 index CountryCode of table
`world`.`city` trx id 6261 lock_mode X locks gap before rec insert intention waiting
Record lock, heap no 652 PHYSICAL RECORD: n_fields 2; compact format; info bits 0
 0: len 3; hex 415554; asc AUT;;
 1: len 4; hex 800005f3; asc   ;;

*** WE ROLL BACK TRANSACTION (2)

The deadlock occurred on November 6, 2019, at 18:29:07 in the server time zone.
You can use this information to see if the information is for the same deadlock as the
deadlock reported by a user.

The interesting part is the information for the two transactions. You can see that
transaction 1 was updating the population of the country with Code = 'AUS':

UPDATE world.country SET Population = Population * 1.1 WHERE Code = 'AUS'

Transaction 2 was attempting to insert a new city:

INSERT INTO world.city VALUES (4080, 'Darwin', 'AUS', 'Northern Territory', 146000)

This is a case where the deadlock involved multiple tables. While the two queries
work on different tables, it cannot on its own prove that there are more queries involved
as a foreign key can trigger one query to take locks on two tables. In this case though, the
Code column is the primary key of the country table, and the only foreign key involved is
from the CountryCode column on the city table to the Code column of the country table
(showing this is left as an exercise for the reader using the world sample database). So it
is not likely that two queries deadlock on their own.

Note   The deadlock output is from MySQL 8.0.18 which added additional
information to the output. This discussion only uses the information that is also
available in previous releases as well. However, if you are still using an earlier
release, upgrading will make it easier to investigate deadlocks.

The next thing to observe is what locks are being waited on. Transaction 1 waits for an exclusive lock on the primary key of the country table:

```
RECORD LOCKS space id 161 page no 5 n bits 128 index PRIMARY of table
`world`.`country` trx id 6260 lock_mode X locks rec but not gap waiting
```

The value of the primary key can be found in the information that follows this information. It can seem a little overwhelming as InnoDB includes all the information related to the record. Since it is a primary key record, the whole row is included. This is useful to understand what data is in the row, particularly if the primary key does not carry that information on its own, but it can be confusing when you see it the first time. The primary key of the country table is the first column of the table, so it is the first line of the record information that contains the value of the primary key the lock is requesting:

```
 0: len 3; hex 415553; asc AUS;;
```

InnoDB includes the value in hexadecimal notation, but also tries to decode it as a string, so here it is clear that the value is "AUS", which is not surprising since that is also in the WHERE clause of the query. It is not always that obvious, so you should always confirm the value from the lock output. You can also see from the information that the column is sorted in ascending order in the index.

Transaction 2 waits for an insert intention lock on the CountryCode index of the city table:

```
RECORD LOCKS space id 160 page no 14 n bits 1368 index CountryCode of
table `world`.`city` trx id 6261 lock_mode X locks gap before rec insert
intention waiting
```

You can see the lock request involves a gap before record. The lock information is simpler in this case as there are only two columns in the CountryCode index – the CountryCode column and the primary key (ID column) since the CountryCode index is a nonunique secondary index. The index is effectively (CountryCode, ID), and the values for the gap before record are as follows:

```
 0: len 3; hex 415554; asc AUT;;
 1: len 4; hex 800005f3; asc     ;;
```

This shows that the value of the CountryCode is "AUT" which is not all that surprising given it is the next value after "AUS" when sorting in alphabetical ascending order. The value for the ID column is the hex value 0x5f3 which in decimal is 1523. If you query for cities with CountryCode = AUT and sort them in order of the CountryCode index, you can see that ID = 1523 is the first city found:

```
mysql> SELECT *
        FROM world.city
        WHERE CountryCode = 'AUT'
        ORDER BY CountryCode, ID
        LIMIT 1;
+------+------+-------------+----------+------------+
| ID   | Name | CountryCode | District | Population |
+------+------+-------------+----------+------------+
| 1523 | Wien | AUT         | Wien     |    1608144 |
+------+------+-------------+----------+------------+
1 row in set (0.0006 sec)
```

So far so good. Since the transactions are waiting for these locks, it can of course be inferred that the other transaction holds the lock. In version 8.0.18 and later, InnoDB includes the full list of locks held by both transactions; in earlier versions, InnoDB only includes this explicitly for one of the transactions, so you need to determine what other queries the transactions have executed.

From the information available, you can make some educated guesses. For example, the INSERT statement is blocked by a gap lock on the CountryCode index. An example of a query that would take that gap lock is a query using the condition CountryCode = 'AUS'. The deadlock information also includes information about the two connections owning the transactions which may help you:

```
MySQL thread id 61, OS thread handle 22592, query id 39059 localhost ::1
root updating

MySQL thread id 62, OS thread handle 2044, query id 39060 localhost ::1
root update
```

You can see both connections were made using the root@localhost account. If you ensure to have different users for each application and role, the account may help you to narrow down who executed the transactions.

If the connections still exist, you can also use the events_statements_history table in the Performance Schema to find the latest queries executed by the connection. This may not be those involved in the deadlock, depending on whether the connection has been used for more queries, but may nevertheless provide a clue to what the connection is used for. If the connections no longer exist, you may in principle be able to find the queries in the events_statements_history_long table, but you will need to map the "MySQL thread id" (the connection ID) to the Performance Schema thread ID which there is no trivial way to do. Also, the events_statements_history_long consumer is not enabled by default.

In this particular case, both connections are still present, and they have not done anything other than rolling back the transactions. Listing 22-10 shows how you can find the queries involved in the transactions. Be aware that the queries may return more rows than shown here depending on which client you are using and which other queries have been executed in the connection.

Listing 22-10. Finding the queries involved in the deadlock

```
mysql> SELECT SQL_TEXT, NESTING_EVENT_ID,
              NESTING_EVENT_TYPE
         FROM performance_schema.events_statements_history
        WHERE THREAD_ID = PS_THREAD_ID(61)
        ORDER BY EVENT_ID\G
*************************** 1. row ***************************
         SQL_TEXT: START TRANSACTION
  NESTING_EVENT_ID: NULL
NESTING_EVENT_TYPE: NULL
*************************** 2. row ***************************
         SQL_TEXT: UPDATE world.city SET Population = Population * 1.10
WHERE CountryCode = 'AUS'
  NESTING_EVENT_ID: 37
NESTING_EVENT_TYPE: TRANSACTION
```

```
*************************** 3. row ***************************
        SQL_TEXT: UPDATE world.country SET Population = Population * 1.1
WHERE Code = 'AUS'
  NESTING_EVENT_ID: 37
NESTING_EVENT_TYPE: TRANSACTION
*************************** 4. row ***************************
        SQL_TEXT: ROLLBACK
  NESTING_EVENT_ID: 37
NESTING_EVENT_TYPE: TRANSACTION
4 rows in set (0.0007 sec)

mysql> SELECT SQL_TEXT, MYSQL_ERRNO,
            NESTING_EVENT_ID,
            NESTING_EVENT_TYPE
        FROM performance_schema.events_statements_history
       WHERE THREAD_ID = PS_THREAD_ID(62)
       ORDER BY EVENT_ID\G
*************************** 1. row ***************************
        SQL_TEXT: START TRANSACTION
      MYSQL_ERRNO: 0
  NESTING_EVENT_ID: NULL
NESTING_EVENT_TYPE: NULL
*************************** 2. row ***************************
        SQL_TEXT: UPDATE world.country SET Population = Population +
146000 WHERE Code = 'AUS'
      MYSQL_ERRNO: 0
  NESTING_EVENT_ID: 810
NESTING_EVENT_TYPE: TRANSACTION
*************************** 3. row ***************************
        SQL_TEXT: INSERT INTO world.city VALUES (4080, 'Darwin', 'AUS',
'Northern Territory', 146000)
      MYSQL_ERRNO: 1213
  NESTING_EVENT_ID: 810
NESTING_EVENT_TYPE: TRANSACTION
```

```
************************** 4. row **************************
         SQL_TEXT: SHOW WARNINGS
      MYSQL_ERRNO: 0
  NESTING_EVENT_ID: NULL
NESTING_EVENT_TYPE: NULL
************************** 5. row **************************
         SQL_TEXT: ROLLBACK
      MYSQL_ERRNO: 0
  NESTING_EVENT_ID: NULL
NESTING_EVENT_TYPE: NULL
10 rows in set (0.0009 sec)
```

Notice that for connection id 62 (the second of the transactions), the MySQL error number is included, and the third row has it set to 1213 – a deadlock. MySQL Shell automatically executes a SHOW WARNINGS statement when an error is encountered which is the statement in row 4. Notice also that the nesting event is NULL for the ROLLBACK for transaction 2, but not for the ROLLBACK of transaction 1. That is because the deadlock triggered the whole transaction to be rolled back (so the ROLLBACK for transaction 2 did not do anything).

The deadlock was triggered by transaction 1 first updating the population of the city table and then of the country table. Transaction 2 first updated the population of the country table and then tried to insert a new city into the city table. This is a typical example of two workflows updating records in different orders and thus being prone to deadlocks.

Summarizing the investigation, it consists of two steps:

1. Analyze the deadlock information from InnoDB to determine the locks involved in the deadlock and get as much information as possible about the connections.

2. Use other sources such as the Performance Schema to find more information about the queries in the transactions. Often it is necessary to analyze the application to get the list of queries.

Now that you know what triggered the deadlock, what is required to solve the issue?

The Solution

Deadlocks are the easiest lock situation to resolve as InnoDB automatically chooses one of the transactions as the victim and rolls it back. In the deadlock examined in the previous discussion, transaction 2 was chosen as the victim which can be seen from the deadlock output:

```
*** WE ROLL BACK TRANSACTION (2)
```

This means that for transaction 1, there is nothing to do. After transaction 2 has been rolled back, transaction 1 can continue and complete its work.

For transaction 2, InnoDB has rolled back the whole transaction, so all you need to do is to retry the transaction. Remember to execute all queries again instead of relying on values returned during the first attempt; otherwise, you may be using outdated values.

Tip   Always be prepared to handle deadlocks and lock wait timeouts. For deadlocks or when the transaction has been rolled back after a lock wait timeout, retry the entire transaction. For lock wait timeouts where only the query has been rolled back, retry the query possibly adding a delay.

If deadlocks occur relatively rarely, you do not really need to do anything more. Deadlocks are a fact of life, so do not be alarmed by encountering a few of them. If deadlocks cause a significant impact, you need to look at making changes to prevent some of the deadlocks.

The Prevention

Reducing deadlocks is very similar to reducing record lock contention in general with the addition that acquiring the locks in the same order throughout the application is very important. It is recommended to read the section "Reduce Locking Issues" in Chapter 18 again. The main points to reduce deadlocks are to reduce the number of locks and how long they are held and to take them in the same order:

- Reduce the work done by each transaction by splitting large transactions into several smaller ones and adding indexes to reduce the number of locks taken.

- Consider the READ COMMITTED transaction isolation level if it is suitable for your application to reduce the number of locks and how long they are held.

- Make sure transactions are only held open for as short time as possible.

- Access records in the same order, if necessary by executing SELECT ... FOR UPDATE or SELECT ... FOR SHARE queries to take the locks preemptively.

That concludes the discussion of how to investigate locks. You may encounter lock cases that do not entirely match the cases discussed in this chapter; however, the techniques to investigate the issues will be similar.

Summary

This chapter has shown you how you can use the resources available in MySQL to investigate lock-related issues. The chapter included examples of investigating four different types of lock issues: flush locks, metadata locks, record locks, and deadlocks. Each issue type used different features of MySQL including the process list, the lock tables in the Performance Schema, and the InnoDB monitor output.

There are many other lock types that can cause lock wait issues. The methods discussed in this chapter go a long way to investigate issues caused by other lock types as well. In the end, the only way to become an expert on investigating locks is experience, but the techniques from this chapter provide a good starting point.

That concludes Part V about query analysis. Part VI is about improving the queries starting out with a discussion of improving performance through the configuration.

PART VI

Improving the Queries

CHAPTER 23

Configuration

Throughout Part IV of this book, there have been several examples of configuration options that influence the behavior of MySQL. These options include the choice of character sets and collations, how to create index statistics, how the optimizer should work, and more. There are also other options that directly or indirectly influence the performance of your queries. This chapter will consider the most commonly used options not covered elsewhere as well as some general considerations when it comes to configuring MySQL.

The chapter starts out with some "best practices" around changing the configuration. Then the following sections are for InnoDB, query buffers, and internal temporary tables.

Best Practices

When you set out to make configuration changes, it is worth having a few principles in mind which can make you more successful at making configuration changes. The best practices that will be discussed include the following:

- Be wary of best practices.

- Use monitoring to verify the effect.

- Change one option at a time.

- Make relatively small incremental changes.

- Less is often better.

- Make sure you understand what the option does.

- Consider the side effects.

© Jesper Wisborg Krogh 2020

J. W. Krogh, *MySQL 8 Query Performance Tuning*, https://doi.org/10.1007/978-1-4842-5584-1_23

It may sound contractionary that the first item of a best practices list is to be wary of best practices. What is meant is that when you see some advice, then you should not jump straight ahead and apply that.

No two systems are identical, so while an advice may in general be good, you still need to consider whether it also applies to your system. Another gotcha is to look at advice that applies to an older version of MySQL or to a time when 8 GiB of memory was a lot. If you Google some setting, it is possible that you can see recommendations that were written many years ago. Similarly, a recommendation that worked well for your system some time ago, may no longer work due to changes in the application workload. Finally, even if a recommendation will improve the performance for your system, there may be side effects such as the risk of loss of committed changes that are unacceptable for you.

Tip   The recommendation to be wary of best practices also applies to the suggestions in this book. Always consider how they apply to your system.

How should you then approach configuration changes? Apply the principles described in Chapter 2. Figure 23-1 recapitulates the steps.

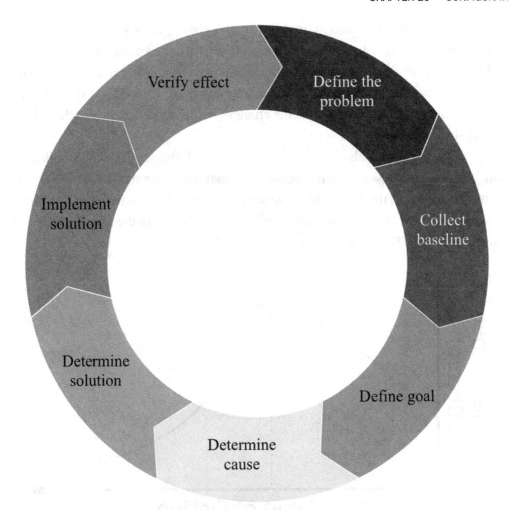

Figure 23-1. *The performance tuning lifecycle*

You start out defining what the issue is and then collect the baseline either through your monitoring system or by timing the query or similar. The baseline may also be a combination of observables. Then you can define the goal of the optimization. It is very important that you define what is good enough, or you will never be done. The next steps are to determine the cause and use that to find a solution. Finally, you implement the solution and verify the effect by comparing to the baseline. If the problem is not solved or you have identified multiple problems, you can start over.

Monitoring is very important in this process as it is used both to define the problem, to collect the baseline, and to verify the effect. If you skip these steps, you have little idea whether your solution worked and whether it affected other queries as well.

When you decide on a solution, make as small a change as possible. This applies both to the number of configuration options that you turn the knobs on and how far you turn the knobs. If you change more than one option at a time, you cannot measure the effect of each change. For example, two changes may cancel each other out, so you think the solution did not work when one of the changes really worked great and the other made the situation worse.

Configuration options also often have a sweet spot. If the setting is too small, the feature the option represents cannot be used enough to make a significant impact. If the setting is too large, the overhead of the feature becomes worse than the benefit. In between, you have the optimal combination of the benefits of the feature while the overhead is limited. This is illustrated in Figure 23-2.

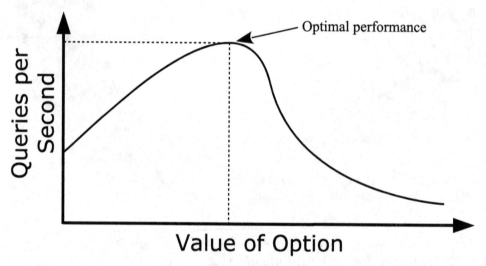

Figure 23-2. *A typical relationship between the option value and performance*

By making small incremental changes, you maximize the chance of finding this sweet spot.

This relates to the next point: small is often better. Just because you, for example, have enough memory to increase a per query or per join buffer does not mean it makes the queries faster to increase the buffer size. It of course depends on the option to what extent this principle applies. For the size of the InnoDB buffer pool, it is better to have a relatively large buffer as it helps reduce disk I/O and serve data from memory. A key thing to remember about the buffer pool is also that memory allocations only happen when MySQL starts and when you dynamically increase the size of the buffer pool.

However, for buffers such as the join buffer that may be allocated several times for a single query, the sheer overhead of allocating the buffer can become a problem. This is discussed further in the section "Query Buffers." In all cases, for options that relate to resources, you need to remember that the resources you allocate to one feature are not available for other features.

The concept of "less is often better" applies both to the optimal value of a configuration option and to the number of options that you tune. The more options you set in the configuration file, the more cluttered your configuration file becomes, and the harder it becomes to keep the overview of what has been changed and why. (It also helps to group the settings by feature, e.g., to have all InnoDB settings together.) If you are in the habit of including options set to their default values, it is still better to leave them out as including the options means that you will miss out of changes to the default values that are implemented as part of optimizing the default configuration to reflect changes to the MySQL internals or to changes in what is considered standard hardware.

Note   In MySQL 5.6 and later, a significant effort has gone into improving the default values for the MySQL configuration options. The changes mainly occur between major versions based on testing by the development team and feedback from the MySQL Support team, customers, and community members.

The recommendation is to start out setting as few options as possible. You will most likely want to set the size of the InnoDB buffer pool, the redo log, and possibly the table caches. You may also want to set some paths and ports, and you may have requirements that some features such as global transaction identifiers (GTIDs) or Group Replication are enabled. Beyond that, only make changes based on observations.

Tip   Start out with a minimal configuration that just sets the size of the InnoDB buffer pool and redo logs, paths, and ports and enable required features. Otherwise, only make configuration changes based on observations.

The last two points in the list are related: make sure that you understand what the option does and consider the side effects. Understanding what the option does helps you identify whether the option is useful for your case and what other effects the option may have. As an example, consider the sync_binlog option. This tells how often updates to the binary log should be synced to disk. In MySQL 8, the default is to sync with every commit which for disks that have poor sync performance can significantly impact the query performance. It may thus be tempting to set sync_binlog to 0 which disables forced synchronizations; however, are the side effects acceptable? If you do not sync the changes, then they only live in memory until something else – such as the memory being required for other uses – forces the sync to happen. This means that if MySQL crashes, then the changes are lost, and if you have a replica, you will have to rebuild it. Is that acceptable?

Even if you can accept potentially losing binary log events, there is a more subtle side effect of using sync_binlog = 0. Just because the sync does not happen at transaction commit does not mean it never happens. The maximum size of a binary log is 1 GiB (the max_binlog_size option) plus the size of the last transaction, and rotating the binary log means the old binary log is flushed to disk. Nowadays that usually means that MySQL will end up writing 1 GiB and then flush it all at once. Even on fast disks, it does take a measurable amount of time to write out a gigabyte of data. In the meantime, MySQL cannot perform any commits, so any connection issuing a commit (whether implicit or explicit) will stall until the sync has completed. This can come as a surprise, and the stall may end up being long enough to upset the end user – who may be a customer. The author of this book has seen commit stalls arising from binary log rotations in the range of a couple of seconds up to half a minute. In short, sync_binlog = 0 gives the overall highest throughput and average commit latency, but sync_binlog = 1 provides the best data safety and the most predictable commit latency.

The rest of this chapter provides some recommendations for the options related to query tuning that most often need to be changed.

InnoDB Overview

Given that all queries involving tables interact with the InnoDB storage engine, it is important to take some time to look at the configuration of the InnoDB parameters. These include the size of the InnoDB buffer pool and the redo log size – two configurations that need to be adjusted for most production systems.

Before discussing the configuration options, it is worth reviewing how the data flows between the tablespaces and the buffer pool and back to the tablespace through the redo log system. Figure 23-3 shows a simple overview of this flow.

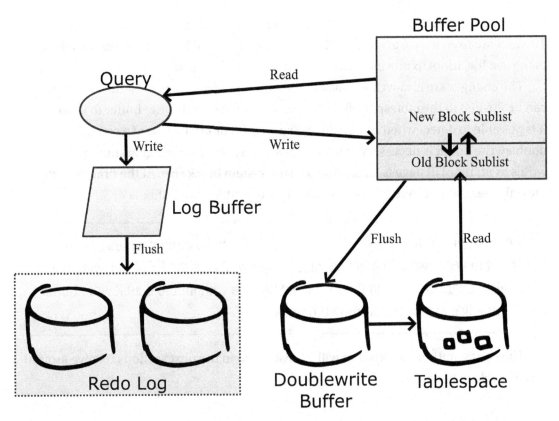

Figure 23-3. *The InnoDB data flow*

When a query requests data, it is always read from the buffer pool. If the data is not already in the buffer pool, it is fetched from the tablespace. InnoDB divides the buffer pool into two parts: the old blocks sublist and the new blocks sublist. Data is always read into the head (top) of the old blocks sublist in whole pages. If data from the same page is required again, the data is moved to the new blocks sublist. Both sublists use the *least recently used* (LRU) principle to determine which pages to expel when it is necessary to create room for a new page. Pages are evicted from the buffer pool from the old blocks sublist. Since new pages spend time in the old blocks sublist before being promoted to the new blocks sublist, it means that if a page is used once, but then left unused, then it will quickly be expelled from the buffer pool again. This prevents large rare scans such as backups from polluting the buffer pool.

When a query updates changes, the changes are written to the in-memory log buffer and from there written and later flushed to the redo log which consists of at least two files. The redo log files are used in a circular fashion, so writes start at the beginning of one file and then fill up the file, and when it is full, InnoDB continues with the next file. The files are fixed in size and with a fixed number of files. When the log reaches the end of the last file, InnoDB moves back to the beginning of the first file.

The changes are also written back to the buffer pool and marked as dirty until they can be flushed to the tablespace files. InnoDB uses the doublewrite buffer to ensure it is possible to detect whether a write was successful or not in case of a crash. The doublewrite buffer is necessary, because most file systems do not guarantee atomic writes as an InnoDB page is larger than the file system block size. At the time of writing, the only file system where it is safe to disable the doublewrite buffer is ZFS.

Caution   Even if the file system is supposed to handle atomic writes of InnoDB pages, it may not work in practice. An example of this is the EXT4 file system with journaling enabled which in theory should be safe without the doublewrite buffer but in practice can cause corrupted data.

The configuration options that will be discussed in the next sections revolve around this lifecycle of the data.

The InnoDB Buffer Pool

The InnoDB buffer pool is where InnoDB caches data and indexes. Since all requests for data go through the buffer pool, it naturally becomes a very important part of MySQL from a performance perspective. There are a few important parameters for the buffer pool that will be discussed here.

Table 23-1 summarizes the buffer pool–related configuration options that you most likely need to change to optimize the query performance.

Table 23-1. *Important configuration options for the buffer pool*

Option Name	Default Value	Comments
innodb_buffer_pool_size	128 MiB	The total size of the InnoDB buffer pool.
innodb_buffer_pool_instances	Auto-sized	How many parts the buffer pool is split into. The default is 1 if the total size is less than 1 GiB and otherwise 8. For 32-bit Windows, the default is 1 below 1.3 GiB; otherwise, each instance is made to be 128 MiB. The maximum number of instances is 64.
innodb_buffer_pool_dump_pct	25	The percentage of the most recently used pages in the buffer pool that are included when dumping the pool content (backing it up).
innodb_old_blocks_time	1000	How long in milliseconds a page must have resided in the old blocks sublist before a new read of the page promotes it to the new blocks sublist.
innodb_old_blocks_pct	37	How large the old blocks sublist should be in percentage of the whole buffer pool.
innodb_io_capacity	200	How many I/O operations per second InnoDB is allowed to use during nonurgent conditions.
innodb_io_capacity_max	2000	How many I/O operations per second InnoDB is allowed to use during urgent conditions.
innodb_flush_method	unbuffered or fsync	The method InnoDB uses to write the changes to disk. The default is unbuffered on Microsoft Windows and fsync on Linux/Unix.

These options will be discussed in more detail in the remainder of this section starting with options related to the size of the buffer pool.

Note   The option key_buffer_size has nothing to do with caching InnoDB indexes. The option got its name in the early days of MySQL when the MyISAM storage engine was the main storage engine, so it was not needed to prefix the option with mysiam. Unless you use MyISAM tables, there is no reason to configure key_buffer_size.

The Buffer Pool Size

The most important of these options is the size of the buffer pool. The default size of 128 MiB is nice for setting up a test instance on your laptop without draining it of memory (and why the default value is so small), but for a production system, you most likely want to allocate more memory. You can benefit from increasing the size until your *working data set* fits into the buffer pool. The working data set is the data that is needed by the queries executing. Typically, this is a subset of the total data set as some data is inactive, for example, because it concerns events in the past.

Tip   If you have a large buffer pool and have core dumps enabled, then disable the `innodb_buffer_pool_in_core_file` option to avoid dumping the entire buffer pool if a core dump occurs. The option is available in MySQL 8.0.14 and later.

You can get the buffer pool hit rate – that is, how frequently a page request can be fulfilled directly from the buffer pool without reading from disk – using the following formula:

$Hit\ Rate = 100 - \left(\dfrac{Innodb\_pages\_read}{Innodb\_buffer\_pool\_read\_requests} \right)$. The two variables

Innodb_pages_read and Innodb_buffer_pool_read_requests are status variables. Listing 23-1 shows an example of how to calculate the buffer pool hit rate.

Listing 23-1. Calculating the buffer pool hit rate

```
mysql> SELECT Variable_name, Variable_value
         FROM sys.metrics
        WHERE Variable_name IN
                ('Innodb_pages_read',
                 'Innodb_buffer_pool_read_requests')\G
*************************** 1. row ***************************
 Variable_name: innodb_buffer_pool_read_requests
Variable_value: 141319
*************************** 2. row ***************************
 Variable_name: innodb_pages_read
Variable_value: 1028
2 rows in set (0.0089 sec)
```

```
mysql> SELECT 100 - (100 * 1028/141319) AS HitRate;
+----------+
| HitRate  |
+----------+
| 99.2726  |
+----------+
1 row in set (0.0003 sec)
```

In the example, 99.3% of the page requests are fulfilled from the buffer pool. This number is across all buffer pool instances. If you want to determine the hit rate for a given period, you need to collect the values of the status variables at the start and end of the period and use the difference between them in the calculation. You can also get the rate from the INNODB_BUFFER_POOL_STATS view in the Information Schema or the InnoDB monitor. In both cases, the rate is returned as per thousand requests. Listing 23-2 shows examples of this. You will need to ensure you have executed some queries to generate some buffer pool activity to get a meaningful result.

Listing 23-2. Getting the buffer pool hit rate directly from InnoDB

```
mysql> SELECT POOL_ID, NUMBER_PAGES_READ,
              NUMBER_PAGES_GET, HIT_RATE FROM information_schema.INNODB_
              BUFFER_POOL_STATS\G
*************************** 1. row ***************************
          POOL_ID: 0
NUMBER_PAGES_READ: 1028
 NUMBER_PAGES_GET: 141319
         HIT_RATE: 1000
1 row in set (0.0004 sec)

mysql> SHOW ENGINE INNODB STATUS\G
*************************** 1. row ***************************
  Type: InnoDB
  Name:
Status:
=====================================================
2019-07-20 19:33:12 0x7550 INNODB MONITOR OUTPUT
=====================================================
...
```

```
----------------------
BUFFER POOL AND MEMORY
----------------------
Total large memory allocated 137363456
Dictionary memory allocated 536469
Buffer pool size     8192
Free buffers         6984
Database pages       1190
Old database pages 428
Modified db pages    0
Pending reads        0
Pending writes: LRU 0, flush list 0, single page 0
Pages made young 38, not young 0
0.00 youngs/s, 0.00 non-youngs/s
Pages read 1028, created 237, written 1065
0.00 reads/s, 0.00 creates/s, 0.00 writes/s
Buffer pool hit rate 1000 / 1000, young-making rate 0 / 1000 not 0 / 1000
Pages read ahead 0.00/s, evicted without access 0.00/s, Random read ahead
0.00/s
LRU len: 1190, unzip_LRU len: 0
I/O sum[6]:cur[0], unzip sum[0]:cur[0]
...
```

What is important to realize is that the hit rates returned directly by InnoDB are for the period since the buffer pool statistics were last retrieved, and they are per buffer pool instance. If you want full control of what period a hit rate is for, you need to calculate it yourself either by using the status variables or the NUMBER_PAGES_READ and NUMBER_PAGES_GET from the INNODB_BUFFER_POOL_STATS view.

You should aim at having the buffer pool hit rate as close to 100% or 1000/1000 as possible. That said, in some cases it is simply not possible as the amount of data cannot possibly fit into memory. In that case, the buffer pool hit rate is still useful as it allows you to monitor the effectiveness of the buffer pool over time and compare to the general query statistics. If the buffer pool hit rate starts to drop with a degradation in query performance, you should look at making provisions so the buffer pool can be increased in size.

Buffer Pool Instances

MySQL has supported multiple buffer pool instances since version 5.5. The reason for introducing it was that typical database workloads had more and more queries running in parallel with the prevalence of more and more CPUs per host. This led to mutex contention when accessing data in the buffer pool.

One of the solutions to reduce the contention is to allow the buffer pool to be split into multiple instances with different mutexes for each instance. The number of instances is controlled with the `innodb_buffer_pool_instances` option. The total amount of buffer pool specified with `innodb_buffer_pool_size` is divided evenly among the instances. Except on 32-bit Windows, the default is to have one instance for a buffer pool size of less than 1 gigabyte. For larger buffer pools, the default is eight instances. The maximum number of instances is 64.

For a single-threaded workload, the optimal is to have all of the memory in a single buffer pool. The more parallel your workload is, the more additional instances help reduce contention. The exact effect of increasing the number of buffer pools depends on the extent the parallel queries request data stored in different pages. If all requests are for different pages, you can benefit from increasing the number of instances toward the number of concurrent queries. If all queries request data in the same page, there is no benefit of more instances. In general, be careful not to make each buffer pool instance too small. If you do not have monitoring data proving otherwise, allow each instance to be 1 gigabyte or larger for buffer pools that are at least 8 gigabytes large.

Dumping the Buffer Pool

One of the common problems with restarts of a database is that the caching does not work well for a while until the cache has been warmed up. This can lead to very poor query performance and poor end user satisfaction. The solution to this is to store a list of the most frequently used pages in the buffer pool at shutdown and read these pages into the buffer pool immediately after a restart even if no queries have requested them yet.

This feature is enabled by default, and the main thing to consider is how much of the buffer pool you want to include in the dump. This is controlled with the `innodb_buffer_pool_dump_pct` option which takes the percentage of pages to include. The default is 25%. The pages are read from the head of the new blocks sublist, so it is the most recently used pages that are included.

The dump just includes a reference to the page that should be read, so the size of the dump is roughly 8 bytes per page. If you have a 128 GiB buffer pool, and you are using 16 KiB pages, there are 8,388,608 pages in the buffer pool. If you use the default of 25% for the buffer pool dump, that gives a dump that is around 16 MiB. The dump is stored in the file ib_buffer_pool in the data directory.

Tip   When you create backups by copying the tablespace files (a physical or raw backup), back up the ib_buffer_pool file as well. You can use the innodb_ buffer_pool_dump_now option to create a new copy of the most recently used pages. This is, for example, done automatically by MySQL Enterprise Backup. However, for logical backups (where the data is exported as an SQL or CSV file), the ib_buffer_pool file is not useful.

If you encounter problems with slow queries after restarting, consider increasing innodb_buffer_pool_dump_pct to include a larger part of the buffer pool in the dump. The main drawbacks of increasing the option are that the shutdown takes longer as more page references are exported, the ib_buffer_pool file becomes larger, and it takes longer to load the pages after the restart. Loading the pages back into the buffer pool happens in the background, but by including more pages it may take longer before all of the most important pages are restored in the buffer pool.

The Old Blocks Sublist

If you have a data set that is larger than the buffer pool, a potential problem is that a large scan can pull in data that is just used for that scan and then not used again for a long time. When that happens, you risk that more frequently used data is expelled from the buffer pool and the queries needing that data will suffer until the scan has completed and the balance has been restored. Logical backups such as those made by mysqlpump and mysqldump are good examples of jobs that can trigger the issue. The backup process needs to scan all data, but the data is not needed again until the time of the next backup.

To avoid this issue, the buffer pool is split into two sublists: the new and old blocks sublists. When pages are read from the tablespaces, they are first "quarantined" in the old blocks sublist, and only if the page has been in the buffer pool for more than `innodb_old_blocks_time` milliseconds and is used again will it be moved to the new blocks sublist. This helps make the buffer pool scan resistant as a single table scan will only read rows from a page in rapid succession and then not use the page again. This leaves InnoDB free to expel the page once the scan has completed.

The default value for `innodb_old_blocks_time` is 1000 milliseconds which for most workloads is enough to avoid scans polluting the buffer pool. If you have jobs doing scans where the job returns to the same rows again after a short while (but longer than one second), then you can consider increasing `innodb_old_blocks_time`, if you do not want the subsequent accesses to promote the page to the new blocks sublist.

The size of the old blocks sublist is set by the `innodb_old_blocks_pct` option which specifies the percentage of the buffer pool that should be used for the old blocks sublist. The default is to use 37%. If you have a large buffer pool, you may want to reduce `innodb_old_blocks_pct` to avoid newly loaded pages taking up too much of the buffer pool. The optimal size of the old blocks sublist also depends on the rate you load transient pages into the buffer pool.

You can monitor the use of the old and new blocks sublists similar to how the hit rate is found. Listing 23-3 shows a sample output using the `INNODB_BUFFER_POOL_STATS` view and the InnoDB monitor.

Listing 23-3. Obtaining information about the new and old blocks sublists

```
mysql> SELECT PAGES_MADE_YOUNG,
              PAGES_NOT_MADE_YOUNG,
              PAGES_MADE_YOUNG_RATE,
              PAGES_MADE_NOT_YOUNG_RATE,
              YOUNG_MAKE_PER_THOUSAND_GETS,
              NOT_YOUNG_MAKE_PER_THOUSAND_GETS
         FROM information_schema.INNODB_BUFFER_POOL_STATS\G
*************************** 1. row ***************************
           PAGES_MADE_YOUNG: 98
       PAGES_NOT_MADE_YOUNG: 354
      PAGES_MADE_YOUNG_RATE: 0.000000000383894451752074
  PAGES_MADE_NOT_YOUNG_RATE: 0
```

```
    YOUNG_MAKE_PER_THOUSAND_GETS: 2
NOT_YOUNG_MAKE_PER_THOUSAND_GETS: 10
1 row in set (0.0005 sec)

mysql> SHOW ENGINE INNODB STATUS\G
*************************** 1. row ***************************
  Type: InnoDB
  Name:
Status:
=====================================================
2019-07-21 12:06:49 0x964 INNODB MONITOR OUTPUT
=====================================================
...
----------------------
BUFFER POOL AND MEMORY
----------------------
Total large memory allocated 137363456
Dictionary memory allocated 463009
Buffer pool size    8192
Free buffers        6974
Database pages      1210
Old database pages 426
Modified db pages   0
Pending reads       0
Pending writes: LRU 0, flush list 0, single page 0
Pages made young 98, not young 354
0.00 youngs/s, 0.00 non-youngs/s
Pages read 996, created 223, written 430
0.00 reads/s, 0.00 creates/s, 0.00 writes/s
Buffer pool hit rate 1000 / 1000, young-making rate 2 / 1000 not 10 / 1000
Pages read ahead 0.00/s, evicted without access 0.00/s, Random read ahead
0.00/s
LRU len: 1210, unzip_LRU len: 0
I/O sum[217]:cur[0], unzip sum[0]:cur[0]
...
```

Pages made young means that a page located in the old blocks sublist is moved to the new blocks sublist. That a page is not made young means it stays in the old blocks sublist. The two rate columns are per second since the last time the data was fetched. The pages per thousand gets are the number of pages made young or kept in the old blocks sublist per thousand pages requested; this is also since the last report.

One possible sign that you may need to configure the old blocks sublist is a decrease in buffer pool hit rate while scans are ongoing. If the rate of making pages young is high and you have large scans at the same time, you should consider increasing innodb_old_blocks_time to prevent subsequent reads to make the page young. Alternatively, consider decreasing innodb_old_blocks_pct to evict the pages from the scan after a shorter time in the old blocks sublist.

Vice versa, if you have few scans and the pages stay in the old blocks sublist (the non-young making stats are high), then you should consider decreasing innodb_old_blocks_time to promote the pages faster or increase innodb_old_blocks_pct to allow the pages to remain in the old blocks sublist for longer before they are evicted.

Flushing Pages

InnoDB needs to balance how hard it works at merging changes into the tablespace files. If it is too lazy, the redo log ends up being full and a forced flush is required, but if it works too hard it can impact the performance of other parts of the system. Needless to say, it is complex to get the equation right. Except during a crash recovery or after restoring a physical backup such as the ones created with MySQL Enterprise Backup, the merging is done by flushing dirty pages from the buffer pool to the tablespace files.

In recent MySQL versions, you do not in general need to do much as the adaptive flush algorithm that InnoDB uses is good at striking a good balance as long as there is enough redo log to work with. There are primarily three options to consider: two for setting the I/O capacity of the system and one for setting the flush method.

The two options for the I/O capacity are innodb_io_capacity and innodb_io_capacity_max. The innodb_io_capacity option is used during normal flushing of changes and should be set to the number of I/O operations InnoDB is allowed to use per second. In practice, it is not very easy to know what value to use. The default is 200 which roughly corresponds to a low-end SSD. Usually high-end storage can benefit from setting the capacity to a few thousand. It is better to start out with a relatively low value and increase it if your monitoring shows that flushing is falling behind and there is spare I/O capacity.

Note   The innodb_io_capacity and innodb_io_capacity_max options are not only used to determine how quickly InnoDB flushes dirty pages to the tablespace files. Other I/O activities such as merging data from the change buffer are also included.

The innodb_io_capacity_max option tells how hard InnoDB is allowed to push if the flushing is falling behind. The default is the minimum of 2000 and twice the value of innodb_io_capacity. In most cases the default value works well though if you have a low-end disk, you should consider reducing the setting to below 1000. If you experience an asynchronous flush (this will be discussed with the redo logs) and your monitoring shows that InnoDB does not use enough I/O capacity, increase the value of innodb_io_capacity_max.

Caution   Setting the I/O capacity too high can severely impact the performance of the system.

The flushing of the dirty pages can be performed in several ways, for example, using the operating system I/O cache or avoiding it. This is controlled using the innodb_flush_method option. On Microsoft Windows, you can choose between the values unbuffered (the default and recommended) and normal. The choice is harder on Linux and Unix where the following values are supported:

- **fsync:** This is the default value. InnoDB uses the fsync() system call. The data will also be cached in the operating system I/O cache.

- **O_DSYNC:** InnoDB uses the O_SYNC option when opening the redo log files (synchronous writing) and uses fsync for the data files. The reason O_SYNC is used instead of O_DSYNC is that O_DSYNC has been proven to be too unsafe, so O_SYNC is used instead.

- **O_DIRECT:** This is similar to fsync, but the operating system I/O cache is bypassed. It only applies to the tablespace files.

- **O_DIRECT_NO_FSYNC:** This is the same as O_DIRECT except that the fsync() system call is skipped. Due to bugs in the EXT4 and XFS file systems, this is not safe to use until MySQL 8.0.14 where a workaround for those bugs was implemented. If the redo log files are located on a different file system than the tablespace files, you should use O_DIRECT instead of O_DIRECT_NO_FSYNC. On most production systems, this is the best option.

Additionally, there are a couple of experimental flush methods that should only be used for performance testing.[1] These experimental methods are not covered here.

It is very complex which flush method will give the best performance. Since InnoDB caches its data itself and does so better than the operating system possibly can (as InnoDB knows how the data is used), it is natural to believe one of the O_DIRECT options will work the best. This is also usually the case; however, life is more complicated and, in some cases, fsync is faster. So you will need to test on your system to know for sure which flush method works the best. Another thing is that when restarting MySQL without restarting the operating system, if you use the fsync flush method, then InnoDB can benefit from the I/O cache when reading the data for the first time.

At the other end of the data flow there are the redo logs.

The Redo Log

The redo log is used to persist committed changes while providing sequential I/O to make the performance as good as possible. To improve the performance, changes are first written to the in-memory log buffer before they are written to the log files.

A background process then merges the changes from the buffer pool through the doublewrite buffer into the tablespaces. The pages that have not yet been merged to the tablespace file cannot be evicted from the buffer pool as they are considered dirty. That a page is dirty means that it has a different content than the same page from the tablespace, so InnoDB is not allowed to read the page from the tablespace until the changes have been merged.

Table 23-2 summarizes the redo log–related configuration options that you most likely need to change to optimize the query performance.

---

[1]https://dev.mysql.com/doc/refman/en/innodb-parameters.html#sysvar_innodb_flush_method

Table 23-2. *Important configuration options for the redo log*

Option Name	Default Value	Comments
innodb_log_buffer_size	16 MiB	The size of the log buffer where redo log events are stored in memory before being written to the on-disk redo log files.
innodb_log_file_size	48 MiB	The size of each file in the redo log.
innodb_log_files_in_group	2	The number of files in the redo log. There must be at least two files.

The remainder of this section covers these options.

Log Buffer

The log buffer is an in-memory buffer that InnoDB uses to buffer the redo log events before writing them to disk. This allows the transactions to keep the changes in memory until the buffer is full or the changes are committed. The default size of the log buffer is 16 MiB.

If you have large transactions or a high number of smaller concurrent transactions, it is recommended to increase the size of the log buffer. You set the size of the log buffer using the innodb_log_buffer_size option. In MySQL 8 (unlike older versions), you can change the size dynamically. Optimally, the buffer should be large enough that InnoDB only has to write out the changes when they are committed; however, this should of course be weighed against what the memory can otherwise be used for. If a single transaction has a large amount of changes in the buffer, it can also slow down the commit as all the data must be written to the redo log at that time, so that is another thing to consider for very large log buffer sizes.

Once the log buffer is full or the transaction is committed, the redo log events are written to the redo log files.

Log Files

The redo log is fixed in size and consists of a number of files – at least two – each of the same size. The main consideration when configuring the redo logs is to ensure that they are large enough to not become "full." In practice, full means 75% of the capacity as at that time an asynchronous flush is triggered. The asynchronous flush blocks the thread that triggered the flush while in principle the other threads can continue doing their work. In practice, the asynchronous flush is so ferocious that it usually causes the system to come to a grinding halt. There is also a synchronous flush, which triggers at 90% capacity and blocks all threads.

You control the size with the two options innodb_log_file_size and innodb_log_files_in_group. The total redo log size is the product of the two values. The recommendation is to set the file size up to 1–2 GiB and adjust the number of files to get the desired total size with a minimum of two files. The reason not to let each redo log file become very large is that they are buffered in the operating system I/O cache (even with innodb_flush_method = O_DIRECT), and the larger the files, the more potential for the redo log to use a large amount of memory in the I/O cache. The total size of the redo log is not allowed to exceed 512 GiB, and there can be at most 100 files.

Note   The larger the redo log, the more changes can be stored that are not yet flushed from the buffer pool to the tablespaces. This can increase the recovery time in case of a crash and the time it takes to perform a normal shutdown.

The best way to determine how large to make the redo log is to monitor how full it is over time through a monitoring solution. Figure 23-4 shows examples of graphs showing I/O rate for the redo log files and the usage of the redo log as measured by the checkpoint lag. If you want to create something similarly, you need to perform an intense write worklog; the employees database can be useful for that. Exactly what is required depends on the hardware, the configuration, which other processes use the resources, and more.

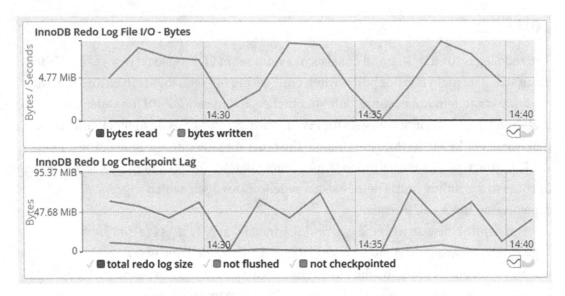

Figure 23-4. *Timeseries graphs for the redo log*

Make sure the part of the redo log that is not checkpointed stays clear of the 75% mark. In this example, the highest peak is at around 73 MiB out of 96 MiB (at 14:37) of redo log which means that almost 76% of the redo log was used for dirty pages. That means there was an asynchronous flush around that time which would have impacted the queries running at the time. You can use the I/O rate for the redo log file to get an idea of how stressed the file system is doing I/O for the redo log.

The best way to inspect the current redo log usage manually is to enable the `log_lsn_current` and `log_lsn_last_checkpoint` InnoDB metrics which allow you to query the current log sequence number and the log sequence number when the last checkpoint was made. The checkpoint lag in percentage of the total redo log is then calculated as

$$Lag\ Pct = 100 * \frac{log\_lsn\_last\_checkpoint - log\_lsn\_current}{\#log\ files * log\ file\ size}.$$

You can get the current values from the `INNODB_METRICS` table from the `information_schema` or the `sys.metrics` view. Alternatively, the log sequence numbers are also available from the `LOG` section of the InnoDB monitor irrespective of whether the metrics have been enabled. Listing 23-4 shows an example of determining the checkpoint lag using these resources.

Listing 23-4. Querying the redo log usage

```
mysql> SET GLOBAL innodb_monitor_enable = 'log_lsn_current',
            GLOBAL innodb_monitor_enable = 'log_lsn_last_checkpoint';
Query OK, 0 rows affected (0.0004 sec)

mysql> SELECT *
          FROM sys.metrics
         WHERE Variable_name IN ('log_lsn_current',
                                 'log_lsn_last_checkpoint')\G
*************************** 1. row ***************************
 Variable_name: log_lsn_current
Variable_value: 1678918975
          Type: InnoDB Metrics - log
       Enabled: YES
*************************** 2. row ***************************
 Variable_name: log_lsn_last_checkpoint
Variable_value: 1641343518
          Type: InnoDB Metrics - log
       Enabled: YES
2 rows in set (0.0078 sec)

mysql> SELECT ROUND(
                 100 * (
                   (SELECT COUNT
                       FROM information_schema.INNODB_METRICS
                      WHERE NAME = 'log_lsn_current')
                   - (SELECT COUNT
                       FROM information_schema.INNODB_METRICS
                      WHERE NAME = 'log_lsn_last_checkpoint')
                 ) / (@@global.innodb_log_file_size
                     * @@global.innodb_log_files_in_group
              ), 2) AS LogUsagePct;
+-------------+
| LogUsagePct |
+-------------+
|       39.25 |
+-------------+
```

```
1 row in set (0.0202 sec)

mysql> SHOW ENGINE INNODB STATUS\G
*************************** 1. row ***************************
  Type: InnoDB
  Name:
Status:
================================================
2019-07-21 17:04:09 0x964 INNODB MONITOR OUTPUT
================================================
...
---
LOG
---
Log sequence number         1704842995
Log buffer assigned up to   1704842995
Log buffer completed up to  1704842235
Log written up to           1704842235
Log flushed up to           1696214896
Added dirty pages up to     1704827409
Pages flushed up to         1668546370
Last checkpoint at          1665659636
5360916 log i/o's done, 23651.73 log i/o's/second
...
```

The required InnoDB metrics are first enabled. The overhead of having these enabled is very small, so it is fine to leave them enabled. The values of the metrics are then queried from the sys.metrics view followed by using the INNODB_METRICS table to calculate the lag directly. Finally, the log sequence numbers are also found in the InnoDB monitor output. The log sequence numbers change very rapidly, so even if you query them in rapid succession, they will have changed if there is any work going on. The values reflect the amount of work in bytes that has been done in InnoDB, so they will be different on any two systems.

Parallel Query Execution

Since MySQL 8.0.14, InnoDB has limited support for executing a query in parallel. This happens by performing a scan of the clustered index or partitions using multiple read threads. The implementation was greatly improved in 8.0.17 which is what is considered here.

The parallel scans happen automatically based on the number of index subtrees that will be scanned. You can configure the maximum number of threads that InnoDB can create for parallel execution across all connections by setting the innodb_parallel_read_threads option. These threads are created as background threads and are only present when needed. If all parallel threads are in use, InnoDB will revert to single-threaded execution for any additional queries until threads are available again.

As of MySQL 8.0.18, the parallel scans are used for SELECT COUNT(*) (multiple tables are allowed) without any filter conditions and for the second of the two scans performed by CHECK TABLE.

You can see the current usage of parallel threads from the performance_schema. threads table by looking for threads with the name thread/innodb/parallel_read_ thread. If you want to try the feature, you can, for example, use the Python mode in MySQL Shell to keep counting the rows in the employees.salaries table:

```
Py> for i in range(100): session.run_sql('SELECT COUNT(*) FROM employees.
salaries')
```

An example of the output of performance_schema.threads with innodb_parallel_ read_threads = 4 (the default) is

```
mysql> SELECT THREAD_ID, TYPE, THREAD_OS_ID
          FROM performance_schema.threads
         WHERE NAME = 'thread/innodb/parallel_read_thread';
+-----------+------------+--------------+
| THREAD_ID | TYPE       | THREAD_OS_ID |
+-----------+------------+--------------+
|        91 | BACKGROUND |        12488 |
|        92 | BACKGROUND |         5232 |
|        93 | BACKGROUND |        13836 |
|        94 | BACKGROUND |        24376 |
+-----------+------------+--------------+
4 rows in set (0.0005 sec)
```

You can try with smaller tables such as the ones in the world database and see the difference in number of background threads.

If you see that all of the configured read threads are in use most of the time, and you have spare CPUs, you can consider increasing the value of innodb_parallel_ read_threads. The maximum supported value is 256. Remember to leave enough CPU resources for the single-threaded queries.

If you see semaphore waits and monitoring of the CPUs suggests there is contention for the CPU resources while there are many parallel read threads present, you can consider decreasing innodb_parallel_read_threads to reduce the parallelism of the queries.

Query Buffers

MySQL uses several buffers during query execution. These include storing column values used in joins, a buffer for sorting, and more. It is tempting to think that more is better for these buffers, but it is not in general the case. On the contrary, often less is better. This section discusses why this is so.

When MySQL needs to use a buffer for a query or part of a query, there are several factors that determine the impact on the query. The factors include the following:

- Is the buffer large enough for the job required?

- Is there enough memory?

- How much does it cost to allocate the buffer?

If the buffer is not large enough, the algorithm cannot perform at its most optimal as more iterations are needed, or it is necessary to overflow to disk. However, in some cases the configured value of a buffer serves as a minimum size rather than the maximum size. This is, for example, the case with the join buffer with the size set by join_buffer_size. The minimum size is always allocated, and if it is not large enough to hold the columns needed from a single row when using it for a join, then it will be expanded as required.

The question about memory is also very relevant. Probably the most common reason that MySQL crashes is that the operating system is out of memory and the operating system kills MySQL. The amount of memory required for the various buffers may not seem to add up to much for a single query, but if you then multiply all of the concurrently executing queries and add the memory required for the idle connections and the global allocations, you may suddenly be closer to being out of memory than you like. This may also lead to swapping which is a major performance killer.

The last point is more surprising to most. Allocating memory has a cost, and often the more memory you need, the more expensive it is per byte. For example, on Linux there are various thresholds where the allocation method changes. These thresholds depend on the Linux distribution, but may, for example, be at 256 KiB and 2 MiB. If you cross one of the thresholds, the allocation method becomes more expensive. This is part of the reason the default value for the options `join_buffer_size`, `sort_buffer_size`, and `read_rnd_buffer_size` is 256 KiB. This means that sometimes it is better to have a buffer that is a little too small, because the benefit of an optimally sized buffer does not improve performance enough to compensate for the overhead of allocating more memory.

Tip   Allocation of buffers is one of the areas where improvements are made, so upgrading can in some cases allow you to use larger buffers without the traditional drawbacks. For example, in MySQL 8.0.12 and later, a new algorithm for the sort buffer is used. This means that on Linux/Unix and for nonconcurrent sorts on Windows, memory is allocated incrementally which makes it safer performance wise to have a large value for `sort_buffer_size`. You still need to consider how much memory a single query is allowed to use though.

The conclusion is that it is better to be conservative with the buffers that are allocated for the duration of a query. Keep the global settings small – the default values are a good starting point – and increase only for the queries where you can demonstrate that there is a significant improvement when increasing the setting.

Internal Temporary Tables

When a query needs to store the result of a subquery, combine the results of UNION statements, and similar, it uses an internal temporary table. MySQL 8 features the new TempTable storage engine which is vastly superior to the MEMORY engine used in previous versions when keeping the table in memory as it supports variable width columns (blob and text columns are supported from version 8.0.13). Additionally, the TempTable engine supports spilling over to disk using mmap, so storage engine conversion can be avoided if the table does not fit in memory.

There are primarily two settings to consider for internal temporary tables in MySQL 8: how much memory is the TempTable engine allowed to use and what should happen if it is necessary to overflow to disk.

You configure the maximum amount of memory used by internal temporary tables using the temptable_max_ram option. This is a global setting which defaults to 1 GiB. This memory is shared among all queries needing internal temporary tables, so it is easy to cap the total memory usage. The temptable_max_ram option can be set dynamically.

If you run out of memory, it is necessary to start storing the temporary tables on disk. How that is done is controlled by the temptable_use_mmap option which was introduced in version 8.0.16. The default value is ON which means that the TempTable engine allocates space for the on-disk data as memory-mapped temporary files. This is also the method used prior to 8.0.16. If the value is set to OFF, InnoDB on-disk internal temporary tables are used instead. Unless you experience problems with the memory-mapped files, it is recommended to use the default setting.

You can monitor the TempTable memory usage using the memory/temptable/physical_ram and memory/temptable/physical_disk Performance Schema events. The physical RAM event shows the memory usage for the in-memory part of the TempTable engine, whereas the physical disk event shows the memory-mapped part when temptable_use_mmap = ON. Listing 23-5 shows three examples of querying the memory usage of the two memory events.

Listing 23-5. Querying the TempTable memory usage

```
mysql> SELECT *
          FROM sys.memory_global_by_current_bytes
         WHERE event_name
               IN ('memory/temptable/physical_ram',
                   'memory/temptable/physical_disk')\G
*************************** 1. row ***************************
        event_name: memory/temptable/physical_ram
     current_count: 14
     current_alloc: 71.00 MiB
 current_avg_alloc: 5.07 MiB
        high_count: 15
        high_alloc: 135.00 MiB
    high_avg_alloc: 9.00 MiB
```

```
*************************** 2. row ***************************
       event_name: memory/temptable/physical_disk
    current_count: 1
    current_alloc: 64.00 MiB
current_avg_alloc: 64.00 MiB
       high_count: 1
       high_alloc: 64.00 MiB
   high_avg_alloc: 64.00 MiB
2 rows in set (0.0012 sec)

mysql> SELECT *
        FROM performance_schema.memory_summary_global_by_event_name
       WHERE EVENT_NAME
             IN ('memory/temptable/physical_ram',
                 'memory/temptable/physical_disk')\G
*************************** 1. row ***************************
                  EVENT_NAME: memory/temptable/physical_disk
                 COUNT_ALLOC: 2
                  COUNT_FREE: 1
     SUM_NUMBER_OF_BYTES_ALLOC: 134217728
      SUM_NUMBER_OF_BYTES_FREE: 67108864
              LOW_COUNT_USED: 0
           CURRENT_COUNT_USED: 1
              HIGH_COUNT_USED: 1
    LOW_NUMBER_OF_BYTES_USED: 0
CURRENT_NUMBER_OF_BYTES_USED: 67108864
   HIGH_NUMBER_OF_BYTES_USED: 67108864
*************************** 2. row ***************************
                  EVENT_NAME: memory/temptable/physical_ram
                 COUNT_ALLOC: 27
                  COUNT_FREE: 13
     SUM_NUMBER_OF_BYTES_ALLOC: 273678336
      SUM_NUMBER_OF_BYTES_FREE: 199229440
              LOW_COUNT_USED: 0
           CURRENT_COUNT_USED: 14
              HIGH_COUNT_USED: 15
```

```
      LOW_NUMBER_OF_BYTES_USED: 0
  CURRENT_NUMBER_OF_BYTES_USED: 74448896
     HIGH_NUMBER_OF_BYTES_USED: 141557760
2 rows in set (0.0004 sec)

mysql> SELECT *
         FROM performance_schema.memory_summary_by_thread_by_event_name
        WHERE EVENT_NAME
              IN ('memory/temptable/physical_ram',
                  'memory/temptable/physical_disk')
          AND COUNT_ALLOC > 0\G
*************************** 1. row ***************************
                    THREAD_ID: 29
                   EVENT_NAME: memory/temptable/physical_disk
                  COUNT_ALLOC: 2
                   COUNT_FREE: 1
    SUM_NUMBER_OF_BYTES_ALLOC: 134217728
     SUM_NUMBER_OF_BYTES_FREE: 67108864
              LOW_COUNT_USED: 0
          CURRENT_COUNT_USED: 1
             HIGH_COUNT_USED: 1
     LOW_NUMBER_OF_BYTES_USED: 0
  CURRENT_NUMBER_OF_BYTES_USED: 67108864
     HIGH_NUMBER_OF_BYTES_USED: 67108864
1 row in set (0.0098 sec)
```

The two first queries request the global usage, whereas the third query asks for per thread usage. The first query uses the sys.memory_global_by_current_bytes view which returns the events that at the time have a current_alloc greater than 0. This shows that the TempTable engine is in use and a part of the data has spilled over to disk using the memory-mapped files. The second query uses the Performance Schema and will always return data for both events even if there currently is no memory allocated to it. The third query shows which threads have allocated TempTable memory. Due to the way the TempTable overflow is implemented, it is not possible to see which threads have files on disk using the Performance Schema.

Summary

This chapter went through the general considerations of configuring a MySQL instance and the options that most commonly need adjustments. When you consider making changes to the configuration, the most important thing is that you think about why you want to make the change, what it should solve, and why it will solve it and that you confirm whether it did work. You can best confirm this by making small incremental changes to a single option at a time.

The three options that are the most likely to benefit from non-default values are the innodb_buffer_pool_size for setting the size of the InnoDB buffer pool and innodb_log_file_size and innodb_log_files_in_group options for setting the size of the redo log. Other InnoDB options that were discussed control the number of buffer pool instances, how much of the buffer pool is included when dumping it, the old blocks sublist, how to flush pages, and the size of the redo log buffer.

In MySQL8.0.14 and later, there is support for executing some queries in parallel. You can limit the parallelism using the innodb_parallel_read_threads option which starting from 8.0.17 specifies the total maximum of parallel threads InnoDB will create across all connections. The parallel execution threads are considered background threads and only exist while queries are being executed in parallel.

Your queries may also benefit from larger per query buffers, but you must be careful as larger values do not necessarily work better than smaller values. The recommendation is to use the default value for these buffers and only increase them for queries where testing proves there is a significant benefit.

Finally, the internal temporary tables were discussed. In MySQL 8 these use the TempTable engine which supports spilling over to disk when the global maximum memory usage is reached. It is also possible to convert the internal temporary table to InnoDB when storing it on-disk.

The next chapter will look into how you can change queries to perform better.

CHAPTER 24

Change the Query Plan

There are several possible reasons why a poorly performing query does not work as expected. This ranges from the query plainly being wrong over a poor schema to lower-level causes such as a nonoptimal query plan or resource contention. This chapter will discuss some common cases and solutions.

The chapter starts out introducing the test data used for most of the examples in the chapter and discussing the symptoms of excessive full table scans. Then it is covered how errors in the query can cause severe performance problems and why indexes cannot always be used even when they exist. The middle part of the chapter goes through various ways to improve queries either by improving the index use or rewriting complex queries. The last part discusses how the SKIP LOCKED clause can be used to implement a queue system and how to handle queries with many OR conditions or an IN () clause with many values.

Test Data

This chapter mostly uses test data specifically created for the examples in the chapter. The file chapter_24.sql in this book's GitHub repository includes the necessary table definitions and data, if you want to try the examples yourself. The script will delete the chapter_24 schema and create it with the tables.

You can execute the script using the \source command in MySQL Shell or the SOURCE command in the mysql command-line client. For example:

```
mysql shell> \source chapter_24.sql
...
mysql shell> SHOW TABLES FROM chapter_24;
```

© Jesper Wisborg Krogh 2020

J. W. Krogh, *MySQL 8 Query Performance Tuning*, https://doi.org/10.1007/978-1-4842-5584-1_24

```
+---------------------+
| Tables_in_chapter_24 |
+---------------------+
| address             |
| city                |
| country             |
| jobqueue            |
| language            |
| mytable             |
| payment             |
| person              |
+---------------------+
8 rows in set (0.0033 sec)
```

The script requires the `world` sample database to be installed before sourcing the `chapter_24.sql` script.

Note   Since index statistics are determined using random dives into the index, their values will not be the same after each analysis. For that reason, you should not expect to get identical outputs when trying the examples in this chapter.

Symptoms of Excessive Full Table Scans

One of the causes for the most severe performance issues is full table scans particularly when there are joins involved and the full table scan is not on the first table in the query block. It can cause so much work for MySQL that it also affects other connections. A full table scan happens when MySQL cannot use an index for the query either because there is no filter condition or there is no index for the conditions present. A side effect of full table scans is that a lot of data gets pulled into the buffer pool, possibly without ever being returned to the application. This can make the amount of disk I/O increase drastically causing further performance issues.

The symptoms you need to look out for to spot when queries perform excessive table scans are increased CPU usage, increased number of rows accessed, low rate of using indexes, and possible increased disk I/O combined with reduced efficiency of the InnoDB buffer pool.

The best way to detect excessive full table scans is to turn to your monitoring. The direct way is to look for queries that have been flagged as using full table scans in the Performance Schema and to compare the ratio of examined rows with the number of returned or affected rows as discussed in Chapter 19. You can also look at the timeseries graphs to spot a pattern of too many rows being accessed or too much CPU usage. Figure 24-1 shows examples of monitoring graphs during a period with full table scans on a MySQL instance. (The employees database is useful if you want to simulate a case like that as it has large enough tables to allow some relatively large scans.)

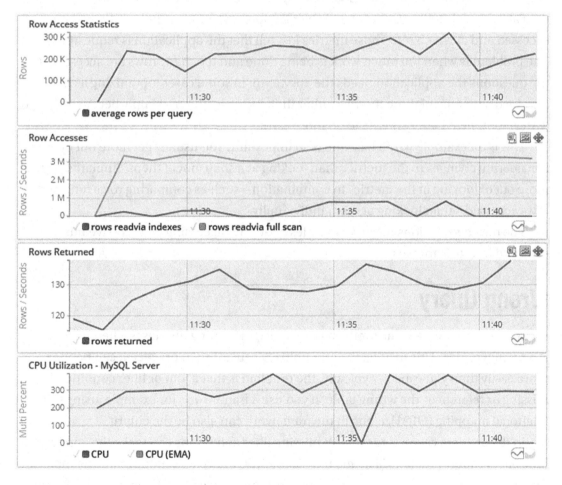

Figure 24-1. *Monitoring graphs while there are queries with full table scans*

Notice how at the left side of the graphs, the rows accessed, row access rate for rows read via full scans, and the CPU usage increase. The number of rows returned, on the other hand, changes very little (in percent) compared to the number of rows accessed. Particularly the second graph showing the rate rows are read via index compared to full scans as well as the ratio between rows read and rows returned suggests a problem.

Tip   Full table scans in connection with joins are not as big an issue in MySQL 8.0.18 and later where hash joins can be used for equi-joins. That said, a hash join still pulls more data into the buffer pool than is needed.

The big question is when there is too much CPU usage and too many rows are accessed, and unfortunately the answer is "it depends." If you consider CPU usage, then all it is really telling is that work is being done, and for the number of rows being accessed and at which rate, those metrics just tell that the application is requesting data. The problem is when too much work is being done and too many rows are accessed for the questions the application needs the answer to. In some cases, optimizing a query may increase some of these metrics rather than reducing them – simply because MySQL with an optimized query is able to do more work.

This is an example why a baseline is so important. You usually get more out of considering changes to the metrics than looking at a snapshot of them. Similarly, you get more out of looking at the metrics in combination – such as comparing rows returned to rows accessed – than looking at them individually.

The next two sections discuss examples of queries accessing an excessive number of rows and how to improve them.

Wrong Query

One of the common reasons for the most poorly performing queries is when the query is written wrongly. This may seem as an unlikely cause, but in practice it can happen more easily than you expect. Typically, the problem is that a join or filter condition is missing or references the wrong table. If you use a framework, for example, using object-relational mapping (ORM), a bug in the framework can also be the culprit.

In the extreme cases, a query with missing filter conditions can make the application time out the query (but not kill it) and retry it, so MySQL keeps executing more and more of the same very badly performing query. This can in turn make MySQL run out of connections.

Another possibility is that the first of the submitted queries start to pull in data to the buffer pool from disk. Then each of the subsequent queries will be faster and faster as they can read some of the rows from the buffer pool and then will slow down when they get to the rows not yet read from disk. In the end, all copies of the query will finish within a short period of time and start to return a large amount of data to the application which can saturate the network. A saturated network can cause connection attempts to fail because of handshake error (the COUNT_HANDSHAKE_ERRORS column in performance_schema.host_cache), and the host the connections are made from can eventually become blocked.

This may seem extreme, and in most cases, it does not become that bad. However, the author of this book has indeed experienced exactly this scenario happen due to a bug in the framework generating the query. Given that MySQL instances nowadays often live in virtual machines in the cloud possibly with a limited amount of resources available such as for CPU and network, it is also more likely that a poor query may end up exhausting the resources.

As an example of a query and query plan where the join condition is missing, consider Listing 24-1 which joins the city and country tables.

Listing 24-1. Query that is missing a join condition

```
mysql> EXPLAIN
       SELECT ci.CountryCode, ci.ID, ci.Name,
              ci.District, co.Name AS Country,
              ci.Population
         FROM world.city ci
              INNER JOIN world.country co\G
*************************** 1. row ***************************
           id: 1
  select_type: SIMPLE
        table: co
   partitions: NULL
         type: ALL
possible_keys: NULL
          key: NULL
```

```
           key_len: NULL
               ref: NULL
              rows: 239
          filtered: 100
             Extra: NULL
*************************** 2. row ***************************
                id: 1
       select_type: SIMPLE
             table: ci
        partitions: NULL
              type: ALL
     possible_keys: NULL
               key: NULL
           key_len: NULL
               ref: NULL
              rows: 4188
          filtered: 100
             Extra: Using join buffer (Block Nested Loop)
2 rows in set, 1 warning (0.0008 sec)

mysql> EXPLAIN ANALYZE
        SELECT ci.CountryCode, ci.ID, ci.Name,
               ci.District, co.Name AS Country,
               ci.Population
          FROM world.city ci
               INNER JOIN world.country co\G *********** 1. row *********
EXPLAIN:
-> Inner hash join  (cost=100125.15 rows=1000932) (actual time=0.194..80.427
                    rows=974881 loops=1)
    -> Table scan on ci  (cost=1.78 rows=4188) (actual time=0.025..2.621
       rows=4079 loops=1)
    -> Hash
        -> Table scan on co  (cost=25.40 rows=239) (actual time=0.041..0.089
           rows=239 loops=1)

1 row in set (0.4094 sec)
```

Notice how both tables have the access type set to ALL and that the join is using the join buffer in a block nested loop. A cause that often has similar symptoms is a correct query, but where the query cannot use indexes. The EXPLAIN ANALYZE output shows that a hash join is used in version 8.0.18. It also shows that a total of almost 1 million rows are returned! The Visual Explain diagram for the query is shown in Figure 24-2.

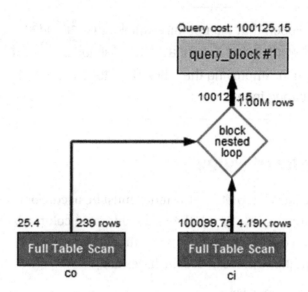

Figure 24-2. *Visual Explain for a query that is missing a join condition*

Notice here how the two (red) full table scans stand out and how the query cost is estimated to be more than 100,000.

The combinations of multiple full table scans, a very high estimated number of returned rows, and a very high cost estimate are the telltale signs you need to look for.

A cause of poor query performance that gives similar symptoms is when MySQL is not able to use an index for the filter and join conditions.

No Index Used

When a query needs to find rows in a table, it can essentially do it in two ways: accessing the rows directly in a full table scan or going through an index. In cases where there is a filter that is highly selective, it is usually much faster to access the rows through an index than through a table scan.

Obviously, if there is no index on the column the filter applies to, MySQL has no choice but to use a table scan. What you may find is that even if there is an index, then it cannot be used. Three common reasons for this are that the columns are not the first in a multicolumn index, the data type does not match for the comparison, and a function is used on the column with the index. This section will discuss each of these causes.

Tip   It can also happen that the optimizer thinks that an index is not selective enough to make it worth using it compared to a full table scan. That case is handled in the section "Improving the Index Use" together with the example of MySQL using the wrong index.

Not a Left Prefix of Index

For an index to be used, a left prefix of the index must be used. For example, if an index includes three columns as (a, b, c), then a condition on column b can only use the filter if there is also an equality condition on column a.

Examples of conditions that can use the index are

```
WHERE a = 10 AND b = 20 AND c = 30
WHERE a = 10 AND b = 20 AND c > 10
WHERE a = 10 AND b = 20
WHERE a = 10 AND b > 20
WHERE a = 10
```

An example where the index cannot be used as effectively is WHERE b = 20. In MySQL 8.0.13 and later, if a is a NOT NULL column, MySQL can use the index using the skip scan range optimization. If a allows NULL values, then the index cannot be used. The condition WHERE c = 20 cannot use the index under any circumstances.

Similarly, for the condition WHERE a > 10 AND b = 20, the index will only be used for filtering on the a column. When a query only uses a subset of the columns in the index, it is important that the order of the columns in the index corresponds to which filters are applied. If you have a range condition on one of the columns, make sure that column is the last one being used in the index. For example, consider the table and query in Listing 24-2.

Listing 24-2. Query that cannot use the index effectively due to column order

```
mysql> SHOW CREATE TABLE chapter_24.mytable\G
*************************** 1. row ***************************
       Table: mytable
Create Table: CREATE TABLE `mytable` (
  `id` int(10) unsigned NOT NULL AUTO_INCREMENT,
  `a` int(11) NOT NULL,
  `b` int(11) DEFAULT NULL,
  `c` int(11) DEFAULT NULL,
  PRIMARY KEY (`id`),
  KEY `abc` (`a`,`b`,`c`)
) ENGINE=InnoDB AUTO_INCREMENT=16385 DEFAULT CHARSET=utf8mb4
COLLATE=utf8mb4_0900_ai_ci
1 row in set (0.0004 sec)

mysql> EXPLAIN
       SELECT *
         FROM chapter_24.mytable
        WHERE a > 10 AND b = 20\G
*************************** 1. row ***************************
           id: 1
  select_type: SIMPLE
        table: mytable
   partitions: NULL
         type: range
possible_keys: abc
          key: abc
      key_len: 4
          ref: NULL
         rows: 8326
     filtered: 10
        Extra: Using where; Using index
1 row in set, 1 warning (0.0007 sec)
```

Notice in the EXPLAIN output that the key_len is only 4 bytes, whereas it should be 9 if the index was used for both the a and b columns. The output also shows that it is estimated that only 10% of the rows that are examined will be included. Figure 24-3 shows the same example in Visual Explain.

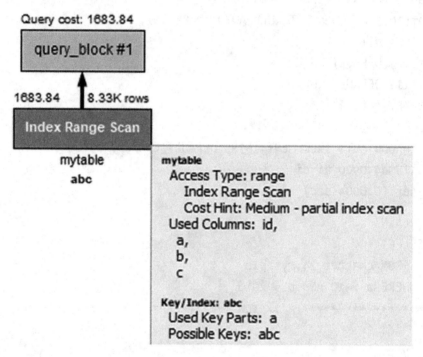

Figure 24-3. *Visual Explain with nonoptimal column order in the index*

Notice that the *Used Key Parts* (near the bottom of the box with additional details) just lists column a. However, if you change the order of the columns in the index, so that column b is indexed before column a, then the index can be used for the conditions on both columns. Listing 24-3 shows how the query plan changes after adding a new index (b, a, c).

Listing 24-3. Query plan with the index in optimal order

```
mysql> ALTER TABLE chapter_24.mytable
         ADD INDEX bac (b, a, c);
Query OK, 0 rows affected (1.4098 sec)

Records: 0  Duplicates: 0  Warnings: 0

mysql> EXPLAIN
       SELECT *
         FROM chapter_24.mytable
        WHERE a > 10 AND b = 20\G
*************************** 1. row ***************************
           id: 1
  select_type: SIMPLE
        table: mytable
   partitions: NULL
         type: range
possible_keys: abc,bac
          key: bac
      key_len: 9
          ref: NULL
         rows: 160
     filtered: 100
        Extra: Using where; Using index
1 row in set, 1 warning (0.0006 sec)
```

Notice how the key_len column now returns 9 bytes and that the filtered column shows that 100% of the examined rows will be included from the table. The same is reflected in Visual Explain as shown in Figure 24-4.

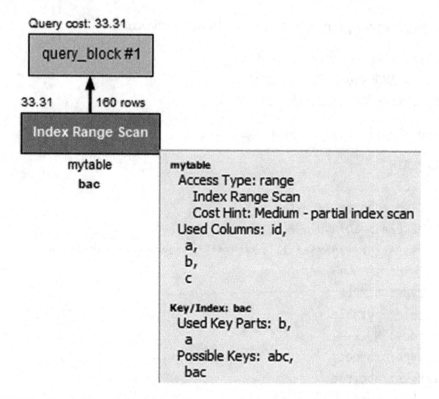

Figure 24-4. *Visual Explain when there is an optimally ordered index*

In the figure, you can see that the number of rows that will be examined is reduced from more than 8000 rows to 160 rows and that Used Key Parts now includes both the b and a columns. The estimated query cost has also reduced from 1683.84 to 33.31.

Data Types Not Matching

Another thing that you need to look out for is that both sides of a condition use the same data type and for strings that the same collation is used. If that is not the case, MySQL may not be able to use an index.

When a query is not working optimally because of the data types or collations not matching, it can be hard to realize at first what the problem is. The query is correct, but MySQL refuses to use the index that you expect. Other than the query plan not being what you expect, the query result may also be wrong. This can happen due to the casting, for example:

```
mysql> SELECT ('a130' = 0), ('130a131' = 130);
+--------------+--------------------+
| ('a130' = 0) | ('130a131' = 130)  |
+--------------+--------------------+
|            1 |                  1 |
+--------------+--------------------+
1 row in set, 2 warnings (0.0004 sec)
```

Notice how the string "a130" is considered equal to the integer 0. That happens because the string starts with a non-numeric character and thus is casted to the value 0. In the same way, the string "130a131" is considered equal to the integer 130 as the leading numeric part of the string is casted to the integer 130. The same kind of unintended matches can occur when casting is used for a WHERE clause or a join condition. This is also a case where inspecting the warnings of a query sometimes can help catch the problem.

If you consider the country and world tables in the test schema for this chapter (the table definitions will be shown during the discussion of the example), you can see an example of a join that does not use an index, when the two tables are joined using the CountryId columns. Listing 24-4 shows an example of a query and its query plan.

Listing 24-4. Query not using an index due to mismatching data types

```
mysql> EXPLAIN
        SELECT ci.ID, ci.Name, ci.District,
               co.Name AS Country, ci.Population
          FROM chapter_24.city ci
               INNER JOIN chapter_24.country co
                    USING (CountryId)
         WHERE co.CountryCode = 'AUS'\G
*************************** 1. row ***************************
           id: 1
  select_type: SIMPLE
        table: co
   partitions: NULL
         type: const
possible_keys: PRIMARY,CountryCode
          key: CountryCode
      key_len: 12
```

```
               ref: const
              rows: 1
          filtered: 100
             Extra: NULL
*************************** 2. row ***************************
                id: 1
       select_type: SIMPLE
             table: ci
        partitions: NULL
              type: ALL
     possible_keys: CountryId
               key: NULL
           key_len: NULL
               ref: NULL
              rows: 4079
          filtered: 10
             Extra: Using where
2 rows in set, 3 warnings (0.0009 sec)
Warning (code 1739): Cannot use ref access on index 'CountryId' due to type
or collation conversion on field 'CountryId'
Warning (code 1739): Cannot use range access on index 'CountryId' due to
type or collation conversion on field 'CountryId'
Note (code 1003): /* select#1 */ select `chapter_24`.`ci`.`ID` AS
`ID`,`chapter_24`.`ci`.`Name` AS `Name`,`chapter_24`.`ci`.`District` AS
`District`,'Australia' AS `Country`,`chapter_24`.`ci`.`Population` AS
`Population` from `chapter_24`.`city` `ci` join `chapter_24`.`country` `co`
where ((`chapter_24`.`ci`.`CountryId` = '15'))
```

Notice that the access type for the ci (city) table is ALL. This query will neither use a block nested loop nor a hash join as the co (country) table is a constant. The warnings (if you do not use MySQL Shell with warnings enabled, you will need to execute SHOW WARNINGS to fetch the warnings) have been included here as they provide a valuable hint to why it is not possible to use an index, for example: *Cannot use ref access on index 'CountryId' due to type or collation conversion on field 'CountryId'*. So there is an index that is a candidate, but it cannot be used because the data type or collation is changed. Figure 24-5 shows the same query plan using Visual Explain.

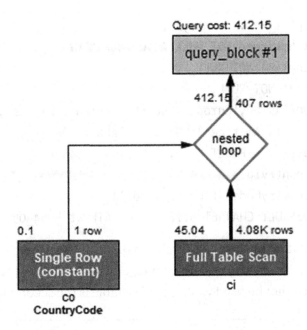

Figure 24-5. *Visual Explain where the data types do not match*

This is one of the cases where you need the text-based output to get all details as Visual Explain does not include the warnings. When you see a warning like this, go back and check the table definitions. These are shown in Listing 24-5.

Listing 24-5. The table definitions for the `city` and `country` tables

```
CREATE TABLE `chapter_24`.`city` (
  `ID` int unsigned NOT NULL AUTO_INCREMENT,
  `Name` varchar(35) NOT NULL DEFAULT '',
  `CountryCode` char(3) NOT NULL DEFAULT '',
  `CountryId` char(3) NOT NULL,
  `District` varchar(20) NOT NULL DEFAULT '',
  `Population` int unsigned NOT NULL DEFAULT '0',
  PRIMARY KEY (`ID`),
  KEY `CountryCode` (`CountryCode`),
  KEY `CountryId` (`CountryId`)
) ENGINE=InnoDB DEFAULT CHARSET=utf8mb4 COLLATE=utf8mb4_general_ci;
```

```
CREATE TABLE `chapter_24`.`country` (
  `CountryId` int unsigned NOT NULL AUTO_INCREMENT,
  `CountryCode` char(3) NOT NULL,
  `Name` varchar(52) NOT NULL,
  `Continent` enum('Asia','Europe','North America','Africa','Oceania',
   'Antarctica','South America') NOT NULL DEFAULT 'Asia',
  `Region` varchar(26) DEFAULT NULL,
  PRIMARY KEY (`CountryId`),
  UNIQUE INDEX `CountryCode` (`CountryCode`)
) ENGINE=InnoDB DEFAULT CHARSET=utf8mb4 COLLATE=utf8mb4_0900_ai_ci;
```

Here it is evident that the CountryId column of the city table is a char(3) column but the CountryId of the country table is an integer. That is why the index on the city. CountryId column cannot be used when the city table is the second table in the join.

Note   If the join goes the other way with the city table being the first table and the country table the second table, then city.CountryId is still casted to an integer, while country.CountryId is not changed, so the index on country. CountryId can be used.

Notice also that the collation is different for the two tables. The city table uses the utf8mb4_general_ci collation (the default utf8mb4 collation in MySQL 5.7 and earlier), whereas the country table uses the utf8mb4_0900_ai_ci (the default utf8mb4 collation in MySQL 8). Different character sets or collations can even prevent the query from executing altogether:

```
SELECT ci.ID, ci.Name, ci.District,
       co.Name AS Country, ci.Population
  FROM chapter_24.city ci
       INNER JOIN chapter_24.country co
            USING (CountryCode)
 WHERE co.CountryCode = 'AUS';
ERROR: 1267: Illegal mix of collations (utf8mb4_general_ci,IMPLICIT) and
(utf8mb4_0900_ai_ci,IMPLICIT) for operation '='
```

This is something to be aware of if you create a table in MySQL 8 and use it in queries together with tables created in earlier MySQL versions. In that case, you need to ensure that all tables use the same collation.

The problem with data type mismatch is a special case of using functions in the filters as MySQL does an implicit cast. In general, using functions in filters is something that can prevent the use of an index.

Functional Dependencies

The last common reason for an index not to be used is that a function is applied to the column, for example: WHERE MONTH(birth_date) = 7. In that case, you need to rewrite the condition to avoid the function, or you need to add a functional index.

When possible, the best way to handle a case where the use of a function prevents using an index is to rewrite the query to avoid the function. While a functional index can also be used, unless it helps create a covering index, the index adds overhead which is avoided with a rewrite. Consider a query that wants to find the details of persons born in 1970 as in the example in Listing 24-6 using the chapter_24.person table.

Listing 24-6. The person table and finding persons born in 1970

```
mysql> SHOW CREATE TABLE chapter_24.person\G
*************************** 1. row ***************************
       Table: person
Create Table: CREATE TABLE `person` (
  `PersonId` int(10) unsigned NOT NULL AUTO_INCREMENT,
  `FirstName` varchar(50) DEFAULT NULL,
  `Surname` varchar(50) DEFAULT NULL,
  `BirthDate` date NOT NULL,
  `AddressId` int(10) unsigned DEFAULT NULL,
  `LanguageId` int(10) unsigned DEFAULT NULL,
  PRIMARY KEY (`PersonId`),
  KEY `BirthDate` (`BirthDate`),
  KEY `AddressId` (`AddressId`),
  KEY `LanguageId` (`LanguageId`)
) ENGINE=InnoDB AUTO_INCREMENT=1001 DEFAULT CHARSET=utf8mb4
COLLATE=utf8mb4_0900_ai_ci
1 row in set (0.0012 sec)
```

```
mysql> EXPLAIN
        SELECT *
          FROM chapter_24.person
         WHERE YEAR(BirthDate) = 1970\G
*************************** 1. row ***************************
           id: 1
  select_type: SIMPLE
        table: person
   partitions: NULL
         type: ALL
possible_keys: NULL
          key: NULL
      key_len: NULL
          ref: NULL
         rows: 1000
     filtered: 100
        Extra: Using where
1 row in set, 1 warning (0.0006 sec)
```

This query uses the YEAR() function to determine the year the person is born in. An alternative is to look for everyone born between January 1, 1970, and December 31, 1971 (both days included), which amount to the same thing. Listing 24-7 shows that in this case the index on the birthdate column is used.

Listing 24-7. Rewriting the YEAR() function to a date range condition

```
mysql> EXPLAIN
        SELECT *
          FROM chapter_24.person
         WHERE BirthDate BETWEEN '1970-01-01'
                             AND '1970-12-31'\G
*************************** 1. row ***************************
           id: 1
  select_type: SIMPLE
        table: person
   partitions: NULL
         type: range
```

```
possible_keys: BirthDate
          key: BirthDate
      key_len: 3
          ref: NULL
         rows: 6
     filtered: 100
        Extra: Using index condition
1 row in set, 1 warning (0.0009 sec)
```

This rewrite reduces the query from using a table scan examining 1000 rows to an index range scan just examining six rows. A rewrite similar to this is often possible where functions are used on dates which effectively extract a range of values.

Note   It can be tempting to rewrite a date or datetime range condition using the LIKE operator, for example: WHERE birthdate LIKE '1970-%'. This will not allow MySQL to use a query and is discouraged. Use a proper range instead.

It is not always possible to rewrite a condition that uses a function in the way just demonstrated. It may be the condition does not map into a single range or that the query is generated by a framework or a third-party application, so you cannot change it. In that case, you can add a functional index.

Note   Functional indexes are supported in MySQL 8.0.13 and later. If you use an earlier release, you are recommended to upgrade. If that is not possible or you also need the value returned by the function, you can emulate functional indexes by adding a virtual column with the functional expression and creating an index on the virtual column.

As an example, consider a query that finds all persons with a birthday in a given month – for example, because you want to send them a birthday greeting. In principle that can be done using ranges, but it will require one range per year which is neither practical nor very efficient. Instead, you can use the MONTH() function to extract a numeric value of the month (January is 1 and December 12). Listing 24-8 shows how you can add a functional index that can be used together with a query that finds all persons in the chapter_24.person table who have a birthday in the current month.

Listing 24-8. Using a functional index

```
mysql> ALTER TABLE chapter_24.person
          ADD INDEX ((MONTH(BirthDate)));
Query OK, 0 rows affected (0.4845 sec)

Records: 0  Duplicates: 0  Warnings: 0

mysql> EXPLAIN
          SELECT *
            FROM chapter_24.person
           WHERE MONTH(BirthDate) = MONTH(NOW())\G
*************************** 1. row ***************************
           id: 1
  select_type: SIMPLE
        table: person
   partitions: NULL
         type: ref
possible_keys: functional_index
          key: functional_index
      key_len: 5
          ref: const
         rows: 88
     filtered: 100
        Extra: NULL
1 row in set, 1 warning (0.0006 sec)
```

After the functional index on MONTH(BirthDate) has been added, the query plan shows that the index used is functional_index.

That concludes the discussion of how to add index support for queries that are currently not using an index. There are several other rewrites that relate to using indexes. These will be covered in the next section.

Improving the Index Use

The previous section considered queries where no index was used for a join or WHERE clause. In some cases, an index is used, but you can improve the index, or another index gives better performance, or indexes cannot be used efficiently because of the complexity of the filters. This section will look at some examples of improving queries already using an index.

Add a Covering Index

In some cases when you query a table, the filtering is performed by an index, but then you have requested a couple of other columns, so MySQL needs to retrieve the whole row. In that case, it would be more efficient to add those extra columns to the index, so the index contains all columns required for the query.

Consider the city table in the chapter_24 sample database:

```
CREATE TABLE `city` (
  `ID` int unsigned NOT NULL AUTO_INCREMENT,
  `Name` varchar(35) NOT NULL DEFAULT ",
  `CountryCode` char(3) NOT NULL DEFAULT ",
  `CountryId` char(3) NOT NULL,
  `District` varchar(20) NOT NULL DEFAULT ",
  `Population` int unsigned NOT NULL DEFAULT '0',
  PRIMARY KEY (`ID`),
  KEY `CountryCode` (`CountryCode`),
  KEY `CountryId` (`CountryId`)
) ENGINE=InnoDB DEFAULT CHARSET=utf8mb4 COLLATE=utf8mb4_general_ci;
```

If you want to find the name and district of all cities with CountryCode = 'USA', then you can use the CountryCode index to find the rows. This is efficient as shown in Listing 24-9.

Listing 24-9. Querying cities by a non-covering index

```
mysql> EXPLAIN
       SELECT Name, District
         FROM chapter_24.city
        WHERE CountryCode = 'USA'\G
```

```
*************************** 1. row ***************************
            id: 1
   select_type: SIMPLE
         table: city
    partitions: NULL
          type: ref
 possible_keys: CountryCode
           key: CountryCode
       key_len: 12
           ref: const
          rows: 274
      filtered: 100
         Extra: NULL
1 row in set, 1 warning (0.0376 sec)
```

Notice that 12 bytes are used for the index (three characters each up to 4 bytes wide), and the Extra column does not include Using index. If you create a new index with CountryCode as the first column and District and Name as the remaining columns, you have all columns you need for the query in the index. Choose the order of District and Name as it is most likely you will use them together with the CountryCode in filters and ORDER BY and GROUP BY clauses. If it is equally likely that the columns are used in filters, choose Name before District in the index as the city name is more selective than the district. Listing 24-10 shows an example of this together with the new query plan.

Listing 24-10. Querying cities by a covering index

```
mysql> ALTER TABLE chapter_24.city
       ALTER INDEX CountryCode INVISIBLE,
        ADD INDEX Country_District_Name
                 (CountryCode, District, Name);
Query OK, 0 rows affected (1.6630 sec)

Records: 0  Duplicates: 0  Warnings: 0

mysql> EXPLAIN
        SELECT Name, District
          FROM chapter_24.city
         WHERE CountryCode = 'USA'\G
```

```
*************************** 1. row ***************************
            id: 1
   select_type: SIMPLE
         table: city
    partitions: NULL
          type: ref
 possible_keys: Country_District_Name
           key: Country_District_Name
       key_len: 12
           ref: const
          rows: 274
      filtered: 100
         Extra: Using index
1 row in set, 1 warning (0.0006 sec)
```

When adding the new index, the old index that just covers the CountryCode column is made invisible. That is done because the new index also can be used for all uses where the old index was used, so there is usually no reason to keep both indexes. (Given the index just on the CountryCode column is smaller than the new index, it is possible that some queries benefit from the old index. By making it invisible, you can verify it is not needed before dropping it.)

The key length is still returned to be 12 bytes as that is what is used for the filtering. However, the Extra column now includes Using index to show that a covering index is being used.

Wrong Index

When MySQL can choose between several indexes, the optimizer will have to decide which to use based on the estimated cost of the two query plans. Since the index statistics and cost estimates are not exact, it can happen that MySQL chooses the wrong index. Special cases are where the optimizer chooses not to use an index even if it is possible to use it or the optimizer chooses to use an index where it is faster to do a table scan. Either way, you need to use index hints.

Tip   Index hints can also be used just to affect whether an index is used for sorting or grouping as discussed in Chapter 17. An example where it can be necessary to use an index hint is when the query chooses to use an index for sorting instead of filtering and that causes poor performance – or vice versa. A case where the reverse can happen is when you have a LIMIT clause and using an index for sorting can allow the query to stop the query early.

When you suspect that the wrong index is used, you need to look at the possible_keys column of the EXPLAIN output to determine which indexes are candidates. Listing 24-11 shows an example of finding information about the people in Japan who turn 20 years old in 2020 and speak English. (Imagine you want to send them a birthday card.) Part of the tree-formatted EXPLAIN output has been replaced by ellipsis to improve the readability by keeping most of the lines within the width of the book page.

Listing 24-11. Finding information about the countries where English is spoken

```
mysql> SHOW CREATE TABLE chapter_24.person\G
*************************** 1. row ***************************
       Table: person
Create Table: CREATE TABLE `person` (
  `PersonId` int(10) unsigned NOT NULL AUTO_INCREMENT,
  `FirstName` varchar(50) DEFAULT NULL,
  `Surname` varchar(50) DEFAULT NULL,
  `BirthDate` date NOT NULL,
  `AddressId` int(10) unsigned DEFAULT NULL,
  `LanguageId` int(10) unsigned DEFAULT NULL,
  PRIMARY KEY (`PersonId`),
  KEY `BirthDate` (`BirthDate`),
  KEY `AddressId` (`AddressId`),
  KEY `LanguageId` (`LanguageId`),
  KEY `functional_index` ((month(`BirthDate`)))
) ENGINE=InnoDB AUTO_INCREMENT=1001 DEFAULT CHARSET=utf8mb4
COLLATE=utf8mb4_0900_ai_ci
1 row in set (0.0007 sec)

mysql> SHOW CREATE TABLE chapter_24.address\G
```

```
*************************** 1. row ***************************
       Table: address
Create Table: CREATE TABLE `address` (
  `AddressId` int(10) unsigned NOT NULL AUTO_INCREMENT,
  `City` varchar(35) NOT NULL,
  `District` varchar(20) NOT NULL,
  `CountryCode` char(3) NOT NULL,
  PRIMARY KEY (`AddressId`),
  KEY `CountryCode` (`CountryCode`,`District`,`City`)
) ENGINE=InnoDB AUTO_INCREMENT=4096 DEFAULT CHARSET=utf8mb4
COLLATE=utf8mb4_0900_ai_ci
1 row in set (0.0007 sec)

mysql> SHOW CREATE TABLE chapter_24.language\G
*************************** 1. row ***************************
       Table: language
Create Table: CREATE TABLE `language` (
  `LanguageId` int(10) unsigned NOT NULL AUTO_INCREMENT,
  `Language` varchar(35) NOT NULL,
  PRIMARY KEY (`LanguageId`),
  KEY `Language` (`Language`)
) ENGINE=InnoDB AUTO_INCREMENT=512 DEFAULT CHARSET=utf8mb4
COLLATE=utf8mb4_0900_ai_ci
1 row in set (0.0005 sec)

mysql> UPDATE mysql.innodb_index_stats
          SET stat_value = 1000
        WHERE database_name = 'chapter_24'
              AND table_name = 'person'
              AND index_name = 'LanguageId'
              AND stat_name = 'n_diff_pfx01';
Query OK, 1 row affected (0.0920 sec)

Rows matched: 1  Changed: 1  Warnings: 0

mysql> FLUSH TABLE chapter_24.person;
Query OK, 0 rows affected (0.0686 sec)
```

```
mysql> EXPLAIN
        SELECT PersonId, FirstName,
               Surname, BirthDate
          FROM chapter_24.person
               INNER JOIN chapter_24.address
                   USING (AddressId)
               INNER JOIN chapter_24.language
                   USING (LanguageId)
         WHERE BirthDate BETWEEN '2000-01-01'
                            AND '2000-12-31'
               AND CountryCode = 'JPN'
               AND Language = 'English'\G
*************************** 1. row ***************************
           id: 1
  select_type: SIMPLE
        table: language
   partitions: NULL
         type: ref
possible_keys: PRIMARY,Language
          key: Language
      key_len: 142
          ref: const
         rows: 1
     filtered: 100
        Extra: Using index
*************************** 2. row ***************************
           id: 1
  select_type: SIMPLE
        table: person
   partitions: NULL
         type: ref
possible_keys: BirthDate,AddressId,LanguageId
          key: LanguageId
      key_len: 5
          ref: chapter_24.language.LanguageId
```

```
           rows: 1
       filtered: 5
          Extra: Using where
*************************** 3. row ***************************
             id: 1
    select_type: SIMPLE
          table: address
     partitions: NULL
           type: eq_ref
  possible_keys: PRIMARY,CountryCode
            key: PRIMARY
        key_len: 4
            ref: chapter_24.person.AddressId
           rows: 1
       filtered: 6.079921722412109
          Extra: Using where
3 rows in set, 1 warning (0.0008 sec)

mysql> EXPLAIN FORMAT=TREE
        SELECT PersonId, FirstName,
               Surname, BirthDate
          FROM chapter_24.person
               INNER JOIN chapter_24.address
                   USING (AddressId)
               INNER JOIN chapter_24.language
                   USING (LanguageId)
         WHERE BirthDate BETWEEN '2000-01-01'
                           AND '2000-12-31'
               AND CountryCode = 'JPN'
               AND Language = 'English'\G
*************************** 1. row ***************************
EXPLAIN:
-> Nested loop inner join  (cost=0.72 rows=0)
    -> Nested loop inner join  (cost=0.70 rows=0)
        -> Index lookup on language using Language...
```

```
        -> Filter: ((person.BirthDate between '2000-01-01' and '2000-12-31')
            and (person.AddressId is not null))...
            -> Index lookup on person using LanguageId...
    -> Filter: (address.CountryCode = 'JPN')  (cost=0.37 rows=0)
        -> Single-row index lookup on address using PRIMARY...

1 row in set (0.0006 sec)
```

The key table for this example is the person table which is joined both to the language and address tables. The UPDATE and FLUSH statements are used to emulate that the index statistics are out of date by updating the mysql.innodb_index_stats table and flushing the table to make the new index statistics take effect.

The query can use either the BirthDate, AddressId, or LanguageId index. The effectiveness of the three WHERE clauses (one on each table) is determined very accurately as the optimizer asks the storage engine for a count of rows for each condition. The difficulty for the optimizer is to determine the best join order based on the effectiveness of the join conditions and which index to use for each join. According to the EXPLAIN output, the optimizer has chosen to start with the language table and join on the person table using the LanguageId index for the join and finally join on the address table.

If you suspect the wrong indexes are used for the query (in this case, using LanguageId for the join on the person table is not optimal and is only chosen because the index statistics are "wrong"), the first thing to do is to update the index statistics. The result of this is shown in Listing 24-12.

Listing 24-12. Updating the index statistics to change the query plan

```
mysql> ANALYZE TABLE
                chapter_24.person,
                chapter_24.address,
                chapter_24.language;
+---------------------+---------+-----------+----------+
| Table               | Op      | Msg_type  | Msg_text |
+---------------------+---------+-----------+----------+
| chapter_24.person   | analyze | status    | OK       |
| chapter_24.address  | analyze | status    | OK       |
| chapter_24.language | analyze | status    | OK       |
+---------------------+---------+-----------+----------+
3 rows in set (0.2634 sec)
```

```
mysql> EXPLAIN
        SELECT PersonId, FirstName,
               Surname, BirthDate
          FROM chapter_24.person
               INNER JOIN chapter_24.address
                   USING (AddressId)
               INNER JOIN chapter_24.language
                   USING (LanguageId)
         WHERE BirthDate BETWEEN '2000-01-01'
                            AND '2000-12-31'
               AND CountryCode = 'JPN'
               AND Language = 'English'\G
*************************** 1. row ***************************
           id: 1
  select_type: SIMPLE
        table: language
   partitions: NULL
         type: ref
possible_keys: PRIMARY,Language
          key: Language
      key_len: 142
          ref: const
         rows: 1
     filtered: 100
        Extra: Using index
*************************** 2. row ***************************
           id: 1
  select_type: SIMPLE
        table: person
   partitions: NULL
         type: range
possible_keys: BirthDate,AddressId,LanguageId
          key: BirthDate
      key_len: 3
          ref: NULL
```

```
         rows: 8
     filtered: 10
        Extra: Using index condition; Using where; Using join buffer (Block
     Nested Loop)
*************************** 3. row ***************************
           id: 1
  select_type: SIMPLE
        table: address
   partitions: NULL
         type: eq_ref
possible_keys: PRIMARY,CountryCode
          key: PRIMARY
      key_len: 4
          ref: chapter_24.person.AddressId
         rows: 1
     filtered: 6.079921722412109
        Extra: Using where
3 rows in set, 1 warning (0.0031 sec)

mysql> EXPLAIN FORMAT=TREE
        SELECT PersonId, FirstName,
               Surname, BirthDate
          FROM chapter_24.person
               INNER JOIN chapter_24.address
                   USING (AddressId)
               INNER JOIN chapter_24.language
                   USING (LanguageId)
         WHERE BirthDate BETWEEN '2000-01-01'
                            AND '2000-12-31'
               AND CountryCode = 'JPN'
               AND Language = 'English'\G
*************************** 1. row ***************************
EXPLAIN:
-> Nested loop inner join  (cost=7.01 rows=0)
    -> Inner hash join...
        -> Filter: (person.AddressId is not null)...
```

```
        -> Index range scan on person using BirthDate...
      -> Hash
        -> Index lookup on language using Language...
    -> Filter: (address.CountryCode = 'JPN')...
      -> Single-row index lookup on address using PRIMARY...

1 row in set (0.0009 sec)
```

This significantly changed the query plan (only part of the tree-formatted query plan is included for readability) which is easiest seen by comparing the tree-formatted query plan. The tables are still joined in the same order, but now a hash join is used to join the language and person tables. This is effective because only one row is expected from the language table, so doing a table scan on the person table and filtering on the birthdate is a good choice. In most cases where the wrong index is used, updating the index statistics will solve the problem, possibly after changing the number of index dives that InnoDB makes for the tables.

Caution   ANALYZE TABLE triggers an implicit FLUSH TABLES for the tables that are analyzed. If you have long-running queries using the analyzed tables, no other queries requiring access to those tables can start until the long-running queries have completed.

In some cases, it is not possible to solve the performance problem by updating index statistics. In that case, you can then use an index hint (IGNORE INDEX, USE INDEX, and FORCE INDEX) to influence which index MySQL will use. Listing 24-13 shows an example of doing this for the same query as before after changing the index statistics back to become outdated.

Listing 24-13. Improving the query plan using an index hint

```
mysql> UPDATE mysql.innodb_index_stats
         SET stat_value = 1000
       WHERE database_name = 'chapter_24'
             AND table_name = 'person'
             AND index_name = 'LanguageId'
             AND stat_name = 'n_diff_pfx01';
Query OK, 1 row affected (0.0920 sec)
```

```
Rows matched: 1  Changed: 1  Warnings: 0

mysql> FLUSH TABLE chapter_24.person;
Query OK, 0 rows affected (0.0498 sec)

mysql> EXPLAIN
        SELECT PersonId, FirstName,
               Surname, BirthDate
          FROM chapter_24.person USE INDEX (BirthDate)
               INNER JOIN chapter_24.address
                   USING (AddressId)
               INNER JOIN chapter_24.language
                   USING (LanguageId)
         WHERE BirthDate BETWEEN '2000-01-01'
                           AND '2000-12-31'
               AND CountryCode = 'JPN'
               AND Language = 'English'\G
*************************** 1. row ***************************
           id: 1
  select_type: SIMPLE
        table: language
   partitions: NULL
         type: ref
possible_keys: PRIMARY,Language
          key: Language
      key_len: 142
          ref: const
         rows: 1
     filtered: 100
        Extra: Using index
*************************** 2. row ***************************
           id: 1
  select_type: SIMPLE
        table: person
   partitions: NULL
         type: range
```

possible_keys: BirthDate
     key: BirthDate
   key_len: 3
     ref: NULL
    rows: 8
  filtered: 0.625
    Extra: Using index condition; Using where; Using join buffer (Block
    Nested Loop)
*************************** 3. row ***************************
      id: 1
  select_type: SIMPLE
    table: address
  partitions: NULL
     type: eq_ref
possible_keys: PRIMARY,CountryCode
     key: PRIMARY
   key_len: 4
     ref: chapter_24.person.AddressId
    rows: 1
  filtered: 6.079921722412109
   Extra: Using where
3 rows in set, 1 warning (0.0016 sec)

This time the USE INDEX (BirthDate) index hint is added for the person table which gives the same query plan as when the index statistics were updated. Notice that the possible keys for the person table only include BirthDate. The disadvantage of this approach is that the optimizer does not have the flexibility to change the query plan should the data change, so the BirthDate index is no longer the most optimal.

This example had three different conditions on the person table (the date range for the birthdate and two join conditions). In some cases, when you have multiple conditions on a table, it is beneficial to do some more extensive rewrites of the query.

Rewriting Complex Index Conditions

In some cases, a query becomes so complex that it is not possible for the optimizer to come up with a good query plan, and it is necessary to rewrite the query. An example of a case where a rewrite can help includes multiple filters on the same table where the index merge algorithm cannot be used effectively.

Consider the following query:

```
mysql> EXPLAIN FORMAT=TREE
       SELECT *
         FROM chapter_24.person
        WHERE BirthDate < '1930-01-01'
           OR AddressId = 3417\G
*************************** 1. row ***************************
EXPLAIN:
-> Filter: ((chapter_24.person.BirthDate < DATE'1930-01-01') or
          (chapter_24.person.AddressId = 3417))  (cost=88.28 rows=111)
    -> Index range scan on person using sort_union(BirthDate,AddressId)
       (cost=88.28 rows=111)

1 row in set (0.0006 sec)
```

There are indexes for both the BirthDate and AddressId columns, but no index that spans both columns. A possibility is to use an index merge, which the optimizer will choose by default, if it believes the benefit is large enough. Usually this is the preferred way to execute the query, but for some queries (particularly more complex than in this example) it can help to split the two conditions out into two queries and use a union to combine the result:

```
mysql> EXPLAIN FORMAT=TREE
       (SELECT *
          FROM chapter_24.person
         WHERE BirthDate < '1930-01-01'
       ) UNION DISTINCT (
        SELECT *
          FROM chapter_24.person
         WHERE AddressId = 3417
       )\G
```

```
*************************** 1. row ***************************
EXPLAIN:
-> Table scan on <union temporary>  (cost=2.50 rows=0)
    -> Union materialize with deduplication
        -> Index range scan on person using BirthDate, with index
           condition: (chapter_24.person.BirthDate < DATE'1930-01-01')
           (cost=48.41 rows=107)
        -> Index lookup on person using AddressId
           (AddressId=3417)  (cost=1.40 rows=4)

1 row in set (0.0006 sec)
```

A UNION DISTINCT (which is also the default union) is used to ensure that rows that fulfill both criteria are not included twice. Figure 24-6 shows the two query plans side by side.

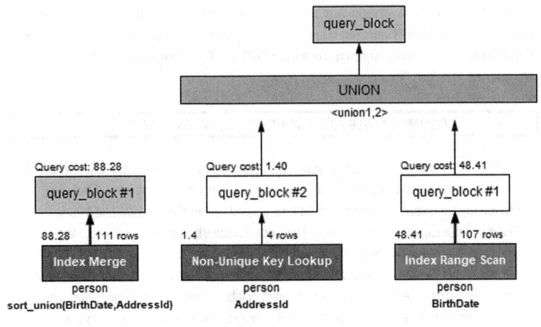

Figure 24-6. *Query plans for the original query and rewritten query*

On the left is the original query using an index merge (the `sort_union` algorithm), and on the right is the manually written union.

Rewriting Complex Queries

The optimizer has by MySQL 8 had several transformation rules added, so it can rewrite a query to a form where it performs better. This means that the need for rewriting complex queries keeps reducing as the optimizer knows more and more transformations. For example, as late as the 8.0.17 release, support was added to rewrite `NOT IN` (subquery), `NOT EXISTS` (subquery), `IN` (subquery) `IS NOT TRUE`, and `EXISTS` (subquery) `IS NOT TRUE` into an antijoin which means the subquery is removed.

That said, it is still good to consider how queries potentially can be rewritten, so you can help the optimizer on its way for the cases where it does not arrive at the optimal solution or it does not know how to do the rewrite on its own. There are also cases where you can take advantage of the support for common table expressions (CTEs – also known as the `with` syntax) and window functions to make queries more effective and easier to read. This section will start out considering common table expressions and window functions and then finish off rewriting a query using `IN` (subquery) to a join and to use two queries.

COMMON TABLE EXPRESSIONS AND WINDOW FUNCTIONS

It is beyond the scope of this book to go into the details of using common table expressions and window functions. This chapter will include a few examples to give an idea of how you can use the features. A good starting point for a general overview is *MariaDB and MySQL Common Table Expressions and Window Functions Revealed* by Daniel Bartholomew and published by Apress (`www.apress.com/gp/book/9781484231197`).

Guilhem Bichot (the MySQL developer who implemented common table expressions in MySQL) also wrote a blog series in four parts about common table expression when the feature was first developed: `https://mysqlserverteam.com/?s=common+table+expressions`. There are also two blogs by other MySQL developers about window functions: `https://mysqlserverteam.com/?s=window+functions`.

For the latest information, the best source is the MySQL reference manual. Common table expressions are described in `https://dev.mysql.com/doc/refman/en/with.html`. Window functions are covered in two parts based on whether the function is a regular or aggregate function: `https://dev.mysql.com/doc/refman/en/window-functions.html` which also includes a general discussion of window functions and `https://dev.mysql.com/doc/refman/en/group-by-functions.html` for aggregate window functions.

Common Table Expressions

The common table expressions feature allows you to define a subquery at the start of the query and use it as a normal table in the main part of the query. There are several advantages of using common table expressions instead of inlining the subqueries including better performance and readability. Part of the better performance comes from support of referencing the common table expression multiple times in a query, whereas an inlined subquery can only be referenced once.

As an example, consider a query against the `sakila` database that calculates the sales per month per the staff member who handled the rental:

```
SELECT DATE_FORMAT(r.rental_date,
                   '%Y-%m-01'
       ) AS FirstOfMonth,
       r.staff_id,
       SUM(p.amount) as SalesAmount
  FROM sakila.payment p
       INNER JOIN sakila.rental r
           USING (rental_id)
 GROUP BY FirstOfMonth, r.staff_id;
```

If you want to know how much the sales changes from month to month, then you will need to compare the sales for one month with that of the previous month. To do that without using common table expressions, you either need to store the result of the query in a temporary table or duplicate it as two subqueries. Listing 24-14 shows an example of the latter.

Listing 24-14. The monthly sales and change in sales without CTEs

```
SELECT current.staff_id,
       YEAR(current.FirstOfMonth) AS Year,
       MONTH(current.FirstOfMonth) AS Month,
       current.SalesAmount,
       (current.SalesAmount
          - IFNULL(prev.SalesAmount, 0)
       ) AS DeltaAmount
  FROM (
        SELECT DATE_FORMAT(r.rental_date,
                           '%Y-%m-01'
               ) AS FirstOfMonth,
               r.staff_id,
               SUM(p.amount) as SalesAmount
          FROM sakila.payment p
               INNER JOIN sakila.rental r
                   USING (rental_id)
         GROUP BY FirstOfMonth, r.staff_id
       ) current
       LEFT OUTER JOIN (
         SELECT DATE_FORMAT(r.rental_date,
                           '%Y-%m-01'
               ) AS FirstOfMonth,
               r.staff_id,
               SUM(p.amount) as SalesAmount
          FROM sakila.payment p
               INNER JOIN sakila.rental r
                   USING (rental_id)
         GROUP BY FirstOfMonth, r.staff_id
       ) prev ON prev.FirstOfMonth
                   = current.FirstOfMonth
                   - INTERVAL 1 MONTH
             AND prev.staff_id = current.staff_id
 ORDER BY current.staff_id,
          current.FirstOfMonth;
```

This hardly qualifies for the query that is easiest to read and understand. The two subqueries are identical and the same as that used to find the sales per staff per month. The two derived tables are joined by comparing the current and previous months for the same staff member. Finally, the result is ordered by the staff member and the current month. The result is shown in Listing 24-15.

Listing 24-15. The result of the monthly sales query

```
+-----------+------+-------+-------------+-------------+
| staff_id  | Year | Month | SalesAmount | DeltaAmount |
+-----------+------+-------+-------------+-------------+
|         1 | 2005 |     5 |     2340.42 |     2340.42 |
|         1 | 2005 |     6 |     4832.37 |     2491.95 |
|         1 | 2005 |     7 |    14061.58 |     9229.21 |
|         1 | 2005 |     8 |    12072.08 |    -1989.50 |
|         1 | 2006 |     2 |      218.17 |      218.17 |
|         2 | 2005 |     5 |     2483.02 |     2483.02 |
|         2 | 2005 |     6 |     4797.52 |     2314.50 |
|         2 | 2005 |     7 |    14307.33 |     9509.81 |
|         2 | 2005 |     8 |    11998.06 |    -2309.27 |
|         2 | 2006 |     2 |      296.01 |      296.01 |
+-----------+------+-------+-------------+-------------+
10 rows in set (0.1406 sec)
```

One thing to notice from the result is that there are no sales data in the months September 2005–January 2006. The query assumes the sales amounts are 0 in that period. When rewriting this query to use a window function, it is shown how to add the missing months.

Figure 24-7 shows the query plan for this version of the query.

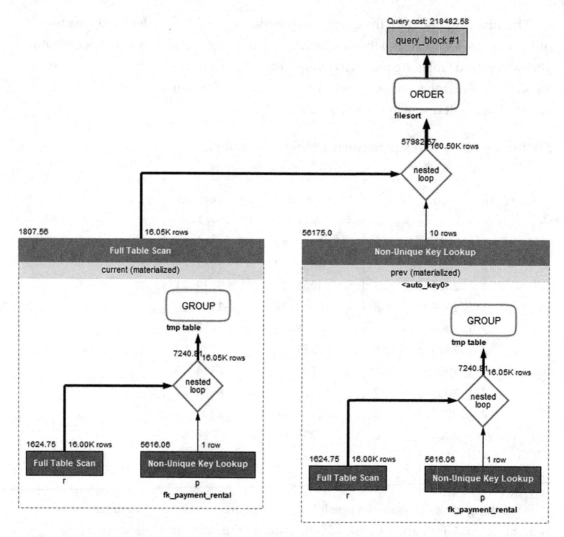

Figure 24-7. *Visual Explain for the non-CTE query*

The query plan shows that the subquery is evaluated twice; then the join is performed using a full table scan on the subquery named current and joined using an index (and auto-generated index) in a nested loop to form the result that is ordered by a file sort.

If you use common table expressions, you can just define the subquery once and refer to it twice. This simplifies the query and makes it perform better. The version of the query using common table expressions is shown in Listing 24-16.

Listing 24-16. The monthly sales and change in sales using CTE

```
WITH monthly_sales AS (
  SELECT DATE_FORMAT(r.rental_date,
                     '%Y-%m-01'
         ) AS FirstOfMonth,
         r.staff_id,
         SUM(p.amount) as SalesAmount
    FROM sakila.payment p
         INNER JOIN sakila.rental r
             USING (rental_id)
   GROUP BY FirstOfMonth, r.staff_id
)
SELECT current.staff_id,
       YEAR(current.FirstOfMonth) AS Year,
       MONTH(current.FirstOfMonth) AS Month,
       current.SalesAmount,
       (current.SalesAmount
          - IFNULL(prev.SalesAmount, 0)
       ) AS DeltaAmount
  FROM monthly_sales current
       LEFT OUTER JOIN monthly_sales prev
              ON prev.FirstOfMonth
                    = current.FirstOfMonth
                    - INTERVAL 1 MONTH
             AND prev.staff_id = current.staff_id
 ORDER BY current.staff_id,
          current.FirstOfMonth;
```

The common table expression is defined first with the WITH keyword and given the name monthly_sales. The table list in the main part of the query can then just refer to monthly_sales. The query executes in around half the time as the original query. An added benefit is that if the business logic changes, you only need to update it in one place which reduces the potential for ending up with a bug in the query. Figure 24-8 shows the query plan for the version of the query using the common table expression.

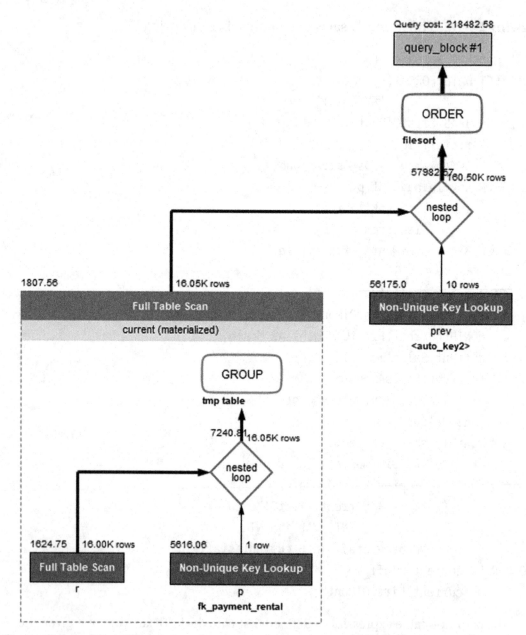

Figure 24-8. *Visual Explain when using a common table expression*

The query plan shows that the subquery is only executed once and then reused as a regular table. Otherwise, the query plan remains the same.

You could also have solved this problem using a window function.

Window Functions

Window functions allow you to define a frame where the window functions return values that depend on other rows in the frame. You can use this to generate row numbers and percentage of a total, compare a row to the previous or next row, and more. Here the previous example of finding the monthly sales numbers and comparing them to the previous month will be explored.

You can use the LAG() window function to get the value of a column in the previous row. Listing 24-17 shows how you can use that to rewrite the monthly sales query to use the LAG() window function as well as add the months without sales.

Listing 24-17. Combing CTEs and the LAG() window function

```
WITH RECURSIVE
  month AS
  (SELECT MIN(DATE_FORMAT(rental_date,
                          '%Y-%m-01'
         )) AS FirstOfMonth,
         MAX(DATE_FORMAT(rental_date,
                          '%Y-%m-01'
         )) AS LastMonth
    FROM sakila.rental
   UNION
   SELECT FirstOfMonth + INTERVAL 1 MONTH,
         LastMonth
    FROM month
   WHERE FirstOfMonth < LastMonth
),
  staff_member AS (
  SELECT staff_id
    FROM sakila.staff
),
  monthly_sales AS (
  SELECT month.FirstOfMonth,
         s.staff_id,
         IFNULL(SUM(p.amount), 0) as SalesAmount
```

```
    FROM month
        CROSS JOIN staff_member s
        LEFT OUTER JOIN sakila.rental r
            ON r.rental_date >=
                    month.FirstOfMonth
            AND r.rental_date < month.FirstOfMonth
                                    + INTERVAL 1 MONTH
            AND r.staff_id = s.staff_id
        LEFT OUTER JOIN sakila.payment p
            USING (rental_id)
    GROUP BY FirstOfMonth, s.staff_id
)
SELECT staff_id,
        YEAR(FirstOfMonth) AS Year,
        MONTH(FirstOfMonth) AS Month,
        SalesAmount,
        (SalesAmount
            - LAG(SalesAmount, 1, 0) OVER w_month
        ) AS DeltaAmount
    FROM monthly_sales
WINDOW w_month AS (ORDER BY staff_id, FirstOfMonth)
 ORDER BY staff_id, FirstOfMonth;
```

This query at first seems quite complex; however, the reason for this is that the first two common table expressions are used to add sales data for each month between the first and last months with rental data. The cross product (notice how an explicit CROSS JOIN is used to make it clear that the cross join is intended) between the month and staff_member tables is used as a base for the monthly_sales table with an outer join made on the rental and payment tables.

The main query now becomes simple as all the information required can be found in the monthly_sales table. A window is defined by ordering the sales data by staff_id and FirstOfMonth, and the LAG() window function is used over this window. Listing 24-18 shows the result.

Listing 24-18. The result of the sales query using the LAG() function

staff_id	Year	Month	SalesAmount	DeltaAmount
1	2005	5	2340.42	2340.42
1	2005	6	4832.37	2491.95
1	2005	7	14061.58	9229.21
1	2005	8	12072.08	-1989.50
1	2005	9	0.00	-12072.08
1	2005	10	0.00	0.00
1	2005	11	0.00	0.00
1	2005	12	0.00	0.00
1	2006	1	0.00	0.00
1	2006	2	218.17	218.17
2	2005	5	2483.02	2264.85
2	2005	6	4797.52	2314.50
2	2005	7	14307.33	9509.81
2	2005	8	11998.06	-2309.27
2	2005	9	0.00	-11998.06
2	2005	10	0.00	0.00
2	2005	11	0.00	0.00
2	2005	12	0.00	0.00
2	2006	1	0.00	0.00
2	2006	2	296.01	296.01

Notice how the months without sales data have been added with a sales amount of 0.

Note   The window does not require the values over which it orders the data to be in sequence. If you omit the month and staff_member expressions, the lag for February 2006 becomes August 2005. This may very well be what you want – but it is a different result compared to the solution found by the original query in Listing 24-14. It is left as an exercise for the reader to change the query and see the difference.

Rewrite Subquery As Join

When you have a subquery, an option is to change a subquery to a join. The optimizer will often perform this kind of rewrite on its own when possible, but occasionally, it is useful to help the optimizer on the way.

As an example, consider the following query:

```
SELECT *
  FROM chapter_24.person
 WHERE AddressId IN (
         SELECT AddressId
           FROM chapter_24.address
          WHERE CountryCode = 'AUS'
            AND District = 'Queensland');
```

This query finds all persons who live in Queensland, Australia. It can also be written as a join between the person and address tables:

```
SELECT person.*
  FROM chapter_24.person
       INNER JOIN chapter_24.address
             USING (AddressId)
 WHERE CountryCode = 'AUS'
       AND District = 'Queensland';
```

As a matter of fact, MySQL makes this exact rewrite (except the optimizer chooses the address table to be the first since that is where the filters are). This is an example of a semijoin optimization. If you come across a query where the optimizer cannot rewrite the query, you can have rewrites like this in mind. Usually the closer you get to a query just consisting of joins, the better the query performs. However, the life of query tuning is more complicated than that, and sometimes going the opposite way improves the query performance. The lesson is always to test.

Another option you can use is to split a query into parts and execute them in steps.

Splitting a Query Into Parts

A last option is to split a query into two or more parts. With the support for common table expressions and window functions in MySQL 8, this type of rewrite is not needed nearly as often as in older versions of MySQL. Yet, it can be useful to keep in mind.

Tip   Do not underestimate the power of splitting a complex query into two or more simpler queries and gradually generating the query result.

As an example, consider the same query as in the previous discussion where you find all persons who live in Queensland, Australia. You can execute the subquery as a query of its own and then put the result back into the IN() operator. This kind of rewrite works best in applications where the application programmatically can generate the next query. For simplicity, this discussion will just show the SQL required. Listing 24-19 shows the two queries.

Listing 24-19. Splitting a query into two steps

```
mysql> SET SESSION transaction_isolation = 'REPEATABLE-READ';
Query OK, 0 rows affected (0.0002 sec)

mysql> START TRANSACTION;
Query OK, 0 rows affected (0.0400 sec)

mysql> SELECT AddressId
         FROM chapter_24.address
        WHERE CountryCode = 'AUS'
          AND District = 'Queensland';
+-----------+
| AddressId |
+-----------+
|       132 |
|       143 |
|       136 |
|       142 |
+-----------+
```

```
4 rows in set (0.0008 sec)

mysql> SELECT *
          FROM chapter_24.person
          WHERE AddressId IN (132, 136, 142, 143)\G
*************************** 1. row ***************************
   PersonId: 79
  FirstName: Dimitra
    Surname: Turner
  BirthDate: 1937-11-16
  AddressId: 132
 LanguageId: 110
*************************** 2. row ***************************
   PersonId: 356
  FirstName: Julian
    Surname: Serrano
  BirthDate: 2017-07-30
  AddressId: 132
 LanguageId: 110
2 rows in set (0.0005 sec)

mysql> COMMIT;
Query OK, 0 rows affected (0.0003 sec)
```

The queries are executed using a transaction with the REPEATABLE-READ
transaction isolation level, which means that the two SELECT queries will use the same
read view and thus correspond to the same point in time in the same way as if you
executed the question as one query. For a query as simple as this, there is no gain from
using multiple queries; however, in the case of really complex queries, it can be an
advantage to split out part of the query (possibly including some joins). One additional
benefit of splitting queries into parts is also that in some cases you can make caching
more efficient. For this example, if you have other queries using the same subquery
to find the addresses in Queensland, caching can allow you to reuse the result for
multiple uses.

Queue System: SKIP LOCKED

A common task in connection with databases is to handle some list of tasks that are stored in a queue. An example is to handle orders in a shop. It is important that all tasks are handled and that they are handled only once, but it is not important which application thread handles each task. The SKIP LOCKED clause is perfect for such a scenario.

Consider the table jobqueue that is defined as shown in Listing 24-20.

Listing 24-20. The jobqueue table and data

```
mysql> SHOW CREATE TABLE chapter_24.jobqueue\G
*************************** 1. row ***************************
       Table: jobqueue
Create Table: CREATE TABLE `jobqueue` (
  `JobId` int(10) unsigned NOT NULL AUTO_INCREMENT,
  `SubmitDate` datetime NOT NULL DEFAULT CURRENT_TIMESTAMP,
  `HandledDate` datetime DEFAULT NULL,
  PRIMARY KEY (`JobId`),
  KEY `HandledDate` (`HandledDate`,`SubmitDate`)
) ENGINE=InnoDB AUTO_INCREMENT=7 DEFAULT CHARSET=utf8mb4
COLLATE=utf8mb4_0900_ai_ci
1 row in set (0.0004 sec)

mysql> SELECT *
         FROM chapter_24.jobqueue;
+-------+---------------------+-------------+
| JobId | SubmitDate          | HandledDate |
+-------+---------------------+-------------+
|     1 | 2019-07-01 19:32:30 | NULL        |
|     2 | 2019-07-01 19:32:33 | NULL        |
|     3 | 2019-07-01 19:33:40 | NULL        |
|     4 | 2019-07-01 19:35:12 | NULL        |
|     5 | 2019-07-01 19:40:24 | NULL        |
|     6 | 2019-07-01 19:40:28 | NULL        |
+-------+---------------------+-------------+
6 rows in set (0.0005 sec)
```

When HandledDate is NULL, then the task has not yet been handled and is up for grabs. If your application is set up to fetch the oldest unhandled task and you want to rely on InnoDB row locks to prevent two threads taking the same task, then you can use SELECT ... FOR UPDATE, for example (in the real world the statement would be part of a larger transaction):

```
SELECT JobId
  FROM chapter_24.jobqueue
 WHERE HandledDate IS NULL
 ORDER BY SubmitDate
 LIMIT 1
   FOR UPDATE;
```

This works well for the first request, but the next will block until a lock wait timeout occurs or the first task has been handled, so the task processing is serialized. The trick is to ensure there is an index on the columns you filter and sort by, and you then use the SKIP LOCKED clause. Then the second connection will simply skip the locked rows and find the first non-locked row fulfilling the search criteria. Listing 24-21 shows an example of two connections each fetching a job from the queue.

Listing 24-21. Fetching tasks with SKIP LOCKED

```
Connection 1> START TRANSACTION;
Query OK, 0 rows affected (0.0002 sec)

Connection 1> SELECT JobId
                FROM chapter_24.jobqueue
               WHERE HandledDate IS NULL
               ORDER BY SubmitDate
               LIMIT 1
                 FOR UPDATE
                SKIP LOCKED;
+-------+
| JobId |
+-------+
|     1 |
+-------+
```

```
1 row in set (0.0004 sec)

Connection 2> START TRANSACTION;
Query OK, 0 rows affected (0.0003 sec)

Connection 2> SELECT JobId
                FROM chapter_24.jobqueue
                WHERE HandledDate IS NULL
                ORDER BY SubmitDate
                LIMIT 1
                  FOR UPDATE
                  SKIP LOCKED;
+-------+
| JobId |
+-------+
|     2 |
+-------+
1 row in set (0.0094 sec)
```

Now both connections can fetch tasks and work on them at the same time. Once the task has been completed, the HandledDate can be set and the task marked as complete. The advantage of this approach compared with having a lock column that the connection sets is that if the connection for some reason fails, the lock is automatically released.

You can use the data_locks table in the Performance Schema to see which connection has each lock (the order of the locks depends on the thread ids which will be different for you):

```
mysql> SELECT THREAD_ID, INDEX_NAME, LOCK_DATA
         FROM performance_schema.data_locks
        WHERE OBJECT_SCHEMA = 'chapter_24'
          AND OBJECT_NAME = 'jobqueue'
          AND LOCK_TYPE = 'RECORD'
        ORDER BY THREAD_ID, EVENT_ID;
```

```
+-----------+-------------+------------------------+
| THREAD_ID | INDEX_NAME  | LOCK_DATA              |
+-----------+-------------+------------------------+
|     21705 | PRIMARY     | 1                      |
|     21705 | SubmitDate  | NULL, 0x99A383381E, 1  |
|     25101 | PRIMARY     | 2                      |
|     25101 | SubmitDate  | NULL, 0x99A3833821, 2  |
+-----------+-------------+------------------------+
4 rows in set (0.0008 sec)
```

The hex values are the encoded datetime values for the SubmitDate column. From the output, it can be seen that each connection holds one record lock in the secondary index and one in the primary key just as expected from the JobId values returned by the SELECT queries.

Many OR or IN Conditions

A query type that can cause confusion when it comes to performance is queries with many range conditions. This typically can be an issue when there are many OR conditions or the IN () operator has many values. In some cases, a small change to the condition may totally change the query plan.

When the optimizer encounters a range condition on an indexed column, it has two options: it can assume all values in the index occur equally frequent, or it can ask the storage engine to do index dives to determine the frequency of each range. The former is the cheapest, but the latter is by far more accurate. To decide which method to use, there is the eq_range_index_dive_limit option (default value is 200). If there are eq_range_index_dive_limit or more ranges, the optimizer will just look at the cardinality of the index and assume all values occur at the same frequency. If there are fewer ranges, the storage engine will be asked for each range.

The performance issues can occur when the assumption that each value occurs equally frequent does not hold. In that case, when passing the threshold set by eq_range_index_dive_limit, the estimated number of rows that match the condition may suddenly change significantly causing a completely different query plan. (When you have many values in the IN () operator, what is really the important thing is that the average number of rows matching the values included is close to the estimate obtained from the index statistics. So the more values you have in the list, the more likely you include a representative sample.)

Listing 24-22 shows an example of the payment table that has a column ContactId with an index. Most of the rows have ContactId set to NULL, and the cardinality for the index comes out as 21.

Listing 24-22. Query with many range conditions

```
mysql> SHOW CREATE TABLE chapter_24.payment\G
*************************** 1. row ***************************
       Table: payment
Create Table: CREATE TABLE `payment` (
  `PaymentId` int(10) unsigned NOT NULL AUTO_INCREMENT,
  `Amount` decimal(5,2) NOT NULL,
  `ContactId` int(10) unsigned DEFAULT NULL,
  PRIMARY KEY (`PaymentId`),
  KEY `ContactId` (`ContactId`)
) ENGINE=InnoDB AUTO_INCREMENT=32798 DEFAULT CHARSET=utf8mb4
COLLATE=utf8mb4_0900_ai_ci
1 row in set (0.0004 sec)

mysql> SELECT COUNT(ContactId), COUNT(*)
         FROM chapter_24.payment;
+-------------------+----------+
| COUNT(ContactId)  | COUNT(*) |
+-------------------+----------+
|                20 |    20000 |
+-------------------+----------+
1 row in set (0.0060 sec)

mysql> SELECT CARDINALITY
         FROM information_schema.STATISTICS
        WHERE TABLE_SCHEMA = 'chapter_24'
          AND TABLE_NAME = 'payment'
          AND INDEX_NAME = 'ContactId';
```

```
+--------------+
| CARDINALITY |
+--------------+
|          21 |
+--------------+
1 row in set (0.0009 sec)

mysql> SET SESSION eq_range_index_dive_limit=5;
Query OK, 0 rows affected (0.0003 sec)

mysql> EXPLAIN
        SELECT *
          FROM chapter_24.payment
         WHERE ContactId IN (1, 2, 3, 4)\G
*************************** 1. row ***************************
            id: 1
   select_type: SIMPLE
         table: payment
    partitions: NULL
          type: range
 possible_keys: ContactId
           key: ContactId
       key_len: 5
           ref: NULL
          rows: 4
      filtered: 100
         Extra: Using index condition
1 row in set, 1 warning (0.0006 sec)
```

In the example eq_range_index_dive_limit is set to 5 to avoid the need to specify a long list of values. With four values, the optimizer has requested statistics for each of the four values, and the estimated row count is 4. However, if you make the list of values longer, things start to change:

```
mysql> EXPLAIN
        SELECT *
          FROM chapter_24.payment
         WHERE ContactId IN (1, 2, 3, 4, 5)\G
```

```
************************* 1. row *************************
...
         key: ContactId
     key_len: 5
         ref: NULL
        rows: 4785
...
```

Suddenly, it is estimated that there are 4785 rows matched instead of the five rows that are really matched. The index is still used, but if the payment table with this condition is involved in joins, then the optimizer may very well choose a nonoptimal join order. If you make the list of values longer, the optimizer will stop using the index altogether and do a full table scan as it believes the index works terribly:

```
mysql> EXPLAIN
       SELECT *
         FROM chapter_24.payment
        WHERE ContactId IN (1, 2, 3, 4, 5, 6, 7)\G
************************* 1. row *************************
...
         type: ALL
possible_keys: ContactId
          key: NULL
...
         rows: 20107
...
```

This query only returns seven rows, so the index is highly selective. So what can be done to improve the optimizer's understanding? Depending on the exact nature of the reason for the poor estimate, there are various possible actions. For this particular problem, you have the following options:

- Increase eq_range_index_dive_limit.

- Change the innodb_stats_method option.

- Force MySQL to use the index.

The easiest solution is to increase eq_range_index_dive_limit. The default value is 200, which is a good starting point. If you have a candidate query, you can test with different values of eq_range_index_dive_limit and determine whether the added cost of doing the index dives is worth the savings from getting a better row estimate. A good way to test a new value of eq_range_index_dive_limit for a query is to set the value in the SET_VAR() optimizer hint:

```
SELECT /*+ SET_VAR(eq_range_index_dive_limit=8) */
       *
  FROM chapter_24.payment
 WHERE ContactId IN (1, 2, 3, 4, 5, 6, 7);
```

The reason relying on the cardinality causes such a bad row estimate in this case is that almost all rows have the ContactId set to NULL. By default, InnoDB considers all rows with a NULL value for an index to have the same value. That is why the cardinality comes out at just 21 in this example. If you switch innodb_stats_method to nulls_ignored, the cardinality will be calculated only based on the non-NULL values as shown in Listing 24-23.

Listing 24-23. Using innodb_stats_method = nulls_ignored

```
mysql> SET GLOBAL innodb_stats_method = nulls_ignored;
Query OK, 0 rows affected (0.0003 sec)

mysql> ANALYZE TABLE chapter_24.payment;
+---------------------+---------+-----------+----------+
| Table               | Op      | Msg_type  | Msg_text |
+---------------------+---------+-----------+----------+
| chapter_24.payment  | analyze | status    | OK       |
+---------------------+---------+-----------+----------+
1 row in set (0.1411 sec)

mysql> SELECT CARDINALITY
         FROM information_schema.STATISTICS
        WHERE TABLE_SCHEMA = 'chapter_24'
              AND TABLE_NAME = 'payment'
              AND INDEX_NAME = 'ContactId';
```

```
+-------------+
| CARDINALITY |
+-------------+
|       20107 |
+-------------+
1 row in set (0.0009 sec)

mysql> EXPLAIN
        SELECT *
          FROM chapter_24.payment
         WHERE ContactId IN (1, 2, 3, 4, 5, 6, 7)\G
*************************** 1. row ***************************
           id: 1
  select_type: SIMPLE
        table: payment
   partitions: NULL
         type: range
possible_keys: ContactId
          key: ContactId
      key_len: 5
          ref: NULL
         rows: 7
     filtered: 100
        Extra: Using index condition
1 row in set, 1 warning (0.0011 sec)
```

The biggest issue with this approach is that innodb_stats_method can only be set globally, so it will affect all tables, and it may have a negative effect for other queries. For this example, set innodb_stats_method back to the default value and recalculate the index statistics again:

```
mysql> SET GLOBAL innodb_stats_method = DEFAULT;
Query OK, 0 rows affected (0.0004 sec)

mysql> SELECT @@global.innodb_stats_method\G
```

```
*************************** 1. row ***************************
@@global.innodb_stats_method: nulls_equal
1 row in set (0.0003 sec)

mysql> ANALYZE TABLE chapter_24.payment;
+--------------------+---------+----------+----------+
| Table              | Op      | Msg_type | Msg_text |
+--------------------+---------+----------+----------+
| chapter_24.payment | analyze | status   | OK       |
+--------------------+---------+----------+----------+
1 row in set (0.6683 sec)
```

The last option is to use an index hint to force MySQL to use the index. You will need the FORCE INDEX variant as shown in Listing 24-24.

Listing 24-24. Using FORCE INDEX to force MySQL to use the index

```
mysql> EXPLAIN
        SELECT *
          FROM chapter_24.payment FORCE INDEX (ContactId)
         WHERE ContactId IN (1, 2, 3, 4, 5, 6, 7)\G
*************************** 1. row ***************************
           id: 1
  select_type: SIMPLE
        table: payment
   partitions: NULL
         type: range
possible_keys: ContactId
          key: ContactId
      key_len: 5
          ref: NULL
         rows: 6699
     filtered: 100
        Extra: Using index condition
1 row in set, 1 warning (0.0007 sec)
```

This will make the query perform as fast as if it had more accurate statistics. However, if the payment table is part of a join with the same WHERE clause, then the row estimate is still off (6699 rows estimated versus seven actual rows), so the query plan may still come out wrong in which case, you need to tell the optimizer what the optimal join order is.

Summary

This chapter has shown several examples of techniques to improve the performance of queries. The first topic was to look at symptoms of excessive full table scans and then look at two primary causes of full table scans: that the query is wrong and that an index cannot be used. Typical reasons an index cannot be used are that the columns used do not form a left prefix of the index, the data types do not match, or a function is used on the column.

It can also happen that an index is used, but the usage can be improved. This can be to convert an index to cover all columns required for the query, that the wrong index is used, or that rewriting a query with complex conditions can improve the query plan.

It can also be useful to rewrite complex queries. MySQL 8 supports common table expressions and window functions that can be used to both simplify the queries and possibly make them perform better. In other cases, it can help to do some of the rewriting that the optimizer usually would do or to split the query into multiple parts.

Finally, two common cases were discussed. The first was to work with a queue where the SKIP LOCKED clause can be used to efficiently access the first non-locked rows. The second is the case of having a long list of OR conditions or an IN () operator with many values which can lead to surprising changes in the query plans when the number of ranges reaches the number set by the eq_range_index_dive_limit option.

The next chapter looks at improving the performance of DDL and bulk data loads.

DDL and Bulk Data Load

From time to time, it is necessary to perform schema changes or to import large amount of data into a table. This may be to accommodate a new feature, restore a backup, import data generated by a third-party process, or similar. While the raw disk write performance is naturally very important, there are also several things you can do on the MySQL side to improve the performance of these operations.

Tip If you have problems that restoring your backups takes too long, consider switching to a backup method that copies the data files directly (a physical backup) such as using MySQL Enterprise Backup. A major benefit of physical backups is that they are much faster to restore than a logical backup (containing the data as INSERT statement or in a CSV file).

This chapter starts out discussing schema changes and then moves on to some general considerations around loading data. These considerations also apply when you insert single rows at a time. The rest of the chapter covers how to improve the data load performance from inserting in primary key order, how the buffer pool and secondary indexes impact performance, configuration, and tweaking the statements themselves. Finally, the parallel import feature of MySQL Shell is demonstrated.

Schema Changes

When you need to perform changes to your schema, it can require a large amount of work for the storage engine, possibly involving making a completely new copy of the table. This section will go into what you can do to speed up this process starting with the algorithms supported for schema changes and followed by other considerations such as the configuration.

© Jesper Wisborg Krogh 2020
J. W. Krogh, *MySQL 8 Query Performance Tuning*, https://doi.org/10.1007/978-1-4842-5584-1_25

Note   While OPTIMIZE TABLE does not make any changes to the schema of the table, InnoDB implements it as an ALTER TABLE followed by ANALYZE TABLE. So the discussion in this section also applies to OPTIMIZE TABLE.

Algorithm

MySQL supports several algorithms for ALTER TABLE with the algorithm deciding how the schema change is performed. Some schema changes can be made "instantly" by changing the table definitions, while at the other end of the spectrum some changes require copying the entire table into a new table.

In the order of the amount of work required, the algorithms are

- **INSTANT:** Changes are only made to the table definition. While the change is not quite instant, it is very fast. The INSTANT algorithm is available in MySQL 8.0.12 and later.

- **INPLACE:** Changes are in general made within the existing tablespace file (the tablespace id does not change), but with some exceptions such as ALTER TABLE <table name> FORCE (used by OPTIMIZE TABLE) which is more like the COPY algorithm but allowing concurrent data changes. This may be a relatively cheap operation but may also involve copying all the data.

- **COPY:** The existing data is copied to a new tablespace file. This is the algorithm with the most impact as it typically requires more locks, causes more I/O, and takes longer.

Typically, INSTANT and INPLACE algorithms allow concurrent data changes which reduces the impact on other connections, whereas COPY requires at least a read lock. MySQL will choose the algorithm with the least impact based on the requested changes, but you can also explicitly request a specific algorithm. This can, for example, be useful if you want to ensure that MySQL does not go ahead with the change, if your algorithm of choice is not supported. You specify the algorithm with the ALGORITHM keyword, for example:

```
mysql> ALTER TABLE world.city
          ADD COLUMN Council varchar(50),
             ALGORITHM=INSTANT;
```

If the change cannot be performed using the requested algorithm, the statement fails with an ER_ALTER_OPERATION_NOT_SUPPORTED error (error number 1845), for example:

```
mysql> ALTER TABLE world.city
          DROP COLUMN Council,
             ALGORITHM=INSTANT;
ERROR: 1845: ALGORITHM=INSTANT is not supported for this operation. Try
ALGORITHM=COPY/INPLACE.
```

You will obviously get the best ALTER TABLE performance if you can use the INSTANT algorithm. At the time of writing, the following operations are allowed using the INSTANT algorithm:

- Adding a new column as the last column in the table.

- Adding a generated virtual column.

- Dropping a generated virtual column.

- Setting a default value for an existing column.

- Dropping the default value for an existing column.

- Changing the list of values allowed for a column with the enum or set data type. A requirement is that the storage size does not change for the column.

- Changing whether the index type (e.g., BTREE) is set explicitly for an existing index.

There are also a few limitations that are good to be aware of:

- The row format cannot be COMPRESSED.

- The table cannot have a full text index.

- Temporary tables are not supported.

- Tables in the data dictionary cannot use the INSTANT algorithm.

Tip   If you, for example, need to add a column to an existing table, make sure to add it as the last column, so it can be added "instantly."

Performance wise, an in-place change is usually – but not always – faster than a copying change. Furthermore, when a schema change is made online (LOCK=NONE), InnoDB must keep track of the changes made during the execution of the schema change. This adds to the overhead, and it takes time to apply the changes that were made during the schema change at the end of the operation. If you are able to take a shared (LOCK=SHARED) or exclusive lock (LOCK=EXCLUSIVE) on the table, you can in general get better performance compared to allowing concurrent changes.

Other Considerations

Since the work done by an in-place or copying ALTER TABLE is very disk intensive, the single biggest effect on performance is how fast the disks are and how much other write activity there is during the schema change. This means that from a performance perspective, it is best to choose to perform schema changes that require copying or moving a large amount of data when there is little to no other write activity on the instance and host. This includes backups which on their own can be very I/O intensive.

Tip   You can monitor the progress of ALTER TABLE and OPTIMIZE TABLE for InnoDB tables using the Performance Schema. The simplest way is to use the sys.session view and look at the progress column which has the approximate progress in percentage of the total work. The feature is enabled by default.

If your ALTER TABLE includes creating or rebuilding secondary indexes (this includes OPTIMIZE TABLE and other statements rebuilding the table), you can use the innodb_sort_buffer_size option to specify how much memory each sort buffer can use. Be aware that a single ALTER TABLE will create multiple buffers, so be careful not to set the value too large. The default value is 1 MiB, and the maximum allowed value is 64 MiB. A larger buffer may in some cases improve the performance.

When you create full text indexes, then you can use the `innodb_ft_sort_pll_degree` option to specify how many threads InnoDB will use to build the search index. The default is 2 with supported values between 1 and 32. If you are creating full text indexes on large tables, it may be an advantage to increase the value of `innodb_ft_sort_pll_degree`.

One special DDL operation that needs consideration is to drop or truncate a table.

Dropping or Truncating Tables

It may seem unnecessary to have to consider performance optimizations of dropping tables. It would seem that all that is required is to delete the tablespace file and remove references to the table. In practice, it is not quite so simple.

The main issue when dropping or truncating a table is all the references to the table's data in the buffer pool. Particularly, the adaptive hash index can cause problems. For that reason, you can greatly improve the performance when dropping or truncating large tables by disabling the adaptive hash index for the duration of the operation, for example:

```
mysql> SET GLOBAL innodb_adaptive_hash_index = OFF;
Query OK, 0 rows affected (0.1008 sec)

mysql> DROP TABLE <name of large table>;

mysql> SET GLOBAL innodb_adaptive_hash_index = ON;
Query OK, 0 rows affected (0.0098 sec)
```

Disabling the adaptive hash index will make queries benefitting from the hash index run slower, but for tables with a size of a couple of hundred gigabytes or larger, a relatively small slowdown from disabling the adaptive hash index is usually preferred over potential stalls occurring because of the overhead of removing references to the table that is being dropped or truncated.

That concludes the discussion of performing schema changes. The rest of the chapter discusses loading data.

General Data Load Considerations

Before discussing how to improve the performance of bulk inserts, it is worth performing a small test and discussing the result. In the test, 200,000 rows are inserted into two tables. One of the tables has an auto-increment counter as the primary key, and the other uses a random integer for the primary key. The row size is identical for the two tables.

> **Tip**   The discussion in this and the next section applies equally well to non-bulk inserts.

After the data load has completed, the script in Listing 25-1 can be used to determine the age of each page in the tablespace file measured in terms of the log sequence number (LSN). The higher the log sequence number, the more recent the page was modified. This script is inspired by innodb_ruby by Jeremy Cole[1] and produces a map similar to the innodb_ruby `space-lsn-age-illustrate-svg` command. However, innodb_ruby does not yet support MySQL 8, so a separate Python program was developed. The program has been tested with Python 2.7 (Linux) and 3.6 (Linux and Microsoft Windows). It is also available in the file listing_25_1.py in this book's GitHub repository.

Listing 25-1. Python program to map the LSN age of InnoDB pages

```
'''Read a MySQL 8 file-per-table tablespace file and generate an
SVG formatted map of the LSN age of each page.

Invoke with the --help argument to see a list of arguments and
Usage instructions.'''

import sys
import argparse
import math
from struct import unpack

# Some constants from InnoDB
FIL_PAGE_OFFSET = 4              # Offset for the page number
FIL_PAGE_LSN = 16               # Offset for the LSN
FIL_PAGE_TYPE = 24              # Offset for the page type
FIL_PAGE_TYPE_ALLOCATED = 0  # Freshly allocated page

def mach_read_from_2(page, offset):
    '''Read 2 bytes in big endian. Based on the function of the same
    name in the InnoDB source code.'''
    return unpack('>H', page[offset:offset + 2])[0]
```

---

[1]https://github.com/jeremycole/innodb_ruby

```python
def mach_read_from_4(page, offset):
    '''Read 4 bytes in big endian. Based on the function of the same
    name in the InnoDB source code.'''
    return unpack('>L', page[offset:offset + 4])[0]

def mach_read_from_8(page, offset):
    '''Read 8 bytes in big endian. Based on the function of the same
    name in the InnoDB source code.'''
    return unpack('>Q', page[offset:offset + 8])[0]

def get_color(lsn, delta_lsn, greyscale):
    '''Get the RGB color of a relative lsn.'''
    color_fmt = '#{0:02x}{1:02x}{2:02x}'

    if greyscale:
        value = int(255 * lsn / delta_lsn)
        color = color_fmt.format(value, value, value)
    else:
        # 0000FF -> 00FF00 -> FF0000 -> FFFF00
        # 256 + 256 + 256 values
        value = int((3 * 256 - 1) * lsn / delta_lsn)
        if value < 256:
            color = color_fmt.format(0, value, 255 - value)
        elif value < 512:
            value = value % 256
            color = color_fmt.format(value, 255 - value, 0)
        else:
            value = value % 256
            color = color_fmt.format(255, value, 0)

    return color

def gen_svg(min_lsn, max_lsn, lsn_age, args):
    '''Generate an SVG output and print to stdout.'''
    pages_per_row = args.width
    page_width = args.size
```

```python
num_pages = len(lsn_age)
num_rows = int(math.ceil(1.0 * num_pages / pages_per_row))
x1_label = 5 * page_width + 1
x2_label = (pages_per_row + 7) * page_width
delta_lsn = max_lsn - min_lsn

print('<?xml version="1.0"?>')
print('<svg xmlns="http://www.w3.org/2000/svg" version="1.1">')
print('<text x="{0}" y="{1}" font-family="monospace" font-size="{2}" '
    .format(x1_label, int(1.5 * page_width) + 1, page_width) +
    'font-weight="bold" text-anchor="end">Page</text>')

page_number = 0
page_fmt = '  <rect x="{0}" y="{1}" width="{2}" height="{2}" fill="{3}" />'
label_fmt = '  <text x="{0}" y="{1}" font-family="monospace" '
label_fmt += 'font-size="{2}" text-anchor="{3}">{4}</text>'
for i in range(num_rows):
    y = (i + 2) * page_width
    for j in range(pages_per_row):
        x = 6 * page_width + j * page_width
        if page_number >= len(lsn_age) or lsn_age[page_number] is None:
            color = 'black'
        else:
            relative_lsn = lsn_age[page_number] - min_lsn
            color = get_color(relative_lsn, delta_lsn, args.greyscale)

        print(page_fmt.format(x, y, page_width, color))
        page_number += 1
    y_label = y + page_width
    label1 = i * pages_per_row
    label2 = (i + 1) * pages_per_row
    print(label_fmt.format(x1_label, y_label, page_width, 'end', label1))
    print(label_fmt.format(x2_label, y_label, page_width, 'start', label2))

# Create a frame around the pages
frame_fmt = '  <path stroke="black" stroke-width="1" fill="none" d="'
```

```
frame_fmt += 'M{0},{1} L{2},{1} S{3},{1} {3},{4} L{3},{5} S{3},{6} {2},{6}'
frame_fmt += ' L{0},{6} S{7},{6} {7},{5} L{7},{4} S{7},{1} {0},{1} Z" />'
x1 = int(page_width * 6.5)
y1 = int(page_width * 1.5)
x2 = int(page_width * 5.5) + page_width * pages_per_row
x2b = x2 + page_width
y1b = y1 + page_width
y2 = int(page_width * (1.5 + num_rows))
y2b = y2 + page_width
x1c = x1 - page_width
print(frame_fmt.format(x1, y1, x2, x2b, y1b, y2, y2b, x1c))

# Create legend
x_left = 6 * page_width
x_right = x_left + pages_per_row * page_width
x_mid = x_left + int((x_right - x_left) * 0.5)
y = y2b + 2 * page_width
print('<text x="{0}" y="{1}" font-family="monospace" '.format(x_left, y) +
      'font-size="{0}" text-anchor="start">{1}</text>'.format(page_width,
                                                               min_lsn))
print('<text x="{0}" y="{1}" font-family="monospace" '.format(x_right, y) +
      'font-size="{0}" text-anchor="end">{1}</text>'.format(page_width,
                                                             max_lsn))
print('<text x="{0}" y="{1}" font-family="monospace" '.format(x_mid, y) +
      'font-size="{0}" font-weight="bold" text-anchor="middle">{1}</text>'
      .format(page_width, 'LSN Age'))

color_width = 1
color_steps = page_width * pages_per_row
y = y + int(page_width * 0.5)
for i in range(color_steps):
    x = 6 * page_width + i * color_width
    color = get_color(i, color_steps, args.greyscale)
    print('<rect x="{0}" y="{1}" width="{2}" height="{3}" fill="{4}" />'
          .format(x, y, color_width, page_width, color))

print('</svg>')
```

```
def analyze_lsn_age(args):
    '''Read the tablespace file and find the LSN for each page.'''
    page_size_bytes = int(args.page_size[0:-1]) * 1024
    min_lsn = None
    max_lsn = None
    lsn_age = []
    with open(args.tablespace, 'rb') as fs:
        # Read at most 1000 pages at a time to avoid storing too much
        # in memory at a time.
        chunk = fs.read(1000 * page_size_bytes)
        while len(chunk) > 0:
            num_pages = int(math.floor(len(chunk) / page_size_bytes))
            for i in range(num_pages):
                # offset is the start of the page inside the
                # chunk of data
                offset = i * page_size_bytes
                # The page number, lsn for the page, and page
                # type can be found at the FIL_PAGE_OFFSET,
                # FIL_PAGE_LSN, and FIL_PAGE_TYPE offsets
                # relative to the start of the page.
                page_number = mach_read_from_4(chunk, offset + FIL_PAGE_OFFSET)
                page_lsn = mach_read_from_8(chunk, offset + FIL_PAGE_LSN)
                page_type = mach_read_from_2(chunk, offset + FIL_PAGE_TYPE)

                if page_type == FIL_PAGE_TYPE_ALLOCATED:
                    # The page has not been used yet
                    continue
                if min_lsn is None:
                    min_lsn = page_lsn
                    max_lsn = page_lsn
                else:
                    min_lsn = min(min_lsn, page_lsn)
                    max_lsn = max(max_lsn, page_lsn)

                if page_number == len(lsn_age):
                    lsn_age.append(page_lsn)
```

```
            elif page_number > len(lsn_age):
                # The page number is out of order - expand the list first
                lsn_age += [None] * (page_number - len(lsn_age))
                lsn_age.append(page_lsn)
            else:
                lsn_age[page_number] = page_lsn

        chunk = fs.read(1000 * page_size_bytes)

    sys.stderr.write("Total # Pages ...: {0}\n".format(len(lsn_age)))
    gen_svg(min_lsn, max_lsn, lsn_age, args)

def main():
    '''Parse the arguments and call the analyze_lsn_age()
    function to perform the analysis.'''
    parser = argparse.ArgumentParser(
        prog='listing_25_1.py',
        description='Generate an SVG map with the LSN age for each page in an' +
        ' InnoDB tablespace file. The SVG is printed to stdout.')

    parser.add_argument(
        '-g', '--grey', '--greyscale', default=False,
        dest='greyscale', action='store_true',
        help='Print the LSN age map in greyscale.')
    parser.add_argument(
        '-p', '--page_size', '--page-size', default='16k',
        dest='page_size',
        choices=['4k', '8k', '16k', '32k', '64k'],
        help='The InnoDB page size. Defaults to 16k.')

    parser.add_argument(
        '-s', '--size', default=16, dest='size',
        choices=[4, 8, 12, 16, 20, 24], type=int,
        help='The size of the square representing a page in the output. ' +
        'Defaults to 16.')
```

```
    parser.add_argument(
        '-w', '--width', default=64, dest='width',
        type=int,
        help='The number of pages to include per row in the output. ' +
        'The default is 64.')

    parser.add_argument(
        dest='tablespace',
        help='The tablespace file to analyze.')

    args = parser.parse_args()
    analyze_lsn_age(args)

if __name__ == '__main__':
    main()
```

The page number, log sequence number, and page type are extracted at the positions (in bytes) defined by the FIL_PAGE_OFFSET, FIL_PAGE_LSN, and FIL_PAGE_TYPE constants for each page. If the page type has the value of the FIL_PAGE_TYPE_ALLOCATED constant, it means it is not used yet, so it can be skipped – these pages are colored black in the log sequence number map.

Tip   If you want to explore the information available in the page headers, the file storage/innobase/include/fil0types.h (https://github. com/mysql/mysql-server/blob/8.0/storage/innobase/include/ fil0types.h) in the source code and the descriptions of the fil headers in the MySQL internals manual (https://dev.mysql.com/doc/internals/en/ innodb-fil-header.html) are good starting points.

You can get help to use the program by invoking it with the --help argument. The only required argument is the path to the tablespace file you want to analyze. Unless, you have set the innodb_page_size option to something else than 16384 bytes, then the default values for the optional arguments are all you need unless you want to change the dimensions and size of the generated map.

Caution   Do not use the program on a production system! There is minimal error checking in the program to keep it as simple as possible, and it is experimental in nature.

You can now generate the test tables. Listing 25-2 shows how the `table_autoinc` table is created. This is the table with the auto-incrementing primary key.

Listing 25-2.   Populating a table with an auto-incrementing primary key

```
mysql-sql> CREATE SCHEMA chapter_25;
Query OK, 1 row affected (0.0020 sec)

mysql-sql> CREATE TABLE chapter_25.table_autoinc (
             id bigint unsigned NOT NULL auto_increment,
             val varchar(36),
             PRIMARY KEY (id)
           );
Query OK, 0 rows affected (0.3382 sec)

mysql-sql> \py
Switching to Python mode...

mysql-py> for i in range(40):
             session.start_transaction()
             for j in range(5000):
                 session.run_sql("INSERT INTO chapter_25.table_autoinc
                 (val) VALUES (UUID())")
             session.commit()
Query OK, 0 rows affected (0.1551 sec)
```

The table has a `bigint` primary key and a `varchar(36)` that is populated with UUIDs to create some random data. MySQL Shell's Python language mode is used to insert the data. The `session.run_sql()` method is available in version 8.0.17 and later. Finally, you can execute the `listing_25_1.py` script to generate the tablespace age diagram in scalable vector graphics (SVG) format:

```
shell> python listing_25_1.py <path to datadir>\chapter_25\table_autoinc.
ibd > table_autoinc.svg
Total # Pages ...: 880
```

The output of the program shows there are 880 pages in the tablespace plus possibly some unused pages at the end of the file.

Figure 25-1 shows the log sequence number age map for the `table_autoinc` table.

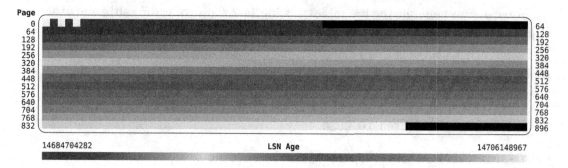

Figure 25-1. *The LSN age for each page when inserting in primary key order*

In the figure, the top left represents the first pages of the tablespace. As you go through the figure from left to right and top to bottom, the pages are further and further into the tablespace file, and the lower right represents the last pages. The figure shows that other than the first pages, the pattern of the age of the pages follows the same pattern as in the LSN Age scale at the bottom of the figure. This means that the age of the pages becomes younger as you progress through the tablespace. The first few pages are the exception as they, for example, include the tablespace header.

This pattern shows that the data is sequentially inserted into the tablespace making it as compact as possible. It also makes it as likely as possible that if a query reads data from several pages that are logical in sequence, then they are also physical in sequence in the tablespace file.

How then does it look if you insert in random order? A common example of random order inserts is a UUID as a primary key, but to ensure the row size is the same for the two tables, a random integer is used instead. Listing 25-3 shows how the `table_random` table is populated.

Listing 25-3. Populating a table with a random primary key

```
mysql-py> \sql
Switching to SQL mode... Commands end with ;

mysql-sql> CREATE TABLE chapter_25.table_random (
             id bigint unsigned NOT NULL,
             val varchar(36),
             PRIMARY KEY (id)
          );
Query OK, 0 rows affected (0.0903 sec)

mysql-sql> \py
Switching to Python mode...

mysql-py> import random
mysql-py> import math
mysql-py> maxint = math.pow(2, 64) - 1
mysql-py> random.seed(42)

mysql-py> for i in range(40):
             session.start_transaction()
             for j in range(5000):
                 session.run_sql("INSERT INTO chapter_25.table_random
                 VALUE ({0}, UUID())".format(random.randint(0, maxint)))
             session.commit()

Query OK, 0 rows affected (0.0185 sec)
```

The Python random module is used to generate 64-bit random unsigned integers. The seed is set explicitly as it is known (by experiment) that a seed of 42 generates 200,000 different numbers in a row so no duplicate key errors occur. When the table is populated, execute the listing_25_1.py script:

```
shell> python listing_25_1.py <path to datadir>\chapter_25\table_random.ibd
> table_random.svg
Total # Pages ...: 1345
```

The output of the listing_25_1.py script shows that there are 1345 pages in this tablespace. The resulting age map is shown in Figure 25-2.

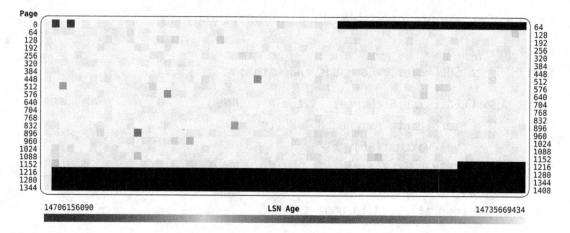

Figure 25-2. *The LSN age for each page when inserting in random order*

This time the log sequence number age pattern is completely different. The age colors for all pages except the unused pages correspond to the colors for the most recent log sequence numbers. That means all of the pages with data were last updated around the same time, or in other words they are all written to until the end of the bulk load. The number of pages with data is 1345 compared to the 880 pages used in the table with the auto-increment primary key. That is more than 50% more pages.

The reason inserting data in random order causes so many more pages for the same amount of data is that InnoDB fills up pages as data is inserted. When data is inserted in sequential primary key order, this means the next row will always be in succession of the previous, so this works well when the rows are ordered in primary key order. This is illustrated in Figure 25-3.

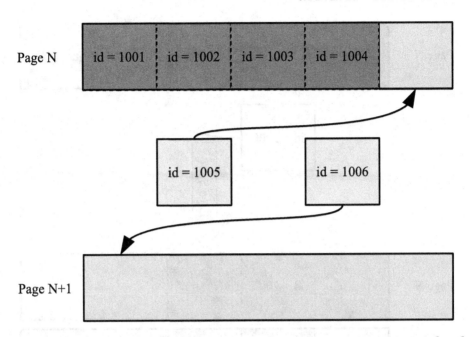

Figure 25-3. *Example of adding a new row when inserting in sequential order*

The figure shows two new rows being inserted. The row with id = 1005 can just fit into page N, so when the row with id = 1006 is inserted, it is inserted into the next page. Everything is nice and compact in this scenario.

When rows arrive in random order, it will sometimes be necessary to insert the row in a page that is already so full that there is no room for the new row. In that case, InnoDB splits the existing page in two with half the data of the original page in each of the two pages resulting from the page split, so there is room for the new row. This is shown in Figure 25-4.

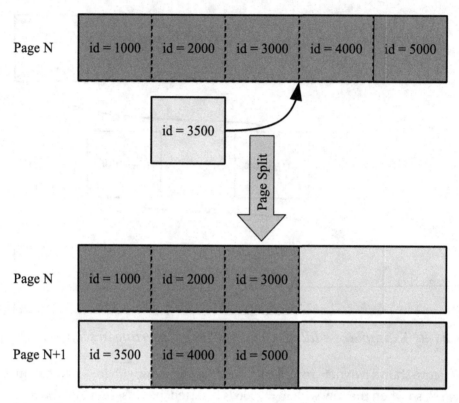

Figure 25-4. *Example of a page split as result of inserting in random order*

In this case the row with id = 3500 is inserted, but there is no more room in page N where it logically belongs. So page N is split into pages N and N+1 with roughly half the data going into each page.

There are two immediate consequences of the page split. First, the data that previously occupied one page now uses two pages which is why the insert in random order ends up occupying 50% more pages which also means the same data requires more space in the buffer pool. A significant side effect of the additional pages is that the B-tree index ends up with more leaf pages and potentially more levels in the tree, and given that each level in the tree means an extra seek when accessing the page, this causes additional I/O.

Second, rows that previously were read into memory together are now in two pages located in different places on the disk. When InnoDB increases the size of a tablespace file, it does so by allocating a new extent that is 1 MiB when the page size is 16 KiB or less. This helps making disk I/O more sequential (to the degree that the new extent gets consecutive sectors on the disk). The more page splits that occur, the more the pages are spread not only within an extent but also across multiple extents causing more random disk I/O. When the new page is created due to a page split, it may very well be located in a completely different part of the disk, so when reading the pages, the amount of random I/O increases. This is illustrated in Figure 25-5.

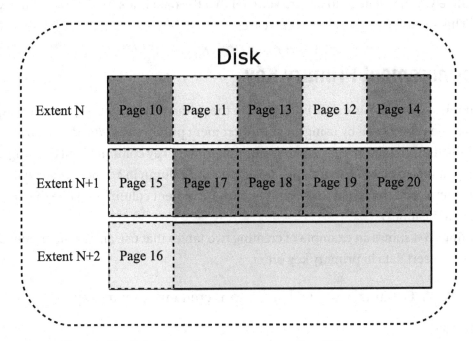

Figure 25-5. *Example of the location of pages on the disk*

In the figure three extents are depicted. For simplicity, just five pages are shown in each extent (with the default page size of 16 KiB, there are 64 pages per extent). Pages that have been part of page splits are highlighted. Page 11 was split at a time when the only later page was page 13, so pages 11 and 12 are still located relatively close. Page 15, however, was split when several extra pages had been created meaning page 16 ended up in the next extent.

The combination of deeper B-trees, more pages that take up space in the buffer pool, and more random I/O means that the performance of a table where rows are inserted in random primary key order will not be as good as for an equivalent table with data inserted in primary key order. The performance difference not only applies to inserting the data; it also applies to subsequent uses of the data. For this reason, it is important for optimal performance to insert the data in primary key order. How you can achieve that is discussed next.

Insert in Primary Key Order

As the previous discussion showed, there are great advantages of inserting the data in primary key order. The easiest way to achieve that is to auto-generate the primary key values by using an unsigned integer and declaring the column for auto-incrementing. Alternatively, you will need to ensure yourself that the data is inserted in the primary key order. This section will investigate both cases.

Auto-increment Primary Key

The simplest way to ensure data is inserted in the primary key order is to allow MySQL to assign the values itself by using an auto-increment primary key. You do that by specifying the auto_increment attribute for the primary key column when creating the table. It is also possible to use an auto-increment column in connection with a multicolumn primary key; in that case, the auto-increment column must be the first column in the index.

Listing 25-4 shows an example of creating two tables that use an auto-increment column to insert data in primary key order.

Listing 25-4. Creating tables with an auto-increment primary key

```
mysql> \sql
Switching to SQL mode... Commands end with ;

mysql> DROP SCHEMA IF EXISTS chapter_25;
Query OK, 0 rows affected, 1 warning (0.0456 sec)

mysql> CREATE SCHEMA chapter_25;
Query OK, 1 row affected (0.1122 sec)

mysql> CREATE TABLE chapter_25.t1 (
         id int unsigned NOT NULL auto_increment,
         val varchar(10),
         PRIMARY KEY (id)
       );
Query OK, 0 rows affected (0.4018 sec)
```

```
mysql> CREATE TABLE chapter_25.t2 (
          id int unsigned NOT NULL auto_increment,
          CreatedDate datetime NOT NULL
                              DEFAULT CURRENT_TIMESTAMP(),
          val varchar(10),
          PRIMARY KEY (id, CreatedDate)
        );
Query OK, 0 rows affected (0.3422 sec)
```

The t1 table just has a single column for the primary key, and the value is auto-incrementing. The reason for using an unsigned integer instead of a signed integer is that auto-increment values are always greater than 0, so using an unsigned integer allows twice as many values before exhausting the available values. The examples use a 4 byte integer which allows for a little less than 4.3 billion rows if all values are used. If that is not enough, you can declare the column as bigint unsigned which uses 8 bytes and allows for 1.8E19 rows.

The t2 table adds a datetime column to the primary key which, for example, can be useful if you want to partition by the time the row is created. The auto-incrementing id column still ensures the rows are created with a unique primary key, and because the id column is the first in the primary keys, rows are still inserted in primary key order even if subsequent columns in the primary key are random in nature.

When you use auto-incrementing primary keys, you can use the schema_auto_increment_columns view in the sys schema to examine the use of auto-increment values and monitor whether any tables are getting close to exhausting their values. Listing 25-5 shows the output for the sakila.payment table.

Listing 25-5. Using the sys.schema_auto_increment_columns view

```
mysql> SELECT *
          FROM sys.schema_auto_increment_columns
        WHERE table_schema = 'sakila'
              AND table_name = 'payment'\G
*************************** 1. row ***************************
          table_schema: sakila
            table_name: payment
           column_name: payment_id
             data_type: smallint
```

```
        column_type: smallint(5) unsigned
           is_signed: 0
         is_unsigned: 1
           max_value: 65535
      auto_increment: 16049
auto_increment_ratio: 0.2449
1 row in set (0.0024 sec)
```

You can see from the output that the table uses a smallint unsigned column for the auto-increment values which has a maximum value of 65535, and the column is named payment_id. The next auto-increment value is 16049, so 24.49% of the available values are used.

In case you insert data from an external source, you may already have values assigned for the primary key column (even when using an auto-increment primary key). Let's look at what you can do in that case.

Inserting Existing Data

Whether you need to insert data generated by some process, restore a backup, or convert a table using a different storage engine, it is best to ensure that it is in primary key order before inserting it. If you generate the data or it already exists, then you can consider sorting the data before inserting it. Alternatively, use the OPTIMIZE TABLE statement to rebuild the table after the import has completed.

An example of rebuilding the chapter_25.t1 table is

```
mysql> OPTIMIZE TABLE chapter_25.t1\G
*************************** 1. row ***************************
   Table: chapter_25.t1
      Op: optimize
Msg_type: note
Msg_text: Table does not support optimize, doing recreate + analyze instead
*************************** 2. row ***************************
   Table: chapter_25.t1
      Op: optimize
Msg_type: status
Msg_text: OK
2 rows in set (0.6265 sec)
```

The rebuild may take a substantial amount of time for large tables, but the process is online except for short durations at the start and end where locks are needed to ensure consistency.

If you create a backup using the mysqldump program, you can add the --order-by-primary option which makes mysqldump add an ORDER BY clause that includes the columns in the primary key (mysqlpump does not have an equivalent option). This is particularly useful if the backup is created of tables using a storage engine that uses so-called heap organized data such as MyISAM with the purpose of restoring it to an InnoDB table (using an index organization of the data).

Tip   While you should not in general rely on the order rows are returned when using a query without an ORDER BY clause, InnoDB's index-organized rows mean that a full table scan will usually (but no guarantees) return the rows in primary key order even if you omit the ORDER BY clause. A noticeable exception is when the table includes a secondary index covering all columns and the optimizer chooses to use that index for the query.

You can use the same principle if you copy data from one table to another. Listing 25-6 shows an example of copying the rows of the world.city table to the world.city_new table.

Listing 25-6. Ordering data by the primary key when copying it

```
mysql> CREATE TABLE world.city_new
          LIKE world.city;
Query OK, 0 rows affected (0.8607 sec)

mysql> INSERT INTO world.city_new
        SELECT *
          FROM world.city
         ORDER BY ID;
Query OK, 4079 rows affected (2.0879 sec)

Records: 4079  Duplicates: 0  Warnings: 0
```

As a final case, consider when you have a UUID as the primary key.

UUID Primary Keys

If you are limited to a UUID for your primary key, for example, because you cannot change the application to support an auto-increment primary key, then you can improve the performance by swapping the UUID components around and storing the UUIDs in a binary column.

A UUID (MySQL uses UUID version 1) consists of a timestamp as well as a sequence number (to guarantee uniqueness if the timestamp moves backward, e.g., during daylight savings changes) and the MAC address.

Caution   In some cases, it may be considered a security issue to reveal the MAC address as it can be used to identify the computer and potentially the user.

The timestamp is a 60-bit value with the number of 100-nanosecond intervals since midnight of October 15, 1582 (when the Gregorian calendar was taken into use), using UTC.[2] It is split into three parts with the least significant part first and the most significant part last. (The high field of the timestamp also includes four bits for the UUID version. The components of a UUID are also shown in Figure 25-6.)

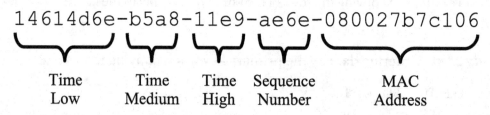

Figure 25-6. *The five parts of a UUID version 1*

The low part of the timestamp represents up to 4,294,967,295 (0xffffffff) intervals of 100 nanoseconds or just under 430 seconds. That means that every seven minutes and a little less than 10 seconds, the low part of the timestamp rolls over making the UUID start over from an ordering point of view. This is why plain UUIDs do not work well for the index-organized data as it means the inserts will largely be into a random place in the primary key tree.

---

[2]www.ietf.org/rfc/rfc4122.txt

MySQL 8 includes two new functions to manipulate UUIDs to make them more suitable as a primary key in InnoDB: UUID_TO_BIN() and BIN_TO_UUID(). These functions convert a UUID from the hexadecimal representation to a binary and back, respectively. They accept the same two arguments: the UUID value to convert and whether to swap the low and high parts of the timestamp. Listing 25-7 shows an example of inserting data and retrieving it using the functions.

Listing 25-7. Using the UUID_TO_BIN() and BIN_TO_UUID() functions

```
mysql> CREATE TABLE chapter_25.t3 (
          id binary(16) NOT NULL,
          val varchar(10),
          PRIMARY KEY (id)
       );
Query OK, 0 rows affected (0.4413 sec)

mysql> INSERT INTO chapter_25.t3
       VALUES (UUID_TO_BIN(
                  '14614d6e-b5a8-11e9-ae6e-080027b7c106',
                  TRUE
              ), 'abc');
Query OK, 1 row affected (0.2166 sec)

mysql> SELECT BIN_TO_UUID(id, TRUE) AS id, val
          FROM chapter_25.t3\G
*************************** 1. row ***************************
 id: 14614d6e-b5a8-11e9-ae6e-080027b7c106
val: abc
1 row in set (0.0004 sec)
```

The advantage of this approach is twofold. Because the UUID has the low and high time components swapped, it becomes monotonically increasing making it much more suitable for the index-organized rows. The binary storage means that the UUID only requires 16 bytes of storage instead of 36 bytes in the hex version with dashes to separate the parts of the UUID. Remember that because the data is organized by the primary key, the primary key is added to secondary indexes so it is possible to go from the index to the row, so the fewer bytes required to store the primary key, the smaller the secondary indexes.

InnoDB Buffer Pool and Secondary Indexes

The single most important factor for the performance of bulk data loads is the size of the InnoDB buffer pool. This section discusses why the buffer pool is important for bulk data loads.

When you insert data into a table, InnoDB needs to be able to store the data in the buffer pool until the data has been written to the tablespace files. The more data you can store in the buffer pool, the more efficiently InnoDB can perform the flushing of dirty pages to the tablespace files. However, there is also a second reason which is maintaining the secondary indexes.

The secondary indexes need to be maintained as the data is inserted, but the secondary indexes do not sort in the same order as the primary key, so they will constantly be rearranged while the data is inserted. As long as the indexes can be maintained in memory, the insert rate can stay high, but when the indexes no longer fit into the buffer pool, the maintenance of them suddenly becomes much more expensive and the insert rate decreases significantly. Figure 25-7 illustrates how the performance depends on the availability of the buffer pool to handle the secondary indexes.

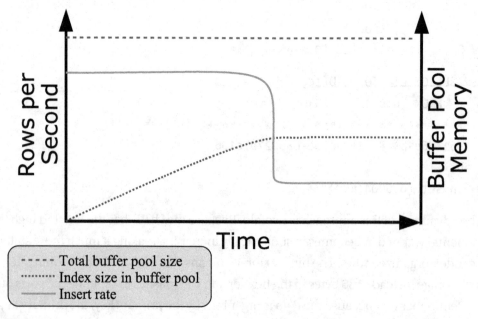

Figure 25-7. *Insert performance compared to the index size in the buffer pool*

The figure shows how the insert rate is roughly constant for a while and during that period more and more of the buffer pool is used for secondary indexes. When no more of the index can be stored in the buffer pool, the insert rate suddenly drops off. In the extreme case of loading data into a table with a single secondary index that includes the whole row with nothing else going on, the drop comes when the secondary index uses close to half the buffer pool (and the remaining for the primary key).

You can use the information_schema.INNODB_BUFFER_PAGE table to determine how much space an index uses in the buffer pool. For example, to find the amount of memory used in the buffer pool by the CountryCode index on the world.city table

```
mysql> SELECT COUNT(*) AS NumPages,
              IFNULL(SUM(DATA_SIZE), 0) AS DataSize,
              IFNULL(SUM(IF(COMPRESSED_SIZE = 0,
                           @@global.innodb_page_size,
                           COMPRESSED_SIZE
                          )
                     ),
                  0
                  ) AS CompressedSize
         FROM information_schema.INNODB_BUFFER_PAGE
        WHERE TABLE_NAME = '`world`.`city`'
          AND INDEX_NAME = 'CountryCode';
+-----------+-----------+----------------+
| NumPages  | DataSize  | CompressedSize |
+-----------+-----------+----------------+
|         3 |     27148 |          49152 |
+-----------+-----------+----------------+
1 row in set (0.1027 sec)
```

The result will depend on how much you have used the index, so in general your result will be different. The query is best used on a test system as there can be a significant overhead querying the INNODB_BUFFER_PAGE table.

Caution   Be careful querying the INNODB_BUFFER_PAGE table on your production system as the overhead can be significant, particularly if you have a large buffer pool with many tables and indexes in it.

Three strategies to avoid a performance hit when the secondary indexes cannot fit into the buffer pool are as follows:

- Increase the size of the buffer pool.

- Remove the secondary indexes while inserting data.

- Partition the table.

Increasing the buffer pool size while the bulk load is ongoing is the most obvious strategy, but also the one that is the least likely to be useful. It is primarily useful when inserting data into tables that already have a large amount of data and you know that during the data load, you can take some memory that is otherwise needed by other processes and use it for the buffer pool. The support for dynamically resizing the buffer pool is useful in this case. For example, to set the buffer pool size to 256 MiB

```
mysql> SET GLOBAL innodb_buffer_pool_size = 256 * 1024 * 1024;
Query OK, 0 rows affected (0.0003 sec)
```

Once the data load has completed, you can set the buffer pool size back to the usual value (134217728 if you use the default).

If you are inserting into an empty table, a very useful strategy is to remove all the secondary indexes (possibly leaving unique indexes for the data validation) before loading the data and then add the indexes back. This is in most cases more efficient than trying to maintain the indexes while loading the data, and it is also what the mysqlpump utility does if you use that to create backups.

The last of the strategies is to partition the table. This helps as the indexes are local to the partition (this is the reason the partition key must be part of all unique indexes), so if you insert the data in the partition order, InnoDB will only have to maintain the indexes for the data in the current partition. That makes each index smaller, so they easier fit into the buffer pool.

Configuration

You can influence the load performance through the configuration of the session that performs the load. This includes considering switching off constraint checks, how auto-increment ids are generated, and more.

Table 25-1 summarizes the most important configuration options related to bulk data performance other than the buffer pool size. The scope is whether the option can be changed at the session level or it is only available globally.

Table 25-1. *Configuration options influencing the data load performance*

Option Name	Scope	Description
foreign_key_ checks	Session	Specifies whether to check if the new rows violate the foreign keys. Disabling this option can improve performance for tables with foreign keys.
unique_checks	Session	Specifies whether to check if the new rows violate unique constraints. Disabling this option can improve performance for tables with unique indexes.
innodb_autoinc_ lock_mode	Global	Specifies how InnoDB determines the next auto-increment values. Setting this option to 2 (the default in MySQL 8 – requires binlog_format = ROW) gives the best performance at the expense of potentially nonconsecutive auto-increment values. Requires restarting MySQL.
innodb_flush_ log_at_trx_ commit	Global	Determines how frequently InnoDB flushes changes made to the data files. If you import data using many small transactions, setting this option to 0 or 2 can improve the performance.
sql_log_bin	Session	Disables the binary log when set to 0 or OFF. This will greatly reduce the amount of data written.
transaction_ isolation	Session	Sets the transaction isolation level. If you are not reading existing data in MySQL, consider setting the isolation level to READ UNCOMMITTED.

All of the options have side effects, so consider carefully whether changing the setting is appropriate for you. For example, if you are importing data from an existing instance to a new instance, and you know there are no problems with foreign key and unique key constraints, then you can disable the foreign_key_checks and unique_checks options for the session importing the data. If you are on the other hand importing from a source, where you are not sure of the data integrity, it may be better to keep the constraint checks enabled to ensure the quality of the data even if it means a slower load performance.

For the innodb_flush_log_at_trx_commit option, you need to consider whether a risk of losing the last second or so of committed transactions is acceptable. If your data load process is the only transactions on the instance, and it is easy to redo the import, you can set innodb_flush_log_at_trx_commit to 0 or 2 to reduce the number of flushes. The change is mostly useful with small transactions. If the import commits less than once a second, there is very little gained by the change. If you change innodb_flush_log_at_trx_commit, then remember to set the value back to 1 after the import.

For the binary log, it is useful to disable writing the imported data as it greatly reduces the amount of data changes that must be written to disk. This is particularly useful if the binary log is on the same disk as the redo log and data files. If you cannot modify the import process to disable sql_log_bin, you can consider restarting MySQL with the skip-log-bin option to disable the binary log altogether, but note that will also affect all other transactions on the system. If you do disable binary logging during the import, it can be useful to create a full backup immediately after the import, so you can use the binary logs for point-in-time recoveries again.

Tip   If you use replication, consider doing the data import separately on each instance in the topology with sql_log_bin disabled. Please note though that it will only work when MySQL does not generate auto-increment primary keys and is only worth the added complexity if you need to import a large amount of data. For the initial load in MySQL 8.0.17, you can just populate the source of the replication and use the clone plugin[3] to create the replica.

You can also improve the load performance by the statements you choose to import the data and how you use transactions.

---

[3]https://dev.mysql.com/doc/refman/en/clone-plugin.html

Transactions and Load Method

A transaction denotes a group of changes, and InnoDB will not fully apply the changes until the transaction is committed. Each commit involves writing the data to the redo logs and includes other overheads. If you have very small transactions – like inserting a single row at a time – this overhead can significantly affect the load performance.

There is no golden rule for the optimal transaction size. For small row sizes, usually a few thousand rows are good, and for larger row sizes choose fewer rows. Ultimately, you will need to test on your system and with your data to determine the optimal transaction size.

For the load method, there are two main choices: INSERT statements or the LOAD DATA [LOCAL] INFILE statement. In general LOAD DATA performs better than INSERT statements as there is less parsing. For INSERT statements, it is an advantage of using the extended insert syntax where multiple rows are inserted using a single statement rather than multiple single-row statements.

Tip   When you use mysqlpump for your backups, you can set the --extended-insert option to the number of rows to include per INSERT statement with the default being 250. For mysqldump, the --extended-insert option works as a switch. When it is enabled (the default), mysqldump will decide on the number of rows per statement automatically.

An advantage of using LOAD DATA to load the data is also that MySQL Shell can automate doing the load in parallel.

MySQL Shell Parallel Load Data

One problem you can encounter when you load data into MySQL is that a single thread cannot push InnoDB to the limit of what it can sustain. If you split the data into batches and load the data using multiple threads, you can increase the overall load rate. One option to do this automatically is to use the parallel data load feature of MySQL Shell 8.0.17 and later.

The parallel load feature is available through the util.import_table() utility in Python mode and the util.importTable() method in JavaScript mode. This discussion will assume you are using Python mode. The first argument is the filename, and the second (optional) argument is a dictionary with the optional arguments. You can get the help text for the import_table() utility using the util.help() method, like

    mysql-py> util.help('import_table')

The help text includes a detailed description of all the settings that can be given through the dictionary specified in the second argument.

MySQL Shell disables duplicate key and foreign key checks and sets the transaction isolation level to READ UNCOMMITTED for the connection doing the import to reduce the overhead during the import as much as possible.

The default is to insert the data into a table in the current schema with the same name as the file without the extension. For example, if the file is named t_load.csv, the default table name is t_load. A simple example of loading the file D:\MySQL\Files\t_load.csv into the table chapter_25.t_load is shown in Listing 25-8. The t_load.csv file is available from this book's GitHub repository as t_load.csv.zip.

Listing 25-8. Using the util.import_table() utility with default settings

```
mysql> \sql
Switching to SQL mode... Commands end with ;

mysql-sql> CREATE SCHEMA IF NOT EXISTS chapter_25;
Query OK, 1 row affected, 1 warning (0.0490 sec)

mysql-sql> DROP TABLE IF EXISTS chapter_25.t_load;
Query OK, 0 rows affected (0.3075 sec)

mysql-sql> CREATE TABLE chapter_25.t_load (
             id int unsigned NOT NULL auto_increment,
             val varchar(40) NOT NULL,
             PRIMARY KEY (id),
             INDEX (val)
           );
Query OK, 0 rows affected (0.3576 sec)
```

```
mysql> SET GLOBAL local_infile = ON;
Query OK, 0 rows affected (0.0002 sec)

mysql> \py
Switching to Python mode...

mysql-py> \use chapter_25
Default schema set to `chapter_25`.

mysql-py> util.import_table('D:/MySQL/Files/t_load.csv')
Importing from file 'D:/MySQL/Files/t_load.csv' to table `chapter_25`.`t_load`
in MySQL Server at localhost:3306 using 2 threads
[Worker000] chapter_25.t_load: Records: 721916  Deleted: 0  Skipped: 0  Warnings: 0
[Worker001] chapter_25.t_load: Records: 1043084  Deleted: 0  Skipped: 0  Warnings: 0
100% (85.37 MB / 85.37 MB), 446.55 KB/s
File 'D:/MySQL/Files/t_load.csv' (85.37 MB) was imported in 1 min 52.1678 sec
at 761.13 KB/s
Total rows affected in chapter_25.t_load: Records: 1765000  Deleted: 0
Skipped: 0  Warnings: 0
```

The warning when creating the chapter_25 schema depends on whether you have
created the schema earlier. Notice that you must enable the local_infile option for the
utility to work.

The most interesting part of the example is the execution of the import. When you
do not specify anything, MySQL Shell splits the file into 50 MB chunks and uses up to
eight threads. In this case the file is 85.37 MB (MySQL Shell uses the metric file sizes –
85.37 MB is the same as 81.42 MiB), so it gives two chunks, of which the first is 50 MB and
the second 35.37 MB. That is not a terrible good distribution.

Tip   You must enable local_infile on the server side before invoking the
util.import_table() utility.

What you can choose to do is to tell MySQL Shell what size to split at. The optimal is
that each thread ends up processing the same amount of data. For example, if you want
to divide the 85.37 MB data, set the chunk size to a little more than half the size, such as
43 MB. If a decimal value is specified for the size, it is rounded down. There are also several
other options you can set, and Listing 25-9 shows an example of setting some of them.

Listing 25-9. Using `util.import_table()` with several custom settings

```
mysql-py> \sql TRUNCATE TABLE chapter_25.t_load
Query OK, 0 rows affected (1.1294 sec)

mysql-py> settings = {
              'schema': 'chapter_25',
              'table': 't_load',
              'columns': ['id', 'val'],
              'threads': 4,
              'bytesPerChunk': '21500k',
              'fieldsTerminatedBy': '\t',
              'fieldsOptionallyEnclosed': False,
              'linesTerminatedBy': '\n'
          }

mysql-py> util.import_table('D:/MySQL/Files/t_load.csv', settings)
Importing from file 'D:/MySQL/Files/t_load.csv' to table `chapter_25`.
`t_load` in MySQL Server at localhost:3306 using 4 threads
[Worker001] chapter_25.t_load: Records: 425996  Deleted: 0  Skipped: 0  Warnings: 0
[Worker002] chapter_25.t_load: Records: 440855  Deleted: 0  Skipped: 0  Warnings: 0
[Worker000] chapter_25.t_load: Records: 447917  Deleted: 0  Skipped: 0  Warnings: 0
[Worker003] chapter_25.t_load: Records: 450232  Deleted: 0  Skipped: 0  Warnings: 0
100% (85.37 MB / 85.37 MB), 279.87 KB/s
File 'D:/MySQL/Files/t_load.csv' (85.37 MB) was imported in 2 min 2.6656
sec at 695.99 KB/s
Total rows affected in chapter_25.t_load: Records: 1765000  Deleted:
0  Skipped: 0  Warnings: 0
```

In this case the target schema, table, and columns are specified explicitly, and the file is split into four roughly equal chunks and the number of threads is set to four. The format of the CSV file is also included in the setting (the specified values are the default).

The optimal number of threads varies greatly depending on the hardware, the data, and the other queries running. You will need to experiment to find the optimal settings for your system.

Summary

This chapter has discussed what determines the performance of DDL statements and bulk data loads. The first topic was schema changes in terms of ALTER TABLE and OPTIMIZE TABLE. There is support for three different algorithms when you make schema changes. The best-performing algorithm is the INSTANT algorithm which can be used to add columns at the end of the row and several metadata changes. The second-best algorithm is INPLACE which in most cases modifies the data within the existing tablespace file. The final, and in general most expensive, algorithm is COPY.

In cases where the INSTANT algorithm cannot be used, there will be a substantial amount of I/O, so the disk performance is important, and the less other work going on requiring disk I/O, the better. It may also help to lock the table, so MySQL does not need to keep track of data changes and apply them at the end of the schema change.

For inserting data, it was discussed that it is important to insert in primary key order. If the insert order is random, it leads to larger tables, a deeper B-tree index for the clustered index, more disk seeks, and more random I/O. The simplest way to insert data in primary key order is to use an auto-increment primary key and let MySQL determine the next value. For UUIDs, MySQL 8 adds the UUID_TO_BIN() and BIN_TO_UUID() functions that allow you to reduce the storage required for a UUID to 16 bytes and to swap the low and high order parts of the timestamp to make the UUIDs monotonically increasing.

When you insert data, a typical cause of the insert rate suddenly slowing down is when the secondary indexes no longer fit into the buffer pool. If you insert into an empty table, it is an advantage to remove the indexes during the import. Partitioning may also help as it splits the index into one part per partition, so only part of the index is required at a time.

In some circumstances, you can disable constraint checks, reduce flushing of the redo log, disable binary logging, and reduce the transaction isolation to READ UNCOMMITTED. These configuration changes will all help reduce the overhead; however, all also have side effects, so you must consider carefully whether the changes are acceptable for your system. You can also affect the performance by adjusting the transaction size to balance the reduction of commit overhead and overhead of working with large transactions.

For bulk inserts you have two options of loading the data. You can use regular INSERT statements, or you can use the LOAD DATA statement. The latter is in general the preferred method. It also allows you to use the parallel table import feature of MySQL Shell 8.0.17 and later.

In the next chapter, you will learn about improving the performance of replication.

CHAPTER 26

Replication

One of the features that has helped make MySQL so popular over the years is the support for replication which allows you to have a MySQL instance that automatically receives the updates from its source and applies them. With quick transactions and a low latency network, the replication can be in near-real time, but note that as there is no such thing as synchronous replication in MySQL except for NDB Cluster, there is still a delay which potentially can be large. A recurring task for database administrators is to work on improving the performance of the replication. Over the years, there have been many improvements to MySQL replication including some that can help you improve the replication performance.

Note   This chapter focuses on traditional asynchronous replication. MySQL 8 also supports Group Replication and its derivative InnoDB Cluster. It is beyond the scope of this book to go into the details of Group Replication; however, the discussion still applies in general. For details of Group Replication, the book *Introducing InnoDB Cluster* by Charles Bell (Apress) (www.apress.com/gp/book/9781484238844) is recommended together with the MySQL reference manual (https://dev.mysql.com/doc/refman/en/group-replication.html) for the latest updates.

This chapter will start out providing a high-level overview of replication with the purpose of introducing terminology and a test setup that will be used for the section on replication monitoring. The other half of the chapter discusses how the performance of the connection and applier threads can be improved and how replication can be used to offload work to a replica.

© Jesper Wisborg Krogh 2020
J. W. Krogh, *MySQL 8 Query Performance Tuning*, https://doi.org/10.1007/978-1-4842-5584-1_26

Replication Overview

Before you dive into improving the performance of replication, it is important to discuss how replication works. This will help agreeing on a terminology and to have a reference point for the discussion in the rest of this chapter.

Note   Traditionally the terms *master* and *slave* have been used to describe the source and target of MySQL replication. In recent times, the terminology has moved toward using the words *source* and *replica*. Likewise, on the replica, the two thread types for handling the replication events have traditionally been called *I/O thread* and *SQL thread*, whereas the current terms are *connection thread* and *applier thread*. This book will to the largest extent possible use the new terms; however, the old terms are still present in some contexts.

Replication works by recording the changes made on the source of the replication after which they are sent to the replica where the connection thread stores the data and one or more applier threads apply them. Figure 26-1 shows a simplified overview of the replication omitting everything related to storage engines and implementation details.

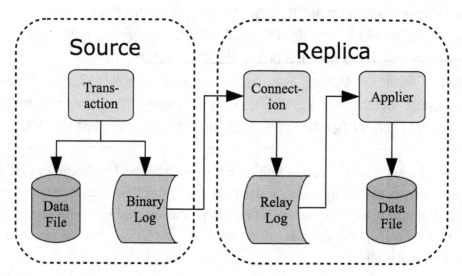

Figure 26-1. *Replication overview*

When a transaction commits its changes, the changes are written both to the InnoDB specific files (redo log and data files) and to the *binary log*. The binary log consists of a series of files as well as an index file with the index file listing the binary log files. Once the events have been written to the binary log file, they are sent to the replica. There may be more than one replica in which case the events are sent to all the replicas.

On the replica, the connection thread receives the events and writes them to the *relay log*. The relay log works the same way as the binary log, just that it is used as a temporary storage until an applier thread can apply the events. There may be one or more applier threads. It may also be that the replica replicates from multiple sources (called multi-source replication) in which case there is a set of one connection thread and one or more applier threads for each *replication channel*. (That said, the most common is a single source per replica.) Optionally, the replica writes the changes to its own binary log which enables it to become a source for a replica further downstream the replication chain. In that case it is common to call it a *relay* instance. Figure 26-2 shows an example of a setup with a replica receiving updates from two sources, of which one is a relay instance.

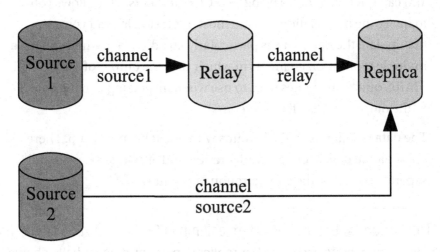

Figure 26-2. *Replication topology with two replication streams*

Here *Source 1* replicates to the *Relay* instance which in turn replicates to the *Replica* instance. *Source 2* also replicates to the *Replica* instance. Each channel has a name to make it possible to distinguish between them, and in multi-source replication, each channel must have a unique name. The default channel name is an empty string. When monitoring is discussed, it will use a replication setup like the one in the figure.

Monitoring

When you encounter replication performance problems, the first step is to determine where the delay is introduced in the chain of steps described in the previous section. If you have been using replication in earlier versions of MySQL, you may jump to the SHOW SLAVE STATUS command to check the health of the replication; however, in MySQL 8 that is the last source of monitoring information to check.

In MySQL 8, the primary source of monitoring information for replication is the Performance Schema which contains several tables describing the configuration and status of the replication at each replication step on the replica. Some of the advantages of the Performance Schema tables are as follows:

- The status tables include much more detailed information about the replication delays in the form of timestamps with microsecond resolution for each step in the replication process and with timestamps from both the original and immediate sources.

- You can query the tables using SELECT statements. This allows you to query the information you are most interested in, and you can manipulate the data. This is particularly an advantage when you have multiple replication channels in which case the output of SHOW SLAVE STATUS quickly becomes hard to use when inspecting it in the console as the output scrolls off the screen.

- The data is split into logical groups with one table per group. There are separate tables for the configuration and applier processes and separate tables for the configuration and status.

Note The Seconds_Behind_Master column in SHOW SLAVE STATUS has traditionally been used to measure the replication delay. It essentially shows how long time has passed since the transaction started on the original source. That means, it only really works when all transactions are very quick and there are no relay instances. Even then it does not provide any information of where the cause of a delay is. If you are still using Seconds_Behind_Master to monitor the replication delay, you are encouraged to start switching to the Performance Schema tables.

When you first start out working with the Performance Schema replication tables, it can feel difficult to picture what the relationship is between the tables and how they relate to the replication flow. Figure 26-3 shows the replication flow for a single replication channel and adds the replication tables corresponding to what information they include. The tables in Figure 26-3 can also be used in a Group Replication setup in which case the group_replication_applier channel is used for the transactions while the node is online and the group_replication_recovery channel is used during recovery.

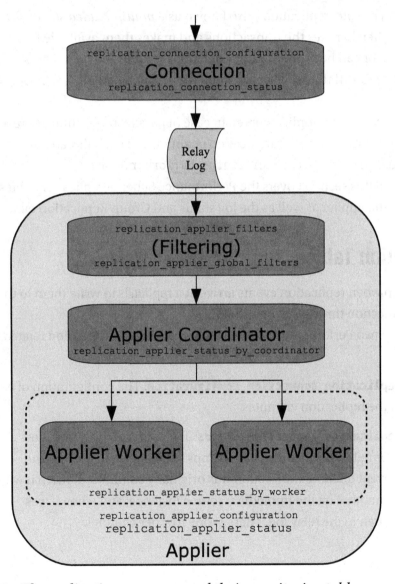

Figure 26-3. *The replication processes and their monitoring tables*

The events arrive at the top of the figure from the immediate source and are processed by the connection thread which has the two tables `replication_connection_configuration` and `replication_connection_status`. The connection thread writes the events to the relay log, and the applier reads the events from the relay log while applying the replication filters. The replication filters can be found in the `replication_applier_filters` and `replication_applier_global_filters` tables. The overall applier configuration and status can be found in the `replication_applier_configuration` and `replication_applier_status` tables.

In case of parallel replication (also known as a *multithreaded slave*), the coordinator then handles the transactions and makes them available for the workers. The coordinator can be monitored through the `replication_applier_status_by_coordinator` table. If the replica uses single-threaded replication, the coordinator step is skipped.

The final step is the applier worker. In case of parallel replication, there are `slave_parallel_workers` threads per replication channel, and each thread has a row with its status in the `replication_applier_status_by_worker` table.

The rest of this section covers the Performance Schema replication tables for the connection and applier as well as the log status and Group Replication tables.

Connection Tables

The first step when replication events arrive at a replica is to write them to the relay log. It is the connection thread that handles this.

There are two Performance Schema tables providing information related to the connections:

- **replication_connection_configuration:** The configuration of each of the replication channels.

- **replication_connection_status:** The status of the replication channels. This includes timestamps showing when the last and current queuing transaction was originally committed, when it was committed on the immediate source instance, and when it was written to the relay log. There is one row per channel.

The replication connection tables include the information related to the connection to the immediate upstream source as well as timestamps when the latest received event was committed on the original source. In simple replication setups, the immediate and original sources are the same, but in chained replication the two are different. Listing 26-1 shows an example of the contents of the two connection tables for the relay channel in the replication setup discussed in the previous section. The output has been reformatted to improve the readability in this book. The original formatted output including the row for the source2 replication channel is included in the file listing_26_1.txt.

Listing 26-1. The replication connection tables

```
mysql> SELECT *
         FROM performance_schema.replication_connection_configuration
        WHERE CHANNEL_NAME = 'relay'\G
*************************** 1. row ***************************
              CHANNEL_NAME: relay
                      HOST: 127.0.0.1
                      PORT: 3308
                      USER: root
         NETWORK_INTERFACE:
             AUTO_POSITION: 1
               SSL_ALLOWED: YES
               SSL_CA_FILE:
               SSL_CA_PATH:
           SSL_CERTIFICATE:
                SSL_CIPHER:
                   SSL_KEY:
SSL_VERIFY_SERVER_CERTIFICATE: NO
              SSL_CRL_FILE:
              SSL_CRL_PATH:
  CONNECTION_RETRY_INTERVAL: 60
     CONNECTION_RETRY_COUNT: 86400
        HEARTBEAT_INTERVAL: 30
               TLS_VERSION:
           PUBLIC_KEY_PATH:
            GET_PUBLIC_KEY: NO
```

```
      NETWORK_NAMESPACE:
   COMPRESSION_ALGORITHM: uncompressed
   ZSTD_COMPRESSION_LEVEL: 3
1 row in set (0.0006 sec)

mysql> SELECT *
       FROM performance_schema.replication_connection_status
       WHERE CHANNEL_NAME = 'relay'\G
*************************** 1. row ***************************
                          CHANNEL_NAME: relay
                            GROUP_NAME:
                           SOURCE_UUID: cfa645e7-b691-11e9-a051-
                                        ace2d35785be
                             THREAD_ID: 44
                         SERVICE_STATE: ON
             COUNT_RECEIVED_HEARTBEATS: 26
              LAST_HEARTBEAT_TIMESTAMP: 2019-08-11
                                        10:26:16.076997
              RECEIVED_TRANSACTION_SET: 4d22b3e5-a54f-11e9-8bdb-
                                        ace2d35785be:23-44
                     LAST_ERROR_NUMBER: 0
                    LAST_ERROR_MESSAGE:
                  LAST_ERROR_TIMESTAMP: 0000-00-00 00:00:00
                LAST_QUEUED_TRANSACTION: 4d22b3e5-a54f-11e9-8bdb-
                                        ace2d35785be:44
 LAST_QUEUED_TRANSACTION_ORIGINAL_COMMIT_TIMESTAMP: 2019-08-11 10:27:09.483703
LAST_QUEUED_TRANSACTION_IMMEDIATE_COMMIT_TIMESTAMP: 2019-08-11 10:27:10.158297
    LAST_QUEUED_TRANSACTION_START_QUEUE_TIMESTAMP: 2019-08-11 10:27:10.296164
      LAST_QUEUED_TRANSACTION_END_QUEUE_TIMESTAMP: 2019-08-11 10:27:10.299833
                   QUEUEING_TRANSACTION:
 QUEUEING_TRANSACTION_ORIGINAL_COMMIT_TIMESTAMP: 0000-00-00 00:00:00
QUEUEING_TRANSACTION_IMMEDIATE_COMMIT_TIMESTAMP: 0000-00-00 00:00:00
    QUEUEING_TRANSACTION_START_QUEUE_TIMESTAMP: 0000-00-00 00:00:00
1 row in set (0.0006 sec)
```

The configuration table largely corresponds to the options that you can give when setting up replication with the CHANGE MASTER TO statement, and the data is static unless you explicitly change the configuration. The status table mostly contains volatile data that changes rapidly as events are processed.

The timestamps in the status table are of particular interest. There are two groups with the first showing the timestamps for the last queued event and the second for the event currently being queued. That an event is being queued means it is being written to the relay log. As an example, consider the timestamps for the last queued event:

- **LAST_QUEUED_TRANSACTION_ORIGINAL_COMMIT_TIMESTAMP:** The time when the event was committed on the original source (*Source 1*).

- **LAST_QUEUED_TRANSACTION_IMMEDIATE_COMMIT_TIMESTAMP:** The time when the event was committed on the immediate source (*Relay*).

- **LAST_QUEUED_TRANSACTION_START_QUEUE_TIMESTAMP:** The time when this instance started to queue the event – that is, when the event was received and the connection thread started to write the event to the relay log.

- **LAST_QUEUED_TRANSACTION_END_QUEUE_TIMESTAMP:** The time when the connection thread completed writing the event to the relay log.

The timestamps are in microsecond resolution, so it allows you to get a detailed picture of how long the event has been on its way from the original source to the relay log. A zero timestamp ('0000-00-00 00:00:00') means that there is no data to return; this can, for example, happen for the currently queueing timestamps when the connection thread is fully up to date. The applier tables provide further details about the event's journey through the replica.

Applier Tables

The applier threads are more complex as they both handle filtering of events and applying events, and there is support for parallel appliers.

At the time of writing, the following Performance Schema tables with information about the applier threads exist:

- **replication_applier_configuration:** This table shows the configuration of the applier threads for each replication channel. Currently the only setting is the configured replication delay. There is one row per channel.

- **replication_applier_filters:** The replication filters per replication channel. The information includes where the filter was configured and when it became active.

- **replication_applier_global_filters:** The replication filters that apply to all replication channels. The information includes where the filter was configured and when it became active.

- **replication_applier_status:** The overall status for the appliers including the service state, remaining delay (when a desired delay is configured), and the number of retries there have been for transactions. There is one row per channel.

- **replication_applier_status_by_coordinator:** The applier status as seen by the coordinator thread when using parallel replication. There are timestamps for the last processed transaction and the currently processing transaction. There is one row per channel. For single-threaded replication, this table is empty.

- **replication_applier_status_by_worker:** The applier status for each worker. There are timestamps for the last applied transaction and the transaction currently being applied. When parallel replication is configured, there is one row per worker (the number of workers is configured with slave_parallel_workers) per channel. For single-threaded replication, there is one row per channel.

At the high level, the applier tables follow the same pattern as for the connection tables with the addition of the filter configuration tables and the support for parallel appliers. Listing 26-2 shows an example of the content of the replication_applier_status_by_worker table for the relay replication channel. The output has been reformatted for improved readability. The output can also be found in the file listing_26_2.txt in this book's GitHub repository.

Listing 26-2. The `replication_applier_status_by_worker` table

```
mysql> SELECT *
         FROM performance_schema.replication_applier_status_by_worker
        WHERE CHANNEL_NAME = 'relay'\G
*************************** 1. row ***************************
                                               CHANNEL_NAME: relay
                                                  WORKER_ID: 1
                                                  THREAD_ID: 54
                                              SERVICE_STATE: ON
                                          LAST_ERROR_NUMBER: 0
                                         LAST_ERROR_MESSAGE:
                                       LAST_ERROR_TIMESTAMP: 0000-00-00 00:00:00
                                   LAST_APPLIED_TRANSACTION:
         LAST_APPLIED_TRANSACTION_ORIGINAL_COMMIT_TIMESTAMP: 0000-00-00 00:00:00
        LAST_APPLIED_TRANSACTION_IMMEDIATE_COMMIT_TIMESTAMP: 0000-00-00 00:00:00
             LAST_APPLIED_TRANSACTION_START_APPLY_TIMESTAMP: 0000-00-00 00:00:00
               LAST_APPLIED_TRANSACTION_END_APPLY_TIMESTAMP: 0000-00-00 00:00:00
                                       APPLYING_TRANSACTION:
             APPLYING_TRANSACTION_ORIGINAL_COMMIT_TIMESTAMP: 0000-00-00 00:00:00
            APPLYING_TRANSACTION_IMMEDIATE_COMMIT_TIMESTAMP: 0000-00-00 00:00:00
                APPLYING_TRANSACTION_START_APPLY_TIMESTAMP: 0000-00-00 00:00:00
                       LAST_APPLIED_TRANSACTION_RETRIES_COUNT: 0
        LAST_APPLIED_TRANSACTION_LAST_TRANSIENT_ERROR_NUMBER: 0
       LAST_APPLIED_TRANSACTION_LAST_TRANSIENT_ERROR_MESSAGE:
     LAST_APPLIED_TRANSACTION_LAST_TRANSIENT_ERROR_TIMESTAMP: 0000-00-00 00:00:00
                         APPLYING_TRANSACTION_RETRIES_COUNT: 0
            APPLYING_TRANSACTION_LAST_TRANSIENT_ERROR_NUMBER: 0
           APPLYING_TRANSACTION_LAST_TRANSIENT_ERROR_MESSAGE:
         APPLYING_TRANSACTION_LAST_TRANSIENT_ERROR_TIMESTAMP: 0000-00-00 00:00:00
*************************** 2. row ***************************
                                               CHANNEL_NAME: relay
                                                  WORKER_ID: 2
                                                  THREAD_ID: 55
                                              SERVICE_STATE: ON
                                          LAST_ERROR_NUMBER: 0
```

```
                            LAST_ERROR_MESSAGE:
                          LAST_ERROR_TIMESTAMP: 0000-00-00 00:00:00
                       LAST_APPLIED_TRANSACTION: 4d22b3e5-a54f-
                                                 11e9-8bdb-
                                                 ace2d35785be:213
    LAST_APPLIED_TRANSACTION_ORIGINAL_COMMIT_TIMESTAMP: 2019-08-11 11:29:36.1076
   LAST_APPLIED_TRANSACTION_IMMEDIATE_COMMIT_TIMESTAMP: 2019-08-11 11:29:44.822024
       LAST_APPLIED_TRANSACTION_START_APPLY_TIMESTAMP: 2019-08-11 11:29:51.910259
         LAST_APPLIED_TRANSACTION_END_APPLY_TIMESTAMP: 2019-08-11 11:29:52.403051
                             APPLYING_TRANSACTION: 4d22b3e5-a54f-11e9-8bdb-
                                                   ace2d35785be:214
         APPLYING_TRANSACTION_ORIGINAL_COMMIT_TIMESTAMP: 2019-08-11 11:29:43.092063
        APPLYING_TRANSACTION_IMMEDIATE_COMMIT_TIMESTAMP: 2019-08-11 11:29:52.685928
           APPLYING_TRANSACTION_START_APPLY_TIMESTAMP: 2019-08-11 11:29:53.141687
              LAST_APPLIED_TRANSACTION_RETRIES_COUNT: 0
   LAST_APPLIED_TRANSACTION_LAST_TRANSIENT_ERROR_NUMBER: 0
  LAST_APPLIED_TRANSACTION_LAST_TRANSIENT_ERROR_MESSAGE:
LAST_APPLIED_TRANSACTION_LAST_TRANSIENT_ERROR_TIMESTAMP: 0000-00-00 00:00:00
                  APPLYING_TRANSACTION_RETRIES_COUNT: 0
       APPLYING_TRANSACTION_LAST_TRANSIENT_ERROR_NUMBER: 0
      APPLYING_TRANSACTION_LAST_TRANSIENT_ERROR_MESSAGE:
    APPLYING_TRANSACTION_LAST_TRANSIENT_ERROR_TIMESTAMP: 0000-00-00 00:00:00
```

The timestamps follow the same pattern as you have seen earlier with information
for both the last processed and current transactions. Notice that for the first row, all
timestamps are zero which shows that the applier cannot take advantage of the parallel
replication.

For the last applied transaction with the global transaction identifier 4d22b3e5-a54f-
11e9-8bdb-ace2d35785be:213 in the second row, it can be seen that the transaction was
committed on the original source at 11:29:36.1076, committed on the immediate source
at 11:29:44.822024, started to execute on this instance at 11:29:51.910259, and finished
executing at 11:29:52.403051. That shows that each instance adds a delay of around eight
seconds, but the transaction itself only took half a second to execute. You can conclude
the replication delay is not caused by applying a single large transaction, but it is rather a
cumulative effect of the relay and replica instances not being able to process transactions

as fast as the original source, that the delay was introduced by an earlier long-running event and the replication has not yet caught up, or that the delay is introduced in other parts of the replication chain.

Log Status

A table that is related to replication is the log_status table which provides information about the binary log, relay log, and InnoDB redo log using a log lock to return the data corresponding to the same point in time. The table was introduced with backups in mind, so the BACKUP_ADMIN privilege is required to query the table. Listing 26-3 shows an example output using the JSON_PRETTY() function to make it easier to read the information returned as JSON documents.

Listing 26-3. The log_status table

```
mysql> SELECT SERVER_UUID,
              JSON_PRETTY(LOCAL) AS LOCAL,
              JSON_PRETTY(REPLICATION) AS REPLICATION,
              JSON_PRETTY(STORAGE_ENGINES) AS STORAGE_ENGINES
         FROM performance_schema.log_status\G
*************************** 1. row ***************************
   SERVER_UUID: 4d46199b-bbc9-11e9-8780-ace2d35785be
         LOCAL: {
  "gtid_executed": "4d22b3e5-a54f-11e9-8bdb-ace2d35785be:1-380,\ncbffdc28-
                    bbc8-11e9-9aac-ace2d35785be:1-190",
  "binary_log_file": "binlog.000003",
  "binary_log_position": 199154947
}
   REPLICATION: {
  "channels": [
    {
      "channel_name": "relay",
      "relay_log_file": "relay-bin-relay.000006",
      "relay_log_position": 66383736
    },
    {
```

```
        "channel_name": "source2",
        "relay_log_file": "relay-bin-source2.000009",
        "relay_log_position": 447
      }
    ]
}
STORAGE_ENGINES: {
  "InnoDB": {
    "LSN": 15688833970,
    "LSN_checkpoint": 15688833970
  }
}
1 row in set (0.0005 sec)
```

The LOCAL column includes information about the executed global transaction identifiers and the binary log file and position on this instance. The REPLICATION column shows the relay log data related to the replication process with one object per channel. The STORAGE_ENGINES column contains the information about the InnoDB log sequence numbers.

Group Replication Tables

If you use Group Replication, then there are two additional tables that you can use to monitor the replication. One table includes high-level information about the members of the group, and the other has various statistics for the members.

The two tables are

- **replication_group_members:** The high-level overview of the members. There is one row for each member, and the data includes the current status and whether it is a primary or secondary member.

- **replication_group_member_stats:** Lower-level statistics such as the number of transactions in the queue, which transactions are committed on all members, how many transactions originated locally or remotely, and so on.

The `replication_group_members` table is most useful to verify the status of the members. The `replication_group_member_stats` table can be used to see how each node views what work has been done and whether there is a high rate of conflicts and rollbacks. Both tables include information from all nodes in the cluster.

Now that you know how to monitor replication, you can start working on optimizing the connection and applier threads.

The Connection

The connection thread handles the outbound connection to the immediate source of the replication, reception of the replication events, and saving the events to the relay log. This means that optimizing the connection process revolves around the replication events, the network, maintaining the information about which events have been received, and writing the relay log.

Replication Events

When row-based replication is used (the default and recommended), the events include information about the row that was changed and the new values (before and after images). By default, the complete before image is included for update and delete events. This makes it possible for the replica to apply the events even if the source and replica have the columns in different order or have different primary key definitions. It does however make the binary log – and thus also the relay logs – larger which means more network traffic, memory usage, and disk I/O.

If you do not require the full before image to be present, you can configure the `binlog_row_image` option to `minimal` or `noblob`. The value `minimal` means that only the columns required to identify the row are included in the before image, and the after image only includes the columns changed by the event. With `noblob`, all columns except `blob` and `text` columns are included in the before image, and `blob` and `text` columns are only included in the after image if their values have changed. Using `minimal` is the optimal for performance, but make sure you test thoroughly before making the change on your production system.

Caution   Make sure you have verified that your application works with `binlog_row_image = minimal` before making the configuration change on production. If the application does not work with the setting, it will cause replication to fail on the replicas.

The `binlog_row_image` option can also be set at the session scope, so a possibility is to change the option as needed.

The Network

The main tuning options inside MySQL for the network used in replication are the interface used and whether compression is enabled. If the network is overloaded, it can quickly make replication fall behind. An option to avoid that is to use a dedicated network interface and route for the replication traffic. Another option is to enable compression which can reduce the amount of data transferred at the cost of higher CPU load. Both solutions are implemented using the `CHANGE MASTER TO` command.

When you define how to connect to the source of the replication, you can use the `MASTER_BIND` option to specify which interface to use for the connection. For example, if you want to replicate from a source at 192.0.2.101 using the interface that on the replica has the IP address 192.0.2.102, then you can use `MASTER_BIND='192.0.2.102'`:

```
CHANGE MASTER TO MASTER_BIND='192.0.2.102',
                 MASTER_HOST='192.0.2.101',
                 MASTER_PORT=3306,
                 MASTER_AUTO_POSITION=1,
                 MASTER_SSL=1;
```

Replace the addresses and other information as needed.

Caution   It may be tempting to not enable SSL to improve the network performance. If you do that, the communication including authentication information and your data will be transferred unencrypted, and anyone who gets access to the network can read the data. Thus, it is important for any setup handling production data that all communication is secure – for replication that means enabling SSL.

Compression is enabled in MySQL 8.0.18 and later using the MASTER_COMPRESSION_ ALGORITHMS option which takes a set of allowed algorithms. The supported algorithms are

- **uncompressed:** Disable compression. This is the default.

- **zlib:** Use the zlib compression algorithm.

- **zstd:** Use the ztd version 1.3 compression algorithm.

If you include the zstd algorithm, then you can use the MASTER_ZSTD_COMPRESSION_ LEVEL option to specify the compression level. Supported levels are 1–22 (both included) with 3 being the default. An example of configuring the replication connection to use either the zlib or zstd algorithm with a compression level of 5 is

```
CHANGE MASTER TO MASTER_COMPRESSION_ALGORITHMS='zlib,zstd',
                 MASTER_ZSTD_COMPRESSION_LEVEL=5;
```

Before MySQL 8.0.18, you specify whether to use compression with the slave_ compressed_protocol option. Setting the option to 1 or ON makes the replication connection use zlib compression if both the source and replica support the algorithm.

Tip   If you have the slave_compressed_protocol option enabled in MySQL 8.0.18 or later, it takes precedence over the MASTER_COMPRESSION_ ALGORITHMS. It is recommended to disable slave_compressed_protocol and use the CHANGE MASTER TO command to configure the compression as it allows you to use the zstd algorithm and it makes the compression configuration available in the replication_connection_configuration Performance Schema table.

Maintaining Source Info

The replica needs to keep track of information it has received from the source. This is done through the mysql.slave_master_info table. It is also possible to store the information in a file, but this has been deprecated as of 8.0.18 and is discouraged. Using a file also makes the replica less resilient to recover from crashes.

With respect to the performance of maintaining this information, then the important option is `sync_master_info`. This specifies how frequently the information is updated with the default being every 10000 events. You may think that similar to `sync_binlog` on the source side of the replication, it is important to sync the data after every event; however, that is not the case.

Caution   It is not necessary to set `sync_master_info` = 1 and doing so is a common source of replication lags.

The reason it is not necessary to update the information very frequently is that it is possible to recover from a loss of information by discarding the relay log and fetching everything starting from the point the applier has reached. The default value of 10000 is thus good, and there is rarely any reason to change it.

Tip   The exact rules when the replication can recover from a crash are complex and change from time to time as new improvements are added. You can see the up-to-date information in `https://dev.mysql.com/doc/refman/en/replication-solutions-unexpected-slave-halt.html`.

Writing the Relay Log

The relay logs are the intermediate storage of the replication events between the connection receiving the replication events and the applier has processed them. There are mainly two things that affect how quickly the relay log can be written: the disk performance and how often the relay log is synced to disk.

You need to ensure that the disk you write the relay log to has enough I/O capacity to sustain the write and read activity. One option is to store the relay logs on a separate storage so other activities do not interfere with the writing and reading of the relay log.

How often the relay log is synchronized to disk is controlled using the `sync_relay_log` option which is the relay log equivalent of `sync_binlog`. The default is to synchronize every 10000 events. Unless you use position-based replication (GTID disabled or `MASTER_AUTO_POSITION=0`) with parallel applier threads, there is no reason to change the value of `sync_relay_log` as recovery of the relay log is possible. For position-based parallel replication, you will need `sync_relay_log = 1` unless it is acceptable to rebuild the replica in case of a crash of the operating system.

This means that from a performance perspective, the recommendation is to enable global transaction identifiers and set `MASTER_AUTO_POSITION=1` when executing `CHANGE MASTER TO`. Otherwise, leave the other settings related to the master info and relay log at their defaults.

The Applier

The applier is the most common cause of replication lags. The main problem is that the changes made on the source are often the result of a highly parallel workload. In contrast, by default the applier is single threaded, so a single thread will have to keep up with potential tens or hundreds of concurrent queries on the source. This means that the main tool for combating replication lags caused by the applier is to enable parallel replication. Additionally, the importance of primary keys, the possibility of relaxing data safety settings, and the use of replication filters will be discussed.

Note   There is no effect of changing the `sync_relay_log_info` setting when you use a table for the relay log repository and use InnoDB for the `mysql. slave_relay_log_info` table (both are the default and recommended). In this case, the setting is effectively ignored, and the information is updated after every transaction.

Parallel Applier

Configuring the applier to use several threads to apply the events in parallel is the most powerful way to improve the replication performance. It is however not as simple as setting the `slave_parallel_workers` option to a value greater than 1. There are other options – both on the source and replica – to consider.

Table 26-1 summarizes the configuration options that affect parallel replication including whether the option should be set on the source or the replica.

Table 26-1. *Configuration options related to parallel replication*

Option Name and Where to Configure	Description
`binlog_transaction_dependency_tracking` Set on the source	Which information to include in the binary log about the dependencies between transactions.
`binlog_transaction_dependency_history_size` Set on the source	How long information is kept for when a row was last updated.
`transaction_write_set_extraction` Set on the source	How to extract write set information.
`binlog_group_commit_sync_delay` Set on the source	The delay to wait for more transactions to group together in the group commit feature.
`slave_parallel_workers` Set on the replica	How many applier threads to create for each channel
`slave_parallel_type` Set on the replica	Whether to parallelize over databases or the logical clock.
`slave_pending_jobs_size_max` Set on the replica	How much memory can be used to hold events not yet applied.
`slave_preserve_commit_order` Set on the replica	Whether to ensure the replica writes the transactions to its binary log in the same order as on the source. Enabling this requires setting `slave_parallel_workers` to `LOGICAL_CLOCK`.
`slave_checkpoint_group` Set on the replica	The maximum number of transactions to process between checkpoint operations.
`slave_checkpoint_period` Set on the replica	The maximum time in milliseconds between checkpoint operations.

The most commonly used of the options are `binlog_transaction_dependency_tracking` and `transaction_write_set_extraction` on the source and `slave_parallel_workers` and `slave_parallel_type` on the replica.

The binary log transaction dependency tracking and write set extraction options on the source are related. The `transaction_write_set_extraction` option specifies how to extract write set information (information about which rows are affected by the transaction). The write sets are also what Group Replication uses for conflict detection. Set this to `XXHASH64` which is also the value required by Group Replication.

The `binlog_transaction_dependency_tracking` option specifies what transaction dependency information is available in the binary log. This is important for the parallel replication to be able to know which transactions are safe to apply in parallel. The default is to use the commit order and rely on the commit timestamps. For improved parallel replication performance when parallelizing according to the logical clock, set `binlog_transaction_dependency_tracking` to `WRITESET`.

The `binlog_transaction_dependency_history_size` option specifies the number of row hashes that are kept providing information on which transaction last modified a given row. The default value of 25000 is usually large enough; however, if you have a very high rate of modifications to different rows, it can be worth increasing the dependency history size.

On the replica, you enable parallel replication with the `slave_parallel_workers` option. This is the number of applier worker threads that will be created for each replication channel. Set this high enough for the replication to keep up but not so high that you end up having idle workers or that you see contention from a too parallel workload.

The other option that is often necessary to update on the replica is the `slave_parallel_type` option. This specifies how the events should be split among the applier workers. The default is `DATABASE` which as the name suggests splits updates according the schema they belong to. The alternative is `LOGICAL_CLOCK` which uses the group commit information or the write set information in the binary log to determine which transactions are safe to apply together. Unless you have several layers of replicas without including write set information in the binary log, `LOGICAL_CLOCK` is usually the best choice.

If you use the LOGICAL_CLOCK parallelization type without write sets enabled, you can increase binlog_group_commit_sync_delay on the source to group more transactions together in the group commit feature at the expense of a longer commit latency. This will give the parallel replication more transactions to distribute among the workers and thus improve the effectiveness.

The other major contributor to replication lags is the absence of primary keys.

Primary Keys

When you use row-based replication, the applier worker processing the event will have to locate the rows that must be changed. If there is a primary key, this is very simple and efficient – just a primary key lookup. However, if there is no primary key, it is necessary to examine all rows until a row has been found with the same values for all columns as the values in the before image of the replication event.

Such a search is expensive if the table is large. If the transaction modifies many rows in a relatively large table, it can in the worst case make replication seem like it has come to a grinding halt. MySQL 8 uses an optimization where it uses hashes to match a group of rows against the table; however, the effectiveness depends on the number of rows modified in one event, and it will never be as efficient as primary key lookups.

It is strongly recommended that you add an explicit primary key (or a not-NULL unique key) to all tables. There is no savings in disk space or memory by not having one as InnoDB adds a hidden primary key (which cannot be used for replication) if you do not add one yourself. The hidden primary key is a 6 byte integer and uses a global counter, so if you have many tables with hidden primary keys, the counter can become a bottleneck. Furthermore, if you want to use Group Replication, it is a strict requirement that all tables have an explicit primary key or a not-NULL unique index.

Tip   Enable the sql_require_primary_key option to require all tables to have a primary key. The option is available in MySQL 8.0.13 and later.

If you cannot add a primary key to some tables, then the hash search algorithm works better the more rows are included in each replication event. You can increase the number of rows grouped together for transactions modifying a large number of rows in the same table by increasing the size of binlog_row_event_max_size on the source instance of the replication.

Relaxing Data Safety

When a transaction is committed, it must be persisted on disk. In InnoDB the persistence is guaranteed through the redo log and for replication through the binary log. In some cases, it may be acceptable on a replica to relax the guarantees that the changes have been persisted. This optimization comes at the expense that you will need to rebuild the replica if the operating system crashes.

InnoDB uses the option `innodb_flush_log_at_trx_commit` to determine whether the redo log is flushed every time a transaction commits. The default (and safest setting) is to flush after every commit (`innodb_flush_log_at_trx_commit = 1`). Flushing is an expensive operation, and even some SSD drives can have problems keeping up with the flushing required from a busy system. If you can afford losing up to a second of committed transactions, you can set `innodb_flush_log_at_trx_commit` to 0 or 2. If you are willing to postpone flushes even further, you can increase `innodb_flush_log_at_timeout` which sets the maximum amount of time in seconds between flushing the redo log. The default and minimum value is 1 second. That means if a catastrophic failure happens, you will likely need to rebuild the replica, but the bonus is that the applier threads can commit changes cheaper than the source and thus easier keep up.

The binary log similarly uses the `sync_binlog` option which also defaults to 1 which means to flush the binary log after each commit. If you do not need the binary log on the replica (note that for Group Replication the binary log must be enabled on all notes), you can consider either disabling it altogether or to reduce the frequency the log is synced. Typically, in that case, it is better to set `sync_binlog` to a value such as 100 or 1000 rather than 0 as 0 often ends up causing the entire binary log to be flushed at once when it is rotating. Flushing a gigabyte can take several seconds; and, in the meantime, there is a mutex that prevents committing transactions.

Note   If you relax the data safety settings on a replica, make sure you set them back to the stricter values if you promote the replica to become the replication source, for example, if you need to perform maintenance.

Replication Filters

If you do not need all the data on the replica, you can use replication filters to reduce the work required by the applier threads and reduce the disk and memory requirements. This can also help the replica to keep up to date with its source. There are six options to set the replication filters. The options can be divided into three sets with a *do* and an *ignore* option as shown in Table 26-2.

Table 26-2. *Replication filter options*

Option Name	Description
replicate-do-db replicate-ignore-db	Whether to include the changes for the schema (database) given as a value.
replicate-do-table replicate-ignore-table	Whether to include the changes for the table given as a value.
replicate-wild-do-table replicate-wild-ignore-table	Like the replicate-do-table and replicate-ignore-table options but with support for the _ and % wildcards in the same way as when writing LIKE clauses.

When you specify one of the options, you can optionally prefix the schema/table with the channel name the rule should apply to and a colon. For example, to ignore updates to the world schema for the source2 channel

```
[mysqld]
replicate-do-db = source2:world
```

The options can only be set in the MySQL configuration file and require a restart of MySQL to take effect. You can specify each option multiple times to add more than one rule. If you need to change the configuration dynamically, you can configure the filters with the CHANGE REPLICATION FILTER statement, for example:

```
mysql> CHANGE REPLICATION FILTER
            REPLICATE_IGNORE_DB = (world)
            FOR CHANNEL 'source2';
Query OK, 0 rows affected (0.0003 sec)
```

The parentheses around `world` are required as you can specify a list if you need to include more than one database. If you specify the same rule more than once, the latter applies, and the former is ignored.

Tip To see the full rules for `CHANGE REPLICATION FILTER`, see `https://dev.mysql.com/doc/refman/en/change-replication-filter.html`.

Replication filters work best with row-based replication as it is clear which table is affected by an event. When you have a statement, the statement may affect multiple tables, so for statement-based replication it is not always clear whether a filter should allow the statement or not. Particular care should be taken with `replicate-do-db` and `replicate-ignore-db` as with statement-based replication they use the default schema to decide whether to allow a statement or not. Even worse is to use replication filters with a mix of row and statement events (`binlog_format = MIXED`) as the effect of a filter can depend on the format the changes replicate with.

Tip It is best to use `binlog_format = row` (the default) when you use replication filters. For the complete rules for evaluation replication filters, see `https://dev.mysql.com/doc/refman/en/replication-rules.html`.

That concludes the discussion of how to improve the replication performance. There is one topic left which is kind of the opposite of what has been discussed thus far – how to improve the performance of the source by using the replica.

Offloading Work to a Replica

If you have problems with an instance being overloaded by read queries, a common strategy to improve the performance is to offload some of the work to one or more replicas. Some common scenarios are to use replicas for read scale-out and to use a replica for reporting or backups. This section will look at this.

Note   Using replication (e.g., using Group Replication's multi-primary mode) does not work as a way to scale out writes as all changes must still be applied on all nodes. For write scale-out, you need to shard the data, for example, as it is done in MySQL NDB Cluster. Sharding solutions are beyond the scope of this book.

Read Scale-Out

One of the most common uses of replication is to allow read queries to use a replica and, in that way, reduce the load on the replication source. This is possible because the replicas have the same data as their source. The main thing to be aware of is that there will even at the best of time be a small delay from a transaction is committed on the source until a replica has the change.

If your application is sensitive to reading stale data, then an option is to choose Group Replication or InnoDB Cluster which in versions 8.0.14 and later supports consistency levels, so you can ensure the application uses the required level of consistency.

Tip   For a good explanation of how to use the Group Replication consistency levels, the blog by Lefred at `https://lefred.be/content/mysql-innodb-cluster-consistency-levels/` is highly recommended together with the links at the top of the blog to blogs by the Group Replication developers.

Using replicas for reads can also help you bring the application and MySQL closer to the end user which reduces the roundtrip latency, so the user gets a better experience.

Separation of Tasks

The other common use of replicas is to perform some high-impact tasks on a replica to reduce the load on the replication source. Two typical tasks are reporting and backups.

When you use a replica for reporting queries, you may benefit from configuring the replica differently than the source to optimize it for the specific workload it is used for. It may also be possible to use replication filters to avoid including all the data and updates from the source. Less data means the replica has to apply fewer transactions and write less data, and you can read a larger percentage of the data into the buffer pool.

It is also common to use a replica for backups. If the replica is dedicated to backups, then you do not need to worry about locks and performance degradation due to disk I/O or buffer pool pollution as long as the replica can catch up before the next backup. You can even consider shutting the replica down during the backup and perform a cold backup.

Summary

This chapter has looked at how replication works, how to monitor and improve the performance of the replication process, and how to use replication to distribute the work across several instances.

The start of the chapter provided an overview of replication including introducing the terminology and showed where you can find monitoring information for the replication. In MySQL 8, the best way to monitor replication is to use a series of Performance Schema tables that split the information out depending on the thread type and whether it is the configuration or status. There are also tables dedicated to the log status and Group Replication.

The connection thread can be optimized by reducing the size of the replication event by only including minimal information about the before values for the updated rows in the replication events. This will not work for all applications though. You can also make changes to the network and to writing the relay log. It is recommended to use GTID-based replication with auto-positioning enabled which allows you to relax the synchronization of the relay log.

The two most important things for the performance of the applier are to enable parallel replication and to ensure all tables have a primary key. Parallel replication can be either over the schema the updates affect or by the logical clock. The latter is often what performs the best, but there are exceptions, so you will need to verify with your workload.

Finally, it was discussed how you can use replicas to offload work that would otherwise have to be performed on the replication source. You can use replication for read scale-out as you can use the replicas for reading data and dedicate the source for tasks that require writing data. You can also use replicas for highly intensive work such as reporting and backups.

The final chapter will go into reducing the amount of work being done by use of caching.

CHAPTER 27

Caching

The cheapest queries are those you do not execute at all. This chapter investigates how you can use caching to avoid executing queries or to reduce the complexity of queries. First, it will be discussed how caching exists everywhere and how there are different types of caching. Then it is covered how you can use caching inside MySQL using cache tables and approximate values. The two next sections consider the two popular products that offer caching: *Memcached* and *ProxySQL*. Finally, some caching tips are discussed.

Caching Is Everywhere

Even if you do not think you have implemented caching, you are already using caching in several places. These caches are transparent and maintained at the hardware, operating system, or MySQL levels. The most obvious of these caches is the InnoDB buffer pool.

Figure 27-1 shows examples of how caching exists throughout the system and examples of how custom caching can be added. The picture – including the interactions – is by no means complete, but it serves to illustrate how common caching is and in how many places it can occur.

© Jesper Wisborg Krogh 2020
J. W. Krogh, *MySQL 8 Query Performance Tuning*, https://doi.org/10.1007/978-1-4842-5584-1_27

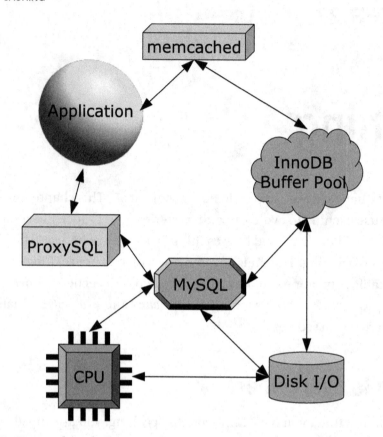

Figure 27-1. *Examples of where caching can occur*

In the lower-left corner, there is the CPU which has several levels of caches that cache the instructions and data used for CPU instructions. The operating system implements an I/O cache, and InnoDB has its buffer pool. All of these caches are examples of caches that return the up-to-date data.

There are also caches that may serve slightly stale data. This includes implementing cache tables in MySQL, caching query results in ProxySQL, or caching data directly in the application. In those cases, you typically define a period to consider the data fresh enough, and when it has reached a given age – *time to live* (TTL) – the cache entry is invalidated. The Memcached solution is special as there are two versions of it. The regular Memcached daemon uses time to live or some application-depending logic to evict the data when it is too old; however, there is also a special MySQL version which works as a plugin and can fetch the data from the InnoDB buffer pool and write data back to the buffer pool, so the data is never stale.

It may seem wrong to use potentially out-of-date data in your application. In many cases, however, that is perfectly fine as exact data is not required. If you have an application that shows a dashboard of sales figures, how big a difference does it make if the data is current as of the time the queries executed or if they are a few minutes old? By the time the user is done reading the figures, they are likely slightly out of date anyway. The important thing is that the sales figures are consistent and get updated regularly.

Tip   Consider carefully what the requirements for your application are and remember it is easier to start out with relaxed requirements to how up to date data must be and make it more strict if needed than convincing a user that they no longer can have up-to-the-second result. If you use cached data that is not automatically updated to the latest values, you can consider storing the time when the data was current and show that to the user, so the user knows when the data was last refreshed.

The next three sections will go through more specific examples of caching starting with implementing your own caching inside MySQL.

Caching Inside MySQL

A logical place to implement caching is inside MySQL. This is particularly useful if the cached data is used together with other tables. The downside is that it still requires a roundtrip from the application to the database to query the data, and it requires executing a query. This section covers two ways to cache data in MySQL: cache tables and histogram statistics.

Cache Tables

A cache table can be used to pre-calculate data, for example, for a report or a dashboard. It is mostly useful for complex aggregations that are needed frequently.

There are several approaches to use cache tables. You can choose to create a table storing the result for the feature that it is used with. This makes it cheap to use, but also relatively inflexible as it can only be used with that one feature. Alternatively, you can create building blocks that need to be joined together, so they can be used for several features. This makes the queries a little more expensive, but you can reuse the cached data and avoid duplicating the data. It depends on your application which approach is the best, and you may end up choosing a hybrid where some tables are used on their own and others are joined together.

There are two main tactics to populate the cache tables. You can either periodically completely rebuild the tables, or you can use triggers to keep the data up to date continuously. Completely rebuilding the tables works best by creating a new copy of cache tables and at the end of the rebuild using `RENAME TABLE` to swap the tables around as it avoids deleting a potentially large number of rows in the transaction and it avoids fragmentation building up over time. Alternatively, you can use triggers to update the cached data as the data it depends on changes. Rebuilding the cache tables is the preferred in most cases if it is acceptable to use not completely up-to-date data as it is less error prone and the refresh is done in the background.

Tip   If you rebuild cache tables in place by deleting the existing data inside the transaction, then either disable auto-recalculation of index statistics and use `ANALYZE TABLE` at the end of the rebuild or enable the `innodb_stats_include_delete_marked` option.

A special case is a cached column that is included in a table that otherwise does not cache data. An example where a cached column is useful is to store the time, status, or id of the latest event that belongs to some group. Imagine that your application supports sending text messages and for each message you store the history such as when it was created in the application, when it was sent, and when the recipient acknowledged the message. In most cases only the latest status and when the status was reached are needed, so you may want to store that with the message record itself rather than have to query it explicitly. In that case you can use two tables to store the statuses:

```
CREATE TABLE message (
  message_id bigint unsigned NOT NULL auto_increment,
  message_text varchar(1024) NOT NULL,
  cached_status_time datetime(3) NOT NULL,
  cached_status_id tinyint unsigned NOT NULL,
  PRIMARY KEY (message_id)
);
CREATE TABLE message_status_history (
  message_status_id bigint unsigned NOT NULL auto_increment,
  message_id bigint unsigned NOT NULL,
  status_time datetime(3) NOT NULL,
  status_id tinyint unsigned NOT NULL,
  PRIMARY KEY (message_status_id)
);
```

In the real world, there may be more columns and foreign keys, but for the example this information will suffice. When the status changes for a message, a row is inserted into the `message_status_history` table. You can look for the latest row for a message to find the latest status, but here a business rule has been created to update the `cached_status_time` and `cached_status_id` in the message table with the latest status and time it was changed. That way, to return to the application details of the message (except when requiring the history), you only need to query the `message` table. You can update the cached columns through the application or a trigger, or if you do not need the cached status to be completely up to date, you can use a background job.

Tip   Use a naming scheme that makes it clear what data is cached and what is not. You can, for example, prefix cache tables and columns with `cached_`.

Another case that you can consider a case of caching are the histogram statistics.

Histogram Statistics

Recall from Chapter 16 how histogram statistics are statistics of the frequency each value is encountered for a column. You can take advantage of this and use the histogram statistics as a cache. It is primarily useful if there are at most 1024 unique values for the column as that is the maximum number of buckets supported, so 1024 is the maximum number of values that can be used with singleton histograms.

Listing 27-1 shows an example of using a histogram to return the number of cities in India (CountryCode = IND) in the world database.

Listing 27-1. Using histograms as a cache

```
-- Create the histogram on the CountryCode
-- column of the world.city table.
mysql> ANALYZE TABLE world.city
        UPDATE HISTOGRAM on CountryCode
        WITH 1024 BUCKETS\G
*************************** 1. row ***************************
   Table: world.city
      Op: histogram
Msg_type: status
Msg_text: Histogram statistics created for column 'CountryCode'.
1 row in set (0.5909 sec)

mysql> SELECT Bucket_Value, Frequency
        FROM (
          SELECT (Row_ID - 1) AS Bucket_Number,
                SUBSTRING_INDEX(Bucket_Value, ':', -1)
                  AS Bucket_Value,
                (Cumulative_Frequency
                 - LAG(Cumulative_Frequency, 1, 0)
                      OVER (ORDER BY Row_ID))
                  AS Frequency
            FROM information_schema.COLUMN_STATISTICS
            INNER JOIN JSON_TABLE(
                histogram->'$.buckets',
```

```
                '$[*]' COLUMNS(
                    Row_ID FOR ORDINALITY,
                    Bucket_Value varchar(42) PATH '$[0]',
                    Cumulative_Frequency double PATH '$[1]'
                )
            ) buckets
        WHERE SCHEMA_NAME = 'world'
              AND TABLE_NAME = 'city'
              AND COLUMN_NAME = 'CountryCode'
    ) stats
    WHERE Bucket_Value = 'IND';
+--------------+---------------------+
| Bucket_Value | Frequency           |
+--------------+---------------------+
| IND          | 0.08359892130424124 |
+--------------+---------------------+
1 row in set (0.0102 sec)

mysql> SELECT TABLE_ROWS
       FROM information_schema.TABLES
       WHERE TABLE_SCHEMA = 'world'
             AND TABLE_NAME = 'city';
+------------+
| TABLE_ROWS |
+------------+
|       4188 |
+------------+
1 row in set (0.0075 sec)

mysql> SELECT 0.08359892130424124*4188;
+---------------------------+
| 0.08359892130424124*4188  |
+---------------------------+
|      350.11228242216231312 |
+---------------------------+
```

```
1 row in set (0.0023 sec)
mysql> SELECT COUNT(*)
          FROM world.city
        WHERE CountryCode = 'IND';
+----------+
| COUNT(*) |
+----------+
|      341 |
+----------+
1 row in set (0.0360 sec)
```

If you think the query against COLUMN_STATITICS looks familiar, then it is derived from the one used in Chapter 16 when listing bucket information for a singleton histogram. It is necessary to collect the histogram information in a subquery as otherwise the frequency is not calculated.

You will also need the total number of rows. You can either use the approximate value from the information_schema.TABLES view or cache the result of SELECT COUNT(*) for the table. In the example, the estimate is that the city table has 4188 rows (your estimate may be different) which together with the frequency for India suggests there are around 350 Indian cities in the table. An exact count shows that there are 341. The deviation comes from the total row count estimate (there are 4079 rows in the city table).

Using histograms as a cache is mostly useful for large tables for a column with at most 1024 unique values, particularly if there is no index on the column. This means that it does not match all that many use cases. It does however show an example of thinking outside the box – something that is very useful when you try to find caching solutions.

For more advanced caching solutions, you need to look at third-party solutions or implement your own in the application.

Memcached

Memcached is a simple but highly scalable in-memory key-value store that is popular as a caching tool. It has traditionally been mostly used with web servers but can be used by any kind of application. An advantage of Memcached is it can be distributed across multiple hosts which allows you to create a large cache.

> **Note**   Memcached is only officially supported on Linux and Unix.

There are two ways to use Memcached with MySQL. You can use the regular standalone Memcached or you can use the MySQL InnoDB Memcached plugin. This section will show a simple example of using both. For the full Memcached documentation, see the official homepage at `https://memcached.org/` and the official wiki at `https://github.com/memcached/memcached/wiki`.

Standalone Memcached

The standalone Memcached is the official daemon from `https://memcached.org/`. It allows you to use it as a distributed cache or to have the cache very close – possibly on the same host – to the application reducing the cost of querying the cache.

There are a few options to install Memcached including using the package manager of the operating system and compiling from source. The simplest is to use your package manager, for example, on Oracle Linux, Red Hat Enterprise Linux, and CentOS 7:

```
shell$ sudo yum install memcached libevent
```

The `libevent` package is included as `memcached` requires it. On Ubuntu Linux the package is called `libevent-dev`. You may already have `libevent` and/or `memcached` installed in which case the package manager will let you know there is nothing to do.

You start the daemon by using the `memcached` command. For example, to start it using all the default options

```
shell$ memcached
```

If you use it in production, you should configure `systemd` or whatever service manager you are using to start and stop the daemon when the operating system boots and shuts down. For testing, it is fine to just start it from the command line.

> **Caution**   There is no security support in Memcached. Limit the cached data to nonsensitive data, and make sure that your Memcached instances are only available in the internal network and use a firewall to restrict access. One option is to deploy Memcached on the same host as your application and prevent remote connections.

You can now use Memcached by storing the data you retrieve from MySQL in the cache. There is support for Memcached in several programming languages. For this discussion, Python will be used with the pymemcache module[1] and MySQL Connector/Python. Listing 27-2 shows how to install the modules using pip. The output may look a little different depending on the exact version of Python you are using and what you have .installed already, and the name of the Python command depends on your system. At the time of writing, pymemcache supports Python 2.7, 3.5, 3.6, and 3.7. The example uses Python 3.6 installed as an extra package on Oracle Linux 7.

Listing 27-2. Installing the Python pymemcache module

```
shell$ python3 -m pip install --user pymemcache
Collecting pymemcache
  Downloading https://files.pythonhosted.org/packages/20/08/3dfe193f9a1dc6
  0186fc40d41b7dc59f6bf2990722c3cbaf19cee36bbd93/pymemcache-2.2.2-py2.py3-
  none-any.whl (44kB)
    |████████████████████████████████
    |████████████████████████| 51kB 3.3MB/s
Requirement already satisfied: six in /usr/local/lib/python3.6/site-
packages (from pymemcache) (1.11.0)
Installing collected packages: pymemcache
Successfully installed pymemcache-2.2.2

shell$ python36 -m pip install --user mysql-connector-python
Collecting mysql-connector-python
  Downloading https://files.pythonhosted.org/packages/58/ac/
  a3e86e5df84b818f69ebb8c89f282efe6a15d3ad63a769314cdd00bccbbb/mysql_
  connector_python-8.0.17-cp36-cp36m-manylinux1_x86_64.whl (13.1MB)
    |████████████████████████████████
    |████████████████████████| 13.1MB 5.6MB/s
Requirement already satisfied: protobuf>=3.0.0 in /usr/local/lib64/
python3.6/site-packages (from mysql-connector-python) (3.6.1)
Requirement already satisfied: setuptools in /usr/local/lib/python3.6/site-
packages (from protobuf>=3.0.0->mysql-connector-python) (39.0.1)
```

---

[1]https://pypi.org/project/pymemcache/

Requirement already satisfied: six>=1.9 in /usr/local/lib/python3.6/site-packages (from protobuf>=3.0.0->mysql-connector-python) (1.11.0)
Installing collected packages: mysql-connector-python
Successfully installed mysql-connector-python-8.0.17

In your application you can query Memcached by a key. If the key is found, Memcached returns the value that was stored with the key, and if it is not found you need to query MySQL and store the result in the cache. Listing 27-3 shows a simple example of doing this querying the world.city table. The program can also be found in the file listing_27_3.py that is included in this book's GitHub repository. If you want to execute the program, you need to update the connection arguments in connect_args to reflect the settings used to connect to your MySQL instance.

Listing 27-3. Simple Python program using memcached and MySQL

```
from pymemcache.client.base import Client
import mysql.connector

connect_args = {
    "user": "root",
    "password": "password",
    "host": "localhost",
    "port": 3306,
}
db = mysql.connector.connect(**connect_args)
cursor = db.cursor()
memcache = Client(("localhost", 11211))

sql = "SELECT CountryCode, Name FROM world.city WHERE ID = %s"
city_id = 130
city = memcache.get(str(city_id))
if city is not None:
    country_code, name = city.decode("utf-8").split("|")
    print("memcached: country: {0} - city: {1}".format(country_code, name))
else:
    cursor.execute(sql, (city_id,))
    country_code, name = cursor.fetchone()
    memcache.set(str(city_id), "|".join([country_code, name]), expire=60)
    print("MySQL: country: {0} - city: {1}".format(country_code, name))
```

```
memcache.close()
cursor.close()
db.close()
```

The program starts out creating a connection both to MySQL and the memcached daemon. In this case the connection parameters and the id to query are hardcoded. In a real program, you should read the connection parameters from a configuration file or similar.

Caution   Never store connection details in the application. Particularly never hardcode the password. Storing the connection details in the application is both inflexible and insecure.

The program then tries to fetch the data from Memcached; notice how the integer is converted to a string as Memcached uses strings for keys. If the key is found, the country code and name are extracted from the cached value by splitting the string at the | character. If the key is not found in the cache, the city data are fetched from MySQL and stored in the cache with the time to keep the value in the cache set to 60 seconds. Print statements are added for each case to show where the data was fetched from.

The first time you execute the program after each restart of memcached, it will end up querying MySQL:

```
shell$ python3 listing_27_3.py
MySQL: country: AUS - city: Sydney
```

On subsequent executions for up to a minute, the data will be found in the cache:

```
shell$ python3 listing_27_3.py
memcached: country: AUS - city: Sydney
```

When you are done testing Memcached, you can stop it using Ctrl+C in the session where memcached is running or by sending it a SIGTEM (15) signal, for example:

```
shell$ kill -s SIGTERM $(pidof memcached)
```

Using the Memcached directly as in this example has the advantage that you can have a pool of daemons and you can run the daemon close to the application, possibly even on the same host as the application. The disadvantage is that you must maintain the cache yourself. An alternative is to use the memcached plugin that comes from MySQL which will manage the cache for you and even automatically persist writes to the cache.

MySQL InnoDB Memcached Plugin

The InnoDB Memcached plugin was introduced in MySQL 5.6 as a way to access InnoDB data without the overhead of parsing the SQL statements. The primary use of the plugin is to let InnoDB handle the caching through its buffer pool and just use Memcached as a mechanism to query the data. Some of the nice features of using the plugin this way are that writes to the plugin are written to the underlying InnoDB table, the data is always up to date, and you can use both SQL and Memcached to access the data concurrently.

> **Note**   Make sure you have stopped the standalone Memcached process before installing the MySQL InnoDB Memcached plugin as they by default use the same port. If you do not, you will keep connecting to the standalone process.

Before you install the MySQL memcached daemon, you must ensure that the libevent package is installed like for the standalone Memcached installation. Once you have installed libevent, you need to install the innodb_memcache schema which includes the tables that are used for the configuration. You perform the installation by sourcing the share/innodb_memcached_config.sql file that is included in the MySQL distribution. The file is relative to the MySQL base directory which you can find through the basedir system variable, for example:

```
mysql> SELECT @@global.basedir AS basedir;
+----------+
| basedir |
+----------+
| /usr/    |
+----------+
1 row in set (0.00 sec)
```

If you have installed MySQL using the RPM from https://dev.mysql.com/downloads/, the command is

```
mysql> SOURCE /usr/share/mysql-8.0/innodb_memcached_config.sql
```

Note   Be aware that this command does not work in MySQL Shell as the script includes the USE command without a semicolon which MySQL Shell does not support in scripts.

The script also creates the test.demo_test table which will be used in the rest of this discussion.

The innodb_memcache schema consists of three tables:

- **cache_policies:** The configuration of the cache policies which defines how the caching should work. The default is to leave it to InnoDB. This is usually the recommended and ensures that you will never read stale data.

- **config_options:** The configuration options for the plugin. This includes which separator to use when returning multiple columns for the value and the table map delimiter.

- **containers:** The definition of the mapping to the InnoDB tables. You must add a mapping for all the tables you want to use with the InnoDB memcached plugin.

The containers table is the table you will use the most. By default, the table includes a mapping for the test.demo_test table:

```
mysql> SELECT * FROM innodb_memcache.containers\G
*************************** 1. row ***************************
                 name: aaa
            db_schema: test
             db_table: demo_test
          key_columns: c1
        value_columns: c2
                flags: c3
           cas_column: c4
   expire_time_column: c5
unique_idx_name_on_key: PRIMARY
1 row in set (0.0007 sec)
```

You can use the name to reference the table defined by db_schema and db_table when querying the table. The key_columns column defines the columns in the InnoDB table that is used for the key lookup. You specify the columns you want to include in the query results in the value_columns column. If you include multiple columns, you use the separator configured in the config_options table in the row with name = separator (the default is |) to separate the column names.

The cas_column and expire_time_column columns are rarely needed and will not be discussed further here. The final column, unique_idx_name_on_key, is the name of a unique index in the table, preferably the primary key.

Tip   The detailed description of the tables and their use can be found in https://dev.mysql.com/doc/refman/en/innodb-memcached-internals.html.

You are now ready to install the plugin itself. You can do that using the INSTALL PLUGIN command (remember this does not work on Windows):

```
mysql> INSTALL PLUGIN daemon_memcached soname "libmemcached.so";
Query OK, 0 rows affected (0.09 sec)
```

This statement must be executed using the legacy MySQL protocol (by default port 3306) as the X Protocol (by default port 33060) does not allow you to install plugins. That is it – the InnoDB memcached plugin is now ready for testing. The simplest way to test it is to use the telnet client. Listing 27-4 shows a simple example specifying the container explicitly and using the default container.

Listing 27-4. Testing InnoDB memcached with telnet

```
shell$ telnet localhost 11211
Trying ::1...
Connected to localhost.
Escape character is '^]'.

get @@aaa.AA
VALUE @@aaa.AA 8 12
HELLO, HELLO
END
```

get AA
```
VALUE AA 8 12
HELLO, HELLO
END
```

To make it easier to see the two commands, an empty line has been inserted before each. The first command uses @@ to specify the container name before the key value. The second command relies on Memcached using the default container (the first entry when sorting alphabetically in ascending order by the container name). You exit telnet by pressing Ctrl+] followed by the quit command:

```
^]
telnet> quit
Connection closed.
```

The daemon uses port 11211 by default as for the standalone Memcached instance. If you want to change the port or any of the other Memcached options, you can use the daemon_memcached_option option which takes a string with the memcached options. For example, to set the port to 22222

```
[mysqld]
daemon_memcached_option = "-p22222"
```

The option can only be set in the MySQL configuration file or on the command line, so it requires a restart of MySQL to make the change take effect.

If you add new entries to the containers table or change existing entries, you will need to restart the memcached plugin to make it read the definitions again. You can do that by restarting MySQL or by uninstalling and installing the plugin:

```
mysql> UNINSTALL PLUGIN daemon_memcached;
Query OK, 0 rows affected (4.05 sec)
```

```
mysql> INSTALL PLUGIN daemon_memcached soname "libmemcached.so";
Query OK, 0 rows affected (0.02 sec)
```

In practice you will mostly be using the plugin from your application. The usage is straightforward if you are used to use Memcached. As an example, consider Listing 27-5 which shows a few Python commands using the pymemcache module. Note that the example assumes you have set the port back to 11211.

Listing 27-5. Using the InnoDB memcached plugin with Python

```
shell$ python3
Python 3.6.8 (default, May 16 2019, 05:58:38)
[GCC 4.8.5 20150623 (Red Hat 4.8.5-36.0.1)] on linux
Type "help", "copyright", "credits" or "license" for more information.
>>> from pymemcache.client.base import Client
>>> client = Client(('localhost', 11211))
>>> client.get('@@aaa.AA')
b'HELLO, HELLO'
>>> client.set('@@aaa.BB', 'Hello World')
True
>>> client.get('@@aaa.BB')
b'Hello World'
```

The interactive Python environment is used to query the `test.demo_test` table through the `memcached` plugin. After creating the connection, the existing row is queried using the `get()` method, and a new row is inserted using the `set()` method. There is no need to set a timeout in this case as the `set()` method ends up writing directly to InnoDB. Finally, the new row is retrieved again. Notice how simple this example is compared to the regular Memcached where you need to maintain the cache yourself.

You can verify that the new row was really inserted into the table by querying it in MySQL:

```
mysql> SELECT * FROM test.demo_test;
+----+--------------+----+----+----+
| c1 | c2           | c3 | c4 | c5 |
+----+--------------+----+----+----+
| AA | HELLO, HELLO |  8 |  0 |  0 |
| BB | Hello World  |  0 |  1 |  0 |
+----+--------------+----+----+----+
2 rows in set (0.0032 sec)
```

There is more to using the MySQL InnoDB Memcached plugin. If you plan to use it, you are encouraged to read the "InnoDB memcached Plugin" section in the reference manual at `https://dev.mysql.com/doc/refman/en/innodb-memcached.html`.

Another popular utility that supports caching is ProxySQL.

ProxySQL

The ProxySQL project[2] is founded by René Cannaò and is an advanced proxy that supports load balancing, routing based on query rules, caching, and more. The caching feature caches based on query rules, for example, you can set that you want to cache queries with a given digest. The cache is automatically expired based on the time to live value you set for the query rule.

You download ProxySQL from `https://github.com/sysown/proxysql/releases/`. At the time of writing, the latest release is version 2.0.8 which is the release used in the examples.

Note   ProxySQL is only officially supported for Linux. For the full documentation including installation instructions for the supported distributions, see `https://github.com/sysown/proxysql/wiki`.

Listing 27-6 shows an example of installing ProxySQL 2.0.8 on Oracle Linux using the RPM from the ProxySQL GitHub repository. The installation process is similar on other Linux distributions using the package command for the distribution (but of course the output will be different depending on the package command used). After the installation has completed, ProxySQL is started.

Listing 27-6. Installing and starting ProxySQL

```
shell$ wget https://github.com/sysown/proxysql/releases/download/v2.0.8/
proxysql-2.0.8-1-centos7.x86_64.rpm
...
Length: 9340744 (8.9M) [application/octet-stream]
Saving to: 'proxysql-2.0.8-1-centos7.x86_64.rpm'

100%[============================>] 9,340,744   2.22MB/s   in 4.0s

2019-11-24 18:41:34 (2.22 MB/s) - 'proxysql-2.0.8-1-centos7.x86_64.rpm'
saved [9340744/9340744]
```

---

[2]https://proxysql.com/

```
shell$ sudo yum install proxysql-2.0.8-1-centos7.x86_64.rpm
Loaded plugins: langpacks, ulninfo
Examining proxysql-2.0.8-1-centos7.x86_64.rpm: proxysql-2.0.8-1.x86_64
Marking proxysql-2.0.8-1-centos7.x86_64.rpm to be installed
Resolving Dependencies
--> Running transaction check
---> Package proxysql.x86_64 0:2.0.8-1 will be installed
--> Finished Dependency Resolution

Dependencies Resolved

================================================================
 Package   Arch    Version Repository                    Size
================================================================
Installing:
 proxysql x86_64 2.0.8-1 /proxysql-2.0.8-1-centos7.x86_64   35 M
Transaction Summary
================================================================
Install  1 Package

Total size: 35 M
Installed size: 35 M
Is this ok [y/d/N]: y
Downloading packages:
Running transaction check
Running transaction test
Transaction test succeeded
Running transaction
  Installing : proxysql-2.0.8-1.x86_64                        1/1
warning: group proxysql does not exist - using root
warning: group proxysql does not exist - using root
Created symlink from /etc/systemd/system/multi-user.target.wants/proxysql.
service to /etc/systemd/system/proxysql.service.
  Verifying  : proxysql-2.0.8-1.x86_64                        1/1

Installed:
  proxysql.x86_64 0:2.0.8-1
```

Complete!

```
shell$ sudo systemctl start proxysql
```

You can configure ProxySQL only through its admin interface. This uses the `mysql` command-line client and has a familiar feel for MySQL administrators. By default, ProxySQL uses port 6032 for the administration interface, and the administrator username is `admin` with the password set to `admin`. Listing 27-7 shows an example of connecting to the administration interface and listing the schema and tables available.

Listing 27-7. The administration interface

```
shell$ mysql --host=127.0.0.1 --port=6032 \
             --user=admin --password \
             --default-character-set=utf8mb4 \
             --prompt='ProxySQL> '
Enter password:
Welcome to the MySQL monitor.  Commands end with ; or \g.
Your MySQL connection id is 1
Server version: 5.5.30 (ProxySQL Admin Module)

Copyright (c) 2000, 2019, Oracle and/or its affiliates. All rights reserved.

Oracle is a registered trademark of Oracle Corporation and/or its
affiliates. Other names may be trademarks of their respective
owners.

Type 'help;' or '\h' for help. Type '\c' to clear the current input statement.

ProxySQL> SHOW SCHEMAS;
+-----+---------------+----------------------------------------+
| seq | name          | file                                   |
+-----+---------------+----------------------------------------+
| 0   | main          |                                        |
| 2   | disk          | /var/lib/proxysql/proxysql.db          |
| 3   | stats         |                                        |
| 4   | monitor       |                                        |
| 5   | stats_history | /var/lib/proxysql/proxysql_stats.db    |
+-----+---------------+----------------------------------------+
```

```
5 rows in set (0.00 sec)
ProxySQL> SHOW TABLES;
+-----------------------------------------------+
| tables                                        |
+-----------------------------------------------+
| global_variables                              |
| mysql_aws_aurora_hostgroups                   |
| mysql_collations                              |
| mysql_galera_hostgroups                       |
| mysql_group_replication_hostgroups            |
| mysql_query_rules                             |
| mysql_query_rules_fast_routing                |
| mysql_replication_hostgroups                  |
| mysql_servers                                 |
| mysql_users                                   |
| proxysql_servers                              |
| runtime_checksums_values                      |
| runtime_global_variables                      |
| runtime_mysql_aws_aurora_hostgroups           |
| runtime_mysql_galera_hostgroups               |
| runtime_mysql_group_replication_hostgroups    |
| runtime_mysql_query_rules                     |
| runtime_mysql_query_rules_fast_routing        |
| runtime_mysql_replication_hostgroups          |
| runtime_mysql_servers                         |
| runtime_mysql_users                           |
| runtime_proxysql_servers                      |
| runtime_scheduler                             |
| scheduler                                     |
+-----------------------------------------------+
24 rows in set (0.00 sec)
```

While the tables are grouped in schemas, you can access tables directly without referencing the schema. The output of SHOW TABLES shows the tables in the main schema which are the ones associated with the configuration of ProxySQL.

The configuration is a two-stage process where you first prepare the new configuration and then apply it. Applying the changes means saving them to disk if you want to persist them and to load them into the runtime threads.

The tables with the runtime_ prefix in the name are for configuration pushed to the runtime threads. One way of configuring ProxySQL is to use a SET statement similar to setting system variables in MySQL, but you can also use UPDATE statements. The first step should be to change the admin password (and optionally the administrator username) which you can do by setting the admin-admin_credentials variable as shown in Listing 27-8.

Listing 27-8. Setting the password for the administrator account

```
ProxySQL> SET admin-admin_credentials = 'admin:password';
Query OK, 1 row affected (0.01 sec)

ProxySQL> SAVE ADMIN VARIABLES TO DISK;
Query OK, 32 rows affected (0.02 sec)

ProxySQL> LOAD ADMIN VARIABLES TO RUNTIME;
Query OK, 0 rows affected (0.00 sec)

ProxySQL> SELECT @@admin-admin_credentials;
+---------------------------+
| @@admin-admin_credentials |
+---------------------------+
| admin:password            |
+---------------------------+
1 row in set (0.00 sec)
```

The value for the admin-admin_credentials option is the username and password separated by a colon. The SAVE ADMIN VARIABLES TO DISK statement persists the change, and the LOAD ADMIN VARIABLES TO RUNTIME command applies the changes to the runtime threads. It is necessary to load the variable into the runtime threads as ProxySQL keeps a copy of the variables in each thread for performance reasons. You can query the current values (whether applied or pending) as you can query system variables in MySQL.

You configure the MySQL backend instances that ProxySQL can use to direct the queries in the mysql_servers table. For this discussion, a single instance on the same host as ProxySQL will be used. Listing 27-9 shows how to add it to the list of servers that ProxySQL can route to.

Listing 27-9. Adding a MySQL instance to the list of servers

```
ProxySQL> SHOW CREATE TABLE mysql_servers\G
*************************** 1. row ***************************
        table: mysql_servers
Create Table: CREATE TABLE mysql_servers (
    hostgroup_id INT CHECK (hostgroup_id>=0) NOT NULL DEFAULT 0,
    hostname VARCHAR NOT NULL,
    port INT CHECK (port >= 0 AND port <= 65535) NOT NULL DEFAULT 3306,
    gtid_port INT CHECK (gtid_port <> port AND gtid_port >= 0 AND gtid_port
    <= 65535) NOT NULL DEFAULT 0,
    status VARCHAR CHECK (UPPER(status) IN ('ONLINE','SHUNNED','OFFLINE_SOFT',
    'OFFLINE_HARD')) NOT NULL DEFAULT 'ONLINE',
    weight INT CHECK (weight >= 0 AND weight <=10000000) NOT NULL DEFAULT 1,
    compression INT CHECK (compression IN(0,1)) NOT NULL DEFAULT 0,
    max_connections INT CHECK (max_connections >=0) NOT NULL DEFAULT 1000,
    max_replication_lag INT CHECK (max_replication_lag >= 0 AND
    max_replication_lag <= 126144000) NOT NULL DEFAULT 0,
    use_ssl INT CHECK (use_ssl IN(0,1)) NOT NULL DEFAULT 0,
    max_latency_ms INT UNSIGNED CHECK (max_latency_ms>=0) NOT NULL DEFAULT 0,
    comment VARCHAR NOT NULL DEFAULT ",
    PRIMARY KEY (hostgroup_id, hostname, port) )
1 row in set (0.01 sec)

ProxySQL> INSERT INTO mysql_servers
                    (hostname, port, use_ssl)
        VALUES ('127.0.0.1', 3306, 1);
Query OK, 1 row affected (0.01 sec)

ProxySQL> SAVE MYSQL SERVERS TO DISK;
Query OK, 0 rows affected (0.36 sec)

ProxySQL> LOAD MYSQL SERVERS TO RUNTIME;
Query OK, 0 rows affected (0.01 sec)
```

The example shows how you can use SHOW CREATE TABLE to get information about the mysql_servers table. The table definition includes information about the settings you can include and allowed values. Other than the hostname, all settings have a default value. The remaining part of the listing inserts a row for the MySQL instance on localhost port 3306 with the requirement that SSL is used. The change is then persisted to disk and loaded into the runtime threads.

Note   SSL can only be used from ProxySQL to the MySQL instance, not between the client and ProxySQL.

You will also need to specify which users can use the connection. First, create a user in MySQL:

```
mysql> CREATE USER myuser@'127.0.0.1'
            IDENTIFIED WITH mysql_native_password
            BY 'password';
Query OK, 0 rows affected (0.0550 sec)

mysql> GRANT ALL ON world.* TO myuser@'127.0.0.1';
Query OK, 0 rows affected (0.0422 sec)
```

ProxySQL does not presently support the caching_sha2_password authentication plugin, which is the default in MySQL 8, when you connect using MySQL Shell (but there is support using the mysql command-line client), so you need to create the user with the mysql_native_password plugin. Then add the user in ProxySQL:

```
ProxySQL> INSERT INTO mysql_users
                    (username,password)
          VALUES ('myuser', 'password');
Query OK, 1 row affected (0.00 sec)

ProxySQL> SAVE MYSQL USERS TO DISK;
Query OK, 0 rows affected (0.06 sec)

ProxySQL> LOAD MYSQL USERS TO RUNTIME;
Query OK, 0 rows affected (0.00 sec)
```

You can now connect to MySQL through ProxySQL. The SQL interface by default uses port 6033. You connect through ProxySQL in the same way as usual except for the port number and possibly the hostname:

```
shell$ mysqlsh --user=myuser --password \
               --host=127.0.0.1 --port=6033 \
               --sql --table \
               -e "SELECT * FROM world.city WHERE ID = 130;"
+-----+--------+-------------+------------------+------------+
| ID  | Name   | CountryCode | District         | Population |
+-----+--------+-------------+------------------+------------+
| 130 | Sydney | AUS         | New South Wales  |    3276207 |
+-----+--------+-------------+------------------+------------+
```

ProxySQL collects statistics in a similar way to the Performance Schema. You can query the statistics in the stats_mysql_query_digest and stats_mysql_query_digest_reset tables. The difference between the two tables is that the latter only includes the digests since you queried the table the last time. For example, to get the queries ordered by their total execution time

```
ProxySQL> SELECT count_star, sum_time,
                 digest, digest_text
            FROM stats_mysql_query_digest_reset
            ORDER BY sum_time DESC\G
*************************** 1. row ***************************
 count_star: 1
   sum_time: 577149
     digest: 0x170E9EDDB525D570
digest_text: select @@sql_mode;
*************************** 2. row ***************************
 count_star: 1
   sum_time: 5795
     digest: 0x94656E0AA2C6D499
digest_text: SELECT * FROM world.city WHERE ID = ?
2 rows in set (0.01 sec)
```

If you see a query that you would like to cache the result of, you can add a query rule based on the digest of the query. Assuming you want to cache the result of querying the world.city table by ID (digest 0x94656E0AA2C6D499), you can add a rule like the following:

```
ProxySQL> INSERT INTO mysql_query_rules
                    (active, digest, cache_ttl, apply)
          VALUES (1, '0x94656E0AA2C6D499', 60000, 1);
Query OK, 1 row affected (0.01 sec)

ProxySQL> SAVE MYSQL QUERY RULES TO DISK;
Query OK, 0 rows affected (0.09 sec)

ProxySQL> LOAD MYSQL QUERY RULES TO RUNTIME;
Query OK, 0 rows affected (0.01 sec)
```

The active column specifies whether ProxySQL should take the rule into account when evaluating rules that can be used. The digest is the digest of the query you want to cache, and the cache_ttl specifies how long in milliseconds the result should be used before it is considered expired, and the result is refreshed. The time to live has been set to 60000 milliseconds (1 minute) to allow you time to execute the queries a few times before the cache gets invalidated. Setting apply to 1 means that no later rules will be evaluated when the query matches this rule.

If you execute the query a few times within a minute, you can query the cache statistics in the table stats_mysql_global to see how the cache is used. An example of the output is

```
ProxySQL> SELECT *
          FROM stats_mysql_global
          WHERE Variable_Name LIKE 'Query_Cache%';
+----------------------------+----------------+
| Variable_Name              | Variable_Value |
+----------------------------+----------------+
| Query_Cache_Memory_bytes   | 3659           |
| Query_Cache_count_GET      | 6              |
| Query_Cache_count_GET_OK   | 5              |
| Query_Cache_count_SET      | 1              |
```

```
| Query_Cache_bytes_IN    | 331           |
| Query_Cache_bytes_OUT   | 1655          |
| Query_Cache_Purged      | 0             |
| Query_Cache_Entries     | 1             |
+-------------------------+---------------+
8 rows in set (0.01 sec)
```

Your data will most likely be different. It shows that the cache uses 3659 bytes and there have been six queries against the cache and, in five of those cases, the result was returned from the cache. The last of the six queries required executing the query against the MySQL backend.

There are two options you can set to configure the cache. These are

- **mysql-query_cache_size_MB:** The maximum size of the cache in megabytes. This is a soft limit that is used by the purging thread to decide how many queries to purge from the cache. So the memory usage may temporarily be larger than the configured size. The default is 256.

- **mysql-query_cache_stores_empty_result:** Whether result sets with no rows are cached. The default is true. This can also be configured per query in the query rules table.

You change the configuration similar to how you changed the administrator password earlier. For example, to limit the query cache to 128 megabytes

```
ProxySQL> SET mysql-query_cache_size_MB = 128;
Query OK, 1 row affected (0.00 sec)

ProxySQL> SAVE MYSQL VARIABLES TO DISK;
Query OK, 121 rows affected (0.04 sec)

ProxySQL> LOAD MYSQL VARIABLES TO RUNTIME;
Query OK, 0 rows affected (0.00 sec)
```

This first prepares the configuration change, then saves it to disk, and finally loads the MySQL variables into the runtime threads.

If you want to use ProxySQL, you are encouraged to consult the wiki on the ProxySQL GitHub project at https://github.com/sysown/proxysql/wiki.

Caching Tips

If you decide to implement caching for your MySQL instances, there are a few things to take into consideration. This section investigates some general caching tips.

The most important consideration is what to cache. The example earlier in this chapter of caching the result of a single-row primary key lookup is not a good example of the type of queries that benefit the most from caching. In general, the more complex and expensive the query is and the more often the query is executed, the better a candidate the query is. One thing that can make the caching more effective is to split complex queries into smaller parts. That way you can cache the result of each part of the complex query separately which makes it more likely to be reused.

You should also take into consideration how much data the query returns. If the query returns a large result set, you may end up using all the memory you have made available for caching for a single query.

Another consideration is where to have the cache. The closer you can place the cache to the application, the more efficient it is as it reduces the time spent on network communication. The downside is that if you have multiple application instances, you will have to choose between duplicating the cache and having a remote shared cache. The exception is if you need to use the cached data with other MySQL tables. In that case, it may be better to keep the cache inside MySQL in the form of a cache table or similar.

Summary

This chapter has provided an overview of caching with MySQL. It started out describing how caching is found everywhere from inside the CPUs to dedicated caching processes. It was then discussed how you can use cache tables and histograms for caching inside MySQL.

The two main sections discussed using Memcached and ProxySQL for caching. Memcached is an in-memory key-value store that you can use from your application, or you can use the special version included with MySQL that allows you to interact directly with InnoDB. ProxySQL combines a router and caching mechanism which stores the result sets transparently according to the query rules you have defined.

Finally, a few considerations regarding caching were covered. The more often you execute a query, and the more expensive it is to execute, the more you benefit from caching. The second consideration is that the closer you can place the cache to the application, the better.

That concludes the last chapter of the journey through MySQL 8 query performance tuning. Hopefully it has been a rewarding journey, and you feel ready to use the tools and techniques in your work. Remember that the more you practice query tuning, the better you become at it. Happy query tuning.

Index

A

Access method
    range, 459, 637
ALTER TABLE algorithm, 854–856
antijoin, 460
auto-increment, 857, 865, 868, 872–874,
        876, 880, 881

B

Benchmark
    tools
        Database Factory, 24
        DBT2, 23
        DBT3, 23
        DVD Store, 24
        HammerDB, 24
        iiBench, 24
        Sysbench, 23–32
    TPC benchmarks
        TPC-C, 22–24
        TPC-DI, 22
        TPC-DS, 22
        TPC-E, 22, 24
        TPC-H, 22–24
        TPC-VMS, 22
Best practice, 19–21, 128, 148, 336, 761–766
Blocked nested loop, 432–436
Build phase, 437
Build table, 437

C

Cache column, 920, 921
Cache table, 919–921
Cardinality, *see* Index cardinality
Character set
    utf8mb3, 286
    utf8mb4, 286, 289
Clustered index, 301–302, 336
Collation
    UCA 9.0.0, 286, 287, 295
Common table expressions, 829–834
Configuration options
    autocommit, 522, 692, 701, 704, 708,
        735, 736
    binlog_format, 913
    binlog_group_commit_sync_delay,
        908, 910
    binlog_row_event_max_size, 910
    binlog_row_image, 903
    binlog_row_value_options, 289
    binlog_transaction_dependency_
        history_size, 908, 909
    binlog_transaction_dependency_
        tracking, 908–909
    cte_max_recursion_depth, 376
    eq_range_index_dive_limit, 387, 845,
        848
    foreign_key_checks, 690, 881, 882
    histogram_generation_max_mem_
        size, 399, 400

947

P

Printed in the United States
By Bookmasters